PUBLICATION NUMBER 16

Duke University Commonwealth-Studies Center

*Economic Systems of the
Commonwealth*

Duke University Commonwealth-Studies Center Publications

Economic Systems of the Commonwealth

|||

Calvin B. Hoover, P. H. Karmel, Maureen Brunt, G. C. Allen,
O. W. Main, Henry M. Oliver, Jr., J. W. Williams,
P. S. Lokanathan, T. H. Silcock, C. G. F. Simkin,
Nural Islam, O. P. F. Horwood, John R.
Burrows, W. Arthur Lewis

Edited by
Calvin B. Hoover

PUBLISHED FOR THE
Duke University Commonwealth-Studies Center
DUKE UNIVERSITY PRESS, DURHAM, N. C.
CAMBRIDGE UNIVERSITY PRESS, LONDON
1962

© 1962, Duke University Press

Library of Congress Catalogue Card number 62-18316
Cambridge University Press, London N.W. 1, England

PRINTED IN THE UNITED STATES OF AMERICA
BY THE SEEMAN PRINTERY, INC., DURHAM, N. C.

ACKNOWLEDGMENTS

The financial support of the Carnegie Foundation to the Commonwealth-Studies Center of Duke University which made these studies possible is gratefully acknowledged. The Carnegie Foundation, however, is not responsible for any of the data or conclusions set forth in these studies.

The contributions which follow have been greatly facilitated by the previous studies, part of the "grand design" for a series of studies of economic systems, under the joint editorship of Dr. Rudolf Frei and Dr. Edgar Salin, published in two volumes by the List Gesellschaft with the financial assistance of the Twentieth Century Fund. These studies, *Economic Systems of the West,* have been available to the authors of the present work and have furnished a series of alternative models. Dr. Salin kindly agreed on behalf of the List Gesellschaft to the use in the present volume of the studies on the economic systems of the United Kingdom and Canada. These two studies have, however, been substantially revised.

Professor Robert S. Smith of Duke University has undertaken the detailed editing of the studies and has supervised the preparation of the index. He has also seen the book through the press. We have indeed been fortunate in having an economist of such stature and an editor of such skill as Professor Smith in charge of these responsibilities.

Dean Alan K. Manchester has administered the considerable financial aspects of these studies with the effectiveness with which he has administered the larger financial affairs of the Commonwealth-Studies Center. For this we are all grateful.

Mrs. Dorothy Moore has handled the extensive correspondence

associated with the studies and has retyped some of the manuscripts with her customary efficiency.

CALVIN B. HOOVER

Durham, North Carolina
  August, 1962

CONTENTS

LIST OF TABLES

Economic Systems of the
Commonwealth

The General Framework of
the Studies

Calvin B. Hoover*

The studies in this volume are part of the research program of the Commonwealth-Studies Center of Duke University.

These studies, titled *Economic Systems of the Commonwealth*, are descriptive analyses of the economic systems of Australia, Canada, New Zealand, South Africa, the United Kingdom, Malaya, India, Pakistan, Ceylon, Ghana, and the West Indies. They represent a further stage in a "grand design" for the study of the diverse economic systems of the world, including those of Soviet Russia and its orbit. This grand design has previously produced *Economic Systems of the West*, published in two successive volumes by the List Gesellschaft in 1957 and 1958 under the editorship of Rudolf Frei and Edgar Salin at my instigation.[1] These studies furnished descriptive analyses of the economic systems of thirteen countries of Western Europe in addition to those of Japan and Canada.

As the initial step in this larger plan, the annual meeting of the American Economic Association in 1953 was devoted to an examination of the economic system of the United States, with particular reference to the controversy among American economists concerning whether or not our economic system has been characterized by a general decline in its competitiveness and by an abandonment of the policy of laissez faire.[2] The *Proceedings* of the annual meeting of the Association, together with the *Economic Systems of the West*, were drawn upon and added to the studies which had previously

---

* James B. Duke Professor of Economics, Duke University.

[1] Rudolf Frei, ed., *Economic Systems of the West*, List Gesellschaft, Kyklos-Verlag, Basel, Vol. I, 1957; Vol. II, 1958.

[2] *Papers and Proceedings of the Sixty-sixth Annual Meeting of the American Economic Association*, *American Economic Review*, Vol. XLIV, No. 2, May 1954.

been made of the totalitarian economic systems. The Twentieth Century Fund supported a research study extending over three years which enabled me to carry out a comparative analysis of these diverse economic systems. The results were then embodied in the study *The Economy, Liberty and the State*, published in 1959.[3]

These studies of the economic systems of eleven Commonwealth countries were then initiated in 1959 in order to carry further the design for the examination of national economic systems. These eleven countries present an extraordinary diversity of cultures, natural and human resources, stages of economic development and political institutions. Consequently, the analysis of their economic systems affords an extraordinary opportunity to observe the interaction of diverse factors in their development.

All of these studies have been carried out by economists resident in the countries concerned, except for Ceylon and Malaya-Singapore, where this was not feasible. Even in the latter cases, the studies were done by economists who had spent substantial periods attached to the universities of these countries and who have kept up their interest and contacts with these countries.

These economists were asked to attempt to answer the questions which the writer had addressed to European economists in the article "The Relevance of the Competitive Laissez-faire Economic Model to Modern Capitalistic National Economies" and which were used as the basis for the studies published as *Economic Systems of the West*.[4] These questions were as follows:

1. What industries have been nationalized (or denationalized) since the beginning of World War II (or other appropriate date)?
2. To what extent have cartel-type agreements in industry increased or decreased in importance during the period?
3. To what extent has concentration in industry been intensified?
4. To what extent have new forms of competition developed and offset oligopolistic tendencies or tendencies toward impairment of traditional forms of competition?
5. What currents and counter-currents with respect to governmental measures to further national economic self-sufficiency have been in operation during the period?

[3] Calvin B. Hoover, *The Economy, Liberty and the State*, Twentieth Century Fund, New York, 1959.
[4] Calvin B. Hoover, "Relevance of the Competitive, Laissez-faire Economic Model to Modern Capitalistic National Economies," *Kyklos*, Fasc. 1, 1955, pp. 54-55.

6. What is the present status and the trend with respect to governmental control of prices (including subsidy arrangements) and production in agriculture?

7. Has the extent to which the government takes responsibility for the stabilization of particular prices and the general price level changed significantly during the period?

8. To what extent has governmental responsibility for the maintenance of full employment affected the character of the system?

9. Are there more or less formal agreements among industry, labor organizations and the government with respect to allowable increases in wages in relation to costs of living or in relation to the general price level or to the level of export prices?

10. Has there been any noticeable trend with respect to the extent to which the managements of industrial corporations act independently of effective control by stockholders?

11. Have there been pronounced changes in the degree of inequality in the distribution of national income and what have been the major causal factors in this change if it has occurred?

12. How substantial have been increases in and extensions of social security benefits during the period?

13. What changes have taken place with respect to the proportion of national income which flows through the governmental budget?

14. To what extent has the government replaced private savers-investors as a source of capital funds for the national economy?

15. As a kind of "catch-all" question: To what extent has the national economy become a more or less "directed economy"?

It was pointed out that some of these questions asked of European economists were not relevant for the studies presently contemplated. It was also stated:

A number of questions apart from those answered by the economist-authors of the studies of European economic systems suggest themselves. To what extent are economic development policies likely to affect the trend towards "statization" of the national economy? Are there constitutional provisions which do or do not imply the socialization of the economy? Are any of the major political parties or movements committed to the socialization of the economy as a matter of principle? Other questions will, of course, occur to you.

Each of the economists co-operating in the present studies was furnished copies of the article referred to above and with the two volumes of *Economic Systems of the West*. There was wide diversity in the way in which the economists who wrote these studies handled their subjects. In consequence, the authors of the present studies had fifteen models from which to choose elements for their own. Once more, diverse methods of description and analysis have resulted. This was expected and has been welcomed.

In the United Kingdom we have an economy in which modern industrial capitalism not only first developed, but which was for a century both the most advanced and the wealthiest in the expanding capitalist world. It was inevitable that the economic institutions developed in the United Kingdom should serve in an important degree as a model for those which developed later in other countries. Furthermore, just as the political institutions of the Commonwealth countries have been particularly influenced by those of the parent country, we would expect their economic institutions likewise to be even more influenced than in the case of other countries.

It is noteworthy, however, that the economic institutions which are being developed in the younger Commonwealth countries do not simply reflect the classic capitalistic model developed in the United Kingdom. There are forces and factors within these countries which would make the adoption of the economic institutions of classic capitalism out of the question. Moreover, as Professor Allen's study of the economic system of the United Kingdom makes plain, old-style capitalism no longer exists there. Some, but not all, of the forces which brought about the modification of capitalism in the United Kingdom also operate in the other countries of the Commonwealth. The newer model of modified capitalism in the United Kingdom also in turn exerts its influence on the development of economic institutions of the younger members of the Commonwealth.

To an economist, it is analytically important that both the old and the new types of "underdeveloped countries" are represented in these studies. It is not generally remembered that until after World War II underdeveloped countries, or "undeveloped countries" as they were more commonly called, meant countries with undeveloped *natural* resources. Thus, the United States was considered an underdeveloped country before the twentieth century because of the relatively low labor and capital resources in proportion to natural resources. Canada, Australia, New Zealand, and South Africa were considered to be still in this category even in the twentieth century.

After World War II, the term "underdeveloped countries" came to mean primarily countries with low ratios of capital and modern technology to labor supply. The ratio of natural resources to these other factors came to occupy a minor role in determining whether a country should be considered underdeveloped or not.

This change in the definition of what should be considered an undeveloped or underdeveloped country coincided with the greatly lessened importance of the output of land and other natural resources as a component of national income and a greatly lessened importance of this factor in economic theory. Indeed, the principle of diminishing returns once considered so basic by all economists is now being called into question.[5]

India, Pakistan, Ceylon, Malaya-Singapore, and the West Indies, of the countries included in these studies, would apparently not have been considered underdeveloped countries according to the old terminology, but certainly would be included under the new terminology. Ghana might have been included under the old terminology and certainly would be included under the new.

The older analysis led to the conclusion that countries such as Australia, New Zealand, and Canada might be expected to turn towards somewhat more socialistic economic institutions as the need for the free enterprise considered so essential for the development of underdeveloped countries lessened. To some degree this has happened, as can be seen from the studies of Professor Karmel and Miss Brunt for Australia, of Colin Simkin for New Zealand, and of O. W. Main for Canada.

Quite a different causation for the inclination towards a more socialistic type of economic system exists in countries such as India, Pakistan, Ghana, and Ceylon. The belief that a collectivist form of economic system is more egalitarian than modern capitalism, is, in fact, not necessarily or even usually true; but such a belief is a factor favoring collectivism in these countries. Apart from the preference for a more egalitarian system, however, is the unwillingness of the political leaders of these countries to depend upon the "natural" process of capital accumulation and entrepreneurial activity of free enterprise capitalism which made possible the industrialization of

---

[5] Professor Theodore W. Schultz has been the leader in calling attention to the diminishing role of land and other natural resources. For a statement of his position and a criticism of it as well as other related matters, see *Natural Resources and Economic Growth*, edited by Joseph J. Spengler. (Resources for the Future, Inc.: Washington, 1961), pp. 1-19.

Western Europe, the United States, and Japan, but which stretched over a number of generations.

This unwillingness to rely upon the past processes of capitalism to bring about industrialization in these countries, unlike Canada, Australia, and New Zealand, means the repudiation of the doctrine that socialism must wait until capitalism has provided a material foundation for the later stage. Paradoxically enough, this fundamentally non-Marxian doctrine of the possibility of dispensing with the capitalistic stage of economic development is supported in these underdeveloped countries most strongly, although by no means exclusively, by those under Marxist influence. This Leninist gloss on Marxism has supplanted the original doctrine.

More fundamental than any doctrinaire causation is the effect of the so-called revolution of rising expectations which leads political leaders in these underdeveloped countries to believe that only by means of state intervention can the necessary resources for the massive capital investment required for industrialization be raised. They further believe that only by state control and intervention can investment be channeled in the directions which are most necessary and productive from the national viewpoint but which are not the most immediately profitable to private investors and entrepreneurs. Implicit is the belief that grants and loans from the more economically developed countries can be relied upon to meet at least the foreign exchange costs of such capital investment.

Professor Lokanathan has pointed out that in India the undertaking of some of the major social-overhead capital investment and some of the direct investment in heavy industry by the state has been essential to the current rate of development of private industry. It is consequently uncertain how much of the development of the state sector has been due to the goal of a "socialistic pattern of society" as set forth by the Parliament of India and how much has been due to sheer necessity, once the decision for industrialization under forced draft has been taken.

In some cases, as Dr. Islam has pointed out for Pakistan, the state sometimes invests in essential new industries because private investment does not take place or takes place at too slow a rate. The state may then withdraw when private capital and entrepreneurial ability have developed sufficiently to take over. In a country where the constitution reflects the choice of a socialist type of economy in preference to capitalism, such a withdrawal of the state in favor of private capital is, however, not to be expected.

In countries like Ceylon and Ghana, the will to collectivize the economy may exist, but the small extent of foreign industries limits the possibility of attaining socialism through the easy channel of the nationalization of foreign holdings. Nationalized industry must, for example, wait upon the development of industry in Ghana, where, as Professor Williams points out, neither large-scale industries, the existence of administrative personnel, nor the psychology of the people as yet renders the matter a practical issue.

Our authors have generally avoided any definite forecast as to whether the trend in these economies is toward greater collectivism or statism. The reluctance to forecast the direction of this trend was also true of the authors of the *Economic Systems of the West*. This reluctance is the natural consequence of the emasculation of the meaning of terms such as "capitalism" or "socialism" in application to existing economic systems.

Almost all so-called capitalistic economic systems are now actually "mixed" systems, with the state playing an important role. The United States, for example, has undergone profound institutional changes, particularly since the Great Depression of the thirties. We no longer have simply an individualistic capitalism. Instead we have an economy of industrial corporations, of labor unions, of agricultural production and prices controlled by government and that government committed to the maintenance of full employment. We have, in fact, developed an organizational economy which has been accompanied by substantial changes in our distribution system.

On the other hand, in the countries of Western Europe, even where and when political parties formally adhering to "socialist" tenets have been in power, the movement towards nationalization of industry has come to at least a temporary halt. This halt had come about not only because of disillusionment with nationalization of industry as a means of bringing about a more equitable distribution of income, but because other means of redistribution of income had proved more effective.

In the major country in which capitalism was overthrown, Soviet Russia, the economic and political system which developed turned out to be in almost total contradiction to that envisioned by almost all socialist philosophers of the past. Thus, substantial progress towards the commonly accepted goals of socialism has been made in some countries without a deliberate move towards socialism or even partial nationalization of industry. On the contrary, where private property was abolished and the powers of the state extended without limit, progress towards the goals of socialism, as these goals were understood in the past, has been least. It is no wonder that our economists writing in *Economic Systems of the Commonwealth* have not wished to prophesy whether "capitalism" was being left behind on the march towards "socialism."

It has not been feasible either to expand or to restrict these studies to correspond with the limits of the Commonwealth as they existed at the moment of publication, since the membership of the Commonwealth is undergoing continual change. Thus, neither Nigeria, nor Tanganyika, nor Cyprus is included. The Union of South Africa and the West Indies are included although the one has now left the Commonwealth, and the expected West Indian Federation has apparently been abortive.

In co-ordinating the publication of these studies of the economic systems of eleven different countries, it has not been possible to insure that the data for each country would have the same terminal date. Most of the manuscripts were written in 1960. It has been possible to "up-date" the material to a limited extent through 1961.

Since these studies have been carried out by mature and distinguished economists, no effort at substantive or comprehensive editing has been undertaken.

2

The Australian Economy

Relevance of the Competitive Laissez-Faire Model

P. H. Karmel and Maureen Brunt*

INTRODUCTION

The Competitive Laissez-Faire Model

Given the physical endowment of an economy and the production possibilities determined by the state of technical knowledge, the pattern of production of goods and services which emerges depends on the manner in which economic decisions are effected. In the competitive laissez-faire model, decisions are made by large numbers of small entities. Decisions are marginal, and the extent to which the decisions of any one entity can affect the total pattern of production is severely limited. The individual producer must take all prices as given and his area of choice is strictly circumscribed. The question of his following one or another policy does not arise.

The principal characteristic of such a model is its automaticity. Within their restricted ranges of choice, producers attempt to maximize profits and consumers attempt to maximize satisfaction. From the independent activities of many separate economic entities there emerges the pattern of goods and services produced. This pattern can, in a broad sense, be regarded as conforming to the preferences

* Professor Karmel and Miss Brunt are members of the Department of Economics of the University of Adelaide. They feel that they should make clear the division of authorship: Miss Brunt owns responsibility for the section on Business Organization and the subsection on Competition and Public Policy, Professor Karmel for the remainder. They wish to thank their many colleagues in the University of Adelaide upon whose expertise they have called and who have been most generous in their help, in particular Dr. K. J. Hancock, Mr. R. R. Hirst, Dr. F. G. Jarrett, Mr. R. H. Wallace, Mr. D. H. Whitehead, and Mr. J. C. G. Wright of the Department of Economics; Dr. Alex. Castles of the Department of Law; and Dr. G. S. Reid of the Department of History and Political Science. They also wish to thank Dr. J. E. Isaac of the University of Melbourne.

of the individual persons making up the economy. Indeed, it can be demonstrated that it is optimal, in the sense that no marginal change in the pattern which emerges can make any one person better off without making others worse off. This is reflected in the equality of prices and marginal costs of production. But a pattern of production which is optimal in this sense is not necessarily optimal with respect to structural changes. In any case this optimal property is by no means unequivocal, since no particular virtue can be attached to the distribution of income which is implied in any given pattern of production.

In a stationary economy the pattern of production, once established, would persist. In a dynamic world the growth of population, the accumulation of capital, and technological progress continuously modify the production possibilities available. The shape of the economy changes, and people are able to choose new combinations of goods and services of quantity and quality not previously available. In the competitive laissez-faire model the modifications to the shape of the economy over time are subject to the same automaticity as is the pattern of production in a given situation. The perfection of the capital market and the use of profit as an indicator for expansion or contraction insures the adjustment of the shape of the economy to the preferences of individuals. Investment decisions, like consumption decisions, are marginal and limited by the "given" market situations which producers face.

On the basis of this model there has developed an elaborate theory of production and price. No one has believed that any real economy could be epitomized in all its essential particulars by the laissez-faire model. But the economic theory which has been developed from this model is generally supposed to be relevant to modern capitalistic economies. It follows that one should ask whether or not this supposition is well founded.

As shown above, the essence of the laissez-faire model lies in the assumption that all decision-making units are small relative to the extent of the market. The nature of modern techniques of production and marketing (e.g., increasing returns to scale) and the likelihood of competition itself breeding stronger firms, mergers, and combinations make this assumption unrealistic over wide areas of modern capitalistic economies. Indeed, even if one started from a fully competitive position, it is probable that large units of decision-making would emerge over the course of time, so that in a modern setting the extreme laissez-faire model would prove unstable. The competitive model does in fact seem to be only one form of market structure and at that a special and rather extreme form. Market structures range from pure competition at one extreme to the total monopolization of a particular industry at the other, and in between lies a rich variety of structures based on numbers and size distribution of firms, product differentiation, conditions of entry, cartelization, and trade agreements. To these forms of market structure the competitive model may not be wholly irrelevant; for competitive oligopoly, competition between industries and potential competition from new entrants, new products and techniques may replace the older concept of large-numbers competition within industries.

When decisions are taken by large rather than small units, they cease to be marginal decisions and become structural decisions. The choices open to producers are very much widened, since the producers themselves can influence prices. Producers can choose this or that policy, and the consequences of the decisions of one producing unit on the economy become appreciable. The pattern of production will differ from that under competitive conditions, prices need no longer reflect marginal costs, the distribution of income will differ, and so on. More important are the consequences on the growth of the economy. In the competitive model the shape of this growth will be in response to consumers' preferences; under non-competitive conditions this shape may be determined by the policies of giant firms. The greater the tendency to the self-financing of expansion by large firms, the more true this is. Capital no longer necessarily flows to the points showing the highest rate of return. Moreover, the sales promotion campaigns of giant firms engineer changes in consumers' preferences, and their research activities determine the nature of the goods available. Under these conditions consumers may still be free to choose what goods they want within a given area of choice, but they may have little influence on how that area is to be widened with economic progress. This is not to say that the outcome of a situation in which large firms predominate is inferior in any sense to that of the competitive model. Whether it be regarded inferior or superior from whatever aspect considered, it is, however, different; and in this respect the competitive model may have little relevance to the real world.

A second factor which may reduce the relevance of the laissez-faire model is the involvement of governments in the production of goods and services. Governments have always been responsible for the provision of those services which must be enjoyed collectively, if they are to be enjoyed at all. In the competitive laissez-faire model their role has been regarded as being limited to this, namely, the provision of defense and law and order and certain public works and institutions. However, they have in fact become responsible to an increasing extent for the provision of services, the consumption of which is regarded as highly desirable on social or political grounds; for example, health and education. Decisions as to the volume of services of these kinds are essentially political decisions, and there is little point in attempting to rationalize them in terms of an economic calculus. Thus, in modern capitalistic economies there is a great range of government expenditure on collective goods and services, which is quite outside the relevance of the competitive laissez-faire model. In addition, governments own and direct many trading enterprises for reasons either of public policy (e.g., industries associated with defense or health), or of political conviction, or because they cannot be run profitably by private enterprise (e.g., many public utilities). These enterprises are almost always in a monopolistic or quasi-monopolistic position, and in any case they are large and their control is highly concentrated. They are certainly not competitive in the traditional sense.

Finally, the governments of most modern capitalistic economies have come to accept a responsibility for insuring that economic activity is kept at a satisfactory level. This does not necessarily imply that governments have to regulate the detailed workings of the economy by direct controls on materials, manpower, and prices. However, if they are serious about maintaining full employment and avoiding inflation, the exercise of control over aggregative spending through budgetary and monetary policy is necessary. Although such economic policy is global in its impact on the economy, it may have a very direct influence on the pattern of production and the shape of the economy. If taxation is to be increased, how will the incidence of the increase be distributed as between personal and business taxes? If spending is to be encouraged, will the emphasis be on consumption, investment, or government expenditure? Moreover, some governments concern themselves with encouraging a high rate of economic growth. With this economic objective, it is difficult to avoid policies which are discriminatory in their effect between different industries and hence affect the future structure of the economy.

The object of this essay is to examine the Australian economy with the special task of determining the extent to which it diverges from the competitive laissez-faire model, both with respect to market organization (see pp. 33-106) and to the activities of government (pp. 107 ff.). Before pursuing these matters in detail, a brief survey of the economic and institutional background of Australia will be made.

Economic Background

Australia, with an area of just under three million square miles, is almost as large as the United States and four-fifths the size of Canada. About 40 per cent of the area receives less than ten inches of rainfall per annum and the great bulk of the central area is unsuitable for settlement. Settlement is heavily concentrated in the southeastern corner of the continent.

With a population of ten and one-half million, the domestic market is limited. This has obvious implications for the structure of manufacturing industry. Nevertheless, the economy is highly industrialized in terms of employment, only 13 per cent of the work force being engaged in primary production, while 28 per cent is engaged in manufacturing. This compares with 12 and 27 per cent, 5 and 37 per cent, and 14 and 26 per cent for the United States, United Kingdom, and Canada, respectively.[1] Over 80 per cent of the work force are wage and salary earners. Of these, three-quarters are in private employment, the remainder being employees of public authorities. Associated with this industrialization is a very strong tendency towards urbanization, just under 80 per cent of the population living in cities. The population is highly concentrated in the larger cities. There are only eight cities with populations over 100,-000, and these account for 57 per cent of the total population. Nearly 40 per cent is contained in the two great metropolises of Sydney and Melbourne alone. For purposes of comparison it may be of

[1] International comparisons, where used, have been derived from: United Nations, *Year Book of National Accounts Statistics, 1957; Statistical Abstract of the United States, 1959;* United Kingdom, *Annual Abstract of Statistics* No. 96, 1959 C.S.O.; Canada, *Year Book, 1959;* International Labour Office, *Year Book of Labour Statistics, 1959;* United Nations, *Statistical Year Book, 1960.*

interest to note that in the United States there are 106 cities with populations exceeding 100,000, and these account for 29 per cent of the total population. The corresponding figures for the United Kingdom and Canada are 46 cities and 51 per cent and 11 cities and 23 per cent.

Although primary production employs a relatively small fraction of the work force, it contributes about one-fifth to the national income and some 90 per cent to Australian exports. With exports standing in recent years between 15 and 20 per cent of gross national product, Australia is essentially an open economy. Moreover, since most exports are primary products, the Australian scene must be viewed against a backdrop of fluctuating export proceeds—fluctuating by reason both of domestic seasonal conditions and of the instability of world prices. Year-to-year movements of up to 30 per cent in export proceeds are not uncommon. This implies a considerable potential for instability in income and employment.

The Australian standard of living is among the highest in the world. Since international comparisons of real income are dubious at their best, it may be sufficient to draw attention to two indicators. In 1959 the number of persons per motor vehicle was 4.0, having fallen from 7.2 in 1949. This compares with 2.6, 8.0, and 3.7, for the United States, the United Kingdom, and Canada in 1957. The mean expectation of life at birth is 67.1 years for males and 72.8 years for females; these figures are almost identical with those for the United States (white population) and the United Kingdom. A further indication is given by the housing situation. At the Census of 1954 the number of inmates per private dwelling was 3.55, having fallen from 3.75 in seven years. Moreover, 63 per cent of private dwellings were owner-occupied, as against 53 per cent seven years earlier.

Some idea of the industrial structure of Australia and of recent changes in that structure can be obtained from Table 1. The trend against agriculture and in favor of secondary production and tertiary services (other than personal services) can be seen.

Since the end of World War II the Australian economy has undergone remarkable development, and its rapid expansion must be regarded as the key feature of the postwar period. This expansion has been based upon a population growth of nearly 2.5 per cent per annum and a rate of capital accumulation amounting to over

TABLE I. *Work Force by Industry, 1933, 1947, and 1954*
(Per cent)

	1933	1947	1954
Primary production, mining, and quarrying	24.3	17.6	15.1
Industrial—manufacturing, utilities, construction	32.1	37.1	38.1
Transport and communication	8.3	10.1	11.3
Commerce and finance	16.7	16.2	17.1
Public administration and professional	8.6	11.5	12.2
Entertainment, sports, and recreation	0.9	1.1	1.0
Personal and domestic service	9.1	6.4	5.2
Total work force	100.0	100.0	100.0

Source: Commonwealth Bureau of Census and Statistics. These figures have been adjusted to give a comparable classification for the three census years.

one-quarter of gross national product. By any standard these are high figures. Thus, for the quinquennium 1951-56, the rate of population growth per annum was 2.28 per cent for Australia, compared with 2.80 for Canada, 1.72 for the United States, and 0.30 for the United Kingdom. The proportion of gross national product devoted to capital formation has in recent years been somewhat higher than for Canada and about 50 per cent higher than for the United States and the United Kingdom. Over two-fifths of the population growth has been due to migration, the rest being accounted for by a level of fertility 60 per cent higher than that obtaining before World War II (the net reproduction rate is currently 1.6). Large-scale migration has been a conscious part of government policy, and the Commonwealth Government has made a determined and successful effort to encourage migration by furnishing financial assistance to bring migrants to Australia, by entering into agreements with the United Kingdom and other European governments, and by providing some accommodation for assisted migrants when they arrive. The current long-term migration target is 125,000 per annum, although it was temporarily reduced in the middle of 1961 as a result of some employment difficulties. This is a rate of more than one per cent of the population.

Table 2 illustrates the magnitude of Australian economic development over recent years. With population growing at nearly 2.5 per cent per annum, real gross national product has grown at about

TABLE 2. *Indexes of Australian Economic Development*
1948-49 to 1960-61
(1948-49 = 100)

	Mean population[a]	Real gross national product[b]	Volume of factory production[c] (excluding power)	Volume of rural output[d]
1948-49	100	100	100	100
1949-50	103	108	104	106
1950-51	106	115	116	100
1951-52	109	114	119	94
1952-53	112	118	113	111
1953-54	114	125	134	112
1954-55	117	132	145	113
1955-56	119	139	153	120
1956-57	122	142	157	120
1957-58	125	145	166	114
1958-59	128	155	176	137
1959-60	131	162	192	133
1960-61	133	166	190	139

Sources: [a] Commonwealth Bureau of Census and Statistics, *Demography Bulletins.*
  [b] Estimates computed by Malcom Cockburn, Department of Economics, University of Adelaide.
  [c] Index published by Australia and New Zealand Bank.
  [d] Commonwealth Bureau of Census and Statistics, *Commonwealth Year Books.*

4.5 per cent per annum. It follows that productivity has also been rising at over 2 per cent. As one would expect in the circumstances, rural output has not kept pace with the general expansion of the economy. The greatest developments have been within the manufacturing sector; and within that sector the well-established and "traditional" trades—textiles and food—have expanded slowly, while the more complex products—metals, machinery, chemicals, and consumer durables—have expanded very rapidly. The pattern of development is illustrated in Table 3.

The rapid development of the past decade has been associated with an almost continuous record of full employment accompanied by inflationary tendencies and balance-of-payments difficulties. The latter have been due not only to the instability of export income but also to the short-term tendency for excess domestic spending to spill over onto imports and to the long-term tendency for the demand for imports to outrun export capacity. A substantial and continuing

TABLE 3. *Changes in Manufacturing Employment, 1948-49 to 1958-59*

Industry group	1948-49 (thousands)	1958-59 (thousands)	Increase (per cent)
Products of non-metallic minerals	33	43	30
Chemicals and allied products	32	43	34
Primary metal industries	42	68	62
Fabricated metal products	42	48	14
Plant, equipment, and machinery (excluding electrical)	79	105	33
Electrical machinery and wireless	39	67	72
Transportation equipment (excluding motor vehicles)	69	69	0
Motor vehicles	62	113	82
Textiles and textile goods	44	45	2
Clothing and footwear	139	129	—7
Food, drink, and tobacco	118	125	6
Timber and timber products	66	76	15
Paper, paper products, and printing	51	68	33
Rubber goods	12	18	50
Fuel, lubricants, light and power	16	23	44
Miscellaneous	46	48	4
Total	890	1,088	22

Source: Derived from Commonwealth Bureau of Census and Statistics, *Secondary Industries Bulletin.*

capital inflow has helped to moderate pressures on the balance of payments, but import restrictions of varying severity have been in operation during almost the whole war and postwar period. In Table 4 is set out the current account position of the balance of payments over the past decade. The figures show considerable variation, and, in interpreting them, the effect of import restrictions in reducing these variations below what they would otherwise have been must be kept in mind.

As far as employment is concerned, Australia has enjoyed brimful employment over this period, except for minor recessions in 1952 and 1956-57 and a somewhat deeper trough beginning in 1961. But even in these periods unemployment did not rise much above 2 or 3 per cent. The numbers registered as unemployed are shown in Table 4. The number of wage and salary earners during the period shown in the tables was about three millions. Also in this table is set out the rate of rise of retail prices. Over the whole period prices rose by about 6.5 per cent per annum. In the first half

TABLE 4. *Unemployment, Prices, and Balance of Payments, Australia, 1949-1960*

	Registered unemployed in June[a] (thousands)	Change in consumer price index June quarter to June quarter[b] (per cent)	Surplus on current account in balance of payments. Year ending June[c] (£ million)
1949	14.4	—	32
1950	12.2	8.7	− 45
1951	9.8	18.0	105
1952	38.3	20.4	−579
1953	53.4	4.3	192
1954	22.4	0.7	− 1
1955	19.1	1.5	−236
1956	31.5	6.4	−212
1957	52.2	3.2	115
1958	67.1	1.0	−154
1959	65.7	1.7	−185
1960	47.2	3.7	−219
1961	111.7	3.2	−369

Sources: [a] Department of Labour and National Service, *Commonwealth Employment Statistics.*
[b] Commonwealth Bureau of Census and Statistics, *Consumer Price Index*, S.B. 837.
[c] Commonwealth of Australia, *National Income and Expenditure*, 1959-60 (Canberra, 1960).

of the period prices rose very steeply, but in recent years the rate of increase has fallen.

Institutional Background

Australia is a federation of six states. The Commonwealth Constitution,[2] which dates from 1901 and which was greatly influenced by the United States model, sets down certain specific powers for the Commonwealth, the residual powers being exercised by the states. The Commonwealth has exclusive power over the imposition of customs and excise duties and over the coining of money; but apart from these two, all other powers of the Commonwealth are exercised concurrently with the states, subject to the supremacy of Commonwealth laws in the event of inconsistency with state laws.

The Constitution lists thirty-nine concurrent powers of the Commonwealth Parliament. Apart from the defense and external affairs

[2] Commonwealth Bureau of Census and Statistics, *Year Book of the Commonwealth of Australia*, No. 46, 1960, pp. 6-23.

powers, which have some economic implications, the powers which are of major relevance from an economic point of view relate to trade and commerce, taxation, bounties, public borrowing, currency, banking, insurance, corporations, social security, migration, and industrial disputes. However, it is important to realize that in many respects these powers are circumscribed, either because they are themselves qualified (e.g., the Commonwealth can acquire property only on "just terms") or because they are subject to the overriding requirement of Section 92 that "trade, commerce and intercourse among the States . . . shall be absolutely free," a requirement to which, it has been held, both Commonwealth and states are subject.

Since federation there has been a continuous history of doubt and litigation on the economic powers of the Commonwealth. Interpretation of the Constitution lies in the hands of the High Court of Australia, subject to appeal to the Privy Council. Over the greater part of the life of the Commonwealth judicial interpretation has favored the powers of the Commonwealth vis-à-vis the states. However, the High Court has in a number of cases changed ground over the years. Therefore, one cannot be categorical as to the precise powers of the Commonwealth. All one can do is to set out what the Commonwealth Parliament is able to do at present, in the knowledge that time and circumstances may alter cases. The discussion which follows is limited to those powers which are generally regarded as weapons in the armory of government economic policy.

In this context government economic policy is taken to include measures aimed at influencing the level of economic activity, the stability of prices, the preservation of overseas reserves, the growth of the economy, and its balance. These objectives can be sought, of course, by both the Commonwealth and the states. However, the Australian economy is so integrated that no individual state could pursue an independent policy with any hope of success. Moreover, it would prove quite impossible for the states to act together, because in practice full agreement between the states is extremely difficult to achieve; and even if it could be achieved, six separate governments could not pursue a single policy with any degree of flexibility. It follows that economic policy, in the sense used here, must be the province of the Commonwealth if it is to be effective at all.

The Commonwealth's ability to regulate the general economic welfare of the economy is based essentially on its powers to tax, to raise loans, and to control banking. Although the states have concurrent powers to levy taxation of all kinds, other than customs and excise, it became clear from the early days of the Federation that the Commonwealth would become the dominant tax-raising authority. The tendency for the financial strength of the Commonwealth to grow at the expense of the states culminated during World War II in the arrangements by which uniform income taxation was introduced. Prior to 1942 both Commonwealth and states levied income taxation on individuals and companies. The varying tax structures of the states limited the capacity of the Commonwealth to raise income taxes and thus interfered with the finance of war expenditure during World War II. In 1942 the Commonwealth passed legislation making grants to the states on condition that they vacated the field of income tax. This legislation was challenged before the High Court and upheld. It was originally to be in force only for the duration of the war, but when the war ended it was re-enacted and survived subsequent litigation. The Commonwealth is thus the sole levier of taxes on income. In return it makes grants to the states on the basis of a formula which varies the grants with annual movements in average wages and in state populations, written up by a "betterment factor." In addition the Commonwealth Government has, since 1933, on the advice of the Commonwealth Grants Commission (a statutory board) made special grants to the financially weaker states to enable them to operate their government services at a standard not appreciably below that of the stronger states. The Commonwealth also makes grants for special purposes, e.g., aid for roads and universities. The net effect is that the Commonwealth raises over 80 per cent of all taxation (including local authority rates), and states and local authorities are dependent on Commonwealth grants to the extent of 45 per cent of their current revenues. The Commonwealth's main sources of taxation are income taxes, sales taxes, customs and excise duties, payroll taxes, and estate duties; the states' main sources are motor taxes, stamp duties, probate and succession duties, land taxes, liquor and racing taxes.

The dominance of the Commonwealth extends also to the raising of loans. In 1927, as a result of constitutional amendment, Commonwealth and state public debts were amalgamated and the Commonwealth Government accepted legal (and some financial) responsibility for the state public debts. At the same time the Australian Loan

Council, which had been established informally a few years earlier, was given constitutional authority to co-ordinate the public borrowings of the Commonwealth and the states. The Loan Council consists of the Prime Minister and one other minister of the Commonwealth and the six state premiers. The Prime Minister is chairman and has a deliberative and a casting vote. Unless five states vote against the Commonwealth, the Commonwealth's will must prevail. The Loan Council determines the volume and distribution of all Commonwealth and state loans, other than for defense. For these reasons and because the Commonwealth has power (through the Reserve Bank) to influence the volume of loan raisings, the control of capital funds has virtually passed to the Commonwealth. The Loan Council also exercises some supervision over the loan raisings of semi-governmental authorities (i.e., publicly owned but independently controlled business undertakings). Moreover, in recent years owing to the large amounts to be raised and the tightness of the capital market, the Commonwealth Government has underwritten state loan programs. This has strengthened its position even more.

The Commonwealth has no direct control over the budgets of the states, although the power of the purse is an effective weapon in influencing these budgets. It cannot make direct expenditures on functions which are not within its constitutional powers, but it can make grants to the states, tied to particular forms of expenditure. Nor can it be sure that the states will pursue policies of expansion or contraction in line with its own policy. Thus, in 1951-52, the Commonwealth budget was sharply contractionary, whereas state works programs were at record levels. In addition, political difficulties arise from the Commonwealth's being the main tax-gathering authority, while the states are the main spending authorities. The states spend money which they have no responsibility for raising and are in a position to blame the Commonwealth for their own budgetary shortcomings. Some idea of the division of revenue and expenditure between the Commonwealth and the states can be obtained from Table 5. The figures for the states include local government authorities, which are relatively unimportant in Australia. Included in public works expenditure is the capital expenditure of government business undertakings.

As a consequence of the almost complete financial domination of the Commonwealth over the states, the Commonwealth is able to

TABLE 5. *Revenue and Expenditure of Public Authorities, 1960-61*

	Commonwealth (£ million)	State and Local (£ million)
Revenue		
Taxation	1,409	276
Surplus of business undertakings	37	126
Other	30	41
Total	1,476	443
Transfers from Commonwealth to State and Local	−382	382
Total after transfers	1,094	825
Expenditure		
Expenditure on goods and services		
War and defense	193	—
Public works	86	499
Law, order, and public safety	1	48
Education	3	146
Health, welfare, etc.	7	91
Repatriation	20	—
Immigration	12	—
Development and conservation of national resources	26	27
Civil aviation	11	—
Other	78	76
Total	437	887
Cash social service benefits	411	4
Interest paid	23	164
Other	7	1
Total	878	1,056

Source: Commonwealth of Australia, *National Income and Expenditure*, 1960-61.

use its budget, in conjunction with the loan program, to influence directly private spending from income and public spending. At the same time its powers over banking enable it to influence at least one component of private spending from borrowed funds. Monetary policy is under the control of the Reserve Bank of Australia, but in the ultimate the Bank is subject to the Commonwealth Government. The Reserve Bank requires the trading banks to keep statutory reserve deposits with it, equal to a given fraction of their deposits. The reserve ratio can be varied at the will of the Reserve Bank (subject to certain requirements about notice when the ratio exceeds 25 per cent), and thus the Reserve Bank can influence the liquidity of the trading banks and their lending policies. In addition the Reserve Bank issues directives to the trading banks from time to time, indicating the desirable trend and allocation of bank advances, and fixes interest rates (see pp. 133-134 below).

The Reserve Bank has full control over foreign exchange, acquiring all foreign exchange earned through overseas transactions and determining the rate of exchange. When this has added to it the Commonwealth Government's power to determine tariffs and impose import controls, it is clear that the Commonwealth is in a position to execute policies to preserve overseas reserves. As far as the tariff is concerned, the necessity for new, increased, or reduced duties and for the granting of bounties is investigated by the Tariff Board before action is taken. The Tariff Board, which is a statutory board on which civil service representation is in a minority, advises the government in matters relating to trade and customs and conducts extensive inquiries into claims for new or additional protection and into claims that existing protection is being abused by particular industries. It publishes its findings.

It will appear from the above that in spite of the division of powers between the Commonwealth and the states, the Commonwealth Government is in a position, through its budgetary and monetary policy, to implement economic policies directed towards the objectives listed earlier. Nevertheless, in at least two respects its actions are severely circumscribed. The first relates to the regulation of aggregate spending and the second to prices, wages, and conditions of employment.

As pointed out above, the Commonwealth Government can, through its budget, directly influence government spending and private spending from income. Through the Reserve Bank it can influence the raising of funds from the banking system. But it cannot influence the borrowing of funds from other sources. It is doubtful whether the Commonwealth can control hire-purchase finance and capital issues in general. In fact it has not attempted to do so, except in periods of war, when its defense powers give it power to do almost anything. Consequently there is an appreciable area of spending over which the Commonwealth cannot exercise control, an area which, with the development of new types of financial institutions, has become of increasing importance in recent years.

The Commonwealth has no power to control prices. As far as wages and conditions of employment are concerned, the Constitution has enabled it to set up an independent authority which has acquired considerable influence. Under the Constitution the Commonwealth has power in respect of "conciliation and arbitration for the prevention and settlement of industrial disputes extending beyond the limits of any one State." Under this power the Commonwealth set up the Commonwealth Court of Conciliation and Arbitration in 1904. The Court, whose senior members must have been barristers and who have the status of judges, conducts its affairs in a manner similar to that of a court of law, although many of its functions are clearly legislative rather than judicial.

The wording of this power in the Constitution would seem to limit quite severely the operations of the Court. However, on a number of occasions, the High Court has interpreted this wording so as to extend its application. A "dispute" has come to mean disagreement over a formal log of claims served on either party by the other, and a dispute is "interstate" so long as a dispute in this sense exists simultaneously in two or more states. With widespread unionism on a federal scale and with the tendency for state industrial tribunals to follow Commonwealth awards, the influence of the Commonwealth Conciliation and Arbitration Commission, as it is now called,[3] has become pervasive.[4] The Commission handles disputes covering a wide range of industrial matters, but from the point of view of economic policy its determinations in respect of the level of the general wage structure and standard hours of work are of major importance. In effect, the Commission can in a single determination modify the general level of money wages throughout Australia (see pp. 42-43 below).

The Commission exercises a considerable measure of control in the field of wages policy. But it must be clearly recognized that,

[3] In 1956 the structure of the Commonwealth Court of Conciliation and Arbitration was extensively modified. The judicial functions of the Court (e.g., enforcement and interpretations of awards) have been separated from the conciliation and arbitration functions. The judicial functions are exercised by the Commonwealth Industrial Court and the conciliation and arbitration functions by the Commonwealth Conciliation and Arbitration Commission. In this essay the term Commission will be used to include the Court before 1956 and the Commission thereafter.

[4] See R. J. Hawke, "The Commonwealth Arbitration Court—Legal Tribunal or Economic Legislature?", *University of Western Australia Annual Law Review*, III (1954-56), 422-478, especially pp. 428-449.

although the Commission is a creation of the Commonwealth, the Commonwealth Parliament itself cannot legislate on matters relating to wages and conditions of work. That the Commonwealth has no control over industrial conditions can be easily seen by the not unusual occurrence of the Commission following a policy in respect of wages at variance with the current budgetary and monetary policies of the Commonwealth; e.g., substantial increases in wages were granted in 1959 at a time when a major objective of Commonwealth policy was to keep costs down. Moreover, the several state parliaments can and do legislate on industrial conditions and sometimes do so with the intention of forcing the hand of the Commission, as occurred in 1947 when the state of New South Wales—the largest state—legislated for a forty-hour week, while a hearing on the matter was still in progress before the Commission.

Apart from the matters discussed above, there are three other major facets of economic policy concerning which the Commonwealth apparently has little power. These relate to nationalization of industries, schemes for orderly marketing of primary products, and the control of monopolies and restrictive practices.

The Commonwealth can, of course, establish its own business undertakings in any of the areas in which it has power (for example, banking or air transport); and it has done so. But it cannot nationalize an industry in such a way as to create a government monopoly. This was shown in the attempt to nationalize air transport in 1947, when the legislation was struck down by the Privy Council after appeal from the High Court. Among other things, such nationalization offends against Section 92, for it would prevent businesses from carrying on trade and commerce between the states. It is also doubtful whether any state parliament could nationalize an industry, unless it were a purely intrastate industry.

As far as the provision of schemes for the marketing of primary products is concerned, such schemes invariably conflict with Section 92. This has not prevented the organization of marketing in some cases. The marketing of wheat by the Australian Wheat Board has been made possible by parallel legislation in the Commonwealth and the six states; but even these arrangements are endangered by Section 92, and it would not be possible to prevent wheat moving from one state to another if a drought in one state made it profitable for private growers to transport wheat to another state, rather than to deliver it to the Wheat Board. Similarly, a scheme exists for the marketing of butter and cheese, but it is based on a voluntary agreement and there are circumstances in which it could also break down. Since marketing of all major primary products must involve interstate transactions, neither the Commonwealth nor the states have, in effect, any power to enforce marketing schemes. In passing, it may also be noted that the regulation of interstate road transport is fraught with constitutional difficulties.

Finally, there is considerable doubt as to the Commonwealth's power to legislate against monopolies and restrictive practices. In 1906 the Australian Industries Preservation Act, modeled on the Sherman Antitrust Act, was passed. This was challenged and certain sections were declared invalid. Moreover, difficulties arose before the High Court when prosecution under the Act was attempted. Even though the Act was amended, it has become a dead letter. While it is true that the states have power in this direction—and indeed New South Wales, Queensland, and Western Australia have at various times legislated against unfair profit-taking and unfair methods of trading—it is quite likely that Section 92 would prevent the states taking action against firms or industries in interstate trade and commerce.

In requiring that "trade, commerce and intercourse between the States . . . shall be absolutely free," Section 92 has been effective in preventing governments, both Commonwealth and state, from interference with and regulation and control of a wide range of economic activities. The nationalization of major industries has been made virtually impossible. Thus, there is preserved in the Australian economy an element of laissez faire in the traditional sense.

During the sixty years of federation there has been a growing recognition that, however appropriate was the Constitution to the conditions of 1901, the economic powers of the Commonwealth are insufficient for the pursuit of economic policy in the modern world. The Australian economy is now so integrated and the economies of the states so interdependent that economic policy can be effective only if indivisible. Moreover, the acceptance of the belief that governments must take responsibility for the general economic well-being of the economy makes questions of economic policy the major political issues of our times. The Commonwealth Constitution can be amended only by referenda. Alternatively, powers may be re-

ferred by the states to the Commonwealth. To be effective this requires identical legislation by all states and no subsequent amendment; and this is not a political practicability. Referenda have in
fact proved very difficult to carry. Altogether twenty-four amendments have been the subject of referenda; only four have succeeded.
Although many attempts have been made to widen the economic
powers of the Commonwealth, the only amendments to these powers
which have succeeded have been in respect of the management of
state debts and the provision of social security services. In 1956 the
Commonwealth Parliament set up a committee of both Government
and Opposition members to review the Constitution. It reported in
1959 and recommended extensive amendments.[5] As far as the economic powers are concerned it recommended marked extension of
Commonwealth powers in relation to the terms and conditions of
industrial employment, restrictive trade practices, organized marketing of primary products, capital issues, and hire-purchase. It is not
possible to forecast whether these extensions will eventuate.

The above discussion has concentrated on the powers of the
Commonwealth, because over-all economic policy can be effective
only if it is in the hands of the one federal authority. However, it
is important to avoid the impression that the state governments do
not play an important role in the economic life of the states. Quite
the reverse. The states have virtually exclusive control of public
utilities, education, and health within their own boundaries. Moreover, the development of resources and the encouragement of industry is one of the major preoccupations of state governments. As
can be seen from Table 5 the states are the major spenders of public
money and their influence on day-to-day economic affairs should not
be underestimated.

Although, as has been pointed out above, the Commonwealth
Government has strictly limited powers of economic control, in wartime its powers under the defense power are virtually without restriction. During World War II, the Commonwealth Government
set up an extensive and effective apparatus of control over the detailed operations of the economy. These controls covered manpower, allocation and use of materials, rationing of consumer goods
(meat, butter, tea, sugar, clothing, and petrol), prices and rents, cap-

[5] Commonwealth of Australia, *Report from the Joint Committee on Constitu-*
tional Review, 1959. For matters discussed in this section, see especially chaps.
xiv-xx.

ital issues, banking, exports and imports, marketing of primary products, building, and transport. Most of these controls were dismantled fairly rapidly after the war, partly because constitutional authority for many of them no longer existed once the emergency was over.

Manpower controls ceased early in 1946. Rationing was over by 1950. Capital issues control was abandoned in the same year, although it was reintroduced temporarily during the Korean War (without a great deal of effect). By the early fifties the only important controls remaining related to banking, imports, prices, and rents. The Commonwealth Government possesses constitutional power over banking and imports, and has always exercised some measure of control over them. However, the techniques of Central Bank control and of import licensing were highly developed during the war and have become familiar features of the Australian economy (see pp. 133-134 below).

As far as price and rent controls are concerned, the Commonwealth Government attempted in 1948 to obtain, by referendum, permanent power to control prices and rents. In this it was unsuccessful, and the responsibility for the fixation of prices and rents was assumed by the state governments. The states attempted to co-ordinate their activities by close collaboration, but the difficulties of achieving unanimity were considerable, and the system gradually began to break down. The area of control steadily diminished, and from 1953 to 1956 all states except Queensland and South Australia abandoned price control completely. Control has now been virtually discontinued in Queensland, and it is not extensive in South Australia. On the other hand, rent controls have been maintained to some extent. Unilateral action by individual states is, of course, possible in the market for house-room. Western Australia, Victoria, and Tasmania have now abandoned rent control. It is still relatively stringent in Queensland and South Australia and is severe in New South Wales. Thus, practically nothing remains of the highly planned and centrally controlled war economy of 1942 to 1945.

Political Attitudes

In Australia there are four important political parties: the Liberal party, the Australian Labor party, the Country party, and the Democratic Labor party. Of these the latter two are relatively minor. The Country party represents the interests of primary producers.

Although arithmetically it frequently holds the balance of power between the two major parties, it is ordinarily allied with the Liberal party. At present the Commonwealth Government is a Liberal-Country party coalition, with the Liberal party as the dominant partner. The Democratic Labor party is a breakaway, predominantly Roman Catholic, from the Labor party. It is aggressively anti-communist, but on economic matters has attitudes similar to those of the Labor party. It has to date had little direct influence in Parliament but, by splitting the Labor vote, has for some years prevented a Labor victory in federal elections.

This section is not intended as a description of Australian politics. Rather, it is aimed to outline the *attitudes* of the main political parties on those economic questions which are the subject of this essay. Accordingly, attention will be concentrated on the Liberal and Labor parties. In theory the economic aims of the Liberal and Labor parties are diametrically opposed, the Liberal party standing for free enterprise and the minimum of government interference, the Labor party for the "democratic socialisation of industry, production, distribution and exchange—to the extent necessary to eliminate exploitation and other anti-social features in those fields."[6] In practice, the actions of the two parties indicate relatively minor differences of policy. This is probably due partly to the limitations of practical politics and partly to the restrictions imposed by the Federal Constitution. The electorate is normally evenly divided between non-Labor and Labor supporters, so that the winning of elections depends on wooing a relatively small number of marginal voters. This naturally leads to a watering down of the more extreme elements in the platforms of both parties. As far as the Constitution is concerned, most of the more radical reforms advocated by the Labor party are *ultra vires* and therefore for the time being beyond the realm of practical action.

It follows from this that the influence of the color of the ruling government upon policy is to be seen rather in a bias of policies one way or another than in the natures of the policies themselves. Both parties advocate and attempt to implement policies for full employment and social security. Perhaps Labor's definition of full employment implies slightly "fuller" employment; and Labor in

[6] This is the objective of the Australian Labor party as set out in the party's platform as last amended in June 1958.

the Commonwealth field has shown itself more willing to use direct controls within the constitutional powers. The Liberal party has a bias towards contributory schemes of social security and perhaps has a somewhat narrower conception of social security than the Labor party (see pp. 123-127 below). Both parties are against means tests and aim to abolish them when possible; but this may have a lower priority with Labor than with Liberal.

Labor advocates the nationalization of a number of industries. As has been pointed out above (see p. 27), constitutional factors bar the way. The Liberal party concedes the necessity for public enterprise when any service or business undertaking cannot be financed and operated efficiently by private enterprise and in fact has been active in maintaining public enterprises. But, in general, the Liberal party is prejudiced against nationally owned undertakings and appears to be unsympathetic towards them and without pride in them (see pp. 113-114 below). On the other hand, the Labor party encourages active competition between public and private enterprise in fields where both exist.

The Liberal party is anxious to keep taxation down and reveals a preference for indirect over direct taxation. The Labor party is more concerned about equality of income distribution, and is more willing to implement progressive income and estate taxes and to have greater taxation generally.

Although the Labor party inveighs against monopolies and the Liberal party stands for free enterprise, neither party has in fact shown much interest in attacking monopolistic and restrictive practices in industry and commerce, although quite recently the Liberal Commonwealth Government has promised to investigate the possibility of legislation against restrictive practices.

Both Liberal and Labor parties are protectionist in flavor, although the Liberal party derives support from both commerce and manufacturing and hence tends to be a little schizophrenic on the question of tariffs. However, since the 1920's the notion of "protection all round" has become accepted and there seems to be a tacit understanding that manufacturers should be protected by the tariff, workers by basic wage awards, and farmers by marketing and price-stabilization schemes. The Liberal, Country, and Labor parties all appear to be privy to this understanding.

In the field of industrial relations both main parties support compulsory arbitration and conciliation, although there are wings in both parties showing signs of interest in collective bargaining along the American pattern. Of course, when the government becomes involved in any industrial matter, a Liberal government reveals itself favoring employers' interests and a Labor government favoring employees' interests. Moreover, the Liberal party is much more ready to include in industrial legislation anti-strike clauses and penal clauses for the enforcement of awards.

Parliamentary members of both parties have, by their membership of the Committee on Constitutional Reform (see p. 29 above), indicated their support for extending the economic powers of the Commonwealth. But the Labor party would go a long way farther than the Liberal party, even as far as clothing the Commonwealth with unlimited powers in all fields, with the authority to delegate powers to the states. Thus the Labor party (at least at the federal level) is unificationist in spirit, whereas the Liberal party is more tender of states' rights.

Both parties have supported rapid expansion and economic development in Australia. Indeed the migration program and a number of important developmental schemes were initiated by the Labor party, which held office in the Commonwealth Parliament from 1941 to 1949, and were carried on and extended by the Liberal party, which has been in office since 1949. However opposed the theoretical platforms of the two parties may appear to be, in practice the difference between them appears to be one of emphasis. This is not to say that, in other times and under other constitutional circumstances, essential divergences in matters of economic policy might not be revealed.

Capital and Labor Markets

Capital Market

As has been pointed out above (see p. 17), over the past decade Australia has experienced a very high rate of capital formation. The manner in which the real resources have been made available for this is set out in Table 6.

From this table it can be seen that the finance of investment has been made up of three roughly equal parts—about one-third has

TABLE 6. *Sources and Uses of Savings, 1948-49 to 1960-61*

Sources	Per cent	Uses	Per cent
Overseas capital inflow	11	Gross private investment	60
Undistributed company profits	12	Public authority investment	29
Depreciation allowances	20	Increase in international reserves	2
Public authorities current surplus	23	Increase in stocks	9
Savings through insurance funds	7		
Personal savings	27		
	100		100

Source: Derived from Commonwealth of Australia, *National Income and Expenditure,* 1960-61, and previous issues.

come from personal savings and savings through insurance funds, about one-third from retained company profits and depreciation allowances, and the balance from the current surplus of public authorities and from capital inflow.

Although Australia's investment program has for the most part been based on domestic resources, capital inflow has played an important role, not only by contributing a significant quantity of resources but also by providing Australia with technical know-how and valuable links with major industrial organizations in the most advanced industrial countries. The newest techniques and the facilities of modern industrial research have been made available from parent company to subsidiary and by way of license. This has occurred because most overseas investment in Australia has been direct investment. Almost all the capital inflow has come from the United Kingdom and North America. The United Kingdom share has been rather more than twice the American. United Kingdom investment has been three-quarters direct investment and American investment has been almost wholly direct. Substantial profits have been earned by overseas countries on their Australian investments. Over the past decade these have amounted to about half the capital inflow, but about half of these profits have been ploughed back. Characteristically, American companies have ploughed back relatively more of their profits than United Kingdom ones.

The savings of both public authorities and persons have been high. About three-quarters of public authority investment has been financed from current taxation revenue. This feature of Australian public finance is discussed in more detail below (see p. 128). Personal savings have constituted, on the average, nearly 12 per cent of persons' disposable income, although there have been sharp year-to-year fluctuations associated with fluctuations in farm income. This figure includes retained profits of unincorporated enterprises and the savings involved in the purchase of motor vehicles for private use.

A considerable fraction of the expansion of business enterprise has been financed from internal sources. A survey of about eight hundred public companies for the years 1957-58 and 1958-59, undertaken by the Reserve Bank of Australia,[7] indicated that this fraction was approximately one-third. Of the balance, about one-sixth came from share issues and the rest from outside borrowing of one sort or another.

Prior to World War II, leaving aside the operations of the stock exchanges, the main financial intermediaries in Australia were the banks, both trading and savings, and life assurance companies, building societies, and to a much lesser extent trustee and pastoral companies. Of these the trading banks were the most important. They were the main providers of working capital to commerce and industry and were also of some consequence in the provision of fixed capital. Although the Central Bank, in its postwar directives to the trading banks, has suggested that the banks should restrain their lending for fixed capital, it is still true that the banks play an important role in the financing of private investment in fixed equipment. This continues to be done by way of overdraft rather than by way of long-term loan or direct participation in share issues.

Trading bank advances have, however, undergone a long-term relative decline in their importance in the economy.[8] This has been due partly to the relative growth of the government sector, which does not rely on this type of credit, partly to the growing tendency towards self-finance in business, and partly to the growth of new types of financial intermediaries. In addition, over the past two decades, there has been a switch in the industrial distribution of advances, finance to the manufacturing and housing sectors having in-

[7] See Reserve Bank of Australia, *Statistical Bulletin, Company Supplement,* Jan. 1961.

[8] See H. W. Arndt, *The Australian Trading Banks* (2nd ed.; 1960), pp. 51-57.

creased at the expense of the agricultural and pastoral ones. This can be explained by the relative growth in the manufacturing sector and population growth on the one hand, and the improved debt position of farmers on the other.

Commercial banking in Australia is heavily concentrated (see Table 7). There are only thirteen check-paying banks, with some thousands of branches and agencies. Of these the six main private banks hold over 75 per cent of total assets and the government-owned Commonwealth Trading Bank holds a further 14 per cent. Commercial banking is, however, highly competitive. There is a great deal of competition in the opening of new branches and agencies, in the seeking of new customers and the attraction of existing ones from one bank to another, and in the provision of auxiliary banking services (e.g., investment advice, travel bureaus, etc.). Competition in rates of interest offered on deposit or charged on loans does not exist, since these rates are fixed by the Central Bank. Moreover, competition in the granting of advances is likely to be inhibited

TABLE 7. *Australian Check-Paying Banks*[a]

	Average assets within Australia, June 1960 (£ million)	Number of branches in Australia, June 30, 1959
Bank of New South Wales	440	676
Commonwealth Trading Bank of Australia	278	537
The National Bank of Australasia	275	564
Australia and New Zealand Bank	236	486
The Commercial Banking Company of Sydney	193	365
The Commercial Bank of Australia	192	409
The English, Scottish & Australian Bank	153	344
The Bank of Adelaide	38	82
Major trading banks	1,805	3,463
Other check-paying banks	132	208
Total	1,937	3,671

Source: Australian Banking Statistics, *Commonwealth of Australia Gazette*, No. 55, 1960, p. 2; Commonwealth Bureau of Census and Statistics, *Finance Bulletin*, No. 50, 1958-59, pp. 89-90.
  [a] The Commonwealth Trading Bank is government owned. The other major trading banks are privately owned. The Australia and New Zealand Bank and the English, Scottish and Australian Bank have their head offices in London, are predominantly owned in England, and have their general policy controlled by boards of directors in London, although their day-to-day direction is exercised by their general managers in Melbourne.

from time to time by Central Bank policy. Further reference to the competitive role of government-owned banks is made below (see p. 110). The control exercised by the Reserve Bank of Australia over the trading banks has already been referred to (see p. 24) and is also discussed later in connection with the implementation of general economic policy (see pp. 133-134 below).

Prior to World War II, the combined assets of savings banks and life assurance companies were roughly the same as those of the trading banks. They now exceed them by quite an appreciable margin.[9] Their main avenues for investment have always been public authority securities and housing loans, although in recent years the assurance companies have been turning towards investment in company debentures, preference shares, and even ordinary shares.[10]

The savings banks are ten in number, (see Table 8), and the number active in any one state varies between only two and five (see p. 110 below), but they compete actively for new accounts. Four are government-owned, and these account for 80 per cent of deposits. The three main private ones are offshoots of private trading banks, formed to gain the same advantages with respect to the winning of new accounts which accrue to the Commonwealth Trading Bank through its association with the Commonwealth Savings Bank.

There are over thirty life offices operating in Australia, but five offices do 90 per cent of the business (see Table 9). Of these, all but one are mutual. Competition for new business is very keen, but as with the savings banks there is no great competition in the granting of loans for housing, the demand for these loans being so high.

Since the end of World War II there has been a remarkable growth of diversified financial intermediaries and of sophistication in the capital market (see Table 10). Perhaps the most dramatic development has been the growth of finance houses, dealing mainly in hire-purchase finance. At the end of the war hire-purchase finance was of little importance. By the end of 1960 the net balances outstanding to hire-purchase companies were over 40 per cent of the level of trading bank advances. The hire-purchase companies were initially financed mainly by bank overdraft. As their demand for

[9] See R. R. Hirst, "The Place of Banking in the Capital Market," in *Fifth Summer School of Business Administration* (University of Adelaide, 1960), p. 37.

[10] See A. R. Hall, "Institutional Investment in Listed Company Securities," *Economic Record*, XXXIV (1958), 375-389.

TABLE 8. *Australian Savings Banks*

	Assets within Australia at the end of June 1960 (£ million)
Commonwealth Government	
Commonwealth Savings Bank of Australia	834
State Government	
The State Savings Bank of Victoria	319
The Savings Bank of South Australia	131
The Rural and Industries Bank of Western Australia	6
Trustee	
The Hobart Savings Bank	15
The Launceston Bank for Savings	13
*Private**	
Bank of New South Wales Savings Bank	149
Australia & New Zealand Savings Bank	82
Commercial Banking Company Savings Bank	47
Total	1,596

Source: Commonwealth of Australia Gazette, No. 55, 1960, Australian Banking Statistics.
*The English, Scottish, and Australian Savings Bank Ltd. began operations September 29, 1961.

TABLE 9. *Australian Life Assurance Companies*

	Total assets at balancing date, 1958-59 (£ million)
Australian Mutual Provident Society	408
National Mutual Life Association of Australasia Ltd.	165
The Mutual Life and Citizens Assurance Company Ltd.[a]	155
Colonial Mutual Life Assurance Society Ltd.	144
Australasian Temperance and General Mutual Life Assurance Society Ltd.	134
Major life assurance companies	1,006
Other	115
Total	1,121

Source: Commonwealth of Australia, *Fourteenth Annual Report of the Insurance Commissioner*, 1960, p. 11.
[a] This company has private shareholders. The other four major companies are mutual.

TABLE 10. *Assets of Certain Financial Institutions*[a]
Australia 1953 and 1958

	June 1953 (£ million)	June 1958 (£ million)
Trading banks	1,548	1,791
Savings banks	1,000	1,358
Life insurance offices	595	851
Pension funds	235	438
Hire-purchase and other instalment credit companies	89	364
Building societies	121	198
Non-life insurance offices	101	168
Pastoral finance companies	129	166
Unit trusts and investment companies	19	51
Friendly and health societies	28	43

Source: Reserve Bank of Australia Report, 1960, p. 18.
[a] Total assets in respect of Australian business.

finance grew and as the Central Bank discouraged the extension of overdrafts to them, they came to rely more and more on the issues of debentures and notes on the open market. Such was the profitability of their business that they could offer high rates of interest. As a result, the monetary authorities were forced to permit the rate on government securities to rise, despite their desire to hold this rate down, thus illustrating the difficulty of attempting to seal off the capital market into watertight compartments. There are over one thousand hire-purchase companies, but nearly 90 per cent of hire-purchase business is handled by the top eight firms (see Table 11). Although the larger firms set the tone of the industry, there is strong competition both for funds and for providing finance to purchasers. This competition extends to rates of interest offered and charged. It is of interest to note that all the major private trading banks have associated themselves with a finance company, not only because of the profitability of hire-purchase business, but also because the connection with a hire-purchase company brings potential customers into contact with the trading bank.

There has also been a considerable growth over the past fifteen years of building and investment societies, of superannuation funds, and of unit investment trusts. The building and investment societies are financed very heavily from bank overdraft, and their investment

TABLE 11. *Australian Hire-Purchase Companies*

	Balances outstanding at balancing date in 1960[a] (£ million)	Major shareholdings	
		Shareholder	Per cent
Industrial Acceptance Holdings Ltd.	88	A.N.Z. Bank	14.3
Custom Credit Corporation Ltd.	84	National Bank	40
Australian Guarantee Corporation Ltd.	66	Bank of N. S.W.	40
Esanda Ltd.	28	E.S. & A. Bank	100
General Motors Acceptance Corporation, Australia	28	G.M.A.C. (United States)	100
Lombard Australia Ltd.	25	Lombard Bank (London)	60
General Credits Ltd.	24	Commercial Bank	45
Commercial & General Acceptance Ltd.	24	Commercial Banking Co. of Sydney	40
Major hire-purchase companies[b]	367[c]		
Other	55		
Total	422		

Sources: Sydney Stock Exchange Research and Statistical Bureau, *Investment Service*; Industrial Acceptance Holdings Ltd., *Annual Report and Accounts 1960*; General Motors Acceptance Corporation, Australia, *Prospectus, 15th July 1960*; Commonwealth Bureau of Census and Statistics, *Retail Hire Purchase Operations of Finance Businesses*, Feb. 1961.

[a] The balancing dates vary from company to company, and hence are not absolutely comparable. Total balances outstanding are as at June 30, 1960.

[b] Six of the eight major trading banks are associated with one or other of the major hire-purchase companies. Of the other two, the Bank of Adelaide has a 40 per cent shareholding in Finance Corporation of Australia Ltd., whose balances outstanding at the balancing date in 1960 were £15m., and the Commonwealth Trading Bank has a sister institution under the aegis of the Commonwealth Banking Corporation, namely, the Commonwealth Development Bank, whose balances outstanding were £18m.

[c] These figures include a small component of loans in a form other than hire-purchase, and are not absolutely comparable with the figure for total balances outstanding.

is almost solely in advances on mortgage for housing purposes. The superannuation funds are split about equally between public authority and private. Of these, the former, with the exception of the New South Wales State Superannuation Fund, invest entirely in the government securities, but the latter have tended to invest in company shares and debentures as well as in the normal "trustee" securities. The unit investment trusts, some of which have trading bank associates, invest in stock securities.

With the general expansion of the Australian economy there has been a growth in the volume of new issues coming on to the stock exchanges, and, associated with this, the development of issuing houses. The demand for equity shares has been high, as means both for avoiding taxation—there is no capital-gains tax in Australia—and for hedging against inflation. As a consequence share prices have risen steadily since the end of World War II, with only minor breaks in the trend. Yields have been bid to low levels. Over the years 1957-58 to 1959-60, there has been a marked switch in company finance to debentures, notes, and deposits; and the annual volume of new money raised by these means has been several times that raised by equity issues, whereas formerly fixed interest issues were of negligible importance. Finance by fixed interest debt has attractions, particularly as interest payments are charged against profits, before tax is assessed.

A wide range of debentures and notes with varying terms and some with rights to convert to shares is now available to the investing public. Nevertheless, the average gearing ratio (or leverage, i.e., ratio of fixed interest debt to equity) of Australian companies probably remains lower than in the United States.[11]

The market for government securities in Australia has been a narrow one. Moreover, there has been no public dealing in Treasury Bills. Several steps have been taken recently to widen this market. The most important of these was the establishment early in 1959 of a short-term money market. Nine discount houses have been approved by the Reserve Bank as money market dealers. These dealers are restricted to investing funds lodged with them (at call or for short periods) in government securities having a maturity of not longer than three years, and they have the right to rediscount these securities with the Reserve Bank up to the limit of the line of credit allotted to them. In the early days of the market, its main source of funds was from the trading banks, but the public has steadily becomes a much larger depositor with the market. The market, which is highly competitive, has grown rapidly and its growth is at present limited only by the shortage of suitable short-term government paper. Not only has this development widened the market for government securities, but it has also helped to divert some funds from the private

[11] See H. W. Arndt, *The Banks and the Capital Market* (E.S. & A. Research Lecture, University of Queensland, 1960), pp. 9-10.

to the public sector. In addition the Commonwealth Treasury has added to the diversity of government paper available by establishing first Special Bonds for the small investor which can be cashed at par or at a small premium according to the time from maturity; and secondly seasonal notes with a ninety-day currency, which are available to the public in the season of flush liquidity (September to March), when export receipts are seasonally high and tax revenues lag behind expenditures.

The recent diversification of the capital market has undoubtedly been in response to the rapid growth of the economy and the need for institutions to mobilize the financial resources required for a high rate of capital formation. The private trading banks, which in the past were the dominant financial institutions, have played an important role in this diversification by expanding their own interests directly into savings banking and indirectly into hire-purchase, unit-trusts, and development banking. In this they have shown vigor— a vigor stimulated by competition from the government-owned Commonwealth Trading Bank. The total effect of these postwar developments has certainly been to increase greatly the competitiveness and to reduce the imperfection of the capital market. On the other hand, there still remain considerable imperfections. The public reporting of company results is of poor quality and often misleading. It is certainly inferior to that in the United States and Canada. This is due partly to the limited requirements of the various Companies Acts (each state has its own act) and partly to the absence of any regulatory body comparable to the United States Securities and Exchange Commission. Decisions of the investing public must usually be based on published reports, often concealing the true profit and asset position of the company. As a result many inexperienced investors prefer market leaders, which consequently obtain an excessive share of the funds flowing into the market. Moreover, the new and small business and the farmer have inadequate access to capital funds. Probably the major imperfection in the capital market lies in this area. In 1946 the Commonwealth Government created the Industrial Finance Department of the Commonwealth Bank to assist in the establishment and development of industrial undertakings. In 1959 the Commonwealth Development Bank was established to take over this work and that of the Mortgage Bank Department, which specialized in long-term loans to primary producers. The Development Bank is intended to take a more active role in the provision of finance to promising enterprises where finance would not otherwise be available. In addition there are private ventures in the field of development banking. The two most important of these specialized institutions have trading banks as shareholders.

In the fifties one consequence of the diversification of the capital market has been the diversion of funds from low-yielding government loans to high-yielding industrial and financial fixed interest securities. Public capital formation would have lagged seriously if there had not been a determined effort to finance the greater part of it from revenue. The increased perfection of the capital market has certainly tended to switch finance to the points of greatest private return. This switch has not necessarily accorded with social priorities. The steps taken to widen the bond market, noted above, are an attempt to rectify this, and they have had a measure of success.

A second consequence has been that monetary policy, operating as it does upon the liquidity of the trading banks, has been working in a steadily decreasing area of the capital market. It is therefore working with greater severity on that part of the market which it can influence. This is perhaps partly cause and partly effect. Monetary policy has on the whole been restrictive in the postwar period. To the extent to which it has clamped down on the trading banks, new institutions for organizing finance have evolved. The Central Bank, by the nature of things, operates on the quantity of money, but it cannot prevent the activation of idle deposits. Indeed the velocity of circulation of money has increased substantially.[12] This suggests that monetary policy ought to operate over the whole gamut of the capital market rather than on the banking system alone. As has been pointed out above (see p. 25), in Australia this involves constitutional difficulties.

Labor Market

Industrial relations in Australia operate in a setting of compulsory arbitration. During the past sixty or seventy years there has developed both on Commonwealth and on state levels an elaborate system of tribunals for handling industrial disputes. Reference has already been made to the Commonwealth Conciliation and Arbitration Com-

[12] See R. R. Hirst, *op. cit.*, p. 47.

mission (see pp. 25-26 above). Similar tribunals operate under state legislation in all states, except in Victoria and Tasmania, where systems of wage boards on an industry basis and including employer and employee representatives have been established.

Many disputes are settled by direct negotiation between the parties involved, but practically all disputes of any magnitude are handled by one industrial tribunal or another. The disputes reach the tribunal either on the motion of one or other party or by way of the tribunal itself taking cognizance of the dispute. Although there is a good deal of emphasis on conciliation in the legislation governing the tribunals, actually they operate more as arbitral bodies. Their determinations are embodied in awards, which are legally binding on the parties subject to them. In practice, this means that an award for a particular industry is binding on all employees and employers in that industry, irrespective of whether any employer or employee is or is not a member of the respective organizations involved in the hearing leading to the award.

The rights of employees to strike are circumscribed. The position differs according to the legislation under which the relevant tribunal is operating. It is commonly illegal to strike against an award or to strike during the hearing of a dispute. In some states certain types of employees (e.g., government employees) may not strike. Restrictions on the right to strike under Commonwealth laws are limited to employees' organizations registered with the Commonwealth tribunal, and the usual way to discipline such an organization is to impose a fine on it. The Commonwealth tribunal also has power to insure that the rules of employee and employer organizations registered with it conform to certain standards and it may, under certain circumstances, conduct an election of office-bearers of a union. In practice strikes take place readily enough and fines are frequently imposed on the unions concerned. The industrial scene has been relatively peaceful during the past few years, less than one-fifth of one per cent of working time having been lost in strikes.

Although a certain amount of direct employer-employee collective bargaining has taken place, particularly in recent years, it is comparatively unimportant (an exception is the metal mining industry at Broken Hill). Even where collective bargaining arrangements operate (for example, in paper, printing, brewing, and building), they operate within the shadow of industrial tribunals and the awards of these tribunals have frequently formed the basis for the agreements.[13] The influence of arbitration is virtually complete. About 90 per cent of all wage and salary earners work under awards. Within this area the Commonwealth Conciliation and Arbitration Commission is of predominant importance, not only because its awards directly cover a large proportion of employees but also because state tribunals frequently follow Commonwealth determinations.

The arbitration system has itself encouraged the rapid growth of both employee and employer organizations, and the establishment of Commonwealth industrial jurisdiction has promoted the development of federal or interstate organizations. In 1901 6 per cent of wage and salary earners were members of unions. This had grown to over 50 per cent by 1921, and the percentage at present stands at 60 per cent: 65 per cent of male and 41 per cent of female employees. In the past decade there has been no great relative growth. Unionism has thus proceeded further than in the United Kingdom or the United States.[14]

Although organization on an industrial basis is an aim of many unions, craft unions persist and many unions cut across industrial divisions. Very often several, and sometimes many, unions are involved in one industry. Unions are of three main classes: local independent, state, and interstate. Virtually all important unions are interstate ones, nearly 90 per cent of union members being members of unions operating in two or more states. Although Australian unions are not large by British or American standards, within the Australian structure large unions are dominant. Three-quarters of union members are members of unions with 10,000 members or more, and one-quarter are members of unions with 50,000 members or more. In total there are 370 unions but the 18 largest contain half the total membership. Within states, most unions are affiliated with a state labor council, usually known as the Trades Hall Council. The THC formulates union policy and concerns itself with the conduct of disputes involving more than one union. On the federal level, all important unions with one exception—the Australian Workers' Union—are affiliated with the Australian Council of Trade Unions.

[13] J. E. Isaac, "The Prospects for Collective Bargaining in Australia," *Economic Record*, XXXIV (1958), 347.

[14] K. F. Walker, "Arbitration in a New Key," *Economic Record*, XXXIII (1957), 60-71.

The main practical function of the ACTU is to control and direct interstate industrial disputes.

On the employers' side many associations exist. Many of these are trade associations and have little interest in industrial relations. Like the trade unions they are organized on a state and federal basis. It is the state and federal bodies which are important in the sphere of industrial relations. The three most important organizations on the federal level are the Associated Chamber of Manufacturers, the Australian Council of Employers' Federations, and the Australian Metal Industries Association. These three organizations, with others, form a national employers' group, whose structure and composition alter from time to time.

The trade union movement in Australia is one of long traditions and great strength and solidarity. From it sprang the Australian Labor party, when the failure of pressure at the industrial level in the latter part of the nineteenth century caused the unions to look to political action as a means for securing their economic objectives. The unions have remained the main support for the Labor party and its main inspiration, and the links between unionism and political labor have remained very close. Indeed, in some areas the unions have made their principal gains through legislative action at state level, for example, in relation to hours of work, workers' compensation, and long service leave. Thus the unions have worked through two main avenues—political action and the system of industrial arbitration. Their influence on the labor market has been within this framework rather than through face-to-face conflict with employers at the factory or company level. This contrasts sharply with American experience.

Continuous and almost automatic resort to arbitration machinery has lowered the sense of responsibility on the part of both unions and employers in the settlement of disputes. The onus for settlement is placed on the industrial tribunal. Both parties are encouraged to make extravagant claims and to take attitudes without any feeling of compulsion towards compromise. When the award does not suit, the tribunal can be blamed. The skills of negotiation combined with a realistic appreciation of the possible limits of bargaining, so necessary in collective bargaining on the American pattern, are replaced by the skills of advocacy. Perhaps this is one of the main reasons why both employees and employers have made little attempt to build up economic and statistical intelligence and research services, and have relied in their major cases on lawyers as their advocates. Whatever the reason, both parties run their organizations "on the cheap," and the unions, in particular, depend on underpaid and underassisted union secretaries.

Traditionally Australian trade unionism has been restrictive in outlook. It has emphasized the conflict between labor and capital and has concentrated on shares of production rather than on the size of production. It has feared technical progress and opposed wage incentives. These attitudes were, no doubt, born out of the struggles of unionism in the 1890's and the high levels of unemployment experienced in Australia in the 1930's. With the modern era of full employment and rapid economic growth, these attitudes have changed in fact, even though some unionists pay lip service to them. Although traditionally against large-scale migration, the trade union movement has supported the migration program. Indeed the program would not have been possible without its support. The trade union movement now tolerates wage incentive schemes, which are quite widespread. The attitude of trade unionism is certainly less restrictive than it has been in the past.

The Australian system of widespread unionism and industrial arbitration has imparted a uniformity into conditions of employment over the Australian economy, which is best exemplified in the way in which the general level of wages is determined. The chief influence determining the general level of wages is the Commonwealth Conciliation and Arbitration Commission. The Australian wage structure is dominated by two concepts: the basic wage and margins. The basic wage is the minimum wage which can be paid to an unskilled worker. Margins are margins above the basic wage for skill or for special circumstances attaching to a particular occupation. These concepts are applied not only to wage earners but to higher paid administrative and professional employees whose margins may be several times the basic wage itself. From time to time the Arbitration Commission holds a basic wage inquiry and determines the basic wage. In these inquiries the leading protagonists are the ACTU (employees) and the National Employers' Organization. Strictly speaking, the Commission's award relates only to the parties to the dispute which initiated the inquiry; but in fact the influence of the award extends to the whole wage structure, with virtually no lags in the case of the basic wage and with lags of up to perhaps one year in the case of margins.

The first basic wage was declared in 1907 by Mr. Justice Higgins at a level which he regarded as appropriate to "the normal needs of the average employee, regarded as a human being living in a civilized community." This set the tone for the determinations for the next twenty-five years, which asserted that "needs" was the principle used in the setting of the basic wage. Moreover, to preserve the real value of the basic wage the Commission provided for its automatic adjustment, at first annually and later quarterly, by tying it to a retail prices index number. Automatic adjustment operated from 1921 to 1953.

In spite of assertions to the contrary, it is clear that the Commission did pay attention to the capacity of industry to pay a given level of wages, even in the early days. In the thirties references to the two principles of "needs" and "capacity to pay" are to be found in the Commission's determinations, but by the fifties it became clear that the Commission was being guided by the capacity criterion. This was made explicit in the 1953 hearing, in which the Commission intimated that it would pay attention mainly to such matters as employment, investment, production and productivity, overseas trade, overseas balances, the competitive position of secondary industry, and retail trade. The Commission has on some occasions felt constrained to take into account the consequences of its actions on the general state of the economy, but at other times it has regarded its main job to be the settlement of industrial disputes. Since 1956 basic wage inquiries have been held annually.

The marginal structure over and above the basic wage is in detail the result of many individual determinations, but the general level of the structure is, in fact, determined from time to time by awards covering the metal trades, since these are regarded as leading cases. Metal trades hearings are conducted quite independently of basic wage inquiries and occur less frequently, the last four major margins awards being in 1937, 1947, 1954, and 1959. Nevertheless, they just as surely affect the general level of wages.

The net effect of the all pervasive influence of the Commonwealth Arbitration Commission in this matter of wages is that, at fairly frequent intervals, the whole structure of Australian wages is shifted bodily, so there is substantially uniform treatment of all wage and salary earners. The consequences of this on price levels and on general economic policy is discussed in detail on pp. 135-136 below.

This uniformity of treatment also extends, in one important sense, to the relative wage structure. This structure is the result of attaching margins of various kinds to particular occupations. It has been built up as a consequence of very many awards relating to individual occupations, although, as pointed out above, the absolute level of margins is usually the consequence of a decision relating to the metal trades. Particular margins are modified from time to time in relation to the "work value" of the job, which presumably reflects the demand and supply situation, or to its onerousness; but changes in margins applied to one industry are usually quickly reflected in changes in similar occupations in other industries, on the grounds of "wage justice." The result is that the relative marginal structure can be modified only gradually and that a given occupation will attract similar award wages in different industries and locations.

The wage rates referred to in the preceding paragraphs are award wage rates; that is, they are legally prescribed minima. Actual wage rates may differ from them because of over-award payments or bonuses; and actual earnings may differ from actual wage rates because of the working of overtime. When labor is plentiful, actual earnings and award rates will be close together, but a shortage of labor in general will result in an upward drift of earnings above award rates. This has in fact happened since the end of World War II: award wages have risen by about 190 per cent, but average earnings have risen by 260 per cent. In real terms, this amounts to an annual rate of increase of about one per cent for award wages and two-and-a-quarter per cent for average earnings. Shortages of particular kinds of labor, or of labor in particular industries, will also cause the relative wage structure to differ from the structure of award wages. Thus, despite the high degree of institutionalization of the Australian wage structure, the ordinary forces of supply and demand do have some impact on the structure, indirectly through their influence on the determinations of industrial tribunals and directly through the divergences which may arise between actual earnings and award rates.

Moreover, in two respects the Australian system may produce a wage structure nearer to that which would obtain in a competitive and perfect labor market than in a system of collective bargaining on an industry or company basis. First, the variability of rates of pay for given jobs tends to be relatively less than under a system of collective bargaining, so that there is a greater tendency for the values of the marginal product of given kinds of labor to equalize. Secondly, it is less likely that employees and employers in particular industries will be in a position to exercise joint monopolistic power against the rest of the community by keeping prices high and sharing out the monopoly profits.

Income Distribution

Nothing definite can be said about the distribution of incomes by size. Information is available for taxation statistics on the nominal distribution of incomes by grade of actual income; but it is dangerous to draw any conclusions from these, both because of tax evasion and because there are various practices as a result of which nominal incomes understate effective incomes (e.g., expense accounts, provision of cars and housing to executives, concessions to farmers, schemes for converting income into capital gains, etc.). These practices appear to have grown in recent years and naturally are more common and more effective in the higher income groups. Moreover, no great meaning can be attached to the size-distribution of income, unless incomes are reckoned *minus* taxation of all kinds and *plus* cash social service benefits and other beneficial government expenditure. Unfortunately, no definitive work on these problems has been done in Australia.

However, there are several factors which must have contributed to a greater equality of income since prewar. First, the elimination of mass unemployment (the percentage unemployed stood at nearly 10 per cent in the immediate prewar years) has removed a large very-low-income segment from the income distribution. Secondly, farm incomes, although falling in recent years, are still somewhat higher than in the prewar period; the relative weight of low-income farmers has thus been reduced (see Table 13). Thirdly, the incidence of direct taxation, which is progressive in character, has increased relatively to that of indirect taxation. This was markedly so between 1938-39 and 1948-49. Since 1948-49 there has been some reversal of this trend. Finally, there has been an appreciable increase in cash social security benefits. The latter two points are illustrated in Table 12. On the other hand, the very high rate of economic devel-

TABLE 12. *Taxation and Cash Social Service Benefits,*
1938-39 to 1960-61
(Per cent)

	Indirect taxes, less subsidies, as a proportion of gross national product	Direct taxes as a proportion of national income	Cash social service benefits as a proportion of national income
1938-39	9.9	6.3	3.9
1939-40	10.0	6.7	3.6
1940-41	10.2	9.5	3.5
1941-42	10.3	11.5	3.8
1942-43	10.2	12.8	3.8
1943-44	8.7	15.1	3.9
1944-45	8.7	18.1	4.2
1945-46	8.9	17.5	5.3
1946-47	10.6	16.0	6.1
1947-48	8.7	14.0	5.3
1948-49	9.7	14.6	5.4
1949-50	9.5	12.8	5.2
1950-51	8.2	15.0	4.7
1951-52	10.8	17.4	5.3
1952-53	9.8	16.1	5.8
1953-54	10.2	14.4	5.8
1954-55	10.3	13.6	5.9
1955-56	10.4	13.7	6.1
1956-57	10.8	13.8	6.0
1957-58	11.6	14.7	6.7
1958-59	11.3	12.9	6.9
1959-60	11.4	12.9	6.7
1960-61	11.5	14.7	6.1

Source: Derived from Commonwealth of Australia, *National Income and Expenditure,*
1960-61, and previous issues.

opment which has obtained during the past decade and the speculative
boom in equities and real estate at the end of the fifties have undoubtedly fostered the creation of many large private fortunes. But
these are unlikely to have amounted to a great deal in the aggregate.

The distribution of national income by factor shares has revealed
an interesting pattern over the past twenty years. This is shown in
Table 13.

The most striking features of this table are the great instability
in the share of national income going to farms and the marked decline in the net rent and interest component. The former reflects

TABLE 13. *Distribution of National Income, 1938-39 to 1960-61*
(Per cent)

| | Share in national income | | | | | | Ratio of wages and salaries to non-farm national income |
	Wages and salaries	Company income	Farm income	Unincorporated business income	Net revenue of public authority business under-takings	Net rent and interest	
1938-39	57.0	10.8	5.6	10.8	4.1	11.8	60.5
1939-40	53.5	11.6	10.3	9.5	4.1	10.9	59.7
1940-41	58.2	11.6	6.5	8.9	4.4	10.3	62.3
1941-42	60.9	10.7	8.3	7.1	4.3	8.9	66.3
1942-43	61.9	9.9	9.8	6.3	4.7	7.5	68.6
1943-44	62.2	10.5	9.7	6.0	4.2	7.3	68.9
1944-45	63.2	10.6	8.5	6.2	3.9	7.5	69.1
1945-46	60.5	10.3	11.4	7.6	2.9	7.3	68.3
1946-47	56.1	11.6	12.6	10.8	1.7	7.2	64.2
1947-48	51.6	10.8	19.9	10.7	1.0	6.0	64.4
1948-49	54.5	10.9	16.3	11.5	0.5	5.7	65.1
1949-50	53.1	10.9	19.3	11.3	0.3	5.1	65.8
1950-51	49.2	12.3	24.1	10.3	—	4.2	64.8
1951-52	58.8	11.5	13.4	11.9	—	4.4	67.9
1952-53	57.8	10.5	15.8	11.2	0.2	4.5	68.6
1953-54	58.2	12.2	12.9	11.2	0.8	4.7	66.8
1954-55	59.2	12.5	10.8	11.5	0.8	5.1	66.4
1955-56	60.3	12.3	10.0	11.3	0.7	5.4	67.0
1956-57	59.3	12.5	10.9	10.8	1.0	5.5	66.5
1957-58	62.0	12.3	7.4	10.8	1.3	6.2	66.9
1958-59	60.2	12.6	9.0	10.4	1.5	6.3	66.1
1959-60	60.1	13.4	8.5	10.1	1.6	6.3	65.7
1960-61	61.3	12.6	8.0	9.5	1.9	6.7	66.6

Source: Derived from Commonwealth of Australia, *National Income and Expenditure,* 1960-61, and previous issues.

the vagaries of the seasons and the swings of world primary produce prices. The latter is the consequence of the wartime legacy of control over interest rates and rents. During the past eight years interest rates have been rising and rent decontrol proceeding. The rent and interest component is rising, but it is still well below its prewar level.

The share of company and unincorporated business income (with the exception of war years) has been relatively steady, with a slight upward trend in the former, and a downward movement over the past six or seven years in the latter. Wages and salaries as a proportion of national income have fluctuated during the period covered by the table, but the fluctuations can be attributed either to the special circumstances of the war economy or to the effect of booms in farm income. There is no evidence of any trend. When wages and salaries are taken as a proportion of non-farm national income, they show remarkable stability from 1948-49 onwards, in spite of the substantial increase in real production over the period and the great inflation of money values.

Does this mean that trade unionism in Australia has not succeeded in securing a greater share of the national income for its members? The difficulties in interpreting the concept of "labor's share in the national income" are well known. Notwithstanding this, it must be recorded that there is, in fact, no convincing statistical evidence of any radical change in this share over the past fifty years during which trade unionism has established its power and authority.[15] Year-to-year fluctuations can be discerned, but no clear trend. In other words, real wages have, on the average, moved with changes in productivity.

Indeed in the present Australian institutional setting it is very doubtful whether the pre-tax distribution of income can be much affected by changes in money wages, except in the short-run. To illustrate this, assume that productivity is unchanging and suppose that money wages in general are increased as the result of an industrial award. This will normally be passed on in higher prices. There are however two sectors which cannot determine their prices freely. One of these consists of industries competing with imported goods, the other of industries selling products (mainly primary products) on the world market. But even in the short-run, competition from imports is likely to be more nominal than real, since the need for equilibrium in the balance of payments must cause the authorities to limit imports either by exchange-rate or tariff manipulation or by import controls. Consequently, at best, it is unlikely that real wages can be increased at the expense of real profits. On the other hand, they can, at least in the short run, be increased at the expense of real farm income. Real income can be shifted from the farm to the wage-

[15] See H. P. Brown, "The Composition of Personal Income," *Economic Record*, XXXV (1949), 18-36; and B. M. Cheek, "Profit Margins and Wages Shares in Australian Manufactures, 1945-55," *Economic Record*, XLIII (1957), 191-215.

earning sector by raising money wages. However, in the longer run this too may affect the balance of payments deleteriously, as the profitability of export production falls. This would require balance-of-payments action which would tend to restore the original distribution of income between the three main sectors of farms, business, and labor.

Nevertheless, it would be quite wrong to suppose that the consolidation of the power of organized labor has had no effect on the distribution of welfare. First, organized labor can and has modified the distribution of income within the labor sector, as between male and female, adult and junior, skilled and unskilled. Thus, over the past decade there has been some evening up of differentials. The female basic wage, which had previously been set at 56 per cent of the male wage, was fixed at 75 per cent in 1950. Between 1947 and 1954 there was a reduction in the inequality of margins for skills as between different degrees of skill, although since 1954 the basic wage for unskilled workers has risen less than other wages. Juvenile wages have also been raised relatively to adult rates. Secondly, organized labor has eliminated pockets of abnormally low-paid labor; in particular, it has rectified the balance of power between weak and ill-organized groups and their employers. The Australian system of compulsory arbitration has especially facilitated this. Weak unions can avail themselves of industrial tribunals as readily as strong unions, and awards apply equally to union and non-union employees. Thirdly, it has made available a comprehensive system for the policing of awards by union officials, so that employers must conform to awards in respect of wages and conditions of employment. Fourthly, it has, through political action, brought about reduced hours of work, improved factory conditions, long-service leave, and other fringe benefits. Finally, it has, again through political action, had an important influence on the structure of the tax system and on social security programs. It is in these directions, rather than through any impact on the nominal distribution of income, that organized labor in Australia has exerted an influence on the balance of power between capital and labor.

Business Organization[16]

Ownership and Control

It has already been stressed that the principal characteristic of the purely competitive laissez-faire model is its automaticity. In such a model the decisions of the firm are constrained by market pressures: the so-called decision-making unit has negligible decision-making powers. In Australia pure competition exists only in agricultural production, but a similar absence of market power is characteristic of much of the small business sector of the economy. It is arguable, indeed, that this small business situation—oligopolistic or not—is the typical non-agricultural market situation of classical economics. In Australia the small business sector consists chiefly of the service trades, the professions, the greater part of retailing, and some sections of building and construction. The usual forms of legal organization are the sole proprietorship, the partnership, and the proprietary (private) company. With some exceptions (chiefly the professions) these are areas characterized by low barriers to entry and a consequent high turnover of firms. Even where markets are oligopolistic there will be a continual pressure on firms to behave in a profit-maximizing (or loss-minimizing) manner: to produce with greatest internal efficiency, given the state of knowledge and the availability of resources, and to choose the "right" price-output policy for survival. Whether this profit-maximizing behavior will be the most socially desirable behavior, in particular whether it will lead to the "best" structure of industry, is another matter. All that is stressed for the moment is the lack of discretionary power in the hands of the individual firm. It follows that in small business, no less than in pure competition, an examination of the pattern of control within the firm is unnecessary to explain its behavior.

The corporate sector of the economy is altogether different. In Australia this is largely made up of manufacturing, mining, finance, large-scale retailing, and large-scale construction; for few public utilities and only some means of transportation are privately owned. The greater part of this corporate sector (in terms of employment or value added) consists of firms in oligopolistic or monopolistic posi-

---

[16] Unless a specific source is given, all tables in this section have been specially compiled for this essay.

tions, protected by high to moderate barriers to entry, firms, more-over, which are frequently large in absolute size and in relation to the total economy. The discretionary power of such firms with respect to investment, pricing and production policy, research and innovation, product variation and advertising, will be considerable. Within quite wide limits the market will permit managements to choose their own ends: profit-maximizing, empire-building, the quiet life, good labor relations, fairness to customers and suppliers, and so on. Yet while the market will permit this, shareholders may not. For the greater the degree of shareholder control, the greater the weight given to "profit maximization," although it must be emphasized that the precise content of this phrase will depend upon the time horizon and attitude to risks of shareholders and upon market circumstances. The question arises, then, as to what extent the managements of Australian joint-stock companies act independently of effective control by their shareholders.

This is one of the few aspects of Australian industrial organization of which a systematic study has been made. E. L. Wheelwright examined the ownership and control of a selection of large companies in 1953.[17] His procedure was to examine the share registers of 102 of the largest public companies registered in Australia, mostly listed on Australian stock exchanges. Some of the largest companies operating in Australia are registered overseas or are unlisted subsidiaries of companies registered overseas. Nevertheless, Wheelwright's 102 companies are an important segment of the corporate sector. If taxable income and dividends declared are reckoned to be a reasonable indication of firm size, then these companies (including subsidiaries) accounted for close to 40 per cent of the corporate sector. In addition their capital amounted to over half the capital of all companies listed on the Sydney Stock Exchange.

Not unexpectedly, Wheelwright found a considerable dispersion of share ownership and a considerable inequality in size of share holdings. For 437 million voting shares there were approximately 490,000 holdings; 99.6 per cent of holdings were of less than £10,-000 in nominal value, and 0.4 per cent of the holdings had 37 per cent of the voting power.[18]

Wheelwright defined control as the "real power to select the

[17] *Ownership and Control of Australian Companies* (Sydney, 1957).
[18] *Ibid.*, p. 71.

directors"[19] and on this basis identified four types of control situation: (i) majority control in which a compact group of individuals owned over 50 per cent of the voting shares; (ii) minority control in which a similar group owned more than 15 per cent but less than 50 per cent of voting shares and in which the remaining shares were widely dispersed; (iii) joint minority-management control in which a small number of large shareholdings totaled more than 5 per cent but less than 15 per cent of voting shares (an indeterminate classification resulting from lack of knowledge as to who "really" controlled the company); and (iv) management control in which ownership was so widely dispersed that no single shareholding (apart from institutional) accounted for more than 5 per cent of voting shares. Where the apparent controlling group was another company, an attempt was made to locate the type of ultimate control; however, the seventeen companies subject to overseas control were simply classified as management controlled. Table 14 shows the results of this procedure. The conclusion made familiar by overseas investigations emerges for Australia also: in the large company ownership is at least partially, often almost entirely, separated from control. Notice, however, that in Australia this is not simply for the familiar reason that large companies have large bodies of shareholders. It is also partly for the reason that a significant number of large companies are overseas-sponsored; the control of these companies is separated from that portion of their ownership which is Australian.

So far as domestic companies are concerned, there is some evidence to suggest that the separation of ownership and control has not proceeded as far as in the United Kingdom and the United States.[20] This is entirely as we should expect in an economy in which the largest companies are relatively small by British and American standards. There is less dispersion of share ownership—even the largest company had only 40,000 shareholders in 1953—and less

[19] *Ibid.*, p. 82. The extent to which the boards of directors of large Australian companies exercise an active power of control is not clear. Some at least, it seems, are relatively passive, not formulating policy, merely rubber-stamping it. A recent investigation of the boards of 340 companies found that only 129 met more frequently than once a month, though it was also true that about two directors out of every five were full-time executives (R. K. Yorston, *Limited Liability Companies in Australia*, Sydney, 1956, pp. 63 and 70). One has the impression, however, that the typical Australian board exercises a considerably greater degree of control than its American counterpart.

[20] Cf. Wheelwright, *op. cit.*, pp. 59-63, 109-110, 120-121.

TABLE 14. *Classification of 102 Large Companies by Type of Control, 1953*
(Per cent)

Type of control	All Companies		Domestic Companies	
	By number	By shareholders' funds	By number	By shareholders' funds
I Majority control	8	5	9	7
II Minority control	28	19	34	23
III Joint minority–management control	11	7	13	8
IV Management control	44	51	33	39
V Unclassified (special cases)	9	18	11	23
Total	100	100	100	100

Source: Wheelwright, *Ownership and Control of Australian Companies*, p. 4.

inequality in the size distribution of shareholdings. Non-voting ordinary shares are rare and until recently the typical company was not highly geared (in the sense of having a high ratio of fixed interest debt to equity). However, we should, of course, expect the situation to become progressively more like the British and American as the economy develops.

Yet in many ways—and certainly in the present context—the most useful question we can ask of a collection of data such as Wheelwright's is not whether it indicates that shareholders lack effective control of directors, but whether it indicates that shareholders and directors lack an identity of interest. For if there is a substantial identity of interest between the non-speculative ordinary shareholders and the board of directors, and if the board exercises an active power of control, then it may be expected that profit-making will rank high in the list of motives which govern the firm's policy. We therefore need to know not only the extent to which shareholders control the directors, but also the extent to which directors are ordinary shareholders. Wheelwright's investigation picked up only the large shareholdings of directors (shareholdings of a nominal value of £10,000 and over), but presumably these are the relevant ones: only when a shareholding is of some significance in relation to the director's personal resources will it serve to remind him of his proprietary interest.[21] The 100 companies for which usable figures are available had roughly 700 directors in all. Only 183 directors held large holdings of ordinary shares. However, these holdings amounted to 11 per cent of ordinary capital for the group, and in three-quarters of the companies at least one director had a large personal holding. The detailed figures are set out in Table 15. They indicate a rather mixed situation. Whereas in 28 companies a majority of the board held large ordinary shareholdings, in 24 companies not one member of the board had a significant personal holding. In 23 per cent of the cases characterized by management control or suspected management control (Categories III and IV) a majority of the board held large ordinary holdings; but in 37 per cent of cases there was not one director who did so. Nevertheless, one might argue, on the basis of this table, that in at least half the companies in Wheelwright's

TABLE 15. *Distribution of 100 Companies According to Proportion of Board with Large Ordinary Shareholdings*[a]

Type of control	Proportion of board with large ordinary shareholdings			
	None	Less than 50 per cent	50 per cent and over	All companies
I Majority control	—	2	6	8
II Minority control	1	21	7	29
III Joint minority—management control	3	4	4	11
IV Management control— (a) Domestic	10	11	7	28
(b) Overseas	8	7	2	17
V Unclassified	2	3	2	7
Total	24	48	28	100

Source: Compiled from Wheelwright, *Ownership and Control of Australian Companies*, chaps. vi-vii and Appendix.

[a] Strictly speaking, these figures refer to voting shareholdings. However, in only six companies do preference shares carry equal voting rights with ordinary shares.

[21] The market value of these shares would generally have been much higher, perhaps of the order of 50 to 100 per cent higher. Even so, it must be conceded that £15,000 or £20,000 would not represent an especially large investment to a wealthy man. It is difficult to know what importance to attach to this consideration in the absence of any knowledge of the size distribution of holdings—and, indeed, of the wealth of directors.

group there would be found a reasonable identity of interest between the non-speculative ordinary shareholders and the board of directors. For thirty-seven of the companies were subject to majority or minority control, and in fifteen of the remainder a majority of the board held large shareholdings. At least for this group of companies one would expect "profit-maximizing" to be the central objective, although there still would be room for differences of opinion as to the time horizon and degree of risk to be taken; and the objective might not be pursued with the ruthlessness constrained by market pressures. Nevertheless, it seems that old-fashioned profit maximization still has some place—at least in the colonies!

However, there would appear to be considerable scope for conflicts of interest between shareholders and directors, perhaps none more sharp than may occur in the overseas-sponsored company. Here there is a clear possibility of conflict between the interests of Australian shareholders and those of the overseas parent. Partly as a result of Australia's chronic balance-of-payments difficulties over the past few years, there has been considerable public discussion of the limited franchises permitted to Australian branches of many overseas principals. An incomplete survey in 1959 found, for example, that of 275 firms with American affiliations which expressed themselves as "interested in export" some 40 per cent were restricted by their principals in the countries with which they might trade.[22] But even without the benefit of figures it is obvious that the most profitable policy for an international group need not be the one which is most profitable for the Australian subsidiary or affiliate—and hence need not be the one which will best serve the interests of Australian shareholders, nor indeed the interests of Australia as a whole. The extent of overseas control of the corporate sector has not proceeded as far as in Canada. In particular, all the leading retailing firms are Australian in origin and ownership. But the figures are quite sufficiently impressive as they stand. Wheelwright has argued persuasively that in 1953 at least one-sixth of shareholders' funds in the corporate sector and at least one-quarter of funds in the manufacturing sector must have been overseas controlled.[23] The dependent economy has its own version of the "separation of ownership and control."

[22] H. W. Arndt and D. R. Sherk, "Export Franchises of Australian Companies with Overseas Affiliations," *Economic Record*, XXXV (1959), 239.

[23] *Op. cit.*, pp. 78-81.

The Concentration of Economic Power

Although the phrase "concentration of economic power" has a high emotive content, it is here used in its technical sense to refer to the extent to which a small number of large firms dominate the whole economy, or at least some substantial segment of the economy, such as manufacturing or retailing. Thus, it is analytically distinct from "market concentration" (the extent to which a small number of large firms dominate an industry).[24] Indeed it is quite conceivable for a considerable concentration of economic power to be associated with a low degree of monopoly (where firms have a very diversified product line) or conversely for a high degree of monopoly to be associated with a low concentration of economic power (where monopoly is achieved through restrictive practices or where markets are quite small in relation to the economy). It follows that this section is not directly concerned with matters of competition and monopoly; it is concerned to discuss, rather, what may loosely be termed "Big Business." The consequences of Big Business in this sense are in many respects more political and social than economic.

There is no doubt that there is a very great concentration of economic power in Australia, although no comprehensive index can be calculated. We do not know the number of firms in Australia, let alone their size. The official statistics are sometimes on an unconsolidated company basis, sometimes on an establishment basis, never on a firm basis. Published financial reports are notoriously uninformative, rarely showing total sales, and in some instances using such conservative valuation procedures as to be positively misleading. Moreover, as already stressed, some of the largest firms are subsidiaries of overseas companies, and for these we have no reports at all. All that one can hope to do by way of measurement is to list a number of rough indexes of the degree of concentration within various sectors of the economy.

(i) In 1959 the first ten manufacturing companies listed on Australian stock exchanges accounted for over 18 per cent of manufacturing fixed assets, the first twenty-five for over 25

[24] The "degree of concentration" is also a technical term, meaning the extent to which a small *number* of units (whether firms or plants) accounts for a large *proportion* of the activity under consideration. It should not be confused with inequality in the size distribution of units nor with the absolute size of units. The "degree of inequality" refers to the extent to which a small *proportion* of units accounts for a large proportion of total activity.

per cent. These figures must be regarded as an underestimate—
and probably a considerable underestimate of the degree of
concentration in manufacturing. First, the figures refer to the
fixed assets which are owned (either directly or through legal
subsidiaries) by the largest companies; even higher percentages
would be effectively controlled by these companies. Second,
the calculation excludes some of the largest companies operating
in Australia, namely overseas-sponsored companies not listed
on Australian exchanges (for which financial reports are un-
available).[25]

(ii) In 1959-60 the four largest retailing organizations handled
approximately 6 to 7 per cent of total retail sales.[26]

(iii) In 1959 the four largest mining firms accounted for roughly 40
per cent of the value of mine output (taken to the stage of
primary treatment).[27]

(iv) In 1958 the four largest financial enterprises owned about 40
per cent of total assets in the financial sector.[28]

[25] The corresponding percentages for 1951 are over 16 per cent and over 24 per
cent. Here "manufacturing" includes newspaper publishing but excludes public
utilities. The "fixed assets" are the depreciated value of land, buildings, plant, and
machinery: for the firms as reported in their balance sheets, for the aggregate as
reported in the factory statistics. The figures have been quoted in the form "over
x per cent" since three of the companies on the lists for both 1951 and 1959 did not
present consolidated balance sheets. One of these companies (Colonial Sugar Refining Co. Ltd.) falls within the first ten. This is another reason (in addition to the
two emphasized in the text) for regarding the figures as an underestimate of the
degree of concentration in manufacturing.
    The figures given appear to conflict with a widely quoted set computed by Edith
Penrose ("Towards a Theory of Industrial Concentration," *Economic Record*,
XXXII, 1956, 65-66); but they are consistent with those presented by A. R.
Hall (*Australian Company Finance*, Australian National University Social Science
Monograph 7, 1956, pp. 21-23).
    [26] This figure must be approximate since one of the organizations does not publish
its sales. The term "organization" refers to parent company plus subsidiaries. For
retailing (unlike manufacturing and mining), effective control of associated companies coincides with legal control. Total retail sales include sales of motor vehicles, parts, petrol, etc.
    [27] Computed on the basis of information published in Department of National
Development, *The Australian Mineral Industry 1959 Review* (Canberra, 1960).
One would like the "firm" to include both legal subsidiaries and associated companies
effectively controlled, but the identification of lines of effective control is particularly
difficult in the Australian non-ferrous metals industries (see pp. 75-77 below).
Consolidated Zinc and New Broken Hill Consolidated have been treated as the one
firm, but other links within the Collins House Group have been disregarded.
    [28] The Australian assets of the leading financial enterprises were obtained for the
most part from published financial reports. For total assets in the financial sector
see pp. 36-40 above.

(v) In 1960 the first 27 quoted public companies accounted for 42 per cent of total market value of ordinary shares quoted on Australian stock exchanges.[29]

A firm may grow to a large absolute size in any one of three different ways: through dominance of one of the larger industries in the economy, through diversification of product line into a series of related fields, and through wide-ranging financial empire-building (where the only connection between companies is that they are controlled by the same investment group). It is a fact of the greatest significance in Australian industrial organization that the high concentration of economic power is largely a reflection of the high degree of market concentration; it is to a much lesser extent the reflection of diversification and financial empire-building. This is not to deny that there are examples of financial holding companies, or that in the last decade the activities of large firms have not become increasingly diversified. It is simply to stress that in Australia over the last twenty-five years Big Business and positions of market dominance have gone hand in hand. The one has served to reinforce the other.

Some evidence for these propositions is offered in Table 16, which shows the activities of the fifteen largest manufacturing and distribution companies listed on Australian stock exchanges in 1959. Here the criterion of size employed is consolidated total assets. It is apparent that thirteen of these firms (all but nos. 6 and 14) possess a high degree of monopoly or monopsony in one or more important markets. From information readily to hand a somewhat different test is also possible. This is to examine the activities of the twenty largest listed manufacturing firms (again, largest in terms of total assets).[30] It turns out that every firm, with the possible exception of Felt and Textiles (number 14 in the table), is a monopolist of a leading

[29] We are indebted to Dr. R. F. Henderson for supplying us with this information. The computation was made for May 31, 1960.

[30] These were The Broken Hill Proprietary Co. Ltd., General Motors-Holdens Ltd., The Colonial Sugar Refining Co. Ltd., Imperial Chemical Industries of Australia and New Zealand Ltd., British Tobacco Co. (Australia) Ltd., Australian Consolidated Industries Ltd., Australian Paper Manufacturers Ltd., Tooth and Co. Ltd., Felt and Textiles of Australia Ltd., Carlton and United Breweries Ltd., Dunlop Rubber Australia Ltd., Electronic Industries Ltd., Olympic Consolidated Industries Ltd., Associated Pulp and Paper Mills Ltd., Davies Coop and Co. Ltd., Email Ltd., Metal Manufacturers Ltd., The Nestle Co. (Australia) Ltd., The Herald and Weekly Times Ltd., and John Fairfax and Sons Proprietary Ltd.

TABLE 16. *Activities of the Fifteen Largest Listed*[a] *Manufacturing and Distributing Companies*
(in Terms of Total Assets at 1959 Balancing Date)

Rank	Consolidated total assets (£ million)	Name	Activity
1.	183.0	Broken Hill Proprietary Co. Ltd.	*Manufacturing.* Monopoly of basic steel; monopoly of wiremaking; associated activities in iron and coal mining, shipping, and the manufacture of steel products. An "associate" has virtual monopoly of ferrous pipes and tubes.
2.	78.3	General Motors-Holdens Ltd.	*Manufacturing.* Dominant firm in production of motor vehicles. (Share of new motor vehicle registrations has ranged between 46-50% in three-year period 1957-59.)
3.	(63.3)[b]	Colonial Sugar Refining Co. Ltd.	*Manufacturing.* Virtual monopoly of refined sugar production;[c] 20% of raw sugar production; industrial chemicals and building materials.
4.	57.1	Imperial Chemical Industries of Australia and New Zealand Ltd.	*Manufacturing.* The largest industrial and heavy chemical firm in Australia (in an industry dominated by four firms) and the sole producer of many chemicals; the sole producer of explosives; one of four leading producers of paints.
5.	48.4	British Tobacco Co. (Australia) Ltd.	*Manufacturing.* Dominant firm in the cigarette industry. (1950-55—about 90% of cigarette market; 1960—about 50% of cigarette market.)
6.	37.2	Reid Murray Holdings Ltd.	*Distribution, finance, real estate, manufacturing.* Diversified range of activities: retailing and wholesaling of dry goods and consumer durables,

[a] These companies are the *largest listed on Australian stock exchanges in 1959.* Some of the largest manufacturing companies operating in Australia are registered overseas or are unlisted subsidiaries of companies registered overseas. In 1960 General Motors-Holdens Ltd. became a wholly owned subsidiary of General Motors Corporation (following the purchase of the Australian-held preference shares). It is now a proprietary (private) company and is no longer listed on Australian exchanges.

[b] Total assets of parent company only (consolidated total assets not available). The bulk of C.S.R. business in 1958-59 was transacted by the parent company.

[c] An independent refinery supplies one-third of the Queensland market.

(Table 16 Cont.)

Rank	Consolidated total assets (£ million)	Name	Activity
			hire-purchase, real estate development, and minor manufacturing.
7.	36.5	Australian Consolidated Industries Ltd.	*Manufacturing.* Monopoly of glassmaking; diversified interests in plastics, cartons and cases, clay products, engineering, and other fields.
8.	35.0	Australian Paper Manufacturers Ltd.	*Manufacturing.* Virtual monopoly of heavy wrapping and printing papers and paper boards.
9.	33.6	Ampol Petroleum Ltd.	*Distribution.* Fifth-ranking distributor of petroleum products (in market dominated by four overseas firms); "associates" in oil exploration, tire manufacture.
10.	32.0	G. J. Coles and Co. Ltd.	*Distribution.* One of two dominant variety chains; recent acquisitions of intrastate grocery chains.
11.	31.5	Woolworths Ltd.	*Distribution.* One of two dominant variety chains; recent acquisitions of intrastate grocery chains.
12.	31.4	The Myer Emporium Ltd.	*Distribution.* The largest department store chain in Australia. (1959-60— nine department stores in six cities, two per cent of total Australian retail sales.)
13.	31.2	Tooth and Co. Ltd.	*Manufacturing and distribution.* The largest brewery in the New South Wales market which is dominated by two firms; owns over 600 hotels.
14.	24.8	Felt and Textiles of Australia Ltd.	*Manufacturing.* Diversified range of activities in textiles, soft floor coverings, footwear (20% of shoe production, 45% of slipper production), clothing, plastics.
15.	24.6	Carlton and United Breweries Ltd.	*Manufacturing and distribution.* Virtual monopoly (over 90%) of Victorian beer production; owns over 100 Victorian hotels; through 1961 takeover, shares Queensland beer market with one other firm.

product or is a leading firm in a fairly concentrated industry (defined below as one in which the first eight firms account for at least 50 per cent of employment).

The question arises as to whether this concentration of economic power has been increasing since prewar. We have no numbers bearing on this matter, only general impressions. There has undoubtedly been an increase in over-all concentration as a reflection of the structural changes which have accompanied increasing industrialization, in particular the relative rise in manufacturing, public utilities, transportation, and communication, and the relative fall in primary production and provision of personal services. (See Table 1 above.) Within the corporate sector generalization is less easy. There is some evidence of decreasing plant concentration in manufacturing (as one would expect with increasing maturity of the economy); but there is no evidence of the extent of multi-plant operations on the part of the individual firm. The largest firms have been growing rapidly, but so has the corporate sector.

Australia, no less than a number of overseas countries, has had a postwar merger movement which reached spectacular proportions in 1954-55 and 1958-60. The effects upon concentration, however, are not altogether easy to assess. The Melbourne Stock Exchange has recorded[31] that over the six years 1955-60 no fewer than 190 companies were delisted as a result of takeovers. (Compare this with the total number of listings which ranged about the 800 mark.) Yet in only 1959 and 1960 was there a net decrease in the number of companies listed, and over the six-year period 289 new companies were added to the list. Further, there have been many small mergers, quite often for defensive reasons, more often for reasons connected with taxation, finance, and management. Of 673 mergers identified in the period 1947-56, all but 68 were quite small (of less than £500,000 value in 1956 purchasing power).[32] On the other hand, a fair number of the mergers in more recent years have been very large: of the 484 mergers identified in 1956-59, 45 were over £600,-000 in value;[33] and two of the largest mergers in Australian history occurred in 1960 when two of the biggest retailing firms made substantial acquisitions. In addition, on quite general grounds we should

[31] *Annual Reports*, 1959, p. 5; 1960, p. 5.
[32] J. A. Bushnell, *Australian Company Mergers 1946-1959* (Melbourne, 1961), pp. 16-18.
[33] *Ibid.*, pp. 180 and 193.

expect the largest firms to enjoy a substantial advantage in takeover operations. They not only have the motivation; they also have the means. They not only have the means; they also can afford to pay a better price. In a growing economy not very many large firms will have a surplus of investible funds and payment will typically be made in shares[34] normally carrying a market value considerably above par. The use of high share premiums does not in itself make an acquisition "cheap," but it may carry with it certain associated advantages. First, in an imperfect capital market such as the Australian, these share premiums are very often an overestimate of the large firm's worth in relation to the small. Second, where this is not the case, the use of the share premium may enable a short-run saving in dividend commitments and hence a preservation of the firm's liquidity. Irrespective of what form the payment takes, however, the large firm has this key advantage over the small: in the consideration offered it is in a position to include a sum representing a partial capitalization of the monopoly, monopsony, and other strategic advantages anticipated from the merger.

So far as concentration within the manufacturing sector is concerned there are two additional considerations. On the side of increasing concentration there is the fact that it is the large-scale heavy sections of industry (especially metals, motor vehicles, and petroleum refining) which have been rising at the relative expense of the smaller-scale light sections of industry (especially food, clothing, and footwear). On the side of decreasing concentration there is the fact that the rapid rate of growth of the sector has permitted the establishment of new firms. (See pp. 95 and 101 below.) It must be concluded that the evidence with respect to manufacturing is indefinite. Only in retailing, it seems, can an easy conclusion be reached. Undoubtedly there has been a considerable increase in over-all concentration here, chiefly through a series of interstate and intercity mergers, partly through a series of intertrade mergers (of which the most important has been the movement of variety stores into food distribution).

The virtues of the laissez-faire competitive model were seen by its admirers to be at least as much political and social as economic. The model was necessarily associated with the existence of a large number of independent centers of decision-making, small in relation

[34] *Ibid.*, p. 19.

to the market and small in relation to the economy as a whole. To a large extent it was this atomistic quality that was attractive—the absence of business power, both in the market place and politics and in the molding of public opinion.

In Australia a handful of firms, certainly no more than a couple of hundred, dominate the private sector of the economy. There are innumerable small businesses, it is true; and in the aggregate their contribution to production would be considerable. But almost by definition these days a small business is no longer an independent business. It is a dependent business, bound to the large firms which act as customers, suppliers, or financiers. These small businesses have their trade associations and their co-operative agencies of one kind and another, and to some extent these constitute a countervailing power. But the membership of many such associations is too large, the interests too diverse, the sanctions too inadequate for them to do more than partially redress the balance. And in any event the vertical relation which exists between big business and small is not solely one of conflict. It is also one of co-operation, and here the trade association may be no more than the instrument of that co-operation (as, for example, in the establishment of standards of workmanship or of resale price maintenance). Nevertheless, it would be true to say that Australian trade associations are a stronger countervailing power than their North American counterparts, chiefly because their activities are quite uninhibited by any kind of controlling legislation.

It would be simple-minded to suggest that it is this handful of large firms which "really" controls government policy and public opinion. For one thing other pressure groups exist, notably labor and agriculture, and to a lesser extent small business. For another, the interests of Big Business are too diverse for there to be a single coherent voice—at least on many concrete issues, if not on the predominantly "free enterprise way of life." Nevertheless, a situation does exist where the success of crucial aspects of government policy may be dependent upon the co-operation of a small number of large firms; and consequently it is not uncommon on a number of issues to find Government and Business (or the relevant section of Business) bargaining on somewhat equal terms. Nor is it fanciful to suggest that, to an unusual extent in a developed economy, a handful of men are in positions of very great economic and political power; and that quite irrespective of how they use that power, they are accountable to no one. Wheelwright established that in 1953 less than two hundred directors and their families owned 10 per cent of the capital in his 102 large firms,[35] and there is no doubt that they would have controlled a considerably higher percentage. As a pointer, these groups constituted a majority on the boards of directors in over one-quarter of the companies concerned (see Table 15). In writings upon the American economy much has been made of the economic and political power possessed by Berle and Means' "handful of individuals," the so-called princes of industry. Whether, or in what sense, this is true does not concern us here. The interesting thing is that in writings upon the Australian economy the possibility that a similar situation might exist has seldom been explored. This may be largely because the dominance of a small number of men ("leaders of the business community" is the usual Australian phrase) both in economic decision-making and political bargaining is so obvious as to be taken for granted. And partly, too, it may be because paternalism in government and paternalism in business are part of the Australian tradition: the Australian is less of a rugged individualist than might be imagined.

One aspect of this situation is the extent to which the communication media are dominated by less than half a dozen firms. Indeed, in 1960 no less than 43 per cent of daily newspaper circulation[36] throughout Australia was controlled by the one firm, The Herald and Weekly Times Ltd. Australia has 14 metropolitan dailies and 35 provincial dailies, seemingly sufficient to provide some diversity of opinion. But the degree of urbanization is such that the 14 metropolitan dailies account for 90 per cent of the total circulation; and the four leading firms, which publish 10 of the metropolitan dailies between them, are thus in a position to handle 75 per cent of total daily circulation. Associated with this is the fact that not one metropolitan daily presents a left-wing point of view. In addition, these four firms publish an extensive list of non-daily newspapers and magazines of which the most important is the *Australian Women's Weekly*, published by Australian Consolidated Press Ltd. This must be rated Australia's foremost national medium of communication, for its weekly circulation implies that it is purchased by one in every three families in Australia. While "only a women's magazine,"

---

[35] *Op. cit.*, p. 118.

[36] All circulation figures quoted in this paragraph are for 1960.

its influence in setting and unifying standards of living is of the greatest importance. In addition to their publications, these four firms control eight of the 16 metropolitan TV stations and five of the 37 metropolitan radio stations. The only other broadcaster of significance is the government instrumentality, the Australian Broadcasting Commission, which operates six TV stations and a dozen radio stations (see p. 109 below.)

The economic consequences of Big Business are seen in its effects upon the availability of business opportunity and upon the nature of the competitive process. Generally speaking, the competitive advantages of the large firm stem chiefly from its financial strength but partly also from the leverage obtained through its presence in more than one market. In Australian manufacturing there are some special factors at work which give this general proposition a rather novel twist.

(i) The characteristic association of Big Business with positions of market dominance gives the large firm ready access, to an unusual degree, to both internal and external sources of finance. Its advantage over smaller rivals is reinforced by the comparative lack of financial institutions catering to small business and the existence of a capital market which is relatively imperfect, certainly more imperfect than the American or Canadian. This ready access to finance has been of great importance in the postwar period when inflationary pressures have resulted in considerable capital erosion.

(ii) The large firm has the advantage of access to new products and new techniques, not in general because of the research facilities employed but because of the links established with overseas firms. Private research departments are operated by only a small number of firms such as The Broken Hill Proprietary Co. Ltd., Imperial Chemical Industries of Australia and New Zealand Ltd., and The Zinc Corporation Ltd. Co-operative research ventures are rare. However, partially redressing the balance, it is possible for firms or industries to commission the Commonwealth Scientific and Industrial Research Organization (see p. 111 below), and to a lesser extent the universities, to investigate their own special problems.

(iii) The large firm enjoys certain advantages in sales promotion not so much because of the absolute costs of sales promotion

—a full page color advertisement in the *Women's Weekly* costs less than £2,000—as because of its access to international brands. Australians are great readers of British and American magazines, including their advertisements; and the overseas product made under license has automatic prestige.

(iv) The international firm may engage in a subtle form of price discrimination whereby the Australian market is called upon to cover only the costs directly attributable to Australian operations. The research and development overheads in particular may be recouped elsewhere. This type of practice has been of especial importance in the motor vehicle, plant and equipment, and chemical industries.

(v) The virtual absence of anti-monopoly legislation means that unfair competitive practices on the part of the larger firm are much more prevalent in Australia than in North America or even, of recent years, the United Kingdom. Tying clauses and full-line forcing are fairly common.

The result of these factors has been to reinforce the large firm's position as market leader. While there is not too much scope for a higher degree of market concentration in manufacturing than already exists (as will be shown directly), the leading firms in a number of strategic industries have established positions of virtually impregnable strength, at least as far as conquest by domestic firms is concerned.

Market Concentration in Agriculture, Mining, and Retailing

It is said that in a nudist colony nakedness goes unnoticed. Similarly, in Australia, structural monopoly and oligopoly, along with Big Business, are so common as to be taken for granted. No systematic study has ever been made of market concentration, not even as it exists in manufacturing industry.[37] It is proposed in this section to take a bird's-eye view of the extent of concentration in three major sectors of private business: agriculture, mining, and retailing. The manufacturing sector will be treated in greater detail in the section following.

It has already been demonstrated (pp. 36-37 above) that the

[37] However, a very recent article by Professor Alex. Hunter presents concentration ratios for 29 manufacturing industries and makes a comparison with similar ratios in the United States and the United Kingdom. See "Restrictive Practices and Monopolies in Australia," *Economic Record*, XXXVII (1961), 33-37.

financial sector is highly concentrated. In commercial banking seven banks hold 90 per cent of total assets; in savings banking four banks (three government owned) hold 90 per cent of total assets; and in life assurance the leading five offices also hold about 90 per cent of total assets. In the provision of hire-purchase finance the first eight companies account for over 85 per cent of the balances outstanding. In every case one does not have to go beyond the largest three firms in order to account for at least 50 per cent of the industry's business.

Agriculture. The general conclusion may be expressed in a nutshell: while agricultural *production* is altogether unconcentrated, there is only one important rural product—but that a very important one—for which *marketing* is unconcentrated. This is explained by the prevalence of marketing boards which have been a long-standing feature of Australian agriculture. Over the last twenty years there has been no discernible trend in this situation one way or the other.

The organization of the great bulk of agricultural production is competitive in the sense that the individual farms are price-takers. However, wool is the only major commodity not subject to production or marketing controls, the only major commodity whose price is competitively determined on both domestic and overseas markets. Nevertheless, it is a *very* major commodity: in postwar years it has consistently accounted for over 40 per cent of the value of exports and over 30 per cent of the value of rural output. While Australia produces over one-quarter of the world's wool and over one-half of the world's fine wool, producers make no attempt to band together to influence world wool prices. Rather, the industry has long been devoted to the auction system (although it should be noted that some doubts have recently been expressed); and currently over 95 per cent of the Australian wool clip is sold at auctions conducted at Sydney, Melbourne, and lesser centers. However, a curious feature of this system is that the six leading wool-broking firms handle approximately 60 per cent of the total clip. The Australian Wool Bureau is not a marketing board in the usual sense: its function is to promote the use of wool by publicity and research. The only other major commodity whose price is competitively determined on the domestic market is meat (though meat prices are controlled in the Brisbane metropolitan area). Exports of meat are regulated by the Australian Meat Board in accordance with the fifteen-year Meat Agreement with the United Kingdom which dates from 1952.

For the rest, agricultural production and marketing are subject to a variety of price support schemes which aim to raise or to stabilize the prices received by primary producers.[38] Apart from these common objectives the schemes cannot be simply described. Unlike the United States or the United Kingdom, Australia has no general system of price supports. Rather the measures have been developed piecemeal in accordance with the exigencies of the particular case. Further, while the schemes are implemented by marketing boards, the constitution and functions of these boards vary. Some are statutory authorities, others are co-operative ventures on the part of producers themselves; and even within each of these categories there is no common pattern. Moreover, there are both Commonwealth and state marketing boards, and the state boards are not always in respect of the same products. However, this much of a pattern emerges: The Commonwealth boards are normally concerned with export and the state boards with intrastate trade; further, all states have boards controlling the marketing of eggs, milk, and fruit.

For commodities entering international trade, home price schemes are very common. Examples are wheat, butter and cheese, dried fruits, sugar, eggs, leather and hides, rice, and canned fruits. In the case of two commodities (milk for butter and cheese manufacture and wheat) the two-price scheme is associated with a government-guaranteed price. Nevertheless, it must not be imagined that the two-price schemes are invariably associated with a high home price. This is another illustration of the *ad hoc* variety of marketing schemes in force. Sometimes the home price has been set higher than the world price in order to benefit producers, other times it has been kept lower in order to benefit consumers; nor has the one commodity always been treated in the one fashion. Where the home price is higher than the world price, the two-price scheme must be associated with some form of import control. There is an embargo on the import of sugar. Protective duties are imposed on butter and cheese, rice, sugar, wine, dried fruit, wheat and flour, eggs and egg products. Production control is not a common feature of Australian

[38] This account of price support schemes has drawn heavily on a mimeographed paper by J. N. Lewis, "Agricultural Price Supports—A Classification of Measures Operating in Australia," Monograph No. 207 of the Economic Society of Australia and New Zealand, New South Wales Branch (Sydney, 1958).

price support schemes. The only important cases are sugar, rice, and dried vine fruits (the last two indirectly by means of rationing of water rights).

So far as overseas marketing is concerned, there are only two commodities which are not sold on the open market: sugar and meat. Sugar is subject to both the International Sugar Agreement and the British Commonwealth Sugar Agreement, and meat to the bilateral agreement with the United Kingdom already mentioned. Australia is a party to the International Wheat Agreement, but there is also a significant free market in wheat. The bulk of rural exports, then, is sold on the open world market. Nevertheless, for every major commodity which enters the open world market, with the important exception of wool, there exists a marketing board which regulates Australian disposal. There are also marketing boards for sugar and meat. The declared aim of these boards is to promote "orderly marketing": namely, to regulate supplies to international markets with a view to obtaining the most advantageous prices, to act as a countervailing power against strong buyers and thus to protect the individual producer from exploitation, to negotiate freight and insurance concessions, and to undertake sales promotion and research into marketing and production methods. In the case of some commodities (dairy produce for the British market, wheat, sugar, and eggs) the relevant board operates an export pool; but in the case of other commodities (meat, canned fruits, dried fruits, apples, and pears) the board relies upon a system of licenses to obtain the observance of minimum export prices.

Mining. The Australian mining industries are highly concentrated. Consider the seven leading industries which account for approximately 80 per cent of the value of output (taken to the stage of primary treatment). These are black coal, iron ore, lead, copper, gold, zinc, and brown coal. In every case one does not have to go beyond the first five firms in order to account for 50 per cent or close to 50 per cent of the industry's production. The details are supplied in Table 17.

On the basis of an examination of these seven commodities we can conclude that *at least* one-fifth of the value of Australian mine production is monopolized in the supposedly old-fashioned sense; and *at least* three-fifths of the value of production is highly concentrated (in the sense of the leading four firms accounting for a

TABLE 17. *Concentration in the Mining Industries, 1959*

Industry	Value of output (mining and treatment) (£ million)	Concentration
Black coal	49.3	The first five firms (three private firms and two New South Wales Government instrumentalities) accounted for 43 per cent of tonnage. As a result of a merger arranged in 1960 this figure may be expected to rise to close to 50 per cent. The leading producer is The Broken Hill Pty. Co. Ltd. (17 per cent of 1959 tonnage).
Iron ore	34.0	The Broken Hill Pty. Co. Ltd. has a virtual monopoly.
Lead	29.8	The largest four companies (as distinct from firms—the unit of control) accounted for 82 per cent of tonnage. The Collins House Group of companies accounted for 80 per cent of tonnage. Outside the Group there are only two producers of any significance.
Copper	25.6	The first four firms accounted for 88 per cent of tonnage. There are only seven producers of any significance.
Gold	15.8	The first four firms accounted for 50 per cent of production (in fine oz.); the first eight for 78 per cent of production.
Zinc	13.0	The largest four companies accounted for 78 per cent of tonnage. The Collins House Group of companies accounted for 90 per cent of tonnage. Outside the Group there are only two producers of any significance.
Brown coal	6.2	The State Electricity Commission of Victoria has a virtual monopoly.
All other mining industries	39.2	Unclassified.
Total	212.8	

Source: Compiled from Department of National Development, *The Australian Mineral Industry 1959 Review* (Canberra, 1960) and Joint Coal Board, *Annual Report, 1958-59* (Sydney, 1959).

minimum of 50 per cent of the industry's production). Of course, in some cases the market power of the producers concerned is more apparent than real. There is brisk competition between the different fuel industries, especially coal and oil. Iron ore may be imported from Pacific sources (and, indeed, is already imported from New Caledonia)—though this would be of greater significance if the ore monopolist and the steel monopolist were not one and the same! Finally, in lead and zinc it is not the Australian market which is relevant so much as the world market, for Australia is one of the foremost world producers and exporters of these commodities.

Not all the producers which dominate the mining industries are private firms. There are state coal mines in Queensland, New South Wales, Victoria (brown), and South Australia. The State Electricity Commission of Victoria has a virtual monopoly of brown coal production; and the state of New South Wales (through two instrumentalities) is currently the second largest producer of black coal (though it should drop to third place following a recent merger).

Nevertheless, about 20 per cent of the value of Australian mining output is produced by a single firm, The Broken Hill Proprietary Co. Ltd.; and a further 15 per cent or so is produced by a closely associated group of private firms, the so-called Collins House Group. A brief account of the scope of the activities of these two dominant houses in the mining sector will give something of the flavor of business organization in Australia.

B.H.P.'s leading position in the black coal industry and its monopoly of iron ore production are based upon its monopoly of basic steel production (smelting, refining, and rolling). This does not exhaust the scope of B.H.P.'s activities (as already indicated in Table 16). The firm is, for instance, the largest private operator of coastal shipping in Australia, and it has extensive interests in steel fabrication (including a virtual monopoly of wiremaking); an associate company (in which B.H.P. has a 42 per cent interest) is holding company for a group with a virtual monopoly of ferrous pipes and tubes. B.H.P. does not produce coal for the market but for its own integrated steel plants. It is sometimes implied or suggested that B.H.P.'s monopoly of iron ore production is based upon control of iron ore leases, but this may be going too far. It is true it holds leases of all the most accessible high-grade ore deposits in Australia, but not of all the workable deposits. Until recently (1960) the export of iron ore was prohibited. Now, with the lifting of the prohibition, a number of independent firms are showing some interest in export possibilities, thus suggesting that in the past the barrier to entry of this industry may have been not so much B.H.P.'s possession of leases as its possession of steel plant.

The Collins House Group is a collection of non-ferrous metal companies linked together in a complex way by interlocking shareholdings and directorates and by common interests. There are, to begin with, five mining companies, all specializing in the lead-zinc field. In no case is there a legal holding company subsidiary relationship; nevertheless the five companies are widely believed to act very closely together, although there is some evidence that the degree of association has been diminishing in recent years. One of these mining companies operates the sole zinc refinery in Australia. The sole lead refinery in Australia is jointly owned by three of them. Until 1959 there was only one copper refinery in Australia capable of casting the metal into commercial shapes, that jointly owned by two of the Collins House mining companies. And to complete the picture, the Collins House Group has extensive interests in non-ferrous metals fabrication. However, the copper mines are independent of the Group in point of ownership and control, though just how much true independence was possible when the Collins House copper refinery had a virtual monopoly is another matter. It is significant that the new copper refinery has been established by the largest of the copper mining firms. In 1960 The Consolidated Zinc Corporation Ltd. (a holding company for one of the Collins House mining companies) and Kaiser Aluminum and Chemical Corporation acquired the Commonwealth Government's two-thirds share in the Australian Aluminium Production Commission, the only producer of primary aluminum in Australia (see p. 112 below). The Consolidated Zinc–Kaiser group holds the lease of the very large bauxite deposits at Weipa in northern Queensland for which they have impressive development plans. Most recently (1961) this group has acquired interests in companies responsible for approximately half the aluminum fabrication in Australia. Whatever the subsequent developments in this very new field of aluminum production and fabrication, Consolidated Zinc has certainly entered on the ground floor.[39]

[39] In June 1961 a further development in the aluminum field was announced. A new company, Alcoa of Australia Propietary Ltd., is to be formed jointly by

Retailing. At first sight Australian retailing presents a picture of unusual concentration. The merger activity of the last fifteen years has been spectacular, culminating in two of the biggest mergers in Australian history. One is constantly informed by the somewhat excitable financial press that the "postwar revolution" in retailing has led to the dominance of large-scale retailing. An American observer has written:

The emergence of a half dozen dominant chains holding among them a substantial part of the dry goods business in every Australian city makes dry goods retailing in Australia more concentrated than in any other developed country. . . . The possible power of the large retailers, if they were to act together, over both customers and suppliers is alarming.[40]

It is true that there have been important structural changes in retailing organization over the last fifteen years:

(i) the development of *national* chains of general merchandise and apparel stores;

(ii) the introduction of planned suburban shopping centers (though there is only one so far which is a regional center of the American type—Chadstone Regional Centre, in Melbourne);

(iii) a significant, though not pronounced, decline in the percentage of retailing conducted in inner city areas;

(iv) the rise of self-service grocery stores of a somewhat larger unit size than previously;

(v) the virtual elimination of the independent grocery store in most urban areas in favor of chain organizations (including co-operative chains);

(vi) the virtual elimination of the traditional independent grocery wholesaler; and

(vii) the expansion of the two leading variety chains into food distribution.

It is also true that a small number of large firms dominate the general merchandise field. These are The Myer Emporium Ltd., David Jones Ltd., and Cox Brothers (Australia) Ltd. (department store chains), and G. J. Coles and Co. Ltd. and Woolworths Ltd.

the Aluminum Company of America, the Western Mining Corporation, North Broken Hill, and Broken Hill South. The last two companies are members of the Collins House Group. The Alcoa group holds the lease of bauxite deposits near Kwinana in Western Australia and plans to establish mining-refining-fabrication operations by the end of 1963.

[40] J. A. Bushnell, *op. cit.*, p. 150

(variety store chains). It is difficult to convey the size of these organizations in the general merchandise field: Woolworths does not disclose its sales, an unknown (though subsidiary) proportion of both Coles' and Woolworths' business is in food lines, and in any event the Commonwealth Statistician does not employ a general merchandise classification in retailing statistics.[41] However, in 1959-60 these five organizations would have handled 7 to 8 per cent of *total* retail sales[42] in Australia. The Myer Emporium and Coles each accounted for 2 per cent of total retail sales—and this was prior to two big Myer's and Coles' takeovers in the latter part of 1960. In view of the expansive vigor of all five firms, it will be surprising if they do not handle over 10 per cent of total retail sales in the near future.

Nevertheless, it must be stressed, when making international comparisons, that what is unusual in Australian retailing is not the degree of selling concentration but the degree of buying concentration, not the degree of monopoly but the degree of monopsony. Of their nature retail markets are local in extent, ranging from the neighborhood catchments of convenience stores to the metropolitan markets for durables and certain types of apparel. The outstanding change in Australian retailing since prewar is in the number of markets in which firms operate; and, while there has been some increase in the size of the individual unit, to a considerable extent this has been balanced by an increase in the size of the relevant market. The degree of monopsony is indeed alarming, especially when it is realized that many of the suppliers in the food, apparel, dry goods, and furniture trades are small. (Compare the concentration estimates presented in the next section.) Further it must be conceded that while there has been little significant increase in the degree of monopoly to date, there may be a significant increase in the future precisely because of the buying power of the larger organizations.

A factor which may be expected to increase the degree of monopsony, though possibly not of monopoly, is the advent of the

[41] In 1956-57 (the year of the most recent census of retail establishments) the Myer organization accounted for 19 per cent of total department store sales. A department store is defined by the Commonwealth Statistician as "an establishment with 50 persons or more working mainly on retail activities, with goods arranged in separate departments, and with Clothing and Drapery constituting the predominant type of goods sold or service rendered."

[42] Total retail sales include sales of motor vehicles, parts, petrol, etc.

TABLE 18. *Concentration in Retailing: Sales According to Type of Market, 1956-57*

Type of Business	Type of Market		
	Large numbers (£ million)	Oligopoly (£ million)	Mixed (£ million)
Food stores			
Grocers			470.2
Butchers		170.9	
Fruiterers		70.0	
Bakers		58.9	
Confectioners and milk bars			72.6
Cafes			14.0
Fishmongers and poulterers		12.8	
Other		18.8	
Hotels and tobacconists			
Hotels & wine saloons		247.9	
Tobacconists and tobacconist hairdressers			24.4
Clothiers and drapers			
Clothiers and footwear stores	468.5		
Drapers & haberdashers			74.7
Hardware, electrical goods, furniture stores			
Domestic and builders' hardware			117.7
Electrical goods, radios, and musical instruments	89.6		
Furniture and floor coverings	82.2		
Business machines		19.1	
Motor vehicle dealers			
Tractor dealers		21.6	
New motor and motorcycle dealers } Garages and service stations		495.1	
Motor parts and tire dealers	27.0		
Used motor vehicle dealers	89.2		
Other			
News agents and booksellers		62.1	
Chemists		64.9	
Sports goods stores			8.9
Watchmakers and jewelers			22.9
Cycle stores	3.8		
Florists and nurserymen		6.6	
Total Classified[a]	760.3	1248.6	805.4

Source: The sales figures are from the Commonwealth Bureau of Census and Statistics, *Census of Retail Establishments,* 1956-57.
[a] Unclassified: trades with sales amounting to £86.6 million.

large regional shopping center of the American type. The declared policy in the selection of tenants for Chadstone Regional Centre was to choose the dominant retailer in each field. It is obvious that this is the most profitable policy for the managers of any such center. But perhaps too much should not be made of this point. Chadstone is the only center of this type in existence (although a second is on the drawing board); only Sydney and Melbourne have the purchasing power to justify the establishment of such centers; and even in these cities the density of purchasing power per square mile and the type of transportation facilities are such as to make the American level of development unlikely.

It was mentioned a paragraph ago that many of the manufacturers in the food, apparel, dry goods, and furniture trades are small. This is not to say that there are not instances of Galbraith's countervailing power (big buyers on the retailing side of the market facing big sellers on the manufacturing side); indeed, just such conscious countervailance has doubtless been one of the motives behind a recent wave of retail grocery mergers (including the formation of co-operative chains). It *is* to say, however, that positions of bilateral monopoly and bilateral oligopoly are not general in the supply of consumer goods. Indeed, if any vertical relationship is to be pointed to as typical in this field it is the asymmetrical one in which a large firm on one side of the market (whether retailing or manufacturing) faces a collection of small firms on the other.

One approach to discussing the degree of selling concentration in retailing is to remark: "Of course, retail markets are local" and leave it at that. Another approach is to examine the structure of the market at the local level and, having special regard to spatial considerations, attempt to classify the various trades according to whether the typical firm is in oligopolistic or large-numbers competition. So, for instance, the typical butcher's shop is in competition with only a few others in the same neighborhood; but the typical furniture shop is in competition with many others, perhaps most others, in the same metropolitan area. Proceeding on this basis (see Table 18), it would seem that 27 per cent of total retail sales in Australia are made by trades which typically sell in large-numbers competition (though not, of course, pure competition); that 44 per cent are made by trades which typically sell in oligopolistic markets; and that 29 per cent of sales are made by trades in which some firms operate in large-numbers markets and some firms in oligopolistic markets.

Market Concentration in Manufacturing

An estimate of market concentration in Australian manufacturing can be made only if one is prepared to use pick-and-shovel methods— that is to say, to use the crude and laborious procedure of investigating the structure of each industry in turn. Not much help can be obtained from official statistics, for these do not go beyond the size distribution of the plants which make up the industry, and in addition the industry classification employed is not very appropriate to concentration work. One of the authors is in the process of making such an investigation and presents certain preliminary results[43] in this section. Since none of these results has been published elsewhere, something will have to be said of the methods employed, though any detailed discussion would clearly be out of place.

The concept of the industry used is that expressed by Stigler in *Business Concentration and Price Policy:*

An industry should embrace the maximum geographical area and the maximum variety of productive activities in which there is strong long-run substitution. If buyers can shift on a large scale from product or area B to A, then the two should be combined. If producers can shift on a large scale from B to A, again they should be combined.[44]

This is a broader concept than has been used in some concentration work, since it stresses the relevance of both cross-elasticity of demand and cross-elasticity of *supply*. An industry is essentially any closely competitive group of plants; and competition proceeds not only through buyers' substitution in their purchases but also through producers' substitution in their output mix. The content of the "industry" will vary according to the time horizon envisaged, especially with respect to substitution on the supply side. The industry, we say, is the area of close competition within the economy; but the nature and degree of that competition will vary from the short-run to the long-run.

[43] The completed study will form one chapter of a volume on the structure of Australian industry which is being edited by Professor Alex. Hunter (of the University of New South Wales) and which is to be published by the Melbourne University Press.

[44] G. J. Stigler, *Business Concentration and Price Policy*, NBER Conference (Princeton, 1955), p. 4.

Here substitution in supply has been limited to what is possible, given existing capital equipment.

In all, 142 meaningful industries have been identified.[45] The 142-industry classification is largely based upon the detailed classification employed by the Commonwealth Bureau of Census and Statistics, though it has been found necessary to break down some industries and to combine others. In 1957-58, the year to which the estimates apply, these 142 industries employed 89 per cent of the manufacturing work force. However the coverage is not as comprehensive as these figures might suggest: it is fairly poor for three groups of industries, namely, fabricated metal products; plant, equipment and machinery; and electrical machinery and wireless. (See Groups D, E, and F in Table 19.)

The measure of concentration employed in any particular study will depend partly upon one's concept of concentration and partly upon the data available. In Australia the information available on market structure is very limited. The only measure of a firm's size which can conceivably be used for a comprehensive survey, it seems, is employment; and the concentration measure must necessarily be of a rather vague type. The method devised was to examine all the material readily at hand on each industry and then to place the industry in one of the following pigeonholes:

(i) *Highly Concentrated:* the first four firms account for at least 50 per cent of total employment in the industry.

(ii) *Fairly Concentrated:* the first eight firms account for at least 50 per cent of total employment in the industry.

(iii) *Slightly Concentrated:* the first twenty firms account for at least 50 per cent of total employment in the industry.

(iv) *Unconcentrated.*

The "firm" in question is the collection of plants operating within the one industry under the same effective control. The aim has been to use the limited information available so that, with greater knowledge, the only possible amendment would be in the direction of higher concentration. Thus the estimates are essentially conservative. The most unsatisfactory estimates are those relating to the food industries (Group K of Table 19). The structure of the Australian

---

[45] Two types of industries have not been identified: (i) small industries (normally those producing less than £1 million of output), and (ii) industries whose employment (i.e., dimensions) it was impossible to estimate, even approximately. In aggregate, (i) is quite unimportant; it is (ii) which causes some trouble.

food industries is something of a mystery and it is probable that greater knowledge would reveal a considerably higher degree of concentration than has been found.

Table 19 summarizes the results for broad groups of industries. Thus, for example, of all the industries producing non-metallic

TABLE 19. *Distribution of Employment by Concentration Class: 142 Australian Manufacturing Industries, 1957-58*[a]
(thousands of employees)

Industry group	Highly concentrated	Fairly concentrated	Slightly concentrated	Uncon-centrated	Not identified	Total
A. Products of non-metallic minerals	16.7	2.3	4.2	11.7	7.3	42.2
B. Chemicals and allied products	24.8	11.1	3.6	—	3.1	42.6
C. Primary metal industries	48.0	—	—	17.3	—	65.3
D. Fabricated metal products	14.4	—	7.1	—	19.6	41.1
E. Plant, equipment, and machinery	14.0	24.3	9.0	23.5	39.0	109.8
F. Electrical machin-ery and wireless	4.0	26.2	—	—	32.9	63.1
G. Transportation equipment	70.2	0.8	—	—	0.2	71.2
H. Motor vehicles	54.0	—	—	57.0	—	111.0
I. Textiles and textile goods	17.1	3.2	23.8	—	2.0	46.1
J. Clothing and footwear	4.9	9.6	—	112.2	4.5	131.1
K. Food	16.4	36.1	19.1	50.1	3.3	124.9
L. Timber and timber products	1.5	0.9	3.3	67.7	3.4	76.8
M. Paper, paper pro-ducts, and printing	26.7	—	2.1	35.7	1.8	66.4
N. Rubber goods	15.0	—	—	3.2	—	18.2
O. Fuel, lubricants, light and power	22.8	—	—	—	—	22.8
P. Miscellaneous	7.4	4.6	14.6	15.4	6.6	48.6
Total	358.0	119.0	86.9	393.8	123.6	1,081.3

[a] While the employment in most industries could be obtained from an official source (Commonwealth Bureau of Census and Statistics, *Secondary Industries Bulletin*, 1957-58), the employment in some industries had to be estimated. The first four columns of the table cover employment in the 142 industries identified. The fifth column covers employment in other industries.

minerals (Group A) those industries which are highly concentrated account for the employment of at least 16,700. One's immediate impression is of a strikingly high degree of concentration, especially when it is recalled how broadly the "industry" is defined. For manufacturing as a whole,[46] highly concentrated industries account for the employment of *at least* 33 per cent of the work force. If we consider the classified segment of manufacturing only, highly concentrated industries employ 37 per cent of the work force and highly *plus* fairly concentrated industries employ 50 per cent of the work force. Further, it is probable that complete coverage of manufacturing would lift these percentages; for the unclassified parts of Groups D, E, and F consist largely of collections of small industries producing specialized products from specialized capital equipment.

Furthermore, these are national concentration ratios, but many markets are regional or local in extent. A number of industries which appear comparatively unconcentrated on a national basis might be found to be much more highly concentrated upon examination of the relevant regional or local markets. To give some indication of the quantitative importance of this consideration, an attempt has been made to distinguish between industries supplying national markets on the one hand and industries supplying regional or local markets on the other. It turns out that there are 45 industries (employing 31 per cent of the work force) for which the proportion of interstate trade is relatively low. Sixteen of these have already been classified as highly concentrated. This leaves 29 industries (employing over 20 per cent of the work force) for which the degree of concentration may be higher than that revealed by the national estimates.

It would seem safe to generalize, then, that highly *plus* fairly concentrated industries employ well over 50 per cent of the work force in Australian manufacturing. But while this is an important result we cannot stop here; for the significance we attach to this finding depends upon the *kind* of industries which make up the 50 per cent. The importance of an industry is dependent not only upon its size but also upon its location in the structure of the economy, upon what has been termed its rank on the "scale of economic sig-

---

[46] The Australian definition of manufacturing includes gas and electricity undertakings, dyeworks and cleaners, as well as trades repairing shoes, tires, motor vehicles, and other transportation equipment.

nificance."[47] Where we place an industry on the scale of economic significance depends upon how vitally its behavior affects the attainment of economic ends.

Table 19 above gives us a broad picture of the incidence of concentration. The industry groups characterized by especially high concentration are chemicals and allied products; primary metal industries; transportation equipment; motor vehicles; rubber goods; fuel, lubricants, light and power; and probably fabricated metal products. Table 20, however, is more useful in this connection. It lists all the large highly concentrated industries which have been discovered—32 industries, producing (with a few exceptions) over £25 million output each, in aggregate employing 28 per cent of the manufacturing work force. For the most part they are industries manufacturing producer goods. Indeed, for manufacturing as a whole, 60 per cent of employment in the highly concentrated sector is accounted for by industries manufacturing producer goods, 21 per cent by industries manufacturing consumer durables, and only 13 per cent by industries manufacturing consumer non-durables.[48]

Generally speaking, the impact of the producer industries on the functioning of the economy must be rated greater than that of the consumer industries. Their organization is vital from the standpoint of an efficient allocation of resources and a rapid rate of growth. So far as resource allocation is concerned, the further back an industry is located in the vertical sequence of processes leading to the consumer, the more its behavior, and in particular its price-cost relationships, will affect the structure of the economy as a whole. A similar importance attaches to the behavior of industries whose output is a significant input for a considerable number of other industries (such as fuel). So far as the achievement of a rapid rate of growth is concerned, it is also the producer-goods industries which are important, more particularly industries producing "basic" materials such as metals and chemicals, construction materials, and plant and equipment (including transportation equipment). In addition, within the producer-goods sector are the investment industries which,

[47] C. Kaysen and D. F. Turner, *Antitrust Policy* (Cambridge, Mass., 1959), chap. ii. Cf. also I. M. D. Little, *The Price of Fuel* (Oxford, 1953), Introduction.

[48] These figures may be biased. They refer only to the highly concentrated industries which have been identified; and, in general, least is known of the structure of those industries which produce consumer non-durables. At the same time, any *large* highly concentrated industry tends to be noticed, no matter what it is producing.

TABLE 20. *Large Highly Concentrated Industries: Australian Manufacturing, 1957-58*

	Value of output[a] (£ million)	Value of production[b] (£ million)	Employment (thousands)
1. Basic steel (smelting, converting, refining, rolling of iron and steel)	230.2	70.4	28.6
2. Mineral oils	163.3	32.7	4.7
3. Construction and assembly of motor vehicles	155.9	67.4	44.0
4. Electric light and power	100.5	55.5	12.9
5. Industrial and heavy chemicals and acids	70.6	30.1	11.3
6. Rubber goods (including tires)	63.0	24.8	15.0
7. Government railway-workshops	61.8	40.7	38.1
8. Newspapers and periodicals	51.4	25.6	14.4
9. Major domestic appliances	47.5	n.a.	14.0
10. Cotton and synthetic spinning and weaving	48.3	19.2	12.5
11. Tobacco and cigarettes	46.7	11.2	4.8
12. Refined sugar	42.2[c]	7.5[c]	1.9[c]
13. Breweries	40.9	17.3	5.9
14. White lead, paints, and varnish	38.9	13.9	5.8
15. Ferrous pipes, tubes, and fittings	37.2	14.0	7.0
16. Motor accessories	29.5	16.9	10.0
17. Glass and glass products	28.5	13.2	8.4
18. Gas works	28.3	10.6	3.8
19. Aircraft (including maintenance)	26.5	17.0	12.6
20. Shipbuilding and repairing, marine engineering	26.1	18.8	15.8
21. Soap and candles	25.4	10.5	3.0
22. Extracting and refining of lead 23. Extracting and refining of zinc }[d] 24. Extracting and refining of copper	80.7[e]	18.1[e]	7.3[e]
25. Newsprint 26. Heavy paper and paper board }[d] 27. Fine and special papers	49.9	23.9	8.1
28. Rolling and extrusion of zinc 29. Rolling and extrusion of copper }[d] 30. Rolling and extrusion of aluminum	43.3	11.2	5.1
31. Steel drums and pails }[d] 32. Tin cans	32.5	n.a.	8.0
Total, Large highly concentrated industries	1,569.2	n.a.	302.9
Total, All manufacturing	4,273.9	1,728.7	1,081.3

Source: With the exception of figures for industries 9, 12, 31, and 32 (which have been

together with the industries producing consumer durables, play such a crucial role in fluctuations of activity. In sum, Australian manufacturing is "highly concentrated" in some economically significant, rather than merely arithmetical, sense.

Table 21 provides still more evidence on this point. It is a commonplace of British and American textbooks that in modern economies single-firm monopoly is virtually non-existent; that is, it is a theoretical type which is a curiosity in practice. And yet in Australia in 1957-58 there were fourteen important cases. These fourteen cases of so-called old-fashioned monopoly accounted for over 8 per cent of gross value added and over 5 per cent of employment in manufacturing; and far more important, it is apparent that these are basic industries occupying a strategic position in the economy. The monopolies listed are the outstanding ones. There are, in addition, little pockets of monopoly or virtual monopoly scattered through the manufacturing sector such as razor blades, matches, car radiators, industrial gases, and big steel drums.

International comparisons of the degree of concentration in manufacturing are fraught with difficulties, both conceptual and practical. The very notion of an *aggregate* degree of concentration can be misleading, certainly without qualification and explanation; and in addition there is the problem of securing comparable measures of concentration and industry classification. The industry classifications should not necessarily be identical *in form*. Indeed, in most cases this would be positively undesirable since the structure of industry (and more especially the structure of cross-elasticities of supply) may be expected to differ from economy to economy. The industry classification should be identical *in principle;* the classifications should be based upon a similar concept of the industry including a similar time horizon.

Kaysen and Turner's survey of concentration in United States

---

obtained from a number of sources) all figures are from the Commonwealth Bureau of Census and Statistics, *Secondary Industries Bulletin,* 1957-58.

Note: (i) Government business undertakings are solely responsible for production in industry 7, almost wholly responsible for production in 4, and partly responsible for production in 18, 19, 20.

     (ii) The following industries supply regional (as distinct from national) markets: 4, 7, 8, 13, 17, 18, 32.

  a Selling value of factory output at the factory door.

  b Value of output less cost of materials, power and fuel, but *not* depreciation charges.

  c 1957 season.

  d Separate statistics for these industries not available.

  e Includes figures relating to extracting and refining of tin and aluminum (both of minor importance).

manufacturing in 1954[49] uses a similar concept of the industry to that employed in this study,[50] but a different measure of concentra-

TABLE 21. *Large National Monopolies;*
Australian Manufacturing, 1957-58

Firm	Industry	Value of output (£ million)	Value of production (£ million)	Employment (thousands)
1. Broken Hill Proprietary Co. Ltd.	(i) Basic steel	230.2	70.4	28.6
	(ii) Wiremaking	15.1	n.a.	2.0
2. Tubemakers of Australia Ltd. (an associate of B.H.P.)	Ferrous pipes, tubes, and fittings	37.2	14.0	7.0
3. John Lysaght (Aust.) Pty. Ltd.	Steel sheets	n.a.	n.a.	n.a.
4. Colonial Sugar Refining Co. Ltd.	Refined sugar	42.2[a]	7.5[a]	1.9[a]
5. Australian Consolidated Industries Ltd.	Glass and glass products	28.5	13.2	8.4
6. Imperial Chemical Industries of Australia and New Zealand Ltd.	Explosives	13.1	5.9	4.0
7. Broken Hill Associated Smelters Pty. Ltd.	Extracting and refining of lead			
8. Electrolytic Zinc Co. (A'sia) Ltd.	Extracting and refining of zinc			
9. Australian Aluminium Production Commission[c]	Extracting and refining of aluminum	[b] 80.7	18.1	7.3
10. Electrolytic Refining and Smelting Co. Pty. Ltd.	Extracting and refining of copper			

[49] *Op. cit.,* chap. ii and appendixes.

[50] In fact the author of this section drew up the classification of industry used in that survey.

(TABLE 21 Cont.)

Firm	Industry	Value of output[a] (£ million)	Value of production[b] (£ million)	Employment (thousands)
11. Australian Newsprint Mills Ltd.	Newsprint			
12. Australian Paper Manufacturers Ltd.	Heavy paper and paper board	49.9	23.9	8.1
13. Associated Pulp and Paper Mills Ltd.	Fine and special papers			
Total (excluding n.a.)		496.8	153.0	67.1

d

Source: All figures (with the exception of those for wiremaking and refined sugar) are from the Commonwealth Bureau of Census and Statistics, *Secondary Industries Bulletin*, 1957-58.

Note: The figures relate to the industries of which the firms listed have (or, in one case, had) a virtual monopoly. The situation in the non-ferrous metal industries requires some explanation. In the case of lead and copper it has been only the refining stage which has been monopolized. Broken Hill Associated Smelters Pty. Ltd. operates the only primary lead smelter-refinery in Australia, but Mt. Isa Mines Ltd. smelts its own lead concentrates, which are exported to Great Britain for refining. In the latter part of 1961 a semi-independent lead-zinc smelter will commence operations. Until 1959 the Electrolytic Refining and Smelting Co. Pty. Ltd. operated the only copper refinery in Australia capable of casting the metal into commercial shapes. While one of the copper mines operates its own refinery, the bulk of its output is sold to E. R. & S. for melting and casting into primary shapes. Two more mines operate their own smelters. In 1959 an in dependent copper refinery began production (see p. 75 above).

[a] 1957 season.
[b] Separate statistics for industries 7-10 not available; includes figures relating to extracting and refining of tin (of minor importance).
[c] In 1960 agreements were reached whereby this public monopoly became a private monopoly (see p. 77).
[d] Separate statistics for industries 11-13 not available.

tion: it is concerned with the extent to which a small number of firms account for a large percentage of sales (including a figure imputed for inter-plant transfers). Nevertheless, let us explore whether any useful comparison can be made. Suppose we list all American industries in which the first eight firms account for 50 per cent or more of total sales. In 1954 these industries together employed 27 per cent of the manufacturing work force. Suppose we do a similar sum for Australian manufacturing, listing all industries in which the first eight firms account for 50 per cent or more of total employment, and adjusting the definition of the manufacturing sector to make it roughly comparable with the American.[51] Then in 1957-58 these industries together employed 47 per cent of the manufacturing work force, but 53 per cent of the work force in classified industries; and it has already been argued that full coverage of the manufacturing sector would raise the index to something above the second figure. Even with this amendment the Australian figure is downwardly biased in comparison with the American. If, in any industry, the first eight firms account for 50 per cent of employment they are likely to account for a considerably higher percentage of sales, because the larger firms are likely to be more capital intensive than the smaller. In addition, it will be recalled that the Australian estimates are minimum estimates. It is difficult to escape the conclusion that an Australian index fully comparable with the American would have a value at the very least of 60 per cent.

Whatever one's misgivings as to the significance of aggregate indexes of concentration, one must attach significance to this result because of the order of magnitude involved. Using comparable definitions, industries in which the first eight firms account for 50 per cent or more of national sales employ 27 per cent of the manufacturing work force in the United States but at least 60 per cent of the manufacturing work force in Australia. Insofar as imports are unimportant and the market is national in scope, a situation in which the first eight firms account for 50 per cent or more of national sales reflects either simple monopoly or tight oligopoly (a *very* few firms are responsible for the bulk of output). In fact, broadly speaking, imports have not been an important source of competition for either economy over the last decade.[52] And in fact, national markets predominate in each economy.[53] It must be concluded that monopolistic

---

[51] This involves eliminating the gas and electricity undertakings, dyeworks and cleaners, and the trades repairing shoes, tires, and motor vehicles.

[52] While Australian imports have been running at the rate of some 15 per cent of gross national product, they have been largely non-competitive with Australian production; for import controls were stringently imposed in 1952 and used with varying degrees of severity for the remainder of the fifties (see p. 134 below). The controls were removed at the beginning of 1960, but whether this will be permanent remains to be seen. In any case, it seems likely that some measure will be used to control the level of imports in the future.

[53] It is suggested above (p. 81) that in Australia, regional and local industries (defined as those for which the proportion of interstate trade is relatively low) account for less than one-third of the manufacturing work force. Kaysen and

and tightly oligopolistic markets are overwhelmingly more important in Australia than in the United States. In support of this conclusion, it has already been established that Australia's highly concentrated industries occupy a strategic position in the economy and include some notable cases of simple monopoly.

No such easy comprehensive comparison can be made with the British and Canadian situations. Nevertheless, it seems safe to generalize that monopolistic and tightly oligopolistic markets are significantly, though not overwhelmingly, more important in Australia. A full-dress comparison with the Canadian case would be of considerable interest since Canada's manufacturing sector is not much larger than Australia's and its composition not so very different. Even without this, one or two points from Rosenbluth's sample investigation of concentration in Canadian manufacturing[54] are suggestive. The ninety-six industries studied covered almost three-quarters of manufacturing output. Although Rosenbluth's concept of the industry appears somewhat narrower than that used in the Australian investigation, there is only one case of simple monopoly cited (aluminum), only two cases of duopoly (nickel and hardwood distillation), and only one case of three-firm oligopoly (cement).[55] Rosenbluth asked how many leading firms were required to account for 80 per cent of employment in any industry. Looking at the less concentrated end of the distribution, in the majority of industries from nine to something over 250 were required; but in industries accounting for the greater part of employment from 35 to over 250 were required.[56]

There are two main reasons for the unusually high degree of concentration in Australian manufacturing: (i) the limited size of the market, and (ii) the advantages of the large established firm in competition with the small. Neither factor has been systematically studied. In public discussion the first is generally emphasized to the exclusion of the second. "Of course," it is said, "if we are to use modern techniques in an economy the size of Australia a high degree of monopoly is inevitable." And the discussion proceeds no further.

Turner (*op. cit.*, p. 36) concluded for the United States that regional and local markets accounted for less than 20 per cent of all manufacturing sales. It is not clear, however, to what extent the criteria employed in distinguishing between regional and national markets are similar for the two studies.

[54] G. Rosenbluth, *Concentration in Canadian Manufacturing Industries*, NBER Study (Princeton, 1957).

[55] *Ibid.*, pp. 111-113.   [56] *Ibid.*, pp. 22-23.

Such a statement is true enough but hardly informative. What is not known is the *extent* to which existing patterns of concentration are explained and "justified" by economies of large-scale production. It is obvious that the typical Australian market is small for an economy which claims to be industrially mature. See, for instance, the figures quoted in Table 22. And it is obvious that high concentration is the only way to secure cheap production in such fields as basic metals, chemicals, paper, glass, motor vehicles, shipbuilding, rubber goods, petroleum refining, and sugar refining. What is not obvious is whether *such* high concentration as exists is necessary, especially in view of the fact that few of the leading firms in these fields operate only one plant. It is this kind of question which has inspired a considerable body of research in the United States in recent years, but it is not one which the average Australian has thought to raise. He is inclined to accept a very high degree of

TABLE 22. *Output in Selected Industries in 1958: Australia, United States, United Kingdom, Canada*

Industry	Units	Australia	U.S.A.	U.K.	Canada
Wheat flour	thousand metric tons	1,246	11,165	3,731	1,868
Motor spirit	thousand metric tons	3,360	149,572	6,859	10,316
Crude steel (ingots and steel for casting)	thousand metric tons	3,213[a]	77,342	19,879	3,955
Cigarettes	millions	14,660	470,067	n.a.	32,778
Motor vehicles (production and assembly)	thousand	240[b]	5,315	1,365	360
Beer	thousand hectoliters	10,294	103,860	39,376	10,649
Paper other than newsprint	thousand metric tons	144	11,966	1,844	809
Caustic soda	thousand metric tons	37	3,623	n.a.	281
Wool yarn	thousand metric tons	21	294[c]	224[d]	18

Source: United Nations, *Statistical Year Book*, 1960.
[a] Ingots only.
[b] Estimate from figures in Commonwealth Bureau of Cenus and Statistics, *Secondary Industries Bulletin*, 1957-58.
[c] Pure and mixed.
[d] Weight of wool fiber consumed by spinners of woolen yarn.

monopoly in manufacturing as part of the order of nature, probably because he has never known anything different. Industrialization (in the sense of the development of manufacturing of a heavy, complex, and diversified kind) began in Australia about the time of World War I. While this was early in relation to the size of the internal market—the population recorded at the 1921 Census was only 5.4 million—it was comparatively late in relation to the maturity of manufacturing techniques. Whatever the importance of economies of scale today (with nearly double the population and a much higher income level) there is no doubt of their historical importance. Historically, economies of scale in relation to the size of the market were such as to establish a monopolistic and oligopolistic structure *ab initio*.

If we ask how today's leading firms achieved both their large absolute size and their positions of market dominance, the answer is largely that they were established early and grew with their markets. While mergers have occurred often enough, they have been less important than in the history of large firms in Britain and America. Some of the large old-established firms were Australian in origin, some foreign. For instance, of the ten largest manufacturing firms listed on Australian stock exchanges in 1959 (see Table 16), three were overseas sponsored and are currently controlled from overseas: General Motors-Holden's Ltd. (established as General Motors (Australia) Pty. Ltd. in 1926), Imperial Chemical Industries of Australia and New Zealand Ltd. (established 1928), and British Tobacco Co. (Australia) Ltd. (established 1904). Not all of today's leading firms are old-established, however. Some have been formed by recent mergers (e.g., metal containers, electrical goods, motor vehicle components). Many have been created recently by overseas parents. For example, over the period September 1945 to July 1953, 292 overseas-sponsored firms were established, of which 189 were sponsored from the United Kingdom and 69 from the United States. Just over 50 per cent of these overseas firms were concentrated in three broad fields: metals and machinery, motor vehicles and other transportation equipment, and chemicals.[57]

That the large manufacturing firm has very great competitive advantages in the Australian setting has already been shown (see pp.

[57] D. M. Hocking, "The Contribution of Overseas Companies to Australia's Post-War Industrial Development," paper presented to Section G, Australian and New Zealand Association for the Advancement of Science, Melbourne, 1955, Table III (mimeographed).

70 above). That these advantages alone would be sufficient to maintain a fairly high degree of concentration, especially in industries characterized by innovation and large absolute capital requirements, seems clear. It remains to be seen if anything can be said as to the current relative importance of economies of scale.

Whatever the firms themselves may know, the outside observer has next to no knowledge of the quantitative incidence of economies of scale, even of economies of large-scale production running with the size of the individual plant. It is sometimes assumed in discussion that these plant economies will be of a similar pattern to those known to exist overseas, particularly in the United States; but there are three general characteristics of Australian production in comparison with American which make any such easy assumption suspect.

(i) Broadly speaking, Australian plants are less capital intensive (reflecting both shorter runs and less costly labor).

(ii) Because of the size of the market, Australian plants are often less specialized. This is especially true in the metal trades.

(iii) Because of the size of the market, Australian plants are sometimes less vertically integrated. Firms may confine themselves to assembling overseas products (e.g., cars, typewriters, sewing machines), thus divesting themselves of the large-scale stage of production.

The three factors listed are essentially devices which diminish the extent of economies to scale of *plant* in relation to the Australian market. There is also this important factor which may diminish the extent of economies to scale of *firm:* that overseas affiliations allow Australian firms to take advantage of research, finance, marketing, and management economies running with the extent of overseas markets. This is a second way (in addition to (iii) above) in which the small dependent economy may divest itself of large-scale activities, short of ceasing production altogether. The effect is to make possible less concentrated industries than would otherwise be the case (though at the same time raising barriers to the entry of wholly Australian firms). For example, the Australian motor vehicle market, which over the five-year period 1956-60 has absorbed on the average only 248,000 new vehicles per year, is currently supporting eight significant producers. There is a high degree of product differentiation, a proliferation of models and makes. In 1960 there were on the market about 90 car models which had been manufactured or assembled in Australia. More significantly, there were seven distinct makes[58] of cars almost wholly manufactured in Australia (about 90 per cent Australian content), and a further 45 or so makes embodying varying degrees of manufacture and assembly in Australia. While less than 5 per cent of vehicles are imported in built-up condition, and over 75 per cent are of substantially Australian manufacture, there is only one truly Australian car—only one car which is Australian both in conception and manufacture, and which is designed primarily for the Australian market. This is the Holden, which, with a production of over 100,000 units per year, is produced in considerably greater quantity than any other make. Yet even the Holden is made by a subsidiary of General Motors, and thus is dependent upon overseas know-how and research.

At the same time, Australian tariff policy has tended to enhance the importance of economies of scale as a cause of concentration. The procedure of the Tariff Board (see p. 25 above), in which the situation of each industry is examined in substantial isolation from the rest, has fostered a very diversified manufacturing structure. Not only, that is to say, is the manufacturing sector small in absolute terms; it also consists of a very large number of different industries. Tariff policy, combined with import controls over the past decade (see footnote 52,) has had two further effects upon the degree of concentration broadly construed. On the one hand, the Tariff Board has established virtually sheltered markets for industries which are, as the formula has it, "efficient and economic" (see pp. 144 below). On the other hand, the existence of high tariffs has encouraged the establishment of branches of overseas firms.

The very rapid rate of growth in the manufacturing sector since the war has widened many markets and reduced the dominance of a number of market leaders. Yet it is by no means clear that the over-all level of concentration has been decreasing. For one thing, growth has created many new industries; for another, it has been associated with structural changes whereby the more concentrated segment of manufacturing has been expanding at the relative expense of the less (see p. 67 above). The postwar merger movement pro-

[58] The term "make" is used to refer to a group of cars with the same basic body and the same basic engine. The figures given refer to the numbers of models and makes in 1960, excluding model make changeovers and excluding models or makes of which less than five units were sold.

vides an additional complication. While only a comparatively small proportion of mergers has had a significant effect upon market structure, and while some have improved the competitive position of smaller firms, on balance the merger movement has been a force making for increased concentration.[59]

The Process of Competition

It has been demonstrated that the degree of concentration which prevails throughout the Australian economy is unusually high. One might almost say that the market organization in general is the antithesis of that which underlies the laissez-faire competitive model. In each of the fields of manufacturing, mining, finance, and retailing, the greater part of activity takes place in monopolistic or oligopolistic markets. While it is true that there are significant areas of large-numbers competition in manufacturing, retailing, construction, and agriculture, only in agriculture is it pure competition; and even in agriculture there are collective marketing arrangements for commodities constituting over one-half of the value of rural output.

Nevertheless, high concentration does not necessarily imply an absence of competition, only of certain types of competition. Even the monopolized industries, by definition not subject to *close* competition, may be subject to some competition from other industries. An important example is the competition now proceeding between glass, metal, plastic, and paper containers. One notices, for instance, that the glass monopolist has been induced both to advertise its product ("Good Things Come in Glass") and to undertake itself the manufacture of plastic goods. Again, the fabricated products of materials monopolized in their basic state are often subject to competition from other fabricated products (e.g., aluminum versus copper products, structural steel versus reinforced concrete); and, as a consequence, it is likely that some indirect pressure may be brought to bear on firms monopolizing the earlier stages. In Australia, as in any technically progressive economy, inter-industry competition is of importance—though whether this is a new form of competition or an old form newly recognized is another matter. Its long-run effect, however, is to break down the old industry barriers (as has been the case in the general area of construction materials) and fashion

[59] J. A. Bushnell, *op. cit.*, chaps. v and viii.

the new. But there appears to be little support from Australian experience for the more extreme versions of the New Competition thesis. In particular, there is scant evidence for the contention that in the modern economy a continuous process of innovation (the "perennial gale") makes industry boundaries so fluid as to destroy the very notion of an industry, and with it the notion of barriers to entry. While industry boundaries are not given for all time, their shifting appears to be patchy and irregular.

Nor does increasing concentration necessarily imply a decline in competition. On the contrary, the emergence of additional market leaders may stimulate competition and lead to improved products and services and lower prices. The best examples of this proposition are to be found in recent merger activity. It is true, for instance, that mergers in retailing have increased concentration in selling markets somewhat and concentration in buying markets a great deal (see above pp. 78-79). But at the same time the general pattern of retail mergers has been the expansion of the vigorous, more efficient retailers using modern techniques into new markets through the takeover of lagging conservative family firms. The chief advantages gained have been the greater utilization of skilled management and economies in buying. For this reason the merger movement in retailing has been accompanied by an increase in efficiency of operations and an increase in competition, at least in the sense of competition to improve services and to supply a better selection of merchandise. So far as the manufacturing sector is concerned, a number of mergers (albeit a relatively small number) has significantly improved the competitive position of smaller firms. Mergers in the petroleum distribution industry, though relatively small in size, have been of particular interest in that they have helped to throw up two Australian firms sufficiently large to offer some challenge to the overseas-sponsored market leaders.[60] It may be, indeed, that some of the most important merger activity of the future will be of this pattern: to effect the union of medium and small domestic firms in industries hitherto dominated by overseas firms.

What then can be said as to the forms of competition within Australian markets? This is not the kind of question which can be answered merely by inspecting the economy at large, especially when such a high proportion of activity takes place in oligopolistic markets;

[60] *Ibid.*, pp. 159-160, 162-165.

and Australia lacks detailed industry studies. Nevertheless, while unable to answer this question in any detail, we can point to two broad characteristics of the economy as a whole which must be considered of enormous importance in determining the competitive climate: on the one hand the prevalence of restrictive practices, but on the other the rapid rate of growth.

Restrictive practices have a long history in Australia and have come to be regarded, by businessmen and consumers alike, as normal business behavior. Indeed, certainly until very recently, the average businessman would have been rather hurt to hear his trade agreements described as restrictive. For instance, the Western Australian Royal Commission on Restrictive Trade Practices and Legislation (1958) reported this exchange as indicative of business attitudes to price agreements.

Question: Can you indicate why you are not in favour of Government control and yet are in favour of private control in regard to price fixation?

Witness: Yes, because firstly we stand primarily for free enterprise and the voluntary conducting of our affairs without being bound by a statute.[61]

The Western Australian Royal Commission is the only public investigation into these matters that Australia has ever had. While most of the evidence tendered was treated as confidential and the findings are hardly specific, the Commission listed 111 known trade associations active in Western Australia and concluded:

Evidence clearly showed that there exists in Western Australia, an increasing tendency to form trade associations for the purpose of—

(a) Mutual self help to members.
(b) Channelling of distribution through its members.
(c) Collective agreement as to price fixation and the enforcement thereof.
(d) Level or collusive tendering.[62]

Quite the most spectacular example of level tendering was supplied by the Western Australian Government Railways. For forty-six listed articles (including such diverse items as cement, electrical

[61] Western Australia, Honorary Royal Commission on Restrictive Trade Practices and Legislation, *Report* (Perth, 1958), p. 14.
[62] *Ibid.*, p. 13.

cables, nails, string, tires and tubes, toilet rolls, spark plugs, and fly wire) whenever tenders are called, said the Railways, the "prices offered are identical."[63]

While just about every restrictive practice known to man is used in Australia (other than those subject to common law restraints), price agreements, both horizontal and vertical, are undoubtedly the most common. For instance, an investigation of the activities of 36 Victorian trade associations found 21 to be operating restrictive agreements of which one-half represented various types of price agreement.[64] A similar investigation of the activities of 75 South Australian trade associations found 43 to be operating restrictive agreements almost all of which contained provisions with respect to price.[65] Level tendering is certainly not confined to Western Australia. The Liberal premier of South Australia, for example, has stated that level tendering is "common" in South Australia and that the "government itself has found this to be so on numerous occasions when it has called for tenders."[66] Australia-wide price agreements (sometimes negotiated and enforced at the state level) are known to exist for the following products and services: pharmaceutical products, chocolate and confectionery, tobacco and cigarettes, automotive parts, tires and tubes, batteries, tire retreading, engine reconditioning, petroleum products, timber distribution, fibrous plaster, plywood, cement, paints, paper products, rope cordage, hardware products, footwear, fluorescent tubes, radio valves, electric lamps, copper wire and cables, bread, and books.[67] State agreements are probably even more common. Moreover, the prevailing degree of concentration is conducive to a very high order of stability in these arrangements. Of course there are exceptions: in some of the food trades characterized by large numbers, for example, the agreements are notoriously unstable. And even a highly concentrated industry with cartel-like

[63] *Ibid.*, p. 15.

[64] R. D. Freeman, "Employers' Associations in Victoria, 1840-1958" (unpublished B. Com. thesis, University of Melbourne, 1959), p. 41.

[65] P. Cook, "Trade Associations in South Australia" (unpublished B. Ec. thesis, University of Adelaide, 1961), pp. 35-38.

[66] Thomas Playford, "Free Enterprise under Changing Economic Conditions," *William Queale Memorial Lecture* (Australian Institute of Management, Adelaide, 1956), pp. 17-18.

[67] See Alex. Hunter, *op. cit.*, pp. 50-52. We are indebted to Mr. P. Cook for additional information.

agreements may revert to price competition when infected by growth and innovation.

The vertical price agreement (whereby an industry-wide price is enforced through withholding of supplies) in itself constitutes a barrier to the entry of low-cost, low-price firms. More general restraints upon entry are also common, sometimes designed to protect the trade association, sometimes the large established firm. For example, only "approved dealers" or "legitimate channels of trade" may be supplied pharmaceuticals, certain toiletries, bicycles, some furniture, Venetian blinds, plywood, timber, hardware, and certain steel products. And, as already mentioned (p. 71), the high degree of concentration is associated with the use of certain practices, which overseas would be termed "unfair practices," such as the tied contract and full-line forcing.

For a small economy such as Australia's, characterized by economies of scale, dominated by large firms, and with negligible legislative restraints upon monopolies and restrictive practices, a rapid rate of growth is the chief prerequisite for entry of new firms into the corporate sector. There is room for all (both for the established firm to expand and the new firm to enter). In addition, special opportunities arise from the innovations associated with growth. Though no adequate statistics exist, it is clear that the rapid rate of growth of Australian manufacturing since the war has made possible the establishment of a very large number of new firms. The entry of overseas-sponsored manufacturing firms has been of special importance in breaking down certain old-established positions of market dominance. The competitive advantages of the established overseas-sponsored firm have already been stressed. Its advantages upon entry are also impressive. It enters as a going concern, with access to overseas innovation and know-how, and with sufficient financial strength to begin on a large-scale, to carry substantial establishment expenses (accounting losses) and, if need be, to buck the existing "channels of trade."[68] Generally speaking, the most important of

[68] The most spectacular example of this has occurred in the cigarette industry where Rothmans of Pall Mall (Australia) Ltd. has succeeded in raising its market share from zero to over 40 per cent in the space of six years (1955-61). In absolute terms, the sales have been achieved partly through market growth and partly at the expense of British Tobacco (Australia) Ltd. which had dominated the market from the turn of the century. In the decade preceding entry, the market trebled. Rothmans came bearing a £1 million establishment loan in the one hand and an overseas innovation in the other (the king-size filter in the flip-top box).

these advantages has been the access to overseas innovations and know-how. A comprehensive investigation of product-innovation in Australia over the years 1939-53 had this as its most important conclusion:

With one or two notable exceptions, it is hardly an exaggeration to say that in every technically dynamic industry practically every major innovation has been introduced since the War by a firm wholly or partly owned by one or more overseas concerns.[69]

While many of these innovations would have been made by well-established firms, many also would have accompanied the entry of newcomers.

Moreover, a rapid rate of growth is in itself a stimulant to internal competition (even without entry), especially if accompanied by the introduction of new techniques and new products. Even a highly concentrated industry may find firms competing vigorously for future shares in a rapidly growing market. At the very least this will be through sales promotion; but often, too, it will be through product and service improvement, and sometimes even through cost and price reduction. Over the last decade, for example, there have been some dramatic improvements in value for money in the products offered by the major domestic appliances industry (one of the most rapidly developing manufacturing industries in the economy). Not only has quality been increased; prices have been substantially reduced. In retailing, the rapid expansion of urban boundaries in postwar years has provoked a number of convenience trades, hitherto characterized by "customary prices," into a flurry of price cutting in outer areas. And low-cost innovators in the grocery trade, introducing large-scale self-service stores and relying upon streamlined chain-store principles of distribution, have cut through the long-standing practice of resale price maintenance.

One symptom of competition in a growing market, so far as manufacturing is concerned, is the tendency of firms to create capacity in advance of the market. Table 23 displays a striking contrast in creation of capacity between the behavior of monopolists and the behavior of all other firms. It has long been recognized that over-capacity is frequently characteristic of large-numbers competition; Australian experience suggests it may frequently also be character-

[69] D. M. Hocking, "Research—The Economic Implications," *Journal of the Australian Institute of Metals* (May 1958), p. 29.

TABLE 23. *Unused Capacity in Large Units of Selected Manufacturing Industries, 1958*[a]
(number of industries)

Market type	Less than 5 per cent	5 per cent and less than 20 per cent	20 per cent and less than 50 per cent	50 per cent and over	Total
			Scope for increased production		
Monopolies	6	2[b]	1	1	10
Highly concentrated oligopolies	1	2	9	6	18
Fairly concentrated industries	—	1	5	8	14
Slightly concentrated and unconcentrated industries	1	—	4	4	9
Total	8	5	19	19	51

Source: Compiled from Department of Trade, *Survey of Capacity in Use,* 1958, mimeographed report issued in 1959.

[a] Fifty-one industries have been classified by market type and unused capacity. While the classification by market type is that of the author, the figures relating to capacity are those of the Department of Trade. The Department of Trade obtained their figures from a sample survey of manufacturing firms. A "unit of production" in this survey was usually the plant or division of plant engaged on manufacture of the type of product concerned. However, in some cases firms submitted combined returns for all plants or divisions of plants producing the one type of product. A "large" unit of production was separately defined for each industry. The figures indicating scope for increased production are at manufacturers' own "preferred level of operations" (including preferred number of shifts), and "assuming adequate demand and no shortages of labour, power or materials."

The "industries" selected from the capacity survey are essentially those to which the concentration estimates may be applied. Their boundaries do not necessarily coincide with the boundaries of the concentration industries. They do not constitute a representative sample of manufacturing, since they include an undue proportion of industries in the fields of metals, machinery, transportation equipment, and construction materials.

[b] One of these is paper. The concentration estimates distinguished three paper industries (see, for example, Table 21), all monopolistic in structure; but it is possible to obtain capacity figures only for the three industries combined.

istic of oligopolistic competition. In interpreting this table it should be noted that while the latter part of the fifties (1957-59) is sometimes referred to as a period of recession this was true only in a very relative sense; for the percentage unemployed ranged between 1.3 and 1.6 per year. It is not suggested that all cases of oligopolistic overcapacity are explained by this kind of competition-for-future-shares, but some certainly are (at least in part), including rubber tires, paints, motor vehicles, and major domestic appliances. In a situation of growth, there is some presumption that even a tightly oligopolistic industry will not behave like a monopolistic cartel. Some degree of overcapacity (though not necessarily the degree which prevails) may be regarded as both normal and socially desirable in the Australian setting. The size of the market is such that the typical plant expands in lumpy fashion; and further, in certain industries, it must stand ready to serve a variety of relatively specialized demands. It may be that the monopolized industries are somewhat out of step; and none is more out of step than the basic steel industry which, for the greater part of the period since the war, has been either unable or unwilling to create sufficient capacity fully to meet the economy's demands.

This raises the question of the extent to which there is "workable" or "effective" competition in Australian oligopolies. A short answer would be that we do not know, since we have little knowledge of the process of competition in particular markets or of the results achieved. Yet there are certain distinctive features of the Australian economy which permit us to say something of the possibilities. The concept of workable competition is not especially precise. Indeed, somebody has remarked that there are almost as many definitions of workable competition as there are working economists. Nevertheless, the core idea may be stated thus: there should be sufficient market rivalry to compel firms to produce with internal efficiency, to price in accordance with costs, to meet the consumers' demand for variety, and to strive for product and process improvement.

It would be overoptimistic to assume that the rapid rate of growth of the Australian economy is sufficient to throw all oligopolistic industries into workable competition. First, not all oligopolistic industries are growing rapidly. Now since in Australia restrictive practices are so widely accepted, oligopolistic agreements are more likely to be overt than tacit. We should thus expect stationary or declining industries frequently to be characterized by such practices as overt price agreements, market sharing, and restrictions on entry. Secondly, even industries which are growing rapidly need not *necessarily* be characterized by rivalrous behavior. If for instance (taking a strong case), firms are of somewhat equal market strength and there is little innovation and high barriers to entry, firms may negotiate agreements as to future market shares. The simplest division of a market is geographic. It is noticeable in Australia that firms in light industry often confine themselves to two or three capital cities, and it is suspected that some of these cases are explained by agreements or understandings among the firms concerned; certainly, such a market-sharing arrangement existed in the biscuit industry for many years and currently exists in the salt industry.

It is generally accepted by economists that the conditions most conducive to oligopolistic rivalry are a rapidly growing market, some uncertainty as to firms' relative market strengths (including the prospects of innovations), and either the threat or the achievement of entry by new firms. Yet, even if these conditions are satisfied, the composition may not be an altogether full-blooded affair. In the first place, some firms may choose to abstain. The sanction for "failure" tends not to be bankruptcy, but merely reduction in market share; for growth of the market as a whole serves to protect the absolute size of a firm's sales and profits. Under such circumstances, a firm's production and selling policies (in particular how vigorously it will compete for its share of the growing market) are partly dependent upon the goals of those who control the enterprise. But perhaps too much should not be made of this point; it has already been suggested (see p. 60) that for many Australian companies ownership and control are sufficiently united for profit-making to be a leading objective. A more important point is that the competition may be diverted from prices and costs to products and advertising. It is certainly not suggested that price competition is the only acceptable form of competition, nor that product improvement, product variation, and advertising are automatically suspect. But competition which is to be regarded as "workable" or "effective" must not be of a one-sided kind. Some degree of price flexibility, (though not necessarily short-run price flexibility) is essential if the price mechanism is to perform its social function, namely to secure the most efficient production of those goods which are most highly demanded. Effective competition requires that prices should reflect costs and that consumers should be given a choice between various combinations of product and price (for example, between high-priced chrome and low-priced utility). One has the impression that in Australia relative prices are not especially flexible in this sense of being subject to the push and pull of the forces of demand and supply. To some extent the lack of flexibility is explained by the importance of monopolies; but to some extent, also, it is explained by the general acceptance of price agreements, so that even in a situation of oligopolistic rivalry, competition often stops short of price. This is not always the case, as has already been stressed. In particular, the introduction of a low-cost innovation or the entry of a new firm is often accompanied by price reduction. It would seem fair to say, however, that the Australian code of business conduct (reinforced by an absence of legislative restraints) is such that the same market situation would be less likely to produce price competition in Australia than it would in the United States.

Whatever the extent of effective competition in Australia it is much less than pervasive; and the results of Australian market organization may be expected to be distinctly less than perfect. Both these conclusions are supported by some financial and cost data recently published by the Tariff Board, a selection of which is presented in Table 24. The data relate to five anonymous manufacturing industries within each of which are produced "essentially similar products," accounting in aggregate for sales of £57 million.[70] The veil of secrecy which surrounds Australian business is rarely lifted. In this instance we catch a glimpse of some extraordinary ranges of efficiency and profitability within the one industry. The Tariff Board drew attention to the wide range in results achieved and commented somewhat dryly that "clearly the need for closer management control is manifest."[71]

TABLE 24. *Financial and Cost Data for Selected Manufacturing Industries, 1959-60*

Industry	Net profit (prior to taxation and interest) as a percentage of total funds[a]		Stocks (including work in progress) as a percentage of sales		Materials as a percentage of factory cost	
	average	range	average	range	average	range
A	10.3	5.3 to 23.3	24.3	16.7 to 33.0	76.0	72.5 to 84.3
B	12.7	3.3 to 67.0	28.0	3.7 to 54.7	43.5	36.5 to 48.0
C	48.0	3.2 to 71.8	17.1	12.5 to 43.7	68.5	17.0 to 69.3
D	8.7	4.3 to 17.0	22.8	17.7 to 32.5	59.0	48.5 to 64.9
E	8.6	loss to 25.2	31.2	17.1 to 49.4	62.1	43.7 to 78.0

Source: Tariff Board, *Annual Report*, 1959-60, p. 35.
 [a] Adjusted in accordance with the Tariff Board's requirements.

[70] Tariff Board, *Annual Report*, 1959-60 (Canberra, 1960), p. 12.
[71] *Ibid.*

The Economic Activities of Government

Government Involvement in Production

Government involvement in the ordinary economic activities of the community can come about through ownership by public authorities of business enterprises and through the absorption of the fruits of production by public authorities for the purpose of providing collective goods and services. In the former case the government is a producer selling its output to private households and firms. For a variety of reasons public authority business enterprises are unlikely to conform to a competitive pattern in their behavior. They are nearly always large units; they are frequently monopolies; they are invariably used, at least to some degree, to serve political ends which, however vital they may be, have little to do with maximizing profits. In providing collective goods and services the government's role is partly that of a producer, when it employs public servants, and partly that of a consumer, when it spends its revenue on the services of these public servants and on the purchase of goods and services from the private sector. Here the independent preferences of individuals are replaced by the scale of values of the government.

Thus, government involvement in the economy has two aspects which may differ considerably in magnitude. It is possible to imagine a situation in which government business enterprise is extensive but the provision of collective goods and services relatively small; alternatively there may be little government business enterprise but an extensive provision of collective goods and services. In the former case there will be a large area of the economy to which the competitive laissez-faire model is unlikely to be applicable. In the latter case the substantial portion of income which will have to be collected in the form of taxation must influence the workings of the private sector, just as the collective demand of the government must affect the pattern of production.

In Australia both aspects of government participation are important. The first can be measured roughly by the proportion of national income originating from the productive activities of public authorities, and the second by the proportion of gross national product devoted to government expenditure on goods and services. Nearly

20 per cent of national income is generated by the public sector. This, however, underestimates the true importance of the public sector. Factor incomes generated in this way include only the wages and salaries of public servants and of the employees of public authority business undertakings plus the relatively small net revenues of these undertakings. They do not include anything corresponding to the "surplus" from which profits and interest payments are paid out in the private sector. In fact, wages and salaries paid out by the public sector constitute nearly 30 per cent of all wages and salaries. Thus, a true measure of the importance of the productive activity of the public sector would probably be between 20 and 30 per cent. On the expenditure side nearly 20 per cent of gross national product is absorbed by the public sector in the provision of collective goods and services, including developmental works.

As far as employment is concerned about one-fifth of the total work force, including employers, is employed by governmental authorities of one sort or another. The proportion of wage and salary earners, other than rural employees and members of defense forces, who are government employees is about one-quarter; but the trend has been slightly upward, having risen from 23½ per cent in 1939 to 26½ per cent in 1952, since when it has remained relatively stable.

Government Business Enterprises

While it is true that nearly 30 per cent of all wages and salaries originate in the public sector, this figure greatly exaggerates the importance of public enterprise in the business field. It does so because it includes the payment of wages and salaries for the provision of collective goods and services and also for public works. The wages and salaries paid by the public authority business enterprises constitute only about one-seventh of the total paid by all business enterprises and this gives a rough measure of the importance of government undertakings in the business field. Moreover, although the relative importance of government activity as a whole has increased somewhat, the relative importance of governments in the business field has not changed since the end of World War II.

Traditionally, public enterprise has always played an important role in the Australian economy. In the field of public utilities and developmental works, government enterprise has always been predominant. The sheer size of the country, the sparsity of population in rural areas, and the distances between the centers of population have rendered projects within this field unattractive to private enterprise; not only because many of them could never be paying propositions without government subsidies, but also because they would involve capital expenditure far beyond the resources of private concerns. Public enterprise is shared between Commonwealth, state, and local governmental authorities, with the states controlling the major part. In recent years the Commonwealth has come to be involved in a number of major developmental projects.

Apart from the production and distribution of electricity and gas, governments have had an almost complete responsibility for public utilities. In the field of transport, governments have a virtual monopoly over railways, tramways, roads, bridges, and ports and harbors; although they share with private enterprise in airlines, shipping, omnibus and road transport services. There is, however, a considerable amount of competition between government and private transport facilities, and the complex relations between government and private activities in the transport industry warrants detailed discussion. Since there have been a number of developments in the transport industry since the end of World War II, which are referred to later in this section, it is convenient to postpone this discussion until after these references have been made.

In communications the government has complete control over posts, telegraphs, telephones, and telecommunications and operates over one-third of the broadcasting and telecasting stations. The national stations do not provide advertising services so that there is no competition between national and commercial stations in relation to advertisers. There is no doubt some competition in the quality of broadcasts and telecasts, and the national stations cater to a somewhat less "popular" audience.

As far as power is concerned, although electricity was first developed mainly by private concerns, there has been over the past forty years a steady trend towards public ownership. This has been due to a number of factors: first, the need for integration and coordination of electricity generation and distribution; second, the need for the electrification of rural areas; and third, the great sums involved in expanding capacity to meet the tremendous increase in the demand for power (production of electricity has increased by nearly five-fold in the past twenty years). Now, substantially all electricity for public consumption is provided by government undertakings. However, the gas industry is in public hands in only Victoria and Western Australia.

Governments (mainly state governments) provide all public water supply and sewerage services and control water resources, dams, and irrigation works. Four-fifths of all forests are government owned, but they are usually exploited by private enterprise under license.

Publicly owned corporations are also important in the field of banking. Until recently there were no private savings banks, all savings bank business being conducted by the Commonwealth Savings Bank which operated in all states and by the State Savings Bank of Victoria, the Savings Bank of South Australia, and two trustee savings banks in Tasmania. In 1956, however, four new savings banks—three of them offshoots from private trading banks and the other an offshoot from a state bank—were permitted to commence business under conditions similar to those under which the government and trustee savings banks operate. The private savings banks have developed rapidly and now hold nearly 20 per cent of all savings bank deposits. As far as trading or commercial banking is concerned, the Commonwealth Trading Bank of Australia (a creation of the Commonwealth Government) and the state banks in New South Wales, South Australia, and Western Australia have assets amounting to one-sixth of all trading bank assets, the Commonwealth Trading Bank being the second largest in Australia.

In banking, competition between public and private enterprise has been of considerable significance. The Commonwealth Trading Bank has, since its inception in 1911, competed with the private banks, although the strength of its competition has varied according to government policy. Until 1959 the Commonwealth Trading Bank (and the Commonwealth Savings Bank) was administered under the Governor and Board of the Commonwealth Bank (i.e., the Central Bank). This gave rise to fears from the private banks of unfair competition. To allay these fears restraint was exercised in competing with the private banks. Nevertheless, the Commonwealth Trading Bank has grown in relative as well as in absolute importance. In 1949 its deposits were 9 per cent of those of the private banks; by 1960 this figure had grown to 18 per cent. In 1960, largely in response to political pressure from the private banks, the trading and savings banks were completely separated from the Central Bank. The Commonwealth Trading Bank is now likely to display even greater competitive vigor. Some of its strength has been derived from its close associate, the Commonwealth Savings Bank, and the entry of the private banks into savings banking has been a direct consequence of this. There can be little doubt that government enterprise has raised the degree of competitiveness in banking.

Governments have also been active in the provision of housing, and since 1945 state housing authorities have been responsible for the erection of almost one-fifth of all houses and flats completed. Their construction has been undertaken by the authorities themselves or has been on a contract basis with private builders. These dwellings have been both for sale and for renting. Since the war state housing authorities have been the main providers of houses for renting, and certainly, in some states, e.g., South Australia, the costs of publicly built houses have been lower than those of privately constructed ones. This has kept housing prices in general lower than would otherwise have been the case, and has led to the promotion of large-scale housing estates by private enterprise. Apart from the direct construction of homes, government instrumentalities have played a significant part in the provision of finance for home building.

Government activity extends in a minor way to many fields of business enterprise, for example, insurance, lotteries, race-course betting facilities, sawmills, brickworks, grain elevators, abattoirs, drugs, and uranium, tin, and coal mining. But in general its influence through these spheres is relatively unimportant.

Mention should be made of the part played by governments in the provision of research services. The main research organization in Australia is the Commonwealth Scientific and Industrial Research Organization, which is financed by the Commonwealth Government. This organization is freely consulted by industry and has made very substantial contributions to Australia's technological progress. Research is also undertaken in a number of other government instrumentalities and in the universities. It is only in recent years that private industry has established any research units and then only the largest concerns have been able to do so. Research remains almost wholly in non-private hands.

Since 1945 there have been a number of major developments in public enterprise. In 1946 overseas telecommunications passed into public control with the nationalization by the Commonwealth Government of the two private companies operating in this field. This was part of an international arrangement involving British Commonwealth countries. During the next few years the long-standing trend towards public ownership of electrical undertakings was virtually completed by the nationalization of the Adelaide Electric Supply Company by the South Australian Government in 1946, and the creation of the Southern Electricity Authority of Queensland in 1952 to take over two private companies. In 1950 the Victorian Government nationalized the main producer and distributer of gas.

These acts of nationalization were essentially tidying-up operations and did not represent any determination to extend public ownership into new fields. However, such a determination was present in the legislation enacted by the Commonwealth Parliament in 1945. This legislation was sponsored by the Labor government, with the object of nationalizing interstate airlines and banking. The nationalization of the airlines was intended to cope with two problems: first, the monopolization of trunk routes by the leading private operator, and second, the provision of more adequate air services; that of the banks was aimed at a greater measure of control over the monetary system than could be brought about by ordinary central banking operations. Nationalization of these industries was in accordance with the political platform of the Australian Labor party. Both these acts of nationalization were challenged before the High Court and Privy Council and both were held to be *ultra vires* under the Constitution.

The Commonwealth Government has been active in the establishment of a number of new government enterprises since the war. The most important of these have been the Australian Aluminium Production Commission (1945) (jointly with the Tasmanian Government) to produce aluminum; Trans-Australia Airlines (1946) to operate air services in competition with the one major private operator; the Snowy Mountains Hydro-electric Authority (1949) to implement a very large scheme for the diversion of water in the Snowy Mountains area for the generation of electricity and irrigation; the Australian Coastal Shipping Commission (1949) to operate interstate shipping services; the Australian Whaling Commission (1949) to establish and develop the whaling industry; and the Atomic Energy Commission (1953), which is concerned with the construction and operation of atomic plant and mining and research. Apart from these, two semi-regulatory authorities have been set up, first, the Joint Coal Board (1947) (jointly with the New South Wales Government) to insure that the coal of New South Wales is conserved, developed, and worked in the public interest and to promote the welfare of the workers in the industry, and second the Australian Stevedoring Industry Authority (1956) to regulate stevedoring. The Joint Coal Board operates a number of mining companies, which were fully owned by the Commonwealth, but with the passing of the postwar coal shortage the Board has felt that it should not continue its producing activities; and in 1957 it sold one of the collieries to private interests and the remaining two to the Electricity Commission of New South Wales. The Commonwealth also established, in 1956, the Exports Payments Insurance Corporation for the purpose of providing insurance against non-payment in overseas trade.

On the other hand, since the accession to power of the Liberal government in 1949, the Commonwealth has handed back certain enterprises to the private sector. The shares of Amalgamated Wireless (Australia) and of Commonwealth Engineering Company (both wholly owned by the Commonwealth) have been sold to the public. Similarly, the Commonwealth's half-share in Commonwealth Oil Refinery Limited has been sold to Anglo-Iranian Oil and the assets of the Australian Whaling Commission have been sold to private interests. In 1960 the aluminum works of the Australian Aluminium Production Commission were sold to private enterprise, although the Tasmanian Government is returning its interest. In total, however, this does not amount to a great deal, and in no case did the government-owned enterprise hold a dominant position in an important industry.

It will be inferred from the above that the national ownership of public utilities and the creation of national enterprises for large-scale development purposes is part and parcel of the pattern of the Australian economy. This is accepted by the public generally and by the two major political parties. Political issues are involved, however, when questions are raised of nationalizing existing industries outside the scope of the traditional public enterprises or of extending government enterprises into fields which private enterprise is prepared to exploit. Although, given the present constitutional limitations, it is extremely unlikely that an attempt to nationalize a major industry would be successful, the Labor party still favors nationalization of certain major industries, while the Liberal party is firmly opposed. At the same time the Liberal party has shown itself willing to sell public enterprises to private interests if they can be properly and efficiently run by them. While it is dangerous to generalize on these matters, it seems that a substantial majority of the general public is against any large-scale nationalization of existing industries, but equally there is a strong feeling against the disposal to private interests of successful government enterprises. This feeling was evidenced only recently when a rumor that the Commonwealth Serum Laboratories might be sold to private interests provoked a storm of public protest.

Many government enterprises suffer large losses in their operations. This is so particularly in the cases of country water supplies and irrigation, metropolitan passenger transportation and state railways. These losses do not necessarily reflect technical inefficiencies, although no doubt in some cases management has not been as efficient as it might have been. They are due partly to the lack of density of demand for the services and partly to the use which has been made of these services to open up new areas. Thus, certain groups of consumers have been heavily subsidized from time to time through the operations of the railways or water supplies. On the other hand, many government enterprises break even on their current operations. This is probably the case for electrical undertakings, metropolitan water supplies, and postal and telephone services. Substantial profits have been made by some enterprises, but generally the enterprises are required to provide their services at cost. This has prevented most from financing capital expansion from profits to the same extent as they would have done if they had been privately controlled. However, some undertakings have been able to adopt a pricing policy which has permitted the retention of profit for capital purposes. The Melbourne Harbour Trust has been doing this for many years, and more recently the State Electricity Commission of Victoria has been following the same policy in an attempt to secure capital funds, having failed to do so on the public market.

Transport provides the most important field in which private and public enterprise compete. The nature of this competition can be seen by examining the development of air and sea transport since World War II.[72]

In domestic civil aviation there was, prior to 1946, only one trunkline operator of significance. This was Australian National Airways Limited. It was controlled by the larger shipping companies operating on the Australian coast and had grown rapidly by absorbing small operators and linking their services into a single network. In 1944 the Commonwealth Labor Government attempted, by referendum, to obtain sufficient powers to nationalize all air services, state and interstate. When this attempt failed, it proceeded with a bill to nationalize interstate operators. As mentioned above (p. 112) this legislation failed when challenged in the High Court and the Privy Council. Defeated in its attempts to nationalize civil aviation the government in 1946 created its own airline, Trans-Australia Airlines, to compete with the private interstate operators. While the policy of nationalizing civil aviation sprang partly from political doctrines, it was also based on defense, national development, and the heavy dependence of the industry on government provision of flight facilities.

Following the establishment of TAA, competition within the industry impinged with great severity on ANA. TAA as a result of wise investment decisions built up a fleet markedly superior to that of ANA. Moreover, TAA had a virtual monopoly of airmail contracts and government business. Although neither TAA nor ANA was indulging in price competition, rates were cut by Ansett Airways, a small but growing competitor. This had more serious consequences for ANA than for TAA because of the inferiority of ANA's fleet and because of the recent deterioration in its safety record. By 1949 ANA faced the dilemma of incurring losses at a time when substantial investment in new heavy aircraft was necessary for its continued existence. In that year ANA approached the government to merge the two major trunkline enterprises. However, with the government's early objective of a public monopoly almost achieved, the negotiations for the merger foundered on the obstacle of personalities. Shortly after, the Labor party was defeated in the elections and the Liberal party gained control of the Federal Parliament. The new government's solution to the industry's problems was to

[72] We are indebted to our colleague, Mr. R. R. Hirst, for supplying us with the material relating to air and sea transport used in this section.

establish "fair and active competition" between the major airlines. This policy required the resuscitation of ANA.

The principle of fair and active competition was implemented in 1952 by the government's negotiating a fifteen-year contract with TAA and ANA, whereby financial assistance was to be provided for the immediate re-equipment of both fleets and their subsequent re-equipment some seven years later. Mail was to be shared equally; travelers with government warrants were free to choose between the airlines; and both operators agreed to a rationalization of routes, timetables, freights, and fares to avoid overlapping and to bring earnings into proper relation with over-all costs. While the rationalization agreement reduced the areas of competition between TAA and ANA, it did not restrict competition in equipment, the most significant form of competition in the industry. Furthermore, both enterprises were subject to price competition from Ansett Airways whose business steadily grew.

Early in 1957 ANA, whose finances were deteriorating again, proposed the formation of a holding company to operate TAA and ANA. This suggestion was rejected by the government, because it was inconsistent with its philosophy of competing airlines. ANA then proceeded to sell the enterprise to Ansett Industries, the new firm taking the name of Ansett-ANA.

The present policy under which the government and private airlines compete is even more restrictive than the conditions of the 1952 agreement: the government through its guarantee of equipment loans now exercises control over the quality as well as the quantity of capital to be provided. The airlines are required to invest in similar aircraft to avoid equipment competition; and a formula has been established whereby each operator purchases sufficient capacity to operate its non-competitive services and to provide for half the estimated traffic on the competitive routes at an optimum load factor. Thus, the industry has evolved a structure that is the antithesis of competition—market sharing, investment control, and the rationalization of fares, services, and timetables. However, structural changes in the industry may still come about through the integration of trunkline and feeder services. Such changes, together with sales promotion, appear to exhaust the scope for competition which now remains.

The Commonwealth Government entered the shipping industry

in the early war years when it built tonnage to supplement private shipowners' fleets which were inadequate for Australia's wartime needs. After World War II the Labor government expanded the National Line, which was controlled by the Australian Shipping Board, until its fleet was the largest on the Australian coast. This was on the argument that a government operator could restrain increases in freight rates and provide orders for the local shipyards which would insure, in a national emergency, adequate shipbuilding facilities to meet defense requirements.

There is little evidence that the Australian National Line does compete actively with the private operators. The industry is not a homogenous one. About 75 per cent of the government ships are engaged in bulk trade, whereas privately operated fleets concentrate on general cargo. For many years the industry has been highly rationalized; committees of shipowners have integrated ships' movements, having regard for the availability of cargoes, their priority, and the avoidance of port congestion. The disposition of government and private ships is determined by mutual agreement in committee, while the booking and stevedoring of their cargoes is left to the private shipowners, who also act as the National Line's agents. Freight rates are determined by a special committee of shipowners; but in practice the Australian Shipping Board and its successor, the Australian Coastal Shipping Commission, have been dominant in that committee and have acted as the regulator of interstate shipping freight rates. Thus the creation of the National Line appears to have been used as an instrument of competition much less than might have been expected. However in the early postwar years the National Line did have a restraining influence on freight rates, as its full costs were lower than those of private operators; the Australian Shipping Board was required to secure only a 4 per cent return on the depreciated value of its assets and was exempt from income taxation.

Shipping policy altered in the 1950's, following the change of government. The Liberal government offered to sell the fleet to private operators on the principle that, if private enterprise could supply shipping services, public money should not be used for this purpose. Failing to find a buyer on its terms, the government decided in 1956 to continue operating the shipping line, but to encourage private shipping. A twenty-year agreement was made with shipowners, in which the Commonwealth Government undertook to use private stevedoring and booking facilities and to limit the rate of growth of the National Line to about 1.5 per cent per annum. The National Line was not to be given favored treatment but was required to pay all taxes and return 6 per cent on its capital. The private shipowners, for their part, agreed to provide the necessary vessels for an economic and efficient interstate service and to order sufficient tonnage to keep Australian shipyards adequately employed. Should they fail to do so, the government might use its own ships to achieve this end. However, it might do this only after confirmation by an arbitrator, an unusual abrogation of authority by a government on what constitutes the national welfare. Thus the government can control the industry's investment policy and the quality of shipping services, while through the operation of the National Line it may also control the industry's pricing policy.

The above discussion relates to direct government participation in industry. Distinct from this is the assistance which governments give private enterprise in order to encourage the establishment of particular industries. This assistance may take several forms. It may involve facilitating finance, by arranging loans or giving bank guarantees. This kind of help is sometimes given by Australian governments, but it has not been extensive. Alternatively, governments (particularly state governments) may provide physical facilities, like water, power or housing, which will be required by the growing industry. This has occurred quite extensively, particularly in the less developed states. Examples of this are associated with the establishment of an oil refinery at Kwinana in Western Australia and of an integrated steel plant at Whyalla in South Australia. Finally the Commonwealth Government may pay subsidies and bounties on certain products or may make special tax concessions. Apart from subsidies to the dairying and shipbuilding industries, and for oil exploration, subsidies and bounties are not being extensively used. Tax concessions are available to the oil and gold mining industries and the tax laws favor rural producers. Between 1946 and 1951, initial depreciation allowances (i.e., accelerated depreciation allowances) for tax purposes were permitted to businesses, but at no stage has any provision been made for investment allowances or similar tax concessions. Recently, the Commonwealth Government announced its intention of making tax concessions to encourage export promotion.

Collective Goods and Services

Since before World War II there has been an appreciable rise in government expenditure on goods and services relative to gross national product. In 1938-39 this expenditure, both capital and current, but excluding all transfer payments, was 13 per cent of gross national product. During the war it rose very steeply, reaching a peak of 42 per cent in 1942-43. It dropped sharply after the war but remained above the 1938-39 figure, being 14½ per cent in 1948-49. By 1960-61 it had risen to 18½ per cent. The omission of defense expenditure does not alter the picture, the percentages excluding defense being 11½ per cent, 12½ per cent, and 16 per cent for the three years 1938-39, 1948-49, and 1960-61, respectively. Thus, over the past two decades (leaving aside the abnormal war years), the public sector has absorbed an increasing proportion of goods and services. The proportion of the gross national product devoted to non-defense government expenditure on goods and services in Australia is almost as high as that for the United Kingdom, higher than that for Canada, and nearly half as high again as that for the United States. When defense expenditure is included, Australia's proportion is less than that of the United States and the United Kingdom.

It is not surprising to find an upward trend in government expenditure after the war. The great extension of government activity left a legacy of services which survived the virtual extinction of defense spending (defense expenditure fell from £536 million in 1942-43 to £20 million in 1947-48) and the dismantling of wartime controls. Many of these services were ones to which people had become accustomed, and there was a general acceptance of the need for greater government expenditures. The movement in expenditure since the war can be explained mainly in terms of four components: defense, education, health, and public works. Table 25 sets out the main items of government expenditure on goods and services for 1948-49 and 1960-61.

The increase in defense expenditure shown in this table must be interpreted with care. After the war, defense expenditure was rapidly

TABLE 25. *Net Expenditure on Goods and Services by Public Authorities, 1948-49 and 1960-61*

	1948-49 (£ million)	1960-61 (£ million)
War and defense	41	193
Public works	142	585
Law and order	13	49
Education	27	149
Cultural and recreational facilities	5	25
Health and welfare	24	98
Repatriation	13	20
Immigration	4	12
Development and conservation of national resources	14	53
Civil aviation	3	11
Other	42	129
Total	328	1,324
Gross national product	2,283	6,778

Source: Commonwealth of Australia, *National Income and Expenditure*, 1951-52 and 1960-61

reduced. However, during the years 1949-50, 1950-51, and 1951-52 it increased considerably, partly because of the deterioration in the international situation and the Korean War and partly as a political anti-communist gesture. However, since 1951-52 defense expenditure has hardly risen in money terms and it has certainly fallen in real terms. As a proportion of total government expenditure it is now about the same as in 1950-51, namely about one-sixth; and although still an important item it cannot be said to be a dominant one. Its decline in importance since 1951-52 and 1952-53 is only partly due to the changing international situation. More important, it reflects the feeling that in Australia's peculiar situation the long-term strength and stability of the country is better served by rapid economic development both in terms of productivity and population. Developmental expenditure on public works has thus been the main consideration. Indeed, many hold the view that substantial cuts in defense expenditure, with expanded effort put into public works, is desirable. In fact, a good deal has been done in this direction by preventing defense expenditure from growing over the past eight years.

Public works expenditure has expanded considerably over the past decade, although it went through a period of relative stagnation from 1951-52 to 1954-55. It is important to emphasize the key position which this expenditure occupies in Australia. As has been pointed out above, transport, communications, and power are almost wholly organized as public enterprises. Their capital expenditure thus comes under the heading of "public works." These industries are the sinews of a modern economy; and growth, whether in the public or private sectors, cannot proceed without their prior development. For the past decade Australia has been growing very rapidly, both because of population growth and because of technological progress. Under these circumstances substantial expenditures on public works (public capital formation) are a *sine qua non* of continued growth.

In recent years gross capital formations has been about one-quarter of gross national product. It might be noted, in passing, that with a capital-output ratio of about four, nearly two-fifths of this (i.e., about 10 per cent of gross national product) would be required for widening investment to keep pace with the growth of the work force. Of gross capital formation about two-thirds has occurred in the private and one-third in the public sectors. It has been commonly argued over the past few years that public investment, even though substantial, has been inadequate to provide a firm foundation for the private sector and to provide satisfactory community amenities. Indeed, in spite of its great importance it has tended to be a residual item, being cut or restrained in periods of inflationary pressure. Private investment, subject only to modifications in banking policy, has in fact been pretty well free to expand as desired. In the earlier postwar years this gave rise to the accusation that Australia was a "milk-bar economy," essential services (like transport and power) being grossly deficient while the fripperies of urban life proliferated. More recently public investment has been expanding, and it is likely to continue to do so as the rate of increase of the work force quickens because of the trend of the birth rate in the forties.

Table 26 gives an idea of the relative importance of the main items included in public works. Expenditure in relation to post office, railways, other transport, fuel and power represents the capital formation of public business enterprises in those fields.

The rapid growth in expenditure on education reflects both the

TABLE 26. *Public Authority Expenditure on Public Works,*
1957-58 to 1960-61

	Per cent
Post Office	6.9
Railways	6.4
Roads	23.6
Other transport	6.8
Fuel and power	20.3
Water supply and sewerage	10.3
Irrigation	2.4
Forestry, land development, etc.	2.3
Dwelling construction[a]	4.0
Schools, etc.	6.9
Hospitals	3.5
All other	6.6
	100

Source: Commonwealth of Australia, *National Income and Expenditure,* 1960-61.
    [a] Includes only expenditure on construction for rental purposes, representing less than 8 per cent of total expenditure for dwelling construction.

growing school population and the tendency for children to stay longer at school. The school-leaving age is sixteen years in Tasmania, fifteen years in New South Wales, and fourteen years in the other states. All children must stay at school until these ages; but full employment and a rising standard of living, together with a growing awareness of the importance of secondary and tertiary education in a technological age, have combined to lead to a rapid decrease in the proportion of children who actually leave at the minimum age. Since prewar, school enrolments have doubled and in the past decade they have increased by above 50 per cent. They will continue to increase rapidly, but the next decade will see the bulge of enrolments advancing into the universities, which expect a 70 per cent increase in their enrolments in the next five or six years. It should be pointed out that while the universities are all government-sponsored institutions, deriving 80 per cent of their revenues from governmental grants (the balance being 15 per cent from fees and 5 per cent from endowment income and private grants), only three-quarters of school children are educated at government schools. The remainder attend private schools, mostly church schools. The main group of these is the Roman Catholic one. This group is heavily subsidized by the Roman Catholic Church. Other private schools are, by and large, self-supporting and charge relatively high fees. Recently a group of private industrialists has made a novel move by proposing to make grants to equip the laboratories of private schools. It is also of interest to note that the relative importance of the private schools has grown slightly over the past twenty years and is now greater than at any time during the past seventy years. New private schools are opening and there is no indication of any change in the dual, private-state, system of primary and secondary education. At present nearly one-fifth of current expenditure on education is financed by the payment of fees to fee-charging institutions.

Expenditure on health and welfare (excluding all cash social service benefits, which are considered below) has also grown with the increase in population and the desire to improve standards. The practice of medicine is in private hands, although payments for doctors' services for old-age pensioners and for those who subscribe to the Medical Benefit Scheme are subsidized by the Commonwealth Government (see p. 125 below). On the other hand the great majority of hospitals are either owned and financed by state governments (state hospitals) or are subsidized by state governments (public hospitals). About three-quarters of the revenues of public hospitals come from state grants, the balance being almost entirely from fees charged to patients. These fees, although not as high as those of private hospitals, are in many cases substantial; but for those who subscribe to the Hospital Benefits Scheme (see p. 125 below) they are largely recoverable, and they may be reduced or dismissed in cases of hardship. It appears that rather more than one-half of all current expenditure on health is met from persons' disposable incomes, the balance being financed from government expenditure. However, because of the voluntary nature of the hospital and medical schemes, the proportion of health expenditure borne by the government varies greatly from person to person.

Social Security

All the items of expenditure referred to in the preceding section involve expenditure on goods and services. Transfer payments are not included. It is now convenient to consider government expenditure in the form of cash social service benefits. In 1938-39 these amounted to 4 per cent of national income; by 1948-49 this had risen to 5.5 per cent and by 1959-60 to 6.5 per cent. This indicates the extent of the growth of the welfare state.

Australia has long been considered a pioneer in social legislation. However true this view in 1900 or 1910, it had certainly ceased to be true by 1940; and the developments since 1940 have represented some attempt to catch up lost ground. In 1908 and 1909 the Commonwealth Government instituted a system of age and invalid pensions, subject to means test. Maternity allowances were introduced in 1912. At the outbreak of World War II the total apparatus of social security consisted of these, together with the war pensions arising from World War I and some arrangements for very meager unemployment allowances operated by the state governments.

Over the period 1941 to 1953, Commonwealth governments of both complexions have built up a substantial framework of social security benefits. In 1941 the Liberal government commenced a system of child endowment by which five shillings per week were paid to mothers for every child under sixteen, except the first. The timing of this particular move undoubtedly aimed at gaining political support, but when a Labor government replaced the Liberal one at the end of the year, a systematic attack on the problems of social security began. In 1942 widows' pensions, subject to means test, were introduced and in 1943 funeral benefits for pensioners. Unemployment and sickness benefits, subject to means test but without limit to period of benefit, came next in 1945.

During this period the Labor government also planned to introduce a comprehensive national health scheme along the lines of that operating in the United Kingdom. The first step was the passage in 1944 of an act to provide pharmaceutical benefits to cover the costs of all drugs prescribed by doctors. This act, which involved the filling in of forms by doctors and the establishment of penalties for improper practices, aroused the opposition of the medical profession, because it was regarded as a precursor to nationalized medicine. It was challenged before the High Court which held that it was *ultra vires* under the Constitution. Under the Constitution the Commonwealth was empowered to legislate for "invalid and old-age pensions," but other social service benefits did not come within the ambit of its power. However, in 1946 a constitutional amendment was carried by referendum. This empowered the Commonwealth to legislate for a wide variety of social service benefits. The Pharmaceutical Benefits Act was re-enacted in 1948, but it never came fully into operation.

Meanwhile the Hospital Benefits Act of 1945 provided for grants to public hospitals on condition that all charges in public wards be abolished and the means test abandoned. The Tuberculosis Act of 1948 provided for free treatment of all tubercular patients and the payment of living allowances to the patients and their relatives. The Commonwealth Parliament passed in 1948 the National Health Service Act, which legislated for the establishment of a comprehensive health scheme. This met with the determined opposition of the medical profession and, despite prolonged negotiations, no progress had been made when the Labor government was defeated towards the end of 1949.

The Labor government had between 1942 and 1949 laid the firm foundation for a welfare program in keeping with the modern trend towards the welfare state. This program was carried on by the succeeding Liberal government, although at a slower pace, and with an increasing emphasis on voluntarism. Pharmaceutical benefits were introduced but limited to a restricted list of life-saving and disease-preventing drugs. In 1950 endowment was introduced for the first child. In 1951 free pharmaceutical and medical benefits for pensioners on full pension and their dependents were established. In the same year grants to public hospitals were no longer made conditional on the hospitals' refraining from charging in public wards.

In 1953 there was established a scheme for hospital and medical benefits. The essence of this scheme is the principle of voluntary contribution: the Commonwealth subsidizes hospital and medical expenses of individuals who contribute to an approved hospital or medical benefits fund. Although the scheme is widely acclaimed and can be judged to have been successful, it suffers from four serious limitations. First, there are ceilings to the benefits payable and these, while adequate for most purposes, are unduly restrictive in the case, for example, of complex surgical treatment. Secondly, and more important, the subscription to the benefit funds is a flat sum and hence regressive in relation to income. Thirdly, since it is voluntary, its coverage is by no means complete. In fact, about two-thirds of the population is covered. However, of these, a substantial proportion would only be very partially covered for hospitalization, as subscribers can exercise an option as to the amount of hospital benefit. Coverage is almost certainly greater, the higher the income group. Fourthly, since the scheme is administered through a relatively large number of organizations, full advantage cannot be taken of large-scale administration, which would enable greater exploitation of modern data processing equipment. This voluntary scheme, by creating a series of hospital and medical benefits organizations with all their vested interests to act as a buffer between the government and the medical profession, has made the wholesale nationalization of medicine most unlikely.

Of all the social service benefits, age and invalid pensions are the most important. They account for 40 per cent of cash social service benefits. Old age pensions are payable to men sixty-five years and over and to women sixty years and over. They are subject to means test both on income and property. Since October 1961 the pension has been £273 per annum and the limit of permissible income, including the pension before the pension begins to be reduced, is £455. An eligible married couple would draw two pensions. These figures should be compared with the basic wage for an unskilled worker of £750 per annum. Since the end of the war the real value of the pension has been more than maintained and the conditions of the means test liberalized. A little less than half the population eligible on an age basis draws the pension. By and large other benefits, through adjustment, have maintained their real value; although child endowment, which was fixed in 1950 at five shillings a week for the first child and ten shillings for each other child, has lost about two-fifths of its real value since that date.

To sum up, the social service benefits fall into three main classes:

(i) Age, invalid, and widows' pensions, unemployment and sickness benefits. These have maintained their real value, but they are subject to means tests, although the latter have in some areas been liberalized.

(ii) Child endowment and maternity allowances. These are not subject to means test but their real value has been allowed to fall over the past decade.

(iii) Hospital and medical benefits. These are on a voluntary basis.

During the past twenty years the foundations of the welfare state have been firmly laid in Australia, but room for further building remains and the extensions in the past five years have been very limited. Its future will depend mainly on the political flavor of the Commonwealth Government. Although, during the office of the present Liberal government, the percentage of national income devoted to cash social service benefits has increased, the Liberals have in three respects reversed important facets of the policy of the previous Labor government: first, in the abandonment of the requirement that public hospitals should make no charges in public wards; second, in the establishment of a *voluntary* hospital and medical benefits scheme; and third, in a decision in 1960 to impose a charge of five shillings per prescription subject to pharmaceutical benefits.

Table 27 sets out the main cash social service benefits paid. This table includes war pensions. These are not subject to means test. It does not include benefits amounting to £8 million for hospitalization and £8.5 million for medical expenses which were paid from voluntary benefit organizations.

TABLE 27. *Cash Social Service Benefits, 1960-61*
(£ million)

Age and invalid pensions	158
Child endowment	74
Maternity allowances	4
Unemployment benefits	4
Sickness benefits	3
Widows' pensions	13
Hospital benefits	21
Medical benefits	10
Medical benefits for pensioners	4
Pharmaceutical benefits	21
Pharmaceutical benefits for pensioners	7
T.B. allowances and maintenance	5
War pensions	74
Other Commonwealth Government benefits	13
State Government benefits	4
	415

Source: Commonwealth of Australia, *National Income and Expenditure,* 1960-61; Commonwealth of Australia, *Budget Speech,* 1961-62.

Government Revenue

The high levels of government expenditure of the past decade have been financed mainly from revenue. Taxation has absorbed about one-quarter of national income, which is a rather smaller fraction than for Canada, the United Kingdom, or the United States. Within the tax field, the proportion of income taxes and estate duties has fallen from 57 per cent in 1948-49 to 51 per cent in 1960-61, perhaps a reflection of the political color of the Commonwealth Government since 1949. The latter figure is not dissimilar to the corresponding Canadian and British figures, but is much lower than the United States figure.

Income taxation, which is the most important form of taxation, is levied both on persons and companies. In 1960-61, 9½ per cent of personal income was taken as personal income tax—a percentage about the same as the Canadian, but much lower than in the United Kingdom or the United States. Personal income tax is levied progressively, the top marginal rate being 13s. 4d. in the £1 which is reached at a taxable income of £16,000 per annum. Deductions on account of dependents and for medical, educational, and assurance purposes are allowed up to certain limits. At 1960-61 rates a man with wife and two children would pay at most 7¼ per cent of his income if it were £1,200 (the current level of average earnings of wage and salary earners) and his marginal rate of tax would be 3s. 10d. If his income were £2,000, he would pay at most 14 per cent of his income and his marginal rate would be 5s. 10d. Capital gains are not taxed. Income taxation is also levied on company income, the standard rate being eight shillings in the £1. Private companies (i.e., companies in which the public is not substantially interested, not being subsidiaries of a public company) pay in addition a tax of ten shillings in the £1 on undistributed income in excess of certain allowable amounts. The table below indicates the importance of the various forms of taxation.

Since 1948-49 very substantial surpluses of revenue over expenditure on current items have been achieved. This has allowed over three-quarters of public capital formation to be financed from these revenue surpluses. The balance has been financed from borrowing from the Australian public. There has been in the aggregate over the period no direct borrowing from the Central Bank, although the

TABLE 28. *Tax Revenue, 1959-60*
(£ million)

Income taxes—personal	442
—company	229
Probate and succession duties	48
Customs and excise	336
Sales tax	164
Land tax	17
Payroll tax	55
Stamp duties, n.e.i.	37
Motor taxes	47
Liquor taxes	9
Racing, lottery, gambling, and entertainment taxes	15
Licenses, n.e.i., and other	12
Total	1,411

Source: Commonwealth Bureau of Census and Statistics, *Commonwealth, State and Territory Taxation Collections,* 1959-60.

Central Bank has indirectly made some finance available through purchases of government securities.[73] The public works program would unquestionably have been severely restricted if it had had to rely on public borrowing for its finance. In financing so much development from its own savings, the government has more than emulated the record of private corporate enterprises.

Budgetary and Monetary Policy

The broad economic objectives, which Australian governments have aimed at since 1945, can be quite simply summarized. They are:

(i) Full employment
(ii) Stability of prices
(iii) Equilibrium in the balance of payments
(iv) A rapid rate of economic development.

These objectives are implied in the programs of both the major political parties and are universally accepted, at least qualitatively, by the community at large. They stem from a paper *Full Employment in Australia* (1945), in which the then Commonwealth Government

[73] See H. W. Arndt, "The Finance of Public Investment," *Economic Record,* XXXIV (1958), 390-411.

pledged itself to pursue policies to maintain full employment. Their confirmation is illustrated by a number of acts of Parliament relating to the Central Bank, in which that institution is directed to exercise its powers in such a way as will best contribute to:

"(a) the stability of the currency of Australia;

"(b) the maintenance of full employment in Australia; and

"(c) the economic prosperity and welfare of the people of Australia."[74]

Of the four broad economic objectives the second and third can be defined precisely enough, but the first and fourth cannot. In Australia, full employment has been interpreted in a more literal sense than in the United States, for example, and the popular view is that full employment means virtually no unemployment. In practice this means that 2 to 3 per cent unemployment is probably the upper limit of unemployment which is politically acceptable. Indeed one hears references from reputable sources (including academic ones) to "slack" in the economy when unemployment is as low as 1 per cent. Moreover, at the first signs of any increase in unemployment, businessmen through Retail Traders' Associations, Chambers of Commerce, etc., become just as vocal as trade unionists. As far as the fourth objective is concerned, it is even more difficult to be exact about the rate of growth at which the economy should aim, but there is little doubt that the general view is that this growth should be as great as practicable.

The four objectives cannot all be completely achieved at the same time. Full employment, defined as more jobs than men or even as a situation with 1 or 2 per cent statistical unemployment, almost certainly means some measure of inflation. Rapid growth may be impossible to achieve without internal full employment. The achieving of balance-of-payments equilibrium may be inconsistent with full employment and rapid growth, which produce a high and expanding demand for imports.

Since all these objectives cannot be totally achieved, it is necessary to approach one less closely in order to approach another more closely. Thus, however much we approve all the objectives individually, we must choose between various feasible combinations of objectives. This means that we must attach priorities or weights to

[74] *Reserve Bank Act 1959*, Section 10.

the objectives. This comes about in the political process. Indeed, it is the very essence of politics in the economic sphere.

The avowed fundamental objectives of the economic policy of the Commonwealth Government have not shifted over the past fifteen years. But there seems to have been a shift in emphasis, a reranking of priorities, particularly during recent years. The implication of the Commonwealth Government's determination after February 1960 to restrain internal activity and avoid a return to import restrictions (see p. 134 below) is that growth and full employment are ranking a little lower and price stability and balance-of-payments equilibrium higher. It is, of course, by no means certain that the rapid growth of the Australian economy of the fifties will be maintained in a situation in which the level of economic activity is restrained sufficiently to produce price stability and balance-of-payments equilibrium.

The objective of rapid growth has been pursued in three main ways. The basis of growth has undoubtedly been the migration program. This has been a conscious act of government policy involving extensive assisted migration schemes, inter-governmental agreements, and active propaganda and recruitment overseas. More than half the total number of migrants since World War II have been assisted by government aid. On top of this governments have undertaken large developmental works programs, although on occasions these have been pruned or restrained when the avoidance of inflation required some cut in spending. Finally, governments have given guidance, assistance, and encouragement to private development plans. With a rate of expansion of the economy of about 4.5 per cent per annum, the objective of rapid growth could be said to have been attained to a high degree. However, unlike the United States, Canada, and even the United Kingdom, the extent to which the structure of industry is conducive to rapid growth has not been an issue of government policy.

Similarly the Australian economy has enjoyed almost continuous full employment over the past decade. Apart from a short period in 1952 and again more recently in 1961, unemployment has never exceeded 2.5 per cent of total wage and salary earners and for much of the period it has been less than 1 per cent. The high level of activity has undoubtedly been due to the general atmosphere of growth and expansion and the confidence with which businessmen and governments have held the expectation of continued growth. This itself has been largely government inspired. Apart from this, the Commonwealth Government has attempted to prevent minor downward fluctuations in activity from deteriorating into serious recessions and to restrain excessive demand from bursting into inflation. It has not been as successful in the latter as it has been in the former attempt.

When one takes into account the backlog of required investment and the accumulation of liquid assets from the war period, the tremendous boom in wool prices in 1951 and the longer-run trend of substantial growth with its implications for capital formation, it is not surprising to find that the major problem for economic policy in Australia for the past decade has been inflation. Associated with this have been balance-of-payments difficulties. Large deficits in the balance of payments on current account have occurred in seven of the past ten years. Four factors have been of importance here. To the extent that excess demand has been present, there has been a spill-over of demand onto imported goods and a worsening of the competitive position of Australian compared with overseas goods. The high level of capital formation has meant a direct demand for imported capital goods. During the past decade there has been a marked deterioration in the terms of trade. Finally there is some reason to believe that the long-run trend is unfavorable to the balance of payments, since the volume of exports (which are still mainly primary products) has grown and is growing more slowly than gross national product and the terms of trade have been moving against Australia while the demand for imports is growing. Moreover, marked year-to-year fluctuations in the world prices of primary products have caused sharp short-term reversals in the balance-of-payments position. Thus Australia has, over the past decade, faced the twin problems of domestic inflation and balance-of-payments disequilibrium.

To tackle these problems the Commonwealth Government has relied on budgetary manipulation, monetary policy, and direct import controls. While government action has sometimes been timid and tardy, nevertheless the Commonwealth Government has shouldered the responsibility for maintaining stability and has shown itself prepared to act. Moreover, a considerable measure of success has been gained in at least one direction, namely the buffering of the economy from the consequences of dramatic change in the value of export proceeds. Both in 1951-52 and 1957-58 there were considerable reductions in export proceeds, but there was no significant cumulative impact on the economy. This was in vivid contrast to the experience of the interwar period.

In implementing budgetary policy the Commonwealth has relied mainly on variations in taxation. Thus, in the face of the inflation associated with the Korean War, the 1950-51 budget contained a scheme for withholding temporarily a part of the high receipts from wool sales and the 1951-52 budget increased direct and indirect taxes. The boom burst in 1951-52 and some unemployment resulted. As a consequence, the 1952-53 budget provided for reduced taxation. However, by 1955 there was evidence of a resurgence of inflationary pressures and a special supplementary budget was brought down early in 1956 to increase taxation substantially. Subsequently, taxation was eased as the economy passed into a state of approximate balance. In 1960 fears of further inflation caused the Commonwealth Government to take a number of tax measures specifically designed to reduce activity. The Commonwealth has also modified government expenditure from time to time, but the great bulk of this expenditure is relatively inflexible. This is less true for works programs, so that in periods of restraint these have tended to be held back. It seems that the impact of restraint has fallen, at the margin, on public investment, personal consumption, and private investment in that order. This, of course, conflicts with the objective of rapid economic growth.

As far as monetary policy is concerned the Central Bank has relied mainly on its power to require the trading banks to keep deposits in special accounts[75] with itself and on general directives to them. It has not operated in the open market to any considerable extent, although it has on occasions supported the market. Open market operations are difficult in Australia, since the market for government bonds is narrow and a small volume of transactions (and hence a small impact on liquidity) can result in a large change

[75] From 1941 until 1960, the Central Bank had the power to require the trading banks to deposit with itself, in special accounts, sums up to certain limits related to the increase in the trading banks' own deposits over a base date. The sums to be held in special accounts were varied from time to time in accordance with the requirements of monetary policy. Since 1960 the power to call to special accounts has been replaced by the power to require the trading banks to keep statutory reserve deposits with itself, equal to a fraction of their deposits, such fraction to be determined by the Central Bank from time to time (see p. 24-25 above).

in the price of the bonds. Nor has it used interest rates to affect spending directly. Rates on advances and deposits have been increased from time to time, but these have followed rather than led the market. The Central Bank has in fact pursued a flexible policy through its operation of the special account procedure and this policy has been integrated with government budgetary policy. In particular there is no doubt that the heavy releases made from special accounts in 1951-52 (when the current deficit on the balance of payments was nearly £600 million), prevented a credit crisis and played the major part in insulating the home economy from violent external effects. On the other hand, the effectiveness of monetary policy has been somewhat limited by the slowness of the reaction of bank lending to changes in Central Bank policy. This has been partly due to the overdraft system of making bank loans, as a result of which there is at any one time a pool of unused rights to overdrafts, which cannot quickly be reduced.

As far as the balance of payments is concerned, import controls have been used freely in order to maintain Australia's international reserves. It is generally agreed (except by some of the manufacturing interests) that import controls should not be used as a permanent measure to mask a long-run disequilibrium in the balance of payments. However, the apparatus of import controls is useful as a short-run measure to meet sharp fluctuations, when international balances are relatively meager. The intensity of restriction has varied a great deal and there has been a general desire to reduce the severity whenever possible. Not only has the existence of import restrictions over the past decade sheltered domestic manufacture from overseas competition, but it has also restricted entry to many activities. After 1945 restrictions were progressively relaxed, until by the end of 1950 imports from areas other than the United States and Japan were exempt from control. The sharp fall in wool prices, combined with a flood of imports in the latter part of 1951, forced the reintroduction of severe restrictions. These were relaxed during 1953 and 1954, but intensified in 1955 and 1956. Since 1956 they have been progressively relaxed. Early in 1960 import restrictions, except for a limited list of consumer non-durables, were completely removed. As a result the flow of imports greatly increased, and the balance of payments went heavily into deficit. At the same time, as has been mentioned above, the Commonwealth Government took steps to reduce the level of economic activity. The demand for imports then fell and by the end of 1960-61 the balance of payments had strengthened. However, a revival of economic activity will almost certainly produce difficulties and there is no sign, as yet, that long-term equilibrium in the balance of payments has been achieved. It might be noted in passing that Australia's balance-of-payments problems have been greatly moderated by the high and steady inflow of overseas capital.

There is no doubt that the Commonwealth Government has directed its energies towards the maintenance of stability both in its internal and external aspects and has intervened on a global, if not a detailed scale, in the working of the economy to achieve this end. Moreover, it seems to have avoided successfully any considerable unemployment, although this has been mainly due to the momentum of a rapidly growing economy. But it cannot claim to have controlled successfully the inflationary tendencies which have been a characteristic of the Australian economy since the end of the war. Prices have risen throughout this period. This might be explained as a lack either of will or of means on the part of the Commonwealth Government. Perhaps it is true that the Commonwealth has not always executed its policies with the requisite rigor—political pressures could easily account for this. But it is certainly true that in some respects the Commonwealth lacks the weapons of policy.

As was pointed out (p. 24 above), the Commonwealth Government can exercise a measure of control over a wide area of aggregate spending, but for constitutional reasons a part of the area falls outside its net, namely, spending from funds borrowed from non-banking institutions. The need for control over such funds is illustrated by the booms of 1955 and 1960, which were largely fed by the rapid expansion of hire-purchase finance. This contributed directly by boosting consumers' expenditure at a time when the economy was already overextended, and when investment should have had priority. Moreover, the entry onto the capital market of the hire-purchase houses as borrowers offering very high interest rates made public borrowing difficult and forced a rise in interest rates generally. More recently there has been a spectacular rise in the volume of debentures and notes issued by commerical and industrial enterprises. The Commonwealth Government can exercise no direct influence to produce an orderly development in these fields.

This means that its actions must either be limited in degree or must fall with exceptional severity on those sectors of spending which it can directly influence.

However, the problem of inflation is only partly one of spending. The sharp increases in prices which occurred during the first half of the fifties can be blamed partly on the existence of an excess demand for goods and services over available supplies, and partly on the rise in world prices resulting from the Korean War. But for the past five years there has been no evidence of any considerable excess demand and overseas prices have been relatively stable, yet prices have continued to rise although at a more moderate rate. It is clear that excess demand has not been the sole cause of rising prices over the past decade.

This leads to the question of the extent to which inflation in Australia has been demand-induced or cost-induced. In a fully competitive economy a quite small excess of demand for goods and services in general over available supplies would result in a general rise in prices. But in a modern economy in which the great mass of producers are price-makers rather than price-takers, this is unlikely to happen. Much more likely is a lengthening of order books and the creation of shortages and queues. Indeed this seems to be the case in Australia. In other words excess demand would have to be substantial and expected to persist before it would directly draw up prices. It may be possible to attribute some of the inflation in prices in the early fifties to excess demand, but only some.

The much more likely explanation is that the inflation has been cost-induced, either through persistent rises in overseas prices affecting the Australian cost level or through persistent rises in wages. Before pursuing this, however, it should be pointed out that government action appropriate to curb demand inflation is not necessarily suitable for dealing with cost inflation. Thus while restraint on aggregate expenditure will eliminate excess demand, it may be effective in preventing costs from rising only if applied to a degree sufficient to produce a great deal of unemployment. Certainly a great deal of unemployment and a reduction in economic activity will reduce the bargaining strength of employees and stiffen the resistance of employers, but most Australians would doubt whether the price of such a policy in terms of wasted resources and inhibited growth would be worth paying. In Australia it seems clear that the amount of unemployment necessary to prevent excessive increases in wages is certainly far greater than that politically acceptable or economically desirable.

In recent years the main cause of increases in costs has been increases in wages. As has been pointed out above (see pp. 26-27), the Commonwealth Conciliation and Arbitration Commission makes determinations from time to time which shift bodily the whole level of the wage structure. Thus, in contrast to a system characterized either by competition or collective bargaining, the Australian system results in changes in practically all wages and salaries, virtually *simultaneously*. Moreover, in practice these changes tend to take place at close intervals. This creates an atmosphere which conduces to a general passing on of increases in wage costs, whatever the degree of competition; there is a general rise in money incomes and the competitive relationships of businesses are unaffected. Similarly, this is something which the consumer has come to accept. The net effect is an upward flexibility in prices and costs which operates to a high degree. While it is theoretically conceivable that the determinations of the Commission may have but followed the market, in fact they seem to have gone further than this and to have imparted autonomous impetuses to the wage level.

It is important to stress that in Australia the formulation of wages policy is in the hands of the Arbitration Commission and not the Commonwealth Government. Constitutionally the Commonwealth Government possesses no powers in regard to wages and conditions of industrial employment, so it cannot directly interfere in these matters. The most it can do is to assist the Commission by presenting to it material on the state of the economy and its views on wages issues. In practice the Commonwealth Government has frequently presented information but, for rather obvious political reasons, has been cautious in giving its views on the desirability of wage changes. Indeed the Commonwealth Government has clearly indicated its own views only once in a basic wage inquiry—that of 1960, when it opposed any increase. Moreover, the Commission itself has vacillated between two notions: first, that its principal job is to settle industrial disputes and hence the state of the economy is not its concern; and secondly, that in the public interest it must take into account the state of the economy. In the event, the Commission has sometimes made determinations that cut across the avowed policy of the Commonwealth Government. Thus there is a lack of co-ordination between the wage determination of the Arbitration Commission and the budgetary and monetary policies of the Commonwealth Government, both of which exercise a powerful influence on prices, employment, and the balance of payments.

Moreover, even if the Commission were to succeed in keeping money wages in line with movements in average productivity per worker, the nature of competition in product markets is such as to give the price level an upward bias. Stability in the general level of prices would require that the prices of the products of those industries in which productivity has risen more than the average should fall, in order to offset the increases in the prices of goods whose productivity has risen less than the average. It is doubtful whether the degree of competition in Australian industries is sufficient to bring about this downward flexibility. Strangely enough, it is this problem, rather than concern with resource allocation, which has been mainly responsible for some revival of interest in the control of monopolies and restrictive practices.

Competition and Public Policy

Australia lacks effective legislation in control of monopolies and restrictive practices. While there is legislation in existence, it is seldom invoked. Moreover, much of it is of an ineffectual kind. There is a federal statute, the Australian Industries Preservation Act;[76] and New South Wales, Queensland, and Western Australia all have legislation of their own. The federal act dates from 1906, and the state acts from 1909 (when New South Wales first legislated in this field). Thus both federal and state legislation have been on the statute books for over fifty years, but the impact upon business has been negligible. In all this time there have been only three prosecutions of any importance and all have failed: the Coal Vend case (1910-13) under the Australian Industries Preservation Act, the Brickworks case (1940) under the New South Wales Monopolies Act, and the Cement case (1957-58) under the Western Australian Unfair Trading and Profit Control Act. The Australian Industries Preservation Act has become virtually a dead letter. In New South Wales, the state Industrial Commission has made a number of in-

[76] A. C. Castles, "Australian Anti-monopoly Legislation," *American Journal of Comparative Law*, XVIII (1959), 82-88.

quiries into monopolies and combinations in accordance with powers first granted in 1912; but in their inquiries the Commissioners appear to have laid greater emphasis upon the preservation of competitors than of competition; and little action has been taken on the basis of the Commission's reports.[77]

There have been three main barriers to effective legislative control of monopolies and restrictive practices. First, there are severe constitutional limitations upon the powers of the federal government to legislate in this field (see above pp. 28-29). Under the Constitution the federal government may make laws with respect to "trade and commerce with other countries and among the States" subject to the condition that interstate trade "shall be absolutely free." While the plain man might think that such words bestow ample powers upon the federal government to regulate interstate trade, in practice they have been very much circumscribed by judicial interpretation. A major stumbling block, currently, is the High Court's narrow interpretation of the scope of interstate trade, so that in Australia the interstate commerce power is very much narrower than in the United States.[78] In 1960 the Commonwealth Government announced its intention to enact anti-monopoly legislation. Following this, the constitutional position has been the subject of intensive re-examination. The government now (1961) appears to be doubtful of its power to enact legislation which would be effective and is proposing joint federal-state legislation. This proposal, one would judge, is unlikely to succeed.

Secondly, the control of Australian monopolies (as distinct from restrictive practices) poses difficult problems. The market for Australian manufactures is so narrow that for many industries a high degree of monopoly must be regarded as the inevitable cost of securing access to economies of large-scale production. While it may be true that the current *degree* of concentration is greater than can be justified by economies of scale, it is also true that a policy of indiscriminate trust-busting after the American model is altogether inappropriate. Yet for much of this century the only well-developed antitrust model available to Australian legislators has been the American. Doubtless it has always been open to Australia to fashion

[77] D. J. Staley, "The Control of Monopoly—New South Wales," *University of Queensland Law Journal*, Dec. 1959, pp. 377-403.

[78] Alex. Hunter, "Restrictive Practices and Monopolies in Australia," *Economic Record*, XXXVII (1961), 45-49.

its own legislation, but such innovation would have needed considerable public support, a support that has been conspicuously lacking. However, in recent years there has emerged a tried alternative to the American model. This is the postwar British legislation which has now been functioning for a sufficient period to have proved itself an effective instrument of control. No longer can monopoly control be dismissed, virtually without discussion, as "impossible in the Australian situation." It is significant that for the first time in almost half a century a federal government is giving serious consideration to anti-monopoly legislation.

The third barrier has just been indicated: legislative control of monopolies and restrictive practices has lacked widespread popular support. Few Australians would value a competitive society as an end in itself, and only some would regard it as a means to a higher standard of living. The pioneering spirit in Australia as been associated not with "individualism" and "rivalry" but with "mateship" and "fair-shares." Paternalism in government and paternalism in business are widely accepted. In such an atmosphere trade agreements have flourished and the "benevolent monopoly" has become an accepted institution. Monopoly, however, has been more suspect than trade agreements. While there have been attempts to amend the Constitution to give the federal government fuller powers to deal with monopolies, it is significant that there has never been an attempt to extend the government's powers to deal with trade agreements. Moreover, while the Labor party has shown little interest in controlling restrictive practices, nationalization of monopolies has long been a plank in the Labor party platform. Nevertheless, Australians' suspicion of monopolies is mainly verbal and seldom results in action. There is no general demand for a continuing scrutiny of the policies of the national monopolies.

Nothing illustrates the tenderness with which Australians view monopolies and restrictive practices so well as the forms of legislation which have actually been employed. The Australian Industries Preservation Act was modeled on the Sherman Act. But (in its original form) it had one important difference—the proviso that contracts and combinations in restraint of trade and that monopolizing or attempting to monopolize were offenses only if there were an "intent" to so act "to the detriment of the public." The New South Wales Monopolies Act (1923), in turn, is partly modeled upon the

Australian Industries Preservation Act. Not only does it retain the proviso concerning intent and public detriment; it also adds this defense: "any combination of producers of any commodity which is reasonably necessary for the maintenance of the industry of such producers shall not be deemed to be to the detriment of the public." While the Queensland Profiteering Prevention Act (1948) includes some tougher provisions designed to control exclusive and discriminatory dealing, boycotts, and the activities of cartels, free use is made of the phrase "of such a nature as to be contrary to the public interest." The Western Australian Unfair Trading and Profit Control Act (1956) embodied an attempt at comprehensive control and included some far-reaching provisions. It lasted only three years. It was replaced in 1959 by a soft act, the Trade Associations Registration Act, whose chief purpose is merely to secure that trade associations and their agreements shall be registered. A "collusive tendering scheme" is prohibited, but this label is to be applied only to arrangements "contrary to the public interest"; and even then, the remedy is the trivial fine of £500.

It is sometimes suggested that government competition is the traditional Australian method of regulating the conduct of private industry. Such a generalization is subject to severe limitations. In the first place, public enterprise is not scattered throughout the economy but is concentrated in certain fields; and further, in only some of these fields is it in competition with private enterprise. This is demonstrated in Table 29. In particular, there are no government enterprises in retailing and only a miscellaneous array of stray examples in manufacturing. Nevertheless, it is true that public and private enterprise exist side by side in a number of important fields. These are transport, broadcasting and television, trading and savings banking, and the provision of housing. However, as has already been shown (pp. 108-119) more often than not the competition is of a limited kind within a clearly delineated framework. Certainly, in recent years, the conduct of public enterprise has stopped short of action which might eliminate private enterprise, or even reduce its profits or market share unduly. One might almost say that there have been in existence "codes of fair competition." In addition the fields concerned are subject to extensive government regulation in accordance with general economic policy.

In aviation there has been the principle of "fair and active com-

TABLE 29. *Public and Private Enterprise in the Australian Economy*

Type of industry	Ownership	Comments
I. *Primary*		
Agricultural and pastoral	Private	Government marketing boards are important in agriculture.
Mining and quarrying	Predominantly private	State coal mines are important, but share production with private enterprise.
Forestry	Mixed	While 80% of forests are government owned, these are usually exploited under license by private enterprise.
Fishing, hunting, and trapping	Private	
II. *Secondary*		
Manufacturing	Overwhelmingly private	There are stray examples of government-owned enterprises in, for instance, sawmills, brickworks, abattoirs, drugs, arms and ammunition, aircraft, shipbuilding and repairing, and printing. In only one of these fields is there a government monopoly, viz., in the production of certain types of arms and ammunition.
III. *Tertiary*		
Electricity, water, and sanitary services	Public	
Gas	Mixed	
Building and construction	Predominantly private	State housing authorities are active in provision of low-cost housing and flats.
Transportation	Mixed	Government has virtual monopoly of railways and tramways; but shares airlines, shipping, bus and road transport.
Communications	Predominantly public	Government has complete control of posts, telegraphs, telephone, telecommunications; but broadcasting and telecasting are shared.
Commerce	Private	
Finance	Mixed	Private enterprise is predominant in trading banking, hire-purchase and mortgage finance,

(TABLE 29 cont.)

Type of industry	Ownership	Comments
		and insurance; but government is predominant in savings banking.
Professional activities	Private	
Education	Predominantly public	
Entertainment, sport, and recreation	Private	
Personal and domestic services	Private	

petition" first laid down in 1952—so fair, it seems, as to guarantee the existence of the leading private operator, so active as to allow the consumer a choice of air hostesses. In shipping, the allocation of the market between the National Line and the private owners has been amicably settled; and freight rates are determined not in the market place but in committee (where the views of the Australian Coastal Shipping Commission have been dominant). In banking, broadcasting, and television, competition has certainly been keen, but it has not been price competition. In housing, the state authorities have been confined to a portion of the industry only, namely, the provision of low-cost housing and flats, though within this field they have been instrumental in keeping down prices and costs. One would not wish to suggest that public enterprise has not performed a useful role. It does need to be stressed, however, that sweeping claims cannot be made for public enterprise as a regulator of private industry.

A somewhat more likely candidate for this role is the Tariff Board, which, with the lifting of import restrictions in February 1960, is becoming considerably more influential. Indeed, the Board is likely to become the principal agent of government in the regulation of manufacturing industry, because an essential feature of the Board's procedure is the detailed scrutiny of costs, profits, prices, products, and marketing of firms applying for protection.

The key principle of tariff making has been expressed by the Board as follows:

The Tariff Board recommends assistance, when necessary, to industries on the basis of their being economic and efficient and showing sound prospects for success.[79]

And again:

In any request for tariff assistance, the Board would usually expect the applicant industry to be able to demonstrate that, because of cost and other factors inherent in the Australian situation and beyond the industry's control, it cannot compete on reasonable terms with imports even although it is an economic and reasonably efficient industry.[80]

The Board has always resisted the invitation to state shortly what is meant by "economic and efficient," preferring to emphasize instead that the criteria employed must be tailored to the circumstances of the particular case. It is thus a matter of principle that their procedures should be essentially *ad hoc*.

Nevertheless it appears from reading the Board reports that whether an industry is to be judged "economic" turns chiefly on two matters: first, on the level of protection which would be necessary to give the efficient Australian producer a marginal advantage in comparison with imports, and second, on the extent to which the industry is to be considered "worthwhile." Over the years the Board has built up a scale of maximum rates considered appropriate for various types of industry, and it will seldom go beyond a British Preferential rate of 27½ per cent. A "worthwhile" industry, for instance, is one which creates opportunities for manufacturing employment, or which uses Australian inputs, or which aids decentralization, or which saves foreign exchange, or which contributes to defense, or whose development is in accordance with government policy.

The concept of "efficiency," on the other hand, is essentially the extent to which firms make best use of the resources available to satisfy the demands of the market. While the Board confines its attention to efficiency within the firm, it has moved beyond a narrow cost-of-production approach. It is concerned not only with costs of production, but with costs of management and marketing, with profit margins, with the effectiveness of marketing procedures, and with

[79] Tariff Board, *Annual Report*, 1958-59 (Canberra, 1959), p. 9.
[80] Tariff Board, *Report on Petroleum Refining Industry*, March 1959, p. 14.

the appropriateness of products produced to meet the Australian demand.[81]

In the past the Board has shown itself prepared to take a tough line with large and small firms alike. It has stressed repeatedly that it will not protect firms from the consequences of their own mistakes (e.g., the creation of over-capacity). It has stated that it is unwilling to underwrite wage and profit rates higher than normal. It has shown itself appreciative of ingenuity, initiative, and innovation. Indeed, the Tariff Board administers a system of rewards and punishments which could become for a considerable section of manufacturing industry a *partial* substitute for the sanctions of the competitive market.

Conclusion

After surveying the Australian economy, one cannot but conclude that in most respects it diverges from the competitive laissez-faire model. It is true that agricultural production takes place under conditions approximating pure competition and that, as in other modern industrial economies, there is a significant small-business sector. Nevertheless the corporate sector, which plays the strategic role in the economy, is dominated to an unusual degree by units which are large in relation to their markets and in relation to the economy as a whole. Thus the structure of the corporate sector, the processes of competition, and the results achieved depart markedly from those of pure competition.

Secondly, public utilities (with only occasional exceptions) are government owned and operated; and government business activity extends into a number of other fields. Moreover, in providing the collective goods and services consonant with a modern welfare state, governments have profoundly influenced the structure of production.

Thirdly, the Commonwealth Government is deeply committed to policies of full employment without inflation and of rapid economic growth. These policies have become the main preoccupation of the Commonwealth Government, and the measures which have been used in pursuing them have largely determined the environment in which the private sector has operated.

[81] R. J. Rechner, "The Economic Validity of Principles Adopted by the Australian Tariff Board" (unpublished B. Ec. Thesis, University of Adelaide, 1961), pp. 8-25.

Governments, economists, and the public generally have shown singularly little interest in the efficiency of resource allocation in the Australian economy. This is reflected in the lack of data relating to market organization and market functioning, and in the almost complete absence of empirical research in these fields. Moreover, government economic policy is conceived in terms of the manipulation of aggregates, like the level of employment or the rate of change of the general price level. Indeed, even economic growth tends to be treated as an aggregate concept, little attention being paid to the manner in which growth is achieved by the exertions of individual persons, businesses, and industries. While micro-economics is studied in the classroom, it is largely the analysis of macro-economics which finds practical application in research and policy. This is partly explained by the Commonwealth Constitution, which, by requiring absolute freedom of trade and commerce between the states, has resulted in a policy of non-interference on the part of government in business affairs; and partly by the fact that Australians seem to have little belief in individualistic competition as a way of life.

However, it would be quite wrong to conclude that there is not a free-enterprise ideology in Australia. Within the private sector there is as passionate a belief in "free enterprise" as can be found elsewhere, but it is a belief in a free enterprise which emphasizes freedom from government intervention and public scrutiny. It is a belief in *private* enterprise in a very literal sense. Thus, although government activity within certain limits is widely approved and pure competition virtually non-existent, there remains in the conduct of business a devotion to laissez faire.

3

The British Economy[1]

G. C. Allen*

Forms of Organization and Their Significance

Professor Calvin Hoover's article in *Kyklos*[2] makes abundantly clear the unhelpfulness of the theoretical models which have been designed as a guide to the complexities of economic organization in the real world. Even in the United States, where inquiry in this field has been conducted systematically for many years, economists are still unable to make up their minds whether the American economy is predominantly competitive or monopolistic, or to interpret, in this context, the trends of recent decades so as to win general consent to their conclusions. There is not only a sharp divergence of opinion among the leading experts. Particular writers of the highest reputation are themselves inconsistent and give different answers at different times. The confusion may have arisen because the definitions of competition (or monopoly) are ambiguous or are unsuited to the needs of practical investigation. It may be that the intricacies of economic organization are such that it is far less easy to distinguish monopolistic and competitive elements than is commonly supposed. Or, perhaps, in respect of the *results* of market behavior, monopolies or oligopolies differ among themselves as sharply as monopoly or oligopoly differs from competition.

This last proposition has doubtless been in the minds of those who have sought to contrast the operations of cartels and those of single-firm monopolies, or to distinguish between the policies of car-

* Professor of Political Economy, University College, London.
[1] This paper is a revised version of one originally published in Rudolf Frei (ed.), *Economic Systems of the West*, I (Kyklos-Verlag; Basel, 1957), 65-99. The author is grateful to the publishers and to the List Society, which sponsored the book, for permission to reprint.
[2] "The Relevance of the Competitive, Laissez-Faire Economic Model to Modern Capitalistic National Economies," *Kyklos*, VIII (1955), 40-58.

tels in the primary industries and those of cartels in the secondary industries. In recent years, when much attention has been directed towards problems of development and innovation, critics of anti-monopoly legislation have noted that the line between progressive and unprogressive industries does not seem to be coincident with the line between monopolized and competitive industries.[3] Few economists would proceed to the conclusion that whether monopolistic or competitive elements predominate in an industry, or in a whole economy, is a matter of minor importance; but there are at any rate reasons for thinking that the significance of monopoly and competition respectively for economic progress, or market behavior, cannot be appreciated without the admission of other factors into the discussion, or without a more subtle analysis of how monopoly and competition work in different situations than is usually provided. Thus an inquiry into the *modus operandi* of a national economy cannot be limited to an examination of "organizational forms."

All this is relevant to conditions in Great Britain at the present time. During the last two generations the typical forms of organization have changed profoundly; the process of price formation in markets both for finished goods and for factors of production has been greatly modified; and the economic functions of the state have been immensely enlarged. Do these changes mean that economic behavior, the motives that determine it and its results, is now so different from that of the past that the "assumptions of traditional economic theory" have been invalidated?[4] Are resources now allocated in ways which that theory ignores? Is the rate of change in the system and also the direction of change determined by means that bear little or no identity to those of a few decades ago? Or, in spite of the changes in organization, are economic forces still operating so as to yield results that conform approximately to the expectations of the traditional, old-fashioned analysis? Professor Hoover has compiled a list of questions the answers to which may be expected to throw light on these difficult problems. So far as Great Britain is concerned, these questions can be most usefully approached by inquiring how present conditions in the several sectors of the economy have evolved, for it is important to discover

[3] Sir Henry Clay, "The Campaign against Monopoly and Restrictive Practices," *Lloyds Bank Review*, N.S. no. 24 (April 1952), pp. 14-29.

[4] Hoover, *op. cit.*, pp. 52-53.

whether a consistent general movement can be detected, despite periodical changes in the underlying economic situation. To begin with, let us consider trends in industrial organization.

The Extension of Monopoly before 1939

During the decade before the outbreak of World War II the organization of British industry was transformed. The older staple exporting industries, where before 1929 competition among numerous producers had ruled, moved into the monopolized area, partly by combination and financial consolidations but mainly by the spread of restrictive agreements among independent firms. In a number of other industries which a generation earlier had passed under the domination of a few great concerns (soap, paper, flour milling, and chemicals), the tendency towards the concentration of production was strengthened, while in several of the newer and most rapidly growing industries (motor vehicles, rubber manufacturing, and rayon) oligopoly was typical. The government and the central monetary authorities played an active part in displacing competition. Rationalization in industries that were suffering from overcapacity was encouraged by fiscal reliefs and by financial help accorded by the Bank of England. In some industries (e.g., coal) producers were compelled by law to set up cartels for fixing minimum prices and controlling output; in others (e.g., cotton spinning in 1939) the decisions of private cartels received, in effect, official and legal endorsement.[5] Outside the manufacturing industries a similar trend could be observed. In agriculture competition was restricted by legislation which imposed quantitative limits on imports and set up marketing boards run by the producers themselves (e.g., the Milk Marketing Board). In transport the competition of the road operators, which had destroyed the monopoly of the railways for many classes of traffic, was damped down by an officially imposed restrictive licensing system.

Restrictive practices were adopted by industry as a defense against depression, and governmental intervention was designed to relieve the distress caused by the decline in the staple trades or as a means of persuading industries to accept schemes of reorganization. But except where the cartels were officially supported, they had com-

[5] It should be added that, because of the outbreak of war, the Act of Parliament that conferred these powers in respect to the cotton industry never came into effect.

paratively mild effects on market behavior, since in a time of deflation the temptation to evade the rules of the cartels was difficult to overcome and those who determined the price policies of monopolies were inclined to caution. The cartel movement, however, probably had a more deleterious effect on technical and commercial progress, for the skill of business leaders was increasingly directed towards devising restrictive measures rather than towards cost-reducing innovations as a means of escape from their financial difficulties. The exceptions, moreover, were important, since they covered such large sectors of the economy as agriculture, transport, coal mining, and, to a large extent, iron and steel. On the other hand, in some large industries cartels and combines exerted little influence. During the thirties one of the most rapidly growing industries was building. Although some local arrangements for controlling tenders had come into existence,[6] in the main this industry, in which the small firm was the typical producer, was keenly competitive. Meanwhile, apart from legislation governing particular industries, the law had become increasingly favorable towards contracts in restraint of trade. By this time the courts were even prepared to enforce such contracts, if considered reasonable, although generally the cartels preferred to police their rules themselves and to apply their own sanctions.

It is not easy to measure the results of these changes in industrial organization, but certain statistical inquiries and estimates deserve a brief reference. Messrs. Leak and Maizels provided some useful information about concentration in a paper read before the Royal Statistical Society in 1945.[7] They showed that about 55 per cent of the 7¼ million persons in the industries surveyed were employed by rather fewer than 2,000 "business units"; and that in a long list of industries or products three "units" accounted for 70 per cent or more of the employment. These products included rayon, vegetable oil, rubber tires, cast-iron stoves, telephone and telegraph apparatus, iron and steel tubes and pipes, soap, photographic apparatus, bicycles, wood screws, cocoa and chocolate powder, railway wagons, cigarettes, linoleum, cement, newsprint, sewing cotton, sewing machines, boot and shoe machinery, lump sugar, gramophones,

---

[6] Notably, the London Builders' Conference. Cf. Monopolies and Restrictive Practices Commission, *Report on the Supply of Buildings in the Greater London Area* (London, 1954), p. 17.

[7] H. Leak and A. Maizels, "The Structure of British Industry," *Journal of the Royal Statistical Society*, CVIII (1945), 142-199.

asbestos, sheet glass, wallpaper, matches, spirits, and a number of chemicals. For some of these products, the proportion of employment given by three firms was above 90 per cent. In some instances, fewer than three firms were responsible for 70 per cent or more. On the other hand, there were large industries in which the degree of concentration was low—under 10 per cent of the total employment—namely, cotton cloth, woolen and worsted cloth, leather and leather goods, most branches of clothing, boots and shoes, finished brass goods, jewelry, printing, woodworking, furniture, pottery, and building.

It is probable that this analysis underestimated the extent of concentration, for the "business unit" was defined as a parent company and its *legal* subsidiaries, and control must have been secured by parent companies over many concerns which did not qualify under the legal definition. In any case, the exercise did not throw light on that part of the industrial field where price leadership and cartels were the agencies of monopoly. Quantitative estimates that attempt to cover the whole area of monopoly are highly speculative. One economist suggested that before World War II about 29 per cent of the total *factory* employment was found in monopolized trades. It was also estimated at that time about 30 per cent of the British export trade in manufactured or partly manufactured goods was directly affected by international cartels in which British firms participated.[8] Monopoly was especially common in producers' goods industries, but the market for consumers' goods also was affected, especially by the wide extension of the practice of resale price maintenance, often buttressed by arrangements for collective enforcement. The Lloyd Jacob Committee accepted the estimate made by the National Institute of Economic and Social Research that, in 1938, approximately 30 per cent of domestic consumers' private expenditure on goods was on articles for which the final prices were fixed or recommended by producers.[9]

In the greater part of the industrial labor market the substitution of nation-wide collective bargaining between trade unions and employers' federations had been completed long before 1939. The membership of trade unions, which was small in the first decade of

[8] Cf. E. H. Chamberlin (ed.), *Monopoly and Competition and Their Regulation* (London, 1954), p. 94.
[9] *Report of Committee on Resale Price Maintenance* (London, 1949), p. 1.

this century, grew rapidly from 1912 to 1920 and, after a decline during the twenties and early thirties, rose to over 6¼ million on the eve of World War II. The same period saw the creation of several huge national unions by amalgamation or federation, and by 1938 seven great unions claimed over two-fifths of the total membership. The public regulation of wages was also widely extended during this time. The tripartite Trade Board procedure, first introduced in 1909, was applied after 1918 to a large number of industries in which trade unions were weak, and Joint Industrial Councils, representative of the two sides of industry, were set up in many other trades. Both the Trade Boards and the Agricultural Wages Boards, established in 1924, had the power to recommend minimum rates of wages which were legally enforceable. During the thirties other weakly organized industries, such as road transport, were covered by officially established wage-bargaining machinery, and the government was empowered to give legal sanction to collective wage agreements in the cotton trade. Sir Henry Clay noted in 1929 that by that time some eight million persons were covered by machinery for collective bargaining, and as the influence of wage agreements extended far beyond the membership of the organizations directly represented, he concluded that "few important gaps" were then "left in the provision for the settlement of wages by collective bargaining."[10] Most of these gaps were filled in the next decade. The extension of unemployment insurance to the greater part of industry in 1920 exerted an important indirect influence on the bargaining strength of trade union negotiators in subsequent years.

Yet, although the classical type of competition was no longer to be found in the labor market, the continued depression in the staple industries and the heavy chronic unemployment in the older industrial areas imposed narrow limits on trade union power. It is plausible to argue that the changes in organization described above had led to the substitution of a "labor standard" for the gold standard, that by the time of the World Depression organized labor was strong enough to resist pressure for wage reductions, and that a point had been reached when equilibrium had to be restored by a depreciation of the monetary standard rather than by wage reduc-

[10] H. Clay, "The Public Regulation of Wages in Great Britain," *Economic Journal*, XXXIX (1929), 324.

tions. But the many substantial changes in relative wages during this period indicate that organized labor was still pliant before the pressure of economic forces.[11] Wage plasticity, though less than in earlier times, had by no means disappeared.

Government Intervention and the Growth of the Public Sector

During the Second World War the retreat from competition was hastened in all sectors of the economy. The introduction of an elaborate system of controls, physical and financial, destroyed the market as a guide to the allocation of resources and converted the entrepreneur into a functionary, an administrator of economic resources under rules drawn up by the government. Labor, no less than materials and capital equipment, was brought under central direction, and the trade unions co-operated with the government in measures to prevent the rise of prices and wages. Consumer rationing of food and clothing was supplemented by the imposition of official specifications for many kinds of manufactured goods under the "utility" schemes and the "austerity" policy. A temporary merging of interests in the manufacturing industries that contracted during the war was enforced by the concentration of production policy, and trade associations and other representative bodies which were set up with official encouragement served as instruments for allotting materials and organizing production according to government plans.

Many of the wartime controls survived into the early postwar period and were even supplemented by others. If this paper had been written in 1950, it would have pointed to a long list of controls which could be regarded as a more or less permanent legacy of the war. At that time price controls over the basic foodstuffs and many other classes of consumers' goods remained in being. Most types of food were still rationed; clothes rationing had been only recently abandoned; and the "utility" clothing schemes were still operated. Nearly all house building was to the orders of the local authorities; other forms of building were strictly limited; and the siting of new factories and the extensions to existing ones were governed by the requirements of the location of industry policy devised to prevent the reappearance of localized unemployment. Land development

---

[11] J. R. Hicks, "Economic Foundations of Wage Policy," *Economic Journal*, LXV (1955), 389-404; and J. H. Richardson, "Wage Policy and a Labour Standard," *Economic Journal*, LXVI (1956), 431-441.

was enmeshed in a complicated procedure introduced in 1947 to insure "the right use of land."[12] The government was still the importer of a wide range of raw materials and foodstuffs. Great Britain then possessed an economy subject in large measure to central direction.

During the next ten years this elaborate structure was dismantled. By the late 1950's quantitative import controls had almost disappeared, state importing had virtually ceased, and the organized commodity markets had been re-established. Price controls and rationing had gone, and a free market had been restored even in agricultural products, although the heavy subsidies to agriculture under arrangements for guaranteed prices remained. Building licensing had been abolished, and the free market in land, subject only to planning controls, had returned. With the relaxation of rent control in 1957 the first step was taken towards bringing back a free market in house property. Later, restrictions on the raising of new capital by private industry were abolished, and foreign exchange controls became very mild. In fact, the government had come to rely mainly on monetary and fiscal measures to achieve its purposes rather than on physical controls or on devices to control particular prices. In all these respects Great Britain had returned to a "free" economy.

Nevertheless, the economic influence of the government has remained far more potent and wide-ranging than in prewar days. In accepting responsibility for maintaining full employment and improved standards of social welfare, the state has permanently enlarged its general economic functions, while the cost of national defense and the social services, and the policy of preserving a flourishing agriculture have kept public expenditure far above prewar levels. In 1938 government expenditure (above and below the line) represented about 20 per cent of the gross domestic product; in 1948 the proportion was 39 per cent and, in spite of the subsequent decline, in the late fifties it was still about 33 per cent.[13] If the extra-budgetary financial activities of the government and its agencies were to be included, notably the transactions of the nationalized industries, the

[12] Cf. *The Control of Land Use: White Paper* (Cmd. 6537; June 1944), p. 1; also *Town and Country Planning Bill 1947, Explanatory Memorandum* (Cmd. 7006).
[13] Committee on the Working of the Monetary System, *Report* (Cmd. 827), p. 16.

proportion would be much higher. This was a permanent legacy of the war and of the social and political changes that attended it.

The government has now lost most of the inhibitions that once deterred it from attempts to influence business decisions and to guide business behavior. Its policy in regard to the location of industry may be taken as an illustration. That policy, which was vigorously applied during the early years of peace, fell into abeyance when it was seen that the former depressed areas were sharing in the general prosperity. In the late fifties, however, the policy was given a new lease on life. Fresh legislation was passed which empowered the government to assist any places (whether within the former depressed areas—so-called Development Areas—or not) that were considered vulnerable to unemployment, and in 1960 its persuasive or coercive powers, reinforced by financial aid, were used to divert new plants in the motor industry from the locations preferred by the manufacturers to Scotland and the Merseyside. Further, when the overlarge cotton industry began to suffer from renewed price competition, the government had no hesitation in providing subsidies for assisting reorganization and the re-equipment of the surviving plants.

The habit of consultation between government and industry (including the trade union side) became firmly rooted during the war, and even after controls were abolished these relations persisted. For instance, informal understandings long continued between government departments and certain representative industrial bodies about the proportion of output to be exported, and for a short period the trade unions agreed to a policy of wage restraint in return for government undertakings concerning the control of prices and profits. At one time it seemed that the wartime methods of consultation and the forms of organization which these fostered would become a permanent feature of the economy. The Working Parties set up by the Board of Trade immediately after the war were at one in recommending the establishment of representative bodies to cover all firms in the industries surveyed.[14] Legislation was passed to give effect to these recommendations, and it was intended that Development Councils, with powers of raising compulsory levies and of undertaking a variety of activities, should be set up in a large

---

[14] The Working Parties were committees of investigation appointed to survey a large number of industries. Their reports were published between 1946 and 1950.

number of industries. But the policy did not enlist industrial support, and very few Development Councils in fact came into being. In this respect also there was a retreat from the conception of a planned and centrally-directed economy that was fashionable in the early postwar years. Nevertheless, relations between government and private industry have remained much closer than hitherto, and there are signs that during the nineteen-sixties they may become closer still. With the recent establishment of the National Economic Development Council the government appears to have accepted the proposition that some form of long-term economic planning is a necessary condition of growth without inflation.

Soon after the war the size of the public sector was much enlarged by the nationalization of a number of basic industries or undertakings; these, by 1951, included the railways, long-distance road transport, electricity supply, gas supply, coal mining and ancillary undertakings, cables and wireless, air services, iron and steel, raw cotton marketing, and the Bank of England. Since 1951 iron and steel, raw cotton marketing, and most of the road transport have been returned to private enterprise. Nevertheless, today about 2¼ million persons are employed in the nationalized industries, nearly a tenth of the total occupied population. This is about six times as many as before the war.

The policy of nationalization had a profound effect on the structure and functioning of the British economy, but its significance may easily be misjudged, especially if the earlier development of the public corporation and of other forms of public enterprise and control is ignored. From the third quarter of the nineteenth century the new public utilities (urban transport, water supply, gas and electricity supply) were a field of municipal enterprise, while undertakings that were built up by private firms were subjected to public control over charges and conditions of service. In the railways an elaborate method of rate control was in operation long before the enforced amalgamation of the main line services by Act of Parliament in 1921. From early in this century public corporations were established by Parliament to run certain enterprises, such as some of the docks and harbors and the London passenger transport system. Centralized control over the generation of electricity was imposed in 1926. In these industries nationalization meant a change in ownership and administration, but it certainly did not represent the replacement of free competition by public monopoly. The same could be said of the coal-mining industry. From 1930 that industry ceased to be competitive, for, as we have seen, it was cartelized by Act of Parliament, and during World War II it was subjected to rigid official controls. Similarly, the Bank of England, though in legal form an institution owned by private shareholders and operated under a charter from the Crown, had long accepted responsibilities as the country's central bank. The cable and wireless service and the air services were also regarded as semi-public undertakings long before nationalization. Even the iron and steel industry had ceased to fall squarely within the private competitive sector, for from 1935 its development was undertaken in consultation with the government and its prices were worked out in agreement with an official agency, the Import Duties Advisory Committee. The denationalization of this industry during the last few years has not, it should be noted, meant the restoration of free competition, for its price and investment policy remained under the general supervision of a statutory body, the Iron and Steel Board. Only road transport and raw cotton marketing among the nationalized trades could be regarded as freely competitive, and these have largely reverted to their former condition. Thus, on a superficial view, it would seem that nationalization had little effect on the character of British industry, since, besides transferring ownership, it did little more than change the form of public control.

This conclusion, however, must be qualified. In fact, the consequences of nationalization have been far greater than a first view might suggest, for the operating policies followed by the controlling boards and the government, and the impact of nationalization on the capital and labor markets, have had far-reaching effects on the economy. As the Radcliffe Committee pointed out, nationalization has altered the balance between public and private investment, and today nearly half the total gross investment is financed by the public authorities, including the local authorities and the nationalized industries. Since public investment does not respond to monetary measures in the same way as private investment, the enlargement of the public sector has raised new problems of monetary control.

The effects on pricing policy have been equally important. The nationalized industries were enjoined by the Acts which created them to follow a pricing policy which would enable them, over a period of years, to earn sufficient revenue to cover costs, although the costs to be covered were not always clearly defined. It is, however, difficult to observe "the commercial principle" when at the same time the operating authorities are expected to have regard to a "national interest" that may at times conflict with it. During the period of inflation, most of the nationalized industries charged their customers less than was necessary to meet current costs, depreciation charges, and interest payments. In some cases, e.g., the railways, this led to their incurring heavy deficits that had to be financed by the Exchequer and so made a significant contribution to inflationary pressure. Even in the expanding and relatively prosperous electricity supply industry, revenue has been insufficient to provide completely for depreciation and for financing expansion.[15] According to one critic, in the nationalized industries as a whole "something like half the sum required to maintain existing capital intact and the whole of the funds required for the expansion of capacity have to be raised as new borrowings."[16] Further, these undertakings have been notoriously guilty of subsidizing some customers at the expense of others. "The cardinal error of the corporations . . . has been their excessive neglect of individual costs which has shown itself in the application of standard charges to groups of widely differing consumers."[17] In the coal industry the practice of averaging costs and proceeds has had the result that some types of coal have been sold for much less than the cost of production and that some pits and areas have subsidized others. The inevitable consequence has been a waste of resources. Types of coal that are expensive to mine have been used for purposes for which less valuable coal would have sufficed. The National Coal Board has tried to secure by administrative action results which would have been achieved by price in a free market; but, to leave aside the question of whether it has

[15] *Report of the Committee of Inquiry into the Electricity Supply Industry* (1956), pp. 87 *et seq.* and 146. See, however, R.S. Edwards, "The Finance of Electricity Supply," *Lloyds Bank Review*, Oct. 1960, where it is argued that it is unreasonable to expect that a nationalized industry *should* finance expansion wholly out of its profits.

[16] P. T. Menzies, "Price Policy in a Period of Continual Inflation," *National Provincial Bank Review*, No. 39 (Aug. 1957), p. 1.

[17] Francis Cassell, "The Pricing Policy of the Nationalized Industries," *Lloyds Bank Review*, N.S. no. 42 (Oct. 1956), pp. 1-18.

succeeded, the process bears little resemblance to that found in competitive industries.

Thus nationalization, or rather the way in which the nationalized industries have been operated, has had important effects on the economy as a whole. Yet the influence has not always been one way. In some cases the policy has probably led to increases in efficiency, as in the gas industry where nationalization, by destroying local monopolies that operated on too small a scale, has brought about a more economical structure. We shall see below that in some respects the enlargement of the public sector has helped to preserve competition in private industry, or at least to provide substitutes for competitive pressures in areas where private monopoly was powerful.

The capital market has been seriously affected by several of the factors discussed above, namely the official control (only recently abandoned) over new issues, the dominance of great concerns in certain fields, and the growth of the public sector. Heavy taxation has made inroads on private savings, while the discriminatory tax on distributed profits has provided a strong inducement to companies to "plow back" a high proportion of their profits, with the result that much new investment has been undertaken without reference to market tests. There is, of course, nothing new in "plowing back" profits, for this was the traditional way in which British industrial firms financed their growth. But in competitive industries the profits earned depend upon the producer's costs in relation to a price set by the market, and only their allocation is left for the decision of the proprietors or directors. In certain monopolized industries the great companies, though they do not necessarily charge according to the textbook criterion of what the traffic will bear, can (and do) fix their prices by reference to the level of profits needed to finance the expansion of capacity which they consider desirable. It is likely that these conditions have come to stay among the strongly entrenched monopolies. On the other hand, the trend is not all one way throughout the economy. In recent years, despite the weight of taxation, the volume of private savings has substantially increased; while the capital market itself has become more technically efficient in consequence of the establishment of new institutions (e.g., the Industrial and Commercial Finance Corporation for financing small businesses) and of improvements in the organization of various savings and investment agencies.[18]

Combines, Cartels, and Public Policy towards Restrictive Practices

We must now consider whether within private industry itself the prewar and wartime trends towards the shrinkage in the area of competition have persisted. We turn first to the question of concentration. The exercise of Leak and Maizels, based upon data drawn from the Census of Production of 1935, has not been repeated for a postwar year in precisely the same form; and Evely and Little, who recently considered the problem, reached the conclusion that it was not possible to say whether industrial concentration as a whole had increased between 1935 and 1951.[19] However, some relevant, if not precisely comparable, information is available. Recent investigations undertaken by the National Institute of Economic and Social Research revealed that in 1953 some 3,000 public companies accounted for 43 per cent of the paid-up capital in all public and private companies. In 1951 these 3,000 companies, which controlled 10,500 manufacturing establishments, provided 46 per cent of the total employment and accounted for 56 per cent of the gross output of manufacturing industry, or perhaps 50-52 per cent of it in terms of "value added."[20] Concentration remained high in the same industries in which it was conspicuous before the war, as was to be expected. Other investigators, who essayed a comparative study, reached the very tentative conclusion that, while in the four ten-year periods before 1939 the tendency towards increased concentration among firms which existed at the beginning of each period had not been offset by the rise of new firms, with the result that the degree of concentration tended to increase, between 1939 and 1950 the trend changed and the degree of concentration diminished.[21] These comparisons apply to "business units." If establishments are considered (and comparisons between the published results of prewar

---

[18] Cf. an illuminating article by Sir Oscar Hobson, "Wanted—A Free Capital Market," *The Three Banks Review*, No. 25 (March 1955), pp. 3-19.

[19] R. Evely and I. M. D. Little, *Concentration in British Industry* (London, 1960), *passim*.

[20] National Institute of Economic and Social Research, *Company Income and Finance, 1949-53* (London, 1956), pp. 7-8.

[21] F. E. Hart and S. J. Prais, "The Analysis of Business Concentration: A Statistical Approach," *Journal of the Royal Statistical Society*, CXIX, Part II (1956), 173-175.

and postwar Censuses of Production are possible here), it appears that the degree of concentration has increased.[22] This means that while trends in the concentration of control since the war are uncertain, the importance of large *plants* has undoubtedly grown.

The conclusion accords with general impressions. It seems quite likely that concentration in the economy as a whole has not increased (notwithstanding the consolidation that has occurred in particular industries), for the buoyant condition of trade and the appearance of many new classes of product have been more favorable to the birth and survival of small firms than was the depression of the thirties. The increased importance of large plants, which is the result of technological changes, is quite consistent with the absence of any such trend among firms. The investigators claimed that since it is the continual appearance of new firms that imposes the main check on increased concentration, the value of maintaining conditions of free entry is underlined by the results of their inquiry. Such conditions have been present in postwar Britain.

It is unfortunate that evidence which would permit more detailed conclusions to be reached is lacking. The proposition that the modern large corporation is immortal can, clearly, be disregarded, for very few of the dominant concerns in contemporary British industry are more than fifty years old! It would be illuminating to survey the industrial field in order to reveal the extent to which the dominant producers of twenty, thirty, or fifty years ago have retained their status in particular lines of production and in industry as a whole. Admittedly, the results of such a survey would not prove the vulnerability or invulnerability of the present-day leaders. But if the inquiry were combined with a study of the means by which past monopolistic positions have been eroded (or sustained), it would at least permit enlightened speculation about the future.

In the absence of such evidence, however, it may be useful to glance at the list of the hundred largest British companies (in order of assets size) recently issued by the National Institute of Economic and Social Research.[23] The majority (as one would expect) consists of firms which were already important in their several fields a generation or two generations ago, or of firms which have been built

[22] *Ibid.*, pp. 184, 190; also *Census of Production for 1951, Summary Tables,* Part I.

[23] *A Classified List of Large Companies Engaged in British Industry* (London, Dec. 1955).

up by formerly leading producers. In general they have risen with the growth of the industries in which they already occupied an important place at the earlier date. But there are some firms among the present-day giants that were quite small a few decades ago; for example, firms in the motor vehicle and motor accessories, rayon, electrical apparatus, and cinema industries, and in the retail trade. This indicates that while over a large area of industry certain great firms have succeeded for a considerable period in sustaining or strengthening their position, usually by taking up fresh products as well as by increasing the output of their original lines, initiative has by no means been confined to well-established firms. Newcomers have played an important part in the newer industries. If one moves down the scale and regards the list of firms which, though substantial, are not in the company of the greatest, one can find in many, though not in all, industrial groups, striking examples of new firms that have been able to force their way into industries already dominated by giants. Some of these have risen to importance since the war. Inspection of the lists does not, of course, reveal cases of declension among the large firms of a generation or so ago; but the structural changes of the intervening period have certainly been attended by movements of that kind. Nevertheless, while this cursory examination shows that British industry has been open to newcomers and that even the older trades have not been the preserve of a charmed circle of established producers, the chief impression is of continuity.

It is equally important to consider whether the prewar trend toward the cartelization of multi-firm industries has been carried into the postwar world. That restrictive practices of some kind are now characteristic of a very large part, probably the greater part, of British industry is a proposition that would be generally accepted. The Monopolies and Restrictive Practices Commission between 1948 and 1956 investigated a considerable cross-section of industry, and its reports, together with those of various *ad hoc* inquiries, official and private, indicate that agreements for common prices, collusive bidding, the allotment of sales or output quotas, the division of markets, exclusive dealing and aggregated rebates or loyalty rebates to customers, were very widespread after the war. The same was true of resale price maintenance and of various devices for collective enforcement. In many industries the cartel provided for sanctions to be imposed for breaches of its rules, and in some of them private courts were set up to try offenders. The practices existed in industries that have become important since the war no less than in those long established. A private investigation into trade associations found that, out of a total of 1,300, about 240 associations were concerned with attempts to suppress price competition.[24] In the Register of Restrictive Practices set up under the Restrictive Trade Practices Act of 1956, there were in 1960 some 2,300 registrations.[25]

The importance of restrictive practices, however, can scarcely be brought out by statistical evidence, for it depends on the success of the cartels in enforcing their rules, on the extent of outside competition, actual or potential, and on the disposition of those who exert the predominant influence over cartel policy. There can be little doubt that the buoyant trade of the postwar period has increased the power of cartels by removing the chief incentives to evasion, which was common in the years of depression. It might have been thought, on the other hand, that in conditions of boom the incentive to resort to restrictive practices would be relatively weak. In many industries, however, especially those with a dismal interwar experience, producers have wished to provide safeguards against a possible return to depression, and have been moved by a belief that unless a strong organization can be created in good times, efforts in bad times to suppress "excessive" competition will be of no avail.

Yet if the disposition of manufacturers and traders towards restrictive practices has been at least as favorable since the war as it was before, the situation has been transformed by a profound change in government policy. This change was foreshadowed in the White Paper on Employment Policy of 1944 where it was argued that a "full employment" policy, to which the wartime Coalition government committed itself, might be frustrated by restrictions designed to limit output and to keep up prices. As a consequence, the Monopolies and Restrictive Practices Act of 1948 was passed as an agreed measure. Under this Act, a commission was appointed to investigate industries and practices referred to it by the government and to propose remedies when the "things done" by a monopolist

[24] Political and Economic Planning, *Industrial Trade Associations* (London, 1957), p. 162.
[25] Many restrictive agreements that existed before 1957 may have been given up when the Act came into force in order to avoid registration.

were judged by it to be contrary to the public interest. The recommendations of the commission, contained in its twenty or so reports, have led to the abandonment of various types of restrictive practice in the industries surveyed, and it is probable that its activities have exercised in general an educative effect on opinion and have resulted in the modification over a wide range of industry of the practices to which the commission has taken the strongest objection.

Further legislation followed. The Restrictive Trade Practices Act of 1956, which embodied in part the recommendations of the commission in its report on Collective Discrimination,[26] prohibited the collective enforcement of resale price maintenance (although it strengthened the power of individual manufacturers to enforce by legal action the retail prices of their own products). It also required the registration of a large number of restrictive arrangements and set up a Restrictive Practices Court to try cases brought before it by the Registrar. The onus of showing that the arrangements are not contrary to the public interest is now placed upon those who practice them, by reference to certain criteria laid down in the Act. These criteria are such as to give the parties to most types of restrictive agreements a poor chance of convincing the court in their favor, as has been demonstrated by the decisions in the cases so far heard. Consequently, during recent years many formal restrictive agreements have been abandoned and a number of price associations wound up. Industry has not been slow to bend its mind to the discovery of new routes to restrictionism now that the old ones have been barred; but it is too early to say how effective the substitutes for the prohibited arrangements will prove to be. For the moment it appears that in industry and trade cartels are in retreat.

The legislative challenge to monopoly has so far been confined to cartels, although the reorganized Monopolies Commission has been given the task of inquiring into single-firm monopolies or oligopolies (defined as firms which produce one-third or more of the total output of a product). The more benevolent attitude towards competition has been demonstrated in other ways. Since the denationalization of road transport, the government has freed the

[26] *Collective Discrimination: A Report on Exclusive Dealing, Collective Boycotts, Aggregated Rebates and Other Discriminatory Trade Practices* (London, 1955).

railways from the legislative restraints which formerly impeded them in their rivalry with the road operators, and although it has not yet abolished the restrictive licensing system imposed on the latter, it has administered the system more liberally. One may conclude that the government now looks to competition rather than to centralized administration to determine the allocation of traffic between road and rail.

A change can also be observed in the government's disposition towards protection. As in other countries, the state has in the past been more often called upon to preserve industries threatened by outside competition than to act as an innovator.[27] The tenderness of the British government towards established interests was frequently demonstrated before the war, and appeals from such interests in more recent times have certainly not been disregarded. Yet the general economic prosperity has strengthened its hand in resisting this kind of pressure, notably the demand that it should sustain the cotton industry against the competition of cheap imports from Asian countries. The problem has now been moved to another plane as a result of the establishment of the Common Market and the European Free Trade Association. Should the United Kingdom join, or become closely associated with, the Common Market, the area of competition would be greatly extended and monopoly and restrictive practices would meet another challenge. It may be concluded, therefore, that competition has secured powerful new allies during the postwar period, and that the tide of restrictionism is no longer flowing so triumphantly as in the past.

The Behavior of Monopolists

Yet monopoly is still powerfully entrenched in a considerable number of industries, and we must now consider whether in modern Britain effective restraints (other than legal restraints) upon the policy of monopolists exist, whether the safeguards which the competitive market is supposed to afford are provided in other ways than by competition, whether, in fact, the behavior of monopolists is in accordance with what general theoretical discussion would lead us to expect.

In the first place, it is clear that there is a wide diversity among monopolists or oligopolists in their behavior and policy. For in-

[27] Except where strategic interests are involved.

stance, the number of independent firms producing private motor cars was reduced from ninety in 1920 to twenty just after World War II, and production is now highly concentrated in five large groups. Yet the appearance of oligopoly has not prevented the most active rivalry, extending to keen price competition, among the few firms. It may be argued that in the long run this is unlikely to endure; but in industries where rapid technical change calls for constant alertness if a producer is to survive at all, and where those in control are combative and enterprising in disposition, attention can be averted without danger from what is likely to happen in the long run. But all industries, even all progressive industries, are not equally well disposed towards rivalry of that type. Where one great producer overshadows the rest and prices are determined by the familiar process of "price leadership," assisted (as in the motor tire industry) by discussions among the several firms, the process of price formation is far removed from that found in competitive markets. Price leaders are sometimes challenged, but since no member of an industry so organized normally wishes to provoke a price war, such a challenge will occur only if one of the "followers" gains an accession of bargaining power as a result of a technical or marketing innovation. In a technically progressive industry this possibility may serve to keep the leader alert. On the other hand, as a general rule the leader's prices may well be fixed at a higher level, out of deference to other producers, than would be the case if he consulted solely his own immediate advantage. Again, although rivalries among oligopolists may sometimes lead to results (forms of market behavior or of innovation) not widely dissimilar from those achieved under classical competition, it has been noted that oligopolists (or monopolists) are inclined to foster those types of innovation in which their special strength can be displayed and which may differ sharply from the types of innovation that would occur under competition.[28]

The importance of a competitive fringe in a monopolized industry may also vary greatly according to particular circumstances. Few, if any, of the industries examined by the Monopolies Commission were found to be covered entirely by the monopolies or cartels that dominated them. Sometimes the existence of outside

[28] Cf. W. J. Corlett, *The Economic Development of Detergents* (London, 1958), pp. 204-205.

competitors may be ignored, or even welcomed and encouraged, by the monopoly (as in the match industry), for it may help to disarm public criticism. On the other hand, small firms, though themselves unable to provide a measure of real competition, may be used as a means of entry into a trade by great firms from other industries who wish to extend their field of operations. The organization of the detergent industry, which for many years was dominated by a single great producer, was transformed in this way. In other industries competitive forces have remained so strong that organized suppliers and traders have been obliged to connive at breaches of their rules. This has occurred in connection with resale price maintenance arrangements in the chocolate and confectionary trade where price-cutting by low-cost distributors has frequently been ignored. When Great Britain was a free-trade country, the power of cartels was always liable to be threatened by foreign competition. This danger has by no means disappeared. For instance, competition from Hong Kong recently rendered largely ineffective the price agreements among British manufacturers of rubber footwear,[29] and British membership of the European Common Market might have the same result in a number of industries now controlled by strong cartels. As commonly happens, the power exercised by certain cartels has been limited by conflicts of interest among the members or by fear of evasion by low-cost producers or "weak sellers." The Monopolies Commission took the view that the restrictive effects of certain agreements in the motor tire trade were mitigated by the establishment of secret distributing companies and the payment of secret allowances to customers by one of the producers.[30]

However dominant a cartel or a monopolist may be in a particular industry, there is always the possibility that competition will arise from outside, either by the "muscling in" of firms from other industries or by the intrusion of substitutes manufactured by other producers. Both forms of competition have been prominent in postwar Britain. The competition between the great chemical firms and the oil refiners in a wide range of products from plastics to fertilizers is well known. Distillers also have penetrated into the chemical industry, which in its turn has overlapped into textiles. An aircraft

[29] Monopolies and Restrictive Practices Commission, *Report on the Supply of Certain Rubber Footwear* (1956), p. 87.

[30] *Report on the Supply and Export of Pneumatic Tyres* (1955), pp. 88-89, 130, 133.

manufacturer soon after the war became for a time a manufacturer of prefabricated buildings. As long as rapid technological change continues to break down the barriers between industries, dominant firms in particular fields will be subject to competitive pressures, or at any rate their conduct must be attuned to the danger. Yet the argument must not be pressed too far, as the following example shows. For many years before World War II the British soap industry had been dominated by a single producer. As already described, with the advent of synthetic detergents another great producer, American in origin, entered the industry as a keen rival. This shows that the industry was not closed to newcomers. But it might have been expected that the chemical firms and the oil refiners, who are the source of materials for detergent manufacture, would also have joined in. The reason they did not appears to be because they lacked the marketing organization appropriate to the sale of detergents for household use.[31] Thus, even when technical conditions favor an extension of the area of competition, the difficulties of solving the marketing problem, in the face of firms with established selling organizations, may be decisive.

So far as competition from substitutes is concerned, there is no lack of evidence of its prevalence in postwar Britain. For instance, the once powerful cartel in the linoleum industry has been much affected by competition from new types of floor coverings manufactured by other trades. The Monopolies Commission report showed that while the market in matches was dominated by two great producers, which agreed together about the division of the market and other matters, the monopolized match industry could not be indifferent to the competition of mechanical lighters.[32] The impact on established positions by outside technical developments has often stimulated innovation in a monopolized no less than in a purely competitive industry. A great firm in the rubber growing and manufacturing industry has been stimulated to devise improvements in the market preparation of its product by the rivalry of synthetic rubber.

[31] W. J. Corlett, *op. cit.*, pp. 192-205.

[32] *Report on the Supply and Export of Matches and the Supply of Match-Making Machinery*, pp. 62-63, 85-86. The duty on lighters is heavy (as it is on matches); moreover, being charged at a flat rate, it discourages the production of cheap lighters. Thus this competition with the monopoly is not as keen as it might be.

One of the merits claimed for the competitive system is that it provides for a rapid adjustment of production and the reallocation of resources in response to changes in demand. But the producer is not to be regarded as the passive partner in the process of economic change. Besides creating new combinations of resources to meet existing wants more effectively, or to adjust supply to altered demands, he is also concerned with *creating* new demands. "Modern industry," it has been said, "actively influences markets . . . in order to mold them according to its requirements."[33] Indeed, in a progressive economy changes are as likely to arise from impulse within industry as from impact upon it. In discharging this function an economic system must provide freedom for experiment and opportunities for innovators; but it does not follow that atomistic competition among numerous firms will be superior in this respect to more highly concentrated forms of organization. A recent study of the British clothing industry has shown that since the war producers in that trade have been active in trying to mold demand in such a way as to justify the use of the advanced productive techniques devised during the period of control which enforced uniformities of style. This industry is in the hands of numerous independent firms. Yet some of the major innovations have been brought about by a very large, multiple retail concern which has striven both to create the market conditions necessary before large-scale manufacturing methods could be introduced and also to reorganize the producing side of the industry to insure that full advantage could be taken of those conditions.[34] Large multiples have also played a leading part in offsetting the trend towards increased market imperfections brought about by the spread of nationally advertised, price-maintained brands of consumers' goods.

In some classes of product the buying power of the great distributors confronts that of large manufacturers, and this provides an illustration of the doctrine of "countervailing power." The Monopolies Commission, in formulating its recommendations, has shown awareness of that doctrine. It has sometimes relied upon the buying power of the government or of the nationalized industries to safeguard the public interest in markets dominated by large combined

[33] H. von Beckerath, *Modern Industrial Organization* (New York, 1933), p. 190.
[34] Cf. Margaret Wray, *The Women's Outerwear Industry* (London, 1957), pp. 157 *et seq.*

suppliers, and in a few cases it has suggested means by which that buying power should be augmented. For instance, the production of mains and supertension cables is in the hands of a very few manufacturers, and price competition is absent. The chief customers, however, are the nationalized industries, notably the British Electricity Authority. The commission stated: "A system of purchasing mains and supertension cables which is in the long term interests of the consumer and the producer will have to be worked out by the BEA with the industry. The present arrangements for the CMA members' costs to be investigated by independent accountants is in the public interest and so long as CMA members act together as sellers of these types of cable, there should be an obligation on them, in the ranges in which no competition exists, to submit their costs to the BEA in order to establish that the prices charged are reasonable. Prices to buyers other than the BEA should bear a distinct relationship to the prices charged to the BEA and this relationship should be reasonable and made known."[35] On the other hand, the commission also recognized the limitations of safeguards of this kind. Thus, for many years there have been agreements between the Post Office and the associated suppliers of telephone and telegraph cables about supplies and prices. The commission expressed some doubts about their results and suggested additional methods of protecting the public interest, including the placing of a proportion of orders with independent concerns.[36] "Countervailing power" has clearly not always proved to be an adequate substitute for the old forms of competition and is sometimes a *pis aller*. But the results of its exercise vary widely according to circumstances. In its inquiries into the insulin trade, the commission found that production was concentrated in a very few firms which collaborated with one another over purchases of materials, technique, and pricing. In this trade, however, the public authorities are not only direct purchasers of considerable quantities of insulin but also exercise control over distribution under the National Health Service arrangements. Here the commission felt that the public interest was adequately safe-

[35] Monopolies and Restrictive Practices Commission, *Report on the Supply of Insulated Electric Wires and Cables* (1952), p. 91. "CMA" stands for Cable Makers' Association.

[36] *Ibid.*, pp. 83-84, 92.

guarded, and it was well satisfied with the way in which the trade was conducted.[37]

While the enlargement of the public sector has increased the opportunities of meeting private aggregations of economic power on equal terms, the great industrial companies have become more sensitive than in the past to public criticism, more amenable to governmental restraints and influences, and readier to accommodate their activities to official policy. We have already shown that a habit of close consultation between the government and the great concerns or trade associations developed during the war and that many of the purposes which the various controls were designed to promote continued to be secured by informal agreement even after those controls were abolished. To a larger extent than in the United States, in Great Britain business firms, especially the large companies, accept public responsibilities, while government departments are inclined to regard the officials of trade associations and the higher administrative officers of the great concerns as useful and necessary instruments of economic policy. This does not exclude the possibility of conflict, but it is significant that, even in the implementation of the Monopolies Commission's recommendations, the Board of Trade preferred to rely upon discussion and agreement with the industries concerned rather than upon the use of the legal powers conferred by the 1948 Act.[38]

While these developments in the relations between business and government may come to inhibit the ruthless exploitation of private economic power, they also reinforce the many other influences that have modified the forms of business behavior characteristic of the old competitive system. The motives and values of businessmen have certainly changed over the last few decades. Marshall once said that "business flourishes most where the aim of the business man is . . . to be held in respect by those who are the best judges of his special form of strength."[39] In the old competitive system "the special form of strength" was demonstrated almost exclusively by profit records. Among those who administer the great concerns of today, profit is only one of several tests of the competence that confers prestige, and the motives and qualities which now attract social

[37] Monopolies and Restrictive Practices Commission, *Report on the Supply of Insulin* (1952), pp. 29-32 and *passim*.

[38] Except in two cases.

[39] Alfred Marshall, *Industry and Trade* (London, 1919), p. 156.

approval differ widely from those of past times. This change in the business attitude has had an effect on the character and operation of the economic system as a whole, and not in every respect a salutory effect. Yet the extent of the change must not be exaggerated. The older attitudes still survive, especially among smaller firms, in spite of such discouraging factors as high taxation, which checks growth from small beginnings.

Organized Labor since the War

Whereas in the markets for goods the prewar and wartime tendencies towards a progressive shrinkage in the area of competition have met with some opposition, and in certain respects may even have been reversed since 1950, in the labor market monopolistic forces have undoubtedly been strengthened. The number of trade unionists grew to about ten million in the late fifties, and the concentration of membership in a few great unions increased. The scope of the public regulation of wages was also enlarged during and after the war. The Trade Boards, now renamed Wages Councils, were given additional powers, and statutory wage regulation was extended to certain "difficult" service industries, such as the catering trades and to the docks where, in the interests of decasualization, tripartite labor boards were set up to determine the number of workers on the dock registers and to supervise conditions of employment. Indeed, it can be said that in mining, manufacturing, agriculture, transport, distribution, and the main service trades, collective bargaining has become practically all-extensive. It would, of course, be an error to suppose that trade union activity and collective bargaining in general have necessarily led to the destruction of a once perfectly competitive market. Many imperfections existed under laissez faire, and organization may often have produced results (for wages and for the distribution of labor) that are nearer to those that would be found under perfect competition than would be reached in the absence of that organization. But such considerations are doubtfully relevant to the conditions brought about by the remarkable growth in the authority of organized labor since the war. The growth has come about mainly through the persistence of full employment and inflation, the wide extension of the social services, and the shift in political power.

It was indicated earlier in this paper that during the war and for some years afterwards organized labor co-operated with the government in its policy of preserving wage and price stability, a policy that was associated with an elaborate system of controls and subsidies as a condition of wage restraint. Since the abandonment of that policy and the reversion to a free pricing system, labor has been free to exert its enhanced bargaining strength. In the industrial disputes of this period the government has made much more extensive use than formerly of its power to refer cases, when the ordinary forms of bargaining have failed, to arbitration either by the Industrial Court set up in 1919, or by the postwar Industrial Disputes Tribunal, which until its abolition in 1959, provided for compulsory arbitration.[40] Many of the wage settlements in the major industries during recent years have been reached in this way. Thus wage determination has become increasingly a matter for nation-wide negotiations and centralized decision.

The establishment of machinery to determine, or to guide, wage policy in industry as a whole would (it has been suggested) consolidate a movement that has been proceeding for many decades. In its most ambitious form, the proposal requires that an annual estimate be made both of the national income for the next year and also of the share in it that could be made available for wages without adding to inflationary pressure. In the light of that information, a wage budget would be drawn up, and the allocation of any aggregate increase would become the function of some central body. Apart from the difficulties of accurate prediction, it is not easy to set out acceptable criteria which a national wages authority might employ. For many years past agreements between trade unions and employers' federations in certain industries have provided that changes in wage rates should automatically follow changes in the official cost-of-living index. But such agreements do not, of course, exclude demands for wage increases on other grounds, and in wage negotiations as a whole there is at any rate a tacit understanding that changes in productivity and profits, as well as in the cost of

[40] A reference to the Industrial Court can be made only if both sides to a dispute agree to it, and the recommendations of the Court are not legally binding. The Industrial Disputes Tribunal was the successor of a Tribunal set up during the war for compulsory arbitration. If one of the parties to a dispute informed the Minister of Labor that ordinary methods of negotiation and conciliation had broken down, and if the Minister accepted that view, then he referred the dispute to the Tribunal, the findings of which were legally binding on both parties.

living, are relevant to the claims put forward. The problem is also complicated by the divergent views held by the unions about the appropriate "differentials" between various classes of workers. At present there is no common agreement on the relative importance of the different criteria in the determination of wages, nor is any such agreement in sight. It is not merely that the trade union movement as a whole is at odds with the employers or the government about them. The trade unions themselves are sharply divided. Each union is intent upon furthering its own interests, and no common wage policy is likely to emerge unless the proposals recently put forward by certain trade union leaders for modifying the structure of the unions and for strengthening the General Council of the Trade Union Congress in relation to the individual unions receive more general support than has so far been accorded to them. Moreover, it is clear that general settlements of the type envisaged would be frequently evaded. During depressions it has certainly become more difficult for employers to reduce agreed wage rates because, in most of the weakly organized industries, legally enforceable *minimum* rates exist. In times of inflation, however, the opportunities for sidetracking bargains reached by central agreement are plentiful. During the period of the wage-standstill, workers found advantages in being members of an unorganized trade, and since then a potent influence in producing wage increases has come from the competition of employers for scarce labor. Even if a national wage policy were put into operation, employers in the more prosperous firms and trades could scarcely be prevented from bidding up wages. Competitive forces expelled from the front door would find their way in from the back. Thus, in spite of the growth of monopoly in the labor market, competitive pressures have not been completely eliminated. Particular wages still tend to accommodate themselves to the structure of demand, irrespective of the machinery used to determine them, although this does not mean that the structure and volume of the demand in this inflationary period have themselves been unaffected by the presence of monopoly and the forms of wage bargaining that now exist.[41]

[41] The "wage pause" introduced by the government in July 1961 as an anti-inflationary weapon was more successful in restraining wage increases than many economists expected, but it has still to be shown whether, in the face of trade union hostility, a policy of restraining wage increases to what is justified by advances in productivity can achieve success in the long run.

Another factor that has powerfully affected the industrial labor market is to be found in the changed conditions in agriculture. In Great Britain during most of the nineteenth century, and in many other countries today (especially those with a large peasantry), the growth of monopoly in the industrial labor market was impeded by the flow of labor from the overpopulated countryside. Even before the beginning of the present century the decline in British agriculture had greatly reduced the size of this reservoir of cheap labor, but up to World War II, in spite of the operations of the Agricultural Wages Board, wages in certain industries (e.g., the railway service) were kept down by the flow of recruits from the rural areas. Since the war, however, agricultural prosperity, derived mainly from lavish subsidies, has raised agricultural wages and has finally destroyed this source of cheap labor. Indeed, the persistent condition of overemployment in the economy as a whole has meant that certain service industries (the nursing service and the railways) can be adequately staffed only by drawing extensively upon workers from overseas, especially from Ireland and the West Indies. The organized workers have not in general been much disturbed by this modest challenge to their monopoly power, but some unions have refused to allow foreigners to be employed in their trades and the generally complacent disposition towards immigrant labor would hardly survive the end of the boom.

Before the war an inquiry was made to discover how far trade union restrictions were obstructive of technical progress and the economical distribution of labor.[42] The conclusions were illuminating. Although many trade unions tried to preserve or to strengthen their monopolistic position by imposing restrictions upon entry, and although some had rules which hampered the adoption of new techniques, it seemed that, except in a few industries, the effect was to delay rather than to prevent the redistribution of manpower in response to changes in the demand for labor, and to make more expensive the adoption of new devices rather than to frustrate their use. Moreover, the restrictive practices were fewer than in the past and were diminishing in importance. In fact, whatever the rules may have been, most industries achieved considerable technical progress in the interwar period and the redistribution of labor was on

[42] John Hilton et al., Are Trade Unions Obstructive? (London, 1935), pp. 334-336 and passim.

a massive scale. Since the war the chronic shortage of labor has increased pressure for the adoption of measures to raise productivity. Leadership in the labor movement has been well disposed, on the whole, towards such measures, and trade unionists have been associated with employers in commending to British industries the lessons learned in the United States by the teams organized by the Anglo-American Council on Productivity. Technical efficiency and labor productivity have made notable advances in most, though not in all, branches of industry. At the same time, even in an era when the danger of technological unemployment seems to have been overcome, there has been obstruction in certain trades to the use of improved methods and new techniques. On occasion, new capital instruments have been inadequately used and production has been held up by jurisdictional disputes among rival unions over the types of workers to be employed on new operations or new materials.[43] The shipbuilding, printing, and building industries have provided examples of this obstructionism. Behavior that impedes technical progress is likely to be more effective and dangerous today, when organized labor is so powerful, than it was before the war when restrictive rules could be more easily circumvented. Management as well as the trade unions must bear some measure of responsibility for these troubles. The system of industrial relations has not yet accommodated itself to the new conditions in the labor market, and effective substitutes for the old pressures are still to seek.

The Present Outlook

To conclude, an attempt must be made to deal with the broad general questions posed by Professor Hoover. It will be readily understood, however, that the intricacies of the situation and the conflicting trends which the above examination has disclosed mean that no simple or downright answer can be given. The elements of monopoly in the British economy are numerous and widely extended. Partly by developments within industry itself and partly through government policy, the area in which the older forms of competition prevail has greatly contracted during the present century. This contraction proceeded rapidly during the thirties and in the course

---

[43] While the growth of large national industrial unions (or federations of unions) increases the rigidity in the labor market, at the same time it provides, for solving jurisdictional problems, opportunities that are not present when the workers are organized in numerous craft or sectional unions.

of World War II. In some respects it was carried even further
during the early postwar period. But since 1950 the trend has been
halted and even reversed. This may apply even to the tendency
noted during several decades before 1939 towards increased concentration of control in private industry; but the most important
factor has been the change in government policy, particularly the
attempt, under the new monopoly policy, to eliminate certain restrictive practices in industry and trade. Few informed observers expect that this policy will go far towards restoring a competitive
economy of the old type, but there is reason to hope that it may
result in a loosening of the rigidity that had come to characterize
many branches of industry. The effect of the policy may be reinforced by the exposure of the British economy to additional outside competition, should it become associated with the Common Market. On the other hand, many of the changes in the structure and
functioning of the economy that were brought about by the increased
activities of the state, notably in the nationalized sector, have come
to stay.

Even when the trend was strongly towards monopoly, a competitive fringe persisted, and monopoly had not been sufficiently
powerful to prevent change and progress or to inhibit the entry of
newcomers in most branches of industry. Indeed, the effects of
monopoly have been more evident in the short run than in the long
run. In a dynamic economy, it seems, monopoly in particular industries may succeed in resisting the pressure of economic forces
for a time, only to give way in the end. When we ask whether
monopoly yields results for market behavior or technical progress
that are widely different from those that result from competition,
no simple answer can be given. Monopolies stand in marked contrast to one another in their origin and operations. Sometimes monopoly replaces conditions of very imperfect competition. In other
cases it has itself been the outcome of the successful competition of
particularly progressive firms. In yet other cases it has undoubtedly
helped to preserve inefficiencies.

Since monopoly is likely to remain powerful over much of the
economy, it is important to consider that restraints are being imposed upon the exercise of monopolistic power and how far new
forms of rivalry have replaced the old. In British industry technological change accompanied by the intrusion of certain great firms

into lines of production hitherto the province of others has made some monopolistic positions less secure and has called forth qualities of alertness and enterprise. The growth in the public sector and the increased importance of the government as a customer have furnished opportunities for the use of "countervailing power," although those opportunities may not always have been adequately seized. Most important of all, the great firms, if they have escaped in some measure from the discipline of a free market, have become exposed to other pressures that have had some considerable influence in sustaining the public interest. The sensitiveness of the industrial leaders to public criticism and their readiness to accommodate their activities to government policy have been noted. Even in industries where there are no dominant firms, trade associations act as a channel for the communication of government policy. Although they often seek to exert pressure on the government, they are also a means, at times, for bringing official influence to bear on individual firms. It must not be imagined that this acceptance of public responsibilities is common to the whole of monopolized industry. Some of the cartels are not by any means ready to accept a role as unofficial agencies of public policy. Nevertheless, in general it seems that as firms escape from free-market pressures they are liable to become exposed to others. This, of course, produces a situation far removed from that found in competitive industry, but it does mean that monopoly is not so free, as is often supposed, to consult merely its own financial interests. In these and other ways, therefore, more or less adequate substitutes are being found for market pressures as safeguards for the consumer, as means of adjustment to changes in technique and markets, and as a stimulus to progress. The adequacy of the substitutes differs widely from industry to industry. To some extent any judgment must depend on whether it is believed that market forces could be expected to work effectively in the absence of these deliberately created monopolistic structures. In some industries, for technical reasons, no real alternative to monopoly or oligopoly exists.

In the field of labor the extension of monopoly has proceeded unchecked. For various reasons set out above, organized labor has increased its power and the area of competition in that market has continuously diminished. No anti-monopoly policy comparable to that introduced for industry and trade has made its appearance. The legal privileges won by the trade unions earlier in the century have not been assailed. Nor does it seem that here the new pressures replacing those of the free market have been very influential. Only for short periods and in special circumstances has the trade union movement co-operated to prevent a full exploitation by labor of favorable market conditions. This is not to suggest that the majority of the trade union leaders lack a sense of public obligation. But when it is a question of accommodating pricing policy to the public interest, they are far more susceptible to pressure from their constituents (or the small active section of them) than are the directors of public companies vis-à-vis their shareholders. The reforms in the structure and organization of the trade union movement now advocated by certain influential leaders might help to deal with this problem, although they might also raise fresh difficulties.[44] Obviously, anything that strengthens the hand of the more statesmanlike trade union leader is likely to be of immense benefit to the functioning of the British economy during the next decade.

Few people would venture to predict how the future will shape. It is possible that the measures against restrictive practices will be strengthened and extended to areas to which they have not yet been applied. At the same time it may well be that the substitutes for competition that have become influential in some parts of the economy will become more effective both by the growth within industries (and trade unions) of a sense of public responsibility in the use of monopolistic power, and also as the result of the dynamic force of technical change. But the issue is in doubt. What remains of the free market is insecure. This is not only because private monopoly may renew its strength. The government, despite the abandonment of the wartime controls, continues to exert a powerful influence over the functioning and development of the economy, and of late years its readiness to intervene in particular business decisions has been frequently demonstrated. If this is so under a Conservative administration, and in a period of prosperity, then there can be little doubt that, with a shift in political power or a deterioration in economic conditions, centralized direction might easily return.

[44] It has been pointed out that for many years past it has been the practice in some large industries for independent unions to be associated in joint negotiations, and that in a few industries federations, which negotiate on behalf of a group of unions, have been formally constituted. From this type of negotiating machinery it is but a step (so it is argued) to co-ordination on a national basis. See A. Birch, *Structure of the British Trade Union Movement* (Manchester, 1957).

4

The Canadian Economy

O. W. Main*

General Structure of the Economy

It would be extremely difficult to apply the general term laissez-faire competition to the complex organization of the Canadian economy, even though it is more free from government restraint and control than most economies in the world. Certainly, there is within the various sectors a strong laissez-faire philosophy which tolerates only a minimum of regulation. Moreover, Canada has always had a Federal Government dedicated to the principles of free enterprise. However, most sectors have looked to the governments at all levels to aid in their development and to provide an atmosphere conducive to growth and full employment.

The reason for the mixture of laissez-faire philosophy and governmental paternalism lies in the nature of the economy. Canada is a relatively new country with abundant resources scattered over a tremendous area, separated by large non-productive regions. Although the total area of the country is larger than that of the United States, the population is small and concentrated in a relatively narrow strip along the border between Canada and the United States where climatic conditions are more favorable for comfortable living. Many of the areas in Canada are dependent upon one resource for their income and are extremely vulnerable to changes in world conditions of price and production. Thus the development of these resource areas and their linkage to the rest of the country have dictated the use of considerable government influence and support, and the maintenance of these areas in the face of wide fluctuations in income has encouraged some governmental control. On the one hand, in order to attract risk capital in sufficient quantities to exploit the

* Professor of Economics and Director, School of Business, the University of Toronto.

areas, a minimum amount of restraint and a maximum amount of concession have been offered. On the other hand, all levels of government have provided extensive services necessary for the development of the country. While there has been a strong desire to be free of government interference, there has been considerable agreement on a wide range of state action, from government ownership of some railways, telephone systems, radio and television communication to the provision of bounties, subsidies, loans, and scientific services for industry and agriculture.[1]

A further complication to a simple description of the Canadian economy is the division of legislative powers between the provincial governments and the Federal Government. When Canada was created as a confederation of the provinces, the British North America Act gave to the provinces considerable specific powers and left to the Federal Government residual powers relating to the country as a whole. Thus, the degree of government ownership or control will vary from province to province. For example, in some provinces telephone service is a government monopoly, but in other provinces telephone service is provided by a privately owned utility subject to regulation. One telephone company whose operations extend over two provinces is regulated by the Federal Government. Such variations may arise from differing conditions in the provinces but also they are the result of differing political philosophies of each of the provincial governments, ranging from modified socialism to conservatism. Further, the division of powers has meant that in many cases government action on a national scale, except in time of national emergency, can be accomplished only by the passage of enabling legislation in each of the provinces.

The Canadian economy can be described as an "open economy" dependent upon foreign trade for a large measure of its prosperity. Exports of goods and services amount to 20 per cent of its gross national product. Of these exports, two-thirds are in a relatively few staples such as newsprint, pulpwood, lumber, wheat, flour, and non-ferrous metals. As an open economy dependent upon staples, Canada is extremely vulnerable to business conditions in other countries and to their trade policies. Not a few of the governmental

[1] J. A. Corry, "The Growth of Government Activities since Confederation," *Report of the Royal Commission on Dominion Provincial Relations* (Ottawa, 1939), Appendix.

controls have arisen as a reaction to changes in conditions and trade policies in other countries. The relation of Canada to the United States is particularly important, since the United States accounts for 60 per cent of all Canadian exports. On the import side, Canada is even more dependent upon the United States, drawing 70 per cent of her imports from that source.

Concern has been felt for many years over the dependence of the country upon the United States. Since 1879 Canada has maintained a protective tariff designed to hasten the industrialization of the country and to preserve its political independence. The structure of the tariff provides for low duties on parts and materials required by Canadian producers and high duties on finished products that compete with those made in Canada. In addition, preference is given to goods imported from Britain and the Commonwealth countries by the use of preferential rates. However, neither the tariff nor the use of British preference has prevented the increasing dependence of Canada upon the United States for markets or sources of supply.

Under the tariff, the industrialization of Canada proceeded slowly until World War II. During the war, Canada was cut off from many products which had to be manufactured at home in order to further the war effort. In the postwar period, industrialization continued under the impetus of a tremendous growth in population and the further development of natural resources. Population increased from 12 million in 1945 to 18 million in 1960, and the gross national product increased by 175 per cent in terms of real output. Today one-third of the national income originates in manufacturing. The significant shift from agriculture to industry has important implications for the competitive structure of the economy and will be discussed in a later section.

Concentration and Competition in Industry

It would be expected that, since Canada furnishes a relatively small market for manufacturing, there would be a high concentration of firms in industry and that the dominant market structure would be that of oligopoly. These expectations have been confirmed by Professor Rosenbluth.[2] He concludes from his study that:

[2] Gideon Rosenbluth, *Concentration in Canadian Manufacturing Industries* (National Bureau of Economic Research, No. 61; Princeton, 1957). See also The

The Canadian manufacturing industries show a wide variation in the degree of concentration, but, on the average, concentration is quite high. In half of the industries studied, 9 or less of the leading firms account for 80 per cent of the employment, and in one-third of the industries less than 5 firms account for 80 per cent of employment. Examples of industries with very high concentration are the primary metals, automobiles, railway equipment, cotton textiles, cigarettes, distilleries and many of the industries processing non-metallic minerals and chemicals, such as glass and compressed gases.[3]

The statement quoted above tends to understate the degree of concentration in the Canadian economy. Some of the industries with a very low concentration have regional markets which are protected from competition by high transportation costs. Even with this qualification omitted, the figures show a startlingly high degree of concentration. The market structure of the economy thus revealed seems to diverge completely from the competitive model of the classical economists.

Statistics on concentration do not give us many clues to the competitiveness within industries or to the ability of competing firms to fix prices and control markets. Some of the industries, such as nickel and aluminum, which are highly concentrated export most of their product and are in such a position in the world market that they have considerable control over price. Other industries, such as copper mining and processing, have high concentration and export their product but are at the mercy of the world markets. High concentration industries with a national market, such as railway equipment, sell to only a few powerful firms and are limited in their control over price and markets. On the other hand, low concentration industries with purely regional markets may exert a considerable influence on price and competition.

Regardless of the degree of concentration, the development of institutions and attitudes among competitors can lessen competition considerably. During the war the Federal Government encouraged association between former competitors, because it was easier to implement wartime control with groups of firms than with each firm individually. Of 164 manufacturing and mining trade associations

Canadian Bank of Commerce, *Industrial Concentration* (a study prepared for the Royal Commission on Canada's Economic Prospects; Ottawa, 1956).
    [3] Rosenbluth, *op. cit.*, p. 15.

recorded in Canada in 1947, 41 were founded in the period 1942-44.[4] The number and strength of these associations have grown since that time but there is no evidence of the degree of success they have had in limiting competition.

Coincident with the problems of maintaining effective competition in a sector marked by high concentration is the equally important problem of the lack of control by Canadians over many of the manufacturing firms. It is estimated that non-residents own over 50 per cent of the capital employed in the manufacturing sector. Further, non-residents control 56 per cent of the capital employed and United States firms account for 80 per cent of non-resident control.

There are two important implications arising from the high degree of foreign ownership. In the first place, these firms are by their very nature management-controlled rather than shareholder-controlled. Even when shares in the foreign-owned Canadian company are made available to the Canadian public, the amount is so small that Canadians have no opportunity to secure even a small share in the management or policy of the company. This situation was serious enough that the Royal Commission on Canada's Economic Prospects in 1956 spent some time in the consideration of the problem of Canadian subsidiaries of foreign companies. It recommended that foreign companies should employ Canadians in senior management positions in their Canadian subsidiaries and purchase in Canada their supplies, materials, and equipment for Canadian operations. Further, it was recommended that Canadian subsidiaries should offer an appreciable percentage of their equity stock to Canadian investors and should include on their boards of directors a number of independent Canadian businessmen.[5] To date, there has been no evidence that the foreign companies have taken any heed of these recommendations. Indeed, the trend to increased foreign ownership and control has continued unabated.

In the second place, Canadian subsidiaries are usually not allowed to seek markets or independent sources of supply in competition with the parent company. These restrictions, where they apply, would prevent Canadian branch companies, no matter how

[4] Dominion Bureau of Statistics, *United States Direct Investment in Canada* (Ottawa, 1949). See also Rosenbluth, *op. cit.*, p. 8.

[5] Royal Commission on Canada's Economic Prospects, *Preliminary Report* (Ottawa, 1956), p. 90.

efficient they might be, from entering the United States market or any other market in which the parent might sell. If the subsidiary were a supplier of the parent, it would normally be prevented from seeking markets with competitors or possible competitors of the parent. Further, it might be forced to buy supplies and equipment from the parent's connections, even though these materials might be obtainable in Canada. Although there are many cases where economic and political reasons also inhibit exports by subsidiaries, the addition of prohibitions as a matter of company policy has acted to impede the growth of exports and has created further resentment against foreign control.[6]

The limitations on the competitive effectiveness of Canadian subsidiaries in foreign markets and the concern over the high degree of foreign ownership have led to agitation for a reversal of the trend. Recent government action imposing a 15 per cent tax on the transfer of profits from Canadian subsidiaries to parent companies has been regarded as the first step in slowing down the trend to foreign ownership.

The high concentration of industry and the lack of competition in many areas has always been a matter of concern for the Canadian government. As early as 1889, the Federal Government passed a law designed to suppress combinations in restraint of trade. The law has been revised many times, the latest revision occurring in 1960. Under the terms of the Combines Investigation Act, suppliers are forbidden to agree to eliminate competition by limiting production, restricting distribution, or fixing prices. Similarly, mergers, trusts, or monopolies are forbidden if there are possibilities that they will operate to the detriment or against the interest of the public. Further, a supplier of goods cannot prescribe prices at which they are to be resold, but may suggest resale prices so long as he does nothing to require the trade to adhere to them. Finally, suppliers may not discriminate among their customers by giving one a preferred

[6] See: J. Lindeman and D. Armstrong, *Policies and Practices of United States Subsidiaries in Canada* (Canadian-American Committee: n.p., 1960). As a result of their study, the authors claim that economic and political factors far outweigh company policy as causes of low exports by subsidiaries. However, since their survey is concerned only with foreign-controlled companies, they made no comparison with the export business of Canadian companies. Excluding those companies set up solely to supply the parent company, e.g., in iron ore, pulp and paper, etc., they found that most of the subsidiaries had some export business but it represented only between 1 per cent and 10 per cent of the total volume, with the majority falling in the range closer to 1 per cent.

price not available to others, and they may not sell at prices lower in one locality than in another, or unreasonably low anywhere if the purpose is to lessen competition substantially or to eliminate a competitor.[7]

Investigations into alleged combines and violations of the Act are carried out by a director of investigation for the Restrictive Trade Practices Commission, which makes formal reports to the Minister of Justice. These reports must be published and made available to the public. Violations of the Act are considered to be criminal offenses, and violators are prosecuted in the courts and are subject to fines and imprisonment. Other remedial measures, such as injunctions, proceedings for the dissolution of an illegal merger, patent impeachment, and tariff reductions may also be used. Although all of these measures are possible, the main weapons have been fines and injunctions.

Much reliance has been placed on the value of publicity as a deterrent. It has always been felt that once businessmen were aware that the anti-combines policy was being applied consistently and effectively, they would abandon practices which had been condemned in the courts. However, there does not seem to be any large-scale abandonment of restrictive practices, as had been hoped. The reason probably lies in the fact that the courts have condemned all price fixing and have refused to determine whether the prices fixed were reasonable or not, or whether the price fixing was detrimental to the public interest. They have consistently held that price fixing and any restraint of trade that has unduly lessened competition is detrimental to the public interest, regardless of how reasonable the actions might have seemed to the business firms involved. Therefore, it has been extremely difficult to convince the businessmen that what they consider good business practice is both illegal and unreasonable. As a result, breaches of the Act have been widespread.

Although the Act has been in effect for many years, it was not until the period following World War II that there was vigorous enforcement of its provisions. After the war there was much concern that the lessons learned in wartime co-operation would be carried into peacetime conditions. The Royal Commission on Prices in 1948 dealt at some length with this problem and recommended

---

[7] Restrictive Trade Practices Commission, *Annual Reports of the Director of Investigations and Research* (Ottawa, 1954-60).

some changes in the Act. In 1952 the Act was revised to provide for imprisonment as well as fines, and made resale price maintenance illegal. Imprisonment has not been used, but the abolition of resale price maintenance has been most effective. By removing the legality of resale price maintenance, the Act has opened up the retail trade to price competition and has led to considerable changes in the structure of the trade, including the rise of discount stores.

In the last ten years some thirty reports on alleged combines have been published. Although some of them have been concerned with local violations of resale price maintenance prohibition, the list of products involved is quite impressive. Included are fine papers, maple syrup, coarse papers, wire fencing, culverts, beer, asphalt products, box-board, sugar, tobacco, electrical wire and cable, transmission and conveyor equipment, and various rubber products. In addition, 25 formal investigations are being carried on at the present time. All of these reports indicate the magnitude of the problem, but there is every indication that the work of the Commission is merely scratching the surface of the problem and that widespread price fixing and agreements are still an important part of Canadian business.

Although the energetic enforcement of the Act and the tightening of its provisions have undoubtedly had some effect upon the development of competition within the Canadian economy, two other factors have been much more important in opening up industry to the breezes of competition. These have been the tremendous postwar growth in the Canadian market and the slow retreat from a protective tariff policy.

The growth of the Canadian market made it difficult for firms to maintain a monopoly position. In many instances, the market grew much faster than the ability or the willingness of the established firms to increase capacity to meet the demands. Moreover, since the market was expanding, there was little incentive to use means to keep out entrants because there was plenty for all. In addition, the growth of the market invited well-established foreign firms to invade the Canadian market and to set up Canadian subsidiaries. These large firms would be difficult to keep out even if the established firms had wished to use competitive means or agreements to do so. In a rapidly expanding economy restrictive trade practices and attempts to keep markets closed proved ineffective.

However, in recent years, as the pace of growth has slackened, pressures on the government to keep out foreign firms and to amend the Combines Act have mounted. In general, these pressures have not been successful but there has been some relaxation to allow firms to co-operate with each other in selling in foreign markets. If the Canadian economy fails to renew its growth, however, there may be considerable change in the government's attitude toward competition and its effectiveness.

In the immediate postwar period, it was recognized that Canada would have to seek to regain its traditional foreign markets and, if it wished to grow, would have to seek new markets. As a result, the Canadian government consistently sought to widen international trade. In a climate of world opinion which favored the reduction of tariff barriers, it was possible for Canada to pursue this policy. Her own rapidly growing market enabled her to reduce tariffs without any serious shock to the economic system. In 1948, Canada became a member of the General Agreement on Tariffs and Trade and has participated in the negotiations since that time. Canada now has trade agreements with sixty-six countries.

The retreat from a protective tariff policy was made more effective by the continued external strength of the Canadian dollar. The depreciation of other currencies made Canadian prices very attractive to foreign shippers, and these higher prices offset to some extent the effect of the tariff. In addition, as world prices rose in the wake of the postwar inflation, specific duties became less protective than formerly. Finally, a relaxation in the customs administration of the duties aided the foreign shipper considerably, because a more general classification of goods to bring them into categories to which a lower tariff applied was just as effective as a general lowering of tariffs.[8]

While the Canadian economy was growing rapidly, ideal conditions for the development of a laissez-faire philosophy were created. Competition, although not high, was increased, and trade shackles were gradually loosened. However, the slackening in the rate of growth and the consequent increase in unemployment has put pressure on the government to reverse its policy. Recent government action in raising tariffs and changing the classification of goods in the tariff schedule and in getting informal agreements with

[8] See G. Blake, *Customs Administration in Canada* (Toronto, 1957).

foreign powers to limit their exports to Canada indicate that the dream of free international trade for Canada is about over. In particular, the development of the European Common Market and the emergence of other trading blocs have threatened Canada's position in the Commonwealth trading system. Canada is torn between close trading ties with the United States and the prospects of being left out of any European trading arrangement. Moreover, the decline in the number of investigations of combines and minor changes in the Combines Act may indicate that even on the domestic scene Canada does not feel that she can afford the luxury of competition where excess capacity exists and the unemployed have an increasingly strong voice.

Agriculture

Prior to World War II, agriculture was the major industry in Canada. Almost a third of the population lived on farms and 29 per cent of the labor force was employed in farming. The country had its roots and traditions deep in the soil and the farm population was loath to accept restraints of any kind. The structure of the agricultural sector was largely that of the traditional model of pure competition. However, the difficulties of the thirties and the changes in the character of the industry since then have moved the agricultural sector away from pure competition to mixed competition marked by considerable governmental control and support.

In the postwar period the gradual drift from the farm, which had been going on during the late thirties, was speeded up. By 1959 only 12 per cent of the labor force was engaged in agriculture and less than 18 per cent of the population lived on farms. This trend was aided by the increased mechanization of agriculture and by an increase in the size of the farm, as well as a decrease in the number of farms. The average size of the farm increased from 224 acres in 1931 to 279 acres in 1951, the last census period. In the same period the number of farms declined from 728,000 to 623,000. The trend to large-scale farming is especially pronounced in the wheat-growing prairie region, where two-thirds of the farms are over 300 acres in size. An indication of the trend is shown by a comparison of farm holding by size in 1931 and 1951 (Table 1 below).

Although the size of the farm has increased, agriculture has not as yet proved suited to operation on the really large scale that has

TABLE I. *Farm Holdings Classified by Size of Farm*

	Per cent of farms occupied	
Size of farm, in acres	*1931*	*1951*
1- 4	2.8	1.5
5- 10	3.3	3.4
11- 50	11.0	9.5
51-100	21.0	19.8
101-200	31.1	27.9
201-299	4.8	6.3
300 and over	26.0	31.6
	100.0	100.0

Source: Dominion Bureau of Statistics, *Ninth Census of Canada,* 1951 (Ottawa, 1953).

been achieved in the manufacturing and commercial service industries to which it sells its products. As a result, the farmer has been faced, over the years, with a steady decline in his bargaining power with those who purchased his products. In addition, the growth of large-scale marketing agencies has reduced the possibility of active competition in the purchase of farm products. The farmer has felt that his failure to share in rising income and prices was caused by his inferior bargaining power and has sought to redress the situation by the development of his own power through organization and through governmental assistance.

During the thirties the farmer abandoned his laissez-faire philosophy and accepted regulation of the marketing of farm products. In 1934 the Federal Government passed the Natural Products Marketing Act, establishing a Dominion Marketing Board to delegate powers to regional boards to regulate the conditions under which farm products would be marketed. Some 19 marketing schemes were put into operation under the Act, but in 1937 the Act was ruled *ultra vires,* since the Federal Government was not empowered to regulate trade within a province. Later, provincial acts replaced the Natural Products Marketing Act.

During World War II the farmer continued to come under governmental control. Under emergency powers, the Federal Government controlled the sale of virtually every farm product. At the end of the period, however, the government dropped its powers, retaining control only over the marketing of grains grown in the prairie provinces. Provincial marketing laws again became operative, and local boards appeared. Most of the provincial marketing legislation now permits the will of a specified majority (usually two-thirds) of the producers to be exerted in the establishment of compulsory marketing schemes for various products. The powers of the boards constituted to regulate the schemes vary considerably from province to province, and their use of power also varies. Some boards are content to negotiate minimum prices with buyers. Others include terms of sale and quality, and a few perform some of the marketing functions.

Although marketing schemes have multiplied, comparatively little use has been made of them except in Ontario and British Columbia, where they have been applied to products in a limited area comprising a number of specialized producers. The reason for their limited use has been found in the limitations on the ability of the boards to enforce regulations, especially when alternative export markets exist and where alternative sources of supply from other regions of Canada and from the United States are open to buyers.

Although governmental action has tried to increase the bargaining power of the farmer through compulsory schemes, only two products, fluid milk and coarse grains, have come under direct and regular participation by the government in marketing. In the case of milk, low prices during the depression and concern about the maintenance of sufficient domestic supplies of milk of good quality led to the passage of milk control acts in several provinces. Although originally designed as emergency measures, the acts have continued in force with some modifications. Provincial milk control boards have the power to fix and enforce producer and consumer prices, limit the number of distributors, and regulate milk marketing. Recently, they have been largely used to assist the producers and distributors in setting producer prices through mediation in the bargaining about contract prices. It was felt that this assistance was necessary to improve the bargaining power of the producers, since the distributors were becoming concentrated into larger and more powerful units.

Efforts to secure government assistance in the marketing of grains, especially wheat, have had a long history in Canada. Wheat is an important export commodity for Canada and is the main source of income for the prairie provinces. As a result, the provinces brought considerable pressure to bear upon the Federal Government to protect the producers from the monopolistic position of the grain buyers. At first, the farmers tried to improve their position by the establishment of producer co-operatives to market wheat. These marketing pools collapsed when wheat prices declined drastically in the thirties. To support the producers, the Federal Government set up a wheat marketing board as an optional marketing outlet and set minimum prices for wheat. After operating on this basis from 1935 to 1943, the Wheat Board became the sole marketing agent for wheat grown in the prairie provinces. In recent years it has also taken over responsibility for the marketing of oats and barley.

As the sole marketing agent, the Board negotiates sales with both private concerns and state trading agencies. Canada is a member of the International Wheat Agreement. It buys grain from the farmers at an initial price set below the expected average price for the coming season. The excess is then distributed to the farmers when the crop is sold, as participation payments. In setting the initial price the Board, in effect, fixes a support price for the grain. If the average price obtained by the Board is less than the initial price, the Board bears the loss. In addition, the government pays the cost of storage for surplus grain under its control.

In addition to support for compulsory marketing schemes and its participation in the marketing of western grains, the Federal Government has also carried on an agricultural price support program. This program arose as a result of the price control policy during the war. Canada attempted to prevent a rapid rise in farm prices by controlling the contract price at which several major farm products were sold to the United Kingdom. In setting relatively low contract prices, the government at the same time encouraged increased production through the provision of subsidy payments. However, the farmers felt that since they had not been able to get any income advantage from the short supply situation during the war, they should be protected from possible declines in prices which might follow the return to normal peacetime conditions. To meet this need, the Agricultural Prices Support Act was passed in 1944 as an emergency measure to meet the transition period. In 1950, however, it was put on a permanent basis.

The Act provided for producers of any farm product, except wheat, to obtain price support if the need could be established. An application for price support was investigated by the Board, which determined the reason for the price decline, determined whether it was temporary or not, and examined the possible long-run consequences of providing support. The Board then recommended to the government whether or not action should be taken and specified the type and the degree of support. There was no mathematical or historical price formula used. Thus, the Act was used as a measure to meet specific conditions, rather than a general support for farm prices. Although many products were supported from time to time, most of the support price losses were incurred by the government in the large-scale buying and selling operations which were undertaken on behalf of hog and cattle producers during the outbreak of foot and mouth disease in 1952.

In 1957 firm government support prices for some farm products were tried when the Conservative party came into power. The lessons to be learned from high support prices were made quickly apparent when surpluses of eggs, pork, and butter began to pile up. At the support prices, the large producers who had taken advantage of the gains in productivity and in mechanization were encouraged to increase production. The increased flow of products could not be sold at the high support prices and the government had to take the surplus. By 1960 the government abandoned the firm price support and let farm prices seek their own level. A limited subsidy program for small producers was substituted. This program enabled the government to meet the needs of the marginal producer without at the same time encouraging a flood of products from the efficient producers.

Many other measures have been used to support the agricultural sector. Among the most important have been the special freight rates on grains moving from the prairie provinces and freight assistance on feed grains shipped to Eastern Canada and British Columbia from the western provinces. Special assistance has also been provided for districts which have suffered crop failures. However, with the exception of coarse grains and milk, government action has been limited to encouragement to the farmer to improve his bargaining position by co-operative marketing. Despite the many post-war changes, the agricultural sector still remains highly competitive.[9]

Labor Organization in the Canadian Economy

Organized labor has developed into an important force in the Canadian economy only in the last twenty years. Before World War II the labor movement was weak and unionism was concentrated in only a few industries. Membership in labor unions numbered 360,000, about 13 per cent of the non-agricultural labor force. Today there are 1.5 million trade unionists, representing about one-third of that labor force. The number of workers under collective agreement has risen to 1.7 million. Agriculture has not yet been affected by the labor movement.

The importance of unions varies considerably from industry to industry. Transportation and communication has 80 per cent of the workers under collective agreement. Manufacturing has 55 per cent, but commercial and service industries have only 9 per cent subject to collective bargaining.

The strength of the labor movement grew considerably during the war. Until that time there had been little legal encouragement to its growth. The Federal Government had passed the Industrial Disputes Investigation Act in 1907, but the Act applied only to industries where continuous operation was of national importance. Provincial governments, which are constitutionally responsible for labor laws, had enacted legislation concerned with workers' compensation for accidents, minimum wages, conditions of work, and apprenticeships, but very little legislation concerned with union recognition and collective bargaining had appeared.

During the war the maintenance of industrial peace became extremely important. Government policy designed to minimize strikes was implemented with the establishment of a Wartime Labour Relations Board. The Board had the power to determine bargaining representatives, to punish for practices regarded as inimical to industrial peace, such as discrimination against unionized workers, and intimidation by unions to force workers to become union members. Both employers and unions were required to bargain in good

[9] For a discussion of the problems of Canadian agriculture, see W. M. Drummond and W. Mackenzie, *Progress and Prospects of Canadian Agriculture* (Royal Commission on Canada's Economic Prospects: Ottawa, 1957).

faith. In this climate labor unions were encouraged to flourish. After the war the Federal Government dropped its emergency measures, but the provincial governments enacted similar legislation, setting up labor relations boards and providing for conciliation and arbitration of labor disputes. Under these laws the workers may choose their own bargaining agents, with whom the employers must negotiate agreements.[10]

The Canadian labor unions have drawn much strength and support from the United States labor movement. Most of the Canadian unions are affiliated with their American counterparts and have drawn on them for assistance in bargaining. A central labor congress, the Canadian Labour Congress, to which most of the unions belong, also has connections with the American central body. These strong ties stemmed from the migration of unions across the border, paralleling the setting up of American branch plants in Canada. However, most of the Canadian unions have maintained a considerable measure of autonomy in their own affairs, although some unions are dominated by American international unions. Needless to say, Canadian unions have been much influenced by the American labor movement and the character of Canadian unionism has been determined by the American structure and development.

Although the unions have achieved considerable success in improving their bargaining position, they are still far from a monopoly position in the economy. In the industries which were experiencing chronic shortages of labor after the war or where the demands for the goods were high, gains were won rather easily. In some export industries which were subject to wide fluctuations in prices, easy victories in the early postwar period were replaced by grim struggles and meager gains as shortages disappeared. As excess capacity has developed, the unions have found that their ability to win gains has diminished and that worker support has grown less enthusiastic.

Three limitations on the growth of unionism have appeared in recent years. One has been the large-scale immigration to Canada. Since 1946 almost two million immigrants have come to Canada, and many have joined the labor force. This continued movement has relieved labor shortages and prevented unions from developing a monopoly position. Another limitation has been the increasing

[10] H. A. Logan, *Trade Unions in Canada* (Toronto, 1948). See also S. Jamieson, *Industrial Relations in Canada* (Toronto, 1957).

development of mechanization in industry. Since labor union power is concentrated in the industrial sector, any shift of the work force from production to service or technical work erodes the power of the unions. Technical and service workers usually have a different view of their role in the business organization and seem less conducive to being organized than the production workers have been. A third limitation has been the effect of foreign competition upon domestic prices. Imports have kept prices down and have prevented the domestic manufacturers from passing on wage increases. As a result, employers have been most reluctant to give in to wage demands. Failure to achieve results in some industries has hampered union growth in those sectors.

Although the Canadian economy has continued to grow in the postwar period, the changing composition of its population has led to an increasing percentage in the labor force. The growth in the number of employed has been paralleled by the growth of the number of unemployed. Unemployment rates have risen from less than 2 per cent to over 6 per cent. Increased unemployment has not had any significant effect on wage rates, which have continued to climb throughout the period. One measure which prevents wage rates from declining is the federal unemployment insurance scheme instituted in 1942. Payments are made for limited periods, depending upon length of previous employment, to unemployed insured workers. The fund is made up of contributions from employers, employees, and the government. While unemployment was low, the scheme was quite successful. As unemployment has grown, the government has used the scheme more and more to provide income for seasonal workers and for workers whose benefits have been exhausted. As a result, the fund has been quickly drained in the last two years. Continued drains on the fund, coupled with increased length of benefit period, will eventually force the government to be responsible for the maintenance of income of the unemployed regardless of the length of their unemployment. Such participation by the government may mean further government intervention in the labor market and increased controls over the labor force.

Government Participation in the Economy

In the preceding sections we have been concerned with the changes in the economy and its sectors and in the government's role in setting the structure within which the economy operates. In general, the policy has been one of trying to improve the power of the weaker sectors and attempting to break down the power of the stronger sectors. This policy has led to the combination of smaller units into larger bargaining units, especially in agriculture and labor, but has not changed the economy significantly. It is still a relatively free competitive economy where the price system still operates, although somewhat imperfectly. In this section we shall discuss the more direct controls of the government as a provider of welfare services, as a purchaser of goods and services, as an owner and regulator of certain industries, and as an agent committed to provide full employment and to maintain stability as well as growth in the economy.

In keeping with the social and political trends in the world, the government has increasingly become committed to a program of welfare services and to a strong national defense policy. These two items have absorbed more and more of the nation's resources. The demand for goods and services by governments at all levels represents about 18 per cent of the gross national product. The level of taxation is over 25 per cent of the gross national product. The difference between these two measures of governmental operations roughly indicates the extent of transfer payments made by the governments to individuals and organizations.

Before the war welfare services were small and largely in the hands of local governments. Increasingly, the Federal Government has taken over the provision of welfare services or has contributed to them indirectly by the provision of grants to the local governments. A large proportion of the expenditure on social services has been in the nature of a transfer of income from one sector of the economy to another. In 1945 the government set up a family allowances scheme which makes monthly payments to parents for every child under the age of sixteen. In 1952 the Old Age Security Act was passed, providing a pension to all persons seventy years of age and over who fulfilled certain residence requirements. These two schemes alone account for 18 per cent of the federal expenditure for non-defense purposes. In addition, the Federal Government provides pensions for veterans, contributes to the unemployment insurance scheme, and is committed to share with the provinces in a national hospitalization plan, which is partly paid by individual contributions but which is largely underwritten by the governments. Finally, the Federal Government makes grants to provinces for relief purposes, pensions for blind and disabled persons and other types of needy persons. It is difficult to estimate the total amount of expenditure on welfare services and of transfer payments, but for the Federal Government alone it amounts to 25 per cent of total expenditures.

The effects of these transfers of income upon the distribution of income has not been systematically studied, but there is no doubt that it has resulted in a more even distribution of income. The progressive nature of the tax structure removes funds largely from those who would save them, and the transfer payments are made largely to those who would use them for consumption purposes. This redistribution of income has undoubtedly affected the consumption-saving pattern of the economy.

In recent years defense has been an important item in the government's expenditure pattern. In 1950 defense expenditures were only 15.7 per cent of total budgetary expenditures. Since then they have risen to 35 per cent of that total. These expenditures are not only related to Canada's own defense needs but are also concerned with the contribution that Canada makes to the various treaty organizations of which the country is a member. Although the expenditures represent only 6 per cent of the national income, they are important in absorbing resources into defense areas rather than into civilian needs and in maintaining industries which would not survive if government needs did not dictate their existence. To this extent defense has affected the structure of the economy.

In its role as an owner, government participation has largely been confined to the fields of transportation, communication, and electrical and water utilities. In most of these areas provision has been made for monopoly control where monopoly would, it is felt, serve the public interest better than competition. In general, it has been the policy to acquire ownership only in those fields where private capital has been unwilling to venture. In some cases the government has pioneered the development by government ownership and then permitted private capital to compete when it appeared profitable. This policy has resulted in a mixture of private enterprise and government ownership in some fields. Government railways serve some areas and private railways serve others. In some sections both types operate in competition. Similarly, airlines, television, radio, telephone and telegraph communications are partly government owned and partly privately owned. Most electrical utilities and urban transit systems are publicly owned at the provincial and municipal level but there are some privately owned systems. Water utilities are exclusively publicly owned. On the other hand, gas utilities are almost exclusively privately owned. All the public utilities are subject to government regulation of rates and franchises.

The railways present an interesting example of the use of government control to influence the structure of the economy. By the use of uniform rates on all lines, the government has favored the development of remote areas, since the light traffic lines enjoy the same rates as the heavy traffic lines. In addition, certain statutory rates on the grain traffic have subsidized the prairie regions, and subsidies on coal movements have aided the maritime regions. Rate regulation of this type and railway subsidies have been used in conjunction with tariffs to foster an east-west movement of trade inside Canada and discouraged the north-south movement across the United States border, which follows more natural geographic lines.[11]

Although governmental ownership and control have been largely confined to transportation, communication, and utilities, governmental participation in the economy has been on a much wider basis. As part of its commitment to provide stability in the economy and full employment, the government has used the traditional fiscal and monetary policy to influence the saving-investment process. Great reliance has been placed on these measures to secure consistent growth in the economy. Recent recessions have tested these policies rather seriously. The results, however, have not been conclusive enough to indicate whether sole reliance can be placed on them or whether the government must resort to more direction and regulation in order to achieve its objectives.

During the war the government used high and discriminatory taxation to buttress the direct controls it used in molding the economy to war needs. In the postwar period, government policy was concerned with raising sufficient revenue to finance defense and increasing demands for welfare services. Budgetary surpluses were achieved in most of the postwar years, partly as anti-inflationary measures

[11] J. C. Lessard, *Transportation in Canada* (Royal Commission on Canada's Economic Prospects: Ottawa, 1956).

but mainly to reduce the burden of public debt imposed by the war. Recent recessions, however, have changed the picture completely. Fiscal policy has been used to a greater extent to buttress the sagging economy. In the 1958 recession, the government ran large deficits, and in the most recent slow-down, deficits and a return to discriminatory taxation are designed to bolster some areas where unemployment has been extremely high.

After the Korean War, heavy reliance was placed on monetary policy to achieve full employment and to curb inflationary pressures. The principal measure was the use of central bank open-market operations to influence interest rate changes and bring about changes in the savings-investment ratios. These operations have revealed several weaknesses in the capital market which prevent the use of price as a regulator of the flow of funds. These weaknesses have dictated the use of more direct controls upon investment in some sectors.

The capital market in Canada has become more institutionalized. Most of the savings of individuals flow through financial intermediaries in the form of bank deposits, premium payments on life insurance, contributions to pension funds, and credit union deposits. The intermediaries have statutory limitations upon the types of investment and loans they may make. In addition, the commercial banks have a legal maximum limit on the interest rate they may charge for loans. These limitations tend to channel funds into certain approved sectors and to dictate the form of the loan and type of security required. Life insurance companies, trust companies, and, to some extent, pension funds, invest primarily in bonds and mortgages. Banks traditionally lend for commercial operations but also invest in government and corporate bonds. Recently, they have invaded the consumer credit field and have been encouraged by the government to give government-insured mortgages on new housing.

Legal limitations as well as tradition have had several effects on the investment process. The conservatism of the institutions has resulted in a dearth of risk capital for large-scale undertakings. Risky ventures have been primarily by foreign interests which have both the technical knowledge and surplus funds for such undertakings. Further, as interest rates rise, those sectors which have sluggish rates tend to lose out in the struggle for funds. The lack of a mortgage market, for example, has made mortgage rates very sluggish, and they are slow to respond to changes in other sectors of the economy. As interest rates rise, institutions slow down their mortgage lending. The resultant slump in construction has forced the government to lend mortgage money directly for the construction of houses to maintain its housing program. The limitations on bank interest rates have even more severe effects. When the banks reach the limit of their lending power, the ceiling on their rates prevents the price system from operating to ration loans. Investment then becomes more a matter of managerial discretion than of economic decision.

Certain features of the capital market also serve to isolate certain types of investment from the effects of government policy. Much of business investment comes from retained earnings, and these earnings are not subject to the test of the capital market. Limitations on investment in the industrial sector are thus determined more by internal availability of funds to each company than by the general availability of funds. Finally, since monetary policy ordinarily does not affect investment of foreign concerns, efforts to control domestic investment are to some extent nullified by free access to foreign capital markets.

The use of monetary policy to maintain stability in the economy has not been very successful. Indeed, recent cyclical fluctuations have pointed up the dangers of sole reliance upon monetary policy. To supplement monetary controls, government action has moved in the direction of more direct controls upon investment through the provision of direct loans for housing, insured bank loans for small businessmen, farm improvement loans, and other devices. Recently, the government has taken steps to discourage the high rate of foreign investment and to encourage more investment by Canadians in equity capital.

Each wave of external pressure, such as war or international tension, and each wave of internal pressure, such as inflationary moves or increases in unemployment, has forced the government to participate more and more in the direction of the economy. Social changes, with increasing demands for welfare, have added to the role of the government. Thus the trend in the Canadian economy has been towards more and more government content in the mixed economy. Relaxation of pressures has stemmed this movement from time to time but has rarely reversed it.

5

The Economy of Ceylon[1]

Henry M. Oliver, Jr. *

The Three Main Sectors

Ceylon's economy is roughly divisible into three sectors: the plantations, 90 per cent dependent on foreign trade; the urban community, which is chiefly the home of government and commerce; and the villages, which in spite of enormous changes retain much of the self-sufficiency that characterized them a century ago. The first two are essentially creations of British rule during the nineteenth and early twentieth centuries; the third has major features derived from the precolonial culture, but the adjective "traditional" only partly applies.

In terms of numbers of people, the village sector is by far the largest, representing over three-fifths of the island's ten million inhabitants. But the distribution in terms of income produced is very different, with the villages' share probably not exceeding a quarter of the total.[2] Although Ceylon's per capita income is relatively high for a South Asian country, being well above Pakistan's and India's, this higher level chiefly reflects the greater percentage im-

---

* The author, who is professor of economics at Indiana University, was Fulbright lecturer in economics at the University of Ceylon, 1955-56.

[1] For a more complete account of Ceylon's economy, see Ceylon government documents: *Ceylon Year Book; The Ten-Year Plan* (Colombo, 1959); *Six-Year Programme of Investment, 1954/55 to 1959/60* (Colombo, 1955); and the following books: H. Howard Wriggins, *Ceylon: Dilemmas of a New Nation* (Princeton, 1960); International Bank for Reconstruction and Development, *The Economic Development of Ceylon* (Baltimore, 1953); W. Ivor Jennings, *The Economy of Ceylon* (Madras, 1951); N. K. Sarkar, *The Demography of Ceylon* (Colombo, 1957); Henry M. Oliver, Jr., *Economic Opinion and Policy in Ceylon* (Durham, 1957).

I am indebted to Messrs. Wriggins, Sarkar, Dharmasena de Silva, and the late I. D. S. Weerawardana for criticisms and suggestions.

[2] Shares of both population and income of course vary with the sectors' definitions. Later pages point out the difficulties of drawing boundary lines.

portance of plantation agriculture and related commerce within Ceylon than within its larger neighbors. Inefficient cultivation and the very small plots which most families till keep peasant output low.

Table 1 shows the officially estimated distribution of the labor force, by type of employment, in 1957, and Table 2 shows the officially estimated distribution of gross domestic product, by source, for the five-year period 1954-1958.[3] The estimate of unemployment, however, is probably much too low, since the 113,000 listed as jobless include only those persons officially registered as seeking work, and the labor-force figures for "other agriculture" and "other services" probably conceal heavy underemployment.[4]

TABLE 1. *Distribution of Labor Force, 1957*
(thousands of workers)

Agriculture		1861
Tea (estates only)	539	
Rubber (estates only)	194	
Coconuts	82	
Other	1046	
Fisheries		79
Industrial employments including cottage industries		291
Construction		105
Electricity		4
Transportation and communications		155
Public administration		181
Other services		719
Unemployed		113
Total		3508

Source: Ceylon National Planning Council, *The Ten-Year Plan*, p. 89.

[3] A small fraction of the jobs attributed to tea and rubber actually represents work in plantation processing plants and various other non-agricultural employments. In Table 2 the value assigned to tea, rubber, and coconut products is chiefly the plantation sector's contribution but includes also the value of transport and trade agencies' services, plus the produce grown on scores of thousands of peasants' plots.
[4] On the basis of a 1953 sample survey the Central Bank of Ceylon tentatively estimated that one-sixth of the island's work force might be unemployed, and another one-seventh seriously underemployed. (*Survey of Ceylon's Consumer Finances*, [Colombo, 1954], pp. 10-14.) Both un- and under-employment are generally believed to have increased since that year, thanks to the rapid increase in population.

By 1961 the number of persons officially registered as unemployed rose to

TABLE 2. *Gross Domestic Product, 1954-1958*
(Yearly Average in Millions of Rupees)

Domestic exports		1655
Tea	1103	
Rubber	297	
Coconut products	227	
Other	69	
Less imported materials used	−40	
Locally produced articles consumed in Ceylon		1371
Rice	334	
Coconut and coconut oil	146	
Tea	44	
Other food crops	316	
Tobacco	10	
Livestock products	145	
Fish	45	
Industrial products	230	
Other	100	
Trade other than in export products		335
Transport other than of export products		244
Professions		70
Personal and domestic services		324
Rent		108
Capital development industries		460
Government		550
Total		5107

Source: *Statistical Abstract of Ceylon.*

The Plantation Sector

The plantations are chiefly the domain of tea, rubber, and coconuts, with the Wet Zone highlands of central Ceylon being the home of the first two commodities and the Wet Zone lowlands along the southwestern coast comprising the principal coconut country. In their processed forms the three crops together constitute a third or more of gross domestic product and earn 95 per cent or more of the foreign exchange which the country wins through foreign trade, or a sum which is consistently greater than the wholesale value of all local produce consumed within the country. Tea is easily the most important of the three, normally providing about two-thirds of the country's total value of exports and more than one-fifth of

more than 150,000. The 1957-1961 rise in this number was steady, not showing a cyclical pattern.

gross domestic product.[5] Rubber is the next most important export crop, winning from a sixth to a fifth of the nation's export proceeds, whereas coconut products win only from an eighth to a seventh. Coconuts, however, contribute somewhat more to real national income, or about 7 per cent to rubber's 6, since they not only move overseas in the form of copra, coconut oil, and desiccated coconut but also enter importantly into domestic consumption, chiefly through kitchen and other household processes. Perhaps one-half of the groves' total output remains within Ceylon.

A few decades ago the island's tea and rubber plantations were almost entirely British-owned, but the nationality of ownership has since radically changed, with the process of Ceylonization being much more pronounced in the case of rubber. Even before World War II Ceylonese planters held more than one-third of the rubber land, and by 1958 postwar purchases of British properties raised this fraction to about five-sixths. At the end of 1957 British proprietors and shareholders still owned one-half or more of the total interest in tea lands,[6] including most of the largest and most profitable plantations.[7] Management of tea and rubber has been somewhat more thoroughly Ceylonized than ownership.[8]

The same general trends characterize the rubber and tea estates' labor force. A few decades ago the bulk of these employees consisted of aliens recruited from the Tamil area of south India, whose descendants today are stateless persons, denied both Ceylonese and Indian citizenship; and as late as 1956 Ceylonese nationals still formed only one-half of the rubber plantations' and only one-fifth

[5] Tea's share of Ceylonese *nationals'* aggregate income is much lower, because of payments to British owners and Indian Tamil workers. Until recently tea's principal contributions to *nationals'* real incomes have been indirect, i.e., benefits from tax revenues and foreign exchange. However, because of a new government policy, which requires the estates to Ceylonize gradually increasing fractions of their labor force, tea's contribution to nationals' wage earnings presumably will grow.

[6] Ceylon-chartered corporations own many of the large tea and tea-cum-rubber estates, and the precise ethnic distribution of shares is not reported.

[7] During the six-year period 1954-59 dividends and interest payable to non-residents averaged 1.7 per cent of gross domestic product. Tea-company dividends formed a very large part of this sum.

[8] Members of the Ceylon Freedom Party, which was the dominant partner in the coalition which ruled the island during 1956-59 and which won the 1960 election, have often argued for the nationalization of foreign-owned estates. The Freedom Party cabinets, however, have repeatedly—and recently—announced that such a measure would not be in the national interest.

of the tea estates' workers. The government, however, is now embarked on a program of gradually Ceylonizing employment and requires a steadily increasing percentage of the estates' labor force to consist of the country's nationals.

Unlike the tea and rubber estates, the coconut groves have been almost entirely a native enterprise from their inception and most of their laborers are Ceylonese. The term "plantation," however, tends to be much more deceptive when applied to coconut farming than when used in conjunction with rubber and tea. Much of the land planted in coconuts consists of very small plots, and three-fifths of it consists of holdings of less than ten acres, whereas only one-tenth of the coconut area takes the form of estates of twenty acres or more. On the other hand, "smallholdings" of less than ten acres form only about one-quarter of the rubber land and one-eighth of the area planted in tea. About one-half of the rubber acreage and four-fifths of the tea lands consist of estates ranging upwards from one hundred acres in size, and one-half of the tea area consists of estates of more than one hundred acres. In the case of both tea and rubber, especially in that of tea, there is a close association between size of the producing unit and efficiency of production. The large estates produce a highly disproportionate fraction of the crops' total value. For this reason the government has taken steps to end the fragmentation of estates which in the past sometimes followed Ceylonese purchase of British properties.[9]

The larger tea and rubber estates are, in effect, company towns. Most of the workers live in compact settlements[10] which the management erected for this purpose and utilize the services of the plantations' own dispensaries, maternity hospitals, day nurseries, bakeries, shops, and schools. The estate hierarchy is not only a chain of business command but a more general aspect of life. Moreover, these larger plantations are not only farming enterprises, but integrated agricultural-industrial units with factories which process raw product and prepare it for shipment to Colombo and export. Many of them purchase much of their raw material from smaller tea and rubber

[9] A recently adopted program, however, calls for the formation of "tea colonies," in which between 1,000 and 10,000 smallholders will each cultivate two-acre plots and sell their output to state-owned tea factories.

[10] This statement applies chiefly to the Indian Tamils, who form most of the larger estates' labor force. About two-thirds of the Sinhalese plantation workers are reported to live in the surrounding villages.

farms without processing facilities. Although Ceylonese official reports exclude such plants from their manufacturing statistics, the
island's nearly one thousand tea factories generate much of the
country's electric power and are easily the single most important
category of manufacturing investment in Ceylon. The plantations'
six hundred rubber mills are simpler, less expensive establishments.

The small-scale nature of most coconut farming, of course, prevents a similar integration of agriculture with factory operations.
Most groves sell their output to the separately owned mills which
dot the coconut country. The 1952 Census of Industry listed seventy-
five such establishments, which then collectively employed seven
thousand persons.

Regardless of the scale of its operations, none of the tea, rubber,
or coconut estates is nearly big enough to influence the prices at which
it sells its output or at which it buys the principal equipment items and
supplies produced on the island or imported from overseas. Similarly,
tea, rubber, and coconut processing plants are so small and so numerous that favorable location and established buyer-seller relationships
appear to be the only significant advantages that any one factory enjoys when it purchases raw product.[11] Various customs and attitudes
which limit labor mobility keep the estates and the separately owned
factories from being atomistically competitive employers, but statutes and labor unions as well as customs and attitudes limit the
discretionary power which management might otherwise possess.
Official boards set minimum wage rates and parliamentary acts
control other conditions of employment. The sector's labor unions
are loosely knit and not very businesslike in their operations but are
channels for the expression of workers' grievances.

Since the plantation commodities finally go overseas, however,
the nature and extent of competition in this sector is largely a question of foreign commerce and, consequently, of governmental policies and the degree of concentration in world distribution channels.
Although some Colombo export houses and shipping agencies are
too big to be atomistic, none is big enough to have a substantial
influence on the prices paid for the plantation factories' output.

[11] Location, however, is sufficiently important for smallholders often to have little
opportunity to sell to more than one or a few purchasers. This helps to explain the
government program, mentioned in n.9, of building and operating tea factories to
which the smallholders can sell their product.

The kind and extent of export-market competition vary among the three crops, with the sale and purchase of coconut products apparently most closely resembling pure competition. Ceylon produces only a very small part of the world's output and provides only about a tenth of the world's exports, hence cannot unilaterally affect price, and the coconut-producing countries have not formed a cartel. The world market is divided among many lands; Ceylonese coconut exports chiefly go to countries where there are multiple purchasers.

The export trade in tea has been a mixture of competition and regulation, with the former element usually predominating. Most sales are at public auction, with the selling brokers representing individual producers and the buying brokers representing individual blenders and distributors rather than syndicates. Trade associations do not act as price-controlling cartels and, although distributive channels within the principal tea-consuming countries are moderately concentrated, they appear to be too numerous and scattered for strong oligopsony models to apply. Ceylon's share of the world export market, about 30 per cent, is big enough for the island's output to have an appreciable effect on current prices, but policy makers have understandably feared that unilateral attempts at market control would not pay. Between 1933 and 1955 the country participated in an International Tea Agreement, which assigned acreage and export maxima, and a Tea Controller still regulates the planting of new areas. The international agreement did not prevent a great postwar increase in output and export sales, however, as Ceylon profited from rising yields, a favorable world market, and the failure of Indonesia to recapture its prewar position. Current regulation of new tea acreage is not intended to bolster export price, but rather to insure a desired use of land. The government urges tea planters to increase yields still further and since 1959 has subsidized the replanting and rehabilitation of smallholdings.

Governmental intervention, both at home and abroad, has been more important in the rubber trade. Although Ceylon produces only about 5 per cent of the world's supply of natural rubber, the Korean War and the Cold War have made its exports strategically important. Since 1952 Peking has contracted to buy a large part of Ceylon's output, chiefly giving rice in return. China initially paid a price far above the "world," or Singapore, level. This level, however, suffered heavily from the United States government's subsidization of synthetic rubber and from rules concerning import and consumption. In accordance with a long-standing international agreement, a Rubber Controller still regulates new acreage in Ceylon; but, as in the case of tea, the regulation's purpose is not to cut output but to achieve a desired use of land. Subsidies which the government offers for the replanting and rehabilitation of inferior rubber acreage are more extensive than those offered for the improved cultivation of tea.

The Urban Community

The urban community, which has nearly half its inhabitants in the Colombo area, derives most of its income from government and trade. Manufacturing provides jobs for only a small fraction of the workers. The 1952 Census of Industry, which excluded tea and rubber processing plants and cottage-industry shops, reported 692 establishments and 53,457 workers, of whom nearly one-third were in engineering and metal working and another third were distributed between coconut products and the printing trades. Although the volume of manufactures has risen by a substantial percentage since that year, total manufacturing employment is still a small fraction of the urban total.

To the extent that its income allows, Ceylon is a "welfare state," which provides tuition-free schooling, free medical services, and modest social-insurance programs and employs a host of extension agents to improve agriculture, industry, and community life. The central government owns many business enterprises, including the railways, the bus lines, the Colombo harbor works, and public power system, a growing number of small factories, the country's largest commercial bank and its most important specialized banking institutions, a life insurance company which monopolizes all new contracts, cottage-industry and agricultural-marketing establishments, and a petroleum-products distribution system. Some of these enterprises are directly managed by the government's regular departments; some are run as separate corporations; some take the guise of co-operative societies. The central government's budget in recent years has been about one-fourth of national income. Between three-quarters and nine-tenths of annual tax revenues has usually come from export duties, import duties, and income taxes, but during 1958-61 the government introduced new taxes on wealth, expenditures, gifts, corporations, resident non-nationals, and professional men as means of reducing consumption, saving foreign exchange, and restricting the size of the budgetary deficit. Directly and indirectly, foreign commerce provides the overwhelming bulk of all such revenues, not merely those coming from import and export duties, since persons and companies dependent on foreign trade contribute most of the proceeds from the income tax and the newer levies.

The pattern of trade within the urban community even more strikingly reflects the island's dependence on tea, rubber, and coconuts. Export houses handle little besides the plantation commodities. Import houses (including governmental agencies) bring in the goods for which these exports pay: that is, about two-fifths of the nation's food supply, the bulk of its manufactured consumer goods, and nearly all its mineral fuels, lubricants, and capital equipment. Since much of the island's output which is not shipped overseas consists of rice and other foodstuffs which the peasant cultivators themselves consume, retail houses are mainly channels for imports.

To even a greater extent than in Western countries, retail markets do not fit neatly into the textbook models. The government is the sole importer of rice and sugar and sells rationed quantities of subsidized rice through officially sponsored co-operative stores, and imports and distributes products through a marketing organization that has the power to impose maximum and minimum prices upon the companies that compete with it. Westernized retail houses with standardized and trade-marked items usually sell their merchandise at quoted prices, but elsewhere bargaining is common. In Colombo and a few other towns outlets range from fairly large department stores to very small shops and stalls in farmers' markets; in most towns all outlets are quite small. Except in Colombo the volume of business transacted within an area is usually so slight as to enforce spatial monopoly or oligopoly, and in many lines even Colombo's sales are too few for multiple sellers. Class divisions and language barriers as well as imperfect knowledge limit both current competition and the entry of new firms; and the lack of a strong tradition of business enterprise plus the relatively low prestige which trade enjoys among the better-educated Ceylonese also tends to keep profits from efficiently fulfilling their textbook functions.

Banking in Ceylon developed as a service to exports and imports and today is still chiefly tied to trade. With the exception of the recently nationalized Bank of Ceylon all the island's commercial banks are branches of overseas institutions; nearly all are British.[12] The Bank of Ceylon, however, now holds about two-fifths of the country's total deposits, and the government has established the State Mortgage Bank, the Agricultural and Industrial Credit Corporation, and the Development Finance Corporation to meet the needs of long-term borrowers. The Agricultural and Industrial Credit Corporation, which has been far more agricultural than industrial in its operations, has helped to finance many Ceylonese purchases of tea and rubber estates. The Development Finance Corporation, an institution recommended by the International Bank's team of experts after their 1951 visit to the island, was initially expected to devote most of its funds and energies to the promotion of private industrial enterprise; but its principal function has been to supply funds and skills for government industrial projects.[13]

Small loans in Ceylon traditionally have been the business of private money lenders, who finance emergencies and unusual consumption and who usually receive high interest rates for their risks and troubles. This small-scale commercial lending is still quite common, but, thanks to government sponsorship, credit unions have in recent years met a large part of the townfolks' and villagers' demands. In 1961 a statute established the People's Bank (also a co-operative) as a further aid to small borrowers.

Apart from the banks, the island's leading financial institutions are the insurance companies, which were chiefly British-owned before a recent statute set up a government life-insurance company which alone can sell new policies. Colombo has a small shares market dealing in the securities of limited liability companies chartered on the island. Ceylonese investors' preference for privately held companies, as well as cost and demand considerations which keep most firms small, serves to limit the volume of stock-market business.

With very few exceptions, manufacturing establishments in Ceylon vary from small-scale to minute. When the government conducted its 1952 Census of Manufactures, most of the 692 plants

[12] Before 1961 the government was the leading shareholder in the Bank of Ceylon but did not dominate its policies. One of the arguments advanced in favor of the bank's nationalization was that, like the British-owned banks, it was too closely tied to foreign trade and did not adequately support other enterprise.

[13] The 1956 election, which ousted the United National party, reversed a short-lived policy of depending chiefly on private enterprise to develop manufacturing industry.

recorded did not deserve the name of "factory." Only 195 employed as many as 50 workers; only 92 employed as many as 100. Recent estimates show that the percentage (although not the absolute) rise in the value of manufacturing output has been substantial since the census, but the general picture has remained the same. Labor-force requirements which new government enterprises have announced have usually ranged between 100 and 400 workers. As befits a capital-poor nation, none of the plants employs these small numbers because of the use of what Western countries would consider capital-intensive methods of production.

Apart from the commodities turned out by plantation-sector processing plants, Ceylon's chief manufactures are inexpensive, simply-made consumer goods, construction materials, and items which service the estates. Most of the factories and many of the small industrial shops depend heavily on import barriers, so that the extent of competition in the sale of their products is largely a function of the kind and extent of protection which the government provides. The small size of the market within the import barriers makes domestic monopoly or oligopoly inevitable in nearly all lines which require factory processes for efficient production. Under the policy which has prevailed during most postwar years, the government has reserved "basic" industries for its own enterprise and defined these to include natural monopolies and industries believed to be of strategic importance in the island's development.[14]   In some other lines governmental action has the effect of conferring a domestic monopoly upon a private firm or a small group of firms. The most obvious example of this is the statute which governs the manufacture of matches and assigns maximum and minimum quotas to the licensed producers, but domestic monopoly also sometimes results from governmental exclusion of foreign firms that wish to commence production on the island and from governmental decisions to grant or to refuse various types of aid which industry-boosting statutes allow.

Since the government nationalized the bus lines a few years ago, commercial land transportation in Ceylon is largely the business of the state; railways have long been an example of government enterprise. Another recent statute has nationalized the Colombo

[14] See Oliver, *op. cit.*, pp. 50-61, 81-87. *The Administration Report of the Acting Director of Industries for 1957* (Colombo, 1958) classified industries according to their state-monopoly, state- and/or private-enterprise, and solely private-enterprise character.

harbor works. Commercial trucking, tourist services, and taxicabs, however, represent private, competitive enterprise; and the state's role in air and sea traffic is limited. Air Ceylon operates by virtue of a contract between the government and the Royal Dutch Airlines, but rival foreign lines carry the greater part of the traffic. The Ceylon Shipping Lines was established with the thought that it would carry all government freight, but the practice of awarding contracts to low bidders was continued.

Just as rubber and tea plantations were chiefly the creation of foreign enterprise, so was the urban community. Both the public service and commerce were slight at the start of British rule, and during most of the century preceding independence British officials held most governmental posts and British and Indian firms dominated trade and finance. As in the plantation sector, however, Ceylonese has gradually replaced foreign capital and management. British urban strongholds still include foreign commerce, engineering, banking, insurance, and the stock exchange, but in all these lines except the last Ceylonese private and/or state enterprise has become important. Indian firms still dominate some trades but have a much smaller share of total business than two decades ago. In both the British and the Indian houses the subordinate staff is largely Ceylonese.

The urban labor force consists chiefly of the island's citizens, although Indian Tamils do much of the more arduous and menial work and most of that with a very low caste status. On the whole, the ethnic make-up of the urban population corresponds to that of the surrounding rural areas, although tens of thousands of Ceylon Tamils live in Colombo and other large towns within the traditional Sinhalese area, where economic opportunities have been more attractive than on the northern and eastern fringes of the island. Government employment especially has encouraged the migration of the better educated to the cities. The "underdeveloped" nature of manufacturing on the island, the lack of a strong commercial tradition, the prestige which the bureaucracy enjoyed during the colonial period, the associated white-collar dignity, and the good salaries which the government pays make a career within the public service very attractive to most Ceylonese. Although planters and urban businessmen receive most of the island's highest incomes, the better government jobs account for a large fraction of the middle-upper incomes, and clerkships provide above-average incomes for the modestly educated. For youths not blessed with large inheritances, good marks at English-language schools and universities have been the chief path to economic and social success. Now that Sinhalese has become the country's only official language and is steadily replacing English in government offices and in the educational system, many Sinhalese leaders hope, and Tamil leaders fear, that good marks in Sinhalese-language curricula will become the main road to income and status.

In 1958-59 the officially reported labor-union membership on the island totaled 821,996, but nearly three-quarters (592,270) of this number belonged to the plantation unions. A classification of the others shows 58,851 in industrial, 56,172 in transportation and communications, 18,914 in clerical, 15,056 in professional, 25,298 in commercial, 689 in administrative and executive, and 54,746 in general unions. Most urban labor organizations are affiliated with Marxist political parties, and strikes appear often to be politically motivated. Postwar labor legislation, including the appointment of wages boards to set minimum wages, narrows the role which business unionism can play.

Unemployment has steadily grown in recent years, with the total number of persons registering at the employment exchanges rising from 36,000 in 1946 to more than 150,000 in 1961, a figure that is generally believed to be much smaller than the actual number of jobless desiring work in that year.[15] The urban-rural distribution of the registrants is not reported, but in 1959 20,869 of the total were classified as professional, technical, and clerical, 13,859 as skilled, 33,723 as semi-skilled, and 59,567 as unskilled. Most of the nation's educated youths are said not to register on the exchanges. The Table I category of "other services," which includes retail trade, paid household services, and many varieties of casual labor, probably conceals much urban underemployment.

The Village Sector

As preceding sections have shown, the villages are not completely separable from the plantations. In the wet highlands they border on or are surrounded by tea and rubber estates, and in the wet low-

[15] For estimates of island-wide unemployment and underemployment, see Central Bank of Ceylon, *Survey of Ceylon's Consumer Finances.*

lands they are part of the same region as the principal coconut country, so that geography helps to explain why scores of thousands of peasants have small patches of tea, rubber, and coconut land and a much greater number of village residents are wage-workers on neighboring estates. Neither is the village sector sharply separable from the urban community. Cottage-industry shops and village boutiques do not differ greatly from tiny manufacturing establishments and stores in the towns; government activities employ townsman and villager alike; tens of thousands of rural families depend on non-governmental urban work.

The heterogeneous nature of village economic life clearly shows in a 1950-51 survey,[16] which reports that of every 100 families covered 40 were principally engaged in village agriculture as owners, tenants, or employees; 7 were chiefly engaged in trade; 5 won most of their income as craftsmen; 17 depended mainly on plantation and other non-village jobs; and 31 derived their income from government employment, charities, and a host of miscellaneous occupations. Because of the rapid population increase, little land available for village expansion in the Wet Zone, and the slow progress of Dry Zone colonization, dependence on non-village sources of income has probably increased greatly in the decade since the survey. Probably all five of the categories listed above have labor forces that are substantially underemployed.[17]

For that plurality of the village population chiefly dependent on village agriculture the growing of rice and other non-export crops is by far the most important activity. The acreage devoted to rice alone vastly exceeds the total area which peasant households plant in the three leading export commodities, and the area sown in "highland crops" is nearly half as great as that planted in rice. It is this rice-plus-vegetables farming that derives most clearly from an earlier Ceylon. Neither the crops nor the methods of cultivation usually employed differ greatly from those of several centuries ago; Buddhist and Hindu teachings as well as poverty and the shortage of suitable land discourage the raising of animals for slaughter. The peasant households themselves consume nearly two-thirds of the rice crop and a very large part of the other foodstuffs which they grow. Before

[16] Ceylon Department of Census and Statistics, *Final Report on the Economic Survey of Rural Ceylon, 1950-51* (Colombo, 1954).

[17] See *Survey of Ceylon's Consumer Finances*, pp. 10-14, and N. K. Sarkar and S. J. Tambiah, *The Disintegrating Village* (Colombo, 1957).

World War II the surplus above local consumption was even smaller.[18]

Village life as a whole continues many of the old traditions. The populace goes back to migrations of centuries or millennia ago; European cultural influences have been much weaker than in the towns and on the estates. This is especially true of the areas more remote from Colombo, the island's capital, only large city, and center of Westernization. Even in these areas, however, today's village culture is far from an unchanged relic of the pre-colonial period. Partly because of legal reform, partly because of Western-type schools, and partly because of the related occupational changes mentioned above, the roles of caste, feudal duty, contract, and money are vastly different from those of a century and a half ago, when British rule was not yet thoroughly established but the coastal lowlands had long known Portuguese and Dutch dominion.[19]   The average levels of education and health are much higher than they were only a few decades ago, just as the degree of economic self-sufficiency is much lower.

Caste still limits economic mobility, especially among the Hindu Tamils and, to a lesser extent, among the Sinhalese of the central highlands, the region last to come under European control. Some of the traditional non-farm occupations usually pass from father to son, most Ceylonese refuse jobs which carry a low-caste stigma, and low-caste villagers find it difficult to enter more favorable lines of work. For that matter the inheritance of property is not entirely separate from caste. Most landholding peasants today ultimately derive their titles from ancestors' caste positions and feudal services. Contract rather than status chiefly governs exchange, however, and for most villagers caste per se does not limit movement nearly so much as education, wealth, enterprise, and ability.[20] A contributing cause here is that the Sinhalese caste hierarchy does not include the equivalent of India's Brahmins and warriors, so that one-half or more of the Sinhalese families (who comprise some 70 per cent of

[18] In spite of the rapid increase in village population, Ceylon is now proportionally less dependent on food imports.

[19] See Bryce Ryan, *Caste in Modern Ceylon* (New Brunswick, N. J., 1953); Ralph Pieris, *Sinhalese Social Organization—The Kandyan Period* (Colombo, 1956).

[20] I. D. S. Weerawardana suggested that lack of economic opportunity may have slowed the disappearance of caste-influenced behavior more than caste itself has limited economic mobility.

the island's population and about five-sixths of the villagers) belong to the highest caste, whose designation of "goyigama" suggests that their ancestors cultivated the soil. In pre-colonial days the chief wealth differential was that between the feudal aristocracy and the lower classes rather than that between the goyigama and lower castes.

Outright economic feudalism, of course, has today all but disappeared. Feudal duties vanished, became extra-legal and ceremonial only, or were transformed into commercial relationships during the nineteenth century. Most tenure became freehold or some variety of share-crop, although a small part of the land has been cultivated in accordance with special joint-ownership rules. The feudal aristocracy, the top class within the goyigama caste, became large landowners, while less exalted goyigama families and others with fairly direct rights in land became peasant proprietors.

Because of the loss of land through debt and because of the rapid rise in village population, in recent decades the percentage of peasants who own the plots which they till has fallen; tenancy and labor for hire have become more common. Table 3 shows the findings of the previously mentioned 1950-51 sample survey with respect to the land owned by the 8,733 agricultural families and 13,349 non-agricultural families covered. Less comprehensive studies indicate that in the ten years since the survey landlessness has become more widespread and landholdings even smaller.[21] Thirty-five per

TABLE 3. *Family Landholdings in the Village Sector*

Amount of land held (in acres)	Agricultural families (per cent)*	Non-agricultural families (per cent)*	All families (per cent)*
No land	26	45	38
Less than 0.5	16	25	22
0.5- 0.99	12	11	11
1.0- 1.99	15	9	11
2.0- 4.99	19	7	12
5.0- 9.99	7	1.5	4
10.0-19.99	3	0.5	1.6
20 and above	1	0.3	0.6

Source: *Final Report on the Economic Survey of Rural Ceylon,* 1950-51.
    * Percentages do not total 100 because of rounding.

[21] Two-thirds of the village families interviewed were landless when a 1955 University of Ceylon team studied a district in the central highlands (N. K. Sarkar and S. J. Tambiah, *op. cit.*).

cent of the agricultural families covered in the survey were owner-cultivators, 18 per cent were tenant cultivators, 45 per cent were hired workers, and 2 per cent were landlords.

As Table 3 helps to show, despite widespread tenancy landlords' holdings are rarely large. Temples control perhaps a sixth or more of the rice fields;[22] a few aristocratic families derive good incomes from their rents; and a number of other landlords hold 10-20 acres; but most village rents go to persons who depend primarily on other sources of income: i.e., to other farmers, businessmen, money lenders, physicians, government employees, and school teachers who have invested a little in land or have acquired their few acres through foreclosure for debt.

This list of petty landlords also indicates some of the non-agricultural occupations in the village sector. Because of the extent to which travel is by foot and by ox cart, because of imperfect knowledge, and because of the resulting small scale of the market, village families often encounter semi-monopolies when they transact business with boutique keepers, money lenders, and purchasers of farm produce. In recent decades, however, government policies have substantially reduced the extent to which villagers face private monopoly. Officially sponsored co-operative societies and the state-established People's Bank advance loans for approved purposes, and governmental agencies sell rationed quantities of rice at below cost and purchase rice and various other food crops at guaranteed prices. Similarly, now that free medical service is available in the larger towns, the villagers are not so dependent upon the neighborhood's ayurvedic physicians.[23]

Cottage industries, another non-agricultural activity, expanded considerably in recent years so that craftsmen probably are now a somewhat larger fraction of the villages' population than the 5 per cent reported in the 1950-51 survey. At the end of 1957 the number of cottage industrial organizations was 1506, of which 307 had been added during the year. Over half of these organizations were textile centers.

Most cottage-industry craft shops, of course, like most peasant

[22] Wriggins, *op. cit.*, p. 38.

[23] These physicians employ medical techniques largely derived from traditional Ceylonese rather than Western sources, but have been influenced by Western discoveries and practices.

farms, are exceedingly small-scale enterprises. It is not helpful, however, to think of either the peasants or the craftsmen as atomistically competitive. In the first place, such a description connotes much more efficiently organized markets and a much more commercial way of life than those of the village sector in Ceylon. Next, the government and the co-operative societies which it creates, sponsors, and supports play major roles in both village agriculture and village manufacturing. As has been stated above, a governmental agency purchases rice and other food crops at guaranteed prices, and officially recognized marketing co-operatives are supposed to perform all the supplementary middleman activities which the program requires. Other state-aided co-operatives help the villagers secure cheaper credit and supplies. Most cottage industries are state-initiated projects, with Colombo not only protecting the craftsmen against foreign competition but also providing technical experts and finance and sometimes selling the products through official distributive outlets.

Moreover, the government's role in the village sector is greater in still other ways than it was before Ceylon gained independence. Just as Colombo pushes the co-operative movement, so it sponsors and gives technical assistance to rural development societies, which have as their purpose the use of underemployed village labor and skills to construct community buildings and schools, improve sanitation facilities, and in other ways raise the community's standards of living. Student enrollment in rural schools has vastly increased. Villagers can secure free medical services in towns which dot most of the island. A recent statute provides at least a small first step towards a crop-insurance program.

A 1958 Paddy Lands Act presumably will result in a still more impressive advance in governmental influence in the villages, since the Act gives the Minister of Agriculture power to regulate land rents and give tenants security of tenure. The Act's significance, however, is still in doubt. Apparently, a large bloc of the legislators who supported it did not intend thereby to promote an economic revolution, and the 1960 election greatly reduced the bargaining strength of the semi-Trotskyist faction largely responsible for the act's passage.

Within the peasant sector the government's over-all role is greatest, not in the villages proper but in the Dry Zone colonies, which owe their existence to state planning and investment and remain for years after their creation largely under the control of a supervisory bureaucracy. In these projects the government decides what land shall be developed, what improvements shall be made, what terms shall be offered potential settlers, who shall become colonists, what level of performance shall entitle the colonists to firm property rights, and the conditions under which transfers of real property may take place.[24] In 1957, however, the colonies' inhabitants numbered only a little over 100,000, or less than 5 per cent of the village sector's population.

STABILITY AND DEVELOPMENT

Unstable Terms of Trade

The plantations which cause Ceylon's real income per capita to be relatively high for a south Asian country also cause it to be relatively unstable. With one-third of gross national product consisting of exports and one-third of gross national expenditure consisting of imports, the island's economic welfare depends heavily on the terms of trade. Effects here are both direct and indirect. A given quantity of output has an unstable real purchasing power; the volume of retail trade, of some other service activities, and of capital formation varies substantially with the volume of imports; price ratios alter profit prospects and thus influence plantation and other production.

The importance of these effects of course depends upon the intensity and duration of the price swings, the foreign-exchange reserves and credit which the country has at its command, and the domestic reserves and credit available to investors and consumers. In the absence of adequate reserves, consumption and investment are highly vulnerable, much more so than agricultural production, which usually does not vary much with price changes,[25] and which depends upon other price-relationships as well as export-import price ratios. Plantation wages, for instance, do not move immediately or proportionally with the import-price index. Village agriculture's costs are chiefly non-monetary and, in the absence of government

[24] See footnote 9 concerning the government's recent plan for the establishment of tea colonies.

[25] An exception here is the sharp rise in rubber output at the start of the Korean War.

price supports, higher prices for food imports would stimulate village production slightly.

Table 4 shows the swings in import and export prices during 1926-59. The record is one of sharp deterioration in the terms of trade during 1926-32, even more rapid improvement during 1932-37, fluctuation during 1937-39, drastic decline during World War II, a roughly offsetting rise between that war and the early part of the Korean War, another sharp drop, recovery, and lesser fluctuation since then. During the great recession of 1926-32 the price indexes revealed the "classical" pattern; that is, export prices fell much more rapidly than import prices, but the latter themselves declined sharply, largely because nearly one-half of the island's overseas purchases consisted of rice and other foodstuffs. Since that time, however, price behavior has rarely displayed this "classical" form. When London's boards set wartime prices and shipping space became very costly, the relative speed of export and import price movements were reversed; goods

TABLE 4. *Indexes of Export and Import Prices*

Year	Export	Import	Ratio	Year	Export	Import	Ratio
	(1934-38 = 100)			1945	205	340	60
1926	193	194	99	1946	226	358	63
1927	169	190	89	1947	300	413	73
1928	141	183	78	1948	305	443	69
1929	127	177	72	1949	324	423	77
1930	105	145	72		(1948 = 100)		
1931	75	117	64	1938	36	26	138
1932	65	106	60	1948	100	100	100
1933	71	98	72	1949	107	96	111
1934	86	101	85	1950	144	98	147
1935	95	104	91	1951	175	116	151
1936	103	97	106	1952	136	125	109
1937	116	99	117	1953	139	114	122
1938	99	102	97	1954	155	100	155
1939	114	101	113	1955	162	101	160
1940	120	120	100	1956	152	113	135
1941	133	147	90	1957	145	105	138
1942	156	220	71	1958	142	95	149
1943	166	315	53	1959	148	104	142
1944	190	349	54				

Sources: Ceylon Ministry of Finance, *Economic and Social Development of Ceylon, 1926-1954;* Central Bank of Ceylon, *Bulletin.*

sent to Ceylon quickly became very expensive, while those that left the island commanded prices that rose at a much slower pace. At the height of the Korean War rubber prices fell precipitately and other exports suffered, while food imports became increasingly costly. During more years than not, export and import prices have moved in the same direction, but the exceptions to this rule are quite important, including not only 1951-52 but also 1932-39 and 1947-50, when import prices remained roughly stable, and 1952-56, when the indexes moved in opposite directions three years out of four.

The percentage of change in the export-import price ratio times the percentage of national income represented by imports and exports of course does not give the percentage by which aggregate income changed within a year, or even within a longer period. Actual income movements reflect not only the changing terms of trade, but also their indirect effects and the effects of other, unrelated or little related forces. Rising population, rising acreage, and improved methods have caused production to show a generally rising trend, which swells the extent of a short period's income rise and at least reduces the size of a short period's income fall. Plantation and village output have varied with weather conditions,[26] and strikes and communal riots have decreased aggregate production in some recent years.[27] During the 1930's tea and rubber prices were supported by multi-country acreage restrictions, so that the export-import price ratio does not adequately describe the "real" terms of trade confronting the owners of tea and rubber resources. Similarly, World War II quantitative controls and subsequent quantitative trade treaties, especially those with mainland China, have caused the price indexes to have rather a different significance from indexes resulting only from competitive market transactions. The government's budget and the banks' lending policies, while usually strongly influenced by export-import price ratios, have not been entirely dependent upon them. Export and import prices per se, as well as their ratio, have had some influence on production.

But while changes in the terms of trade and changes in aggregate income have not always been in the same direction, and certainly have not been proportional, the former have been quite important

[26] Drought and floods made the 1956-57 rice crop much smaller than that of 1955-56. By 1958-59 yields had climbed to a record level.
[27] Because of harbor strikes, the port of Colombo handled less traffic in 1956 and 1957 than in preceding years.

for the latter. During the postwar period, for which comparable estimates of gross national product are available (Table 5), improved terms of trade account for much of the 1947-51, 1952-55, and 1956-58 rises in real per capita income; worsened terms of trade account for much of the 1955-56 decline and most of the 1951-52 fall. For the prewar period, the indexes of volume of trade (Table 6 tell the same general story. Imports per capita fell substantially during the Great Depression and rose substantially during the subsequent recovery. During World War II very low levels of imports accompanied very unfavorable price ratios. Except for the wartime figures, the fluctuations in imports probably understate somewhat the period's fluctuations in real income.

A long-run partial solution to the problems of unstable terms of trade is to make the economy less dependent on exports and im-

TABLE 5. *Indexes of Real Income and Real Product Per Capita*

Year	Real Income per Capita (1948=100)				Real Product per Capita (1953=100)		
	A	B	C	D	E	F	G
1938	78	98	76	112			86
1947	81	96	97	101			95
1948	100	100	100	100			100
1949	102	106	104	107			102
1950	113	126	124	133	97		110
1951	125	129	135	127	103		113
1952	119	117	131	113	104		117
1953	114	116	125	120	100		110
1954		127	128	140	100		111
1955			140	150	104		
1956			133	127	96	100	
1957			129	136	100	98	
1958			135	156	102	100	
1959			132	143	103	101	

Sources: *A.* Ceylon Planning Secretariat, *Six-Year Programme of Investment, 1954/55 to 1959/60.*
B. W. Rasaputram, "Gross National Product of Ceylon at Constant (1948) Prices," Central Bank of Ceylon, *Bulletin,* January, 1956.
C. Gross national product deflated by cost-of-living index.
D. Gross national product deflated by import-price index.
E. United Nations Statistical Yearbook (gross national product, market prices).
F. Annual Report of the Monetary Board (gross national product, factor-cost prices).
G. Calculated from estimates in W. Rasaputram, *loc. cit.*

TABLE 6. *Indexes of Population and Foreign Trade*

Year	Population (1938=100)	Export volume (1934-38=100)	Import volume (1934-38=100)
1926	85	97	84
1929	89	116	97
1932	92	102	84
1933	93	99	81
1937	98	102	104
1938	100	103	98
1939	102	103	103
1942	106	127	65
1943	108	124	69
1946	118	127	87
1947	121	118	108
1948	124	129	110
1949	128	128	119

ports. Such structural change is often proclaimed as a policy goal. One of the motives is political; Ceylonese governments have wished to make their country less dependent on foreign powers. But this political motive obviously ties in with the economic purpose of greater self-sufficiency: i.e., to make real income less dependent on business-cycle movements and other market changes overseas. Moreover, Ceylonese policy makers usually link the goals of greater self-sufficiency and higher real income. They look on them as complements rather than alternatives; the thought is not to decrease exports by transferring resources to rice, other domestically-consumed foodstuffs, and manufactures, but instead to expand production along all lines by employing resources more fully and more efficiently. The next section briefly discusses such problems of economic development.

Short-run policies which the government has employed to reduce or offset changes in the terms of trade include agreements with other exporting countries, steps to secure new markets for Ceylonese exports, and monetary and fiscal measures. The first two are intended to reduce price fluctuations and also to raise the trend level of income. Monetary and fiscal policies are regarded as offsets to unstable terms of trade and also as tools of development.

The international tea and rubber agreements are examples of cartel-like policies. During the 1930's these served to boost commodity prices above their competitive levels. Even before the tea agreement expired in 1955, however, it had little effect on world output; quotas assigned the member countries were very generous. Similarly, the long-lived rubber agreement has had little restrictive effect in recent years. Obstacles to successful cartels include synthetic rubber, competition among beverages, clashing interests of exporting countries, and importing countries' interest and influence in some exporting and potentially exporting lands. Indonesia has not yet recovered its prewar trade position; African lands hope to expand their acreage and output quite substantially; British and American firms have given thought to new sources of supply.

Steps which the government has taken to make Ceylon's exports less dependent on traditional markets include advertising and other sales promotion and trade treaties with various countries, especially those of the Communist bloc. As in the case of the drive for greater self-sufficiency, one of the purposes is political, to make Ceylon less dependent on Western powers, but this motive obviously relates closely to the economic goal of market diversification, less dependence on market changes in English-speaking lands. So far, trade with most Communist countries has been quite minor; but mainland China has taken much of the island's rubber and supplied much of the imported rice, and the 1952 rice-rubber treaty substantially bettered the terms of trade.

Monetary policy can be a fractional but not a major offset to changing terms of trade. In order to stabilize consumption-plus-investment, the Central Bank of Ceylon must curtail expenditure rises when the terms of trade improve and decrease expenditure falls when the terms of trade decline. It must not only keep the commercial banks' changing reserves from accentuating cyclical swings but must cause the banking system to work in the opposite direction. But, although the Central Bank has legal powers resembling the United States Federal Reserve authorities', the volume of expenditure in the country does not substantially depend upon the monetary policies usually stressed in American banking literature. The Island's monetary supply depends chiefly on the balance of payments and fiscal policy. The commercial banks traditionally hold large cash balances, do not form part of an active, well-organized securities market, and, with the important exception of the state-owned Bank of Ceylon, are branches of foreign banks and thus have potential sources of reserves apart from the Central Bank. Moreover, consumption and investment on the island are little responsive to ordinary changes in interest rates. Drastic shifts in the terms on which credit was made available to would-be investors doubtless would produce some corresponding variation in the use of Ceylon's underemployed resources but would also wreck development policy and invite waste.

The success of countercyclical fiscal policy thus depends heavily on the management of Ceylon's foreign-exchange reserves, which change automatically with the terms of trade. If the government is to stabilize the real volume of domestic consumption and investment, while shifting price ratios greatly alter the value of the island's real output, during export booms it must achieve large enough payments surpluses to cover sizeable payments deficits during export slumps. To some extent fiscal policy can stabilize Ceylon's economy even when foreign-exchange reserves are not thus managed. Reductions in export duties, for instance, keep some plantation acreage and labor from being unprofitable during slumps. But, just as production and employment do not respond vigorously to ordinary changes in interest rates, so they do not rise or fall much because of moderate changes in taxes; income-tax cuts would chiefly stimulate imports. A cyclically varied program of public works can directly alter the number of jobs. But, unless import barriers are simultaneously raised, the multiplier effects of budgetary deficits will chiefly be felt abroad; and, if barriers curtail the inflow of goods, the deficits' multiplier effects will chiefly alter the price level.

Ceylonese policy analysts recognize this, and official documents list the requirements of effective countercyclical fiscal action. During export booms the government should raise export duties, let progressive income taxes absorb much of the rise in income, and adjust public works and other expenditures so that they are somewhat below a normal-trend level. After the island has acquired a comfortable foreign-exchange reserve, during export slumps the government should lower export duties and otherwise act so that the budgetary deficit is sizeable but not too large. To a considerable extent, actual policy has followed this advice. Actual swings in consumption and investment, however, have been much greater than a reading of official policy statements might lead one to expect. The impediments to "correct" fiscal action are quite substantial. First, there is the matter of accurate prognostication. For instance, almost no one foresaw the sharp decline in the terms of trade which occurred in the middle of the Korean War. Next, Ceylon is a poor country with ambitions to develop its resources, and public sentiment demands a "welfare state," so that restraint during an export boom is difficult. Stability is not the only objective, and the general public does not understand its requirements.

Rising Population, Underemployment, Low Incomes

Ceylon's inhabitants have approximately doubled in number since the start of the Great Depression and increased by roughly one-half since the postwar anti-malaria campaign. Before 1940 the average annual rate of increase was 1.5; during the past decade it rose to 2.5. There is little likelihood that this growth rate will decline much in the near future; further medical advance may make it rise. Ceylon thus has faced and still faces three major tasks:

to amass capital, improve skills, and mobilize underemployed resources rapidly enough to defeat the law of diminishing returns and raise average income, which, although high for south Asia, has been and is far below the goal of Ceylonese ambitions;

to achieve such a distribution of rising income and pattern of resource use that the number of extremely poor families declines and the volume of unemployment and severe underemployment decreases;

to expand the acreage suitable for peasant farming, to boost per-acre yields, and in other ways to raise the incomes and alleviate the land hunger of a badly overcrowded, rapidly increasing village population, whose current surplus and new additions cannot be fully absorbed in urban employments in the near future, whose mass migration to the towns would greatly accentuate housing and sanitation problems, and whose traditions make them prefer the status of cultivators.

The development policies which Ceylonese cabinets have followed during the postwar period reveal certain swings and trends. From the election of the first Parliament in 1947 to the foreign-exchange crisis of 1953, the ruling United National party proclaimed its belief in "practical socialism," reserved "basic" industries for state enterprise, heavily subsidized low-income families' consumption of food, and otherwise pursued a welfare-state program. After the 1953 crisis it moved to the Right, slashing consumer subsidies, placing greater reliance on private enterprise, and looking more favorably on foreign firms. The 1956 election brought in the People's United Front,[28] which reversed post-1953 trends and increased the scope of state enterprise and egalitarian paternalism. Related financial policies have also changed. Before 1954 the government relied almost entirely on taxes, sterling reserves, and domestic borrowing to pay for its program. Beginning in 1954, a series of foreign loans and grants covered a sizeable portion of the development policies' foreign exchange costs. Sources of aid and/or credit include the governments of the United States, Commonwealth countries, Russia, and mainland China, the International Bank for Reconstruction and Development, and the London money market.

The central characteristics of Ceylonese policy, however, have remained largely the same since the attainment of independence. Despite the 1953-56 swing to the Right, this is true even of the general role assigned the state. Apart from the great cut in consumer subsidies, the Rightist move actually brought about no major change. The newer attitudes towards private and foreign enterprise chiefly concerned the "basic" industries earlier reserved for the state; these industries were never more than a very small fraction of the economy; and the planned transfers from state to private operation never took place. The newer official attitudes were just beginning to influence administrative actions as well as general statutes and policy statements when the 1956 election ousted the cabinet that proclaimed these views. Moreover, during 1953-56 the United National party continued to express its faith in a comprehensive program of state leadership, which included heavy government spending and the guidance of private investment and productive effort. Similarly, as in earlier years, tax policies favored low-income families; much fiscal redistribution continued, even though consumer subsidies were slashed. Export duties, import duties, and income taxes supplied about nine-tenths of annual revenue. The first were chiefly a burden on plantation owners; the second chiefly hit luxury and semi-luxury imports; the last were steeply progressive, and the various tax concessions offered did not greatly diminish their aggregate impact.

[28] The Front was a coalition consisting of the Ceylon Freedom party, which essentially represented Sinhalese "communalist" ambitions, and semi-Trotskyite auxiliaries. Policy disputes split the Front in 1959. In July, 1960, the Ceylon Freedom party won a new election.

Thus, when the People's United Front came into power, the economic measures which it adopted chiefly accentuated the "practical socialism" and welfare-statism which earlier cabinets had introduced and which remained largely in force at all times. Both before and after 1956 the government offered private investors tax concessions, loans, some partnership arrangements, and official aid in securing the assistance of foreign firms, managers, and technicians. Similarly, throughout the period the state tried to direct and assist private enterprise via import barriers and producer subsidies, agricultural, industrial, and market research, the teaching of improved production methods, sponsorship of cottage industries, co-operative societies, and rural development societies, state regulation of tea and rubber acreage, and other rules concerning the use and purchase of public lands. The percentage of national income represented by government spending rose by only a few points, i.e., from more than one-fifth of one-fourth of the over-all figure.

Except for consumer subsidies, which varied enormously, the distribution of government spending among major areas likewise remained fairly constant. The general lines of activity which earlier cabinets financed most heavily were those which later budgets stressed. Income transfers, social services, and public administration have together usually absorbed more than two-thirds, capital formation less than one-third of public expenditure. Of the capital outlay, which has averaged about 7 per cent of gross national product, roughly one-third has usually gone to public utilities, another third to agriculture, from a seventh or a fifth to health, education, and housing combined; manufacturing capacity has received only a very small fraction. Much of the sum spent on public utilities has gone to develop hydroelectric power, which is the mineral-poor island's alternative to imported fuels. Capital expenditure on agriculture largely represents irrigation and related projects making new areas in the Dry Zone suitable for peasant colonization.

A fairly high degree of constancy also characterized Ceylonese policies concerning revenue sources and overseas capital flow. Although foreign loans and grants were much more important during 1954-59 than in earlier years, taxes covered five-sixths or more of the budget; and domestic borrowing covered much of the remainder. Moreover, thanks to Ceylonese purchase of British-owned plantations and other properties, capital imports continued to be much smaller than capital exports; exchange controls did not stop the outflow. During 1955-57 the country's net capital loss amounted to $72 million.[29]

There has been much debate concerning the effects of policies' central characteristics and more specific features, the ways in which and the extents to which they have served and disserved development goals. The record obviously does not show what would have happened if different policies had been followed, and the record itself is not clear. Unemployment, underemployment, landlessness, and near-landlessness have become increasingly serious problems, but the surveys which have been made do not allow confident estimates of the extents of these evils at any one time, much less a measurement of trends. The distribution of income is highly unequal and, in spite of welfare-state measures and the trend rise in average income discussed below, the number of very poor families very possibly has increased, especially among the village population; this is the logical accompaniment of the unemployment, underemployment, landlessness, and near-landlessness mentioned above. A 1953 sample survey showed that, among the 1,708 income recipients covered, the top 1 per cent and the bottom 50 per cent received approximately the same fraction of the total income received, a little less than one-fifth, while the bottom 10 per cent of the income recipients received 1.4 per cent of the total.[30] But while this survey imputes value to goods produced by a family for its own use, it does not attempt to measure the money value of state-provided medical and educational services or the increment of real income represented by consumer subsidies and price controls; and, of course, it does not give information concerning earlier or later years.

Apparently the most favorable part of the Ceylonese postwar record has been the general upward trend in income per capita, which has had to overcome the rapid rise in the island's population. Regardless of the price index which is used to deflate gross national product, real purchasing power per capita (Table 5) was substantially greater in the late 1950's than a decade earlier, and it probably was very much higher than in the immediate prewar period, when probably the best year's real income was not very far above the

[29] *Economic Survey of Asia and the Far East, 1959* (Bangkok, 1960), p. 87.
[30] *Survey of Ceylon's Consumer Finances*, pp. 15-16.

1938 level. (See Tables 4-6.) Even the record of per capita income, however, looks more favorable at first glance than after examination. Higher post-1949 incomes are largely attributable to a great improvement in the terms of trade, and the upward trend consists chiefly of a sudden jump with later fluctuations around the new and higher level. Although real *product* per capita (Table 5) probably rose substantially during the war and first several postwar years, it changed little thereafter and is believed to have reached its peak in 1952 or 1955. The latter was the most prosperous year, thanks to exceptionally favorable terms of trade.

As Ceylon remained chiefly an agricultural land throughout the period, most of the increase in aggregate income consisted of a rise in the value of its crops. Acreage expansion helped improved terms of trade achieve this rise, but higher plantation and village yields contributed much more than new acreage. In the late 1950's the area planted in tea was very little greater than in the immediate prewar years, but production was nearly two-thirds greater; rubber acreage was up by only 10 per cent, but average annual production was up by more than one-half; during the two decades ending in 1958-59 the output of rice may have doubled, while the area devoted to it increased by perhaps one-sixth. Rubber's improved yield reflects the abnormally low output of the late 1930's as well as a longer-run trend rise, and its rising trend did not continue throughout the 1950's; production was greater during the early stages of the Korean War than in subsequent years. Rice harvests also have been irregular, with unfavorable weather making 1956-58 crops especially interrupt the upward trend. Tea's per acre yield, however, has risen fairly steadily and the trend upward has accelerated; its percentage increase during the 1950's was much greater than that during the preceding decade.

Within the non-agricultural segment of the economy, the post-1939 rise in aggregate income has been widely distributed, but the most sizeable increases appear to be those in construction and government services. The percentage rate of growth has been high in non-plantation manufactures, motor transport, and electric power, but none of these yet contributes more than a small fraction of aggregate product.

The Need for and the Obstacles to Industrial Expansion

If Ceylon is substantially to raise real income per capita—perhaps even if it is to maintain the present level—then, unless the terms of trade continually improve, its traditional pattern of economic activity must change. A much higher percentage of the labor force must enter factories. Much agricultural expansion is still possible—and, indeed, is an essential part of a development program, since manufacturing and its accessory industries cannot expand nearly rapidly enough to absorb all job seekers and to provide the desired additions to national income, since a mass movement to the towns would magnify health and housing problems, and since traditions make most Ceylonese prefer the status of cultivator. But, unless the aggregate value of urban manufactures increases enormously, the island's economic future may be bleak.

Agricultural output can still increase through two general routes, acreage expansion and higher yields. At least within the near future, the latter seems to be much more promising. Tea, rubber, and coconut acreage appear to be very close to the limits set by geography and the other factors influencing costs and markets. Government-financed irrigation works can continue long to make new areas in the Dry Zone suitable for peasant colonists; but, so far, Dry Zone colonization has been a very slow process, absorbing at most only a few thousand families within a year, and there is little likelihood that it can soon be greatly speeded.[31] On the other hand, replanting, other rehabilitation, and more careful attention to quality can substantially raise the value of small-holders' tea, rubber, and coconut crops. Similarly, more intensive and better informed farming methods can greatly increase village harvests; rice yields per acre are not nearly as high as in Japan. Although observers repeatedly stress peasants' resistance to change, acreage and production estimates reveal a strong upward trend in village yields.[32]

Ceylon's population explosion, however, makes even the most favorable guesses concerning acreage expansion and rising yields

[31] The most complete study of this is B. H. Farmer, *Pioneer Peasant Colonization in Ceylon* (London, 1957).

[32] The increased size of the village labor force does not chiefly account for this. The surplus above village consumption substantially increased, so that the island became proportionally less dependent on food imports, in spite of the rapid population increase.

not nearly favorable enough. Employment as well as income considerations provide a strong argument for industrial development. Even if improved farming methods would quickly and greatly raise crop yields, they would only fractionally provide work for the 80,-000 new job seekers who leave the schools every year; they might not even fully utilize the energies of villagers who are now underemployed. Certainly, neither higher yields nor Dry Zone colonization will provide jobs for a rising urban population or satisfy the white-collar ambitions of the educated youth, who each year form a larger fraction of the island's inhabitants. For these, and for much of the rural surplus of unskilled labor, the principal hope must be manufacturing plus ancillary industries.

Obstacles to industrial expansion, however, are many and serious. These relate to Ceylon's mineral wealth, the scale of potential markets, the labor force's skills and attitudes, managerial experience, and "enterprise." The precise distribution of wealth also is not optimally helpful. Those persons who now command or can fairly easily raise large sums of capital, do not coincide with the persons most eager to build factories and most likely to run them well; government loans are only a fractional remedy. In the long run, an aggregate shortage of capital may seriously hamper industrial growth, as it now limits the over-all development program. Low incomes mean that the marginal propensity to spend additional income is high, and customs such as spending heavily on weddings and other ceremonies help the "demonstration effect" of richer neighbors' opulence keep this marginal propensity from dropping. Foreign funds are not likely to flow into the country on a massive scale; the island's strategic position is hardly such as to provoke governmental subsidies rivaling Washington's to Korea and Formosa, and the general political climate as well as "normal" cost and market considerations serves to discourage foreign private capital.

But good progress in manufactures *now* does not require *aggregate* savings beyond the island's capabilities; nor does it require much shift of the island's resources from other uses. As is stated above, Ceylon has been a net exporter of capital throughout most of the postwar period. Sums which have gone to purchase British properties could have provided most of the foreign exchange which a much more ambitious industrial program would have required. Similarly, the country's reserves of unemployed and underemployed labor could, if properly mobilized, substantially decrease the amount of domestic saving that manufacturing expansion would otherwise involve. Other obstacles have prevented the full use of the capital potentially available for manufactures, rather than aggregate capital itself being a bottleneck.

Ceylon does not have a broad natural resource base. Hydroelectric power and imported fuels are its substitutes for the coal and petroleum deposits which it lacks; and, because of irregular rainfall, the island's streams cannot generate as plentiful and cheap a supply of power as once was hoped. With the exception of clay, stone, and salt, the country's mineral wealth consists of small bodies of minor ores which apparently can add little to national income. Thus, with such exceptions, Ceylonese factories must process imported materials, forest products, or the produce of domestic agriculture.[33] These natural-resource lacks, however, are not as important as they may seem at first thought. Overseas transport to and from Ceylonese factories is not as costly as inland transportation between sources and markets in many countries. Both rubber and coconuts are major industrial raw materials, and recent government programs have planted new areas in sugar cane and cotton.

At least within the near future, the island's narrow resource base seems a less significant handicap than narrow markets which rule out the economies of large-scale production. Ceylon's domestic market for most factory products is small and will be small until incomes are much higher; this is the familiar vicious circle. Foreign markets for most Ceylonese manufactures are likely to be even smaller, thanks to the competition of such other Asian countries as India, Hong Kong, and Japan, and to the trade barriers which most governments impose in order to promote and protect home industry. Such market considerations are especially important in the case of rubber, since the industries which most heavily consume it flourish only where both sales and skills allow large-scale production and expensive research. For manufacturing, generally, the combination of narrow markets and a narrow resource base not only makes initial expansion more difficult but also weakens the multiplier and derived-demand effects which make continuing industrial development a semi-automatic process in countries blessed with more favorable sup-

[33] Nevertheless, with the aid of Russian loan funds and technical assistance the government is now constructing a small-scale steel mill.

plies of natural resources and with market demands which justify large-scale production.

Other major reasons why initial manufacturing costs are likely to be high are inexpert management and a labor force which is both unskilled and unaccustomed to the industrial discipline. Here again, of course, is the familiar vicious circle. Managerial expertise and laborers' skills and work habits are largely the result of experience. Some observers, however, believe that basic features of Ceylonese culture accentuate the inevitable difficulties. They argue, for instance, that business activity's low prestige keeps the better brains and more ambitious spirits from devoting their energies to industry and trade to the same extent as in Europe, North America, and some Asian lands. Also, that the white-collar tradition, the disdain for mechanical and other hand-dirtying tasks, prevents managers and potential managers from acquiring basic production skills which the top man, or at least, his top lieutenant must supply when an enterprise is small-scale and in a developmental stage. Similarly, observers remark that Ceylonese workers are less ready than Indians, and much less ready than the Japanese at the start of their industrial effort, to pay ceaseless attention to detail and adjust their thoughts and movements to factory routine. Such cultural lags—if that is what they are—are greater obstacles to industrial development after competitive producers have already acquired the suitable skills and attitudes than when a country or a region is an industrial pioneer. Also, they seem to be greater obstacles after labor unions, statutes, and mass opinion demand much job security, minimum wage rates, and other measures which soften the relationship between work performance and a worker's real income.[34] Governmental enterprises' labor costs tend to be especially high.

The relative weight to assign inexpert management is a subject of much controversy. A frequently expressed judgment is that "lack of enterprise" much more seriously retards industrial development in Ceylon, i.e., that the necessary administrative and production skills are already on hand or could be quickly learned if investors would only display initiative and willingness to take entrepreneurial risks. Managerial expertise and the spirit of enterprise are hard to

[34] The language employed and the conclusions drawn here do not imply value judgments. "Pre-capitalistic" attitudes may be considered preferable to those which speed industrial development. Welfare-state goals may be valued more than industrial development.

separate, however. Both inexpertness and lack of enterprise seem to have their principal origins in the lack of a commercial tradition and the relatively low value which the Ceylonese culture assigns business activity. Similarly, knowledge, determination, and administrative competence are likely to stimulate initiative and confidence, just as these two characteristics are likely to provide new opportunities for the growth of the former three. Ceylonese planters were not unenterprising when they developed the commercial groves during the early decades of this century. The tasks involved in growing coconuts, however, were easier and more familiar than the chores facing most would-be manufacturers, and the status of landed proprietors has traditionally been quite high.

Much Ceylonese opinion sees the lack of a strong spirit of *private* enterprise as a conclusive argument for government leadership, not only via assistance and guidance, but also via state ownership and management of much manufacturing industry. Egalitarian and humanitarian arguments support the conclusion. Steeply progressive income taxes cut into the savings available for private capital formation and decrease the incentive to invest. Tax concessions and government loans, even if magnificently administered, cannot fully offset these effects. But if the spirit of private enterprise is weak, tax policies which do not make capital accumulation much more difficult and the hope of entrepreneurial reward much less bright, must largely serve to stimulate luxury consumption and inflation of land values. Much of the intellectual support for state enterprise is pragmatic rather than ideological; it emphasizes businessmen's failure to develop manufacturing industry rapidly enough, instead of a Marxian or Fabian concept of the state.

So far, however, government industrial enterprise has done little to justify the high hopes often expressed for it. Although state ownership and operation of "basic" industries became official policy during World War II and has remained official policy during most subsequent years, and although a long period of study and supposed "planning" preceded the wartime policy declaration, the over-all scope of the government manufacturing program has remained quite small.[35] Moreover, the state-owned factories that have been built have usually not lived up to expectations. Costs have been much

[35] The hydroelectric system intended to supply the power needed for industrial expansion also has lagged far behind its planned schedule.

higher, production lower than the initial estimates; breakdowns have been too frequent. Reasons given for earlier poor performances include the makeshift nature of emergency plants hastily assembled during World War II, the departmental, excessively bureaucratic administration of the factories before they were put under semi-independent government corporations during 1955-56, and the political motives which sometimes controlled plant location. On the whole, the factories' record has been better in recent years, after reorganization, some relocation, and much reconstruction; but costs, volume of production, and continuity of production have remained unsatisfactory.[36]

The Ceylonese political Left[37] argues that state-owned industry has made little headway because the parties in power have not wished it to: that, being dependent on planters' wealth and villagers' votes, cabinets have feared a rising urban proletariat's future strength. The political Right[38] sees in the same record the need for the state to sell its factories, slash income taxes, and otherwise give business a much freer hand. Some argue even that state assistance to and guidance of private investment and production has been harmful, that it has stifled rather than encouraged the spirit of enterprise. Obviously, policy consistent with this advice would represent a sharp reversal of both longer-run and recent trends. None of the parties that campaigned in 1960 favored this reversal, and the Ceylon Freedom Party,[39] which won the election, has raised taxes and has increased the scope of state enterprise, state control of private business, and social-security and redistributionist measures.

[36] Perhaps the most notable example of this is the cement plant at Kankesanturai. Thanks to breakdowns, production fell 40 per cent between 1956 and 1957 and did not quite return to its earlier level until 1959.

[37] The Left chiefly consists of two semi-Trotskyite parties and the much smaller Communist party.

[38] As defined here, the Right is a wing within the United National party but does not control its statements and policies. UNP policy moved in this direction during 1953-56.

In early 1962 a group of army officers and police officers believed to represent extreme Right elements plotted a coup d'etat but were quickly arrested.

[39] The Ceylon Freedom Party was the largest unit within the People's United Front, which won the 1956 elections, but its alliance with semi-Trotskyist auxiliaries ended in 1959.

6

The Economy of Ghana

J. W. Williams[*]

As an underdeveloped country, Ghana has most of the features and faces most of the problems of other underdeveloped countries. The economy is developing from what is usually called a "dual economy" in which the traditional and modern sectors have only a few points of contact. Unlike many other underdeveloped countries, Ghana is not overpopulated. With a population of 6½ million and an area about the same as that of Great Britain, it has a population density of about 70 to the square mile. There are areas where the density of population is a good deal higher but no areas where there is a real scarcity of land. It is predominantly a rural country, and only about 15 per cent of the population lives in towns of 5,000 or more. The modern sector is small and has been advancing rather slowly during the past ten years.

Ghana became formally independent in 1957, but it has had effective self-government in internal and most external affairs since 1952. The present government is socialistic in outlook and has stated that it intends to introduce a socialist form of economic organization in as short a time as possible. The ruling party is strongly supported, and there is little opposition to its policies. It is not clear what form of socialism the economy is intended to take. There is a strong desire to adopt an independent line, and it is not likely to follow a communist or indeed any rigid pattern. The systems of India or Israel appear to be more like the models which will be followed. As foreign capital and foreign enterprise are still required and urgently desired, it is likely that a mixed economy will prevail for some time. There are also numerous economic institutions and patterns of thought in the country which cannot easily be absorbed into a collectivist economy.

[*] Professor of Economics, University of Otago, New Zealand; formerly (1949-61) Professor of Economics, University College, Ghana.

The most recent expression (at the time of writing) of government policy was given by President Nkrumah in a broadcast of October 9, 1960, in which he said:

I now wish to reaffirm and to clarify beyond any doubt the government's economic policy. In my message to the National Assembly of the 2nd September this year, I defined the respective roles of the capital which is available within Ghana and of capital which comes from abroad. I stated that the economic structure is divided into four different sectors. First, the State-owned sector, second, the Joint State-owned Private Enterprise sector; third the Co-operative sector and fourth the Private sector.

The point is, however, what is to be the relative importance of the various sectors? In this essay I attempt to assess the economic forces which are likely to work in the direction of enlarging the first three sectors at the expense of the fourth and those which may result in the private sector's remaining a large one for some time to come. I cannot avoid discussing to some extent sociological and political matters, as the economic system exists in a sociological and political framework. I have no judgment to make on the merits or otherwise of the economic philosophy of Ghana, but the discerning reader will no doubt be able to detect my own particular prejudices.

The Traditional Economy

Ghana was a British colony for some eighty years, and the country has been in contact with Europeans since the seventeenth century. This contact has influenced and modified the traditional economy, partly through trade and partly because the European pattern of life has provided a model and a goal to be sought after by the more enterprising members of the community. Nevertheless, the traditional economy has proved to be remarkably resistant to change, and it still represents the pattern of life of the great majority of the population.

The traditional economy is often called a subsistence economy. If this means that each family supplies its own needs, then the description does not apply to Ghana; but it is true in a rather wider sense in that each household could supply nearly all its basic needs and in fact supplies most of them. There is a good deal of trading even in basic foodstuffs, and a market is a feature of even small villages. While most buyers and sellers are from the same small area, the market is a point of contact with the outside world. Buyers come to take away the surpluses to the towns, and imported luxury goods are offered for sale. But in the traditional economy in its pure form the supply of farm produce for sale is not responsive to outside demand; it is largely an undesigned surplus which is sold.

The essentials of life are fewer in the tropics than they are in colder climates, and in Ghana where land is not scarce they are not difficult to supply. Houses made of earth are quickly and easily built and give adequate shelter. Life is lived largely out of doors, and a stool or two is the only furniture required. No fuel is needed for heating the house. Even clothes are a luxury which can be largely dispensed with. In the North, which is dry, wooded savannah country and which depends on grain for its basic food, there are times when food is short; but in the South, where four-fifths of the people live, the basic food crops grow easily and can be stored for future use. Such a situation is not, of course, a state of bliss. Although it is not difficult to get a living, there are plenty of unpleasant things to contend with. Rainfall is badly distributed over the year, and a good supply of drinking water is one of the problems of the countryside both in the north and the south. Rivers carry bilharzia and river blindness, and water has often to be carried for long distances. The tsetse fly infests large parts of the country, and cattle cannot be raised in these parts. There is a consequent shortage of protein in the diet. The usual tropical diseases are endemic; and malaria, yaws, hookworm, and other parasites add to the burden of life. The climate is not severe by tropical standards, but it is hot and humid enough to make hard work unpleasant. Most of these things are not inevitable, although they are often accepted as such by the rural population. Europeans have shown that it is possible to be as healthy in tropical as in temperate countries, even in rural areas. Better water supplies, better sanitation, and the supply of medical services would undoubtedly raise standards of health a great deal. The application of existing knowledge to the raising of crops would increase their output several fold. Rural electrification would do a great deal to raise the standard of comfort. To have some of these needs only a knowledge of what to do and the willingness to do it. Knowledge is being spread and self-help is not entirely lacking, but there is little real drive originating within the rural community itself and no real conviction that disease is caused by external conditions rather than by witchcraft. What has been accomplished has been largely the work of the central government, which has initiated and kept going schemes of community development. Under the stimulus of mass-education teams and a moderate amount of government money local roads may be built, but a year or so afterwards they will have reverted to forest. Other improvements need money, a lot of money, though not a fabulous sum. As we shall see, money has been and is currently available but it has not been spent in these directions.

The traditional economy in its pure form has reached a state of balance or long-run equilibrium. In the recent past population has been stationary or growing very slowly. Farm technique was such that land was free and under the system of shifting cultivation did not even earn a situation rent. Little capital was needed—hoes and matchets are the only useful tools in forest areas—and the marginal productivity of capital had fallen to zero. Change in such a stationary economy is always suspect—it may do some harm and cannot do any obvious good. It is reasonable to suppose that this attitude in economic life was carried over to changes in methods and standards of living. Population growth has, however, been rapid in the last few decades and, it might be thought, would introduce a disturbing factor into the traditional economy. Undoubtedly continued rapid growth could and will do so, but there has been little change yet. Part of the rural population has emigrated to the towns, which have grown faster than the population. The labor supply in the rural areas may well have reached a point where the marginal productivity of labor is zero. This, however, need not affect long-run stability, as the income of each individual in this type of economy depends not on his marginal but on his average productivity. In other words, the work is shared out among more people who each takes an average share of the proceeds.

Cocoa is by far the most important cash crop in Ghana and accounts for 20 per cent of the national income. It is grown entirely by peasant farmers on small farms of an acre or so in open forest. The typical farmer has, however, a number of farms and he nearly always has sharecroppers who get one-third of the proceeds. Sharecroppers can also raise their own food and are provided either with a house or the facilities for building one. Cocoa is a tree crop which is easily grown and needs the minimum of attention except at harvest time. Even if the sharecropper gets only £20-£30 cash each year, he is not badly off, as his basic needs are already met; while the owner who takes the other two-thirds (or splits it with his creditors, as is very often the case) can live well by local standards without doing much work. One would imagine that such a large addition to the cash resources of the traditional economy would have encouraged its break-up and moved it nearer to the modern sector. To some extent this has happened but not nearly to the extent that might be supposed. A well-qualified observer comments:

. . . at the back of even the urban mind is the feeling that money, with all its existing possibilities, was not made to be squandered on basic necessities. Money is a luxury and meant to be spent on life's greater gratifications particularly the enhancement of prestige.[1]

The stability of the traditional economy has been a proof against the disruptive force of easy money.

Some of the additional income has been used to raise the level of consumption in the form mainly of clothes, bicycles, gramophones, and motor cars. Some has gone into the hire of labor, mainly migrant labor, added to what might be thought to be an already adequate supply or to buy food which would otherwise be grown. Large sums have been spent on funerals, litigation, and travel. Sending sons or nephews to be educated abroad is a favorite use of money. Educated men never, of course, return to rural occupations, so this expenditure is a net cost to the rural community except for remittances which may come back to it. There is also some genuine investment. One form is house-building, either for use or for renting but often only as a prestige symbol in the form of large partly-occupied houses in small villages. Trucks for a transport business are another form of investment, but only too often they are operated at a loss as the market is oversupplied. The most useful form of investment has been the planting of new farms and the extension of old ones. Many of the trees in the old areas have been attacked by the virus disease of swollen shoot, and production could not have been maintained at its present level—at any rate with existing techniques—without considerable extension into new areas and further plantings in old areas. In fact, the net return from cocoa has been less than appears if this capital consumption is taken into account.

[1] M. J. Field, *Search for Security* (London, 1960), p. 32.

It is difficult not to take an attitude of moral disapproval in examining what appears to have been "unproductive" use of resources. However, moral approval or disapproval is not the essential point: it is that the influx of cocoa money has done little to change the basic standards of the traditional economy. To quote again Dr. Field:

An industrious and fortunate cocoa farmer may make up to thousands of pounds in a year but seldom is any of this spent in raising the basic standard of living. He may have [various luxuries] but he lives and eats as his fathers did in a squalid yard where women cook on the ground and naked children swarm, crawl and eat dirt . . . . they have yaws, worms, ringworms and deficiency diseases as freely as other children.[2]

It is significant from our point of view that the educated Ghanaian tends to despise the traditional economy and regards it as hopeless to expect any evolution from within. This opinion is usually shared by the visiting expert. The prevailing view is that increased production in agriculture needs a revolution in methods and, as the traditional farmer is incapable of carrying through this revolution, it must be imposed from outside. As the educated man has no intention of taking up farming and the establishment of plantations by foreigners is strongly discouraged, the only organization which can do anything is the state. The graduate in agriculture from the University thinks only of a career as a government agricultural officer or a research worker, and even a man who has some training in scientific methods at a lower level expects a white-collar supervisory job in government service.

The inability—or alleged inability—of the farmer to save and invest in productive ways is one of the arguments which is used to justify the marketing-board system for cocoa. The Cocoa Marketing Board was established shortly after the war and is the sole buyer and exporter of cocoa. The original purpose of the Board was to stabilize the price paid to the farmer and to accumulate funds so as to maintain prices in bad years. It has become in recent years an overt instrument of taxation and has accumulated large funds which have been lent to the government and used for general development purposes. Government nominees now dominate the Board, and its policy is very largely government determined. There was a pretense in the earlier years that expenditure by the Board was for the benefit of

[2] *Ibid.*, p. 32.

cocoa farmers, but "benefit" has been interpreted in such a wide sense that it has been used to justify expenditure in all sorts of ways which are only indirectly beneficial to him.

It is interesting to speculate on what might have happened if there had been no marketing board. Up to the 1930's there were some large African firms which bought cocoa from the farmer and established shops to sell him imported goods in return. Most of them could not withstand the depression, and the rest went out of business during the war. Under the marketing-board system buying firms operate on a commission, which is too small to allow much accumulation of capital. If there had been no marketing board, we might have seen the growth of substantial African firms based on the profits of the cocoa trade, which would probably have been high, as prices were rising greatly during the fifties. As it is, African firms have remained small and have not been able to compete with large-scale foreign firms.

Economic growth in all countries has been based mainly on surpluses in agriculture. Who has managed to get hold of that surplus has largely determined who shall initiate and carry through the building up of a modern economy. It seems to me that the opportunity which the state has had of using the agricultural surpluses for its own purposes has been and will continue to be the most important factor in the growth of a socialist economy. If there had been no such system, it would have been necessary to invent one.

The picture I have drawn is not, of course, of universal application, and there would be exceptional cases even in the middle of backward areas. Cocoa growing, though widespread in the most populous areas, exists in only part of the country. The North has been largely isolated from outside contact, except for a trickle of trade and the depredations of slave raiders since the decay of the civilizations of the western Sudan. The principal contribution it makes to the more advanced South is the supply of unskilled labor. There is a large migratory movement, estimated by one writer at 300,000 a year, from the north of Ghana and from the French-speaking countries further north (which from this point of view are part of the Ghana economy). The migrants work on farms, in the mines, and in the cities where they are mainly engaged on building and construction work of all kinds. The North has a number of primitive village industries—metal working, leather working, dyeing, cotton spinning—which are absent in the South. It is more adapted to mechanization of agriculture. It is possible that the traditional economy in the North would be less resistant to change than that of the South, but it has not yet been put to the test. The great handicap is the lack of a cash crop of anything like the value of cocoa. Apart from cocoa, the production of timber and minerals in the southern areas probably provides more cash income than is available to the whole of the North. The most promising possibility is improved methods for raising and feeding cattle. With adequate water and better cattle, meat might even be an export commodity.

The traditional society is obviously not a capitalistic one, as it is not motivated by the search for profit or the desire for expansion. On the other hand, it can hardly be described as socialistic. Although each family has its own land, or rather has the use of what land it requires, as the idea of individual ownership of land is not really part of the social philosophy and does not need to co-operate with the rest of the community in raising crops, the techniques of production and what is considered desirable use of consumable goods are regulated by custom. The political system in the traditional society was a democratic one. The chief ruled with a council of elders and, though the position of chief was the prerogative of certain clans, he could be deposed if he were not acceptable to the community, and he often was. There has never been in Ghana a ruling class descended from foreign invaders. Even today a class structure in the usual sense of the word hardly exists. The basic unit is the clan or extended family, and the loyalty of the individual is to his family. The British colonial system did not destroy the traditional political system, but since independence the power of the chiefs has been very much reduced, and the central government dominates local government both through departmental control of local authorities and through the institution of regional commissioners who are party political appointees.

It is apparent that the traditional system, because of its strong resistance to change, would not be easy to incorporate in a centralized collectivist system. As long as subsistence production continues, much of rural life will probably remain outside the modern economy, as indeed it does to a large extent in more developed economies. Dualism is a matter of degree and a completely integrated exchange economy is rare. A recent project which may set the pattern for the future, at any rate for cash crops, is the establishment by the government of rubber plantations and curing plants in rural areas. These are intended partly as commercial production units and partly as demonstration farms. It is intended that individual farmers in the vicinity should grow rubber on contract for the central unit. They would be helped with the planting and with the collection of rubber, at any rate in the early stages. More or less the same plan has been proposed for coffee. A good deal of concern has been felt about the extent to which exports are dependent on a single crop, and there is no doubt that the government will try to develop others to as great an extent as possible. The Agricultural Development Corporation was set up partly for this purpose. It has acted so far mainly as a marketing organization concerned with the buying and export of crops other than cocoa—fruit, palm nuts, etc. There has been talk of the Corporation's taking over the internal marketing of foodstuffs, but no positive steps have been taken in this direction. Internal marketing at the present time is in private hands, mainly those of the itinerant "market mammy" who operates cheaply, seeks out surpluses and brings them into the larger markets, and also travels between one small market and another, evening out supplies. As petty trading is one of the major occupations of women in Ghana, one would not imagine that they would give up their position at all willingly. In the larger markets there also exist wholesalers who send out agents to farmers and also buy truck loads which may be sent in by farmers. There are complaints against these middlemen, who are accused of exacting monopoly profits, but they appear to provide a useful service. The fish trade is entirely in the hands of women traders who very often also own canoes and nets which they hire out to the fishermen.

The Colonial System and the Modern Sector

Until quite recently no clear distinction existed in the mind of the average Ghanaian between the colonial government and expatriate private enterprise in Ghana. They were both part of the white man's economy and comparatively few Ghanaians shared in it.[3]

[3] To save constant qualifying phrases I use the terms Ghana and Ghanaian to refer to the country and its inhabitants both before and after independence. For the same reason I have used the present and the past tenses rather unsystematically, even in the same sentence, when referring to institutions and circumstances which are still fundamentally the same today as they were in the colonial era. Unless it

The colonial government saw its job as primarily that of maintaining law and order, and it tried to act where possible through what it conceived to be native institutions. Towards trade and industry it adopted a laissez-faire attitude in general. It is often alleged by "anti-imperialists" that there was a deliberate policy of discouraging the growth of local trade and industry in the interest of the home traders and manufacturers. I have seen no evidence of this, but I must admit that I am not in sympathy with what might be called the "great conspiracy" school of historical and political analysis. It should be remembered that there were never any preferential tariffs for British imports into the Gold Coast. In practice colonial admin-istrators were often rather unsympathetic towards expatriate trading firms' interests. The cocoa marketing system was set up well before independence, and the opportunity for more than normal profits in buying cocoa was lost to expatriate as well as to native firms. Strict control of immigrants, which was possibly aimed mainly at keeping out Asiatics, restricted the number of overseas employees which expatriate firms could have and in effect was administered in such a way as to reserve retail trade expansion to native firms. A sub-stantial rate of income tax on firms was imposed, but as under a double taxation agreement they were allowed to claim taxation paid in Ghana against taxes due in Britain, income tax was mainly at the expense of the British revenue rather than at the expense of the firms.

There have never been any white "settlers" in Ghana. While the ownership of long leases of land was not forbidden to Europeans, it was discouraged, except for the erection of factories or business premises. A small number of Lebanese families who are engaged in retail trade may be counted as residents and probably look on Ghana as their home. Missionaries also have spent long periods in the coun-try. Other non-Africans normally regard their time in Ghana as a tour of duty, as it is called, and do not regard themselves as perma-nent residents although there are "old coasters" who have worked in the country for thirty years or more.

The colonial government went quite a long way in building up the social overhead—the infrastructure as it is now unfortunately often called. It was necessary to start from scratch, and all con-

---

is otherwise apparent from the context, or specifically stated to the contrary, terms such as the "colonial system" refer to the recent past.

struction was financed from local resources which were not very great in the days before the postwar cocoa boom. Before independence the state-owned railway system and the network of main roads had been constructed. An artificial harbor had been built at Takoradi. There was a postal system, an efficient police system, and other instruments of administration. There were government hospitals in the main towns though not perhaps as many as were desirable. Although the infrastructure was not as extensive as it might have been, it was at least a "going concern" which was handed over at independence.

Most Europeans not employed in the civil service were engaged in trade, mining, or in the timber industry. An estimate of the value of private foreign capital at present invested in Ghana is £135 million. The largest proportion is British, but Swiss, French, Dutch, and American investment has been substantial.

Mining for gold, manganese, and bauxite is entirely a European activity. Almost half the diamonds produced are from European-owned mines, and the other half is produced by African diggers using simple equipment and primitive methods. The gold mines are on a large scale. All the output of the mines except a small amount of gold used for jewelry making is exported. Except for labor—mainly unskilled—and timber, all requirements are imported. Work in the mines is not popular and is often undertaken when nothing else is available or until something better turns up. Many of the workers are migrants, and labor turnover is high. Mining as it is carried on in Ghana has few links with the rest of the country. It provides employment, and the wages paid by the mines are the source of demand for local food. Taxation paid by the mining companies is an important source of government revenue. The mines do not produce raw materials for use by other industries and they do not use the products of other local industries. Profits are for the most part remitted abroad. The lack of a permanent and settled labor force does not encourage the growth of prosperous towns in the vicinity of the mines. A proportion of the wages paid is in fact sent by migrants to other parts of West Africa. The techniques used are rather specialized and do not provide very useful training for other industries.

A number of gold mines are close to the end of their useful life at the present price of gold. The government was paying a subsidy to some of them to maintain production. The recent establishment of a basic minimum wage higher than the existing rate and the intention to withdraw the subsidy led to the announcement of their abandonment. As this would have meant the loss of the remaining gold, hasty legislation was passed to enforce heavy penalties on operators who closed down mines without permission. However, this was quickly followed by a very generous offer to buy out the shareholders of the mines concerned. This action should reassure shareholders who fear nationalization of other industries. It seems unlikely that the government will nationalize the other mines, and I think we must regard the incident as a special case.

Timber felling and the sale of logs and sawn timber is an industry similar to mining. The bulk of the timber is exported but a good deal is used locally for furniture and building. The large operators are foreign firms, but there are a number of small and medium-sized Ghanaian firms in the trade. In recent years the proportion of sawn timber relative to logs has substantially increased. A large veneer plant has recently gone into operation. The Industrial Development Corporation established a sawmill some years ago; it has not been very successful financially. The forest in Ghana is partly reserved forest under the control of the Department of Forestry and partly unreserved. As in most new countries, cutting out in the uncontrolled areas has been wasteful and there has been no replanting. The unreserved area will be cut out in about ten years at the present rate of exploitation. In the reserved area, which has not yet been commercially exploited, it is intended that cutting should be closely controlled so as to insure a steady supply of timber and the perpetuation of the forest. This will mean strict supervision by the Forestry Department and will probably mean the end of the small man in the trade. In the prevailing political climate it seems inevitable that the state will expand its activities as a timber miller and exporter, as this will be the easiest way to insure proper forest management. On the marketing side a government-owned timber marketing company which operated in competition with other firms was unsuccessful and had to be wound up at a considerable loss. The moral drawn from this experiment was not that the state should keep out of the timber marketing business but that it should not be subject to competition. The marketing company has been replaced by a Timber Marketing Board, which will operate on the same lines as the Cocoa Marketing Board, with a monopoly of the export trade. In the meantime it is confining its activities to certain kinds of timber only. One reason given for setting up the Board was that the small timber supplier was not getting a fair deal and was sometimes being cheated over the measurement of his timber. It might seem that these difficulties could have been overcome in a less expensive way.

The import of consumers' goods in the colonial era and to a large extent today is in the hands of six large firms, two British, two French, one Swiss, and one Cypriot with English backing. The United Africa Company, a subsidiary of Unilever, is by far the largest and still accounts for about one-half of the import of non-government consumers' goods. The Firms, as they are commonly called in Ghana, also import producers' goods, but in recent years specialist firms have taken over to a considerable extent. The larger car agencies are also in their hands. The oil companies are the only other large foreign organizations. There have always been some African importers, but until recently their scale of operations has been very small. In the past few years there has been a rapid growth of Ghanaian importing firms, and they now handle an appreciable proportion of the import of food. In total, however, any loss by the Firms has been compensated by the increased trade in consumers' durables—refrigerators, air conditioners, motor vehicles—and in construction machinery and equipment and materials in which Ghanaian firms have usually neither the resources nor the technical knowledge to compete. In recent years there has been a proliferation of manufacturers' agents, commercial travelers, and trade missions from every country in the world, offering goods of all sorts for sale in Ghana. Despite this competition for a share of the Ghana market, there is some substance in the often repeated complaint that the Firms act in a monopolistic manner. Branded goods play a very important part in the market. The consumer is very brand conscious and is not easily shifted to brands with which he is not familiar. In a largely illiterate country advertising is not so effective as it would otherwise be. The larger firms have all the best brands, and even when they are available to others the larger firms seem to be able to get the first and largest share. This is perhaps not a very serious matter in the long run, but it is felt to be a great handicap by the growing Ghanaian firms.

The ordinary Ghanaian buys his requirements—other than expensive consumers' durables—in the markets which exist in every town and village and which in the cities are very large and extensive. In Accra it is estimated that there are 38,000 market and street traders in addition to the shops. Most of them are very small traders selling a few shillings worth of goods a day. Women predominate in petty trade and many regard it as a social rather than a commercial activity. Some dealers in the market are, however, quite large, especially in textiles, where their turnover may exceed £60,000 a year. The markets draw their supplies partly from the wholesale departments of the trading firms, partly from African wholesale importers, and in the case of food from the farmers. In the latter case the market trader will normally either herself or in partnership with others or through family connections collect her own supplies. There are many formal and informal associations in the market which fix or try to fix prices. The very small traders appear to follow the price leadership of the larger sellers. The price to the farmer appears to vary little throughout the year and only slowly from year to year, and the sellers absorb or profit from the changes in prices with changes in demand and supply. The market traders endeavor to buy from the farmer only those quantities which they expect to sell at what they consider to be a reasonable price from their own point of view. If the demand has fallen, the farmer may be left with his supplies, but for staple foods this may not matter, as they can be stored and sold later. The typical farmer, as I have pointed out earlier, is selling a surplus from his subsistence production and, though he may want money for personal expenditure, he has no cash expenses for his farming business and his output need not be affected. Market prices quickly respond to an increase in demand but do not fall nearly as fast to a decrease or to an increase in supply. In the short run competition is far from perfect but, with so many traders and with comparative ease of entry, in the long run it is much more nearly perfect. There appear to have been no serious shortages of food in the market, despite the rapid growth of towns and the fact that commercial farming is still in its infancy.

Between the market and the large importing firms with their department stores and chains of retail stores are the small and medium-sized independent shopkeepers. Ghanaian traders are on the whole small. They are mainly general storekeepers selling a wide range of goods. In the cities there is more specialization, and in recent years Ghanaian traders have been more prominent in the wholesale field. Some of the larger firms have been handling government contracts for cement and other building materials. On a rather larger scale are a number of Lebanese traders and a small number of Indian firms. The Lebanese and Indians are prominent in the textile and fancy goods fields; some of them also handle general goods and hardware. Their growth has been restricted in recent years by the control of immigration. During the past few years the Firms have been giving up their smaller retail shops, especially outside the cities. A common practice has been to sell them to the former managers. In many cases the firms retain a large financial interest in these shops and the new "owner" may be one in name only, remaining closely tied to the wholesale firm; in other cases he is completely independent. The Firm's name is normally retained in all cases, as it carries considerable good will.

The Ghanaian trader and shopkeeper faces many difficulties. He finds it difficult to raise capital and has to rely on his own savings or those of his close relatives. The firms are either one-man concerns or small partnerships; limited liability companies are almost unknown. If funds can be borrowed at all, very high rates of interest have to be paid. Interest rates in Ghana are determined by the insatiable demand for consumption loans for which rates of 50 per cent are common. Ghanaians who have money to lend can see no point in taking shares in companies for a return of say 10 per cent, with considerable risk of loss. One gets the impression that every Ghanaian is in debt up to the extreme limit of his credit. This cannot really be true, as someone must also be lending. There is little doubt, however, that millions in state money which has been lent for the purpose of trade and agriculture has found its way into consumption loans. Once embarked on business, perhaps with some help from the banks, the trader or small manufacturer faces a further series of hurdles if he tries to expand. Each member of an extended family—which may consist of hundreds of people—has a very strong moral obligation to help the rest of the family when they are in difficulties or, today, even to provide benefits—such as medical attention—which were once luxuries but have now become necessities. The more enterprising and successful find their funds continually eaten away in this fashion. The necessity for prestige symbols is a further drain on the trader's capital. As soon as possible a successful trader must build as large a house as is consistent with his position. Fortunately, the rapid growth of cities has made investment in houses profitable and they can be used as security for bank loans. In many cases, however, it is thought necessary that a large house be constructed in the trader's home town or village where there is no demand for this sort of accommodation. The writer knows of many cases where Ghanaian traders have been desperately short of working capital and yet have most strongly resisted the suggestion that they should raise it by selling one of several houses which they own. To do so would apparently involve great loss of face. The Ghanaian business rarely survives the retirement or death of its founder. Nearly all those in existence today were started since the war. The successful man rarely brings up his sons to follow him but prefers to send them to universities in Ghana or abroad to train as professional men or civil servants. With these handicaps and attitudes it is doubtful that most Ghanaian trade, even when it is on a fairly large scale, should be included as part of the modern sector at all. It may be laissez faire but it is hardly capitalistic in spirit. I venture to quote from a paper I wrote some years ago:

The family group was big enough in most cases and the village group in every case to secure the advantages of the division of labour which in any case were soon exhausted. . . . Under these circumstances trade was a luxury, I might even say an amusement. If it was something of a gamble then that only added to the excitement. I think there is still a large element of this attitude in the Gold Coast. More important still the object of trade appears to be in most cases simply to make money. . . . in other countries to the small business man money is the means to an end, that of building up his business. . . . If business is regarded as a speculation, if the object is simply to make money and to drop that particular line of business if something more profitable turns up then there is some sense in putting accumulated profits into real property on the principle of not having all one's eggs in one basket.[4]

The Ghanaian shopkeeper and small manufacturer present something of a problem to the government. The government would naturally like to see trade in Ghanaian private hands rather than in

[4] *Proceedings of the Third Annual Conference of the West African Institute of Social and Economic Research* (Ibadan, 1956).

foreign private hands if it has to choose between the two. On the other hand it does not want to see the rise of a strong commercial middle class of traders and importers. The consequence has been a policy of sometimes coming to the aid of local businessmen and of other times remaining indifferent to their interests. The Bank of the Gold Coast was set up in 1952 as a state-owned bank to make loans to African traders who, it was thought, were not properly catered to by the existing banks. In 1958 a committee to consider methods of helping Ghanaian businessmen was set up. The committee spent several months hearing evidence and produced a long report which has, however, not been published and on which no action appears to have been taken. Recent proposals envisage the formation of co-operatives in trade.

Manufacturing industry in Ghana is at a very early stage of development. Nearly all which is of any size is foreign owned and operated. There are now two breweries, a tobacco processing plant, a biscuit factory in co-operation with the Industrial Development Corporation, vehicle assembly plants, manufactures of enamel ware, and industries bottling and packaging various goods. The IDC operates a match factory, a furniture factory, a distillery, and a number of small factories making other goods. Growth has been a good deal faster during 1960. The Industrial Development Corporation, set up in 1951, at first operated as an industrial finance institution making loans to established small industries and to craftsmen to establish new ones. The policy had little success owing to the difficulty of finding suitable entrepreneurs and to the lack of supervision of the subsequent disposal of the money loaned. The policy is a relic of the days when it was thought that capital could be pumped into a developing economy in a mechanical fashion with satisfactory results. The IDC then turned to the establishment of new industries in partnership with local or foreign entrepreneurs. Today advances are still made to small industry though on a very small scale, and partnership arrangements are still being continued. However, the tendency is for the IDC to have a bigger share than formerly and also to run more factories of which it is the sole owner. It was intended at one time that the IDC should dispose of its factories to private enterprise, once they had been established, and use the funds thus released for the establishment of new ones. In fact this has not been done and it is not now government policy to do so.

The government has voted £10 million for the use of the IDC but expenditure to date has been £6 million. Most of the enterprises have so far lost money. The IDC, as a pioneer, has had to find out all the difficulties of judging the market, insuring supplies, and finding efficient managers. It has run up against most of the things which have hindered organizations of this sort in other under-developed countries—pressure for quick results, a board with little or no industrial experience, reluctance to pay market rates for first-class managers, civil service methods of control, insufficient attention to market research, pilot schemes before embarking on full-scale production, and similar troubles. This type of organization belongs essentially to a transitional phase and is likely to alter in character with the development of a socialistic structure of industry. Proposals have already been made for the setting up of an Industrial and Agricultural Bank to take over the financing functions of the IDC. It seems likely in this case that the individual concerns now subsidiaries of the IDC will become more independent.

There is, unfortunately, a rather insecure base for industry in Ghana. There is no coal, a little iron ore of doubtful quality, no deposits of salt, and little useful lime or other raw materials for local industry. The principal minerals produced, gold and manganese, are likely to continue to be exported. The climate is unsuitable for the preparation of chocolate from the main crop, cocoa. There is little mechanical ability or craftsmanship derived from village industries. Even the wheel was not known until it was introduced by Europeans. In some countries, such as India, industries have grown up from the mechanical ability developed in servicing farm machinery and equipment, but in Ghana this does not exist. It is surprising, for example, that a small foundry has not been developed for the manufacture of iron implements, cooking stoves, etc. Again we are forced to conclude that the initiative for non-foreign manufacturing enterprises must come from the state. There appears to be no other source from which it might come. Village crafts are better developed in the North and, as with agriculture, it is possible that this is the area towards which we should look for this sort of development. Unfortunately, the North is poor and remote from the center of government. It is relatively underpopulated and would provide a poor local market.

A development which might make a great difference to the North, however, is the Volta River scheme. The scheme consists of a dam on the Volta river for a hydroelectric plant with a capacity of about 800,000 kilowatts. There is also to be an aluminum smelter which will take a good deal of the power produced, the rest being fed into a national grid. A very large lake would be formed behind the dam, running well up into the northern region. A supplementary power scheme would also provide additional power in the North. Finance to build the dam is to come partly from the country's own resources and partly from overseas loans. The aluminum plant would be operated by foreign private capital.

Construction work—roads, public buildings, housing, harbors, and bridges—has been the main development activity. Except for some private housing and a little road work, nearly all construction has been undertaken by overseas firms. A few Ghanaian firms have made rapid growth in this field, but they are still much smaller than the smallest overseas firms. A joint Ghana-Israeli firm is, however, now of moderate size and is still expanding. The Ghanaian capital was provided by the government. The best prospect for Ghanaian firms in this field is in private housing.

Commercial banking in Ghana is largely in the hands of two British banks—Barclays D.C.O., which also trades extensively in other parts of Africa, and the Bank of West Africa, which has affiliated banks in other countries. Ghana from the point of view of these banks is part of the British branch-banking system in that the resources to make advances in Ghana do not depend on the cash position in the country. Resources can easily be diverted from other areas if conditions in Ghana are particularly favorable or diverted from Ghana if conditions are more favorable elsewhere. Furthermore, the banks earn most of their revenue from the finance of imports and exports and from dealing in foreign exchange. They have in consequence a very conservative policy in lending for internal trade. They have been accused of discriminating against Ghanaian firms, but this discrimination appears to be against poor banking risks rather than against Ghanaians as such. Ghanaians have in a sense to compete for loans against the rest of Africa and other parts of the world where the banks operate. The Bank of the Gold Coast—now the Ghana Commercial Bank—adopted a more liberal policy towards small traders and has introduced a good deal more competition into the market. The Bank's policy of spreading the money it had available by making a large number of small advances was perhaps not the best one and it has more recently tended to pay more attention to supporting larger firms which appear to have good prospects of expansion. The recent transfer of all the business of statutory bodies, including the large account of the Cocoa Marketing Board, has led to an economizing of reserves and given the Bank greater funds for financing industry.

Trade unionism in the colonial era was not well developed and its growth was slow. The only really strong union was the mine workers' union. The normal form of union organization was the company union with the United Africa Company union, as might have been expected, the strongest. The largest public employees' union was in the railways. The Convention Peoples party, the government party, tried to bring the unions in as direct party supporters but without much success, especially with the large and only effective unions. In 1960, however, labor legislation was put into effect which made membership of unions compulsory for every worker and forced the existing unions to join the Trades Union Council—a party-dominated body—as a condition of recognition. This body has considerable power to control individual unions and receives a large proportion of members' subscriptions. Provision is made for deduction of union fees by employers. Recent legislation provides for the fixing of minimum-wage rates by the government and, in some industries, for scales of wages. There is also provision for compulsory arbitration, which has not yet been much used. A number of obstacles have been put in the way of strike action. Although this legislation is new, the wage-fixing provisions do not much alter the *de facto* position. The state has always been by far the largest employer of wage labor, and government rates have normally set the pace for other employers.

The Future of Socialism and Laissez Faire

If my interpretation of the significance of recent events in Ghana is correct, it seems evident that the state-owned sector is likely to grow. Its growth will be mainly determined by the rate at which new development can take place, which depends partly on the availability of funds and partly on the availability of managerial and technical abilities. State-owned farms are likely to be established where plantations can be operated economically or where mechanized agriculture is feasible. The size of the joint state-owned private enterprise sector will depend on the extent to which large-scale factories are set up. A recent example is an agreement between the government and an Italian firm to set up an £8 million oil refinery. As we have seen, the tendency is for the state to take over from private enterprise its share in such ventures. A recent example is the Black Star Shipping Line, which was originally started in partnership with an Israeli company but which is now state-owned. Another is the taking over of all the shares in Ghana Airways, formerly owned with British Overseas Airways Corporation. The state-owned private enterprise sector may at times be relatively important in terms of the size of industries, but it is unlikely to be allowed to grow in the long run.

The co-operative sector is an unknown quantity. It is apparently the intention of the government to encourage the establishment of consumers' co-operatives on a scale large enough to take over most of the importing of consumers' goods. In the past consumers' co-operatives have, despite a great deal of nursing by the Department of Co-operation, all been failures. To be successful in the future they will undoubtedly need at first a great deal of help from the state, both financially and on the management side. A possibility seems to be the buying out of one of the large importing firms which would give them a going organization. In the early years at any rate it might be difficult to distinguish the consumers' co-operatives from state-operated enterprises. Cocoa marketing co-operatives have, on the other hand, been very successful. They now buy about 20 per cent of the annual crop. They have received a good deal of help from the government in the form of guarantees to the banks for their finance and advice on management problems and audit from officers of the Department of Co-operation. Nevertheless, they were genuine independent societies run by the members themselves. In 1960 they were brought under the control of the Co-operative Council, which is a party-dominated organization. There are also proposals for producers' co-operatives in village crafts, but the system does not yet appear to have been worked out. Co-operative farms are also proposed. Presumably, they could be useful only for plantation crops and where mechanization is possible.[5]

The relative importance of the private sector in the near future is also difficult to forecast. The state has neither the financial nor the management resources to reduce it substantially for some time to come, but there is no doubt of the desire to keep it as small as possible and to insure that it is relatively unimportant in the long run. As long as the traditional economy continues to exist, and I have suggested that it is very tenacious of life, there must be private enterprise of a sort in agriculture. The present structure of cocoa production with a large number of small farms under forest cover can hardly be anywhere else than under private ownership. Replantings may on the other hand work very well in plantations which could be state-owned or co-operative. I cannot see the markets disappearing in the near future. They are efficient and occupy a large number of women who have considerable political power. It is quite possible, however, that the state will provide the link between the farmer and the markets by setting up a buying organization and setting the level of buying prices to the farmer and selling prices to the market traders. The growth of light industry would no doubt reduce the numbers in the market by providing alternative jobs for women. If the consumers' co-operatives are successful, then the small shopkeeper is likely to be squeezed out of business, at any rate in the cities and towns. Some foreign enterprise will undoubtedly remain for a long time—perhaps indefinitely. It would appear that the days of the large importing firms are numbered. It is conceivable that they will be bought out by the state, but in any case a large state-supported wholesale co-operative organization will provide competition which will be hard to withstand. Specialized firms and particularly those providing technical services will probably survive. Foreign manufacturing firms are likely to grow in numbers and importance, as Ghana needs the capital and the know-how which they can provide. I should think that in the future they will be the largest elements in the modern private enterprise sector.

Were the trends I have described inevitable and is there any likelihood of their being reversed? The fact that Ghana is now

[5] It is difficult to be precise about co-operation as no comprehensive indication of its intentions has been issued by the government. There is constant discussion along these lines in party circles, but these are strictly speaking unofficial views.

developing on socialist lines is partly an accident of personalities and politics. Dr. Nkrumah, the president and life chairman of the Convention Peoples party, has a socialist background. The CPP is a popular party which broke away from the leadership of middle-class nationalists, who formed the chief opposition to the colonial government before independence. Socialism has always been part of the party's policy, but in the early days of its rise to power it appears to have been identified with "anti-imperialism" rather than with "anti-private enterprise" by members and supporters of the party. In other words, the CPP was a nationalist party first and a socialist party second. Its adherents were not attracted by socialism, which, though not hidden, was not much mentioned in the first few years. It is very unlikely that the "traditionalists" of the Gold Coast Convention could have won mass support, but it is possible that a vigorous and able leader could have won support for a party of moderates, which has happened in Nigeria.

Although the present government came to power by constitutional means and with the consent of the colonial power, it is in one sense a revolutionary party. The real revolution was not the break with colonialism, which can only be described as evolutionary, but the break with the traditional political system; it was the revolt of the young men against the old, of the modernists against the traditionalists. The new government inherited the prestige of the colonial government and, naturally enough, took over whatever was modern and progressive in that government. It seems quite certain that whatever had been the political complexion of the new government, other than a "return to traditionalism," the state would have played an important part in economic life. With no readily available source of capital and facing the competition from foreign firms, private enterprise without government aid on a large scale would have had little chance of development.

To someone like the writer, rather tired of cities and skeptical of some of the benefits of a good deal of modern civilization, the traditional way of life could be, if facilities such as good water, drainage, health services, and electricity were available, the choice of a reasonable man. But it is obvious that the young and progressive will have none of it. With the lack of faith in the possibility of a good life under the traditional system goes a loss of faith in the traditional form of democracy.

Indigenous private enterprise in Ghana is at best in a transitional stage. It is not attracting the best brains or the most energetic men. The great handicap to the rapid socialization of the economy is the lack of enough educated men to run state industries and trading organizations. The length of the transition will depend on how quickly this handicap can be overcome.

7

The Indian Economic System

*P. S. Lokanathan**

INTRODUCTION

The dominant feature of the Indian economic system today is the assumption by the state of over-all responsibility for economic development. Government-sponsored economic growth is not new; Germany and Japan in the late nineteenth and early twentieth centuries are examples of such growth, and, more recently, the economic growth of communist countries has been engineered by the state. There has been, in fact, a virtually universal trend towards an extension of state authority in the economic sphere. But the real impellants of government intervention in India are to be found in the special features of Indian underdevelopment. As a preliminary consideration, therefore, it may be useful to place the new role of the state in perspective. For this purpose we may first recount the principal features of the Indian economy on the eve of independence and then, briefly, indicate the factors that have led the state to assume its present wide economic and social responsibilities.

India was (and continues to be) a predominantly rural economy, having a traditional agrarian structure which in significant respects and over large areas was basically feudal. A class of landlords—*zamindars, jagirdars,* and *inamdars*—with proprietory and revenue-collecting rights was interposed between the state and the cultivators; and this set-up, which covered about 40 per cent of the country, encouraged absentee landlordism and deprived the cultivator of a secure tenancy. Owner cultivation as a system was robbed of its vitality because the peasant-proprietors farming tiny plots of land

* Director General of the National Council of Applied Economic Research. The writer wishes to acknowledge the assistance he had from his colleagues, Dr. A. Vaidyanathan, Mr. P. E. Daniel, and Mr. N. Venkataraman in the preparation of this paper.

were economically very weak and were continually in debt to the usurious money-lenders. Thus both the landlord and the money-lender were in a position to exploit the cultivator and appropriate the major fruits of his labor. This scheme of things strongly discouraged investment in agriculture, for on the one hand it left the cultivator with little ability or incentive to increase the productivity of land, and on the other it nourished a rural aristocracy of landlord, trader, and money-lender whose interests were urban-centered.

Agricultural productivity, therefore, was very low, and agricultural problems were too serious to go unnoticed. But the official response to the situation was grossly inadequate. A few large irrigation works, minor (and mostly ineffective) tenancy reforms, and cheap but insignificant government loans made up the sum of state policy. There was no attempt to alter radically the organization of production in agriculture and thus increase the productivity of land; and in the absence of a radical reorganization, which could effect a substantial increase in agricultural inputs, no significant improvement of the rural economy was possible. Meanwhile, a relentless increase in the population—which rose from 248 million in 1921 to 357 million in 1951—was causing a rapid deterioration of this situation. For the bulk of the increase had to be absorbed by agriculture, and the continuous rise in the demand for land that followed led to a progressive reduction in the size of holdings and a steep increase in agricultural rents. Both of these developments further depressed agricultural productivity.

The industrial sector was too small and slow-growing to be able to relieve appreciably the pressure of population upon land. Not only the size of the industrial sector but also its structure operated as a limiting factor in this respect. Most industrial activity was of the traditional handicrafts variety, organized largely on a household basis and, as these occupations were mostly hereditary in character, they could not offer much scope for the employment of the fast-multiplying labor force in the agricultural sector. Modern industry was very limited.

It is true that a few big business houses showed remarkable enterprise and pioneered a few modern industries. With the fortunes and experience gained in commerce, these entrepreneurs ventured into industries closely related to their commercial activities. Thus in the latter half of the nineteenth century British trading interests established the jute and tea industries, and the Indian cotton merchants pioneered the cotton textile industry. After 1920 the policy of protection provided some stimulus, and a few more industries—iron and steel, sugar, paper, and matches—were developed. But these industrial beginnings did not gather momentum, and though the growth in the established industries was appreciable, it was not sufficient to spearhead an industrial revolution. Industrial development was lopsided and had no spread effect on account of lack of economic and social overheads.

For one thing the investment effort was too small to raise productivity significantly and thus push the economy out of its massive stagnation and, secondly, it was not designed to be a systematic and integrated attempt to industrialize the country. Private capital, in pursuit of quick and assured profits, was drawn into a pattern of investment dominated by consumer goods, particularly those with a foreign market, and such ancillary lines as banking, railways, and coal. There was thus no effort to realize the country's potential for balanced industrial development.

Table 1 brings out the preponderance of agriculture and the insignificance of industry in terms of income, and more so, in terms of employment. Contributing about half the national income, agriculture supports nearly 80 per cent of the population, and the large-scale underemployment that exists in spite of the use of primitive and relatively labor-intensive techniques is reflected in an exceedingly meager per capita output. This low productivity in agriculture severely limited the size of the home market and was one of the decisive factors which arrested the feeble and lopsided in-

TABLE I. *Output and Occupation Structure of the Economy, 1948-49*

	Net Domestic Output		Working Force	
	Rs. billion	*Per cent*	*Millions*	*Per cent*
Agriculture	42.5	49	100.5	72.4
Mining and manufacture	14.8	17	15.1	10.9
Tertiary activities	29.4	34	23.2	16.7
Total	86.7	100	138.8	100.0

Sources: Cabinet Secretariat, Statistical Organisation, *Estimates of National Income, 1948-49 to 1959-60* (New Delhi, 1961); Ministry of Finance, Department of Economic Affairs, *Final Report of the National Income Committee* (New Delhi, 1954).

dustrial effort. Such scanty gains as accrued from the investment in agriculture and industry were soon swallowed up by the increase in population. There was no increase in per capita income, which had remained stagnant, if it had not actually declined, over the first half of this century. A recent study[1] of long-term trends in output and income suggests that during the preceding six decades per capita agricultural production definitely fell—perhaps by a third; and while per capita income rose from Rs. 325 to Rs. 340 during the three decades 1896 to 1925, it fell sharply during the next thirty years to Rs. 280. As a result, India at the time of her independence stood at the bottom of the scale even among the low-income economies.

Although India presented a picture of stark poverty with all the essential characteristics of an underdeveloped economy, there were certain positive features, for the country was fairly advanced in other respects. There was a rather well-developed system of indigenous banking, and although the various money markets were not integrated into a single national market, each had evolved a fairly efficient complex of institutions and financial instruments. The trading classes have for long been of great importance in the economy, and commerce was well developed with a fairly advanced set of commercial practices. The country was also well endowed with natural resources. The known resources may appear poor in an international comparison on a per capita basis, but, such as they are, these resources can support a more rapid pace of industrialization than has actually taken place. Besides, the discovery of natural resources is a continuing process, and as new deposits are being uncovered from time to time, India's deficiency in certain resources may not be as great as is now imagined. Further, we inherited from the British a dependable administrative framework, an efficient machinery for revenue collection, and a wide network of railways, all important prerequisites for development. By 1945 the attitude of the British administration underwent a marked change, attributable largely to the gathering force of political compulsions within the country, and some program for the reconstruction and development of the economy was formulated. The end of foreign rule in 1947, therefore, left us with a legacy of incomplete projects and blueprints which with a few additions were strung together to form our First Five-

[1] S. J. Patel, "Long Term Changes in Output and Income in India, 1896-1960," *Indian Economic Journal*, XXXVIII (1958), 246.

Year Plan. All these features constituted a considerable potential for development, and the persistent prevalence of poverty in spite of these advantages made rapid economic development an immediate and overriding objective.

Not only the small size of the national income but also its chronic maldistribution invites attention. The acute poverty of rural and urban slums contrasts sharply with the opulence of the few. Statistically speaking, it is estimated that in urban India the top 5 per cent of households get as much as 31 per cent of the aggregate income, while the bottom 10 per cent obtain only 1.5 per cent; more than half the income accrues to about 15 per cent of the households, and the share of the remaining 85 per cent of the households is 42 per cent of the income.[2] Similar data for rural India are not at present available, but some indication of rural inequalities is provided by the distribution of land holdings. Over 74 per cent of rural households own less than 5 acres each, and their share in the total adds up to only 16.8 per cent; whereas the top 5 per cent, owning 25 acres and above each, account for 41 per cent of the total acreage owned by rural households.[3]

These glaring inequalities in income and wealth originate in part from a semi-feudal organization of agriculture; and in part they stem from the super-imposition on this structure of a small capitalist sector of commerce and industry in which there is much concentration of control. Industrialization, in particular, served to widen the gap between the urban and the rural sectors. Such a gap is not peculiar to India, and, in fact, is necessary to bring about the shift in employment and output that characterizes economic development. In India, however, this gap was specially pronounced. Another important aspect of inequality was the disparity in the economic development of different regions. Further, whole sections of the population, such as the backward tribes and scheduled castes, were far below the social and economic level of the general community. Social inequalities worsened the situation created by economic differentials, and opportunities for personal advancement were highly unequal in a social structure frozen by the caste system. Along with

[2] National Council of Applied Economic Research, "Note on Composition and Distribution of National Income" (preliminary and confidential).

[3] Ministry of Finance, Department of Economic Affairs, New Delhi, *National Sample Survey Report*, No. 10, p. 14.

poverty, illiteracy and disease were ubiquitous. When the British left India, five out of six Indians could neither read nor write, and the life-span of the average Indian was twenty-eight years.

It is in this context that we must view the leading role now played by the state in the nation's economic life. For the assumption by the government of a major role in, and over-all direction of, economic activity is the result primarily of pragmatic considerations. Ideology, important though it is, was of only secondary significance in this regard. Even the West European type of capitalism has long since passed over from a "free" system to a well regulated one, and the government in these countries has found it necessary to influence both the level of employment and the composition of the national product. Indeed, the need for state leadership in economic development was first felt in Western Europe, and state-sponsored economic growth began there. In India the need for state action was particularly compelling.

Experience had shown, as the foregoing pages have indicated, that private enterprise left to itself cannot promote a rapid rate of economic development under Indian conditions. It also becomes clear that this inability was not wholly accounted for by the fact that the state has to provide the general climate for investment in the shape of socio-economic overheads and protected markets. What is needed for rapid industrialization is massive and concerted investment in several directions simultaneously. This cannot be expected of private enterprise. For private enterprise, by its very nature, cannot secure the pattern of investment most appropriate for development as this would involve venturing into fields in which there are little or no immediate prospects for profits. Further, individual entrepreneurs cannot command sufficient resources for such capital-intensive projects as a steel plant. Therefore, the state has to enter the industrial field and provide the leadership for balanced industrialization. These considerations gave rise to the policies of an expanding public sector and of economic planning when a national government assumed power.

But the ideological ground for state intervention had been prepared much earlier. In the struggle for independence one finds the intermixture of the political, the social, and the economic. The evolution of Congress ideology had filled the goal of independence with much economic content, and Congress thinking on the subject was strongly influenced by socialist philosophy. As early as 1938 the Congress appointed a National Planning Committee which in its report, submitted after the war, outlined the policy of a public sector in large-scale organized industry. The Election Manifesto of 1945 postulated the prevention of concentration of control and economic power as a major objective. But the system envisaged was one of a mixed economy as evidenced by the Industrial Policy Resolution of 1948. These ideas are crystallized in the Constitution which, although it represents a compromise of diverse points of view, lays down the objective of a welfare state, standing for economic democracy and social equality. The Directive Principles of State Policy, enunciated in Articles 36 to 51 of the Constitution, define clearly the welfare state and visualize the economic and social pattern of life to be attained through proper planning. The Directives to the state grant that all citizens have the right to an adequate means of livelihood; that the state, within the limits of its economic capacity, should endeavor to provide adequate opportunities to work, to secure the right to education and the right to public assistance in case of unemployment, old age, sickness, or disablement. In order to achieve these objectives, the state should insure that the ownership and control of material resources in the country are best distributed for common good and that the operation of the economic system does not result in a close concentration of wealth and factors of production. In an egalitarian society all workers, agriculturists, industrialists, and others, should have the right of a living wage, decent conditions of work, and full enjoyment of leisure and social and cultural opportunities. Also, the state should, within ten years from the beginning of the Constitution, provide free and compulsory education to all children between five and fourteen years. Further, it should promote the welfare of the weaker sections of the population, especially the scheduled castes and scheduled tribes.

The Directives do not prescribe any rigid economic or social order but merely provide the guide-lines of state policy. Planning in India, it was expected, would always follow these guide-lines in order to attain the desired pattern of social life. Under this mandate Parliament adopted national planning as the major technique, and the establishment of the Planning Commission in 1950 was a natural consequence.

The functions of the Commission are to assess the nation's resources and the ways in which they may be augmented, to formulate plans for the effective utilization of these resources, to indicate the conditions necessary for the successful implementation of these plans, and to evaluate the progress achieved in their implementation. In the performance of these tasks the Commission is required to work in close consultation with the cabinets of the Central and state governments. Although the Planning Commission was thought of as an advisory body, through its close connections with the cabinet,[4] it has become the supreme policy-making body of the country. The deputy chairman and the members of the Planning Commission are often invited to the cabinet meetings whenever the development programs are discussed. No major expenditure is possible by any government department, either in the states or the Center, without the prior approval of the Planning Commission. The Planning Commission is really meant to be such an important organization, because in India planned development is essentially linked with the objective of human welfare and with the concept that the state has the moral obligation of achieving the social transition. As such, the virtual unanimity of views of the Planning Commission and the government on different policy matters is unavoidable.

Some introductory lines of the First Five-Year Plan reveal that the Planning Commission has accepted these Directives of the Constitution.

The central objective of planning in India at the present stage is to initiate a process of development which will raise living standards and open out to people new opportunities for a richer and more varied life. Economic planning has to be viewed as an integral part of a wider process aiming not merely at the development of resources in the narrow technical sense, but at the development of human faculties and the building up of an institutional framework adequate to the needs and aspirations of the people.

The emphasis in the other two plans is not far different.

In December 1954 the Parliament adopted as the main objective of planning in India the goal of a "socialistic pattern of society" wherein the values of socialism and democracy were brought together. No rigid policy was set to achieve this objective because the approach would be largely pragmatic. Though the concept of a

---

[4] The Prime Minister is the chairman of the Planning Commission. The Finance Minister and two other ministers are members.

"socialistic pattern of society" has never been defined in clear terms so far, the socialist goal has undoubtedly had a definite sense of direction. The declaration of the "Industrial Policy Resolution" of 1956 indicated the predominant role the state would be playing to achieve the goal of a socialist society. Social gain rather than private profit is to be the basic criterion for deciding the lines of development, and economic policy must be directed not only at a rapid increase in national income but also at a more equal distribution of that income and also of wealth.

It may be added that the emergence of the state as the prime agent of economic development has been facilitated in certain respects. Although India before independence was dominantly laissez faire, there was a strong paternalistic element, and this paved the way for the present assumption by the state of wide economic and social responsibilities. Further, the framework of controls exercised during World War II was fairly comprehensive, and thus the ground was prepared for the administration and acceptance of the present system of controls, many of which are continuations and extensions of wartime regulations. These features have enabled the state to discharge its new socio-economic functions with greater efficiency and less friction.

Some preliminary indications may now be given of the importance of state activity and its evolution over time.

A first figure in this connection is the proportion of national income that is taken by the state through taxation. The proportion of tax revenue to national income has risen from 6.9 per cent in 1948-49 to about 8.9 per cent in 1960-61. Another useful measure is the share of government in total investment in the economy; this rose from 46.4 per cent during the First Plan period (1951-56) to 54.1 per cent over the period of the Second Plan (1956-61). Finally, we may consider the share of government in the generation of national income, which gives an over-all picture of the quantitative importance of state activities. The net output of state enterprises and government administration expressed as a proportion of net domestic product rose from 7.4 per cent in 1948-49 to about 10.4 per cent in 1959-60; in absolute terms the rise was from Rs. 6.4 billion in 1948-49 to Rs. 13.4 billion in 1959-60. These figures provide some idea of the magnitude of the new role of the state. The nature of state intervention, the points at which controls are exercised, and their effect upon the direction and pace at which the economy is changing will be discussed in the following sections. Before entering into a more detailed examination, however, it is necessary to outline briefly the approach that is being adopted.

A description of the Indian economic system is complicated by the fact that India is in the process of development from a traditional economic organization to an industrialized economy with the capacity for self-sustained growth. Rapid changes are taking place in the economic system both as cause and effect of this transition; old institutions and relationships are being modified and new ones are coming up. The first part of this analysis, therefore, describes the present structure in some detail in order to bring out the special features and causes of underdevelopment. With this as the background, the future system outlined by the planning authorities and the measures adopted to achieve the transition will be discussed. In the discussion of these two aspects of the present economic system, the economy will be divided into its two principal sectors. There is a big gulf between the agricultural system and the industrial system —agriculture is largely carried on through relatively primitive techniques whereas factories generally employ "continuous process" and often advanced techniques. The differences resulting from this are so pronounced that a meaningful study must adopt a sectoral approach. Further, as indicated earlier, social considerations exercise a dominant influence and the Constitution calls for economic policies with a social objective. This important element of economic policy, therefore, is discussed separately. Finally, there will be some attempt to view the economy and economic policy as a whole. In this concluding synthesis the important features of government intervention are brought together in order to assess their impact on the economic system.

AGRICULTURE

i

Even in the highly developed economies the role of the state in the agricultural sector has been positive and significant. State intervention was not only protective but aimed at developing agriculture by substantial public investments in research and development. In a country like India which had inherited, on independence, a system of agricultural production which suffered from serious institutional and structural weaknesses, the need for state action was paramount. It is not surprising, therefore, that government resorted to a series of land reforms designed to remove impediments to agricultural production and efficiency, to create conditions for evolving an agrarian economy with higher levels of efficiency and productivity. Both aspects of government actions are designed to serve the common purposes of raising agricultural production from its present lowest levels of efficiency and to provide incentives to the farmer to improve agricultural productivity.

The most important of these is the abolition of *zamindari*—a system of land ownership which prevailed in over 40 per cent of the country. The enactment of laws in this direction and the requisition of the areas controlled by *zamindars*, *jagirdars*, and *inamdars* progressed rapidly during the First Five-Year Plan, and by the end of the Second Plan this feudal setup had been dismantled. As a result of this reform over 20 million tenants have been brought into a direct relationship with the state, which has also acquired considerable forest and waste lands. Much remains to be done, however, in the payment of compensation, survey and settlement of tenants, and the preparation of records of rights.

While *zamindari* abolition broke up the very large estates, ownership of land continued to be concentrated in the hands of a relatively small number of people. A redistribution of land is considered by the government to be essential both for bringing about greater equality and to promote the incentive for the small cultivators and landless workers. The idea of a ceiling on land ownership has been discussed for a long time, but it was only recently that the idea had been given concrete legislative form. Although these measures have aroused intense controversy, they are not likely to make any drastic change immediately in the pattern of land distribution. For the long lag between the time when the principle of ceilings was accepted and its implementation has provided ample time for the large holdings to be transferred or divided. Moreover, the level of ceilings has been rather high; hence the surplus available for redistribution is only marginal.

Legislation providing security of tenure has been enacted in a number of states in order to prevent eviction of tenants and to insure that resumption of land for owner cultivation takes place only in genuine cases and does not entirely deprive the tenant of land. In this connection the Planning Commission recommended that land owners having more than a "basic holding" (defined as one-third of the family holding) may resume land only after allowing for a prescribed minimum area for the tenant and, further, that the state government should provide land to these tenants who are rendered landless as a result of resumption by the owners. A period of five years has been fixed by the Planning Commission, after which no resumption will be allowed. The actual provision of the law varies from state to state; in some no resumption is permitted, in certain others resumption is permitted up to the level of the prescribed ceiling on land holdings, while a third category of states has avoided these extremes and assured the tenant a certain minimum area. Ultimately, ownership rights are to be conferred on tenants working non-resumable land, and this process has already begun. Apart from insecurity of tenure, the tenant was also exploited through exorbitant rents, the customary rates often being half the produce and sometimes even more. The Planning Commission recommended that rents should not exceed one-fourth of the produce, and a number of states have prescribed a legal maximum for rent accordingly.

"Thus, programmes for abolishing intermediary tenures, giving security to tenants and bringing tenants into direct relationship with the state with a view to conferring ownership upon them are steps which lead to the establishment of an agrarian economy based predominantly on peasant ownership."[5] In the short run these legislations may be detrimental to production.

The importance of the community development movement and the introduction of co-operatives in agriculture should be evaluated from this angle. The community development movement was launched in 1952 for assisting the 65 million families in the countryside in their efforts to bring about a substantial improvement in all aspects of life. The aim is to reorganize the village life in such a way as to meet the demands of scientific agriculture on the largest scale possible, of course, implying thereupon certain important changes in attitudes and outlook on life as a whole. The basic considerations here are not purely economic. Non-material values and social gains are equally important. "The movement stands for

[5] Planning Commission, *Second Five Year Plan* (New Delhi, 1956), p. 179.

human values. The aim is to make men and women with a sense of both individual and joint responsibility so that they may rise individually to a full personal life and collectively to a full social life."[6]

In spite of these measures the pattern of landholding remains basically unchanged. In any case the small farms will continue to be a dominant feature of Indian agriculture. In this context the question of appropriate organizational devices by which the limitation of small size may be overcome assumes great importance. One of the important measures in this direction is the consolidation of landholdings. Land consolidation intended to create compact holdings has made rapid enough progress. During the last decade the program has covered 23 million acres, or 7.2 per cent of the crop area, and by the end of the Third Plan, 66 million acres, or only 20.8 per cent of the area, would be covered. There are, however, differences concerning the proper form of agrarian organization whereby the efficiency of production could be insured. One view is that proliferation of small holdings is the real cause of inefficiency, and unless the size of the farm is increased through co-operative or joint farming, the maximum efficiency cannot be achieved. However, there is obviously much resistance on the part of the peasants to such arrangements, so that as a matter of necessity the program for encouraging co-operative and joint farming has to be greatly slackened though not necessarily abandoned. In practice the Third Plan only aims at setting up 300 to 400 such farms on an experimental basis.

Though co-operative farming may not be acceptable to the vast majority of peasants, the need for Service Co-operatives, that is, co-operatives for the supply of credit, seeds, and fertilizers, and the marketing of agricultural produce is generally recognized, as these constitute an important means of helping the farmers to secure fertilizers, seed, and finance at reasonable terms and to enable them to dispose of the produce at more favorable prices.

The credit movement has expanded at a phenomenal rate in recent years. In 1951 the total value of medium- and short-term co-operative credit was of the order of Rs. 229 million. By 1961 the outstandings of the primary co-operatives had increased to Rs. 2,000 million, and the proportion of the credit requirements of farmers that is met by co-operative organizations increased from 3 per

[6] V. T. Krishnamachari, *Planning in India* (Calcutta, 1961), p. 60.

cent in 1951 to an estimated 10 per cent in 1959-60. The provision of medium- and short-term credit is planned to be increased to Rs. 5,290 million by 1965-66. In the matter of long-term credit also considerable progress has been registered by co-operatives; the amount of loans outstanding increased from Rs. 130 million to Rs. 340 million over the years 1956 to 1961 and is expected to reach the figure of Rs. 150 crores* in 1965-66. The progress in co-operative marketing is not so impressive. The total value of sales[7] by farming units rose from Rs. 24.5 crores in 1956-57 to Rs. 46.6 crores in 1959-60 but still accounts for less than 2 per cent of total farm produce marketed in the country.

ii

The basic problem of Indian agriculture is its backwardness and low productivity. The available resources of cultivable land are so meager in relation to population and the per-acre yields are so poor that production is barely sufficient to meet even the present low standards of domestic consumption.

With a population of 438 million, India has a total crop area of 360 million acres or 0.8 acre per capita. By comparison, the per-capita availability of arable land for the world as a whole works out to two acres. The limitations imposed by shortage of arable land can no doubt be overcome by achieving high yields. But Indian yields per hectare of practically all major crops are among the lowest in the world.

At present (1959-60) India produces nearly 72 million tons of food grains, 7.6 million tons of sugar cane,[8] 6.35 million tons of oil seeds, 8.5 million bales of cotton and jute, 7.25 million pounds of tea, and 48,000 tons of coffee. There is a fairly large export trade in plantation crops, jute and to a small extent cotton and oil seeds, but in respect of food the country has an average annual deficit of 2 to 3 million tons. The net supply of food and clothing per head of population in India compares very unfavorably both in quality and quantity with that in other countries.

* One "crore" equals ten millions. The rupee is equal to 21 cents at the official rate of exchange.

[7] The Planning Commission estimates the agricultural business conducted by marketing societies at Rs. 200 crores in 1960-61.

[8] In terms of *Gur*.

The root cause of low productivity is technological backwardness. The lack of irrigation facilities, the meager application of fertilizers and pesticides, and the primitive nature of equipment used are indicative of the backward state of the agricultural practices in the country.

In 1958-59, India consumed artificial fertilizers containing 257,-000 tons of nitrogen, 39,000 tons of phosphoric acid, and 13,000 tons of potash. Japan, with a total crop area of 5 million hectares, compared to 160 million hectares in India, consumes more fertilizers. The United States, where crop area is 188 million hectares, uses 10 times as much nitrogen, 80 times as much P_2O_5, and more than a hundred times as much potash as India. No doubt large quantities of organic manures are applied to the soil; but on the whole it is believed that the manures and fertilizers applied by farmers are barely sufficient to replace the nutrients absorbed by the crops.

Rainfall varies from region to region and from year to year; over large tracts it is insufficient—about 26 per cent of the country receives less than thirty inches of rain—and in general the monsoon is notoriously uncertain. The availability of irrigation facilities to insure an adequate and timely supply of water has thus a vital bearing on the productivity of land. Although the water resources are quite large—the exploitable surface resources alone are estimated to be sufficient to irrigate 175 million acres, or 54 per cent of the crop area—only a small fraction has been harnessed. The area under irrigation is about 70 million acres, which constitutes 22 per cent of the net cropped area.

In other respects also the techniques of cultivation prevailing in India are deficient; most of the draft force is obtained from bullocks and buffaloes; the use of mechanical power is negligible. Crop rotations, methods of irrigation, and such other details of cultivation practices have congealed into a pattern sanctioned by tradition. While they perhaps represent the best adaptation of methods to the prevailing environment possible with the knowledge of a by-gone age, modern technology has opened up vast new vistas of development which have barely touched Indian agriculture.

Ignorance on the part of the farmer is doubtless a major handicap to technological progress, but no less important is the predominance of small units of cultivation. The cultivated area is distributed over some 66 million households, giving on the average 4.72

acres per household. Actually, about 70 per cent of the cultivating families have less than this average, which is itself very small in comparison with that of more advanced countries. The fact that even these small holdings are not in compact blocks but in numerous scattered plots further lowers their productive efficiency.

Not only are small holdings unsuited to the effective application of several modern techniques, but they reduce the capacity and the incentive for farmers to adopt even those improvements which can be introduced with profit. Changes in crop pattern and cultivation methods often require resources and involve risks beyond the capacity of peasants living precariously on the margin of subsistence. The average income of the farmer is hardly sufficient to meet the costs of cultivation and the basic needs of his family. He is so close to the margin of subsistence that a drought or a fall in agricultural prices is apt to upset his budget seriously. Moreover, in the absence of proper organization, the peasants' bargaining power both in securing productive resources and in disposing of the produce is very weak.

Even the modest surplus over the essential requirements for seed and for food in the family has to be disposed of soon after the harvest, when prices are relatively low. Ignorance of conditions over the wider market and the lack of finances necessary for holding stocks place the small farmer at a considerable disadvantage in relation to the trader, who often is also his creditor.

Farmers' Capacity to Borrow. Given his meager income, the farmer's capacity to borrow is also limited. Much of his debt is incurred to meet consumption needs, rather than to augment his productive capacity. And since he has to get practically all his needs from the money-lender or trader, the terms are also stiff. According to a recent survey, about 75 per cent of the borrowings of cultivators was from money-lenders or landlords, the proportion for the small cultivators being substantially higher. The rate of interest on state loans varies between 2½ and 8 per cent, and co-operatives charge between 6¼ and 12½ per cent. Money-lenders, on the other hand, seldom levy less than 12 per cent, and rates as high as 50 per cent are not uncommon.

A rising productivity of land is absolutely essential to meet the progressively increasing requirements for food and raw materials for domestic consumption as well as exports. It is estimated that at current rates of population growth, if per capita income were to be raised by about 65 per cent over the next 15 years, the country would need to increase its food-grains output to 136.10 million tons by 1975-76 (or about 79 per cent above the 1960-61 level), oil seeds by 12.14 million tons (71 per cent), and cotton by 9.53 million bales (about 86 per cent).[9] Considerable changes in the pattern of food production would be necessary to rectify the existing imbalances in the diet. The outputs of sugar, oilseeds, and fibers would have to be increased even more in order to provide for exports.

Expansion of agricultural output is also important because it has a direct bearing on the living standards of the rural population. At present, owing to excessive pressure of population on land, the low level of yields, and the weak bargaining power of the farmers, the standard of living in rural areas is below the national average, which is itself pitifully inadequate. In 1952-53 the per capita income in rural areas was estimated at Rs. 225 compared to the national average of Rs. 267 and to Rs. 468 in the urban areas. A rough notion of the relative position of people in rural and urban areas in respect of certain essential items of consumption may be seen from Table 2. If, as is expected, the entire natural increase in population will hereafter be supported by industries and tertiary activities, the expansion in farm output of the order visualized would roughly

TABLE 2. *Consumer Expenditures in Rural and Urban Areas*

Items	Per person (in Rs. per month)		Per cent of total expenditure	
	Rural	Urban	Rural	Urban
Food grains	8.70	6.14	40.57	20.66
Milk and milk products	1.35	2.46	6.30	8.27
All food items	13.54	14.81	63.15	49.83
Clothing	1.54	2.44	7.18	8.21
Fuel and lights	1.16	1.62	5.41	5.45
All non-food items	7.90	14.91	36.85	50.17
Total (all items)	21.44	29.72	100.00	100.00

Source: Department of Economic Affairs, *National Sample Survey Report* No.14 (Fourth Round) (New Delhi, 1952), p. 8 adapted.

[9] National Council of Applied Economic Research, *Long-term Supply of and Demand for Selected Agricultural Products in India* (to be published shortly).

double the per capita income of the agricultural population over 1955-56 levels.

An increase in total agricultural output and income alone is not sufficient. It is also necessary, in the interests of equity and of political stability if not also as an incentive to greater effort, to insure a more even distribution of income. Some notion of the degree of inequality is given by the fact that in 1958-59 the top 10 per cent of rural households accounted for more than a quarter of the total expenditure by such households, whereas the share of the bottom 10 per cent was only 3.24 per cent.

There are basically two aspects to rural inequalities. In part they arise from the unequal distribution of land, to which reference has been made earlier. But in considerable part they also stem from the relentless pressure of population increase on land which has created a large labor surplus. This is reflected in both inefficient employment of manpower and extensive underemployment. It is difficult to determine precisely the volume of underemployment; it would differ according to the definition that is used. One approach is to estimate underemployment with reference to certain norms of working hours per day, but this presents several difficulties in practice. A second criterion is the extent of additional work that an individual is willing to take up under the prevailing rates and other terms of employment. This concept has been adopted in recent investigations of the National Sample Survey, and underemployment has been reckoned to be of the order of 15-18 million.

The incidence of underemployment falls most heavily on the class of landless laborers and those who own such small pieces of land that their chief means of livelihood is wage labor. It is these sections which bear the brunt of the burden of rural poverty. Perhaps it would be socially more meaningful to have some notion of the large numbers whose actual earnings are less than any reasonable minimum by modern standards. According to the data presented by the National Sample Survey in another round, the average monthly per capita expenditure on consumer items in the rural areas is Rs. 22.84, and it is significant that for about a fourth of the rural population the individual consumption is less than half this figure. These inequalities in consumer expenditure reflect a wider inequality in income distribution, for it is well known that households at the bottom of the income scale generally live on a deficit budget while those at the top have some savings.

iii

The extension of irrigation facilities, soil conservation programs, establishment of fertilizer factories, distribution of improved strains of seed, and the organization of a National Extension Service to educate the farmers in improved techniques are the most important steps taken by the government to increase the productive capacity of land.

During the last decade about Rs. 15,510 million has been spent on these programs, which represents 23.6 per cent of the total outlay on development projects under the auspices of the state. During the Third Plan period it is proposed to spend an additional Rs. 17,508 million, or 23.3 per cent of total public sector outlay, on agricultural development.

As a result of these investments, an additional irrigated area of 19.5 million acres has been created; soil conservation measures have been adopted over 2.7 million acres. New land reclaimed for cultivation is 3.9 million acres, of which 19.8 per cent is under food grains; the indigenous production of fertilizer has risen from virtually nothing to 230,000 tons of nitrogenous fertilizer and 70,000 tons of P_2O_5 by 1961. About 67 per cent of the villages are now covered by the National Extension Service[10] and the Community Development Programme. The facilities for research in problems of agricultural development have been greatly increased and strengthened.

The facilities created by the government have, however, not been uniformly effective. For instance, the use of fertilizers has grown with such unexpected rapidity that the domestic production has been found quite insufficient to meet the requirements. Large quantities have to be imported. The experience in respect of irrigation is strikingly different: a large portion of the irrigation potential created during the past decade remains unutilized. Thus, while the irrigation (major and medium works) potential has increased by 13.2 million acres by 1960-61, the actual irrigated area has risen by only 10 million acres. The reasons for the underutilization are

[10] National Extension Service is the continuation on a more concentrated scale of the services provided by Community Development programs in a limited area.

numerous; in part, it is the result of faulty planning of the main project but equally important are the difficulties experienced in getting farmers to construct fields channels and, having done that, to use the water. Further important limitations are presented by the deficiencies in the technical knowledge of the farmer, his meager resources, and perhaps also the reaction on the part of the farmers to the water rates and betterment levies. Similarly, the effectiveness of the extension services has been much less than hoped for because of the diffusion of effort both over functions and the area of operation.

Besides investments to increase the productive capacity of agriculture, as seen earlier, the state is trying to put through a wide variety of measures designed to eliminate the vestiges of exploitation of the small farmers, landless laborers, and other poorer segments of the rural society and to bring about a more equitable distribution of land.

In practice, however, these tenancy reforms have proved largely ineffective. Laws providing for security of tenure have in considerable measure been defeated by large-scale eviction under the guise of "voluntary surrender" by the tenants. Realizing this loophole, the Planning Commission recommended in the Second Plan that all transfers should be registered with revenue officers, but legislative and administrative action in this direction has fallen far short of this recommendation. In the matter of rent regulation also legislation has been evaded, and customary rates of rent persist owing to the inadequate enforcement of the law. Consequently, even the Planning Commission conceded that over the last decade "the impact of tenancy legislation on the welfare of tenants has been in practice less than was hoped for."[11]

Another section of the rural population which is economically very weak is agricultural labor, but the effect of government programs to improve its condition is extremely limited. There has been little progress in the fixation of minimum wages and still less in the matter of enforcing them. Under the community development schemes some efforts have been made to mobilize local manpower for local projects, but the success of these schemes in bringing forth the initiative and participation of the people is hardly impressive. While the total volume of work on the farms has increased with

[11] Planning Commission, *Third Five Year Plan* (New Delhi, 1961), p. 224.

the expansion of agricultural production, the growth of population has multiplied the numbers demanding work. It is, however, hard to say whether on balance the conditions of agricultural laborers have improved at all during the last decade. Such evidence as is available suggests that their economic position has worsened, if not absolutely at least in relation to the position of other classes.

Agricultural development programs have greatly increased the supply of water, fertilizer, improved seeds, and other ingredients of increased productivity, while the extension services have taught the farmer new and better methods of agriculture. The process of education is slow. Meanwhile, in order to insure the effective application of these physical inputs and the new knowledge, the farmer must be offered sufficient incentives. Organizational reforms have to a rather limited extent given him a stake in the success of the business of agriculture, and the expanding domestic market offers an opportunity to increase his income. In this connection, the return which the farmer gets for his efforts assumes importance, and this is determined both by his bargaining power in relation to the trader (who is also often his creditor), the degree of stability of agricultural prices, and their relation to the prices of manufactures.

Recent improvements in the supply of agricultural credit and the extension of co-operative marketing facilities have tended to reduce the disproportionately large share of the price of agricultural commodities hitherto appropriated by the trader. But agricultural prices have fluctuated considerably during the decade 1951-61; the agricultural price level declined over the major part of the First Plan period (1951-56), particularly in the year 1953-54, whereas the next five years were characterized by a persistent rise. In the interests of increased production it is obvious that the farmers must be protected against any sharp fall in prices. Price support is in fact provided by the state in the case of certain commercial crops, particularly sugar cane and cotton, but the government did not take timely action in the case of the decline in food grain prices referred to above. On the other hand agricultural prices cannot be permitted to rise excessively, both from the viewpoint of the interests of the consumer and in order to minimize inflationary pressures.

A policy of price stabilization designed to keep fluctuations within defined minimum and maximum limits is, therefore, essential. Some attempt has been made to even out fluctuations in the price of food grains through state trading, and, although the program of purchase of domestic production to build up stocks ran into several difficulties, the large-scale import of United States food grains under Public Law 480 helped to stabilize prices towards the end of the Second Plan. It is now accepted that a definite policy of open market operations, whereby the government undertakes to buy food grains when prices fall and sell when they tend to rise, is necessary to eliminate temporal and regional fluctuations. Accordingly, buffer stocks are being built up, and while at present these depend heavily on imports it is hoped that in future the major reliance will be on domestic production.

Two further aspects of price policy require serious consideration. While the over-all level of agricultural prices is of great importance, the relationship between the various prices in the agricultural price structure has a special significance at the present stage in our economic development when it is not only an increase in the total agricultural output that is required but also a change in the composition of that output. However, sufficient attention has not been given to the question of relative prices. Nor has much thought been bestowed upon the price relationship between agricultural products on the one hand and manufactured commodities on the other. This aspect of price policy is of special interest, for it has a direct bearing on the real resources provided by agriculture for industrial expansion.

THE INDUSTRIAL SECTOR

The need for rapid industrialization in India is now well recognized. Apart from the economic context of chronic backwardness, it has been reinforced by the political implications of an increasing volume of urban unemployment and rural underemployment. However, it is useful to begin a discussion of the industrial sector with some consideration of the role of industrialization in economic development. This will clarify the relationship between industrial and economic growth and thus help towards an appreciation of the basic industrial problem and the strategy evolved for its solution.

Operating at a low level of productivity, the bulk of the Indian population has been engaged in producing food, the raw materials required for a minimum of clothing and housing, and a few export crops for the satisfaction of basic import needs. On the demand side the low level of real incomes generated a low demand for manufactures and hence for workers in industry. Starting from this low-level equilibrium, economic growth requires a decline in the proportionate contribution of agriculture to economic welfare, while the combined contribution, both in absolute and relative terms, of industry and other sectors must increase. Thus it is not only an increase in the national income but also a change in the composition of that income that is required. This change in income composition has its counterpart in a change in the employment structure, and as development proceeds there is a shift in employment from agriculture to industry which is particularly pronounced in the initial stages. Economic growth, then, requires an increase in the absolute and relative contribution of industry to the national income and an increase in the proportion of the working force engaged in industries; and in this sense economic growth may be identified with industrialization.

However, this identity is limited. It may be more useful to think of the two as distinct processes with a complex inter-relationship, for industrialization may be viewed as both a cause and a result of economic development. The relationship is more significant than the identity because it brings out not only the results that may be expected of industrialization but also the preconditions of the process and the causal interactions involved and thus provides the basis for policy.

A rapid increase in per capita real income requires a corresponding increase in productivity, which, in agriculture as well as in industry, calls for an increase in the use of manufactured producer goods such as machine tools, cement, and fertilizer. It is true that in an economy where 70-80 per cent of the population are employed in agriculture, the task of increasing productivity is mainly one of increasing agricultural productivity, and this cannot assume a capital-intensive form owing to the abundance of labor. But even here there must be an increase in the supply of such industrial products as fertilizer and improved steel implements. Further, a concomitant expansion of other forms of activity—construction and transport, for example —must take place, and this again requires an expansion of the industrial sector. Thus economic development requires a rapid growth of industries. On the other hand, an increase in incomes leads to a more than proportionate enlargement of the market for industrial goods, for as income rises there is a change in the expenditure pattern, the demand for industrial commodities rising more rapidly than that for primary products. In this way economic development offers a powerful stimulus to industrial expansion. Moreover, the process of development also increases the productive capacity of an economy through a general improvement in technical skills and the building up of an infrastructure. With increased productive ability and expanded markets the rise of industries is virtually assured.

Thus industrialization is a major causal factor in the process of growth and is inevitable in a developing country. But the pace and strategy of industrialization ultimately depend upon the structure of the economy. In this regard foreign trade is a major factor making for modifications. There are plantations and mineral economies which, although they are not really industrialized, enjoy relatively high income levels through a large volume of foreign trade. It is theoretically possible for an economy to employ 70-80 per cent of its population in agriculture and yet have a per capita income of $1,000. But the surplus of primary products and the requirement for industrial imports will be very large at such high levels of productivity and income, and it is estimated that the required volume of foreign trade (exports plus imports) must roughly equal the gross national product.[12] Such an economy would be severely exposed to fluctuations in the world market and would be unstable in the extreme. In practice it is not possible for a country to have such a large volume of international trade. Foreign trade, therefore, cannot significantly affect the ultimate shift in the disposition of the working force and, to a lesser extent, the composition of the national product that must occur as an economy moves on to an advanced stage of development. On the other hand, a limited volume of foreign trade precludes the possibility of attaining high income and productivity levels through the large-scale import of manufactured producer and consumer goods. In India the need for rapid industrialization is heavily underlined by the fact that the total volume of foreign trade is only about 12 per cent of the national income and the scope for an expansion of exports is marginal.

[12] United Nations, *Economic Bulletin for Asia and the Far East*, IX, No. 3 (1958), p. 5.

Structure

The organization of industrial activity in India may be classified into three groups. There is a sector of large-scale enterprises which employs modern technology; this sector covers several industries. Cotton and jute, textiles, sugar, paper, matches, cement, and iron and steel were all fairly well established modern industries by the first half of this century; while heavy chemicals, production of machinery and electrical equipment, and other capital goods are still in their infancy. Apart from being capital-intensive, this sector is also well integrated, and the organization for finance, marketing, and the procurement of supplies is modern and efficient. In some of these industries there is also a large number of small enterprises. Small enterprises in these and other industries fall into two categories. There is a limited sector of small-scale industrial units which use modern techniques to produce modern goods, both finished commodities and components in such industries as bicycles, sewing machines, soap, hosiery, flour milling, and leather manufactures. With the encouragement and special assistance of the government in finance, marketing, and other services, this sector has been growing fast, particularly in the light engineering field, in recent years.

The major part of manufacturing activity, however, is to be found in the small-scale sector of traditional handicrafts, which covers a wide field of processing activities, including handloom cloth and hand-pounded rice. Consisting of a vast number of small, mostly cottage, enterprises, organized largely on a family basis and spread out all over the country, this sector is totally unorganized. The techniques used and the commodities produced go back to the era before the Industrial Revolution, and the methods of organization and finance are survivals of the same age. Thus the modern and traditional sectors stand in striking contrast to each other and are quite unrelated. The extent of the latter illustrates the peripheral impact of modern industry on the economy as a whole and the absence of any widespread technological revolution.

Small-scale establishments dominate the pattern of manufacturing activity. As may be seen from Table 3, such establishments are far more important than large-scale enterprises in the structure of industrial employment. At present, organized factories and mines employ some four million persons and contribute about 8 per cent

TABLE 3. *Employment Structure in Manufacturing Industries*

Description	Definition (number employed in each establishment)	Average Daily Employment in 1956 (in millions)
1. Household enterprises and small workshops	Less than 10	11.1
2. Small factories	10- 49	1.2
3. Medium factories	50-499	1.0
4. Large factories	500 and more	1.7
Total		15.0

Source: P. N. Dhar and H. F. Lydall, *The Role of Small Enterprises in Indian Economic Development* (Bombay, 1961), p. 8.

of the national income, whereas small-scale enterprises contributing about the same proportion of the national income employ thrice as many persons.

From the predominance of small-scale establishments in the structure of industrial employment it may be inferred that the investment per worker in India is very small. Some idea of just how low it is when compared with an advanced economy is provided by certain figures presented in the United Nations *Bulletin on Industrialization and Productivity*, which are reproduced in Table 4. As a consequence, the over-all productivity of industrial labor is extremely low. But even in the sector of large-scale modern industry, productivity in certain Indian industries compares poorly with that in other countries. Labor productivity in the cotton textile industry, for instance, is lower in India than in Japan,[13] and an Indian mill

TABLE 4. *Capital Per Person Employed*
(in thousands of dollars at 1950 prices)

Industry	United States	India
Bread and bakery products	5.0	3.5
Flour and grist mill products	39.1	5.6
Cotton yarn and cloth	8.7	1.8
Iron and steel	32.1	5.7
Sugar refineries	26.8	2.6
Wood pulp, paper and paper products	10.2	6.6

Source: United Nations, *Bulletin on Industrialization and Productivity*, No. 1 (1958).

[13] George Rossen, *Industrial Change in India* (Bombay, 1959).

employs almost thrice as large a labor force as a Japanese mill of the same size.[14] In the small-scale sector the widespread adoption of even relatively minor improvements of technique is held up by the shortage of credit and the technological backwardness of the country.

It is sometimes considered that the stage of industrialization which an economy has achieved may be judged by the ratio between the output of the consumer-goods and producer-goods industries, for in an advanced stage the two are roughly equal. From this point of view it is clear that India is still in the initial stages of industrial growth.

The capacity to produce capital goods is very limited, and consumer-goods industries predominate in the structure of manufacturing production. Modern industry, drawing its major impetus from the policy of protection adopted by the British government, was largely confined to those goods in the production of which the country offered exceptional advantages. And with the exception of steel these fell chiefly in the sphere of consumption goods. The extent of the imbalance is indicated by Table 5. It will be seen that the ratio of consumer-good output to producer-good output was approximately 2:1 in 1954. Food and textiles accounted for about 62 per cent of the value added in manufacture, the share of textiles alone being about 50 per cent. Metallurgical and engineering industries provided only 23 per cent of manufacturing output, as compared with over 33 per cent in Japan and about 40 per cent in the United States. This structure of production reflects the pattern of investment that prevailed under a system of laissez-faire private enterprise. During the British period foreign capital went into the export industries and railways and coal, while domestic capital was, with a few exceptions, generally "shy" and content to follow into fields pioneered by the British. Thus the development of chemical, metallurgical, and engineering industries was neglected.

Another striking feature is the heavy concentration of modern industries in a limited area, principally in and around the chief ports of Bombay, Calcutta, and Madras and a few inland centers such as Ahmedabad and Coimbatore. One of the chief objectives of early railway development was to connect the major ports with the in-

---

[14] M. Mangal Das, "The Japanese Cotton Textile Industry," *The Textile Digest*, XIV, No. 3, 12 (quoted in Rossen's *Industrial Change in India*).

TABLE 5. *Percentage Shares in Value Added by Manufacturing Industries*

Industry	India (1954)	Japan (1955)
A. *Consumer goods*		
Food, beverages, tobacco	11.0	11.7
Textiles	50.7	16.2
Leather, rubber, wood products	2.7	18.5
Total consumer goods	64.4	46.4
B. *Producer goods*		
Chemical and non-metallic minerals	12.5	19.0
Metals	13.3	15.6
Machinery	9.8	19.0
Total producer goods	35.6	53.6
Total A + B	100.0	100.0

Source: United Nations, *Economic Bulletin for Asia and the Far East,* IX, No. 3 (1958) 10, Table 4.

terior areas producing raw materials. These ports became the major commercial centers, and when a few leading business houses turned from commerce to industry, they offered an economic and convenient location. The localization of industries in a few areas had, therefore, historical origins, but it was later intensified by the rise of external economies, which resulted in a general tendency for new industrial units, both large-scale and small-scale, to cluster around these major centers. Thus in 1939 Bengal and Bombay employed 52 per cent of the industrial working force in the country and consumed 69 per cent of the power supplied to industries. Subsequently there arose certain factors which favored a dispersion of industries. With the rapid increase in the demand for land and labor in the early centers, there was a sharp rise in rents and wages. As these centers became less attractive, the further development of railways and hydroelectric power favored certain inland regions.

The development of business ability and capital outside the port-centers of commerce was another vital factor leading to the rise of new centers of industrial activity. Although these "deglomerating" factors have been in operation for some time, the resulting geographical spread of industries is very limited, and the early centers continue to dominate the locational pattern, as shown in Table 6. In 1958, more than half (53.73 per cent) of the industrial workers in the country were employed in Bombay and Bengal, which together accounted for 52.5 per cent of the industrial consumption of power.

While the existence of external economies justifies some concentration, there can be no doubt that such heavy concentration as we have had has retarded the progress of the country as a whole. For it cannot be expected that industrial growth confined to a few localities would automatically permeate the rest of the economy; indeed it has been argued that the industrialization of an area attracts capital and skills from neighboring regions, leading to their further impoverishment.[15] However, it is clear that the localization

TABLE 6. *Percentage Share of the States in All-India Factory Employment and Industrial Consumption of Power, 1958*

States	Employment	Electricity Consumption
Bombay	32.70	29.4
West Bengal	21.03	23.1
Madras	10.00	8.7
Uttar Pradesh	8.52	4.9
Andhra Pradesh	6.81	2.0
Mysore	N.A.	9.3
Bihar	5.61	9.3
Madhya Pradesh	4.94	1.7
Punjab	3.19	2.2
Assam	2.30	Neg.
Delhi	1.81	1.9
Rajasthan	1.62	.2
Orissa	.80	1.4
Kerala	.52	5.9
Andaman, Nicobar Islands	.06	N.A.
Tripura	.06	N.A.
Himachal Pradesh	.03	Neg.
Total	100.00	100.0

Sources: Ministry of Labour and Employment, Labour Bureau, *Labour Yearbook 1959* (Simla, 1960); Directorate of Industrial Statistics, *13th Annual Report of Census of Indian Manufactures*, 1958 (Calcutta, 1960).
Note: Figures for Mysore and Kashmir not available; for Manipur, negligible.

[15] Gunnar Myrdal, *Economic Theory and Underdeveloped Regions* (London, 1957).

of industrial development in India has left large regions of the country practically unaffected by the forces of industrialization.

Arising fundamentally from the scarcity of entrepreneurial talent in the country, there has emerged a considerable degree of concentration of control in the large-scale sector of modern industry. This has been largely achieved through the managing agency system— a somewhat unique institution peculiar to India. In the conditions of transport and communications that prevailed in the nineteenth century, business enterprises incorporated in the United Kingdom found it difficult to manage their industrial enterprises in India and hence appointed local British firms as their agents to manage their undertakings on a commission basis. These managing agents soon extended the sphere of their activities to cover the three vital functions of promotion, finance, and management, and the facilities which the institutions offered for the spread of scarce entrepreneurial ability and risk capital over a wide area of industrial activity led to its adoption also by the Indian business houses. Thus modern industry in India was in large measure pioneered and run by a few managing agency houses. While the majority of managing agencies control only one company each, there is an important group of large managing agency houses, most of which manage several companies.

A measure of the concentration of control in the hands of managing agencies in five important industries can be studied from Table 7. The proportions of industry totals in respect of paid-up capital, net fixed assets, and total assets controlled by the three largest managing agencies are used as indicators. These figures are suggestive rather than accurate because the analysis is confined to a part—although a significant part—of each industry; if the coverage were

TABLE 7. *Index of Oligopoly, 1956: Per Cent Controlled by Managing Agencies*

Industry	Paid-up capital	Net fixed assets	Total assets
Cotton textiles	14.7	19.0	16.3
Jute	27.0	31.7	28.3
Tea	25.5	18.9	25.4
Sugar	21.0	18.5	20.7

Source: National Council of Applied Economic Research, *The Managing Agency System* (Bombay, 1959), p. 111, Table 2 (adapted).

complete, the relevant proportions would be smaller. Particularly in view of this qualification it would appear that the degree of concentration, while significant, is not dangerously high in terms of oligopolistic control.

None of the established industries, with the exception of cement and possibly paper, shows a marked concentration in this respect. In the case of the cement industry approximately half the productive capacity has for some time been accounted for by a single enterprise. But in this industry (as in certain others) the price is determined by the Tariff Commission; and it is interesting to note that the existence of this giant company, through its operational economies, has tended rather to *lower* the price of cement. A similar situation prevailing in the paper industry was irksome enough to move many of the smaller units to request the Tariff Commission to exclude the largest company—Titaghur Paper Mills—in its estimation of the average cost of the industry. In order to find a monopolistic or oligopolistic structure one has to turn to the new industries. Some indication of the degree of concentration and its variation over time in these industries is provided by Table 8. These figures merely indicate the high degree of concentration, for two or more factories may be owned by a single firm and, hence, the actual concentration may well be greater than suggested.

It is significant that in spite of this tendency towards understatement the analysis reveals a high degree of concentration in the new industries. Here, owing to the limited domestic demand for certain goods and the over-all scarcity of resources, the licensing mechanism of the government has restricted the entry of new firms.

TABLE 8. *Changes in Industrial Concentration, 1954-58: Output Concentration in Selected Industries*

Industry	Total number of factories		Percentage of total output produced by the 3 largest factories	
	1954	1958	1954	1958
Soap	46	28	77.31	79.21
Electric fans	22	20	77.26	70.13
Electric lamps	10	10	66.25	68.75
Sewing machines	9	21	96.08	91.59

Source: NCAER Studies (unpublished).

Thus the aluminum foil industry is today a monopoly. But inasmuch as these market situations are created by the government they are under the control of the government and hence fall in a separate category. A wasteful competition must be avoided in order to maximize the growth of the economy, and this larger issue has relegated the monopoly problem to a place of relative insignificance. Nevertheless, recent government policy is to insure that in each major new industry at least three or more firms operate.

There are, further, historical reasons for the relative unimportance of monopoly in India. Whereas the combination movement in Western countries proceeded through the absorption and amalgamation of existing concerns, the development of concentration in India, particularly in the initial stage, occurred through pioneering and entrepreneurial activity and reflected a basic shortage of these abilities in the economy. Even where business groups have expanded by bringing operating enterprises under their control, there is a significant difference. In contrast to the trend towards industrial concentration in the West, the spread of control in India has not been determined by technical considerations but by financial opportunities. As a result an industrial group under one authority does not represent an economic integration, either horizontal or vertical, but rather a financial integration. The growth of giant corporations in the West had as its objective the elimination or restraint of competition. In India the major business entities consist of a heterogenous collection of generally unrelated enterprises, the objective being an extension of the area of control. Hence the problem in India is rather one of the concentration of economic power than of monopoly. It is the abuse of this power through malpractices, such as the transfer of profits and losses and the anti-social use of intercorporate investments, and not the restraint of production, which has been the subject of public concern. Indian legislation has been primarily interested in safeguarding the interests of the shareholder, the protection of the consumer being a secondary issue.

A recent study[16] has pointed out that a corporate group, defined as consisting of units subject to a common decision-making authority, cannot under present circumstances be identified with the managing agency. For one thing, each of the major groups now maintains

[16] R. K. Hazari, "Ownership and Control—A Study of Inter-Corporate Investment," *Economic Weekly*, Nov. 26, Dec. 3 and 10, 1960.

several companies acting as managing agents. Further, the declining importance of the managing agency system with the many legal restrictions placed upon it and the high incidence of taxation have combined to produce different forms of control—interlocking directorates, creation of trusts, and appointment of nominees as managers—some of which have a tenuous basis and are highly elusive. In fact, there are certain companies which have the managing agents of one group but are controlled by another. This study confirms the existence of heterogeneous enterprises in each group and underlines the distinction between industrial concentration in India and the West, but it suggests that the actual area of control is even wider than estimated hitherto.

There are certain factors which make for a low level of operational efficiency in Indian industry. World War II generated an abnormally large demand for industrial goods and at the same time restricted the volume of imports. This situation brought out forcefully the basic imbalance in the country's industrial structure. The consumer-goods industries, particularly cotton textiles, extended their productive capacity to obtain the maximum output, but the shortages of capital equipment and intermediate producer goods were serious limitations. One result of these shortages was that the equipment in the established industries was, at the time of Independence, technologically obsolete and physically overworked. The general inability to produce or import capital equipment led to a large accumulation of replacement needs. This may be illustrated by the case of cotton textiles where even as late as 1952 much of the equipment was of pre-1910 vintage, and the program of modernization had not yet been completed.[17]

Another impediment to efficiency is the existence of units of uneconomic size. In certain industries (cotton textiles and paper, for instance) uneconomic size and antiquated equipment often go together. The importance of this factor varies from industry to industry and, as expansion takes place, from time to time. But it is significant that in 1953 there were an estimated 150 uneconomic units in the cotton textile industry.[18] At present the number of units

---

[17] Ministry of Commerce and Industry, Government of India, *Reports of the Working Party on Cotton Textile Industry 1952*, and *Report of the Working Group for the Cotton Textile Industry*, National Industrial Development Corporation (Bombay, 1960).

[18] Planning Commission, *Programmes of Industrial Development 1951-56*, p. 210.

of uneconomic size in the paper, cotton, textile, and sugar industries is quite large. Further, uneconomic location has also raised the cost structure in certain cases. In 1953 the Planning Commission pointed out that high transport costs resulting from an adverse location were responsible in part for the high costs of cement production. The development of the sugar industry ignored the advantages of economic location; the industry is concentrated in Uttar Pradesh whereas Maharashtra and, to a lesser extent, Southern India offer a more favorable location.

The Problem, the Objectives, and the Strategy

We have in India, against a background of rich and varied natural resources, a broad range of scarcities. There is the proverbial scarcity of capital, which ranks extremely high as a limiting factor in industrialization. This results from the limited capacity to save out of low per capita incomes. In industrially advanced countries the ratio of savings to national income is 15 per cent or more; in India after ten years of planned development the Planning Commission estimates savings to be about 8 per cent of national income[19] and hopes to raise it during the next five years to 12 per cent. Foreign capital has permitted investment in the economy at a higher level (11 per cent of national income in 1960-61), but it is domestic saving which plays the decisive role in economic development and therefore must be increased. This is so vital that economic growth is sometimes conceived in terms of increasing the ratio of savings to national income, from 5 per cent (the level in most underdeveloped countries) to 15 per cent. Another aspect of the scarcity of capital is the limited technical capacity to produce capital goods. Technological backwardness has also resulted in a scarcity of efficient labor in a labor-abundant economy. Labor skilled in traditional crafts is, of course, quite plentiful among the artisans, but owing to the absence of a widespread technological revolution that labor force did not acquire the skills and the attitude required of industrial labor. For the same reason skills and efficiency are scarce at practically all levels. Another major limiting factor is the scarcity of entrepreneurial ability. Entrepreneurship has for long been limited to a few families in a few communities, and although there have

[19] The NCAER estimates savings to be higher, at 9.5 per cent.

been some new entrants to this field in recent years, the base continues to be very narrow. There is little growth of entrepreneurs from the small- and medium-scale enterprises to the large-scale level. The fundamental problem is ultimately a question of allocating these exceedingly scarce resources in order to obtain the maximum rate of industrialization.

While the major objective is to bring about a rapid industrial growth, there are also other important goals. As has been pointed out earlier, large areas of the country have not experienced the impact of industrialization and, consequently, their economic and social life is organized in a traditional manner. In order to develop these areas a satisfactory regional distribution of industries is necessary.

Apart from regional inequalities, we have already observed the existence of striking inequalities in income and wealth. In the context of a socialist pattern of society which the country is trying to evolve, a major objective is progressive reduction of the concentration of incomes, wealth, and economic power.

Finally, there is the growing volume of unemployment. The large investment effort of the Second Plan was unable to absorb the increase in the labor force during that period and as a result the Third Plan starts with a backlog of unemployment larger than that at the beginning of the Second Plan. Hence the provision of expanding employment opportunities has a high priority among our objectives, for success in more than one direction hinges largely upon this.

Partly owing to the economic structure of the country but more because of the social objectives of economic policy (which are discussed later) the public sector and co-operative and small-scale enterprise have an important place in the future pattern of industrial organization that is envisaged.

In the strategy of industrialization, the major emphasis is placed upon producer goods, particularly the "heavy" industries, and an increase in the supply of essential consumer goods which, where possible, are to be manufactured in the sector of small-scale enterprises.

A rapid expansion and diversification of industrial activity requires a substantial increase in the supply of capital goods. The need for a large supply of capital goods in order to maintain a high level of industrialization is illustrated by the fact that in advanced countries the output of producer goods and the output of consumer goods are roughly equal. For an increase in the supply of capital machinery and intermediate producer goods there must either be a large increase in imports or a rapid growth of producer-goods industries. Any large increase in capital imports is not feasible owing to the small and inelastic volume of our exports. The basic pattern of our exports has remained unchanged for decades, and world demand for these goods is more or less stationary. It will take some time before industrialization can have an impact on this export pattern and thus open up scope for a substantial increase in exports.

At present, therefore, the scope for an increase in exports is marginal, and it follows that a large increase in imports is not possible. Foreign loans have indeed helped us to import more than we export and have thereby made a significant contribution to the growth of the economy. But in view of the large investment requirements of the economy, capital imports based on aid cannot support a rapid rate of growth unless the basic imbalance of the industrial structure is rectified. Therefore, the policy that has been adopted is one of a rapid expansion of the industrial base, and considerable investment has taken place in fuel, power, and the heavy industries—metallurgical, engineering, and chemical.

The rising demand generated by developmental expenditure requires an expansion in the production of consumer goods and therefore considerable attention is also given to consumer industries, particularly those producing wage goods. Several arguments have been put forward for the emphasis on small-scale industries in this sphere. The development of these industries is expected to expand employment, conserve capital, diffuse economic power, reduce income inequalities, and act as a seedbed for the growth of entrepreneurship. Of these the "entrepreneurial" argument is probably the strongest. Small industrial units have increased rapidly during the last few years.

Economic Policy

Economic policy has succeeded broadly in securing the pattern of investment indicated by the forementioned strategy. In Table 9

TABLE 9. *Investment in Industries, 1951-66*
(Rs. crores)

(1) Industries	(2) 1951-56 (actual)	(3) 1956-61 (actual)	(4) 1961-66 (proposed)
Metallurgical industries (iron and steel, aluminum, ferro-manganese)	61.0	770.0	748.4
Engineering industries (heavy and light)	46.0	175.0	525.2
Chemical industries (heavy chemicals, fertilizers, drugs, etc.)	27.0	140.0	517.5
Cement, electric porcelain, refractories	17.5*	60.0	85.0
Petroleum refinery	45.0	30.0	73.5
Paper, newsprint, security paper	12.0	40.0	105.5
Sugar	5.0	56.0	100.0
Cotton, woolen, jute, silk cloth, and yarn	20.0**	50.0	34.5
Rayon and staple fiber	8.0	34.0	75.0
Food industries (vegetable oil)	N.A.	N.A.	19.0
Electric power generation and distribution (private sector)	32.6	N.A.	N.A.
Others	18.9	115.0	168.0
Total	293.0	1,470.0	2,451.6

Sources: Col. 2: Planning Commission, *Programmes of Industrial Development*, 1956-61, p. v.
    Col. 3: *Third Five Year Plan*, p. 456.
    Col. 4: *Third Five Year Plan*, Annexure III, pp. 503-509,.
  * Refers only to cement.
 ** Refers only to cotton.

the industrial investment that has taken place in the economy during the decade 1951-61 and that proposed for the next five years are classified according to major groups of industries. A rigorous classification of industrial investment in the relevant categories of capital goods and industrial machinery, intermediate producer goods, and consumer goods is not possible owing to the absence of readily available data for the entire period. However, the figures presented do indicate that consumer-goods industries have absorbed only a small portion of total investment. Although the engineering and chemical industries include certain consumer items, such as bicycles and soap, the bulk of the investment is in the category of capital and producer goods.

In the engineering industries, for example, out of a total investment of Rs. 525 crores in the Third Plan industrial machinery is to account for Rs. 344.5 crores and shipbuilding for a further Rs. 32

crores. A detailed breakdown of the remaining Rs. 148 crores is not yet available, but a good part of this is for the production of such items as earth-moving equipment, agricultural implements, and electric motors, and only a portion is directed towards the manufacture of durable consumer goods.

The Instruments of Policy

Both the public and the private sectors are responsible for the execution of planned industrialization, and the Industrial Policy Resolution of 1956 defines broadly their respective spheres of activity. Although the principle of division of industrial activity between the public and private sectors was accepted long before Independence, the present demarcation is significantly different, as it is determined not only by what private enterprise cannot or will not do but also by what it should not do from the standpoint of certain social objectives.

The resolution of 1956 divides industrial activity into three spheres. The first is to be the exclusive preserve of the state and comprises such industries as defense, atomic energy, rail and air transport, iron and steel, heavy plant and machinery required for mining, machine tool manufacture and steel production, and heavy electrical plant; other basic industries as may be specified by government; major extractive industries, including mineral oils, coal, iron ore and minerals related to atomic energy; the mining and processing of certain important minerals in which India is deficient, for instance, copper, lead and zinc; aircraft manufacture and shipbuilding; telephone, telegraph, and wireless apparatus (excluding radio-receiving sets); and the generation and distribution of electricity.

The second category consists of industries which are to be progressively owned by the state; here the state will take the initiative but private enterprise is expected to supplement these efforts. This sphere covers mining not included in the first category, non-ferrous metals, and tool steels; machine tools, intermediate products for the chemical industry, such as dye-stuffs and plastics; fertilizer, synthetic rubber, and coal carbonization; essential drugs and road and sea transport.

The third group which is defined by exclusion consists of the remaining industries, and here industrial development is to be left to the initiative of the private sector. This sphere is made up largely of consumer-goods industries.

It is explicitly stated that this division of industries is not rigid and watertight. In the first category, while rail and air transport, defense industries, and atomic energy will be developed as Central Government monopolies, the expansion of existing privately owned units and the co-operation of private enterprise in the establishment of new enterprises by the state is not precluded. Wherever it is appropriate, a private enterprise will be allowed to produce an item falling within the exclusive sphere of the state for meeting its own requirements or as a by-product. For example, industries like coal and electricity which are in the first category have been allotted to the private sector to a limited extent. If appropriate projects in this area are proposed by the private sector, it is possible that government may grant permission. Industrial development in the third category will be encouraged by the state through economic overheads, fiscal measures, and financial assistance. On the other hand it is open to the state to start any industry in the field left for private enterprise. But the likelihood of the state's moving into unscheduled industry becomes less probable with every new private investment. The state has plenty to do with its resources in the category I industries, and also in the pure infrastructure area.

Table 10 shows the distribution of investment during the First and Second Plans and planned investment during the Third Plan between the public and the private sectors of industry. It will be observed that investment in the public sector is growing faster than that in the private sector, so much so that while four-fifths of the investment between 1951-56 took place in the private sector, during the next five years investment in the public sector exceeded that in the private sector, and this gap is expected to grow between the years 1961-66.

The Public Sector

The emphasis on the public sector in industrial policy has, as was pointed out earlier, a complex motivation. Accelerated economic development requires the promotion of industries in various fields, some of which are immediately unprofitable, while in others invest-

TABLE 10. *Share of Public and Private Sectors in*
New Industrial Investment
(Rs. crores)

	1951-56 (actual)	1956-61 (actual)	1961-66 (proposed)	1951-66
Public Sector	57 (19.65)	770 (52.36)	1,330 (54.38)	2,157
Private Sector	233 (80.35)	700 (47.64)	1,125 (45.62)	2,058
Total	290	1,470	2,455	4,215

Source: *Programme of Industrial Development*, 1956-61, p. iv; *Third Five Year Plan*,
pp. 455, 456, 459.
Note: Figures in parentheses indicate percentages.

TABLE 11. *Number and Paid-up Capital of Government*
and Non-Government Companies, 1955-56 to 1959-60
(Rs. crores)

Year ended March 31	Govt. Companies		Non-Govt. Companies		Total	
	No.	Paid-up Capital	No.	Paid-up Capital	No.	Paid-up Capital
1956	61	66.0	29,813	958.2	29,874	1,024.2
1957	74	72.6	29,283	1,005.0	29,357	1,077.6
1958	91	256.8	28,189	1,049.5	28,280	1,306.3
1959 (provisional)	103	424.2	27,376	1,085.6	27,479	1,509.8
1960 (provisional)	125	468.4	26,796	1,124.7	26,921	1,593.1

Source: R. K. Nigam and N. C. Chaturvedi, *The Corporate Sector in India*, Department
of Company Law Administration, Ministry of Commerce and Industry (New
Delhi, 1960), p. 12.
Note: Statutorily, the category of government companies came into being with the new
Company Law on April 1, 1956.

ment is required on a scale which only the state at present can provide. Moreover, an expanding public sector is implicit in the objective of a socialist pattern of society; it reduces the concentration
in the ownership and control of the means of production and prevents an intensification of income inequalities. As a result of these
considerations there has been a rapid growth of this sector both in
size and in the area of operation. The capital owned by the public

sector has grown from Rs. 2,840 crores in 1952 to Rs. 5,866 crores in 1958, and the share of the state in total reproducible wealth has risen from 14 per cent in 1949-50 to over 23 per cent in 1958-59.[20] Of greater significance is the expansion in the area of state economic activity. Prior to 1947 the public sector was not only negligible in size, but also narrow in its scope, which was confined to the field of defense industries and public utilities, the principal public undertakings being the munition factories, railways, posts, and telegraphs, the mint, and a few opium and salt factories. Since then the state has widened its sphere to include industries, mining, shipping, air and road transport, banking, and insurance. In the industrial field in particular the state has been playing a leading part, and, as has been observed, investment was higher in public industry than in private industry during the years 1956-61. Public enterprise has, therefore, grown faster than private enterprise in the corporate sector.

It must be emphasized that this expansion of the public sector has not taken place as the result of any major acquisition of assets from the private sector. On the contrary, it represents the role of the state as entrepreneur in the initiation of new industries. The broad *directions* of industrial investment in the public sector are indicated in Table 12. Programs for the manufacture of consumer goods (with the exception of drugs) in the public sector occupy a rather minor position in terms of direct investment in organized industries, and most public sector enterprises are in the category of

TABLE 12. *Investment by Industrial Classifications*

(Rs. crores)

	1951-56	1956-61*	1961-66
Metallurgical	7.85	350.00	586.95
Mechanical engineering	22.90	34.45	243.19
Electrical engineering	4.19	21.75	118.65
Chemical	10.77	41.00	140.08
Oil refining	—	—	73.50
Others	9.12	54.50	162.40

Sources: 1951-56: *Review of First Five Year Plan*, pp. 204-205.
1956-61: *Second Five Year Plan*, pp. 417-419.
1961-66: *Third Five Year Plan*, pp. 493-500, Annexures I, II.
* The figures for proposed investment in the Second Plan exclude investment by the National Industrial Development Corporation.

[20] Nabagopal Das, *The Public Sector in India* (2nd. ed., Bombay, 1961), p. 66.

"heavy" and "basic" industries producing capital and producer goods. Three new steel plants have been established, three major projects for the production of industrial and mining machinery and electrical equipment have been set up, the foundations of a heavy chemical industry have been laid, and there has been considerable progress in the manufacture of scientific and other precision instruments.

With the relative growth of the public sector the area of the economy over which the state has direct control has been increasing. This by itself should facilitate the implementation of the national plans for economic growth, but certain serious problems are being encountered. The major problem pertains to the organizational form most appropriate for public enterprise and centers upon the issue of striking a balance between the conflicting demands of an adequate measure of public control and sufficient scope for managerial initiative and enterprise. At present public sector enterprises are organized in three forms. In descending order of importance from the point of view of the degree of formal ministerial control these are the departmental undertaking, the statutory corporation, and the government company. Most industrial enterprises are organized in the form of a company constituted under the Companies Act, like any other company, but with 51 per cent or more of the share capital subscribed by government. But even here the degree of bureaucratic control is considerable, as in most cases the officers of the ministry concerned are ex officio members of the board of directors, and official approval is required for all capital expenditures exceeding Rs. 10 lakhs and appointments to posts carrying a monthly salary of Rs. 2,000 and over. The process of parliamentary scrutiny often involves the discussion of day-to-day decisions, so that ministers find it necessary to ask for advance knowledge and approval of all decisions. In the face of this ministerial intervention, the management of an enterprise has little of the independence and flexibility so necessary for efficient conduct. The result has been a bureaucratic rather than a business outlook, with efficiency construed to be the avoidance of errors rather than the reduction of costs. Apart from organizational defects there is, further, an acute shortage of managerial talent in the administrative cadres of government. Most managing directors are taken from the ranks of the civil service, and while many civil servants are excellent administrators none of them has much experience in industrial management. In the preliminary stages, when the state has to initiate new enterprises, a high degree of ministerial supervision and control is no doubt necessary. But later, when the question is one of operation with maximum economy, this intervention powerfully inhibits such business enterprise as may exist in professional administrators. Several industrial enterprises have been established during the Second Plan period, and the question of maximum operational efficiency has come into the forefront. But the system of organization and management has not yet been fully evolved to meet this need.

In capitalist and communist countries alike, economic developments have been financed in large measure by the profits of industrial enterprises. While profits depend to some extent on operational efficiency, the major determining factor is the price policy that is followed, because state enterprises are often monopolistic. The latter consideration is a primary issue in the conduct of public enterprises in India today. There are, broadly, three lines of thought. It has for long been held that state enterprises should break even, making neither profits nor losses. A second view, holding that a public good provides simultaneously both utility to the individual buyer and general welfare to the community, suggests that the price should be below the cost of production and that the enterprise should be subsidized by the general revenues. A third school strongly recommends the pursuit of profits by a public enterprise so that it may generate a surplus not only to finance its own expansion but also for investment elsewhere. The Planning Commission has declared that the surpluses of public enterprises in a developing economy constitute a ready and increasingly important source for financing investment, and in the scheme of finance outlined for the Third Plan, credit has been taken for the sum of Rs. 550 crores[21] from this source (including the depreciation and other internal funds). Whether this large sum will materialize or not is an open question—the actual net savings of all public sector undertakings amounted to Rs. 165.32 crores during the years 1956-57 to 1958-59 or an annual average of about Rs. 55 crores—but the inclusion of this source of finance indicates the adoption of a profit-making price policy by some of the public enterprises.

[21] This includes Rs. 100 crores of railway surplus which is net after depreciation.

Private Enterprise—The Framework of Control

A large part of the industrial field—some capital and producer-goods industries and the entire field of consumer goods—has been left open to private enterprise. Industrial growth in the private sector has to be regulated in accordance with the priorities laid down in the five year plans, and private enterprise has to be fitted into the over-all economic and social pattern evolved by the planners. Accordingly, the government has assumed wide powers of control over private industry. The over-all framework for the regulated development of private enterprise is quite comprehensive; and, although in the very nature of things it has to be for the most part negative in character, there are also certain positive features. In what follows the principal features of control over private industry are briefly outlined.

First, there are certain important allocative controls set up to secure a distribution of scarce resources according to the priorities of planned development. The Industries (Development and Regulation) Act contains an elaborate list of industries and requires all existing undertakings in these fields to be registered with government. Further, the establishment of new industrial undertakings as well as the expansion of, or the manufacture of new articles by, existing units cannot take place unless a license is obtained from the Central Government. These licenses may also stipulate the size and location of industrial units. Both license and registration may be revoked under special circumstances. A similar control is exercised in the matter of capital issues. All capital issues in India and those of Indian companies operating abroad require official approval, and so does the renewal or postponement of payment of any security payable in India. From the *Annual Report of the Ministry of Commerce and Industry* (1959-60) it would appear that 75 per cent of the applications for industrial licenses were accepted. In the matter of capital issued, between 80 and 90 per cent of the total capital applied for has been sanctioned. Inasmuch as the rejections of applications for both industrial licenses and capital issues are determined by the requirements of the economy, they may be regarded as indicating the extent to which the diversion of resources to undesirable projects has been prevented. Among the most scarce of our resources is foreign exchange, which is subjected to comprehensive control by the government, acting through the Reserve Bank of India. All transactions in foreign currencies must take place through authorized dealers who are under the surveillance and control of the Reserve Bank and must obey the latter's directives. The government also has the power to order all owners and holders of foreign currencies and securities to sell their command over foreign exchange to the government at a price fixed by it.

A major instrument for securing the desired allocation of resources is the system of price control. Wide powers in this regard are vested in the government. In certain industries—for instance cement, steel, and paper—the Tariff Commission, appointed by the government, fixes the price of the finished product on the basis of the average cost of production in the industry and an adequate return on capital. Under the Essential Commodities Act the government may issue orders for the regulation of the production, supply, and distribution of an essential commodity with a view to securing its equitable distribution and availability at fair prices. Further, the Industries (Development and Regulation) Act empowers the government to regulate the supply, price, and distribution of any article "relatable" to any of the industries listed by the enactment. Moreover, by the same enactment any order made in exercise of this power is legally unchallengeable. Thus the planning authorities have wide powers of price control, and the coverage of such control is fairly extensive. According to a recent estimate, direct price controls cover commodities with 25 per cent of the total weightage in the wholesale price index, while on a rough estimate about half the weights in the wholesale price indices are influenced directly and indirectly through the present system of control and regulation. Some of the most important raw materials are subject to price control and, in certain cases, distribution control. Among the more important articles subject to maximum ex-factory or ex-works selling-price controls are coal, steel, pig iron, tinplate, cement, petroleum products, rubber, electricity, sugar, paper, caustic soda, zinc, fertilizer, and raw cotton. In addition to these controls the government may also adjust the rates of excise duty from time to time in order to alter the relationship between particular prices. The most striking use of the fiscal agency in this direction is the cess on mill-made cloth, the proceeds of which have been used to subsidize the handloom industry. This alteration of relative prices helped to realize the policy objective of encouraging the small-scale sector.

Steel and cement are basic materials upon which the expansion of the entire economy depends; therefore the price policy that is followed in respect of these commodities is of vital importance. Prices in these industries, among others, are determined by the Tariff Commission, and there has been a vigorous controversy between the representatives of the industries and the Commission. In the case of steel, there are two prices; the price paid to the producer—or the retention price—is lower than that charged the consumer, and the difference goes into the Equalisation Fund. This fund is used to subsidize imported steel, the price of which exceeds that of Indian steel. It is the retention price that matters from the point of view of production, and it has been pointed out that this price, fixed in 1955, has proved too low, as it was based on tentative costs of capital construction and production assumptions which were not entirely fulfilled. Representatives of the industry also consider the price formula to be rigid, in spite of the introduction of an escalator clause to compensate the producers for increases in costs, because some of the factors making for higher costs—such as the increasing ash contents of coal—did not exist in the period when the formula was evolved. Owing to the increased costs of production it has been argued that the prices fixed have yielded an insufficient margin for the development and expansion of the steel industry. An analogous position prevails in the cement industry, which has represented to government that the price determined by the Tariff Commission yields an inadequate profit margin for expansion and ultimate increase in supply.

There is another aspect to the policy of fixing low prices in order to stimulate industrial demand. Where there is already a shortage, this tends to accentuate the existing imbalance between demand and supply. In such circumstances certain industrial consumers find it more profitable to sell their allotment of, say, steel in the black market than to use it for production. On the whole, in spite of the large powers taken by the government, they have been used rather sparingly. The Government of India is not eager to fix prices of various commodities nor has it taken on the more difficult task of importing goods and setting up distribution controls. Pragmatism dominates.

In addition to price control, there are other measures adopted by the government to influence production. In a number of industries development councils have been established to fix targets for production and overcome the specific problems that arise in the realization of these targets. In certain industries, notably cotton textiles, spheres of production for the large-scale and small-scale sectors are marked off. A strong deterrent to any sharp fall in the quantity and quality of the output of an industrial enterprise exists in the power of government to take over such a concern. Such action may also be taken if there is an unjustifiable increase in price. In view of the adverse psychological repercussions that such action could have on private industry, the government has understandably exercised considerable restraint in this matter, and the number of cases of take-over is very small. For example, in 1959, only three sugar factories and one engineering concern were being managed through authorized controllers and boards of management appointed by the Central Government.[22]

In the past a lack of sufficient confidence in the country's capacity for industrial development inhibited the growth of the capital market, and the burden of financing industries fell upon the entrepreneurs themselves. Thus the managing agents were the chief providers of capital. The dominance of a single source of financing has many weaknesses, and different devices are necessary from the point of view both of the industrial enterprises and of the investors. Nothing has demonstrated more clearly the importance attached by the government to the role of private enterprise in the industrialization of the country than the setting up of several financial institutions in order to develop the capital market. The first of these institutions was the Industrial Finance Corporation, which provides medium- and long-term credit to public-limited companies and co-operative societies. Established in 1948, the Corporation had by June 1959 advanced a total sum of Rs. 66.69 crores, about two-thirds of which went to new enterprises. As the counterpart at the state level of this all-India organization, twelve state financial Corporations have been instituted. These provide long-term loans and working capital to medium- and small-sized enterprise, in addition to being underwriters. Among the new institutions the Industrial Credit and In-

[22] Ministry of Commerce and Industry, *Annual Report, 1959-60* (New Delhi, 1960).

vestment Corporation of India is unique in that it provides equity capital and loans in foreign currencies, although the scale of the latter in particular is modest. Underwriting facilities are also provided by the Corporation, which has been left with substantial holdings of securities. Another important institution is the Refinance Corporation set up to stimulate medium-term lending by the banking system. This institution grants loans to certain selected banks against advances made by them to medium-sized enterprises.

Certain powerful fiscal devices have been employed to encourage industrial growth. New industrial enterprises are granted a tax holiday for the first five years. During this period not only are the profits of the company, up to 6 per cent of the total capital employed, exempted from the corporation tax but also the dividends from such profits in the hands of shareholders are exempted from both the income and supertaxes. A more powerful incentive is the development rebate which, together with the depreciation allowance, enables established as well as new undertakings to deduct from income before taxes, over a period of time, 125 per cent of the actual capital expenditure on plant and machinery. This is, in effect, a subsidy on investment amounting to the tax on 25 per cent of the cost of all new plant and machinery (40 per cent in the case of ships). Perhaps the most valuable fiscal encouragement is the exemption from supertax of dividends arising from the intercorporate investment in certain specified industries. The scope of this provision has recently been broadened to include a number of items of industrial machinery. All these fiscal incentives add up to a strong stimulus to industrial expansion.

An appreciable effort is being made in the field of scientific and technological research, and the Ministry of Scientific Research promotes such studies and provides grants to scientific associations. A number of industries—e.g., cotton textiles, jute, and sugar—have their own research organizations which together with the Council of Scientific and Industrial Research explore the possibilities of applying science to industry. Research for the metallurgical, engineering, chemical, and mining industries is carried on, along with studies of a more fundamental nature, in a chain of national laboratories. The utilization of the results of scientific research in commercial production is promoted by the National Research Development Corporation. At present there is a considerable time-lag between the availability of the results of scientific research and their application to industry, and a large proportion of the inventions made in the country remains unexploited.

Apart from these efforts to accelerate and regulate the growth of private industry, certain wider economic controls exercised by the government have a bearing upon industrial enterprises. Only the more important of these are here touched upon so far as they impinge upon private industry.

Through the Companies Act of 1956, one of the most all-encompassing laws in the world, the government has acquired considerable powers to influence both the organization and the conduct of corporate enterprise. An important part of the enactment deals with the managing agency system and represents an attempt to deal with the system as a whole rather than an effort to tackle individual cases of malpractice and error. A managing agency firm is one that directs and manages usually more than one company, in which it might or might not hold considerable financial interest. Some of these firms work part-time for many companies and have created a series of quasi-monopolistic enterprises within the country, receiving profits out of all proportion to the management services and without real control by the shareholders. The utility of the managing-agency system, although considerable during the early industrialization of the country, has declined sharply with the changed conditions, and considerable odium surrounds the institution owing to the concentration of power within an enterprise in the hands of managing agents and the not infrequent abuse of this power. With the new law the power of managing agents has shrunk. Their term of office has been reduced, a ceiling has been placed on their remuneration, and their subordination to the board of directors is emphasized. These measures have influenced the institutional set-up in the private sector, as the trend among new companies is in favor of director management and away from the managing-agency system. An attempt has also been made in the company law to improve the conduct of business, principally through an increase in the power of shareholders, the responsibilities of directors, and the supervision and control of government. Several matters now require the approval of government, which has certain important powers including the authority to investigate the affairs of a company and to appoint the directors of a company to prevent mismanagement.

Controls over the country's foreign trade have an obvious impact on private industry, and a comprehensive system of import and export controls prevails in India. All imports have to be authorized by licenses. These are issued fairly liberally in the case of the sterling area, but license to import from the dollar area is granted only if it is established that the goods in question are essential and not available from domestic sources. Priority is given to the import of raw materials, components, and machinery, while imports against foreign investment or medium-term credit have precedence over imports requiring cash payment. Import of those items, the domestic production of which has expanded, is either banned or generally reduced. With the growth of industries there has been substantial increase in the requirements of imported raw materials and intermediate goods. Owing to the scarcity of foreign exchange in relation to the priorities and needs of the plans, however, some of these items could not be imported and therefore production in certain lines is below capacity. In order to expand exports and rectify this situation a special licensing scheme has been introduced. Under this scheme exporting textile units are issued special licenses up to a certain percentage of their export earnings for the import of dyes and chemicals. The import of raw cotton continues to be rigorously licensed, but exporting mills are given a certain proportion under the direction and supervision of the Textile Commissioner.

It is now widely recognized that industrial peace is an essential prerequisite for industrial progress. Problems in this sphere are chiefly concerned with wages, and the immediate aim of policy is to secure to the worker a fair or living wage and to provide a system for the settlement of wage disputes. For this purpose, the Minimum Wages Act empowers the government to fix minimum wages in certain specified occupations. But progress in the fixation of minimum wages has been slow and often ineffective. The Industrial Disputes Act of 1947 introduced the principle of compulsory arbitration and provided for a three-tier machinery for adjudication consisting of a Labour Court, an Industrial Tribunal, and a National Tribunal. The government can refer disputes to the above organs of its own accord or on application by the parties, and provision is made for the enforcement of the awards of the courts. Strikes and lockouts may be prohibited during the consideration of a dispute, and in certain circumstances they are illegal under the enactment.

In outlining the Second Five-Year Plan, the Planning Commission recommended tripartite wage boards as the most suitable method for the settlement of wage disputes in large industries. Hitherto such boards have been set up in the cotton, jute, sugar, cement, and plantation industries. Both employers and workers have agreed that the unanimous recommendation of wage boards should be fully implemented. As a result, the minimum wages of industrial workers have been considerably increased in these industries. But wages are still low by international standards. Monthly minimum wages range widely; for example, in the engineering industries unskilled workers get from $17.85 to $25.83; semi-skilled, $24.68 to $32.55, and skilled from $42.50 to $52.50. The highest paying industry is oil, followed by rubber products, transport equipment, and basic metals. These are also industries where foreign participation is to be found.

Good industrial relations require an atmosphere of co-operation between employers and workers for their mutual benefit, and in this respect a strictly legalistic approach has its limitations. A Code of Conduct and Discipline was therefore drawn up and accepted by workers and employers in 1958. This lays down the specific obligations of labor and management in the promotion of constructive co-operation and requires disputes and grievances to be settled through mutual negotiations and voluntary arbitration. Both parties have agreed under the code to avoid lock-outs and strikes. Although not a legal act, infringements of the codes are investigated by the Ministry of Labour and the violations publicly exposed. The three major management associations and the four major trade unions have voluntarily agreed to abide by its provisions. As a result partly of the code and partly of the pragmatic and realistic approach of the government to labor problems, and partly because of the growing maturity of both trade-union leadership and of the workers themselves, labor-management relations have greatly improved in the past few years. The number of man-days lost because of strikes has been falling since the Code of Discipline was created.

At present the formulation of a code of efficiency and welfare is also being considered in order to promote productivity. The beginnings of social security for workers are to be seen in the establishment by law of the Employees Provident Fund Act of 1952 and the Employees State Insurance Corporation, applicable to industry and to public employment.

Small-Scale Industry

An important place has been assigned to small-scale industries (both traditional and modern) in the programs of both industrialization and rural development. The Industrial Policy Resolution of 1956 points out that in relation to some of the problems that need urgent solutions these industries offer distinct advantages. They present opportunities for the creation of immediate and large-scale employment at low capital cost, offer a method for a more equitable distribution of the national income, and facilitate mobilization of certain resources such as capital and skill which might otherwise remain unutilized. They can also break the concentration of entrepreneurial power and bring about a wider dispersion of entrepreneurship.

With these objectives in view the government has set about the task of developing these industries with much vigor, and an elaborate framework of assistance has been evolved for the broad purposes of expanding production, increasing productivity, and improving the bargaining power of the small producer. A three-tier organization now exists, consisting of the Ministry of Commerce and Industry of the Central Government, all-India boards for various industries, including the National Small Industries Corporation, and at the level of the state government there are departments of industries and boards. Further, industry officers have been appointed at the district and block (comprising one hundred villages) levels. This organization formulates and implements programs of assistance in the fields of technology, organization and management, finance, and marketing.

Under the Industrial Extension Service institutes have been established in all the states and extension centers in various towns. These provide technical counsel to small industrialists and prepare technical bulletins, designs, and model schemes. Foreign consultants are engaged by these institutes, and Indian technicians are sent abroad to "import" the latest processes of production. The institutes are equipped with workshops to impart practical training in the towns while mobile demonstration workshops serve the rural areas. Prototype production-cum-training centers have been established to design and develop the production of machines and machine tools which are at present imported. In addition to technological assistance these institutes conduct economic surveys of selected industries and areas and provide expert counsel on the opportunities for new industries and the assistance available from official agencies. Commercial advice on management and marketing problems is also given, and the institutes provide training in the techniques of business management. As regards organization, considerable efforts have been made to organize small-scale industries along co-operative lines.

Much has been done to maintain and expand the market for small industries. Where such industries compete with large-scale industries, differential taxation and subsidies have been employed to alter the relative prices of the products in favor of the former. Another technique has been the reservation of spheres of production. The most frequently cited example of such measures is the hand-loom industry.

In the First Five-Year Plan, the principle of a common production program[23] was recommended, as it was thought that a large variety of items could be encouraged for production on a small-scale basis. A common production program, i.e., reservation of certain percentage of production, was laid down for bicycles, sewing machines, and storage batteries, certain varieties of agricultural implements, tanning and leather industry, radio receivers, bifurcated rivets, furniture, small hand tools, sports goods, and pencils. It is possible that the common production program will be extended to numerous other articles and stores, following a recommendation of a working group of experts.[24]

Further, a marketing system of mobile shops, wholesale depots, and sales emporia has been set up. The National Small Industries Corporation assists these industries to secure government contracts at prices up to about 15 per cent higher than the products of large-scale units; and large-scale enterprises are persuaded to purchase their components from small units. The corporation supplies ma-

[23] The concept of the common production program relates to those products which are or can be produced by both large and small-scale establishments.

[24] Ministry of Commerce and Industry, *Small Scale Industries Programme of Work for the Third Five Year Plan* (Report of the Working Group), (New Delhi, Dec. 1959), p. 138.

chinery under a system of hire purchase; the initial down payment is only 10 per cent of the cost of machinery.

Financial assistance is provided by government under the State Aid to Industries Act, but the objective is that the credit requirements of village and small-scale industries should in increasing measure be met by the normal channel of banking and financial institutions. The state finance corporations, co-operative banks, and the State Bank of India are the chief financial agencies that help these industries. The State Bank has a scheme for the co-ordinated provision of credit to these industries, and the credit limit sanctioned by the end of March 1961 was Rs. 9 crores. Two other notable measures have recently been taken in this sphere. The Reserve Bank provides special facilities to central co-operative agencies to meet the working capital requirements of the handloom industry. A guarantee scheme has been introduced under which the government shares with certain financial institutions the risks incurred by the latter on loans granted to small-scale industries.

The government program of establishing industrial estates is a pioneering and unique experiment. These estates bring together small workshops operated by different individuals within a compact area and provide a wide range of basic facilities. This grouping of small-scale units promotes co-operation among the industrialists and the pooling of experience. In all, sixty industrial estates have been set up during the period 1956-61, and this organization of small-scale industry has made it more convenient and less expensive for the government to render the various forms of assistance that have been outlined. The total expenditure on the entire program of assistance to small industries was about Rs. 43 crores between 1951-56 and nearly Rs. 180 crores in the period 1956-61.

As a result of this massive and many-sided assistance and the dynamism displayed by hundreds of new entrepreneurs, small-scale industries have recorded substantial progress. The number of industrial co-operatives has increased from 7,105 in 1951 to about 29,000 in 1959-60. Production of Khadi (handspun and hand-woven cloth) increased from 7 million yards in 1950-51 to about 48 million yards in 1960-61, while the output of handloom cloth rose from 742 million yards in 1950-51 to 1900 million yards in 1960-61. But the most remarkable feature has been the upsurge of small-scale industrial activity in the light engineering fields. In spite of short-ages in basic raw materials, the increase in production in many lines—for example, sewing machines, bicycles, and electric fans—is impressive, being as much as 25 to 50 per cent per annum.

Government assistance to and emphasis on small-scale industries has played a significant role in the growth of entrepreneurship. For these industries have provided an opportunity for a large number of gifted entrepreneurs who are handicapped by meager resources to enter industry and has thus widened the base of entrepreneurship. They also provide a training ground for young entrepreneurs, who may eventually grow into big industrialists. However, the forms in which assistance has been provided have been both negative and positive. Particularly in the early phases, considerable emphasis was placed on subsidies, differential taxation, and reserved markets. A positive approach emphasizing an increase in productivity through improvements in the techniques of production and management is more constructive, and this has now been recognized. In this connection it has been realized that small-scale units should be developed in lines of production which are ancillary to large-scale industries, and the area in which the two are complementary is being developed.

SOCIAL OBJECTIVES AND MEASURES

It would be difficult for an outsider to understand the government's action in the economic and social spheres without appreciating the deep feeling in the country that social and economic inequality, however brought about, should be reduced as quickly as possible. The mainspring of government's activities is dominated by this deep urge. Government is not unaware of the fact that some of its social measures might have an immediately adverse effect on economic production and growth. But the Welfare State of India is deeply committed through the Directives of the Constitution to the reduction of social inequalities, and most of the government's actions, for example, land reform, efforts to reduce regional inequalities, investments in cottage and small industries, development of small power industries, are motivated by this broader objective. State intervention is considered necessary in the sphere of social welfare on account of the fear that without it social inequalities might be accentuated.

These inequalities can be classified into different types: first, inequalities in income and wealth, already referred to; second, regional disparities on account of unequal endowments of natural and other resources for development; and, third, differences on account of uneven utilization by the people in those states and areas of facilities provided for education, health, housing, and other social welfare measures.

Regarding the first, fiscal measures have of course a double objective in India, as indeed in other countries as well. Besides seeking to mobilize the country's economic resources for investment, they are also designed to reduce inequality to the extent possible.

A steeply progressive income tax, coupled with a tax on wealth, places virtually a ceiling on increases in income and wealth. To these taxes may be added the taxes on gifts and expenditure, all of which, however, operate mainly in the urban sector. These taxes barely touch the rural sector. In the non-agricultural sector as a whole, the income per engaged person increased from Rs. 1,225 in 1952-53 to Rs. 1,311 in 1956-57 and further to Rs. 1,392 in 1958-59. Against this, income per income-tax assessee fell from Rs. 13,410 in 1953-54 to Rs. 12,428 in 1957-58, but rose to Rs. 12,531 in 1959-60;[25] even within the income tax-paying group, there is a reduction in concentration of wealth. The Lorenz ratio of concentration, which was .32 in 1953-54, fell to .30 in 1959-60. The contribution of the top 1 per cent of the income-tax assessees to the total income assessed was 14 per cent in 1953-54, and it dropped to 10 per cent in 1959-60. The reliability of these figures, however, is not absolute. Allowance must be made for the rather widespread system of tax avoidance and tax evasion as well as the large business expenditures, especially for entertainment, travel, and so on, which escape taxation. To some extent this is borne out by the proportions of direct and indirect taxation to the total tax revenues. The share of direct taxes decreased from 36 per cent in 1950-51 to 29 per cent in 1960-61, while that of the indirect taxes increased from 64 per cent to 71 per cent, thereby showing that no firm conclusion

[25] The one-year difference in the two sets of figures is due to the fact that the assessment in 1953-54 returns refers to the income of 1952-53, and so on.

Source: Central Board of Revenue, Income Tax Statistics, and Central Statistical Organisation, National Income Statistics.

can be reached regarding reduction in concentration; but the data partly explain the widespread feeling that in certain sections of the community concentration of wealth and income has perhaps increased.

The government has recently appointed a high-level committee to look into the question of variations in income and distribution during the last ten years. The report is likely to throw much light on the changes in the income structure of the different classes of people under the impact of numerous development programs and huge investments in the country.

There is a widening gap between rural and urban incomes, which stems primarily from the different levels of productivity. With greater accent on investment in large industrial projects, this inequality of income between rural and urban sectors persists, notwithstanding the large investments in the rural areas through community development programs, irrigation, and other economic and social overheads. The inevitable effect is an imbalance in the development of the two most important sectors of the economy, viz., agriculture and industry. But within the agricultural sector there persist even wider inequalities of income. The fact that the top few of the agricultural class control a major share of land area and consequently agricultural output clearly testifies to this inequality. The abolition of the *zamindari* system and the introduction of land reform and other tenancy legislation in all the states in the country are steps in the direction of reducing the inequalities and increasing the share of the poor farmer in the total agricultural output. The Community Development movement which depends for its success on voluntary co-operation and self-help among the masses, was launched in 1952 for resurrecting rural India, where 65 million families live. With all these positive steps of the government towards the reduction of inequalities, the results are not encouraging. There is little evidence to show that the rural-urban inequalities have decreased. The same is true within the agricultural sector.

The concentration of power in the industrial sector is sought to be reduced by various legislative and other measures. The government effectively controls the development of large-scale industries through the Industries Development and Regulation Act of 1951. The Industrial Policy Resolution of 1956 clearly demarcates the spheres of public and private sectors. Since most of the highly capital-intensive producer-goods industries will ultimately be the monopoly of the public sector, the concentration of economic power and the control of basic industries by a small group of people will be prevented. The impetus given to the development of small-scale industries is another line of action for a more decentralized industrial structure. The possibility of a labor-intensive small-scale sector without detriment to productivity has a special economic advantage in the present shortage of capital.

Balanced regional development, while partly an economic problem, is basically social and political. The Government of India is fully aware of the dangers of an uneven development among the different states. The main objective of the government in encouraging balanced development is the need to bring up the backward and undeveloped regions to a reasonable level and not let them slide behind. Though certain economic concentration due to the developing industrial complexes is unavoidable, it is possible by a proper provision of economic and social overheads and the adoption of proper fiscal measures to bring development to undeveloped areas. There is still need to provide such undeveloped areas with an adequate transport system and ample power supply—the two important economic overheads which attract investment. Here again social objectives may run into conflict with the economic goal in the short run, but planning priorities are not clearly established in favor of economic ends.

The most pressing and seemingly intractable social problem stems from acute unemployment and underemployment in both rural and urban areas, underemployment predominating in rural areas. No reliable estimate of underemployment is available, though the Planning Commission estimated roughly that it would be of the order of 15 to 18 million.[26]

At the end of the First Plan, the backlog of unemployment was estimated at 5.3 million. Additions to the labor force during the Second Plan were estimated at 10 million. However, during the Second Plan the additional employment opportunities created amounted to only about 8 million, of which about 6.5 million were outside agriculture. The backlog of unemployment at the end of the Second Plan was reckoned at 9 million. This is partly due to a larger increase in labor force during the Second Plan (an addition of 1.7 million) than had been visualized earlier.

[26] *Third Five Year Plan*, chap. x, p. 156.

The supply of labor depends both on the backlog of unemployment and the new additions to the labor force. According to the provisional estimates of the census, the total increase in population may be of the order of 187 million in the period 1961 to 1976, of which the labor force may constitute 70 million. It is estimated that during the Third Plan period the additions to the labor force would be of the order of 17 million. The Third Plan provides for an additional employment of 14 million, of which 10.5 million would be in the non-agricultural sector. It is evident, therefore, that the Third Plan would not be able to absorb even the additions to the labor force (17 million) let alone the backlog of unemployment (9 million at the beginning of the Third Plan). Assuming that the Third Plan program will be implemented in full, by 1966 the unemployment situation will have become acute and there will exist an army of unemployment numbering about 12 million.

The state, according to the Constitution, is to provide employment opportunities to all able citizens. There is increasing recognition that the success or failure of democratic ideals hinges on a solution of this problem. Even on humanitarian grounds there is need to create part-time, low-paid jobs as relief measures calculated to secure a minimum income to the individual. It is reasonable to conclude, therefore, that bolder labor-intensive programs should be put through during 1966-76 if the country is to create employment opportunities to the tune of 79 million and thus satisfy one of the basic urges towards the social welfare goal. Unemployment could become a most serious threat to economic and political stability of the country, and this partly explains the country's acceptance of the continuance of cottage and other unorganized industries.

The provision of the social overheads such as education, health, and social welfare facilities for the development of human resources is one of the major objectives of any welfare state. The state in India has assumed in recent years responsibilities of a large magnitude in fulfilling these objectives. An outlay of Rs. 12,890 million was incurred on social service during the 10 years 1951-61. The needs, however, are much greater, and the government is aware of these needs. The lack of adequate financial resources alone is in the way of a larger expenditure.

Education can be considered as the most important single factor in achieving rapid economic development and technical progress and in bringing about a social order based on the values of freedom, justice, and equal opportunities. The total outlay on education during the first two plans amounted to Rs. 3,410 million. The Third Plan has a provision of Rs. 4,180 million, of which Rs. 2,090 million (or 50 per cent) is earmarked for elementary education.

In a country where a literate is defined as a person who can read and write a postcard in any one of the Indian languages, the importance of primary education cannot be overemphasized. About 61 per cent of the children in the age group of six to eleven and 23 per cent of the children in the age group of eleven to fourteen received primary education in 1961. It is expected that the respective percentages will increase to 76 and 29 by 1966. The schooling of the children has suffered because of the extreme backwardness of certain areas and certain sections of the population, which have yet to develop a proper attitude toward education; lack of trained and qualified teachers; "wastage" due to parents taking the children away from school to do odd jobs for supplementing family income; and difficulty in getting girls to schools due to age-old social attitudes. The demand for personnel in the middle and lower grades in many branches of economic life like rural development, commerce, industry, etc., and in administration and professions will be met mostly by the products of secondary schools. With the expansion of secondary education, the demand for higher education has also increased. Scientific and technical education is given due importance by the planners.

One of the directives to the state policy lays down that the state shall endeavor to provide free and compulsory education to all children up to fourteen years within ten years from the commencement of the Constitution. Even by 1966 only 76 per cent of the children in the age group six to eleven and 29 per cent of children between eleven to fourteen years would benefit by educational facilities, according to available indications.

This reveals a need for greater concentration of effort in the field of primary education, if social and economic progress is to be achieved. Schooling of children in the urban and rural sectors is marked by a large difference. The All-Indian Educational Survey (conducted between 1957 and 1959) indicated that in 1957 about 29 per cent of rural households and 17 per cent of the rural population were not served by any school whatever.

The economic effects of general education will be apparent only after a long gestation period of, say, ten to twenty years. "Input" of education today will increase national "output" at a considerably later date. Though education is a true social overhead capital in this sense, its effects are indirect and delayed. The key to equality of opportunity will be free and equal access to education for everybody. A socialist pattern of society has necessarily to put a premium on this overhead, even if it can be realized only in the remote future of fifteen to twenty years. It is beyond doubt that a high proportion of national expenditure must therefore flow into education.

The public health program is important as a social measure because it aims at progressive improvement in the health of the people by guaranteeing them a certain minimum of physical well-being and by the creation of conditions favorable to the inducement of greater efficiency and productivity. Special emphasis has to be laid on sanitation, rural and urban water supply, eradication of contagious diseases, training of medical personnel, maternal and child welfare, and health education. The total outlay on public health schemes during 1951-61 comes to Rs. 3,650 million. The proposed Third Plan outlay of Rs. 3,420 million is certainly a recognition of the importance of public health.

A most promising aspect of the public health program is the emphasis on planned parenthood. The main objective of the state in supporting the spread of family planning is the immediate need to control the explosive growth of population revealed by the 1961 census. India is one of the few countries in the world where family planning receives active government support. An outlay of Rs. 300 million has been proposed for the Third Plan as against a mere Rs. 30 million during the Second Plan. The program proposed would involve intensive education, provision of adequate medical supplies, services, and advice coupled with demographic and medical research on the largest scale possible. Family planning has to assume the dynamic character of a nation-wide movement which should embody a basic attitude towards a better life for the individual, the family, and the community.

With the enormous and persistent increase in the population, coupled with a continuous and large exodus from rural to urban centers, the provision of housing facilities is a challenge to the community. Private housing is largely left in the hands of individuals, although through the co-operatives, government help is not insubstantial. However, the housing program had its beginning during the First Plan in most of the states. This was directed mainly towards housing the industrial workers and low-income groups. The program was later expanded to cover slum clearance, plantation-labor housing, and village housing. The implementation of these schemes entailed an expenditure of Rs. 800 million during 1951-56. In addition, specific schemes were set afoot for the benefit of backward classes and tribes. The Union and state governments undertook housing schemes on a considerable scale. During the Second Plan about 500,000 houses were constructed, and the total outlay was about Rs. 2,500 million. But all these schemes do not meet even part of the problem, and the growth of the slums on the periphery of cities bears out this point. Between 1951 and 1961 urban population in the country has probably increased by 40 per cent. The shortage of houses in urban areas might increase from 2.5 million in 1951 to 5 million in 1961. During the Third Plan, the provision for housing is only Rs. 4,000 million.[27]

Satisfactory working conditions, safety of the workers, and promotion of labor welfare have been somewhat insured through labor legislation. The social security measures have, however, just begun to operate. The Employees' State Insurance Scheme will cover about 1.7 million workers during the Third Plan period. The Employees' Provident Fund Scheme now covering fifty-eight industries will be further expanded during 1961-66. The government has accepted the principle of increasing its contribution from 6.25 per cent to 8.33 per cent. Much remains to be done yet to provide a decent living for the workers in their old age.

The state has accepted the responsibility to insure minimum wages for certain sections of workers, both in industry and agriculture, who are economically weak. The Minimum Wages Act provides for the fixing and revision of wage rates in certain occupations. In most of the industries the wages are determined on the basis of collective bargaining, conciliation, arbitration, and adjudication. The Indian trade unions, though divided because of different ideological and political affiliations, are still a strong force in cer-

[27] In the private sector it is difficult to estimate the magnitude of construction. It is, however, estimated that about Rs. 19,000 million would have been spent during 1951-61 and a further sum of Rs. 11,250 million would be spent during the Third Plan.

tain industries, of which textiles, steel, and railways are worth mentioning. As stated earlier, the Second Plan recommended the setting up of wage boards as a suitable method of settling wage disputes, and wage boards were appointed for cotton and jute textiles, sugar, cement, and plantation industries. A board will shortly be set up for the iron and steel industry and for other industries as and when need arises.

The setting up of joint management councils will have a great impact on the productivity of labor, as the workers thus get a sense of belonging. So far twenty-three such councils have been set up. During the Third Plan an attempt would be made for progressive extension of the scheme to new industries. This will be an important step whereby the private sector will fit into the framework of a socialist order.

The Constitution guarantees to the weaker sections of the community, particularly scheduled castes and tribes, an assurance in the matter of their economic and social interests. According to the 1951 census, the population of scheduled tribes was estimated at 22.5 million and that of scheduled castes at 55 million. During the decade 1951-61 an outlay of Rs. 1,090 million was incurred for programs related to the welfare of backward classes in order to raise their standard of living and to enable them to fit gradually into the framework of the progressive part of the population. During the Third Plan an outlay of Rs. 1,140 million is to be spent to continue the program started during the previous decade. The situation, however, does not show enough signs of improvement. Much more sweeping changes to raise the general standard of life would be necessary to meet the situation adequately; the impact of government efforts so far has not been perceptible.

The development outlays incurred during 1951-61 were considerable and were supposed to contribute a fair share in the achievement of social equality. Though the state is wedded to the concept of a socialist pattern of society, where the maximization of the people's welfare is the main criterion, conflicts cannot be avoided between short-run social and economic objectives. To attain a self-sustained growth, the fulfilment of economic objectives needs preference over social objectives. But India, unlike the industrialized countries which created a welfare state long after development, has started with an initial welfare state although her economy is one of the poorest in the world. Her fast developing social conscience is not matched by an equal economic capacity to satisfy it.

In India today the state has, by virtue of historical circumstances and present compulsions, become a major employer, a major industrialist, a major commercial banker, a major insurer, a major trader. These responsibilities are so heavy that the need for a very large number of trained personnel to carry out these various functions has become very urgent and apparent. In turn, this has thrown upon the government a further responsibility of training many thousands of persons in different fields. The supply of technical and other trained personnel has also become an added responsibility of the Indian Government.

Obviously, the number of officials and experts is growing in such large numbers that a sort of privileged and power-centered bureaucratic class might emerge which will detract from a democratically functioning society. So far this danger has not been evident. But it is conceivable that where so much of economic, social, and other powers are concentrated in the hands of government officials and where the public is so dependent upon the government or bureaucracy, the democratic structure might be weakened and a bureaucratically run society might dominate. The danger of misuse of its power by this so-called privileged class has, however, not materialized.

India faces a challenge. Should she choose a number of social reforms for a large section of the society at the cost of economic development? Can she afford to risk her economic progress to usher in social reforms that would inevitably come in due course in the wake of higher production from factories and fields? On the other hand, it may be that economic progress is conditioned by these necessary social changes. The question is not easy to answer, but on the right choice of priorities depends the rate of growth of the economy as well as increased levels of living.

CONCLUSION

What of the future? It is hazardous to prophesy. Nevertheless, there are clear indications that the state will be called upon to play an increasingly prominent role in the nation's economic life. On the one hand, it is imperative to accelerate the pace of development not only to insure an appreciable improvement in the living standards of a rapidly growing population but also to maintain at least India's relative economic, and hence political, position in the world. This would mean a rapid increase in the rate of investment. And to the extent that the economy fails to generate the requisite volume of savings spontaneously, the state must take appropriate measures to raise the necessary resources. Equally strong pressures for greater state intervention are likely to arise from the need to further the social objectives of promoting a greater measure of equality and welfare in the society.

Until now the government has interpreted the "socialist pattern of society" in a realistic and rather pragmatic manner. So much so that critics are not wanting who say that India is far less socialistic than the United States or the United Kingdom. But such comparisons, which are often based on the percentage of national expenditure controlled by the government, are not quite relevant. For the motivation and content of state intervention in India are quite different from those in other countries. There is great faith in government action as the solution for many of the country's economic and social ills. Even where there is a doubt regarding the efficacy of the government's role in specific matters, public opinion is in favor not of less but more governmental action. Even if in certain situations when the wisest course of action would be inaction and non-intervention there is a tendency to resort to some kind of action, be it unsound or unfruitful. The pressure for action of any kind has become irresistible.

There is a widespread concern that a decade of planning has done little to improve the lot of the common man, in spite of the emphasis given to the reduction in inequalities of income and wealth and of providing wider opportunities for all members of the community. A 16 per cent increase in the per capita income is hardly sufficient to make a strong impression on the minds of the people, especially when their expectations are rising. The situation is made worse by the fact that the increase in income has not been distributed evenly. In fact, there is a belief that the stronger sections of the community have benefited most from the plans and that inequalities have, if anything, increased. One evidence in support of this is the inability of the economy to provide full and reasonable remunerative jobs to even the natural increase in the labor force. Unemployment in the economy has increased appreciably over the last five years. The fact that the regional rates of development differ, often to the disadvantage of the poorer regions, lends further strength to this belief.

However inevitable these tendencies towards accentuated inequalities may be in the initial stages of development, the fact remains that they create tensions in society whose political implications cannot be overlooked. For this reason, the government may be compelled to take drastic action to redress the situation.

There are already some signs that thinking is veering in this direction. For instance, a committee recently appointed by the Ministry of Community Development to suggest measures for promoting the welfare of the weaker sections of the community has put forward some quite radical recommendations. Among other things, it suggests that the government should accept the obligation to provide a guarantee of employment to all people in rural areas who want work. It further suggests that the present system of land ownership which keeps agriculture and cultivators in a chronically depressed condition must be completely scrapped and the ownership and management transferred to the village authority and not be left to individual ownership and management. Voluntary co-operative farming is regarded by many as likely to be a slow and long drawn-out business, and some element of compulsion is regarded as necessary and legitimate.

The Third Plan has committed itself to the definite goal of bringing about a breakthrough in agriculture and food production by increased investments and better organization and administration in the rural sector. But doubts arise as to whether the goal will be achieved, because a mere continuation of the present patterns of investment, without equal regard to action designed to change the system of social values in the villages, will not bring about the desired end. Much hope is rested on the Village Panchayats and Village Co-operatives to bring about the necessary transformation of the economy, but if this hope is frustrated, as well it might be, then government will be driven to more drastic intervention.

In the industrial and urban sectors of the economy the private and public sectors are increasingly coming to terms, and in recent years there is a better understanding and appreciation of the value of the mixed enterprise system. Notwithstanding the expanding public sector, there has been no threat to the expansion of the private sector. Indeed, the latter had expanded faster during the Second Plan.

The private sector has taken full advantage of the opportunities provided by foreign aid and of the favorable climate for its expansion. In a sense it has been strengthened by foreign aid and foreign private investment, by whose contact its own efficiency has improved; also recognition of the value of foreign private investment has naturally brought about a welcome change in the attitudes of those who were previously hostile to the domestic private sector. Even so, the social problem created by growing unemployment and growing inequalities may disturb a proper relationship between the two sectors. Whether the country will be content with this balanced system of mixed enterprise or will embark upon a more full-blooded socialism no one can foresee. Much will depend upon the performance of the private sector and upon its adjustments to the socially ordered society which is the accepted national goal. More, and not less, government action and intervention will be called for.

If the present government fails in its tasks, the alternative will not be a government favoring more free enterprise but rather one which will be more radical and more wedded to socialism. On present reckoning, the chances of either a socialist party or a communist party coming into power in the near future are slim. But much depends upon the next five years. How the challenge and threat posed by the stark and naked poverty of the masses of the people who have not substantially improved their lot during a decade of planning are met will determine the shape of the state and the government in the years to come. The economic system of the country will undoubtedly be a much more publicly ordered and socially oriented system than it is. But whether it will be a democratic one or will have to resort to greater regimentation, the future alone can tell.

8

The Economy of Malaya
Relevance of the Competitive Laissez-Faire Model

T. H. Silcock*

In applying to the economy of Malaya tests of the relevance of the competitive model, it has seemed desirable to use the following method. First, there is a brief sketch of the character of the economy and its relations with the rest of the world. Next, an attempt is made to discuss the present position and the trends in certain main branches of economic life with special reference to price fixing by large aggregates or by the government. This involves some consideration of the actual political aims of the governments, past and present. Finally, some brief comments on the theoretical significance of the facts about this particular economy are presented.

For the purpose of this study the economies of the Federation of Malaya and Singapore are grouped together, though politically they are separate, and even if they are merged in the Greater Federation of Malaysia, are unlikely to be completely integrated economically[1] Much of the ownership both of European and of Chinese business is common to both political areas,[2] there is a common currency,[3] and fiscal policies are discussed between the two governments.[4]

* Emeritus Professor of Economics, University of Malaya.

[1] International Bank for Reconstruction and Development, *The Economic Development of Malaya* (Baltimore, 1955), chap. ii and *passim;* T. H. Silcock, *Towards a Malayan Nation* (Singapore, 1961), pp. 96-112.

[2] F. C. Benham, *The National Income of Malaya, 1947-49* (Singapore, 1951), p. i; J. J. Puthucheary, *Ownership and Control in the Malayan Economy* (Singapore, 1960), chaps. ii, vi.

[3] F. H. H. King, *Money in British East Asia* (Colonial Research Studies no. 19; London, 1957), pp. 26-27. Negotiations in February 1960 led to small revisions of detail within the same system. See *Straits Times*, 3rd Merdeka Anniversary Special Feature, Aug. 31, 1960.

[4] These discussions are informal and up to the present appear to have taken place both at ministerial and at civil service levels. Presentation of the bedgets is approximately synchronized.

Common policy in tariff protection and in other measures to promote industrialization is under discussion.[5] In other respects the economies are separate, with a tariff wall between them. Singapore is almost a free port, living by entrepôt trade, manufacture, and a market-oriented agriculture;[6] while the Federation of Malaya is still predominantly an economy of primary production and semisubsistence agriculture.[7] National income per head is about twice as high in Singapore as in the Federation of Malaya.[8]

Taken as a whole, Malaya has an economy strongly oriented toward primary production for export markets. It is characterized by extreme instability, both because it is unusually dependent on only two products—rubber and tin—and because these are products of unusual price-instability.

Rubber and tin together accounted in 1960 for 65 per cent of Malaya's total export trade. About one-third of this was entrepôt trade in, and processing of, these two products.[9] In the 1959 *Annual Survey* of the United Nations Economic Commission for Asia and the Far East the average annual fluctuations in the prices of these two products since the war were given as 29.4 per cent and 13.8 per cent, respectively.[10]

Moreover, the proportion of Malaya's total income derived from trade is unusually high. Statistics of income by industrial origin are inadequate, but a rough indication of this dependence can be given by comparing the gross national product in 1953, the year before the International Bank Mission's visit, with the total value of exports of domestic produce in the same year. The former was Malayan $5,780 million, the latter M$1,486 million. To the latter figure must be added the difference between c.i.f. cost of imports for re-export and f.o.b. value of re-exports, namely M$160 million, a

---

[5] F. J. Lyle, *An Industrial Development Programme* (Legislative Assembly, Singapore; Cmd. 5 of 1959). Preliminary discussions between the Federation and Singapore were held in 1960 on the basis of a modified program of a "Commodity Common Market" (*Straits Times, loc. cit.*). The matter was also discussed at the 1960 meeting of the U.N. Economic Commission for Asia and the Far East.

[6] F. C. Benham, *Economic Survey of Singapore, 1957* (Singapore, 1957).

[7] International Bank for Reconstruction and Development, *op. cit.*

[8] Benham, *Economic Survey of Singapore* and *National Income of Malaya*; International Bank for Reconstruction and Development, *op. cit.* No separate figure for the Federation is available, though an estimate is being prepared.

[9] Chief Statistician, *Malayan Statistics* (Singapore, Dec. 1961), Table 10.3; *Malayan Statistics, External Trade* (Singapore, Dec. 1960), pp. 173, 178.

[10] Economic Commission for Asia and the Far East, *Economic Survey of Asia and the Far East, 1957* (Bangkok, 1958), chap. v.

rough estimate of the gains from entrepôt trade.[11] Just under 30 per cent of gross national product is derived from trade.

The situation is thus one in which very large fluctuations in the national income are caused by changes in the world price of two products. Roughly a quarter of this income varies more or less directly with the price of rubber, and this has an impact throughout the economy. Tin is much less important, but its violent fluctuations influence government revenue and the balance of payments.

Macroeconomic implications of this instability are interesting and important, but are not treated in the present study.[12] We seek rather to inquire whether such instability has generated concentrations of economic power for the sake of protecting incomes or capital assets against competition, as has happened so frequently elsewhere. Have governments or associations of traders or producers established institutions which hamper the movement of factors and the mutual adjustment of supply, demand, and price?

Broadly, the picture that emerges is one of an economy heavily dependent on exports of primary products, in which we find standard grading and competitive bids in a number of markets linked throughout the world;[13] these markets play an important role in Malaya's economic life, but the responses to such markets do not wholly conform to standard economic theory. They have been modified by pressures from governments, both colonial and independent, in the interest of political and economic stability[14] and of a number of other non-economic or semi-economic objectives;[15] and also by the owners of assets, in the interest of preserving capital values.[16]

Yet reactions to instability, though important in Malaya, are not the only factors which cause it to diverge from the competitive, laissez-faire model. We must also consider the institutional effects

[11]International Bank for Reconstruction and Development, *op. cit.*, pp. 14, 16.

[12] *ECAFE, Economic Survey, 1957*, chap. v; J. P. Meek, *Malaya: A Study of Government Response to the Korean Boom* (Ithaca, N. Y. 1955). A brief review of macroeconomic aspects can be found in T. H. Silcock, ed., *Readings in Malayan Economics* (Singapore, 1961), part iii.

[13] Joan Wilson, *The Singapore Rubber Market* (Singapore, 1959), chaps. i, iv; K. E. Knorr, *Tin under Control* (Stanford, 1945), pp. 29, 63.

[14] T. H. Silcock, *The Commonwealth Economy in Southeast Asia* (Durham, 1959), chap. ii.

[15] Sir A. McFadyean, *History of Rubber Regulation* (London, 1944), chap. ii; J. W. F. Rowe, *Studies in the Artificial Control of Raw Material Supplies: Rubber* (London, 1930).

[16] J. K. Eastham, "Rationalisation in the Tin Industry," *Review of Economic Studies*, IV (1936), 13-32.

of politics and ideology.[17] Malaya is a plural society made up of the descendants of four economically distinct groups—the distinctions partly coinciding with, and partly crossing, racial lines.[18] It is also a society in which the reaction of different groups to socialist ideology, mainly introduced from overseas, has some influence on economic organization, though this influence is extremely complex.

These divergences from the standard model mean that for some purposes in economic analysis, interpretation, and measurement, this model is inadequate. But it is by no means clear that Malaya provides a case for searching for an alternative economic model. It may rather provide a justification for using other than economic techniques—combined in general with economic analysis using existing models—in interpreting its economy.

In rubber, Malaya's most important product, there are two types of production: large-scale estates and smallholdings. The great majority of the former are owned by predominantly European, limited companies; of the latter, by Malay peasants. There are, however, two other types of holding that have some importance: estates owned by Chinese and Indians, mainly on an individual or family basis; and smallholdings owned by Chinese and Indians, which are usually rather larger than the Malay ones and usually employ some hired labor.[19]

The approximate orders of magnitude of the different types of ownership during the postwar period are as follows.[20] Some two million of the three and a half million acres under rubber are on estates of over one hundred acres. Nearly three-quarters of these

[17] T. H. Silcock and Ungku A. Aziz, "Nationalism in Malaya" in W. L. Holland, ed., *Asian Nationalism and the West* (New York, 1953), pp. 267-345; L. W. Pye, *Guerrilla Communism in Malaya* (Princeton, 1956), pp. 55-58.

[18] T. H. Silcock, "Migration Problems of the Far East," in B. Thomas, ed., *Economics of International Migration* (London, 1958), chap. xviii; N. Ginsberg and C. F. Roberts, Jr., *Malaya* (Seattle, 1958), esp. chap. iii.

[19] *Report of a Mission (Chairman F. Mudie) of Enquiry into the Rubber Industry of Malaya* (Kuala Lumpur, 1954), pp. 24-35; R. Ma and You Poh Seng, "Economic Characteristics of the Population of the Federation of Malaya, 1957," *Malayan Economic Review*, V, no. 2 (1960), 38; P. T. Bauer, *Report on a Visit to the Rubber Growing Smallholdings of Malaya* (Colonial Research Publications no. 1; London, 1948), pp. 9, 77-79; Federation of Malaya, *Census of Agriculture 1960* (Kuala Lumpur, 1960-62), vols. vii, viii. There is much inconsistency in the data and fuller interpretation of the Census of Agriculture is needed.

[20] See Federation of Malaya, Department of Statistics, *Rubber Statistics Handbook, 1959* (Kuala Lumpur, 1960), p. 10, for estates, and Mudie, *op. cit.*, for smallholdings.

are estates of one thousand acres or more, mostly public limited companies; on these large estates three acres are owned by Europeans for every one owned by Asians. The remaining quarter is mainly in individual or family ownership, and only about one-seventh of them are European owned. Of the smallholdings, totalling rather more than a million acres, some two-thirds are owned by Malays, mainly in small units of less than five acres, operated by family labor or sharecroppers. The remainder are owned mainly by Chinese and Indians, and often operated by wage labor or labor contractors[21]

There is a good deal of concentration in the European section of the industry. The actual number of estates, even over one thousand acres, is large (nearly six hundred), but the number of independent units of control is much smaller. This is because the estates are controlled by managing agencies and secretarial companies, each of which normally controls a number of different estates.[22] Financial investment by different rubber companies in one another's shares and interlocking directorates limit the independence of action of the different companies. It is doubtful, however, whether there is sufficient cohesion to make the competitive model inappropriate in interpreting normal price formation, however significant this cohesion may be politically. Even the five largest managing agencies, controlling three-quarters of a million acres among them, would not be able to affect output on more than 10 per cent of world acreage.[23] The rubber market is a world-wide one, with close interaction between Singapore, London, and New York; and there can be little doubt that producing companies in normal times accept the price of rubber as a datum and adjust the scale of their output to it in the way that will maximize their profits.

Yet, though the structure of control probably does not influence the volume of output, it may well influence the technical methods of the industry. Planters commonly say that the overheads in processing, packing, and shipping are inflated by the fact that many of the managing agencies have individual interests in auxiliary services which differ from the interests of the rubber companies for which they are nominally acting. Bauer has shown that these costs fluctuate

[21] See Bauer, *Report on a Visit*, pp. 9, 77-79, for character of holdings.
[22] Puthucheary, *op. cit.*, pp. 27-50.
[23] P. T. Bauer, *The Rubber Industry: A Study in Competition and Monopoly* (London, 1948), p. 9.

appreciably with changes in the price of rubber;[24] and this might well indicate that such costs were deliberately inflated in good times. Moreover, the greater adjustment of smallholders' tapping practices to price changes[25] may reflect a greater willingness to adjust quantity, as a result of the absence of any smallholder interest in packing, shipping, etc.

All these, however, are relatively minor influences of the structure of ownership on the competitive pattern. It is through governmental restriction of output, based on the estates' political power, that consolidation of control has had its chief effect.

The pattern of ownership of the small estates and the smallholdings modifies the competitive picture very little. The use of labor contractors instead of direct payment of labor has some influence, which will be considered later. Many of the smaller farmers are sharecroppers and some are also in debt to shopkeepers.[26] Sharecropping systems vary from place to place, but there has as yet been no comparative study to determine the relation (if any) between the systems and the relative scarcities of land and of labor. Indebtedness to dealers certainly introduces an element of monopsony, which affects the price received by the producer. Rubber is not a seasonal crop, and where this indebtedness exists it may be the result either of advances during the waiting period between planting and first tapping, or of overspending during a boom. It is, on the whole, much less serious than the seasonal credit shortage which causes heavy indebtedness among rice producers.

Apart from the combination of shopkeepers, rubber dealers, and money-lenders who trade directly with the smallholders, the marketing of rubber conforms reasonably well to the competitive pattern.[27] There are minor elements of monopoly or monopsony: for example, the legal requirement (mainly in the interest of quality) that rubber dealers and rubber packers must be licensed, and the comparatively

[24] P. T. Bauer, "Rubber Production Costs during the Great Depression," *Economic Journal*, LIII (1943), 361-369.

[25] P. T. Bauer, "The Working of Rubber Regulation," *Economic Journal*, LVI (1946), 391-414; P. T. Bauer, "Notes on Cost," *Economica*, N.S. XII (May 1945), 90-100; T. H. Silcock, "A Note on the Working of Rubber Regulation," *Economic Journal*, LVIII (1948), 228-235.

[26] U. A. Aziz, *Survey of Five Villages in Nyalas* (mimeographed; University of Malaya, 1957). J. W. L. Bevan, *Report on the Marketing of Smallholders' Rubber, with Special Reference to the First Buyer Level*, Kuala Lumpur Rubber Research Institute, Research Archives Document 7, 1956.

[27] See Wilson, *op. cit.*, chap. v, for a brief account of the market structure.

small number of manufacturers' representatives on the Singapore Rubber Market. These things may slightly affect trade margins but not the basic character of competition.

Rubber smallholders who are not in debt normally have a choice of dealers to whom they can offer their rubber. The dealers can usually gain something by juggling with weights or grades; and if they are shopkeepers to whom the smallholder is in debt, they give a lower price; but competition, actual or potential, keeps these margins fairly small.[28]

These dealers again have a choice of wholesale channels, a choice not normally exercised because of trade credit, family ties, and social relationships, but implicit nevertheless and acting to limit the margin of profit. There are many wholesale dealers on the Singapore rubber market and there is adequate control of grading. The importance of grading and technical classification of rubber has been increasing as a result of the competition of synthetic rubber.[29] At the same time the existing methods for insuring reliable grades, which rest on foreign control, are politically vulnerable. A court decision in 1958,[30] which in effect destroyed the legal basis for enforcement of contracts in Singapore's market in rubber futures, has increased the vulnerability of the rubber market. The Federation of Malaya has also recently enacted legislation (February 1962) to set up its own rubber market in Kuala Lumpur. If this market can match or improve the grading and hedging arrangements of Singapore it will no doubt take over much of the business in time. But if it fails to do so a damaging struggle between economic and political forces may result.

This throws into relief the political background of the rubber industry. Because of its dominant position in the life of Malaya it has naturally attracted a good deal of attention from governments; and some of the actions taken by governments are distinctly relevant to the competitive model which we are discussing, even though in most

[28] See J. W. L. Bevan, *op. cit.*; and also K. R. Chou, "Report on the Credit System of the Distributive Trade of Sarawak," in Appendix B of T. H. Silcock, *Fiscal Survey Report of Sarawak* (Sarawak, 1956) for a brief account of a similar structure.

[29] See C. Gamba, *Synthetic Rubber and Malaya* (Singapore, 1956) for an analysis of the development of competition from the synthetic rubber industry.

[30] S. E. Mizrahie v. Stanton Nelson & Co. Ltd. (1958). See *Malayan Law Journal*, XXIV (1958), 97; T. H. Silcock, "A Note on Futures Trading and the Singapore Rubber Market," *Malayan Economic Review*, III, no. 2 (1958), 63. Legislation to regularize existing Singapore practice and render it enforceable is at present under consideration in Singapore.

cases the economic aspects of these actions can be described and analyzed fairly accurately within the framework of a competitive economy, with minor adjustments. It is in criticism and appraisal (in the Malayan context) that the model seems least adequate. In more technical language, the model needs only minor, and manageable, adjustments for positive economics. For normative economics, and still more for political economy, it is seriously inadequate.[31]

The first government measures in this industry were, of course, the introduction of the seeds, the experimental working-out of appropriate tapping systems in the Botanic Gardens, and the efforts, mainly by Ridley as Director of the Botanic Gardens, to stimulate the interest of existing planters (of sugar, coffee, etc.) in this crop.[32] The motives behind this activity are easily intelligible in practical terms but do not fit at all neatly into economic categories. They are not explicable in terms of furthering the wealth of either Great Britain or Malaya, whether considered as political or geographical entities. There was a general desire to found a new industry that might be profitable, some interest in fostering an Empire source of a product mainly produced in foreign territory, and some desire to "open up" the country for the sake of increased revenue and power. There was no desire to favor—for example—British at the expense of Chinese or French planters, or planting in Malaya at the expense of planting in Sumatra. For complex reasons there was some discouragement of independent planting by Malay smallholders; and the attitude to immigration of labor for the rubber industry was not explicable by treating the laborers either as potential citizens or as an external resource to be acquired as cheaply as possible.

Government policy in the development of the industry from 1900 to 1918 cannot be at all adequately explained in terms of attempting to maximize anything, either by acting or by refraining from action. So far as maximizing considerations had any impact they operated through the belief that free trade, accompanied by government provision of essential services, would in some undefined way increase the wealth of the businesses in Malaya and its government revenue. The interests of laborers were considered not in terms of maximizing their income, but of insuring freedom of contract, honest migration con-

[31] P. T. Bauer, *Economic Analysis and Policy in Underdeveloped Countries* (London, 1957), chap. i.

[32] G. C. Allen and Audrey G. Donnithorne, *Western Enterprise in Indonesia and Malaya* (London, 1957), pp. 109-110.

ditions, and healthy surroundings.[33] Smallholders' interests were considered in terms of maintaining a stable way of life and secure food supply.

The result of this policy, at the end of World War I, was an industry very much more developed than it would have been if income per head of the local population had been the main consideration, though less developed than if profit and revenue alone had been the factors borne in mind.

At this stage, after a short postwar boom, a sharp decline in the world price of rubber threatened the solvency of the rubber companies and of the newly developed Chinese banks, and also the revenue of the Federated Malay States government. This inclined the governments to listen to appeals from the planters to introduce compulsory restriction of the export of rubber. On the advice of a committee under the chairmanship of Sir James Stevenson an automatic scheme was introduced throughout the British Empire territories.[34]

This scheme, which lasted until 1928, and a subsequent international regulation scheme which lasted from 1934 to 1942, have been criticized[35] on the ground that the quotas allotted to smallholders were unfair in relation to their productive capacity. Quotas were, in effect, transferable; and at very low prices of rubber the smallholders were net sellers, because labor costs were a higher proportion and overheads a lower proportion of their costs.[36] At medium and high prices they were buyers; and even in spite of this their average output per acre was reduced under restriction. There appears, therefore, to be some ground for the view that the government was less than fair to smallholders.

It is, however, at least doubtful whether such criteria can be applied in relation to the circumstances then prevailing. They imply an attitude to economic development, by a colonial government in the early twentieth century, which does not fully conform to the facts and is of doubtful value even as normative economics.

No doubt the government was ignorant of the potentialities of rubber cultivation by smallholders. But this was true largely because it

[33] W. L. Blythe, "History of Chinese Labour in Malaya," *Journal of the Malayan Branch of the Royal Asiatics Society*, XX (June 1947), 64-114; Lennox A. Mills, *British Rule in Eastern Asia* (London, 1942), chap. vi.

[34] McFadyean, *op. cit.*, chap. ii.

[35] Bauer, *Report on a Visit to the Rubber Growing Smallholdings of Malaya* and "The Working of Rubber Regulation," *loc. cit.*

[36] Silcock, "A Note on the Working of Rubber Regulation," *loc. cit.*

had not been government policy actively to encourage this industry at all. Rubber was a new and speculative crop. It was also one which took long to mature; the length of life of the tree was unknown, and research into tapping methods and bark renewal was fairly new. It was believed—erroneously, as Bauer has shown[37]—that smallholders' unscientific methods were producing a quick revenue at a cost of destroying their assets. The fact that this did not happen was due to good luck, rather than either experience or scientific knowledge.[38] Moreover, the policy of the administration toward the Malays tended to be protective rather than to favor encouraging them to take unknown risks. In Malaya, in the main, rubber growing was being substituted not (as in Sumatra and Borneo)[39] for shifting cultivation but for cultivation of rice by traditional methods.[40] The change brought increased income, but at some cost in commercial risk and social disorganization. The official attitude, as expressed in land alienation and other administrative measures, was one of discouraging too much diversion from rice to rubber, while in principle using the increased revenue derived from rubber to strengthen the economic and political structure of the Malay states.

The restriction schemes should be regarded as measures undertaken mainly to maintain the capital value of reasonably run estates,[41] in conditions of adversity, while trying as far as possible to treat smallholders fairly. The official ignorance of smallholders' economy is much less culpable than is often supposed, since it must be judged in the whole context of policy towards the impact of a commercial world on an economically unsophisticated, traditional Malay society.

Broadly speaking, the political influence of the rubber industry was exercised through the trading and estate-owning interests, at

[37] Bauer, *Report on a Visit*, pp. 74-77; "Working of Rubber Regulation," *loc. cit.*; "Economics of Planting Density in Rubber Growing," *Economicia*, N.S. XIII (1946) 131-135.

[38] Estate practice had been based on an extended period of research; see Allen and Donnithorne, *op. cit.*; smallholders' practice was not based on adequate study (see Bauer, *Report on a Visit*, pp. 42-45) and did not reproduce natural conditions or conditions found in any other country. In view of the time taken in maturing a rubber tree and the absence of systematic research into smallholding conditions, data for a reasonable judgment were hardly available when restriction was introduced.

[39] Bauer, "Working of Rubber Regulation," *loc. cit.*

[40] It must be emphasized that it is labor not land that is transferred from rice to rubber, making the output of rice fall when rubber prices are high. See *Report of the Rice Cultivation Committee* (Kuala Lumpur, 1931), p. 15.

[41] MacFadyean, *op. cit.*, chap. iii.

least in the spheres of promotion, export regulation, control of trade channels, etc.[42] The government's attitude to Malay smallholders and to immigrant laborers was conditioned by several different political pressures, but it did not regard them primarily as economic agents to whom normal maximizing criteria should apply. We may, however, inquire how far the economist can apply such criteria in judging or influencing government policies. This question will be considered after other industries have been explored.

The peculiar structure of ownership in the industry has led to a separation between the influences emphasizing income from rubber and those emphasizing the capital value of the estates. In the absence of a share market and a well-developed system of safeguards against fraud and misrepresentation, even an estate making good profits will not readily find a buyer. The agency houses and secretarial companies specialize in providing the verification, confidence, and continuity that will make a rubber-estate company seem a reasonable investment on the London Stock Exchange.[43]

The majority of individual planters have been short-term operators interested in making a fortune quickly. This can be done only if the estate, once developed, can be sold, or at least partly sold, to a limited company. It is clear that the firms which have been able to build up a reputation for integrity, resources, and concern for shareholders' interests in the Far East have been able to secure for themselves a considerable share in the ownership and control of enterprises developed by others. It is these firms which have been able to exert considerable pressure both on the Colonial Office in London and on colonial governments.

An important recent trend in the industry has been the fragmentation of estates into smallholdings.[44] This is partly an unintended result of a government replanting scheme. The prospect of early political independence led many of the poorer estates to neglect replanting with up-to-date, high-yielding trees. Hence the government, to counter the threat of synthetic rubber, introduced a scheme

---

[42] Puthucheary, op. cit., chap. ii; Allen and Donnithorne, op. cit., chap. ii; Kathleen M. Stahl, The Metropolitan Organisation of British Colonial Trade (London, 1957), chaps. iii-iv.

[43] Stahl, op. cit.

[44] See U. A. Aziz, "Land Disintegration and Land Policy in Malaya," Malayan Economic Review, III, no. 1 (1958), 22-29; also two recent graduation exercises at the University of Malaya, which produced new information on this question, by A. Degani and R. K. Mamajiwala.

of compulsory levies on the export of rubber to finance replanting. For technical and political reasons a higher rate of payment was offered for smallholdings than for estates. In addition, smallholders are naturally exempted from the fairly costly social obligations to labor (e.g., in housing, health, crèches, etc.) which government regulations impose on estates. These conditions, together with politically motivated undervaluation of rubber estates on the London Stock Exchange, facilitated take-over bids by syndicates for the sake of breaking up estates into smallholdings.

It is possible that the syndicates retain some control over the holdings, by agency or other means, at least in some cases, so that time must elapse before the effect of this on the control structure of the industry becomes apparent.

There has also been a considerable increase in Chinese purchase of shares in the former European companies, as a result of profits made in the Korean war boom and of political independence.[45] It is doubtful, however, whether this has yet had any considerable influence on the units of control, the managing agencies, and secretarial companies.

The second major export industry of Malaya, the tin industry, has a structure of ownership and control broadly similar to that of rubber but with rather more integration on the European side.[46] Some three-fifths of the industry is owned by European public companies. Most of the remainder is in the hands of small Chinese businesses with a complex structure of finance and labor organization.[47] Some 2 per cent of the tin is produced by dulang washers—individual producers who concentrate the ore by hand, using a circular tray in the beds of streams. Almost all of these are Chinese, though a few aborigines also do this collecting.

The structure of the European side of the industry is one of concentration of control through ownership, interlocking directorates, mining agencies, and secretarial firms. In addition there are only

[45] Puthucheary, op. cit., pp. 136-137.

[46] U.S. Senate, Preparedness Subcommittee of the Committee on the Armed Services, Stockpiling of Tin and Rubber, Hearings (Washington, 1951); Senate Subcommittee of the Committee on the Armed Services, Sixth Report on Preparedness (Washington, 1951).

[47] Siew Nim Chee, Labour and Tin Mining in Malaya (Ithaca; Cornell University Southeast Asia Program Data Paper, 1953; mimeo.); Yip Yat Hoong, "The Marketing of Tin-Ore in Kampar," Malayan Economic Review, IV, no. 2 (1959), 45-55.

two smelting firms, and the extent to which competition between them is effective cannot be clearly determined.[48] The scope for joint action makes it relatively easy to bring Malaya in as a unit in any negotiations for restriction of output.[49]

About three-quarters of the output of the European mines—only a little less than half Malaya's output—is produced by firms controlled by three large agencies, among which there is considerable interlocking of interests.[50] One of the two tin smelters is also linked to these groups. Some of the big general agency houses also control tin companies, and the output not controlled by one or other of these large aggregates is little more than 10 per cent of the European production.

The financial structure of the two-fifths of the industry controlled by Chinese is largely unknown. In the main the mines are owned by individuals or small syndicates. There are individually wealthy men with interests in many different mines; some of the small mines are financed by ore dealers who use this as a means of obtaining supplies at low prices; some are owned, in whole or part, by one of the smelting companies or by the Chinese interests which largely control them; some are partly financed by the workers who work on a share basis, demanding only food and pocket money and a subsequent share in the proceeds. There are some six hundred separate Chinese mines, and a large number of these must enjoy substantial independence of action.

Competition between the two smelting companies for marginal supplies of ore is keen; but it appears to take the form of competition for influence rather than rivalry on price margins. There has been joint consultation between them on price margins at least since 1940. Prices paid for ore by the smelters are based on the current London price, though sellers of ore often deliver it without selling, speculating on a rise in the price. The margins deducted are based on assay and quantity delivered, and are uniform between the smelters, though actual competition for business and potential price rivalry probably keep them low.

Generally speaking, Malaya is a low-cost tin producer.[51] Not

[48] Yip, "The Marketing of Tin-Ore," *loc. cit.*
[49] J. K. Eastham, "Rationalisation in the Tin Industry," *Review of Economic Studies*, IV (1936), 13-32.
[50] Puthucheary, *op. cit.*, ch. iv.
[51] Sir Lewis L. Fermor, *Report upon the Mining Industry of Malaya* (Kuala

merely are average costs low, because the tin is alluvial and transport is cheap compared to Malaya's chief competitors; marginal cost is even lower, because the European section is very capital-intensive, while the Chinese section, with a higher labor content, employs its labor mainly on a profit-sharing basis.

In tin, even more than in rubber, however, the concentration of control, through agencies and smelters, insures that political influence is exerted mainly in the interest of maintaining capital values, and not only in Malaya. The European interests in Malaya are associated with tin interests in Bolivia, Nigeria, and elsewhere, where costs are higher. This fact led to active Malayan participation in international schemes for the control of tin exports before World War II, at a time when this meant more serious restrictions on Malaya's capacity than on that of its rivals and virtually no restriction on some of the newer rivals, such as Thailand.[52]

Whenever an important part of an economy is subject to a control scheme, interest attaches to the determinants of decisions about the amount and distribution of quota allocations and also the extent to which they are transferable and the terms on which transfer takes place. There has been no study of the tin industry comparable to Bauer's study of rubber, in which a sequence of prices of export rights and evidence of the direction of transfer is set out. Allocations in Malaya have been made by a government committee with representatives of all sections of the industry and have been based on current production capacity, rather than on production at the base date—which is (subject to bargaining in different schemes) the international basis of allocation.[53] The intention has been to preserve capacity in the long run by encouraging reallocation of quotas among firms under a common control—since such a control was presumed to be willing and able to maintain capacity, even when allocating output to the most efficient units—rather than allowing sale of quotas through the open market. Yet, though pressure in this direction has encouraged concentration of control in larger units among

---

Lumpur, 1959), Part B, x; Eastham, "Rationalisation in the Tin Industry," *loc. cit.*

    [52] Eastham, *op. cit.*

    [53] Siew Nim Chee, "The International Tin Agreement, 1953," *Malayan Economic Review*, II, no. 1 (1957), 35-53; Yip Yat Hoong, "The Domestic Implementation of the 1953 International Tin Agreement in Malaya," *Malayan Economic Review*, V, no. 2 (1960), 59-65.

the Chinese mines, it has proved difficult to prevent direct or indirect sale of quotas. In the main quotas appear to have been sold by European mines to Chinese ones. In the earlier, prewar control schemes, it also proved impossible to prevent considerable smuggling of tin from Malaya, where restriction was severe, to Thailand, where it was light. Attempts to control this led to limitations on the holding of tin stocks in mines, which probably aggravated instability.

Not only the structure of ownership in the industry but the price inelasticity both of demand and of supply, the high capital intensity of tin production, and its importance in war, all favor some control over production. From 1931 to 1942 control schemes operated continuously. During World War II there was strict rationing of tin. Shortly after the removal of these restrictions the Korean War led to high prices again, and the subsequent sharp fall led to renewed demands for a scheme to stabilize prices. In the scheme which operated from 1956 to 1960 there was increased consumer representation and greater emphasis on stabilization, rather than on price maintenance. Quotas were abandoned—no doubt only temporarily—in 1960.[54]

The structure of rice growing is in some respects more important to Malaya's economy than that of the tin industry. Tin is important as an export and source of government revenue and accounts for about a tenth of the national income, but its contribution to employment is small. Rice makes up the greater part of the subsistence sector of the economy even though it contributed only 4.5 per cent of the national income of Malaya in 1949.[55] In the 1959 census some 400,000 people listed as rice (or mainly rice) producers were 18.4 per cent of the working population.[56]

Until recently it was usually believed that rice growers were mostly peasants owning their own land, even though it was recog-

---

[54] Siew, op. cit.; Yip, op. cit.; Lim Chong Yah, "A Reappraisal of the 1953 International Tin Agreement," Malayan Economic Review, V, no. 1 (April 1960), 13-24.

[55] Benham, National Income of Malaya, pp. 119-120.

[56] Federation of Malaya, Department of Statistics, Population Census Reports, 2-12, 1957 (Kuala Lumpur, 1959), table 13 and appendix B. The corresponding figure in 1947 was 25.2 per cent. The difference, however, probably does not indicate any trend because the two censuses were taken in different seasons and the reporting was not accurate enough to allow for this. The number working part-time at rice production would, of course, be much greater.

nized that indebtedness to shopkeepers was important.[57] Restrictions have for many years been imposed on the alienation of land from Malays to non-Malays in most of the areas in which rice is grown.[58] Recent studies have shown, however, that about half the rice land is rented under systems of fixed or variable rent, in cash or rice, or farmed under crop-sharing systems.[59] This does not significantly affect the competitiveness of the market in which rice is sold. The market for rice land, though affected by some rigidities and almost certainly weighted against the farmer by the restrictions on sale to non-Malays, seems sufficiently flexible to respond readily to the influences of scarcity and productivity.

Probably more important than these primitive survivals are the measures taken by the government to maintain the production of rice and also the impact of government policy, during and immediately after the war, on the international rice market in Southeast Asia. Both of these influence in some degree the competitive pattern of the economy.

Broadly, we may say that for nearly forty years the official policy toward rice production was one of encouraging higher productivity and eliminating specific abuses within the general framework of subsistence agriculture, and opposing the spread of commercial attitudes among rice farmers.[60] The policy can be traced to four sources. First, there was the desire to protect the Malay way of life and culture, a result partly of the close relations between the British civil service and the Malay aristocracy, and a genuine nostalgia of Edwardian English gentlemen for a leisured and ceremonial culture, partly of the current fashion of indirect rule and a sense of treaty obligations to the sultans under British protection.[61] Next, there was a political emphasis on the stability of a peasant culture as contrasted with transitory migrant peoples.[62] There was, in addi-

[57] Federation of Malaya, *Report of the Rice Production Committee* (Kuala Lumpur, 1953), pp. 21-22, 41.

[58] Mills, *op. cit.*, pp. 250-251; C. H. Meek, *Land Law and Custom in the Colonies* (London, 1949), pp. 41-42.

[59] T. B. Wilson, *The Economics of Padi Production in North Malaya* (Federation of Malaya Ministry of Agriculture; Kuala Lumpur, 1958), p. 11.

[60] Federated Malay States, *Rice Cultivation Committee Report* (Kuala Lumpur, 1931), pp. 19, 20-22.

[61] Sir F. Swettenham, *British Malaya* (London, revised edition, 1948), chaps. x, xi, xv.

[62] R. Emerson, *Malaysia, A Study in Direct and Indirect Rule* (New York, 1937), pp. 17-19 and chaps. iv, v, vii.

tion, some appreciation of the fact that on commercial grounds rice growing could not compete and would decline in importance if the traditional subsistence agriculture ceased to prevail; while the attraction of rubber and other commercial crops was felt to be spurious because it put the commercially unsophisticated Malay peasant in the power of the shrewd, hard-working, and commercially fluent Chinese shopkeeper. Finally, after the rice riots at the end of World War I there was a rather obsessive concern with increasing Malaya's self-sufficiency in food, which took the form of exaggerated anxiety about desertion of their rice fields by Malay peasants.[63]

This official policy led not only to Malay reservations. Land for rice growing was alienated on special terms, and special obligations in cultivating practices were imposed. Local administration took an active interest in the maintenance and improvement of rice cultivation to the neglect of other crops. Even education policy was affected, the design of Malay education being adapted to maintaining and improving peasant agriculture.[64]

Though recent trends in rice policy have been increasingly toward attempting to make rice-growing a commercially profitable undertaking,[65] the prewar policy is important not only because of its effect on the present distribution of land and structure of the economy, but also because a protective attitude toward the Malay rice cultivator as such is still an important element in current right-wing political thought in Malaya, and exercises a distinct influence on policy.

Rice was the most important product subjected to rationing during the war and postwar shortages. The Japanese tried ineffectually to ration it, but the black market supplies organized by the Chinese, mainly from Thailand, were far more important than the government supply network. During the period of the International Emergency Food Control it was generally believed that about 50 per cent

[63] Federated Malay States, *Rice Cultivation Committee Report*, p. 14.
[64] Ho Seng Ong, *Education for Unity in Malaya* (Penang, 1952), pp. 49-52. Though there is little doubt that by the 1930's education policy was influenced by the desire to keep the Malays (other than the most able ones) from wanting to leave their padi fields, it is only fair to note that R. O. Winstedt, who first introduced a rural and vocational bias, was also the first to secure any keen Malay participation in education. See D. D. Chelliah, *A Short History of the Educational Policy of the Straits Settlements* (Kuala Lumpur, 1947), especially pp. 58-79.
[65] Federation of Malaya, *Final Report of the Rice Committee* (Kuala Lumpur, 1956), especially chaps. ii-iii.

of the supplies in Malaya came through the black market.[66] The price margin was initially high because of distribution costs, since there were no legal sources of extra-ration rice. In effect, however, all the governments of Southeast Asia at this time were making claims, based on population and needs, for the allocation of limited supplies allocated by the Control; while at the same time they were all partly dependent on the efficient organization of smuggling, to which they turned a blind eye. The free market was therefore never effectively suppressed; and as soon as the Thais were allowed by the Control to offer those who handed over their rice a proportion of it (initially 3 per cent) to sell without restriction, the distribution cost fell dramatically. Wholesale dealers were enabled to arrange open retail distribution (nominally of "3%" Thai rice) and left virtually unmolested.

The chief effect of the period of ineffectual government monopoly on the present rice market is the existence of a number of large rice mills in government ownership and the persistence of a demand that government should subsidize rice production by a guaranteed minimum price for locally produced rice, a demand rejected in the majority report of the Rice Committee in 1956.[67]

The present market is highly competitive at the wholesale and retail levels, though the grading of local varieties of rice is still inadequate. The purchasing of rice, however, is heavily dominated by indebtedness. It has been estimated that four-fifths or more of the seasonal credit requirements are met by loans against the growing crop, which bind the rice farmer to sell to a particular buyer.[68] The majority of these rice buyers are also shopkeepers who supply consumption goods to the peasants. The co-operative movement has been a little more successful in rice than in other sectors of the economy,[69] but its impact on indebtedness is still small.

In part this indebtedness must be regarded as the result of a government policy, which hinders the alienation of land while doing

[66] See Malayan Union and Singapore, *Joint Wages Commission, Interim Report* (Kuala Lumpur, 1947), appendix D, where some specimen laborers' budgets are given.

[67] Federation of Malaya, *Final Report of the Rice Committee, 1956*, pp. 68-70, and *Minority Report*, pp. 102-103. See also Federation of Malaya, *Rice and Sugar Decontrol: Working Party Report* (Kuala Lumpur, 1954).

[68] Federation of Malaya, *Final Report of the Rice Committee, 1956*, pp. 12-15.

[69] Federation of Malaya, *Annual Report, 1957* (Kuala Lumpur, 1958), pp. 452-455.

little or nothing to educate the peasants to a level of economic sophistication at which they could effectively resist the commercial skills of an economic system introduced from outside. If peasants are to be protected from being either proletarianized or collectivized, the result will not be helpful to economic development unless they are given sufficient education to become entrepreneurs themselves. Absentee landlords, and creditors who merely depress the price of the crop without gaining control of farming methods, give neither the advantages of a ruthless market economy nor those of effective peasant agriculture.[70]

Market structure is easier to discuss in the three major industries already covered than in the smaller industries covering the rest of the economy, where diversities based on race or historical origin make a more confused pattern. Traces of agency house control, leading to some emphasis on maintenance of capital values, traces of government interference with the process of economic development on grounds that are not easily defined by economic categories, and traces of monopsonistic structure based on credit, can be found in many parts of the economy, but the pattern varies. Vegetable oils— coconuts and palm oil—mixed vegetable gardening, fishing, and saw-milling are probably of sufficient importance to be worth describing briefly.

Coconuts are far more important than oil palms in the Malayan economy, but the former are on the whole a declining, the latter an expanding, sector.[71] In their contribution to exports oil palms are now about 50 per cent more important than coconuts, but the coconut is in addition a most important contributor to local consumption, about a third of the crop being used as fruit, cooking oil, or soap, locally produced in the villages.[72] Moreover, since the coconut is mainly a smallholders' crop (some three-quarters of the acreage is in holdings of under 100 acres, the average size being under four acres),[73] its contribution to employment and to local income is much higher than that of the oil-palm, all of which is planted on some 60 estates employing about 15,000 workers in all.

[70] P. T. Bauer and B. S. Yamey, *Economics of Underdeveloped Countries* (London, 1957), chap. xii.

[71] International Bank for Reconstruction and Development, *op. cit.*, pp. 189-192.

[72] Benham, *National Income of Malaya*, pp. 30-31.

[73] T. B. Wilson, *The West Johore Coconut Survey* (Federation of Malaya, Ministry of Agriculture, Kuala Lumpur, 1958), p. 7.

The coconut smallholder has no need of seasonal credit like the rice planter; and he has a shorter period to wait from planting to first crop than the rubber grower.[74] Nevertheless, indebtedness to dealers is important in the marketing of this crop.[75] Standards of productivity have declined severely, and the industry needs a replanting program if it is to survive.[76] This is due in the main to neglect by the government (especially during the war and the communist insurrection) of proper drainage and flood prevention and neglect by the smallholders themselves of proper protection measures to maintain the value of the holding.

Poor practices and inadequate maintenance on coconut holdings lead to falling numbers of trees per acre and nuts per tree and, hence, to low incomes and indebtedness. The process is thus cumulative, especially as there are often restrictions on alienation of the land. In general, however, the quality of the nuts is not affected, and indeed the copra from some of the very poor holdings actually commands a premium in price.

With oil palms the situation is different. The process of extracting the oil is capital-intensive, and delay or neglect can damage the quality severely.[77] Proper drainage and harvesting are also important to quality. Considerable intervention by the government would therefore be necessary to make it a suitable crop for smallholders. The International Bank Mission suggested a detailed study of the possibilities of smallholder production, in view of the fact that the fruit of wild palms is collected by small independent producers in West Africa. The estate side of the industry has, however, so far successfully obstructed its extension to smallholders except in one Federal Land Development Authority scheme in Johore, where a co-operative processing plant is to be established. The suggested use of estate processing facilities would, it is said, be possible without adverse effects on the quality of the product only if a high level of productive efficiency could be achieved.

Although the proportion of the oil palm products produced by the three largest companies is probably fairly high, there is no reason to suspect any monopolistic tendencies. Almost all the crop is ex-

[74] D. H. Grist, *Outline of Malayan Agriculture* (Kuala Lumpur, 1936; reprinted 1950), chap. x.

[75] Federation of Malaya, *Annual Report, 1957*, p. 451; Grist, *op. cit.*, chap. v.

[76] Wilson, *West Johore Coconut Survey*, pp. 41-42.

[77] International Bank for Reconstruction and Development, *op. cit.*, pp. 191-192.

ported, and Malaya is only a comparatively small producer in a competitive world market.[78]

Apart, therefore, from some monopsony due to credit in coconut production and some concern by the estates (on apparently reasonable grounds) to prevent the cultivation of oil palms by smallholders, the competitive pattern applies fairly well to the vegetable oil industry.

Mixed vegetable farming is predominantly a Chinese industry.[79] The holdings vary greatly in efficiency, access to markets, and security of tenure. There is less evidence of monopsonistic tendencies based on credit in this than in most other rural industries, but competition in transport is often ineffective,[80] and the transport operators have normally better market information than the often illiterate and isolated farmers. This leads to important bargaining advantages in so variable a market; but in the absence of better education among the farmers, it is difficult to see how any great improvement can be achieved. It is certainly not a market with standardized products sold under perfect competition, but a framework of competition exists. There is no export market.

The fishing industry is another fairly important industry in which credit, sometimes reinforced by restricted transport licenses, introduces some degree of monopsony, with rather large price margins, into the distributive system.[81] About two-thirds of the fishermen are Malays, and their traditional systems of capital formation and maintenance have been undermined by the impact of a money economy, which has increased (by social competition) the burdens of hospitality that were part of the system.[82] Distribution has passed almost wholly into the hands of Chinese, but they do not appear to be gaining control of the boats and gear in the Malay section, even though mechanization is making the industry more capital-intensive.[83]

[78] Puthucheary, *op. cit.*, p. 48.

[79] H. J. Simpson and Lau Sing Nam, "Chinese Market Gardening," *Malayan Agricultural Journal*, XXII (1934), 119-124; D. W. Le Mare, "Pig Rearing, Fish Farming and Vegetable Growing," *ibid.* XXXV (1952), 156-166.

[80] Information based on unpublished surveys carried out by students of the Economics Department of the University of Malaya, Singapore.

[81] Some studies of marketing practices at different stages (at present available on microfilm only) have been undertaken under the supervision of Ungku A. Aziz, now of the Economics Department of the University of Malaya in Kuala Lumpur.

[82] R. Firth, *Malay Fishermen: Their Peasant Economy* (London, 1946), chaps. v-vi.

[83] Federation of Malaya, *Report of the Committee to Investigate the Fishing Industry* (Kuala Lumpur, 1956).

The chief reason is extensive government assistance, through the Fisheries Department and the Rural and Industrial Development Authority, rather than that Malays in this sector are any more able than elsewhere to match the economic skill of the Chinese.

Saw-milling, a mainly Chinese industry, conforms more closely to standard competitive models in its organization. It is a comparatively risky industry, for both the local and export markets have been unstable, while fairly expensive equipment in relation to turnover is needed. In spite of this the large number of competing enterprises has been sufficient to prevent restrictive practices from developing. There are some four hundred separate saw-mills, and only a small proportion of these are owned by the two or three largest firms.[84]

There is, however, an interesting and quite considerable departure from the competitive model in government policy towards forestry products. This results from the fact that, under the colonial regime, policy with regard to the alienation of forest land was largely influenced by the Forestry Department, which was simultaneously responsible for conservation measures (in the interest of maintaining soil and climatic conditions) and for developing the forests to produce a revenue from them. This has led to the application of a curious hybrid policy, a mixture of conservation and economic self-sufficiency, applied not merely to the protective but to the productive forests.[85] Attempts are made both to preserve self-sufficiency in timber, not only for Malaya as a whole but for each separate state, and also to use the Department's powers of reservation to protect areas of forest in which money has been spent on development in the past, regardless of whether population developments and new access facilities have greatly increased its potential value as agricultural land.

The problem of the optimum economic control of tropical rain forest in countries where population is growing rapidly is one to which economists have given less attention than its importance merits.[86] Few economists would be disposed to deny that the long time-

[84] Puthucheary, op. cit., p. 106; International Bank for Reconstruction and Development, op. cit., pp. 203-204.

[85] For a recent expression of this policy, see G. G. K. Setten and J. Wyatt Smith, "Rural Development and the Forest Department," The Malayan Forester, XXIII (October 1960), 250-254.

[86] See a brief discussion of the subject in Silcock, Commonwealth Economy in Southeast Asia, pp. 35-37.

horizons involved and the considerable external economies and diseconomies resulting from the clearing of forests may point toward some interference with unrestricted private enterprise. But if anything approaching either competitive bidding or even rational planning is to develop, it is obviously important that the agency which makes the decisions should have the kind of structure which enables it to balance both the direct and the indirect gains from alternative uses of land, so that in effect all forests, protective or productive, would be debited with a rent based on their alternative uses and credited with the direct and indirect gains which accrue from them. This is far from being the situation in Malaya, where independence has had little effect so far on the effective control of forest areas.

This general survey of the market conditions in the main industries reveals a situation in which the departures from the competitive laissez-faire model are relatively minor ones that do not fit any simple alternative economic model. Two contradictory trends are observable. On the one hand some of the modifications of competition that depended on conservation of elements in the national life or culture, that appeared to be menaced by capitalist economic development, seem to be diminishing in importance; attitudes to rice growing and to the role of the rubber smallholder appear to be less affected than before by non-economic preoccupations, though there is little evidence of development in the attitude to forest land. On the other hand, divergences from competition based on a desire for better regulation of quality have made some advance in the rubber and pineapple industries and maintained their position in the palm-oil industry. There has been no very marked trend towards competition in those parts of the economy where competition has been modified by monopsony based on credit and transport or on the desire to preserve the value of (mainly foreign-owned) assets. The political conditions which favored these modifications have changed with the growth in the political power of peasants, but this has as yet had no visible effects on the market power of Chinese dealers or European agency houses.

It is worthwhile to inquire to what extent it is legitimate for the economist to attempt to apply criteria based on economic maximization to the activities of governments which had no such objectives in view; for Malaya is certainly a country where this question arises. If we are to apply such criteria, fairly simple ones may well be adequate, for we cannot in any event expect a very exact fit. But if a government chooses to regard its forests not as economic assets but as trusts for the preservation of timber supplies, wild life, etc., for each separate region; if it treats its peasants not as citizens whose income per head should be raised but as subjects of sultans (with whom it has treaties) whose traditional ways ought to be preserved; if it regards its immigrant laborers neither as resources to be hired from abroad as cheaply as possible nor as potential citizens whose income per head it should maximize, but as subjects of an allied government to whom it has limited economic obligations—has the economist any ground on which to criticize these attitudes?

The problem arises because there would certainly be some difference of opinion as to whether the citizens themselves wished for maximization of their incomes. In using such criteria one would be identifying oneself with a quantitative approach to welfare and a dynamic attitude to economic development which, in any obvious sense of the words, are not shared by large sections of the local population.[87]

Probably the best answer to this question is merely to say that the economist must follow his own profession. The criteria of maximization and free economic choice apply only for those who accept these criteria; but, as a result of both population pressure and education introduced from elsewhere, attitudes toward economic life are changing and increasing numbers are thinking of economic life in terms of raising incomes and of governments as having a function of furthering this process.[88] The economist may identify himself with those to whom his analysis can be useful and criticize other policies by these criteria, since such criticism may have the effect of making the implicit valuations of politicians and businessmen more precise; but this can be done effectively only if he recognizes that other, non-economic approaches are also necessary. It will not be worthwhile to elaborate the criteria in economies like that of Malaya beyond the point at which they are readily intelligible. For they provide at best only a rough sketch of certain aspects of the economy.

[87] Silcock, *Commonwealth Economy in Southeast Asia*, chap. v.
[88] J. H. Boeke, *Economics and Economic Policy of Dual Societies* (Haarlem, 1953), especially Part II, and Benjamin Higgins, "The Dualistic Theory of Underdeveloped Areas" (Djakarta, *Ekonomi dan Keuangan*, Feb. 1955, reprinted in *Economic Development and Cultural Change*, IV, no. 2 [1955-1956], 99-115).

This implies not that we should abandon any attempt to modify the standard economic models used in more developed economies, but that we should not expect any economic models, however modified, to give completeness and rigor in the description of the economy, or completely valid criticisms of, or prescriptions for, economic policy. Practical economic policy needs to be clarified by the analysis of other specialists also, notably political scientists and social anthropologists.

This may be illustrated by considering the impact on the economy of Malaya of some of the more important facts in its current political situation. The main political forces are those related to immigration and assimilation of the different groups in the population and those related to various forms of socialist ideology. Both of these political forces influence the structure of the economy and the possible forms which economic development can take.

Malaya is a plural society,[89] with different groups differentiated by race, culture, and country of origin. Some of the characteristics of the different groups, which have been widely discussed elsewhere, have economic importance, but here it may be more profitable to consider four different types of population in terms of their economic relation to the country. These are, first, those who are in Malaya because they were born and grew up there, knowing no other country and having to adapt themselves economically to whatever they could find to do in Malaya. This is by no means a culturally homogeneous group, since it contains members who were born and brought up in different traditions, and these traditions give access to different occupations. Nevertheless, it can be distinguished from three distinct types of migrant. The most important of these is migrant labor, usually brought in under some scheme intended to supply a particular functional need in the economy on an *ad hoc* basis. Large numbers of South Indians on estates,[90] of Chinese doing various kinds of contract work,[91] and of Indian[92] and junior

[89] J. S. Furnivall, *Colonial Policy and Practice* (Cambridge, Eng., 1948), especially pp. 303-312.

[90] Hon. S. Srinivasa Sastri, *Report on Conditions of Indian Labour in Malaya* (New Delhi, 1937); Mills, *op. cit.*

[91] W. L. Blythe, "History of Chinese Labour in Malaya," *Journal of the Malayan Branch of the Royal Asiatic Society*, XX (June 1947), 64-114.

[92] S. Nanjundan, *Indians in Malayan Economy* (Office of Economic Adviser, Government of India, New Delhi, 1951), pp. 40-41.

European mercantile assistants[93] came on these terms, the employer or agent arranging the migration and trying—with varying degrees of success—to secure for himself an appreciable share of the advantage accruing from recruiting labor cheaply in one place and employing it in another where it was more scarce. The second migrant group is made up of those coming to Malaya on a permanent basis, intending to settle and make their permanent home there because of marked differences in economic opportunity between their homeland and Malaya. Many people of Malaysian origin, from Sumatra, South Borneo, and elsewhere,[94] many Chinese small businessmen,[95] and some professional or semiprofessional workers from Ceylon, South India,[96] Hong Kong, and the Philippines are migrants of this type. Finally, there are the international entrepreneurs to whom Malaya as a small country is one field among many for their trading interests in the whole region.[97] These include mainly Chinese and European merchants.

One of the problems of Malaya is that those who have been born and brought up in Malaya are more or less closely related in race or culture to one or another of the migrant groups, with cultural ties and language conflicting with the loyalties of birth and environment. Many of these cultural ties have been reinforced by economic function, and this tends to react on the developing economic structure.

The labor market at all levels is influenced both by pockets of racial specialization and by pressures depending on conflicting attitudes to migration and to migrants. Racial specialization may begin with a special aptitude or contact but tends to be maintained by social and cultural pressures, making it difficult for a newcomer to find acceptance or for an employer to take on a stranger. South Indian check-roll workers on estates, Cantonese tin miners, Sikh night watchmen, Hainanese catering workers—all these form homogeneous groups, with vacancies filled by imported (or locally born) members of the same racial group. Quite marked differences in earnings are needed to break these racial, cultural, and linguistic barriers. New

---

[93] J. S. Fforde, *An International Trade in Managerial Skills* (Oxford, 1957), chap. vii.

[94] Sir R. O. Winstedt, *The Malays: A Cultural History* (London, 1947), chap. viii.

[95] J. K. T'ien, *The Chinese of Sarawak* (New York, 1957), chaps. ii, iv.

[96] K. A. Neelakandha Aiyer, *Indian Problems in Malaya* (Kuala Lumpur, 1938), chaps. iii, vi.

[97] Stahl, *op. cit.*

migration, however, is strictly controlled,[98] mainly owing to political pressure designed to prevent a shift in the racial balance but often reinforced by the members of existing professions, e.g., recent medical opposition to government efforts to recruit foreign doctors.

The chief way in which migration patterns influence the structure of the economy is through generating latent opposition between the government and the actual institutions of a market economy. Most European businesses are organized in such a way that it is very difficult for any but Europeans to hold the key positions, the structure having been built up with members of different races occupying different positions and dependent for the internal balance on European control.[99] Similarly, Chinese businesses are dependent on Chinese clan and family contacts throughout Southeast Asia;[100] they conduct their business in Chinese and do not easily recruit workers of other races. The political situation, however, is one in which political power is likely to be held, at least for some years, by Malays. This creates a situation in which, in spite of a government in the Federation markedly favorable to private enterprise, most of the developments of business that would most naturally take place are likely to be politically vulnerable. Because the government favors development by private enterprise it is likely to continue giving tax reliefs and tariff protection to new industries, and to go ahead with industrial research, industrial sites, and the creation of credit institutions;[101] but every such gesture will be a hostage to fortune, weakening the government's hold on the Malay electorate and compelling more costly and elaborate gestures to the rural population to win it back. Unfortunately, the shortages in the rural areas are shortages of information and properly trained staff, so that waste and disillusionment are almost inevitable.

This introduces consideration of the role of socialist ideas in Malaya and their probable effect on the structure of the economy. To what extent are nationalization, state trading, and administrative planning—as distinct from financial and other global controls—likely to result from the constellation of ideas and social forces in Malaya?

[98] Federation of Malaya, *Annual Report, 1953* (Kuala Lumpur, 1954), p. 9.
[99] These problems are discussed more fully in Silcock, *The Commonwealth Economy in Southeast Asia*, especially pp. 86-91.
[100] Cf. J. K. T'ien, *op. cit.*, chaps. ii-viii.
[101] Federation of Malaya, *Report of the Industrial Development Working Party* (Kuala Lumpur, 1957), especially chaps. viii and x.

Superficially, two circumstances seem markedly favorable to national planning. On the one hand the educational influences all seem to predispose Malaya in that direction. Most current literature in the main national languages of Malaya comes from communist or socialist countries: Chinese material, Indonesian material, South Indian material. Moreover, the leaders among the English educated have virtually a choice between colonial ideas and an English socialist reaction against them.[102] Since an independent country is virtually compelled to offer an ideological reaction against its colonial past, the dice would appear to be heavily loaded in favor of socialist ideas. At the same time the influence of the colonial period has created an attitude of mind rather timid towards voluntary action for social goals (always in danger of being labeled political) and expecting all changes to be initiated by the government. This would appear to favor expanded activities by an independent government.

In the short run it is unlikely that these influences will have a very marked effect on practical politics. The balance of social forces is not such that socialist ideas are likely to command strong mass support, or that the government is likely to dominate the economy increasingly because of lack of private initiative toward development. This situation is unlikely to come to an end until there is a closer political integration of the Federation and Singapore than seemed likely under the present Malaysia proposals and much greater success (in the Federation itself) in the program of fostering a unified education system and a single national language.[103]

The reason is that in the separation of the Federation from Singapore, that part of the economy in which left-wing social forces have some chance of success has been isolated and given a sector of the country in which the economic opportunities for left-wing policies are very limited. Singapore enjoys reasonable racial homogeneity, urban conditions, and the kind of industrial situation in which militant unions can flourish. The Federation, with its mining wealth and large estates, would give far more economic scope for socialist policies; but the left is disorganized not only by the memory of a long and unsuccessful communist insurrection but by lack of a common

[102] Attempts, for example by the United States Information Service, to present a rival picture of competitive American capitalism as an alternative to European and colonial monopoly capitalism appear to have had little impact on Malayan thinking so far.

[103] T. H. Silcock, *Towards a Malayan Nation*, pp. 28-43, 76-90.

language. Trade unions are largely run by English-speaking officers, who are also the delegates at regional and national conferences.[104] It is certainly not impossible for these to gain a following in different trades; but they do not enjoy sufficient advantages, either in acceptance by the people or in capacity to draw them together, to offset the prestige of the Malay aristocrats and Chinese commercial leaders, acting together through the medium of English.

Singapore governments are unlikely to pursue policies of confiscation of assets or other extreme left-wing measures for two reasons: fear of aggravating Federation suspicions and the dependence of Singapore on the trade contacts of individual merchants for its diverse and important entrepôt trade. The former is politically more important and would be likely to influence any government with enough political insight to win power. The latter, however, is also bound to weigh with any government that has competent economic advisers.

It would, therefore, be surprising if there were major shifts to government ownership in either the Federation or Singapore within the next few years. Socialist ideology will insure that steps, short of major institutional changes, must be taken to promote economic development, especially rural development and obvious gestures to industrialization. But in the short run the will is likely to be lacking in the Federation for anything more, and in Singapore, the power.

It is not easy to forecast longer-run effects with any confidence. If a democratic system survives and if a reasonably united nation emerges, it seems on the whole probable that left-wing influences will increase rather than diminish, because of the intellectual contacts of Malaya and a rather marked inequality in the social structure. But no one can foresee in much detail what would be the incidental effects of the process of nation-building or of the economic forces that may develop. Nor can survival of democratic institutions or success in nation-building be taken for granted.[105]

If we assume that government impacts on the economy are unlikely to be massive or drastic, we may nevertheless try to anticipate the steps that may be taken.

Largely as a result of pressures generated by the Colombo Plan

---

[104] Alex Josey, *Trade Unionism in Malaya* (Singapore, 1954), chap. iv; C. Gamba, "Trade Unionism in Malaya," *Far Eastern Survey*, XXIII (1954), 28-30.
[105] T. H. Silcock, *Towards a Malayan Nation*, pp. 58-75, 96-112.

organization,[106] the different states of Southeast Asia now tend to express their economic policies in terms of development plans for periods of five years or so. This is done whether there is an economic secretariat with detailed information about the economy or not.

In Malaya information has not been sufficiently detailed for the plans to be based on budgeting of real resources or detailed forecasting of income, demand, balance of payments, etc. It must be emphasized that detailed forecasting of income in so volatile an economy as that of Malaya might not justify the necessary additional use of its scarce resources of skilled manpower, but the existence of development plans should not be taken as evidence of a greater degree of planning than actually exists. A very small secretariat was built up within the Prime Minister's office during the period of the 1956-60 plan, and more recently some expansion has been reported, mainly designed for day-to-day supervision of the speed of accomplishment of targets set in the 1961-65 plan. It is doubtful, however, whether this faces the real difficulty which is at least partly one of defective knowledge: inadequate statistics and inadequate preliminary research. A great deal will therefore depend on the intelligence and flexibility shown by the Deputy Prime Minister, Tun Abdul Razak, and his few senior advisers, in responding to the information that the actual working of the plan brings to light.

There have been three development plans in all. None of them has been based on detailed economic analysis, though there has been progress in this direction. The first was a six-year plan,[107] covering the years 1950-55 inclusive, and not usually included in the series. Started as a ten-year development program after World War II in accordance with Colonial Office directives, it was a basis for requests for rehabilitation aid under the Colonial Development and Welfare Act. It was later modified to suit the requirements of the Colombo Plan, but many schemes included were continuing schemes started before 1950 under the former plan. It included very rough forecasts of production, but made no attempt to relate these and the plans for government expenditure to real resources available. In the event most of the schemes ran seriously behind, in spite of the

---

[106] The Colombo Plan for Co-operative Economic Development in South and South-East Asia, *Report* and *1st.* to *9th Annual Reports of the Consultative Committee* (London, H.M.S.O. 1950-61; Cmd. 8080, 8529, 9016, 9336, 9622; Cmd. 50, 315, 610, 920, 1251).

[107] *Federation of Malaya Draft Development Plan* (Kuala Lumpur, 1950).

great increase in revenue as a result of the Korean War, because of the emergency caused by communist terrorists.[108]

The first plan for an independent Malaya[109] was drawn up by the elected government in 1956 as a consequence of the International Bank Mission's Report, and in preparation for the financial talks in December 1956 and January 1957 between the Malayan and British governments leading to the achievement of independence in August 1957. Like the 1950-55 plan, it was based on plans put forward by the various government departments; but it had as a basis the International Bank Mission's Report, and the ultimate plan as published had been pruned in accordance with estimates of real, as well as financial, resources by the Economic Adviser. The 1961-65 plan is not a detailed year-by-year program but a set of over-all targets for the whole period. Like its predecessors, it is a response of government policy to current symptoms. On this occasion the loss of rural votes in the 1959 election has led to a crash program of agricultural development. For the first time, however, there is an attempt to assess manpower available and to co-ordinate public and private investment, with an estimate of an over-all rate of growth of 4 per cent in total output.

If the detailed expenditure shown in these plans is studied, it becomes clear that Malaya is very much a private enterprise economy. The government expenditures are expenditures on economic research and training, on the rubber replanting scheme, on communications and power supplies, and on educational and medical development.

Even in the latest plan there is little increase in unorthodox types of government expenditure, although the total amount of public development expenditure is doubled. The provision for direct land settlement and government subscription to Malayan Industrial Development Finance Ltd.—rather more radical departures from private enterprise—will be less than 10 per cent of total public development expenditure.

In accordance with the recommendations of the International

[108] Member for Economic Affairs, *Progress Report on the Development Plan of the Federation of Malaya, 1950/52* (Kuala Lumpur, 1953), pp. 1-2.

[109] Federation of Malaya, *Report on Economic Planning in the Federation of Malaya, 1956* (Kuala Lumpur, 1957).

[110] Federation of Malaya Information Department, *The Second Five Year Plan, 1961/65* (Kuala Lumpur, 1961).

Bank Mission,[111] assistance to industrialization is to be limited to some medium-term finance, provision of industrial sites and research aid to Malaya's many small-scale industries—handicrafts, raw-material processing, biscuits, brewing, engineering workshops, soap, building materials, furniture, rubber goods, etc.—and tax concessions to pioneer industries.[112]

Since it is unlikely that very drastic measures will be taken to change the ownership of factors of production, development is likely to be influenced, in the near future as in the past, by changes in the quantity of factors available. In such an open economy as that of Malaya interest naturally attaches to the steps which governments can take to influence these quantities. We may consider separately the supplies of labor, skill, and capital.

The attitude of Malayan governments to labor supplies and the labor market has undergone great changes during the last seventy years. At the beginning of this period the government found a system not far removed from slavery in operation and tried by regulating it to mitigate its harshness.[113] Systems of indenture were enforced which bound the worker to a particular employer for a period of years in consideration of payment of his passage. At this time the government intervened mainly to insure that conditions were not too harsh and that the immigrant had some chance of gaining his freedom.

In respect of Indian labor the government introduced, in 1907, a scheme by which it raised a cess from all employers of Indian labor and used the proceeds to finance Indian immigration and the return of migrants to India itself.[114] The flow of labor was consciously adjusted to maintain, in certain key areas, a level of wages based on standard budgets of laborers' needs, worked out by officials of the Labour Department, and allowing some margin for savings and remittances to dependents in India. Wages in other than key areas were allowed to be determined by competition, so as to avoid arbitrary fixing of wage margins.

This system, together with regulation of conditions of work and

---

[111] International Bank for Reconstruction and Development, op. cit., pp. 301-316.

[112] Federation of Malaya, Report of the Industrial Development Working Party (Kuala Lumpur, 1957), pp. 7-9.

[113] Blythe, op. cit.; Mills, op. cit., chap. vi.

[114] Straits Settlements, Report of the Controller of Labour (C. Wilson) 1938 (Singapore, 1940), Part I.

obligations of employers under an elaborate Labour Code (administered by the Labour Department with advice from an agent of the Government of India) continued until the termination of migration of Indian laborers to Malaya by the Indian government in 1938. It is necessary to emphasize that systems of debt slavery among the Malays[115] and of a form of indenture among the Chinese[116] were already in existence when the government undertook their regulation and reform. The attitude of the government was protective, within the limits of an existing and developing economic system; attempts were made to reform particular abuses and improve particular practices but not to treat the workers as citizens whose conditions the government wished to transform as rapidly as possible into those of workers in more prosperous countries.

It has already been mentioned that for Malays the objective was primarily to protect and improve existing systems of peasant agriculture, handicrafts, and fishing. For the Chinese immigrants a protectorate was established, which later became the secretariat for Chinese affairs, that was chiefly concerned with eliminating from the indenture system those elements of bondage to a particular employer that were most akin to slavery. In 1914 indenture was abolished altogether, though in practice the free laborers continued to be indebted for their passage, and this restricted their mobility until the debt was paid off. In the unhealthy conditions prevailing in the pioneer work for which Chinese were mainly recruited in the early twentieth century, many died before their debts were paid.

On the whole, however, the government attitude to Chinese labor was less protective than to Indian labor. The immediate employers of most Chinese were Chinese contractors, and it was far more difficult to regulate the conditions of work which they offered.[117] It was generally assumed that Chinese labor was better able to look after itself, and that beyond correcting the worst abuses of the indenture system, no government interference was desirable. There was no attempt to maintain a particular rate of wages by adjusting labor supplies. Restrictions on the numbers of male (and for a few years on female) Chinese immigrants, in the last decade before

---

[115] B. Lasker, *Human Bondage in Southeast Asia* (Chapel Hill, N. C., 1950), chaps. i, iii.

[116] Blythe, *op. cit.*

[117] See Singapore, *Report of the Commission (C. Gamba, Chairman) on Contract Labour* (Singapore, 1960), for general survey of conditions.

World War II, were designed to prevent unemployment rather than to regulate wages.[118]

The chief changes in the government attitude to labor introduced by World War II were a much greater encouragement of trade unionism and collective bargaining and a much stricter control over immigration. The causes of these changes, however, were political rather than economic.

There was some evidence of increased willingness to encourage collective bargaining, just before World War II.[119] A Trade Union Ordinance was actually introduced in 1940, though not properly implemented until after the war. Colonial policy, ever since the Labour government of 1929-31 in the United Kingdom, had shifted towards encouraging constitutional trade unions in colonial territories; and in Malaya a number of factors contributed to the change. Political propaganda beginning with the visit of Mr. Nehru, the appointment of the Sastri Commission from India to investigate charges of exploitation of Indian labor in 1937,[120] and the sudden banning of Indian emigration by the Indian government in 1938 created some of the political conditions; shortage of labor and inflationary pressures after the outbreak of war in Europe, and 100 per cent Excess Profits Duty on companies registered in the United Kingdom (reducing the incentive to resist wage demands)[121] gave economic conditions suitable to trade union pressure; and a visit by a Colonial Office labor officer, Major G. St. J. Orde Browne, discouraged a repressive approach.[122] The trade-union legislation of 1938-40 was not, however, implemented by the registration of trade unions as such until after the Japanese Occupation. A good many—some based on Chinese trade guilds, some multi-racial and Western in outlook—had been registered under the Societies Ordinance (legislation for the control of secret

[118] Straits Settlements, *Report of Controller of Labour, loc. cit.*; M. V. del Tufo, *Malaya: A Report on the 1947 Census of Population* (London, 1949), chap. ii.

[119] G. St. J. Orde Browne, *Report on Labour Conditions in Ceylon, Mauritius and Malaya* (London, H.M.S.O., Cmd. 6423, 1943).

[120] S. Sastri, *Report on the Conditions of Indian Labour in Malaya* (New Delhi, Government of India, 1937).

[121] Bauer, "Working of Rubber Regulation," *loc cit.*; Silcock, "Note on the Working of Rubber Regulation," *loc. cit.*

[122] Browne, *op. cit.*, pp. 109-113.

THE ECONOMY OF MALAYA 363

societies), but the main development of trade unionism came after the war.[123]

The growth of an official policy of active promotion of trade unions came about partly as a result of the election of a Labour government in the United Kingdom and partly because it was necessary to counter communist pressures. Some change in the legislation already on the statute book would have been required without either of these events; for Malaya badly needed help from the Colonial Development and Welfare Fund for reconstruction, and a provision governing the disbursement of this fund—introduced by the wartime Coalition government—had imposed conditions rather more favorable to labor than those of the 1940 Malayan legislation on colonies receiving such help. Nevertheless, if there had not been a Labour government in office in the United Kingdom, any new legislation would almost certainly have been administered by a regular officer of the Labour Department; and if there had been no communist pressure it would have been administered within the framework of that Labour Department, with all its traditions of paternal protection and formal impartiality. Yet the actual development of trade unionism owes almost everything to the appointment of a trade unionist, John Brazier, with enthusiasm and an intuitive genius for organizing Asian labor, and to the establishment of a special Trade Union Adviser's Department in which he could work with direct access to the High Commissioner, who in general accepted the administrative anomalies of this situation with sympathetic equanimity.[124]

The communist guerrillas used the brief interregnum after the Japanese surrender and before the British Military Administration achieved complete control to establish a General Labour Union (later divided into the Malayan Federation of Trade Unions and the Singapore Federation of Trade Unions) through which it attempted to build up communist-dominated subsidiaries in every trade and industry.[125] It was a time of high expectations, limited supplies, and inflation. Employers—both European and Chinese—had little pre-

[123] S. S. Awberry and F. W. Dalley, *Labour and Trade Union Organisation in the Federation of Malaya and Singapore* (Kuala Lumpur, 1948), esp. pp. 20-28.

[124] Josey, *op. cit.* A fuller assessment of the work of John Brazier will be found in a forthcoming book, *The Origins of Trade Unionism in Malaya*, by C. Gamba.

[125] Pye, *op. cit.*, pp. 75-79.

vious experience of collective bargaining, and they and the Civil Service were too ready to treat all economic and political grievances as communist-inspired.

It was essential to create a trade-union movement that would win genuine benefits by organization on non-communist lines. The creation of a Trade Union Adviser's Office, from which (in effect) strikes were fostered, and aid given to organized workers—even organized civil servants in dispute with the government—led to a much more rapid growth of trade-union structure than could otherwise have been attained. In the plantations, in nearly all the government services, and in several smaller industries well-developed unions with machinery for collective bargaining, grievance procedure, and arbitration have now grown up.[126] In the Federation, though the unions as such remain politically neutral, their increasing strength is one of the few factors supporting a non-communist, left-wing opposition.

In Singapore, the People's Action Party government has introduced a system of compulsory arbitration, which includes machinery for recognizing particular unions as representing the workers for the purpose of negotiating legally binding agreements. This has introduced a tendency toward consolidation of unions. No doubt this had two purposes, to strengthen the political hold of the party over the unions through the Trade Unions Congress and to reduce the number of industrial disputes. Until the recent split between the unions supporting the People's Action Party and the mainly communist-controlled unions supporting the Barisan Sosialis, this policy was fairly successful.

While the unions have, of course, favored increased use of collective bargaining in the fixing of wages, their attitude to government control, for example through the provisions of the Labour Code, has been opportunist. Not being, in general, strong enough to impose, themselves, all the conditions that they desire for their members, they are willing to accept government regulation of conditions and to press for its extension, for example, to contract labor. This does not, however, imply any consistent use of political machinery; rather, many of the unions have shown skill in bringing pressure to bear on the government by representing themselves as

[126] C. Gamba, "Staff Relations in the Government Services of Malaya," *Malayan Economic Review*, II, no. 2 (1957), 12-32.

instruments of reasonable negotiation, particularly during the period of the Emergency when direct pressure on employers was difficult.

The change in the government attitude to immigration was far simpler than the change in the attitude to collective bargaining. Before the war immigrants were accepted, provided there was no pressure of unemployment.[127] There was no restriction except on deck passengers, and for them control was unselective, a certain crude number of passages for each sex being allotted to the shipping companies. After the war the racial tensions that developed with the increase in Malay political awareness led to restriction of immigration, first of Chinese and Indians and later of all races.

At first the emphasis in this policy was purely political. The Malays as the dominant group wished to preserve their political superiority. More recently an economic emphasis has been added. There is some alarm—especially in Singapore, but to a lesser degree in the Federation, too—at the rate of population increase, and hence the restriction of immigration is regarded partly as a measure to prevent aggravation of this problem. Increasingly, local workers have felt themselves threatened by the competition of immigrants from India, Hong Kong, etc., and demands have arisen to raise the economic levels at which immigrants can be admitted. Discretion can still be exercised for some categories of commercial, industrial, and professional workers; but only if they have promise of employment at salaries of about the equivalent of U. S. $400 a month.

This shift has of course been accompanied by a great increase in the facilities for the training of local labor at all levels. Trade schools have been expanded and secondary schools with a vocational bias introduced; a national apprenticeship scheme has been developed, with provision for requiring apprenticeship as a condition of skilled employment in certain scheduled trades; most government departments and many businesses have sent trainees overseas; a Polytechnic has been established in Singapore; and the number of university students both in Malaya and in overseas universities has expanded rapidly.

The chief problem in the creation of a skilled labor market is likely to be a cultural and linguistic one. It seems likely that training conducted through the medium of English will continue to be more accessible to non-Malays—with their urban habitat—than to

[127] Mills, *op. cit.*

Malays.[128] At the same time there is increasing pressure to give some preference to Malays, so that the conditions of shortage that at present prevail for administrative officers, rural teachers, and extension workers (where preference must be given to Malays or Malay-speakers) are likely to spread to other occupations. The same scarcity is at present preventing the expansion of Malay translation and Malay secondary education, which might help to solve the problem by developing technical education in Malay. In the meantime, the need to produce a high proportion of technically trained Malays from the multi-racial English schools is bound to involve major distortions of the skilled labor market.

We turn next to the development of government attitudes to the market for land. Here, as we have already seen, the policy has been one of protecting particular groups or techniques, within a general framework of alienation for private development. Malay peasants, particularly rice growers, have been protected from alienating their land to non-Malays as a result of indebtedness; forest land has been protected, not only for reasons of soil and climate, but to protect the timber industry from having to pay for its land what the land could otherwise earn in rent.

This protection has averted genuine evils. Malay peasants do tend to get into debt and lose their land, and would probably do so even more if more enterprising races could acquire their land; forests need protection against wasteful felling, and it is economical (within limits) to allow the protecting agency to earn a forest revenue. The disadvantage is that the policy is a reaction to symptoms, rather than an attempt to pursue a rational long-run economic goal; for example, training the Malay peasants at the same time as protecting them for the sake of their own maximum long-run interest; or calculating the external economies and the costs of forest protection policies.

There has been a marked change in the direction of increased land development, especially since the 1959 elections;[129] but the new policy also bears the mark of being a reaction to symptoms, especially to the defection of Malay rural votes as a symptom of Malay rural discontent. The new policy of treating rural develop-

[128] Federation of Malaya, *Report of the Commission (Sir Alexander Carr-Saunders, Chairman) on University Education in Malaya* (Kuala Lumpur, 1948), chap. iv.

[129] *Straits Times*, Third Merdeka Anniversary, Special Feature, Aug. 31, 1960.

ment as an emergency measure, with strong pressure on every district officer to develop new rural schemes, is certainly cutting through much of the tangle of administrative delay. But there are real shortages, of trained men and hence of relevant skills, of research workers and hence of relevant knowledge; and the emergency scheme has not overcome these. It is probably reasonable to hope that the waste due to incompetent work, ill-thought-out sites, etc., will be less than the waste due to torpor and inactivity; but the resultant disillusion may be greater.

The free market in some measure trains farmers by success and failure and at the same time selects, by success and failure, the farmers who will gain control of most land. It is possible, given sufficient knowledge, both to train and to select by more rational and less ruthless methods; but to attempt to do it without adequate knowledge—selecting settlers, for example, on broadly political criteria and limiting drastically the alienation of their land—may be very wasteful. Yet nothing like a free market in land (which would rapidly transfer a great deal of land to Chinese hands) is politically possible in Malaya, nor is there enough knowledge for rational selection and training for all the settlement that is being planned.

The trend in the market for capital probably exemplifies most clearly a change towards the standard capitalist model; though whether this is a laissez-faire model is obscure, simply because the concept of laissez faire loses all clarity as we approach the realm of money or capital.

The pattern of credit in Malaya until recently was one in which small producers, retailers, and consumers met their credit needs through Chinese or Indian intermediaries,[130] most of whom obtained a large part of the funds directly or indirectly from European merchants or banks with access to the London money market.[131] This does not, of course, mean that most of the "real" capital came from outside Malaya. Cash balances in Malaya were all backed—usually to the extent of over 100 per cent—by sterling assets, and the banks also held substantial assets in London against liabilities

[130] C. Gamba, "Poverty and Some Socio-Economic Aspects of Hoarding, Saving and Borrowing in Malaya," *Malayan Economic Review*, III, no. 2 (Oct. 1958), 33-62.
[131] Lim Tay Boh, *Problems of the Malayan Economy* (Singapore, 1956), chap. vi; Puthucheary, *op. cit.*, pp. 64-66.

in Malaya.[132] This represented a considerable investment by Malaya in London, in real terms, to offset any real capital inflow on a short-term basis.[133] As for long-term capital, the total volume of overseas holdings in Malaya's rubber and tin companies (valued at issue prices) greatly overestimates the sum of the unfavorable balances on current account that were, at any time, financed by capital transfers; for in both industries large capital gains were made between the construction of the asset and the initial issue of shares in London,[134] and the securities so created were held in London by entrepreneurs resident in Malaya who ultimately left Malaya to return home. In one sense, of course, their capital gains can be regarded as part of the cost of creating the rubber estates and tin mines, since these were a part of their inducement for doing business in Malaya. But if this point of view is adopted, the remittance of profits from Malaya must be greatly increased, in striking a balance.[135]

It should be emphasized, therefore, that the contribution of foreign capital was at least as much a technological contribution—a change in the institutional forms of lending and borrowing—as an additional supply of a factor of production. The introduction of the different successive forms of gold and sterling exchange standards[136] made it possible for a supply of currency to be acquired, not in the form of an outright sacrifice of a corresponding amount of goods, but in the form of a loan to the London market, which could be offset by a similar short-term loan to Malaya (for example through a commercial bill) without anyone's being worse off. Similar institutions generating long-term confidence—for example, accounts, audit,

[132] P. A. Wilson, "Money in Malaya," *Malayan Economic Review*, II, no. 2 (Oct. 1957), 53-66.

[133] A. D. Hazlewood, "Notes on Sterling Balances and the Colonial Currency System," *Economic Journal*, LXII (1952), 942-945; Ida C. Greaves, "Sterling Balances and the Colonial Currency System, A Comment," *Economic Journal*, LXIII (1953), 921-923.

[134] D. M. Figart, *The Plantation Rubber Industry in the Middle East* (United States Department of Commerce, Trade Promotion Series, no. 2; Washington, 1925); Eastham, *op. cit.*

[135] T. H. Silcock, *The Economy of Malaya* (Singapore, 1956), p. 16; Puthucheary, *op. cit.*, p. 43. Mr. Puthucheary's main criticism is concerned with the continued retention of control by the agency houses—an important distinction, depending on his emphasis on ownership and mine on receipts. His analysis alludes incidentally to an element in the supply of capital which is often overlooked, and to which I draw attention in the text above.

[136] J. O. Anthonisz, *Currency Reform in the Straits Settlements* (London, ca. 1905), chaps. ii-iii; Sir B. Blackett, *Report on the Malayan Currency* (Kuala Lumpur, 1934); King, *op. cit.*

and formal commercial structure—made it possible for a given real prospect of profit to have a higher commercial value and for this (in a sense) to accrue abroad in part payment for entrepreneurial services.

The credit derived from superior credit institutions and economies of scale, together with that based on superior resources of capital, have given a limited degree of monopoly or monopsony to the European firms in key positions; but they have strengthened even further the hands of those Chinese and Indian firms which can in one way or another substantiate their credit worthiness to the European agency houses or banks and use the credit so obtained to create monopolies and monopsonies for themselves.

The capital market has shown two different but related trends in recent times. On the one hand, there has been a tendency for local Chinese firms to develop, largely on Western lines, and to take over some of the financial roles formerly confined to Europeans. On the other hand, the forms of the financial institutions themselves have shown some tendency to develop in the direction of using more objective methods of verification and protection, so that credit can become more competitive.

The former tendency is exemplified by the growth of Chinese banks[137] and insurance companies, increasingly since World War II but going back even before World War I; also the growth, especially since the Korean War boom, of Chinese buying of shares in companies organized on Western lines and appointment of Chinese to their boards of directors.[138]

The latter tendency, the change in the form of institutions, is also partly exemplified by the Chinese banks, insofar as these have supplied credit which was previously obtained from trade suppliers. The lending policies of these banks, however, still differ widely from those of Western banks, and the new Central Bank has tried unobtrusively to strengthen them by advocating more formal procedures through its inspection system.[139] The Central Bank is also taking steps to establish a money and capital market in Kuala Lumpur.[140]

[137] Tan Ee Leong, "The Chinese Banks Incorporated in Singapore and the Federation of Malaya," *Journal of the Malayan Branch of the Royal Asiatic Society*, XXVI (July 1953), 113-139.

[138] Puthucheary, *op. cit.*, pp. 136-137.

[139] Bank Negara Tanah Melayu, *Annual Reports* (Kuala Lumpur, 1959), pp. 12-13; (Kuala Lumpur, 1961), p. 23.

[140] *Ibid.*, 1961, pp. 20-21.

A market in bills of exchange and a rudimentary share market have existed for many years in Singapore.[141] But the aim in Kuala Lumpur is to develop a short-term money market, with more emphasis on local funds, and a long-term market based on a stock exchange, supported by insurance companies, agency houses, and other institutional investors, and with reliable advisory and reporting services. Steps are being taken also, in the University and in the Polytechnic, to expand the training of local accountants and financial executives— a branch of the economy hitherto largely confined to Europeans or these trained abroad.

In addition the government has taken a hand in the supply of capital, mainly to small enterprises. An Apex bank has been established as a channel through which government funds can give credit to co-operatives, especially in the rural areas.[142] The Rural and Industrial Development Authority has made loans to small and medium rural industries.[143] In Singapore an Industrial Promotion Board, established for some years, has since independence been greatly expanded.[144] In 1961 this was absorbed in the new Economic Development Board.

Taking the whole pattern of governmental operations on the supplies of resources, it is difficult to detect a trend either towards or away from a laissez-faire economy. There is considerable intervention in the markets for all the main factors. Generally the degree of interference with the labor market has changed little, but its character has changed a good deal. Some of the functions of maintaining conditions of work and wages have been handed over to trade unions, while interference with migration has notably increased. There has also been a considerable shift in policy in relation to land, with much more interest in development and opening-up for its own sake. This has involved a shift away from individual alienation to bloc alienation, but the former alienation was not conducted on any principles of laissez faire or maximization. The trend in the capital

[141] G. M. Watson and Sir Sydney Caine, *A Central Bank in Malaya; Report on the Establishment of a Central Bank in Malaya* (Kuala Lumpur, 1956), pp. 4-6.
[142] Federation of Malaya, *Annual Report, 1954* (Kuala Lumpur, 1955), p. 395; *Annual Report, 1955* (1956), p. 412.
[143] D. Fiennes, *Report on Rural and Industrial Development Authority, 1950-1955* (Kuala Lumpur, 1957), pp. 11-14, 41-45.
[144] Singapore, Ministry of Culture, *One Year of Peaceful Revolution* (Singapore, 1960).

market is toward special credit institutions granting loans against regular security and for interest only, and away from trade credit as a basis for monopsony and monopoly; but the change has not yet gone very far.

We may turn, finally, to consider how well Malaya and Singapore fit into the general pattern of a competitive laissez-faire economy. For this purpose it is necessary to distinguish some of the purposes for which a theoretical model of this kind can be used. Obviously, it would serve no useful purpose merely to set up a man of straw, in the form of a traditional model with perfect competition in the sale of all products and all factors (homogeneous products, perfect knowledge, negligible effects of any one producer's output on the price, etc.,) merely for the sake of knocking it down and proposing something more complex and nearer to reality. But we may inquire whether, for a number of different purposes, a competitive laissez-faire model can be useful.

First, it should be fairly obvious that as a framework for reasonably simple and intelligible description of the Malayan economy, no competitive laissez-faire model would give a useful summary of the facts. Many key interventions by government in the main industries and main supplies of factors of production must be described to give an intelligible account. They can be related to a competitive model but not described by it. It has been indicated,[145] however, that several of the aims of the governments, even within areas of policy that seem economic, are difficult to sum up in economic terms at all. No case is established for seeking an alternative economic theory. Rather, we must accept the fact that in describing the economic life of the country a number of important non-economic motives must be described.

The competitive economy may be a useful model for welfare decisions; it may help us to understand the general allocation and pricing of factors of production; or it may help us to pick out relevant elements in the pricing process, so as to form a basis for special theories dealing with public finance, interest policy, international trade, etc. In discussing its adequacy to Malaya we are mainly concerned with whether—within the general field of economic prescription or analysis—the model gives a good enough fit to be useful in these special contexts.

[145] *Supra*, pp. 336-338, 344-345, 350, 351-352.

Suppose there are large aggregations of economic power, devoting an appreciable part of their effort to limiting the supply of (or demand for) a whole class of potentially competing products for the sake of affecting the price at which they sell. Plainly, then, the prices of those products will not represent even approximately the long-run or short-run marginal cost to society of producing them, in terms of alternative products that available resources might have produced instead. Suppose, further, that these aggregates are exceptional and that in the rest of the economy individual economic units are too small (in comparison with the whole market which consumers treat as homogeneous) to influence the price of their own product. It may then be sound policy to break up the aggregates more or less indiscriminately, on the ground that this will in general bring prices more into line with marginal social costs.[146] Similarly, if this is the situation, it may often make good sense for the government to use market prices in assessing projects. Is Malaya an economy in which this situation prevails?

On the one hand the orientation towards export suggests that it is such an economy. Something like perfect competition prevails in the sale of the main export products. There have been government policies of restriction in the interest of stabilization, but these can be assessed in terms of a competitive model. They are open restrictions, for a definite and limited objective, intelligible in simple economic terms and operated by the state.

It is in the market for factors of production that the economy departs most widely from the competitive model. Not only is there a reasonably well-developed trade-union movement; the marketing of the produce of peasants and fishermen and the development of land resources also require a different approach. Moreover, as in all underdeveloped economies, welfare judgments based on static analysis are likely to give too little weight to the aspirations of the people generally toward rapid economic change. Finally, in any complete assessment of the relevance of the competitive model in welfare analysis, account would have to be taken of a comparative absence of fixed prices and prevalence of individual bargaining in retail distribution of most consumers' goods. This is consistent with a fairly high degree of competition; and it can indeed be argued that,

[146] See I. D. M. Little, *A Critique of Welfare Eocnomics* (Oxford, 1950), chaps. viii-ix for an analysis of the limits within which this procedure is rational.

with the extreme diversity of tastes and locations in consumers' markets, our Western fixed prices imply some loss of welfare in effective allocation, offset by simplification of business practice.[147] Nevertheless, an economy of widespread haggling, even within fairly narrow price limits, implies some adjustment in welfare economics.

If we turn from prescription to interpretation, the competitive model still fulfills fairly adequately certain limited objectives. If we wish to seek a wood without too much distraction by trees, we can probably neglect many monopolistic elements as falling within the limits of error imposed by the non-economic variables. It is possible to consider the effects of the land scarcity induced by the Emergency and by the inefficiency of state governments in competitive terms; to look at wage rates at different levels of skill in relation to migration and training opportunities without too much preoccupation with union economics; or to interpret the phenomena of rice production in terms of rival uses of peasants' time. No sane person would try to build a detailed model in which elasticities could be calculated with precision from the statistics and used to give accurate forecasts in these fields. But it is at least doubtful whether anything more complex, attempting to allow for the different elements of monopoly and monopsony, would give enough increase in accuracy to offset the increased complexity. For the still massive impact of influences that call for analysis in terms of other disciplines makes the quest for a more comprehensive economic representation rather hazardous.

[147] See T. H. Silcock, "More Monopolistic Competition Theory," *Malayan Economic Review*, III, no. 2 (Oct. 1958), 14-24, for a brief discussion of this question.

9

The Limits of Competitive Enterprise In New Zealand

C. G. F. SIMKIN*

Stages in Collectivism

A new country provides strong, if not compelling, reasons for much economic activity by the state. In the beginning of colonization in New Zealand the state had to acquire land from a large, formidable Maori population and to regulate its sale or lease to settlers. It was also obliged to construct some roads, bridges, ports, and public buildings and to open a Post Office. When self-government was obtained, however, it soon became clear that the new democracy had no objection to extending *state enterprise* beyond what was strictly necessary. In 1865 a Telegraph Department was set up and a savings bank added to the Post Office. Posts and telegraphs have always been state monopolies, and direct competition with the Post Office Savings Bank has always been limited to such few trustee savings banks as the government authorizes. But the next two state enterprises, the Government Life Insurance Office in 1869 and the Public Trust Office in 1872, were set up to compete with private enterprise and succeeded in promoting cheaper and better services.

State enterprise, however, was of less importance than the assumption of a continuous responsibility for *economic development*. The electors strongly approved, in 1870, an ambitious scheme of borrowing to finance immigration and basic transport facilities on a scale, and at a rate, far beyond the meager resources of private capitalists in a small and scattered population. This scheme added railways to state enterprises, but is significant mainly because its success established an unbroken tradition of state borrowing for development.

* Professor of Economics at the University of Auckland.

The tradition was, of course, checked by the long depression of the eighties, but even then began to extend. An agricultural branch was added to the Lands Department as soon as refrigeration made dairy exports possible and became a separate department in 1892. Its first great activity was assistance to dairy farmers and co-operative dairy factories, but services quickly spread to all types of farming. Even more important aid was given by the State Advances to Settlers Act of 1891, which set up a new department for lending money raised overseas to farmers at low rates of interest and on a new system of instalment repayments.

This act was passed by the reforming Liberal-Labour government that held office from 1891 to 1912. It created further state enterprises when it set up state coal mines in 1901 and a State Fire Insurance Office in 1905. When, moreover, it began to build, in 1910, the first state hydroelectric station, it started a development towards a virtual state monopoly. But this government's most notable work was social legislation creating what we now term the *welfare state*. It established old age pensions (initially at £18 a year) and, in 1911, both added widows' pensions and set up a National Provident Fund to help private saving for retirement as well as to provide the usual range of benefits offered by friendly societies. More impressive, at the time, were new acts controlling working conditions in factories, shops, offices, and ships and the creation of a Department of Labour to enforce them. They were complemented by the Industrial Conciliation and Arbitration Act for preventing strikes or lockouts, as the Arbitration Court soon became an instrument for controlling, in great detail, wages and labor conditions through its power of registering industrial agreements with the Supreme Court.

Succeeding conservative governments were forced to do something about the comparative stagnation of the 1920's but were reluctant to enlarge the state's direct powers over the economy. They found a compromise solution in what Professor C. Weststrate has accurately described as "corporatism," i.e., the creation of producers' organizations with powers, conferred by the state, to promote their own interests. The Meat Producers' Board was set up in 1922 and the Dairy Produce Control Board a year later, followed by similar boards for most farm products with the notable exception of wool. They had a variety of powers to control marketing, regulate production, or foster improvements. Dislike for state control was also shown when the State Advances to Settlers Office was replaced in 1934 by a Mortgage Corporation, having private as well as government directors, and by the similar constitution of the new Reserve Bank.

A Labour government came to office in 1935 and held power until 1949. It immediately reversed this check to state enterprise by nationalizing the Reserve Bank and replacing the Mortgage Corporation by a State Advances Corporation, to which was added an important Housing Division for managing the new state houses the government began to build on a very extensive scale. A National Broadcasting Service was given a monopoly of both ordinary and commercial transmission, and in 1940 all but three large private coal mines were bought out for the State Coal Mines Department. After the war the government took over existing airlines for a National Airways Corporation, and also nationalized the Bank of New Zealand (which had been half-owned by the state since the banking troubles of 1895).

This is not an unimportant list, but Labour came to find nationalization much less effective than the spread of *state regulation* over industry, transport, trade, and finance. The Industrial Efficiency Act of 1936 sought to prevent "undue" competition in a number of manufacturing industries and retail trades by licensing new entrants. It was supplemented by a Motor Spirits Licensing Authority and by Transport Licensing Authorities. An exchange crisis just before the war led to a complete system of licensing for imports, exports, and foreign exchange, to which were soon added controls over bank advances, deposit rates of interest, and capital issues. The National Government of 1949-57 made some attempts to reverse this system, but immediately Labour returned to office it was fully restored. Comprehensive price or profit control was introduced at the outbreak of war and has also survived with an additional function, given in 1958, of checking restrictive practices by trade associations. Building controls were finally lifted in 1956, but rent controls have survived in a modified form.

The Scale of Government Activity

Net national income at market prices was recorded as £1,008 million in 1957-58 so that the figures in the government accounts, summarized in Table 1, may be conveniently interpreted as percentages of national income. They show that 37.7 per cent of national income passes through state and local authorities, that current outlays by these authorities on goods and services amount to 11.5 per cent, and their gross capital formation to 11.1 per cent, of national income. Current transfers, including all interest payments on public debt, come to 12.9 per cent or, together with subsidies, to 14.3 per cent. In New Zealand, therefore, government handles more than a third of the national income, and uses this, in roughly equal proportions, to finance its own current activities, its own capital formation and to effect redistribution within the private sector. This reflects, well enough, the economic power of the state, its energy in promoting economic development, and its concern for social security.

Direct taxes are at the high level of 15.5 per cent of national income, or 17.4 per cent of private income, while social security benefits and pensions amount to 7.1 per cent of private income. The

TABLE I. *Government Outlays and Receipts, 1958-59*
(£ million)

Central Government

Consumption outlays	104	Trading income	22
Subsidies	14	Indirect taxes	91
Transfers	124	Direct taxes, etc.	155
		less Saving	−26
Total current outlays	242		
Gross capital formation	74	Saving	26
Net capital outlays of public		Depreciation allowances	8
corporations	2	Capital sales, etc.	9
Purchase of real estate, etc.	2	Borrowings	20
Loans	7	Decrease of cash balances	21
Total capital outlays	84		
Total outlays	326		

Local Government

Consumption	34	Trading income	10
less Transfers from central		Indirect taxes	1
government	−23	Direct taxes	20
Interest payments	5	less Saving	−15
Total net current outlays	16		16
Gross capital formation	35		
Total net outlays	51		

Sources: Department of Statistics, *Accounts of the Government Sector,* 1960; *Official Estimates of National Income and Expenditure,* 1959.

modest initial old-age pension of £18 a year has risen now to £234 a year and has had added to it not only a widows' pension but also orphans', miners', sickness, and unemployment pensions, together with an unconditional payment, "universal superannuation," of £156 a year to everyone over sixty-four years and another unconditional "family benefit" of £39 for each child. These monetary benefits, together with benefits provided to everyone for medical and hospital services, as well as for medicines prescribed, are paid from a special Social Security Fund. The Fund receives the entire proceeds of the social security tax of 1s.6d. levied on each pound of private income, together with a grant of £14 million from the Consolidated Fund. Expensive as it is, and although monetary benefits are now twice the percentage of national income that they were before the war, neither political party is prepared to reduce social security; political pressures are rather always for extension. It should be noted, however, that direct taxes paid by individuals, as distinct from companies, were £122 million, or, if the proportional social security tax is excluded, £62 million. Progressive taxes on individuals thus came to less than indirect taxes net of subsidies at £77 million, and Weststrate has found from a limited statistical investigation that indirect taxes are regressive although not sufficiently so as to prevent the whole system of taxation from having a considerable egalitarian influence.[1]

Consumption outlays of the central government include the medical benefits of the social security scheme (£17 million). We may also regard as welfare expenditures the £7 million spent on public health services, the £15 million transferred to Hospital Boards from the Consolidated Fund, and the £26 million spent on education. Social services would then amount to 57 per cent of state consumption, or to 27 per cent of state current spending. It should be mentioned in this connection that the Department of Health has extensive responsibilities for public health and preventive medicine, controls the registration of doctors, nurses, dieticians, and pharmacists, and insures the provision of public hospital services by Hospital Boards for whose activities the state assumes full financial responsibility. The Department of Education is responsible for primary and

[1] His example relates to four families, having in 1952-53 incomes of £520, £1040, £2080, and £4160. Income taxes altered the ratios of these incomes from 1/2/4/8 to 1/1.85/3.31/5.36, but taxes as a whole to 1/1.89/3.46/5.71. C. Weststrate, *Portrait of a Modern Mixed Economy: New Zealand* (Wellington, 1959), p. 210.

post-primary schools, all of which are "free, secular and compulsory" (up to age fifteen), although it also approves private schools which take 12 per cent of the primary pupils and 11 per cent of the post-primary pupils. Universities are state-financed, but independently governed.

Some state consumption outlays, moreover, are connected with economic development. The official classification lists £10 million for "development of primary and secondary industries," which is a little less than one-half of the annual appropriations for the Departments of Lands and Survey, Agriculture, Scientific and Industrial Research, Industries and Commerce, Mines, Transport, Tourist and Publicity, Civil Aviation and Meteorological Services, and the Forest Service. Between them the Departments of Agriculture and Scientific Research give extensive aid to farmers by advisory services for soil management, crop and pasture production, farm management, farm engineering, dairy farming and processing, fruit growing, bee-keeping, and market gardening; also by research into animal nutrition, breeding and diseases, crops, grasslands, plant diseases, wheat, hops, and tobacco. The Department of Scientific and Industrial Research has begun to help manufacturers with their research problems, but most of the comparatively meager aid they receive is provided by the Department of Industries and Commerce. This department advises on a variety of matters—location, processing, and design—but mostly upon overseas markets through the trade-commissioner service that it operates for the state.

The bulk of government activity in development, however, is connected with capital formation. Central government capital formation is 7½ per cent of national income, and one-third of this is financed from revenue. Local government capital formation is another 3½ per cent of national income, and more than one-third of this is financed from revenue. In 1938-39 total government capital formation was not much different at 10 per cent of national income, and it was then somewhat greater than private capital formation, whereas now it is almost one-quarter less. It appears, however, that public investment is not very far short of private investment and, as the government has come to borrow very little overseas for development and overseas direct investment in industry was only £12 million, the local capital market is usually strained and has long been controlled by a Capital Issues Committee which rations finance.

The largest single item for state capital formation was electric supply development, £20.4 million. Roads accounted for £8.3 million, railways for £6.7 million, post and telegraph extensions for £6.3 million, land development for £4.1 million, and forest development for £1.7 million. State housing took £8.1 million, education buildings, £7.2 million, and public buildings, about £3 million. Most of the remaining £9 million would be spread over state enterprises, including public corporations.

No information is available about the breakdown of the £35 million spent by local authorities on capital formation. But the types of expenditure are indicated by the variety of these authorities. Besides the basic local government units of city, town, borough, and county councils, there are hospital, fire, harbor, transport, drainage, water-supply, electric-supply, gas, and milk boards; also catchment, river, land drainage, rabbit, and Nasalla tussock boards. One-half of their capital formation is financed from revenue, but nearly one-half of local revenue comes from state grants, mainly for hospitals (£15.6 million) and roads (£4.8 million).

Table 2 sets out information about public enterprises. The list is not quite exhaustive because it excludes most state and municipal factories which, in this year, had a value of output equal to £4.9 million (and an added value of output equal to £2.9 million); but two important industrial establishments, the railway workshops and the government printing office, have been included in the table. Nor does it include the two small mixed enterprises, New Zealand Woolpack and Textiles Ltd. and Dominion Salt Ltd. The former produces one-third of the woolpacks used, but only because of stringent protection through import licensing. Dominion Salt processes by evaporation of sea water and, after overcoming many initial difficulties, now supplies one-fifth of local requirements. Mention might also be made of British Petroleum Ltd., formed in 1947 as a partnership of the state and the Anglo-Iranian Company, but becoming a complete subsidiary of Anglo-Iranian when the national government sold its shares in 1955.

There are eighteen state enterprises listed here, but it is not perhaps correct to regard three of them in this light. The Land Settlement Board, which administers Crown lands, is more concerned with development than profit. Crown land is usually offered at valuation and by ballot, and much of the Board's work is concerned with

TABLE 2. *Public Enterprises, 1958-59*

Enterprise	Revenue (£ million)	Relative Importance
A. Central Government		
Crown lands	1.0	42.9% of occupied land area
State forests	3.0	66.0% of merchantable forest
State coal mines (36)	6.6	62.5% of tonnage produced
Electricity Department	15.7	88.0% of power generated
Railways:		
(a) rail services	29.8	Monopoly
(b) road services	2.9	7.5% of revenue for aggregate road services
National Airways Corporation	3.7	Virtual monopoly as carrier
Post Office		Monopoly of post, telegraph,
	23.4	telephone, and cable services
Post Office Savings Bank		82% of savings bank deposits
National Broadcasting Service	2.2	Monopoly (including television)
Reserve Bank (gross profit)	3.9	Monopoly of central banking
Bank of N.Z. (gross profit)	5.2	48.3% of trading bank assets
Govt. Life Insurance Office	6.3	22.2% of ordinary policies in force
State Fire and Accident Insurance Office	2.8	16.9% of premiums for fire insurance; 12.2% of premiums for accident insurance
Public Trust Office	.9	14.2% of estates passing for duty
State Advances	1.6	36% of new mortgages granted state houses (9.6% of dwellings)
Printing and Stationery Dept.	1.3	Small share of market
Tourist and Publicity Dept.	2.5	Bulk of tourist sales
Tourist Hotel Corporation	.7	13 hotels only but in scenic resorts
B. Local Government		
Electric power boards (43)	15.2	Complete retail monopoly
Gas works (22)	1.3	29.6% of output generated
Urban transport (11)	3.8	Monopoly in larger cities
Harbor boards (41)	5.5	Monopoly

Source: New Zealand Official Year Book, 1960.

bringing land into cultivation (128,000 acres in 1957-58). Commercial activities are quite subsidiary to the conservation and development work of the State Forest Service. By far the most significant exploitation of its large merchantable forest has been undertaken by the Tasman Pulp and Paper Company, formed in 1952, and now a mixed enterprise of government with local and overseas capitalists. The sales of the Printing and Stationery Department also represent a minor part of the work of this department.

The important state enterprises are in power, transport, communications, banking, and finance. Electricity is virtually a state monopoly, as are the post, telegraph, telephone and cable services, broadcasting, and rail transport. The Electricity Department is efficient, retailing power at the low price of 0.35d. a kw-h. but making little profit; legislation passed in 1957 will allow charges to be raised after 1960 so as to finance from revenue some of the heavy capital expenditures of this rapidly growing basic utility. State coal mines, on the other hand, are languishing, their loss being nearly one-half of their revenue from sales. The Railways Department also has its difficulties, making a loss equal to 18 per cent of gross revenue. The National Airways Corporation makes a small profit, as does Tasman Empire Airways, formed originally by the governments of the United Kingdom, Australia, and New Zealand, but after 1954 equally owned by the Australian and New Zealand governments until 1961 when the New Zealand government took over completely. The Post Office pays its way, and also the Broadcasting Service, mainly from commercial stations. The Reserve Bank is naturally profitable in a period of inflation, as is the Bank of New Zealand. The two insurance offices set low premiums and distribute profits as bonuses to policyholders. The State Advances Corporation makes a small profit, although its lending rates are fixed by the Minister of Finance, and state rentals are set below either market values or cost. The Tourist and Publicity Department operates an efficient internal travel agency in competition with several private concerns, and has shown a profit since it passed over its hotels to the new Tourist Hotel Corporation.

Local government enterprises are nearly all monopolies. Electric power boards make substantial profits, which they need to finance expansion, but municipal, like private, gas works run at a loss. All but one transport service have losses, mostly substantial and recovered from ratepayers. Harbor boards, as a whole, have an excess of non-capital expenditures over income, but not all of them.

The commercial as well as the non-commercial activity of government is thus very important in New Zealand. An indication of the scope left for private enterprise may be gained from the statistics of employment. These show, on April 15, 1959, 615,000 people, including working proprietors, employed in all occupations save farming, fishing, and hunting; the 1956 Census returned 15.7 per cent of the occupied population in these excluded categories so that total employment would be about 730,000. Central government employment comes to 14.4 per cent of this total, and local government employment to 9.8 per cent; employment in state enterprises is 10.5 per cent of the labor force and employment in local government enterprises, 2.5 per cent. Private enterprise has thus about two-thirds of the labor force, and, if farming is excluded, has only 4½ times the workers employed in government enterprises. Government enterprise, moreover, has a monopoly in the fields of railway transport, air transport, urban transport, communications, broadcasting, and electrical power supply.

Corporatism in Agriculture

Before 1914 farmers used to complain about shipping companies and overseas meat concerns, but they did not appreciate the possibilities of centrally controlling exports until they had experienced wartime arrangements following the intergovernmental agreement that Britain would take all of New Zealand's export surpluses of wool, meat, butter, and cheese. Prices rose sufficiently with wartime inflation to make farmers satisfied with these arrangements. But when, soon after the war, the bulk purchase agreements were terminated, meat and dairy prices fell so drastically that farmers sought ways of improving their position.

Meat producers held discussions with the government in 1921, with the result that a Meat Producers' Board was set up, including one government representative and having powers to control the preparation, storage, and shipment of meat. The board confined itself to regulating shipments, with a view to avoiding gluts or shortages on the British market and to negotiating agreements about freights and insurance. Dairy farmers were more ambitious. They first sought to set up a co-operative marketing company with monopoly powers. When the government refused, a Dairy Produce Control Board was established in 1923. During the 1926-27 season this board tried to make its London office the sole agent for selling butter and cheese in the United Kingdom and to fix prices by agreement with other distributors in this market. Trade hostility, however, bad selling conditions, and dissension among farmers themselves led to the abandonment of the bold experiment at the end of the season. Thereafter the Dairy Board followed the Meat Board by regulating shipments and negotiating freights, although low prices during the Great Depression led to discussion about another trial of centralized marketing in the hope of easing the position of dairy farmers.

Similar boards followed for other primary producers. A Honey Export Control Board was formed in 1925 because of a threat to the quality of exports and, after a voluntary organization had collapsed, took over exports in 1930, but without much success. A Fruit Export Control Board began in 1925 to regulate shipments of apples and pears and did much to improve quality as well as to lower marketing costs. In the wheat industry speculation had aggravated instability of prices and excess capacity had led to cut-throat competition among millers. Growers and millers, accordingly, combined to establish the Wheat Marketing Agency Ltd., with which both were expected to deal. An immediate improvement resulted, and the government in 1933 agreed to set up a Wheat Purchase Board, renamed the Wheat Committee two years later; it is the sole purchaser, importer, and seller of wheat. A Poultry Board was also set up in 1933, aiming only at the promotion of efficiency, followed by a Tobacco Board in 1935, having powers to adjust the previously fluctuating local crop to the unenthusiastic demand of the few processing firms.

When Labour came to power there was a strong swing away from corporatism towards full state control. This was most marked in connection with dairy products, following the introduction of a guaranteed price scheme such that unchanging prices were fixed by the government for each season on the basis of a fair return to the ordinary farmer (i.e., on the basis of costs of production). Dairy exports were then completely taken over by a state Marketing Department, together with the internal distribution of eggs, fruit, and honey; a milk marketing division was also added in 1944 to control town milk supplies. One major addition, however, and two minor additions were made to corporatism. A Wool Council, renamed the Wool Board in 1944, was established by producers to co-operate with similar bodies in Australia and South Africa in meeting the threat from synthetics by undertaking extensive advertising and research.

The first minor addition was a Raspberry Marketing Committee, set up by the government for Nelson in 1940, and followed ten years later by committees for Canterbury and Otago, together with a Central Council of Raspberry Growers; raspberry producers were thus empowered to negotiate wholesale contracts, to control retail prices, and to arrange seasonal labor and wages. The second minor addition was a Hop Marketing Authority, set up in 1939, to control both local and export sales of hops.

On the outbreak of World War II the New Zealand and the United Kingdom governments again made bulk purchase agreements for dairy produce, meat, wool, and tallow. The Marketing Department then also took over exports of meat and, by agreements reached with farmers in 1942, pay-out prices were linked to costs. Surplus realizations over contract prices, for all exports, were to be paid into new industry reserve funds which soon became substantial. Wool reverted to free marketing in 1946, but bulk purchase contracts for the other main exports were annually reviewed up to 1954.

After the war farmers showed increasing dissatisfaction with state control, contract prices, and stabilization funds to which no individual had a claim and which were all invested in government securities. The Dairy Board succeeded, in 1947, in having a separate Dairy Products Marketing Commission with four producer members to three government nominees. A year later the Meat Board took over the purchase and shipment of meat exports and participated in the annual bulk purchase negotiations with the United Kingdom.

When the Labour government was replaced by a National government there was a steady reversion to the corporate arrangements of the interwar period. It began modestly with a Potato Board, set up in 1950 with equal representation of growers and merchants, to make contracts with growers and to promote an adequate supply for the home market at remunerative prices. An Egg Marketing Authority followed, having four producers to three government members, in order to regulate the marketing and distribution of eggs and egg pulp. A Citrus Marketing Authority, set up in 1953, attempts to sell lemons at prices covering growers' costs and to process any surplus crop. A Honey Marketing Authority was also given full control over the processing and sale of honey. An Apple and Pear Board was revived to control marketing of fruit under a guaranteed price scheme to growers, and a monopoly of imports was given to an association of trade interests, Fruit Distributors, Ltd. The internal, as well as the external, work of the Marketing Department was thus completely transferred to industry organizations.

New arrangements were also made for prices. A Wool Commission was established in 1951 to fix, with the consent of the minister, a schedule of minimum prices for each season and to insure these by intervening at auctions; the minimum prices have been set at low levels but any deficit would be met from the commission's fund, created by transfers from former stabilization funds. In 1955 a more generous scheme of floor prices was introduced for meat. A new Meat Export Prices Committee, in which producers are equally represented with the state, fixes a schedule of minimum prices for each season and the Meat Board would meet any consequent losses by drawing upon the Meat Industry Reserve Account. Dairy farmers secured a similar arrangement two years later with the Dairy Products Prices Authority to fix the season's price after having determined costs. For the first season the price was to be not less than 95 per cent of cost and later was to be no more than 5 per cent below the maximum price for the previous season. When, however, dairy prices fell drastically in 1958 this limitation was removed, and the guaranteed price fell by 10 per cent. Both the industry and the Labour government (which was returned in 1957) came to accept that price must be adjusted to overseas realizations rather than to internal costs. The main pillar of Labour's old scheme for insulating the economy from overseas fluctuations (or influences) was thus finally broken.

Table 3 attempts a summary of the present complex of producer-government organizations concerned with the production or marketing of farm products. The range is almost complete, covering not only the major export staples but almost every type of livestock or agricultural product; the only significant exception to corporate control seems to be grass and clover seed (exports of which were £1,-518,000). Functions, in the main, are regulatory and promotional; only the Dairy Products Marketing Commission, the Apple and Pear Board, the Honey Marketing Authority, and the Wheat Committee directly engage in trading, and only the Honey Marketing Authority engages regularly in processing. They leave scope, therefore, for private enterprise in processing and trading. Such enterprise is controlled so as to promote farmers' interests, but subject to

TABLE 3. *Corporate Authorities in Farming Industries, 1957-58*

Authority	Membership	Main Functions	Value in £ million of Production	Exports
Meat Producers' Board	2 Government 6 Producers 1 Dairy farmers	Regulation of shipments Promotion of exports Deficiency payments	108	73
Meat Export Prices Committee	2 Government 2 Meat Board Agreed Chairman	Fixes minimum export prices for season		
Dairy Board	1 Government 5 Producers 2 N.Z. Co-op. Dairy Co. Ltd.	Promotes efficiency Controls bobby calf pools Assists Pig Producers' Council	86	55
Dairy Products Marketing Commn.	3 Government 2 Dairy Board 2 Dairy Conference	Exports dairy products Regulates local sales of butter and cheese		
Dairy Products Prices Authority	2 Government 7 Members of D.P.M.C.	Fixes payout prices for butter and cheese per season Disposes of trading surplus		
New Zealand Milk Board	2 Government 3 Producers 1 Vendors 1 Consumers 1 Municipal Assn.	Advises on fixed retail price Supervises town milk supplies		
Wool Board	3 Government 6 Producers	Research and promotion	85	80
Wool Commission	2 Government 3 Producers	Fixes floor prices for season and operates scheme		
Apple and Pear Marketing Board	2 Government 2 Producers Agreed Chairman	Markets harvest so as realize minimum price to growers fixed by government	5.2	2.3
Honey Marketing Authority	1 Government 5 Producers	Packing and marketing of all honey	.8	.2
Hop Marketing Authority	1 Government 5 Producers	Controls marketing Arranges seasonal labor and wages	.23	.02

(TABLE 3. Cont.)

| | | | Value in £ million of | |
Authority	Membership	Main Functions	Production	Exports
Egg Marketing Authority	3 Government 4 Producer members of Poultry Board	Controls marketing Administers subsidy	2.5	.01
Poultry Board	2 Government 4 Producers	Registers poultry runs Promotes efficiency		
Citrus Marketing Authority	1 Government 4 Producers	Sells lemon crop at "cost" and processes surplus	—	—
Fruit Distribtrs.	Trade Interests	Imports all citrus fruits, bananas, and pineapples	—	1.1 (imports)
Wheat Committee	As Minister decides	Purchases harvest Arranges processing and sale of output Imports all wheat Operates compulsory insurance	2.3	5.8 (imports)
Potato Board	1 Government 3 Producers 3 Merchants	Contracts with growers Appoints wholesalers Promotes adequate supply	3.38	.06
Tobacco Board	1 Government 4 Producers 4 Manufacturers	Licenses growers and sales Operates compulsory insurance Promotes efficiency	1.0	—
Raspberry Marketing Committees	1 Government 4 Producers	Negotiate prices Arrange seasonal labor and wages	800 tons	
Central Council of Raspberry Growers	1 Government 6 Producers	Co-ordinates R.M. Committees Fixes minimum retail prices Equalizes supply		

Sources: New Zealand Official Year Book, 1960; C. Weststrate, op. cit.

such check as government representatives impose in regard to the "public interest" and, even more important, subject to the conditions set by highly competitive export markets. It should, however, be mentioned that private exporters have been increasingly restricted by both the Dairy Commission and the Meat Board.

Regulation of Industry, Trade, and Finance

Labor conditions. The earliest and most complex regulation of industry is concerned with labor conditions. Minimum standards here are set by a number of acts and enforced by a vigorous Department of Labour. Their provisions may be briefly summarized.

(i) The normal working week in factories, shops, offices, and ships is forty hours, and "overtime" has to be paid at "time and a half," i.e., at a rate of 50 per cent above the minimum rate. Restrictions are placed on the overtime that juveniles and women can work. Shops cannot trade on Sundays without official permissions, save in tobacco, sweets, dairy produce, motor spirits, and a few other goods. All workers, permanent or casual, in any occupation must be paid for an annual holiday of two weeks a year, as well as for seven statutory holidays.

(ii) Minimum rates of pay are prescribed by law and varied by order-in-council; they were set, in October 1959, at 5s.1d. an hour for men and at 3s.5d. an hour for women.

(iii) There are comprehensive provisions for safety, health, and welfare measures, covering machinery, noxious gases, dangerous liquids, limits on loads, first aid appliances, fire precautions, ventilation, heating, drainage, sanitary conveniences, drinking water, canteens, seating facilities, clothes lockers, and, in the case of farm workers, accommodation.

(iv) There is a full scheme of workers' compensation for personal injury, and employers must take out special accident insurance against this liability.

In many respects, however, higher standards are set in the awards made by the Court of Arbitration. There are over six hundred of these awards, covering not only minimum wages but also hours, overtime, holidays, safety, and welfare measures. The standard rates set by the court in 1960 are 5s.4d. an hour for unskilled workers, 5s.6d. to 5s.9d. for semi-skilled, and 6s.2d. for skilled; i.e., at least 3d. over the legal minimum wage. The Court, in fact, has been more active than Parliament in developing labor codes and has been mainly responsible for adjusting minimum wages together with margins for skill. It has power to make "standard wage pronouncements" at six-month intervals, stating the rates it would apply to awards coming before it for amendment, and has also power to make "general wage orders" adjusting comprehensively wage-rates set out in existing awards. In making such orders the Court is required to consider changes in retail prices, in the incomes of different sections of the community, and in general economic conditions. The frequent occasions when the Federation of Labour applies for a new order usually provide an interesting, if not very expert, review of the whole economy and some probing of official policies. But there is little evidence that postwar wage orders have done more than follow the wage increases already paid by employers in a chronically inflated labor market.

The Court is not the only wage-fixing authority. Industrial peace on the waterfront has been such a problem as to have led to a Waterfront Industry Tribunal which, unlike the Court, fixes actual, not minimum, wages. There is, similarly, a Coal Mines Council fixing miners' wages. Within the public service there are a variety of authorities for adjusting civil servants' pay: a Public Service Tribunal, a Post and Telegraph Staff Tribunal, and a Government Railways Industrial Tribunal. Wages for employees of Hospital Boards are fixed by the Minister of Health on the advice of special committees.

Protection. Employers, as well as workers, accept this complex of legislation and approve the Court. They do, of course, complain about the effects on labor costs, but usually seek compensation by way of state protection against competition, external or internal. At the recent Industrial Development Conference, for example, the secretary of the Manufacturers' Federation presented data to show that hours are shorter and wage-rates higher in New Zealand than in the United Kingdom and many other countries, and went on to argue that local industry must have adequate and permanent protection to safeguard "the standard of living, the livelihood, of all those engaged in industries." This, indeed, is largely common ground for politicians, trade unionists, and manufacturers, and the greatest of all impediments to a competitive economy in New Zealand.

Tariff protection has long been accorded, but at quite modest levels by world standards. A comprehensive review of the tariff, in 1934, led to duties on 5.2 per cent of imports and at an average rate of 34 per cent; the highest ad valorem duty is 60 per cent and most range from 20 to 25 per cent. Few changes were later made, until a new review, begun in 1956, led to a complete revision that was to come into force in July 1962.

Since the introduction of import controls, however, the tariff has become only a subsidiary instrument of protection. Originally imposed to meet the exchange crisis of 1938, import controls quickly developed into a deliberate method of fostering the growth of most types of manufacturing. They succeeded up to a point; the contribution of manufacturing to national income has risen from 18 to 25 per cent and the share of consumer goods in total imports has fallen from 27 to 18 per cent. But manufactures (excluding processing) still make a negligible contribution to exports, and manufacturers' demands for materials and equipment have actually raised imports from 23 to 26 per cent of national income.

The original regulations prohibited the import of any goods without a license or exemption, and since 1941 this licensing has been prescribed by annual schedules relating to items in the customs tariff. Licenses are issued by the Customs Department, after receiving advice from the Department of Industries and Commerce about manufacturers' requirements and the extent to which various imports may be admitted without damage to their markets. Soon after the National government came to office in 1950 it released one-third of the tariff items from licensing, admitted token imports to test price and quality of local manufactures, and charged a new Board of Trade with a wholesale revision of the tariff in the hope of replacing import control as a means of protection. This first bold move, however, was upset by a speculative flood of imports, connected with the Korean War boom, and was followed by another exchange crisis. This was met, not by a reimposition of import controls, but by an exchange allocation scheme administered by the Reserve Bank. The Board and the government went a bit further in exempting items from import control and, at the end of 1954, the exchange allocation scheme was removed. An attempt was now made to keep down the strong demand for imports by a credit squeeze. Trouble recurred, however, in 1958 when a fall in dairy prices and speculation about a reimposition of import controls if Labour won the election led to a third exchange crisis. Labour did win the election and met the crisis by a full restoration of import controls.

Manufacturers welcomed this restoration and plans were announced for new investment of £74 million leading to a £68 million increase of production. They were emphatic, at the Industrial Development Conference of 1960, that industry needed protection and that the existing tariff was obsolete and inadequate. A new tariff, they admitted, would improve their situation, but must have the disadvantage of raising prices and they doubted its ability to cope with dumping, discriminating raw material prices charged by overseas suppliers, competition from countries with substantially lower wage costs, or difficulties over the balance of external payments. The only disadvantages they saw in import control were that the severity of licensing, and hence its protection, varied with the level of exchange, that the complexity of licensing caused administrative problems, and that "out-of-line" decisions could result from this or from the political influence of pressure groups. Their conclusion seemed to be that "a properly designed tariff supplemented by a flexible system of quantitative import licensing is a necessity . . . in a country where there is a high wage structure and shorter working hours." This view is, of course, accepted by the Labour party, and the National party seems either to have accepted it also, or to have become resigned to it as a political necessity.[2]

[2] The dual purposes of import control, differently emphasized at different times, have always been to conserve overseas funds and to protect local industry. Decisions about a safe level of private imports derive from forecasts of the balance of payments, made initially by the Reserve Bank but scrutinized, and perhaps revised, by a committee of officials from Treasury, External Affairs, Industries, and Commerce and Statistics. In the end, of course, the decision is made by Cabinet, which also decides upon any changes recommended in the form of licensing.

As practiced in 1960, licensing allowed importers a choice between allocations for individual tariff items, or global allocations covering tariff items within some fifteen individual groupings. In either case, licensing was on a replacement basis; importers were allowed an initial license for one-half of their 1959 imports and, after the goods covered by this initial license had been landed, could be granted a second, and then a third license of equal value. Since 1959 there has been no discrimination against imports from the dollar area, although before that there was fairly consistent discrimination in accordance with the requirements of membership of the sterling area.

The 1959 allocations had derived from 1956 allocations and these, of course, to some extent, from much earlier licensing. Importers, however, who felt that their own imports had been unduly low could appeal to the Customs Department, and any firm wishing to enter importing could also apply to it for a new importer's entitlement. The minister may refer such appeals to the Board of Trade, which has the principal function of advising him on matters relating to external trade,

Internal controls. The state has also tried to regulate internal competition. A Bureau of Industry, set up in 1936, was supposed to promote "new industries in the most economic form," but settled down to licensing entry into a number of specified industries thought to be in danger of disorderly competition. Many of these industries were exempted by the National government, which closed down the Bureau in 1956, after transferring control over the distribution of motor spirits to the Transport Department, control over chains of pharmacies to a new Pharmacy Authority, and control over the manufactures of pulp, paper and board, multi-walled paper bags, paua shell, and rubber tires or tubes to the Department of Industries and Commerce. Transport licensing has fully survived changes of government; special authorities in each district control public road services and a Transport Charges Appeal Authority fixes rates or fares.

Liquor licensing has a different purpose and dates almost from the beginning of government in New Zealand. Today a Licensing Control Commission supervises existing licenses for the sale of alcoholic liquors, which may be sold retail only by hotels and some ten restaurants, and sparingly grants new licenses. Prices for beer are fixed by the price control division of the Department of Industries and Commerce. Picture theaters, similarly, must be licensed by the Chief Inspector of Films, and auctioneers, land agents, money lenders, or pawnbrokers all require a license issued by a magistrate.

Other restraints are imposed in regard to finance. The Capital Issues Committee, controlling new finance raised by companies and set up during the war, has long hampered private enterprise by limiting competition against the state for current savings. (The Local Government Loans Board still restricts local authorities.) But the government continues, by orders-in-council, to regulate hire-purchase

---

tariffs, import licensing, and protection. In these ways attempts have been made to make licensing flexible and to avoid conferring monopoly advantages upon established importers.

Earlier allocations, however, had largely hardened the pattern of importing into one of strong protection for local industries. The enthusiastic discharge by the Department of Industries and Commerce of its duty to advise Customs of manufacturers' needs for imports and for protection against import competition is indicated by the drastic fall in the proportion of imports of consumers' goods to total imports. Since 1950, however, there have been variations in "token" licenses, designed not only to permit continued contact between local importers and overseas suppliers but also to keep both consumers and manufacturers alive to the variety, quality, and cost of some imported consumer goods.

credit and to fix rates of interest paid on deposits by trading banks, savings banks, building and investment societies, stock and station agents, or trading companies. Banks are also restricted in charging interest on advances or overdrafts; the average rate must not exceed 5½ per cent. This, however, is a comparatively trivial control for trading banks. They cannot be set up except by a special act, are forbidden to conduct a savings bank business, and are obliged to keep statutory deposits at the Reserve Bank which has so adjusted them in recent years as to keep trading bank advances almost constant.

Interest controls were designed to keep down prices, limit property incomes, and to cheapen public borrowing. The first two objectives were also aimed at by rent and price controls. A Fair Rents Act was among the first measures passed after the Labour victory of 1935 and was tightened considerably in 1942. Some relaxations were made by the National government, and especially by the Act of 1955. This allows a tenant or landlord to have a fair rent fixed by a magistrate on the basis of current values and, if an agreement is then registered embodying this rent, the landlord may regain possession unhampered by the clauses of the Tenancy Act requiring him to prove greater hardship or to provide alternative accommodation. Such control has practically stopped private building of houses for rental and has also restricted the number of existing houses offered for rental.

Price control, established during World War I, was scrapped after it but revived in the Prevention of Profiteering Act in 1936. A Price Investigation Tribunal followed and was given tremendous powers when wartime regulations prohibited any increase of prices without official sanction. These regulations were consolidated in the Control of Prices Act of 1947, which empowered the Price Tribunal to fix maximum or minimum prices for any goods or services it saw fit. Under the National government, however, there was a marked shift of emphasis from price stability to the prevention of profiteering. Many items were decontrolled and in 1955 general control with specific exemptions was replaced by control of specified items only. At present the list stands at sixteen foodstuffs, gas, school uniforms, rubber, footwear, cars, petrol and tires, cigarettes, tobacco, beer, cinema admissions, hotel tariffs, and sea freights.

The Tribunal has stated criteria for price control. It regards control as necessary if goods are subsidized (butter, milk, eggs, flour, bread, and gas), if they are in short supply, or if impediments to competition have arisen through import control, industrial licensing, restrictions on finance, monopoly conditions, or restrictive practices.

Restrictive Practices

In 1954 the Minister of Industries and Commerce made a strong statement about restrictive practices, recognizing the way they had been fostered by state controls. Many trade associations, he charged, operated a virtual licensing system and also a system of price control. "With a tightly controlled economy and import control there was a natural tendency for trade groups to combine in their dealings with the Government, and out of that had grown the practice of trade groups to combine to their mutual advantage and overlook the person who really counted, the consumer." This charge was repeated, at the Industrial Development Conference in 1960, by the Secretary of the Department: ". . . there are restrictive trade arrangements in most of the countries of the Western World, but it would be difficult to find another country with as rigid and pervasive limitations on competition as those that have existed in New Zealand."

A Trade Practices Act, accordingly, was passed in 1958, requiring trades associations to register agreements concerned with price maintenance, limitation of sales outlets, zoning, ring tendering, and the like, and setting up a commission to investigate such practices and with power to make orders prohibiting or amending them. By March 1961 some 818 agreements had been registered, and the commission had held ten public hearings concerned with a pool for glazing contracts, uniform prices for wire mattresses, uniform profit margins for wire netting, minimum pricing of phonograph records, price collusion for aerated waters, fixing of hairdressing charges, fixing of retail margins for a wide range of groceries, exclusion of one firm from the Wholesale Plumbers' & Merchants' Guild, and an agreement about charges for funeral services. The commission either prohibited these practices or accepted an assurance that they had been abandoned, but two cases went on appeal to a Trade Practices Appeal Authority, also set up by the Act, and the commission's rulings were upheld. So far there is little sign of restrictive agreements being cancelled merely because official inquiries are likely, but the

commission has said it is selecting a cross-section of cases that traders
may draw proper conclusions and take action without waiting for the
commission to intervene. An amendment in 1961 removed the obligation to register agreements, and also made alterations in the
commission's procedures.

Collusion through trade associations is undoubtedly a much more
important factor in limiting competition than is business concentration, although statistical information relating to concentration is
deficient in that it refers to "establishments," more than one of which
may be under the control of a single "firm." Table 4, for what it
is worth, gives information about the character of business organization in manufacturing and retail establishments. In manufacturing,
at least, the discrepancy between establishments and firms may not
be very serious except for public companies, because (in 1956-57)
some 5,495 establishments came under private companies and income-
tax returns gave 5,597 such companies engaged in manufacturing;
but there were 1,356 establishments coming under public companies,
government, municipal, or co-operative concerns, and only 681 such
concerns in the income-tax statistics.

Information about the size distribution of establishments in manufacturing, retailing, wholesaling, and services is given in Table 5,
from which it would appear that the relative degree of concentration
is most marked in wholesaling, about the same in manufacturing
and services, and much less in retailing.

TABLE 4. *Establishments by Type of Firm, 1957-58*

Sector	Indi- vidual (per cent)	Partner- ship (per cent)	Private Company (per cent)	Public Company (per cent)	Co-op- erative and Misc. (per cent)	Muni- cipal and Govt. (per cent)	Totals
Manufacturing:							
Number	11.7	6.2	66.3	9.9	4.8	1.2	8,529
Output	1.5	1.0	48.4	34.0	14.4	0.8	£645m.
Added value	2.0	1.4	53.2	37.9	4.1	1.3	£227m.
Employment	2.9	1.7	58.0	32.7	3.1	1.6	162,985
Retail trade:							
Number	43.8	15.0	35.3	4.1	1.8		26,876
Turnover	18.3	8.5	50.2	19.5	3.5		£599m.
Stocks	12.8	5.6	57.5	21.1	3.0		£97m.

Source: New Zealand Official Year Book, 1960.

TABLE 5. *Establishments by Size of Added Value or Turnover, 1957-58*

Sector	Under £5,000 (per cent)	£5,000 to £9,999 (per cent)	£10,000 to £19,999 (per cent)	£20,000 to £49,999 (per cent)	£50,000 to £99,999 (per cent)	£100,000 to £249,999 (per cent)	£250,000 to £499,999 (per cent)	£500,000 and over (per cent)	Totals
Manufacturing:									
Number	28.0	27.0	21.3	15.1	4.7	3.2		0.7	8,529
Added value	3.4	7.3	11.3	17.4	12.0	23.9		24.8	£227m.
Retail trade:									
Number	19.4	26.7	28.9	17.8	4.1	2.4	0.5	0.2	28,876
Turnover	2.6	8.8	18.4	23.6	12.6	15.3	8.6	10.0	£599m.
Wholesale trade:									
Number	6.2	8.2	11.1	21.5	17.7	25.0	2.5	7.1	2,595
Turnover	0.1	0.4	1.1	4.3	7.6	16.8	19.9	49.9	£433m.
Services:									
Number	75.4	12.7	6.8	3.4	1.1	0.7			2,702
Turnover	20.9	13.1	13.8	15.6	11.6	25.0			£18m.

Source: New Zealand Official Year Book, 1960, PP. 602-605.

More detailed information about relative industrial concentration in manufacturing establishments is provided by Table 6. The high degree of concentration shown for the food industries is accounted for by the meat works, which constitute the largest 5 per cent of establishments and which employ an average of 445 persons each. The even higher degree of concentration in tobacco manufacturing is connected with branch establishments of large overseas concerns. The paper and pulp industry is dominated by two giants, New Zealand Forest Products Limited, a private concern, and the Tasman Pulp and Paper Company, a mixture of government, local, and overseas capital; this industry is controlled by the Licensed Industries Committee of the Department of Industries and Commerce which regulates outputs for the local market, but is subject to strong competition in its important and growing export markets. These cases apart, the table does not suggest any very marked degree of concentration in spite of the small local market to which most industries are practically confined. The typical New Zealand industrial establishment is quite small-scale, so that technical conditions seldom limit competition. Limits arise mainly from state controls and from restrictions imposed by trade associations, which have themselves been fostered by state controls.

TABLE 6. *Estimated Concentration of Employment in Manufacturing Establishments, 1958-59*

Group	Firms	Employees	Per cent of Employment in Largest 5 per cent of firms	10 per cent of firms
Food	749	29,835	58.7	72.1
Beverages	120	2,322	39.7	54.9
Tobacco	7	1,184		73.9*
Textiles	179	8,671	34.0	53.4
Footwear	1,058	25,474	—	25.8
Wood and cork	1,110	12,401	26.0	39.2
Furniture	524	5,112	23.3	38.0
Paper and pulp	103	4,858	40.9	54.1
Printing, publishing, etc.	405	10,102	44.4	59.1
Leather	93	1,465	32.0	46.8
Rubber	85	2,805	48.1	73.0
Chemicals	216	5,076	32.7	51.3
Petroleum and coal	42	375	16.0	27.4
Non-metallic minerals	547	6,541	41.5	54.2
Basic metals	84	850	23.4	38.1
Metal products	389	7,902	32.5	50.7
Machinery	505	8,963	39.5	51.9
Electrical machinery	135	4,081	27.8	46.5
Transport equipment	1,954	21,994	37.8	49.3
Miscellaneous	224	2,974	37.3	47.0
Total	8,529	162,985	44.3	55.0

Source: *New Zealand Official Year Book*, 1960, pp. 602-605.
  * In two largest firms.

The Recent Weakening of Collectivism

The preceding survey shows how state control has developed in New Zealand into a pervasive complex of economic regulation. But it has also shown that, after reaching a peak during the first Labour administration, state control has recently weakened in many ways. This administration made some efforts to fulfil the traditional socialist aim of nationalization, but the succeeding National government reversed the process and the second Labour government seemed content with the reversal; there was, certainly, no mention of nationalization in Labour's program for the 1960 election. State enterprise has come to be discussed in terms of the contribution it should make to the country's economic growth. Both parties accept that public investment is in danger of lagging behind requirements for power, transport, communications, and land development, and both believe that such a lag should be prevented.

There has also been a considerable easing of state regulation. The second Labour government accepted further the passing of control over marketing of farm products from the state to producer boards, even to the extent of giving up the idea, long important in their policy, of guaranteed prices for dairy products. Industrial licensing is now mostly concerned with a few inevitably monopolistic industries. Price control no longer aims at stabilizing prices and has become directly limited to only a few commodities. We have, instead, a new attempt at preventing trade associations from exploiting consumers.

The most durable controls are the oldest, governing wages and working conditions. They have been supplemented, in the postwar period, by an official policy of maintaining "full employment," which New Zealand politicians are led to interpret quite literally. This objective has been achieved with remarkable consistency, but the result owes less to deliberate policy than to failure to control inflation.

Official policy has, in fact, been directed to checking aggregate demand rather than to stimulating it, because if inflation is good for employment it is bad for prices and the balance of payments. The state, of course, has powerful weapons for this purpose. Public finance controls more than one-third of the national income. Both taxes and state expenditures have been varied in attempts to check inflation, and public loans have been raised overseas to ease strains on the balance of payments. Controls over bank credit and hire-purchase finance have been used in the same way. But, in conditions of fine electoral balance, it is difficult to apply fiscal or monetary measures with sufficient rigor to protect external funds against large changes in export or import prices; for, if pushed hard, they would endanger 100 per cent full employment.

The import controls which Labour introduced as an *ad hoc* measure to meet an exchange crisis have thus become widely accepted as a necessity for full employment. They are, as we have seen, also supported by manufacturers and unions as a means of protecting local industries against countries having less generous labor conditions. None of Labour's innovations has proved more durable, and none, as politicians themselves recognize, has proved a more serious impediment to competitive, as distinct from private, enterprise.

Emphasis on egalitarianism has also begun to decline. There was, between 1938 and 1958, little change in the share of either salaries and wages (60 per cent) or of company income (7 per cent) in disposable private income. Social security incomes, however, rose from 4 to 9 per cent, and there has been some decline in the share of incomes from rent and interest. The ratio, moreover, of skilled to unskilled wages, as set by the Court of Arbitration, has declined a little from 118 to 116 per cent. But it seems to have become accepted that there is little scope for further attacks on inequality, and political emphasis has been shifting to a concern about rewards for enterprise and margins for skill. To quote only one example, the 1960 Economic Survey presented by the Minister of Finance, after drawing attention to a falling rate of increase for real national income, says:

A willingness to take risks and also to provide incentives for skill and enterprise is a factor typically associated with rapid rates of growth in other countries. To the extent that these have not been emphasized in New Zealand a slower rate of expansion and development may have occurred.

Little has yet been done to provide greater incentives or margins, although state salaries were adjusted comprehensively in 1960 and both the 1960 and 1961 budgets gave some encouragement to saving.

The reversal of nationalization, the easing of controls, and now the emphasis on incentives have all followed similar developments in other countries. They raise the interesting, if still open, question whether New Zealand, which used to boast of leading the world in socialist legislation, has not come to follow a general swing towards a reformed type of capitalism. Encouragement was given to such a belief by the 1960 general election, which returned the National party to office with a very comfortable majority. But serious difficulties over inflation and the balance of external payments have obliged the National government to move slowly so that, up to mid-1962, it did little to reduce the formidable network of controls that still applied to business in New Zealand.

10

The Economic System of Pakistan

*Nurul Islam**

INTRODUCTION

Pakistan is an underdeveloped, low-income country with a population in 1961 of about 93.8 million on a total land area of 233 million acres, of which about 26 per cent is under cultivation. The per capita income is 250-260 rupees per annum.[1] During the last ten years or so the rate of growth of national income has varied between 2 and 3 per cent per annum, as is evident from the following:[2]

Year	National income at constant prices (Rs. million)	Per cent increase over previous year
1949-50	17,238	—
1954-55	19,857	15.2
1959-60	21,897	10.2

The absolute increase in aggregate income has not been significantly different between the two five-year periods, but with a lower base in 1949-50 the percentage rate of growth during the first five-year period was higher. National income figures include the effects of changes in terms of trade, which have undergone a substantial long-run decline over the years.[3] Indexes of the terms of trade for 1949-59, on the April 1948–March 1949 base, are as follows:

1949	106.2	1952	103.5
1950	118.0	1953	75.0
1951	124.5	1954	81.0

* Dr. Islam is Professor of Economics, Dacca University.
[1] Government of Pakistan, *The First Five Year Plan, 1955-60* (Karachi, 1957), pp. 9-11. $1 equals approximately 4.8 rupees.
[2] Ministry of Finance, Economic Affairs Division, *Hand Book of the Second Five Year Plan (1960-65)* (n.p., 1961), Table 2.
[3] *The First Five Year Plan*, p. 179; State Bank of Pakistan, *Report on Currency and Finance, 1959-60* (Karachi, 1960), p. 188.

1955	75.6	1958	54.0
1956	65.5	1959	52.4
1957	63.0		

The rise in gross domestic product has been higher but has been partially offset by the persistent declining trend in terms of trade. Similarly, the increase in national income has been partly offset by an increasing population, with the result that the per capita income rose by 5.6 per cent in the first five-year period as against 2.8 per cent in the second period. However, as the preliminary results of the 1961 census show, the assumed rates of growth of population on which these estimates of per capita income are based are lower than the actual rates. The new census reveals that population has grown by 23.7 per cent between 1951 and 1961 as against the growth of national income between 1949-50 and 1959-60 by 27 per cent. The rise in per capita income is thus about 3 per cent over the past ten years. However, even assuming that the final results of census may eventually show a rate of growth of population of about 2 per cent per year, it appears that while per capita income might have risen by about 1 per cent per annum during the first period, it has remained more or less stationary in the second period.[4]

More than 90 per cent of the population, which is estimated to increase at the rate of 2.37 per cent per annum, lives in villages. The percentage distribution of the total labor force by occupations in 1955 follows:[5]

	Per cent
Agriculture	64.7
Manufacturing	10.6
Public utilities and construction	2.2
Transport and communications	2.0
Trade and commerce	7.0
Services	11.1
Other	2.4

Agriculture is the source of employment for the bulk of the people. Services provide a source of employment almost equal in importance to that of manufacturing. Trade, commerce, and services together

[4] Government of Pakistan, Population Census Commission, *Census Bulletin*, no. 1, preliminary release (Feb. 1961), p. 1, Table 1.

[5] Government of Pakistan, *Report of the I.L.O. on Manpower Survey in Pakistan* (Karachi, 1958), pp. 19-26. The percentage of rural population reported here is based on the 1951 census. The figures for 1961 are not yet available.

absorb between two and one and a half times the labor force in manufacturing occupations.

Agriculture is not only the most important source of employment but also provides the bulk of the gross national product. Though in recent years there have been changes in the relative importance of the major sources of national income, agriculture continues to occupy a predominant position, as is seen in Table 1.

TABLE 1. *Sector Shares of Gross National Product at Constant Prices*
(per cent)

	1949-50	1954-55	1959-60
Agriculture	61.3	59.3	54.7
Manufacturing	7.0	10.3	13.6
Government	4.7	5.0	6.2
Services	8.6	8.0	7.1
Trade	9.4	9.0	8.6

Sources: The First Five Year Plan, Table 7, pp. 27-28; *The Second Five Year Plan,* 1960-65 (Karachi, 1960), Table 12, p. 45. National income figures are at the average of prices for the period 1949-50 to 1952-53.

In agriculture food crops cover about 85 per cent of the cultivated area. Two major cash crops, jute and cotton, contribute about 80 per cent of the country's total foreign exchange earnings, and the customs revenue from these exports contributes a major portion of the government's income. In the earlier years trade was more important than manufacturing, but with the quickened pace of industrialization it has recently yielded place to the latter.

A comparison of Table I with the percentage distribution of the total labor force given above reveals the existence of significant differences in the productivity of labor as between different sectors of the economy. The low productivity of labor in agriculture is evidenced by the fact that in 1955 65 per cent of the total labor force, which is engaged in agriculture, produced only 59 per cent of the gross national product, yielding per head an average output of Rs. 729. Higher productivity in trade is reflected in the fact that 7 per cent of the labor force employed in trade produced 9 per cent of national product, whereas in the field of services 11 per cent of the labor force produced 8 per cent of output.

The increase in the relative importance of the government sector as a source of income is a reflection of the growing importance of the government's participation in economic activity. Pakistan started her independent political and economic existence in 1947 with virtually no industrial base and with no private industrialists worth the name. The special circumstances of the initial period needed vigorous state initiative in various fields. In the course of these years there has gradually emerged in Pakistan a mixed economy where both private and public enterprises coexist in different areas of economic activity. The interrelations between different forms of enterprise have still been unfolding, with a changing emphasis on their relative roles with the passing of years. Pakistan represents a dual or a mixed economy in yet another sense. Though a quantitative estimate is difficult to obtain, a certain portion of the gross national product does not pass through the market mechanism at all. According to one estimate 80 per cent of food crops and 20 per cent of livestock are consumed on the farm.[6]

Organization of Production and Marketing in Agriculture

Agricultural production is undertaken on small and fragmented holdings by individual cultivators using on the whole traditional methods and implements. Large-scale commercially organized or mechanized farming is an exception rather than the rule. Inheritance laws, coupled with an increasing population, have resulted in a progressive subdivision and fragmentation of holdings into tiny plots of land scattered around a village. In East Pakistan the average size of cultivators' holdings works out at 3.5 acres. However, the average size of cultivators' holdings differs as between different types of cultivators, as is shown in Table 2.

The extent of fragmentation in East Pakistan can be guaged from the fact that the number of plots per acre of holding varies between 2.28 and 4.[7] In West Pakistan the average holding of an owner-cultivator has been estimated at 3.9 acres and that of a tenant-cultivator at 3.8 acres, whereas 51.1 per cent, 37.8 per cent, and 50 per

[6] M. Huq, *Deficit Financing in Pakistan, 1951-60* (Institute of Development Economics, Karachi, 1961), appendix F, p. 68.

[7] Dacca University Socio-Economic Survey Board, *Rural Credit and Unemployment in East Pakistan* (Karachi, 1956), p. 43.

TABLE 2. *Size and Distribution of Agricultural Holdings in East Pakistan, 1960*

Type of holding	Per cent of total holdings	Area operated		Average size of cultivator's holding:	
		Per cent of total area	Per cent of cultivated area	Total (acres)	Cultivated (acres)
Owner-cultivator	62.1	55.9	54.1	3.2	2.7
Owner-cum-tenant	35.6	42.5	44.1	4.2	3.8
Tenant	2.3	1.6	1.8	2.5	2.3
Total	100.0	100.0	100.0	3.5	3.1

Source: Government of Pakistan, *First Agricultural Census: Preliminary Report, East Pakistan* (Karachi, 1960), Table 1.

cent of the holdings in the 0.5, 5 to 10, and 10 to 15 acres groups, respectively, are estimated to be split into tiny fragments.[8]

The institutional arrangements governing the relation of a cultivator to the land, which determine the distribution of income originating from land as well as the system of incentives to cultivators, can be seen from the classification of land workers in 1951 (Table 3).

However, there are cultivators who own part of the land they till, the rest being rented. Similarly, some of the tenants supplement their income by working for hire. This is evident from an analysis of a detailed classification of the total of cultivators (owning or renting land) as distinguished from land workers (Table 4).

Tenants hold and cultivate land owned by landlords under various arrangements regarding the sharing of produce and the provision of implements and cattle, leaving the tenants often with a bare minimum income for subsistence and, consequently, with no incentive or

TABLE 3. *Percentage Distribution of Total Land Workers*

	Land owners	Tenants	Landless labor
East Pakistan	76.0	9.7	14.2
West Pakistan	56.3	41.4	2.3
All Pakistan	69.0	21.0	10.0

Source: Census of Pakistan, I (Karachi, 1951), 110.

[8] Government of West Pakistan, *Report of the Land Reforms Commission* (Lahore, 1959), pp. 16-17.

TABLE 4. *Percentage Distribution of Cultivators Owning or Renting Land in 1951*

	Owning all land tilled	Owning part and renting part	Renting all land tilled	Renting and also working for hire
East Pakistan	41.05	47.64	6.80	4.51
West Pakistan	44.00	13.56	38.08	4.36

Source: Census of Pakistan, I (1951), 110.

funds for capital investment or improvement of production. The relative importance of different classes of cultivators has undergone some recent changes, especially in East Pakistan, consequent on the introduction of land reforms in the fifties.

The distribution of land ownership is very unequal, especially in West Pakistan. In some areas, such as Sind in West Pakistan, 1 per cent of the owners own 30 per cent of the total area, the average holding being more than 500 acres; whereas 60 per cent of the owners own 12 per cent of the total area, in average units of less than 15 acres.[9] The great inequality of the distribution of land ownership in West Pakistan, as revealed in Table 5, needs no comment.

Similar data are not available for East Pakistan. Indirect evidence suggests that the degree of inequality of the ownership of land may be much less, owing partly to the emigration to India of big landlords, who were mostly Hindus, and partly to the recent acquisition by the government of the rights of rent-receiving intermediaries in East Pakistan. Recent sample surveys throw some light on the distribution of farming families according to the size of their cultivated holdings, which include land both owned and rented by the

TABLE 5. *Distribution of Land Ownership in West Pakistan*

Average area owned (acres)	Per cent of owners	Per cent of land owned
5 or less	64.6	15.0
5 to 25	28.5	31.7
25 to 100	5.7	22.4
100 to 500	1.1	15.9
500 and above	0.1	15.0

Source: Government of West Pakistan, *Report of the Land Reforms Commission*, appendix I.

[9] Government of Pakistan, *First Five Year Plan*, pp. 308-309.

farmers. Of the total families surveyed in 1956, in four widely dispersed areas of East Pakistan, only 0.5 to 4 per cent of the families cultivated holdings constituting 10 acres or more. The proportion of families cultivating holdings of 0.5 to 10 acres varied between 3 and 16 per cent in different areas. From 32 to 56 per cent of the families cultivated holdings ranging from one to five acres.[10] Insofar as the farmers cultivate land not owned by them and landowners parcel out land for its cultivation by others under various arrangements for the distribution of the produce of land, this may not indicate any index of the inequality of ownership. This distribution may be said to reflect distribution of earned income from land, whether owned or rented, or both, among the farming families. The upper income group is revealed to be a rather small one.

The landlords were mostly absentee landlords who not only often physically resided in urban centers but also lacked on the whole initiative or interest in undertaking improvements on land or in bringing new and uncultivated land under cultivation. The tenants in certain areas of West Pakistan did not have security of tenure and had generally low bargaining power, in view of a large and increasing rural population pressing upon a limited supply of land. They were left, consequently, with inadequate resources to undertake any agricultural improvement.

Recent legislation on land reforms has attempted to rectify many of the shortcomings of the system of land tenure. In East Pakistan, where legislative enactments for land reforms have been more far-reaching, an Act of 1950 provided for the acquisition by the state, on payment of compensation, of the rights of landlords, i.e., rights to receive rents from tenants (actual cultivators) for the use of land owned by the former. There was to be no intermediary between the cultivator and the state, the latter retaining the sole right to receive rents. Moreover, it provided for the grant of permanent, transferable, and alienable occupancy rights to cultivators, who were now to be tenants of the state only. In 1956 the government of East Pakistan acquired all intermediary rights. As far as owner-cultivators were concerned, it fixed a ceiling on land ownership at 33 acres per family, which is now under consideration for a revision upward to a range of 100 to 125 acres, depending upon the nature of soil and its productivity. Mechanized farms, dairy farms, and tea and sugar plan-

[10] *Rural Credit and Unemployment,* p. 42.

tations have been exempted from restrictions on size, mainly in the interest of efficient cultivation. The progress in the acquisition of excess land and in the payment of compensation has been slow because of administrative difficulties involved in working out a schedule of rates of compensations as well as actual procedures for their payment. Under the Act the subletting of land retained by owners for the payment of a rent is prohibited, but sharecropping under which an owner can have his land cultivated by others in exchange for a share of the produce of land is permitted. Measures are under consideration to regulate sharecropping. The West Pakistan government decided to adopt more conservative measures and accordingly enacted in 1959 a law to abolish (a) all *jagirs*, i.e., land held free of any rent payable to the government, (b) to cancel certain classes of intermediate interests, and (c) to fix ceilings on ownership of land at 500 acres for irrigated land and 1,000 acres for unirrigated land, the excess to be acquired by the government on payment of compensation and to be sold to new cultivators. The cultivators settled on newly acquired land and certain classes of existing tenants, called occupancy tenants, are to be conferred full proprietory rights. Insofar as other classes of tenants of private landlords holding land below or up to the ceiling continue to exist, various measures are being worked out to insure their greater security of tenure and a more equitable distribution of produce. The West Pakistan government has also assumed powers to issue directions to cultivators, in case land remains uncultivated for a period of two years or more, to bring such land under cultivation within a definite time, failing which the government may requisition land for management and utilization. In some cases the government has defined the size of (a) subsistence and (b) economic holdings. Measures to prevent further subdivision of such holdings as well as to encourage an amalgamation of fragmented holdings, if need be by compulsion, are being devised.

The land reforms in West Pakistan have some redistributive effects. As is evident from a reference to the pattern of distribution of ownership of land discussed earlier, it has affected six thousand people owning land to the extent of five hundred acres or more, i.e., the highest income group among the landowners, constituting about 0.1 per cent of the total landowners. However, the redistributive effects are partly modified insofar as landowners are allowed to retain a maximum of 150 acres of orchards in addition to the permissible limit of cultivable land and also are given the option to transfer to their heirs a certain amount of land prior to the assessment of their land for the purpose of the new law, in case they have not done so in the past ten years. Again, since the landlords are given the right to choose the portions of their total holdings to be surrendered to the government, they have surrendered mostly uncultivated land, a major portion of which is cultivable waste land which cannot be brought under cultivation without a further investment of capital. The existing inequality among the rest of the landowners remains unaffected. The ceiling on land ownership in West Pakistan represents a cautious approach towards a modification of the existing socio-economic structure. Whatever may be the form and distribution of land ownership, the typical size of an agricultural enterprise in Pakistan is small. About 50 per cent of owner-cultivators in West Pakistan and 60 per cent in East Pakistan operate on less than subsistence holdings, which keep on growing in numbers with a rising population.[11]

The marketing of agricultural products suffers from such drawbacks as lack of standardization, lack of a proper system of weights and measures, as well as inadequate grading, transportation, and storage facilities. There usually exists a chain of intermediaries from the level of the village grower up to the level of the final consumer, i.e., manufacturer or exporter, with their number at lower stages being usually large enough for a fair degree of competition among buyers. That the number of intermediaries at various stages and the chain of intermediaries from the producer to the final consumer are usually large is partly the result of an absence of an adequate system of communication and transportation facilities. Middlemen often undertake functions which are usually performed by such facilities elsewhere, and thus constitute in fact a substitution of labor-intensive methods for capital-intensive ones. Dissemination of knowledge about prices and qualities, standardization of quality, proper grading, regular and safe transport so that goods in transit need not be accompanied by a representative of buyers or sellers, and an efficient system of telephonic or postal communications enabling maintenance of quick and easy contact between final purchaser and grower—all

[11] Government of Pakistan, *Credit Enquiry Commission Report* (Karachi, 1959), p. 79.

these would obviate the need for the intervention of middlemen, at least in some functions and at some stages of the marketing process. At lower stages the scale of marketing operations is usually very small, partly because a majority of growers produce small quantities each and partly because a lack of roads and good transport facilities limits the consignments for sale to small trickles, often carried in bullock carts or country boats. A small man with little capital finds it relatively easy to establish himself in the trade which has usually no institutional barriers to entry and which needs little managerial or business experience. Moreover, absence of alternative means of livelihood in agriculture often induces a small man to try his luck in this easily accessible field of trading activity.

In the case of some major commercial crops price is usually determined by haggling and bargaining in the primary village market or at the grower's doorstep, where itinerant buyers go around buying small lots from individual farmers. The market equilibrium at this stage resembles Marshallian short-period phenomenon, in which a market price emerges out of the open bargaining process and total output of each seller is sold or cleared off the market at that price. Moreover, a grower has usually little holding power, owing to a lack of credit and storage facilities. Inadequate transport facilities do not enable sales by growers in distant markets in search of better price. All these factors limit their bargaining power vis-à-vis the intermediaries. At the higher stages of marketing open haggling diminishes in importance, and parties to the transactions get fewer on each side. Moreover, the scale of operations of each intermediary gets larger, and monopolistic or monopsonistic market practices tend to develop. Transactions tend to take place at fixed prices rather than at prices evolving out of open bargaining between buyers and sellers, as in the village market. A recent study of the marketing of jute seems to corroborate these hypotheses. While the intermediaries at the lowest level in direct contact with growers run to more than forty thousand, at the highest stages of marketing there are only fourteen domestic mills consuming raw jute and seventy-three shippers undertaking their export.[12] In 1958, 10 per cent of the shippers exported 25 per cent and 33 per cent of the shippers exported 60 per cent of the total exports, respectively, whereas four mills owned

[12] Dacca University, Socio-Economic Research Board, "Report on the Survey of Jute Marketing in East Pakistan, 1959" (manuscript), pp. 38-39.

62 per cent of total looms and accounted for the bulk of domestic consumption. In the export market six countries imported 60 per cent of total exports in 1958.[13]

While the framework presented above holds broadly true for such crops as jute, cotton, sugar, tobacco, and similar cash crops grown on small-scale farms, the details of production and marketing organization usually differ as between different crops. The organization of the production of tea represents an exceptional case, in which production takes place in large commercially managed gardens or plantations run, with the help of hired labor, by big managing-agency firms, mostly foreign, which are themselves organized into a strong association called the Pakistan Tea Association. There is a remarkable concentration of production in a few large gardens, insofar as eight gardens produce 82 per cent of the total output of tea produced by the members of the Association, the combined output of non-members not exceeding 2 per cent of the total output of tea in the country. The Association often acts as a buying agency for the purchase of equipment, materials, and other requirements of the individual gardens and provides scope for a joint or collusive action on the part of the members.[14] The tea traders, i.e., brokers and dealers, are organized on the other hand into the Tea Traders Association, which manages and supervises the sales of tea in auctions, regulates the entry of new brokers into the business, and fixes the terms and conditions of services of brokers, of which there are only two main firms at present. Though there are as many as eighty-eight buyers of loose tea in the auctions, there are only three blenders who control an overwhelming percentage of the total amount of tea distributed for final consumption within the country.[15] The concentration of business in a few hands at the final stage in the processing of tea enables monopolistic manipulation of price and quantity.

The development of co-operative societies in the field of agricultural production, marketing, and finance has been very slow and inadequate. Its progress has been mainly retarded by the lack of an effective leadership, an absence of a wide understanding of basic principles and responsibilities of co-operation, inefficiency of manage-

[13] Government of East Pakistan, *Monthly Summary of Jute Statistics*, Dec. 1959.
[14] Pakistan Tea Association, *Annual Report* (Chittagong, 1958), appendixes C, D, pp. 1-38.
[15] Tea Traders Association of Chittagong, *Annual Report for the Year 1957-58* (Chittagong, 1958), pp. 1-28.

rial staff, and inadequacy of financial resources. A few co-operative marketing societies which have been established in the case of sugar cane and wool, for example, have foundered on an insufficient finance; whereas jute co-operative marketing societies, in the absence of private initiative, have been virtually run by government officials with government funds. The emphasis in the co-operative movement has been on the supply of credit to agriculture, even though co-operatives provide a very insignificant portion of rural credit, the bulk being provided by such sources as friends and relatives, landlords, and marketing intermediaries. The conditions of loans by the latter diminish the bargaining strength of the farmer and often involve a transfer of land. Institutions have not yet been developed to link the supply of credit to an efficient organization of production and marketing so as to insure a productive use of loans resulting in an increased output and a remunerative price for the product—all insuring as a consequence regular repayment of loans. It is increasingly recognized that small and fragmented holdings need to be reorganized into efficient and economical units, maybe under some form of joint cultivation. In view of the prevailing legal and social structure, the prevalent opinion seems to be that as between various forms of joint cultivation, ranging from collective farming to common service co-operative societies, prospects of immediate success probably lie in the organization of co-operative, common service societies which may develop into full-fledged co-operative farming societies in the course of time.

Industrial Structure and Organization

The industrial structure of Pakistan presents a picture of a variety of forms and methods of organization. While a large percentage of industry is family owned and operated, the predominant form of organization among the bigger enterprises is the managing-agency system, under which a firm is placed in charge of the management of an industrial or commercial enterprise or a number of such enterprises engaged in different fields. A managing-agency firm frequently serves as a promoter of new ventures and often provides a large part of the initial capital, both short and long term. However, at a later date it often throws open shares of such enterprises for public subscription, while the agency still retains control and management in its hands and remains a source of supplementary finance. This has enabled a most economical use of the limited financial, managerial, and entrepreneurial resources available in the country and in the process has provided a medium of vertical and horizontal integration, in terms of management and control, of firms operating in the same or different fields.

Small-scale and cottage industries, which use little or no power or employ less than 20 persons, coexist with modern large-scale and mechanically operated industry. Some of these enterprises are carried on in the homes of the workers, often with the help of the members of their families. The importance of small-scale enterprises in Pakistan can be gauged from the fact that in 1956 only one-sixth of the total industrial labor force in West Pakistan and one-eighth in East Pakistan were engaged in establishments employing more than twenty persons.[16] Among the cottage and small-scale industries surveyed in 1956, 78 per cent of all establishments in West Pakistan and 66.6 per cent in East Pakistan had from one to six workers, 15.6 per cent in West and 22.1 per cent in East had seven to twelve workers, and 6.4 per cent in West and 11.3 per cent in East had between thirteen and nineteen.[17] The relative importance of large-scale industry has increased through time because of a proportionately higher rate of growth in the large-scale manufacturing. The following division treats as large-scale all establishments employing more than twenty persons and using power:[18]

	Per cent of all manufacturing			
	1950-51	1954-55	1959-60	1964-65 (plan)
Large scale	24.47	64.80	63.50	69
Small scale	75.53	35.20	36.50	31

However, at the same time the absolute income from small-scale industry is expected to increase by 25.2 per cent during the period of the Second Five Year Plan (1960-65), as compared with 10.7 per cent in the First Plan and 19 per cent in the ten years since 1950-51.[19]

[16] Government of Pakistan, *Report of the I.L.O. on Manpower Survey in Pakistan*, pp. 12-13.
[17] *Ibid.*, Tables 21, 23.
[18] State Bank of Pakistan, *Report on Currency and Finance, 1958-59*, Table 2, p. 89; *Second Five Year Plan*, Table 12.
[19] *Ibid.*

The relative importance of small-scale enterprises differs as between different industries. The greatest proportion of the small-scale enterprises occurs in (*a*) food and textile and (*b*) chemicals, metal, and machinery industries, which either mainly produce simple types of products and small parts or are repairing and servicing establishments. The percentage of small enterprises falling in the first group is around 42 per cent, while in the second group it varies between 23 and 26 per cent. The footwear, furniture, and wood industries claim 12 to 19 per cent and leather, rubber, printing, and publishing trades, 5 to 8 per cent of all the small enterprises.[20] The small-scale enterprises sometimes cater to special tastes or fashions of a small clientele and hence have a limited market. In some cases they specialize in certain branches of production and thus avoid a direct competition with large enterprises which coexist in the same broad field of activity. However, an integrated pattern of industrial structure in which small enterprises engage in the earlier or later stages of production, leaving the intermediate stages to large-scale enterprises, has not yet been developed to any significant scale. In a number of cases small-scale enterprises with less efficient methods and higher levels of costs continue to survive in the same line of production as that of more efficient large-scale firms. They survive partly because the difficulties in the way of expansion of large-scale enterprises, owing to shortages of foreign exchange and of other key inputs, insulate to a certain extent the small enterprises from a vigorous or effective competition. Moreover, the existence of a highly protected internal market keeps out a strong competition from imports. There is a scarcity and a large unsatisfied demand in the domestic market for many products, so that at the resultant high prices some small enterprises, even when they are less efficient, can find a market.

Many small enterprises, especially those which are run not by the employment of hired wage-labor but by the members of a family in their homes, operate on a very low margin of profit and yield an income to the participants which is barely enough to maintain them at a subsistence level. They often require a relatively smaller quantity of imported material and a lower level of technical and organizational skill. In view of the scarcity of these resources in Pakistan development of such enterprises often provides, at least in the short

[20] *Report of the I.L.O.*, Table 20, p. 78.

run, a quicker and easier means of (a) spreading an industrial milieu, i.e., industrial knowledge and experience, over wider areas and a larger population beyond the confines of a limited number of urban centers and (b) providing employment for a larger population, in view of high labor-capital ratio in many such small enterprises. The first and second five-year plans have provided for the expansion of those small-scale enterprises in which the capital-output ratio is small and employment-capital ratio is high and which could eventually develop into larger and more efficient units through a reinvestment of profits and an acquisition of greater skill in management and technique. Not all small-scale enterprises possess such advantages. For example, a comparison of small- and large-scale enterprises in eighteen industries in Karachi reveals that four of the smaller ones have higher capital-output ratios than their corresponding large-scale enterprises in the same field, while three of them have the same or higher capital employment-cost ratios than the latter.[21] Again, while large-scale enterprises have, on the whole, a lower ratio of employment cost to the "value added," it tends to be high in those cases which employ a greater proportion of highly paid executives and professional employees.

In some cases small enterprises are especially handicapped, as in the case of the hand-loom textile industry's producing plain and standard cloth for mass consumption. It has been decided to grant protection to the hand-loom industry against competition by large-scale modern cotton textile industry in order to prevent a sudden mass unemployment and dislocation. In 1956 an agreement was reached between large mills and the hand-loom industry, under the guidance of the government, for excluding mills from the production of certain types of cloth.[22] Delimitation of fields cannot be expected to provide a final solution, because mills may again come around to producing at some stage types and varieties which would provide very close substitutes to hand-loom products at a cheaper

[21] This is based upon an analysis of the census of small-scale manufacturing industries in Karachi in 1958 and of the census of large-scale enterprises in 1957 (Government of Pakistan, CSO, *Statistical Bulletin*, Feb. 1960, Table 80, and *Census of Manufacturing Industries, 1957*). The above conclusions are subject to the qualifications that the sample is small, that products grouped together for comparison are not perfectly homogeneous, and that the concept of capital-output ratio as estimated here takes no account of the degree of utilization of capital equipment and capacity, which varies between different industries.

[22] *The First Five Year Plan*, pp. 471-478.

cost, and thus render protection partially ineffective. This may serve
as a temporary cushion to ease the strain of hand-loom industry's
eventual adjustment to change. The long-run solution seems to consist in the modernization of techniques in smaller enterprises.

The efficient operation and/or subsequent expansion of small-
scale enterprises into larger ones are often greatly hampered by
various handicaps such as (a) finance, (b) supply of materials, and
(c) markets.[23] The difficulties of small-scale enterprises in obtaining
adequate credit facilities can be illustrated by the fact that supply
of both short- and long-term finance is heavily concentrated towards
bigger businesses in industry and trade. The limited amount of total
available credit implies that borrowers at the other end face acute
scarcity. Sixty-three per cent of total bank credit in 1959 was locked
up in only 222 loan accounts, ranging between Rs. 10 and Rs. 50
lakhs (i.e., 5 million rupees) and above. Insofar as a number of
firms are controlled by the same individual or family, the actual
concentration of bank credit may be even greater than the small
number of loan accounts suggests.[24] Attempts are being made by the
government to overcome partially some of these difficulties. The
second Five-Year Plan envisages the development of small-scale industries so as to bring about a complementary relationship with large-
scale industries. Furthermore, it is intended to stimulate them in
the processing of indigenous raw materials, preferably in the rural
areas, and in the production of implements and equipment for agricultural production.

In the field of large-scale manufacturing industry there is a considerable degree of concentration of total output in a few hands, as
shown in the census of manufacturing industries (Table 6).

It appears that a small percentage of total establishments, i.e.,
the relatively bigger ones among them, control a disproportionately
large percentage of total output, whereas a large number of small
ones taken together contribute a small percentage of the total output of manufacturing industries. About 6 per cent of the total establishments control about 51 per cent of the total output covered
in the census of 1957. About 87 per cent of the total establishments

[23] *Report of the I.L.O.*, Table 24; 37 per cent of the cases reported difficulties
in the field of finance as the main reason preventing an expansion, whereas 31 per
cent considered inadequate supply of raw materials as the main obstacle.

[24] *Credit Enquiry Commission Report*, pp. 5 and 117.

TABLE 6. *Concentration in Large-scale Manufacturing Industry, 1957*

Persons employed	Per cent of total establishments	Per cent of total output
Less than 20	44.15	6.22
20- 49	32.10	12.66
50- 99	11.10	11.81
100-249	6.70	18.39
250-499	2.13	9.28
500-999	1.82	9.60
1,000 and over	1.92	32.02

Source: Government of Pakistan, CSO, *Census of Manufacturing Industries,* 1957 (Karachi, 1960).

have less than 100 employees each. However, the degree of concentration as well as the predominant size of firms varies as between different industries.

The degree of concentration is very great in such industries as tobacco, footwear, paper products, non-metallic minerals, and basic metal industries in which a single firm produces 56.52 per cent, 57 per cent, 83.25 per cent, 24.41 per cent and 38.14 per cent of total output of the respective industries. Similarly, in the manufacture of wood products only three firms produce 64 per cent, and in rubber products two firms produce 62.43 per cent of total output.[25] If only homogenous, or at least very closely similar products, are considered, even fewer firms of comparatively large size would appear to control a major part of the output of the different industries. In jute manufacturing, for example, out of a total of fourteen firms one firm controls 29 to 35 per cent of the total loomage and four firms control about 62 per cent of the total loomage in the industry. In such industries as cement, wood, fertilizer, paper and paper products, and fans, etc., there are only a few producers in each line of production. For example, there is only one mill producing paper for ordinary stationery purposes and only one newsprint factory in the whole country. There are only three or four straw board and paper board mills, five cement plants, and ten fertilizer factories of all varieties within the country.[26] There are, therefore, a number of products which are produced by outright monopolies and a few other industries which are oligopolistic. In the rest of the

[25] *Census of Manufacturing Industries, 1957.*
[26] *Ibid.*

TABLE 7. *Degrees of Concentration in Different Industries, 1957*

Industry	Persons employed	Per cent of total establishments	Per cent of total output
Food manufacturing industries other than beverages	500 and less than 1,000	2.74	18.99
	100 and over	12.79	66.29
Beverage industries	100 " "	7.14ᵃ	27.26
	50 " "	28.56	64.50
Tobacco manufactures	1,000 " "	9.09ᵃ	56.52
	100 " "	54.54ᵉ	98.58
Textile manufactures	1,000 " "	7.81	74.65
	250 " "	14.58	90.01
Manufacture of footwear, etc.	1,000 " "	1.02ᵃ	56.95
	100 " "	6.12ᵉ	79.85
Manufacture of wood and cork	100 " "	25.00ᶜ	63.58
	20 " "	50.00ᵉ	74.49
Electrical machinery	250 " "	4.41ᶜ	24.89
	100 " "	13.23	66.69
Transport equipment	500 " "	3.33ᶜ	29.05
	100 " "	14.44ᵍ	69.68
Manufacture of fixtures and furniture	100 " "	1.61ᵇ	34.79
	50 " "	7.83ᶜ	35.73
Manufacture of paper and paper products	1,000 " "	7.14ᵃ	83.25
	500 " "	14.28ᵇ	91.50
Leather and leather products	100 " "	6.10ᵈ	35.97
	50 " "	24.39	63.32
Rubber products	250 " "	5.88ᵇ	62.43
	50 " "	14.70ᵈ	84.34
Chemicals and chemical products	500 " "	3.19ᶠ	16.13
	100 " "	14.60	58.86
Non-metallic minerals	1,000 " "	1.47ᵃ	24.41
	500 " "	8.82ᵉ	54.60
Basic metal industries	1,000 " "	1.44ᵃ	38.14
	100 " "	14.40	68.57
Metal products	250 " "	1.36ᵈ	15.02
	50 " "	16.97	57.81
Machinery, except electric machinery	500 " "	1.38	11.10
	50 " "	13.47	42.28

Source: Census of Manufacturing Industries, 1957.

  ᵃ One firm.   ᵉ Six firms.
  ᵇ Two firms.   ᶠ Seven firms.
  ᶜ Three firms.   ᵍ Thirteen firms.
  ᵈ Five firms.

industrial field a few big firms produce a very large part of the total output, and the remainder is produced by a large number of small-sized firms. Thus there is scope for the big producers to exercise a certain measure of price leadership. There are no data available on the extent of vertical or horizontal integration in industry. However, indirect evidence suggests that it exists on a significant scale and that prevailing circumstances in the field of manufacturing provide an ample scope for it. For one thing, the managing-agency system which prevails widely among bigger enterprises serves as a ready medium for integrating managerial and financial control. Moreover, a larger part of the growth in capital investment in manufacturing industries in recent years has taken place through a reinvestment of profits generated in the existing enterprises and, consequently, often through their extension into different lines of production.

The existence of a protected domestic market maintained by strict quantitative and exchange restrictions, reinforced in some cases by tariffs, has provided scope for a monopolistic or oligopolistic market structure within the economy. Because of the limited size of the domestic market, in many industries a few large firms of an economical size can produce enough to meet the existing demands, leaving little room for new firms of large size. The narrow domestic market is due to a low level of income. Even when existing demand is far in excess of domestic production and an addition to total output made by new firms is not likely to be so large as to bring about a significant fall in prices or profits, restrictions on the entry of new firms are often imposed by the scarcity of foreign exchange necessary to import equipment and materials and in some cases by the scarcity of domestic capital and enterprise. This is true of a number of industries producing consumers' goods, of which there is an excess demand and shortage in the economy. As is well known, the low level of income not only inhibits the growth of market but also works in a vicious circle to restrict the supply of foreign exchange and domestic savings. The export market has been severely limited by the high cost and relative inefficiency of nascent domestic industries. The protected domestic market often leaves the existing industries with little inducement to reduce costs or improve efficiency.

The public enterprises have often been of much larger size than private enterprises, equipped as they are with the most modern techniques and methods of organization. They have access to larger financial and technical resources, both domestic and foreign. This is evidenced in the paper and paper products industry, jute, cement, chemicals, fertilizers, sugar, etc., where public enterprises occupy a prominent position and where the number of large concerns as well as the degree of concentration is higher. In the course of the transfer of public enterprises to private control those which are of monopolistic nature in their respective fields become private monopolies, as in the case of the paper industry, which has recently been transferred to private hands. Moreover, the government seeks to allocate resources between different branches of the private sector by regulating the entry of new firms by means of industrial and import licensing. The government policy tends to emphasize the need to husband scarce resources and to avoid duplication, with the result that additional firms are not encouraged just for the sake of increasing the degree of competition. The usual tendency on the whole is to let the existing firms run to their full capacity by allowing them adequate imports of materials and equipment before any new ones are allowed to compete for such scarce resources as foreign exchange, though this principle has not always been observed. While the exercise of control over free entry conserves scarce resources from a static point of view, it may hinder the dynamic development of more efficient enterprises in competition with existing ones. The growth of more efficient new firms utilizes fewer resources per unit of output and thus in the long run releases resources for other uses, even though in the short run it may involve some wastage or dislocation of resources already invested in a particular line of production. Thus, under a system of priorities administered by government controls it is not easy for new firms to obtain a free entry in a field in response to large profits earned by existing firms, as under a system of free competition. This suggests that the Schumpeterian model, wherein a few innovating entrepreneurs open up new lines of activity, earn temporarily high monopolistic profits and thus attract a train of followers in a given field of activity, does not work itself out so smoothly in an underdeveloped economy like that of Pakistan.

The organization of the credit market and of financial institutions reveals a similar pattern of concentration and a consequent imperfection of competition among the various sections of the market. There is little contact and competition between the modern organized banking system on the one hand and unorganized financial market on the other, which consists primarily of indigenous moneylenders and of non-scheduled banks, i.e., banks whose operations and practices are not as much under the supervision and control of the central bank as the scheduled banks. In 1958 eight out of a total of thirty-four scheduled banks, Pakistani and foreign, held 62.2 per cent of combined time and demand deposits of all banks and supplied 69 per cent of the total advances made by all of them.[27] The rates of interest on loans vary from a minimum of 3 per cent to a maximum of 10 to 12 per cent in urban areas where mainly the scheduled banks are engaged in the financing of trade and industry, whereas in the rural areas and in the financing of agriculture the money rates of interest, insofar as monetary forms of interest prevail, vary between 25 and 60 per cent.[28] Though the rates charged by government-sponsored financial institutions and co-operative societies engaged in the financing of agriculture vary between 5 and 9 per cent, they constitute a very minor source of rural credit.[29] The very wide range of interest rates not only within various sectors of the economy but also between various agencies supplying credit in the same sector, as well as the existence of non-monetary forms of interest in rural areas, emphasizes the widespread prevalence of imperfections in the credit market and lack of mobility of funds between its various sections.

Large-scale trade and industry are organized into associations and chambers of commerce, of which there were forty-nine in 1958. In view of the large degree of control and regulation which the government exercises over trade and industry, these associations serve as a common forum for the representation of their interests and for the formulation of a common policy vis-à-vis the government. In some cases the government has given these associations lately some regulatory powers over its members with respect to export trade.[30] The government actively encourages the formation of such associations, since they facilitate its dealings with trade and industry. In 1958 under government instructions the various associations have been reorganized so as to insure that (*a*) each trade or industry has only one association, (*b*) each area or urban center has one consolidated chamber of commerce and industry representing all interests in the area, and (*c*) there is one federation of chambers of com-

[27] State Bank of Pakistan, *Banking Statistics of Pakistan, 1958-59*, Table IV.
[28] *Ibid.*, Table XIV, p. 47, Table XV, p. 49; *Rural Credit and Unemployment*, appendix B, Table 15 (a) and p. 43.
[29] *Banking Statistics of Pakistan, 1958-59*, Tables XIV-XV; *Credit Enquiry Commission Report*, p. 55.
[30] *Pakistan Trade*, X (Jan. 1959), 1-8.

merce and industry for the whole country. These measures, abolishing multiplicity of organizations in each field and in each area, are expected to add considerably to the strength of each of the links in this linear hierarchy which is being built up. This may strengthen the role of these organizations vis-à-vis other sections of the economy. In the formulation and execution of its program and policies for trade and industry the government is likely to be in a better position to obtain a representative opinion and to fix responsibility unequivocally for decisions and actions of trade and industry, instead of trying to decide which of the many organizations truly represents them. Similarly, the prospect of their effective co-operation in the execution of the government's policy may be enhanced insofar as institutions embracing all interests under a unified organization may be more successful in insuring compliance by its members with the policies of the government. The development of more effective associations also implies that the scope for common action and business agreements or deals regarding price and output policy in order to restrict the scope of competition between various units of the same industry as well as between similar industries may be increased *pari passu*. Correspondingly, however, the government is tending to increase its regulatory powers over trade associations. It has recently assumed powers to fix the numbers, terms of office, and composition of different officers of the various chambers and associations.

There is an additional factor peculiar to the geography of Pakistan which restricts the degree of competition between different units of the same industry located in different wings, separated as they are by one thousand miles of foreign territory. The long distance and limited transportation facilities, resulting in high costs of movement between the two wings, partially insulate at least in the short run the industrial enterprises in one wing from competition by those in the other wing.

An important feature of economic development in Pakistan has been a very unequal rate of growth as between the two wings of the country, which is especially evident in the field of industrialization. Only one-fourth of national income originating in the industrial sector arises in East Pakistan and three-fourths in West Pakistan.[31] Moreover, in 1957 only about 20 per cent of the total number of

[31] *Report of the Panel of Economists on the Second Five Year Plan (1960-65)* (Karachi, 1959), p. 14.

large-scale manufacturing establishments were located in East Pakistan and produced only 26.5 per cent of the aggregate gross value of manufactured output in the country.[32] Excepting food, beverage, wood, printing, paper, and leather industries, the share of East Pakistan in the major large-scale manufacturing industries is between 6 and 20 per cent of the total number of establishments and between 4 and 24 per cent of the gross value of total output. The relative distribution as between the two parts of Pakistan of some major industries in respect of (a) number of establishments and (b) gross value of output is shown in Table 8.

While the share of East Pakistan in almost all the industries is below, and often substantially below, that of West Pakistan, her share in basic heavy industries is proportionately much smaller than in light consumers' goods industries. The differences in the state of development of the two wings of the country are due partly to the fact that the west wing started with a higher per capita income in 1947-48,[33] a larger stock of social overhead capital in the form of

TABLE 8. *Proportion of Industry in East Pakistan*

Industry	Per cent of total establishments	Per cent of total gross output
Basic metal industries	4	2
Electrical machinery	6	2
Other machinery	8	5
Footwear, etc.	7	4
Non-metallic minerals	15	13
Rubber products	12	15
Metal products	15	21
Transport equipment	16	not available
Tobacco	18	"
Textile	11	24
Chemicals and chemical products	20	26
Printing and publishing	34	19
Beverage	29	20
Food	40	23
Leather and leather products	43	37
Wood and cork	41	51
Paper and paper products	50	84

Source: Census of Manufacturing Industries, 1957.

[32] *Census of Manufacturing Industries, 1957.*
[33] R. H. Khondkar, "The Pattern of a Divided Economy," *Journal of the Royal Statistical Society*, CXVIII, Part I (1955), 51-55.

power, transportation, and communication facilities, and a higher ratio of natural resources to population. Subsequently, a number of related factors coupled with the favorable initial conditions contributed to a higher rate of growth in West Pakistan. The latter had a larger pool of private enterprise, mainly immigrant from India, as well as a greater managerial and technical ability, which was augmented by its larger expenditure on the development of skill. Moreover a higher income provided a wider market and a larger flow of savings and investment in the private sector. Private investment guided by considerations of short-run profitability found advantageous location in the West. There has been a tendency in the West for a cumulative process to set in, though its absolute magnitude has not been commensurate with the needs of an increasing population. The comparative or competitive advantages of the eastern wing remain undeveloped, according to the familiar pattern postulated in the "infant industry" hypothesis. The location of public investment expenditure in the past, financed by both domestic and foreign resources, was not directed towards redressing the regional disparities. It was conspicuously higher in the West. During the first plan period combined public and private investment in West Pakistan was double that in the East.[34] Mobility of population between the two wings has been strictly limited, owing to a long distance, high costs of transport, and differences in physical, social, and cultural environments, with the result that the benefits of a greater development in one wing have not spread to the other.

Organization of Labor Market

The total labor force constituted 31.8 per cent of the total population in 1955-56 and is predominantly rural and agricultural. Landless agricultural laborers constituted 10 per cent of the total rural labor force in 1951.[35] There is a considerable degree of seasonal unemployment among agricultural laborers. The "casual" labor, i.e., labor employed for specific operations, especially in peak seasons, is often migratory and moves from one area to another in search of odd jobs in busy seasons. A study of unemployment among farming families in East Pakistan in 1956 reveals that the extent of

[34] *Report of the Panel of Economists*, p. 15.
[35] *Second Plan*, p. 331; *Census of Pakistan*; F. Andrus and A. A. F. Mohammed, *Economy of Pakistan* (London, 1958), p. 429.

visible unemployment, defined as the excess of potential annual man-days (assumed to be 250 days) over the actual man-days spent in work, varies between 10 and 40 per cent of potential man-days over the year as a whole.[36] However, visible unemployment seems to disappear during the peak seasons, when there is an additional employment of hired labor on the farms. This measurement does not include unemployment among landless laborers. It is most likely that even during peak seasons there is a certain excess of supply over demand for landless laborers, as evidenced in the net drift of labor to urban areas. These measurements are all based upon prevailing techniques and organization in agricultural production, without any reference to the intensity of work done in a working day.

Money wage rates in urban and industrial occupations are higher than those in the agricultural sector and in 1953 were found to be about 70 per cent higher than the wage rates of landless agricultural laborers[37] in East Pakistan. Moreover, industrial employment has other advantages, such as security and stability of jobs. The higher money wage rate is a compensation partly for the loss of an elementary social insurance system implied in village joint families and partly for higher costs of housing and transport in urban areas and for the loss on the part of the rest of the family, i.e., wives and children, consequent on migration, of whatever additional sources of income they could tap in sundry occupations in the villages. The existence of organized trade unions among industrial workers also plays a part, especially in the case of major industries or major industrial centers. However, collective bargaining for the determination of wages and conditions of employment is far from widespread among industrial workers. In a large number of cases there still prevails a system of contract labor, under which labor is not recruited directly by the employer but indirectly through an intermediary who, being some sort of labor-supply contractor, negotiates with the worker as to the terms of employment and makes deductions from his wage rate for such services. Even when labor is directly recruited, a worker is usually employed on the recommendation of a jobber, who is invariably a person with long experience in factory work, such as a trainer or supervisor of labor, and who acts as an intermediary

---

[36] *Rural Credit and Unemployment,* p. 133.

[37] A. F. A. Husain, *Human and Social Impact of Technological Change in Pakistan* (Dacca, 1956), pp. 140-143.

between labor and management.[38] Inadequate development of employment exchanges, illiteracy, and lack of familiarity with urban ways and industrial life account for the continued existence of such intermediaries in the labor market.[39]

The membership in the trade-union movement is limited to a fraction of the total industrial labor force. Agricultural labor is by and large unorganized. This can be attributed to the pressure of an increasing population on land, prevalence of unemployment among agricultural laborers, seasonality of their employment, their scattered locations, and illiteracy. Trade unions exist in a relatively few enterprises, among which they vary greatly in strength. The number of registered trade unions increased from 181 in 1948-49 to 600 in 1958, and a total of 484 unions had a membership of 500,000 in 1958.[40] The hostility of employers and intermediaries, the poverty, apathy, and illiteracy of workers, and manipulation of trade unions by outsiders or politicians for their particular ends have all contributed to the slow and restricted growth of a trade-union movement. The poverty and apathy of the workers have acted in a vicious circle. While low wages discourage them from making regular and substantial contributions to union funds, weakness of unions owing to the scarcity of funds aids the continuance of low wages, even when productivity is high enough to warrant higher wages. Recently various unions have been amalgamated with active government help and encouragement into two federations, one in each wing of the country, which together form a nationwide confederation. However, collective bargaining, insofar as it occurs, is mainly conducted on the basis of an individual company or firm. There is as yet no countervailing organization or power developed among industrial workers to parallel the industry or area-wide organization among employers and industrialists.

The intervention of the government in the labor market has been so far mainly directed towards the maintenance of certain minimum working conditions, including the minimum age of industrial workers, hours of work, rest periods, holidays, and safety and health

---

[38] *Ibid.*, p. 130.

[39] The first report of the ILO manpower survey in 1953 noted that out of a total of 98 categories of employers covered in the survey, 58 cases reported employment of contract labor.

[40] *Second Plan*, p. 378.

conditions inside the factories, as well as the employment of women and child labor. The Industrial Employment Act of 1946 requires that these terms and conditions of employment, as certified by government officials, should be posted in prominent places for the information of workers. The administrative machinery for the enforcement of these regulations remains, however, very inadequate.[41] The government encourages the growth of trade unionism among workers and provides for their compulsory recognition by employers in cases where union membership comprises at least 10 per cent of workers. However, in recent years it has assumed wide powers for the prevention of strikes and for facilitating settlement of disputes by negotiation and conciliation or arbitration. Strikes without notice of at least six weeks are illegal in a large number of industries which are declared public utilities by the government. When a notice of strike is served or a strike is threatened, conciliation officers appointed by the government hold conciliation proceedings, failing which any party to a dispute can refer the case to an industrial court consisting of officials and non-official members representing the interests of employers and employees, all of whom are appointed by the government. The decision of the court is legally binding. If neither party refers a case to the court, even after the failure of conciliation proceedings, the government, if it so desires in a particular case, can refer the case to the court and thus can compulsorily adjudicate a dispute.[42]

These are the rather sweeping powers assumed by the government since 1959, in view of an intense and continuous unrest in major industrial centers which resulted in a significant disruption of production. The declared aim of the public policy is that benefits of an increased production through industrial peace will eventually flow to the industrial workers in the form of expanded social services and better amenities of wages, housing, health, and sanitation. In the statement of a new labor policy in 1959 the established commercial and industrial concerns were originally exhorted but now are required by the government to provide houses for at least 25 per cent of their permanent labor force in the course of the next five years.[43]

[41] Husain, *op. cit.*, pp. 286-292.

[42] "Industrial Disputes Ordinance," *East Pakistan Labour Journal*, II (Dacca, Dec. 1959), 134-147.

[43] "Revised Labour Policy," *East Pakistan Labour Journal*, II (Dacca, June 1959), 39-45; also *Pakistan Observer* (Dacca, March 2, 1961), p. 1. The govern-

There is as yet no general attempt on the part of the government to fix a minimum wage level for the economy as a whole or for a large number of industries. However, there seems to be a general recognition of the principle that the government should restrict its intervention in the fixation of wages or in the laying down of a minimum wage level to a few carefully selected cases which employ sweated labor and have an especially low wage level. So far only the East Pakistan Government has passed a Minimum Wages Act (1957), providing for the establishment of a Minimum Wages Board for a number of specified industries and consisting of the representatives of the government, industrialists, and workers. The industries covered under this Act include for the present textiles, sugar, matches, paper, rubber manufactures, and tea. The scope of the Act can be extended at the discretion of the government. Since 1957 a few industries, such as printing, matches, and textiles, have been referred to the board. In each case an attempt has been made to lay down a minimum wage based on some sort of rough judgment about productivity of labor, its minimum physical requirements, and the cost of living in industrial cities. Moreover, it has been left to the individual firms to try, on the basis of criteria and principles indicated by the Wage Board, to evolve a rational wage structure in terms of different skills and occupations. Admittedly, the available data regarding the existing wage structure as well as other factors bearing on the determination of wages are far from adequate to permit any refined analysis.[44] The fixation of minimum wages in some industries without reference to or separately from other industries or sectors of the economy may have indirect repercussions on the costs of production and hence on relative rates of investment and of growth in different industries. It will also have effects on the relative supplies of labor and its productivity in different industries as well as on its mobility as between different occupations. Since the fixation of minimum wages in Pakistan has so far been restricted to a very few selected cases of obviously sweated labor, these complications, which may become important once the scope of the legislation is extended, have not yet arisen.

---

ment has already promised stern action against non-fulfilment of this requirement within the remaining two years.

[44] M. Shafi, *Labour Code of Pakistan* (Bureau of Labour Publications, Karachi, 1958), pp. 464-465.

Social security measures for industrial workers in Pakistan are still underdeveloped and are largely confined to workmen's compensation and maternity benefits. The government's policy is based on the assumption that social welfare is a function of both the state and the private enterprises and that, accordingly, both should jointly bear the expenses. However, it is recognized that a substantial extension of social welfare measures financed either by the private industry or by increased taxes may cut into individual and institutional savings available for capital formation in the immediate future. This may in turn conflict with a rapid progress towards industrialization, except where such measures contribute in the short run to an increased productivity of workers. In many cases under the existing system of organization, institutions, and incentives of production there appears to be a conflict in the short run between demands of a greater social or redistributive justice and a higher rate of investment and output. The economic policy of the government also seems to reflect a recognition of this dilemma and an admission that the inequalities of income and wealth in the commercial and industrial sectors pose a difficult problem, since businessmen and industrialists, while performing a very useful social function, extract sometimes an unduly high price or profits for their services, which to the extent that they are not dissipated in conspicuous consumption lead to increased saving and investment. Recent measures for more strict tax assessment and imposition of estate duties are expected to reduce inequalities somewhat. A more equitable distribution of industrial and commercial licenses and an encouragement of newcomers in the field of commerce and industry may in course of time partially offset a further accentuation of inequalities. Inequalities of income insofar as they reflect inequalities of natural talents and services provide necessary incentives to effort, enterprise, and acquisition and improvement of skills. They are accordingly considered desirable within limits. However, as the First Five Year Plan points out, "these limits are necessarily wide in a country where talents are yet underdeveloped and technical knowledge and administrative experience and ability fall short of actual needs."[45]

[45] *First Five Year Plan*, pp. 3-5.

THE STATE AND ECONOMIC ACTIVITY

Direct participation

The role of the government in economic activity extends from the regulation and control of private enterprises in trade, industry, and agriculture to a direct participation in certain specific fields. The importance of the government's income and expenditure in the aggregate income-and-expenditure flow of the economy is evidenced from the fact that its revenue receipts (tax and non-tax revenue) and expenditures (revenue and capital) constituted, on an average, 8 to 9 per cent and 18 to 19 per cent of national income, respectively, in the years from 1949-50 to 1959-60.[46] A substantial proportion of total resources of the economy are channeled through the government either for investment or for consumption purposes. Its relative importance vis-à-vis the extent of mobilization of resources in the private sector is shown in Table 9.

The ratio of public expenditure to gross national product has been about 16 per cent in the last few years and is expected to increase to 19 per cent during the second plan period. The rise in the proportion of investment to G.N.P. has been in the past, and is expected to be in the future, mainly due to a large increase in public investment. A substantial amount of foreign aid and loans, which is available only on the government account, has added to its growth. Often

TABLE 9. *Private and Public Consumption and Investment*
(in millions of rupees)

	(1) Public consumption	(2) Public investment	(3) Private consumption	(4) Private investment	(5) Government expenditure (1) + (2)	(6) Total private expenditure (3) + (4)	(7) Gross national product (current prices)	Government expenditure ÷ GNP (per cent)	Inflow of foreign resources	Total investment (2)+(4)÷(7) (per cent)
1955-56	2,000	770	14,860	900	2,770	15,760	18,200	15.2	330	9.2
1959-60	2,500	1,680	21,475	1,000	4,180	22,475	25,430	16.6	1,225	10.5
1960-65 (Second Plan period)ᵃ	14,000	13,000	117,490	6,000	27,000	123,490	141,490	19.0	9,000	13.4

Source: Second Five Year Plan, Table I, p. 26.
ᵃ The Second Plan figures are in constant prices of 1959-60. "Foreign resources" figures exclude the expenditure of Rs. 700 million for Indus Basin replacement works.

[46] The percentages are computed from the figures on government receipts and expenditure (both central and provincial) and figures on national income as given in the following sources: Andrus and Mohammed, *op. cit.,* Tables XLVI, XLVIII, XLIX, L, LI; Government of Pakistan, National Planning Commission, *First Five Year Plan,* pp. 143-144; *Second Five Year Plan,* chap. ii, Tables I, XII.

the character of public projects is more appropriate for the use of foreign aid than for private foreign investment in search of quick returns. The comparative growth of public and private investment is shown in Table 10.

The operations of the government have an impact on the generation and sectoral allocation of savings by diverting savings generated in one sector to investment elsewhere. Private savings are transferred to the public sector either by means of borrowing or by sale of public assets. The magnitude of such transfer for investment purposes can be seen in Table 11.

Public investment during the First Five Year Plan was financed substantially by means of resources transferred from the private sector and partly by foreign aid and loans, since there was no public saving. Deficit financing in the public sector is one of the methods by which command over real resources is transferred from the private to the public sector. During the Second Five Year Plan it is expected that the proportion of public investment to be financed by resources transferred from the private sector would decline from 57 per cent to 34 per cent if the total amount of contemplated saving in the public sector materializes. Savings transferred from the private to the public sector are not necessarily all completely utilized in the public sector but some part may be redirected to the private sector. For example, 13 per cent of the resources planned to be transferred to the public from the private sector during the second plan are expected to be put back into the private sector in the form of loans to finance corporations and to selected private enterprises. The rationale

TABLE 10. *Private and Public Investment*

	Million Rs.		
	Private	Public	Per cent private
1951-55	2,372	2,601	45.7
1955-60	4,830	5,950	44.8
1960-65 (plan)	6,000	13,000	31.5

Sources: First Five Year Plan, p. 133; Andrus and Mohammed, *op. cit,* Table XLIII and pp. 288-289. Public investment figures are indirectly derived from public expenditure financed by capital receipts, deficit financing, utilization of foreign exchange holdings, and foreign aid and loans to the public sector. The estimates are very rough approximations.

TABLE 11. *Public Investment*[47]

	Million Rs.			Per cent	
Total public investment program (1)	Resources originating in public sector (2)	Resources transferred from private sector-deficit financing (3)		Ratio of (3) to (1)	Foreign resources $\frac{1-(2+3)}{1}$
1955-60	5,950	—	3,410	57.30	42.70
1960-65 (plan)	13,000	3,060	3,040	34.15	53.07

Sources: First Five Year Plan: Preliminary Evaluation Report (Karachi, 1960), p. 10; *Second Five Year Plan*, pp. 26-39.

of these operations lies in the fact that savings originating in some branches of the private sector may not necessarily flow into investment and, even if they do, they may not flow into those sections where increased investments are considered desirable in the light of the over-all priorities of the plan but where sectoral savings may not be sufficient to meet the needs of increased investment.

The government also influences the allocation of investment as between different sectors of the economy. The government directly affects the allocation of investible resources in the public sector. The major proportion of public investment is concentrated in social overhead capital, i.e., water and power development, transport and communications, housing, training, etc., the percentage of total public investment in such sector during the periods of two five-year plans being respectively 71.2 per cent and 68.4 per cent. The sectoral allocation of private investment is different. The major portion of the private investment that took place in the first plan and is expected for the second plan is in immediately profitable projects rather than in low-

[47] Resources originated in the public sector include surplus on the revenue account of the budget and the undistributed profits which are generated in the semi-public sector (i.e., autonomous public corporations) and which are available for investment in that sector. The public sector includes both the operations of the government departments as well as semi-autonomous public corporations engaged in trade and industry. Resources transferred from the private sector for investment in the public sector include such items as small savings and the unfunded debt of the government, depreciation funds of the state undertakings, such as railways and posts and telegraphs, sale of public assets, and borrowing from the banking system. This definition follows the one adopted by the First Five Year Plan (*First Five Year Plan*, pp. 140-141). For the semi-autonomous public corporations, similarly, absorption of private savings would consist of private participation in the capital of public corporations and of loans from the banking system.

yielding projects of long maturity and gestation lag.[48] The allocation of public and private investments in the two five-year plans
is shown in Table 12 below.

As is evident from Table 13 (p. 439), 53 per cent of the private
investment in the first plan and 53.4 per cent during the second plan
were expected to be in the fields of industry, fuels, and minerals, as
against 13.3 per cent and 15.4 per cent of public investment, respectively, allocated to these fields during the two five-year plans. It is
apparent from the above that the predominant role of public investment activity arises partly out of a need for the provision of overhead
facilities, which in their own turn constitute a precondition to the development of private enterprises in various directly profitable fields
of activity.

The extent and pattern of direct participation by the state in
economic activity have not been decided on any rigid doctrinaire
considerations. The relative role of public and private enterprise
has been mainly guided by the overriding consideration of accelerating the rate of economic growth. The first statement of government
policy in 1948 with respect to its participation in industrial activity
indicated that monopolies and public utilities were peculiarly suitable
for nationalization, so that the main communications and transport
services such as posts, telegraphs, telephones, wireless, broadcasting,
railways, and air transport should be owned and operated by the
government. In road transport, where both public and private enterprise coexisted at that time, and in river transport, which was entirely operated by private enterprise until then, the prospect of their
eventual nationalization was not ruled out. Excepting three other
specific fields of activity, namely, (a) arms and munitions of war, (b)
generation of hydroelectric power, and (c) manufacture of railway
wagons, telephones, telegraphs, and wireless apparatus, private enterprise was left free to operate in any other field. The government,
however, reserved the right to "take over or participate in any other
industry vital to the security or economic well being of the State."
Moreover, it was decided that if in any particular industry of national
importance adequate private capital did not come forward, the government might set up "a limited number of standard units as a meas-

[48] *Preliminary Evaluation Report*, pp. 12-13; *Pakistan Trade*, XI (Feb. 1960),
23. *Second Plan*, Table 2, p. 12.

TABLE 12. *Public and Private Expenditures, First and Second Plans*

	First Plan (million Rs.)						Second Plan (million Rs.)			
	Estimated public expenditure	Per cent	Expected private expenditure	Per cent	Expected public expenditure	Per cent	Expected private expenditure	Per cent	Total public and private expenditure	Per cent
Agriculture and village aid	970	15.5	Included elsewhere		2,520	15.5	900	13.3	3,420	14.8
Water and power	1,770	27.9	11		4,330	26.7	60	0.9	4,390	19.1
Industry, fuels, and minerals	840	13.3	1,435	53.0	2,490	15.4	3,630	53.4	6,120	26.6
Transport and communications	1,450	23.0	45	13.6	3,140	19.3	910	13.4	4,050	17.7
Housing and physical planning	740	11.7	80 (Including agriculture, water, and power)	24.4	2,280	14.0	1,130	16.6	3,410	14.9
Education and training	400 } 8.6				950	6.0 } 9.1	100	1.4 } 2.4	1,050	4.5 } 6.9
Planning and manpower	140 }		30		490	3.1	70	1.0	560	2.4
	6,310		3,300		16,200		6,800		23,000	

Sources: Pakistan Trade, Feb. 1960, p. 23; *Second Five Year Plan*, Revised Estimates, November 1961. Estimated figures for private investment are not available for the First Five Year Plan. Only the figures as proposed in the First Plan are available. In the case of public expenditures figures of actual expenditures made during the First Five Year Plan are available.

ure of attracting private enterprise than for any other object."[49] In the restatement of industrial policy made in 1959 a greater emphasis is placed upon private enterprise.[50] It pledges to give maximum scope to private enterprise for the development of the resources of the country within the framework of the national five-year plans. The fields reserved for public enterprise in this restatement of policy are again (*a*) arms and ammunition, (*b*) railways, air transport, and telecommunications, and (*c*) production of atomic energy. River transport is left free for private enterprise without any threat of nationalization. Road transport is to continue to have both private and state enterprise. The general provision that the government may take over any industry considered essential or vital has been removed. Where private enterprise is inactive, the government will establish such industries as are essential to the life of the community through especially constituted corporation, which will be transferred to private enterprises as circumstances permit. In fact, the government has been of late actively following a policy of transferring state enterprises to private hands.

The rate and pattern of economic development are to be guided by a series of five-year plans, inaugurated in 1955. The National Planning Commission, which was established in 1953, fixes the over-all and specific targets for various sectors of the economy in the light of an assessment of resources of the economy, both domestic and foreign, and in the light of a feasible and stipulated over-all rate of growth. The plan lays down targets for various branches of economy both in the public and the private sectors. The size and allocations of the investment program in the private sector are not under the direct control of the government. Therefore, targets in this sector are viewed more as an expression of the objectives and priorities rather than as specific programs of action centrally determined. They are intended to serve as guides to the private industrialists as well as to various government agencies entrusted with regulating directly or indirectly private investment decisions. There were serious shortfalls in the achievement of the First Five Year Plan. It was difficult to achieve a correspondence between plans and actual amounts of private investments, especially in those sectors where the unit of

[49] Government of Pakistan, "Statement of Industrial Policy," April 2, 1948 (press release).

[50] "New Industrial Policy," *Pakistan Trade*, X (Jan. 1959), 8-12.

investment was small and requirements of foreign exchange were negligible. Moreover, the administrative agencies were lax in enforcing the priorities laid down in the plan, not only in the private but also in the public sector. The shortfall in the implementation of the public investment program was mainly due to a rise in non-development expenditure, which reduced the amount of resources available for investment, an unexpected shortfall in resources, particularly foreign exchange, a rise in the costs of investment projects, a lack of key personnel, administrative inefficiency, and an ineffective co-ordination between different government agencies.[51]

The public sector program is administered either directly by government departments or by semi-autonomous public corporations. Railways, posts, telegraphs, telephones, social service facilities, schools, hospitals, water supply, sanitary or conservation services, and defense and other exclusively community-type installations are mainly run by government departments directly. Public corporations operate in such fields as manufacturing, air lines, road transport, electricity, water and power development, development of ports and towns, marketing and provision of finance in the fields of agriculture and industry. The public corporations, which often draw their finances both from the government and private sectors, entrust the decision-making power to a board of directors, which is appointed by the government but which combines representation from the government, public officials, private businessmen, and industrialists. The criteria governing their operations are not intended always to be immediate and short-run profitability. In addition, they are expected to take into account external economies and indirect benefits to the economy as a whole. However, at the same time the Second Five Year Plan stresses that "their policies be so framed as to promote maximum efficiency and growth" and that "their price policy should, no doubt, be guided by considerations of social gain, but the need for financing their future expansion out of their own resources must also be given due weight."[52] During the second plan 25 per cent of the total investment program in the public sector is expected to be undertaken by the public corporations. Fifty-three per cent of their total investment would be in the field of industry, and 31 per cent would be in such fields as communications, transport, town

[51] *Preliminary Evaluation*, p. 13; *Second Plan*, pp. 1-3.
[52] *Second Plan*, p. 38.

planning and development, and the rest would be in miscellaneous other activities including electric supply, housing for industrial workers, etc.[53]

The most important public corporation which has played a leading role in the industrial development of the country is Pakistan Industrial Development Corporation. Its initial capital was wholly provided by the government. Finances for various projects undertaken by it from time to time are derived from (a) annual budgetary grants of the Central Government, (b) such private capital as it is able to attract, and (c) foreign aid and loans. The government reserves the ultimate right of approval in the final selection of projects to be set up by the PIDC and on the terms on which the PIDC enterprises may eventually be sold to private parties. While on matters of broad policy its operations are subject to the directives of the government, in internal matters it is intended to be autonomous.[54] During the Second Five Year Plan, more than 89 per cent of the total public investment in large-scale industry is expected to be undertaken by the PIDC either in its own factories or in private enterprises or enterprises with private participation.[55] The main objectives of PIDC have been to promote and establish industrial undertaking in the fields in which private enterprise is either wholly unable or unwilling to come forward or do so to an adequate extent. It has initiated pioneering ventures in many new fields of industry and has supplemented private enterprises by establishing additional units where the existing number of private units is insufficient in relation to demand. It has borne the initial risks and high costs in the early years of experimentation of hitherto untested fields of enterprise. It has not only showed the way but also provided opportunities for investment to private investors who, while unwilling or afraid to invest in purely private undertakings, are encouraged to entrust their funds to enterprises run by the PIDC with all the backing of financial resources, technical know-how, and managerial talent which a government-sponsored institution can command. It has supplemented private enterprise by participating in the share capital of private firms which have been initiated and are run by

[53] *Second Plan*, p. 39, Table 9.
[54] M. Ayub, *The Role of Private and Public Enterprise in the Industrial Development of Pakistan* (PIDC, Karachi, 1958).
[55] *Second Plan*, pp. 245-246.

private entrepreneurs but which have failed to attract sufficient capital from private sources.

The PIDC in its original charter is entrusted with responsibility of developing the following twelve industries: jute, paper, heavy engineering including iron and steel, shipbuilding, heavy chemicals other than fertilizers, sugar, cement, textiles, natural gas, chemicals, pharmaceuticals and dyestuff, and development of power from Sui gas. Except in cotton textile and sugar, the PIDC since its establishment in 1952 has taken the initiative in establishing the pioneering ventures in almost all the other lines of production listed above. It has devoted special attention to those industries which (*a*) require heavy initial investment, (*b*) take a long time to be constructed and to mature, and (*c*) involve complicated processes necessitating high technical knowledge and operating experience. The industry-wide percentage distribution of the total PIDC investment in the projects sponsored by it either wholly or in cooperation with private capital is as follows: 22.3 per cent in paper and paper products, 15.2 per cent in gas transmission and distribution, 15 per cent in chemicals, 14.2 per cent in ship- and dockyards, 11 per cent in jute, 9.4 per cent in sugar, and 8 per cent in cement.[56] The PIDC has also attempted to attain a more balanced regional distribution of industries as an antidote to an excessive concentration of private industry in one wing of the country or in certain specific urban centers. At the end of 1958 the total investment in the PIDC projects was Rs. 408.90 million and Rs. 333.95 million in East and West Pakistan, respectively.[57] Since private enterprise in East Pakistan is relatively less developed as compared to West Pakistan, it is intended that the PIDC should play a more active role during the Second Five Year Plan in accelerating industrial development in the East, if private initiative were lacking.

The PIDC projects have provided an important medium for the joint participation of both private and public capital in the same ventures. The private industrialists have often felt induced to participate in new joint ventures along with the PIDC, partly because it insures an easy access to foreign capital and technical assistance, since

[56] M. Ayub, *Public Industrial Enterprises in Pakistan, 1960* (Karachi, 1960), Annexure, pp. 1-32.

[57] Government of Pakistan, Ministry of Finance, *Government Sponsored Corporations* (Karachi, 1959), appendix I, p. 37.

the PIDC can directly negotiate for or receive foreign assistance. There is an additional inducement in that the PIDC, being a government organization, can more successfully and speedily secure the necessary government sanctions of facilities or deal more expeditiously with various government regulations and red tape. The relative position of private and public investments in all the PIDC projects taken together can be seen in Table 13.

TABLE 13. *Industrial Development Corporation Investment*
(millions of rupees)

Period	Total investment in PIDC projects	PIDC investment	Private investment
Up to 1955	257.06	128.18	128.88
Up to 1959	1,033.42	758.56	274.86

Source: PIDC, *Annual Report*, 1955-56, pp. 12-16, and 1958-59.

While in 1955 the PIDC and private investments in the projects sponsored by the PIDC were equal in magnitude, the share of the PIDC investment greatly increased by 1959. This is owing to the fact that a large number of projects were newly started by the PIDC during the period of the First Five Year Plan, and in the initial years a large part of the investment came from the PIDC. Many of these enterprises have been sold to private individuals or industrialists, either partially or completely. The transfer of an enterprise to private hands after it has successfully overcome teething troubles and stood on its feet has facilitated the development of private enterprise and the mobilization of private savings. Moreover, it enables the most economical and fruitful use of limited resources at the disposal of the PIDC in serving as a sort of revolving fund for initiating new and difficult ventures in cases where private initiative is not likely to step in. The extent of the gradual transfer of the PIDC enterprises to the private hands can be gauged from the fact that as of 1958 eighteen out of thirty-seven PIDC projects were already transferred to private management and control, though PIDC had still some investment left in these enterprises. In the jute industry out of twelve mills initially established by PIDC, either singly or in combination with private enterprise, ten were already under private management and control. In the paper industry three out of four mills were under private management by 1960.[58]   In many projects, even when the PIDC has retained substantial investment, rights of management have been given over to private firms or vice versa. The extent of transfer to private management and also the participation of private capital have been relatively meager in the industries which involve complicated processes, greater technical know-how, and high initial costs of investment.[59] The process of disinvestment by PIDC reflects the government's policy of providing scope for private enterprise whenever the latter is willing and able to take over. The provision in the Second Five Year Plan for a large public investment program in the field of industry is admittedly made on the assumption that private enterprise may not be available to an adequate extent. It is even suggested that if in the course of the next five years private enterprise is found ready and capable of undertaking any or all of the industrial investment indicated in the plan for the public sector, there should be no hesitation in allowing the private sector to do so.[60]   It is partly a recognition of the fact that in view of the large and growing responsibilities of public agencies, which are already handicapped by the inadequacies of a limited administrative machinery, assignment to them of tasks which can very well be performed by private enterprise may restrict the pace of development.

Questions have often been raised regarding the relative efficiency of private and public enterprises in industry. An attempt at a comparison can be made from two angles: (a) comparative efficiency of the same enterprise in two situations, i.e., first under PIDC management and, secondly, when it is transferred to private management, and (b) relative efficiency of PIDC and private enterprises which coexist in the same industry at the same time. Available data are not adequate to provide a conclusive answer to these questions. However, some broad considerations and factors bearing on this problem can be mentioned. Regarding the first kind of comparison, it is clear that circumstances surrounding an enterprise in its early years of

[58] Ayub, *Public Industrial Enterprises in Pakistan, 1960*, pp. 6-16; PIDC *Annual Report, 1957-58*.
[59] PIDC, *Annual Report, 1957-58*; Ayub, *Public Industrial Enterprises in Pakistan, 1960*, Annexure II.
[60] *Second Plan*, pp. 225-226.

teething troubles and experimentation, especially in the hitherto
unknown branches of industry, are quite different from those confronting the same enterprise after it has successfully overcome the
initial handicaps and has gained experience in techniques, management, and marketing. It is only at this later stage that an enterprise
initially developed by the PIDC has been and usually is transferred
to private hands. The PIDC by the very nature of its being a promoter and a pioneer in the field of industrialization has to embark
on projects which in an undeveloped industrial milieu may not for
some years reach a condition of profitability by the usual commercial
standards. They may, however, indirectly contribute to the generation of external economies, as in the case of investment in gas, power,
etc. Again, while considering the possible differences in efficiency
of the same enterprise in two time periods, it is important to re-
member that conditions regarding supply and demand, i.e., cost of
factors and markets, may change; and this makes a correct appraisal
rather difficult.

The second kind of comparison, i.e., comparison between private
and the PIDC enterprises coexisting in the same field, raises different
issues. Insofar as private enterprises antedate public enterprises
in the same line of production, depreciation costs of the former are
often much smaller than those of the latter, partly because prices of
imported capital equipment have gone up steadily through the years
with the result that the new PIDC enterprises incur a much higher
capital cost. Furthermore, in many cases older private enterprises
may have largely written down the value of their capital equipment.
The PIDC enterprises often have larger establishment and overhead costs because economy in a large government organization is
not always observed on the same scale or as strictly as in a private
firm. The PIDC, being a state-financed institution, is generally expected to act on the whole as a model employer, offering additional
benefits and facilities to employees. Insofar as this is not counter-
balanced by a higher productivity it adds to the costs of the PIDC
enterprises. Moreover, in the location of the PIDC enterprises the
considerations of least cost are modified by the need to attain a more
widespread distribution of industries between different areas or regions, in view of a limited mobility of labor and of undesirable
social and human consequences of overconcentration.

The State and the Private Sector: Assistance, Regulation, and Control

While a large segment of the economy has been left to the care of private enterprise, the government seeks on the whole to retain a general control and supervision over the private sector of the economy. Direct and indirect measures have been adopted to influence the amount and direction of private investment to help and assist private enterprises in the areas in which an accelerated development is considered desirable to meet recognized social needs, or to moderate their undesirable social effects.

The government provides assistance to private enterprise over a wide field and in many forms. In the field of industry, for example, the provision of state assistance to private enterprise has been of significant importance in one respect, i.e., supply of finance through a number of state-sponsored financial institutions which derive their funds either wholly from the government or jointly from the government and private sources with a view to providing credit facilities to private industries. The Pakistan Industrial Credit and Investment Corporation is authorized to borrow from abroad, and it lends both domestic and foreign currency and also participates in the share capital of private enterprises. It thus serves as a medium for associating private with public capital as well as foreign with domestic capital.[61] During the years 1955-59 the average annual credit granted by such agencies was Rs. 60 million, as against Rs. 94 million advanced by all the commercial banks together. During the period of the second plan the state-sponsored institutions are expected to provide 40 per cent of the total credit to be advanced by all the credit agencies, including commercial banks and stock exchanges.[62] Additional measures of assistance to private industries consist of the establishment of industrial estates and the provision of tax incentives, both designed to encourage investment in the private sector. Industrial estates provide private firms with such social overhead facilities and common services as land furnished with road, water, power, communication, sewerage, transport, etc. Small-scale and cottage industries have been the recipients of special financial and technical assistance provided through the medium of a number of "small scale industries corporations" established by the government

[61] Government of Pakistan, Ministry of Finance, *Government Sponsored Corporations* (Karachi, 1959), pp. 87-91.
[62] *Second Five Year Plan*, pp. 64-69.

in the various parts of the country. They are intended to provide technical and management services regarding methods of production, business management, industrial surveys and research, and pilot projects to demonstrate new lines of production. These corporations will also establish design centers and common facilities centers as well as provide credit in kind or cash for the purchase of equipment and materials and for marketing. They will undertake direct imports of materials and equipment and arrange for their distribution among small producers. They are also expected to serve as intermediaries for marketing, sales, and distribution of products of small producers. These corporations, established very recently, are only beginning to expand their operations and hence as yet have a very limited impact.

There are other direct measures of control and regulation exercised by the government, such as a control over the allocation of foreign exchange, manipulation of tax rates, and regulation of domestic credit facilities. Moreover, the government controls the location of industry and the allocation of materials in short supply. Since 1955 government intervention in these fields is to be co-ordinated within the framework of over-all national five year plans. Before establishing an industry an investor has to register his company, secure the government's permission to set up the specific industry, depending upon whether it falls within the set of priorities laid down by the government, obtain a sanction of the controller of capital issues, and secure a permit from the controller of imports and exports for the import of materials and equipment. These various kinds of permits are administered by various agencies and not always without delays and inconveniences for a private entrepreneur engaged in dealing with multiple government agencies. The extent of co-ordination between different agencies and departments with different and often overlapping authorities and at various levels of the government has not been very successful.

The existence of the various kinds of controls implies that a free and unrestricted entry into the field of industry as conceived in the theoretical model of competition does not exist. As reported in the ILO survey mentioned earlier, more than 20 per cent of the large-scale industries considered government controls as one of the main obstacles to the expansion of their respective industries. The restrictions imposed by the government on entry which arise from a shortage of foreign exchange are reflected in this figure. This does not necessarily denote that newcomers do not enter into the field of industry. As a matter of fact the avowed policy of the government in recent years is to encourage the entry of newcomers. However, the development of new enterprises is regulated and controlled as to the amounts and directions of investment by the government. The controls are necessitated by the government's policy to guide and direct the optimum use of scarce capital and foreign exchange resources in the light of over-all priorities. It has been alleged that the grant of industrial licensing for the establishment of new enterprises during the first five years did not always follow the criteria or priorities laid down by the plan. The discipline warranted by the provisions of the plan was in some cases ignored by arbitrary administrative decisions or political pressures. Moreover, there was a lack of sufficient co-ordination among the different agencies concerned with the regulation and control of different aspects of industrial development. In an attempt to mitigate the inconvenience arising from a division of responsibility among multiple agencies, a new agency called the Investment Promotion Bureau was established in 1959. This new organization is expected to disseminate information among prospective investors, both domestic and foreign, about investment opportunities in Pakistan, receive and co-ordinate all investment applications and proposals from private investors, process the applications and channel them through the appropriate government departments, and finally help in obtaining speedy decisions on them. Moreover, it would assist private investors in obtaining power, water, land, building materials, licenses for imported equipment and materials, appropriate technical help and advice, and other facilities for which the approval or sanction of the different government departments is necessary. It is, in short, expected to act as a sort of clearinghouse for the various problems confronting private investors.

In the field of agriculture the direct responsibility of the government includes such projects as the reclamation of land, provision of drainage and irrigation facilities, and prevention of waterlogging and salinity through a large public investment program executed in some cases by semi-autonomous public corporations. The important forms of government assistance to individual private farmers consist in the provision of credit facilities, supply of fertilizers at subsidized prices, and supply and development of improved seeds and implements. The extent of such assistance in each of these fields is to date rather limited and its impact on agricultural development is restricted. In the sphere of financial assistance to private agriculture, the government grants loans to farmers either directly or through the government-sponsored financial institutions, though the total credit supplied by them is meager. They concentrate on more credit-worthy farmers with an adequate security to offer. A large number of farmers, often below subsistence level, do not qualify for their credit and hence are outside the range of government operations.

The principal government institution entrusted with the task of improvement of agriculture and village life in general is the Village Aid Organization (i.e., community development projects). The basic unit is a development area consisting of 150 to 250 villages under the control and guidance of a development officer aided by village workers as well as specialists in various subjects affecting the productive activities in a village. It is intended to be a medium through which financial and technical assistance from the government can be used to "draw forth the resources of skill, energy and money which exist in the villages, to channel them into productive uses and to create means by which they can be progressively enlarged."[63] The village aid extension workers, being in continuous contact with the villagers, are expected to help farmers understand and solve their problems, appraise their opportunities, and take advantage of the services of specialists and government funds in such matters as farm management, animal husbandry, co-operation and marketing, health, education, sanitation, etc. The areas in which village aid workers are active are increasing in number, but the progress to date has been rather slow even though the Second Five Year Plan expects a considerable enlargement of the organization. By 1959 only 18,000 villages had been covered, comprising merely 14 million villagers.[64] The progress is limited by a lack of trained personnel with necessary qualities of leadership and also with specialized knowledge, both of which can be developed only through time-consuming training. The methods of self-help taught to villagers seem to fritter away after a time, if continued interest cannot be maintained in worthwhile projects leading to some immediate tangible results in one or other aspects of village life.

[63] *First Plan*, p. 197.   [64] *Preliminary Evaluation*, pp. 35-37.

The government has also undertaken more direct measures of control and regulation of the production of different agricultural crops, such as jute, cotton, tea, and sugar. The acreage of cultivated land under jute was controlled until recently by means of licensing of jute growers. Each year the total permissible area under jute was fixed by the government as a certain percentage of the total acreage under jute in the base year, i.e., 1940, on the basis of some rough judgment as to the competing supply, stocks, and demand for jute, both at home and abroad. The rationale of the regulation of the jute acreage was to maintain and stabilize the price of raw jute via the restriction of output or the prevention of overproduction. The purpose was to achieve a better balance and adjustment between demand and supply than could otherwise be achieved. The uninformed and unorganized farmers have no means at their disposal of estimating demand or forecasting export demand. The unrestricted free-market reaction or adjustment of production to current prices often accentuates the fluctuation of prices, according to the familiar pattern of the well-known "cobweb" theorem, since there is a time lag in the process of production and marketing. In the years of overproduction or fall in demand jute growers have traditionally suffered heavy losses. Fluctuations in jute prices cause fluctuations in foreign exchange earnings, since jute is one of Pakistan's principal exports. This has important destabilizing effects on the capacity of import and consequently on capital investment. To achieve a better adjustment of supply to demand was one aim of the regulation of jute acreage; the other related objective was to exercise monopoly power to raise price via the restriction of output. This was based on the assumption that in 1940 the then undivided India had a monopoly of the supply of raw jute and that demand for jute was on the whole inelastic. However, it is generally agreed that licensing regulations have not been effective and in fact have not even been rigorously enforced, except in one or two years. The area actually cropped as a percentage of the area licensed has varied between wide limits, i.e., between 83 and 128 per cent. An FAO study reveals that both before and after the introduction of the licensing system the actual area cropped each season has been mainly determined by the ratio of the price of jute to that of rice, which is the main substitute crop that can be grown on the same land.[65] Since actual acreage in the majority of years has in fact been determined by the price mechanism, an ineffective regulation is more a nuisance and administrative burden than a help. Moreover, jute is no longer a monopoly of Pakistan, with India being a powerful competitor. Over the past ten years the share of Pakistan in the total world supply of raw jute has declined. India, among others, has considerably expanded the production of raw jute to feed her own jute manufacturing industry. This has meant a higher price elasticity of demand for raw jute from Pakistan, accentuated in certain uses by the rise of alternative packing materials. These considerations, coupled with a growing emphasis in recent years on price mechanism, led to the abolition of the system of regulation in 1960.

The regulation of the production of cotton has a much narrower scope, as it is mainly designed to regulate the relative outputs of different varieties of cotton and to prevent their intermixing. The cotton-growing areas are divided into zones, in each of which a particular variety is allowed to be grown and in which government agencies distribute pure seeds for that variety. However, there were years, such as 1952-53 and 1953-54, when the government restricted the acreage under cotton in an attempt to encourage the production of summer grains and to relieve food shortage. But when again in 1955-56 a grow-more-cotton campaign was launched to meet the needs of increased domestic consumption and export, reliance was placed not on direct regulation or control but on public exhortation and subsidized distribution of fertilizers, improved seeds, and water supplies.[66] The direct intervention in and regulation of production of tea by the government are very recent phenomena and are intended mainly to increase production with a view to boosting exports. The Pakistan Tea Board, a government agency appointed to guide and regulate production and trade in tea, has been entrusted since 1960 with the responsibility of establishing, with the help of government funds, new tea gardens and of acquiring or rehabilitating derelict tea gardens which, after being properly developed or rehabilitated, may be offered for sale to private enterprises. It is expected to render assistance for the development of private tea

[65] R. Clerk, "The Economic Determinants of Jute Production," *F.A.O. Bulletin of Agricultural Economics and Statistics* (Rome, Sept. 1957).
[66] Andrus and Mohammed, *op. cit.*, pp. 66-67.

gardens in such forms as loans at concessional rates for the expansion or the improvement of tea gardens. It may even issue compulsory directives to private tea gardens to plant or replant tea in such minimum areas as may be specified by it from year to year.[67]

In the field of agricultural marketing the government has intervened by means of direct state trading, as in the case of jute and cotton and by the exercise of over-all regulatory powers over the conditions of marketing. The jute and cotton boards constituted by the government in the early years of Pakistan were originally authorized to fix minimum prices of jute and cotton and to intervene, if necessary, by means of open market operations to ensure that such minimum prices were effective. The boards were also empowered to supervise trading practices in these commodities, including all matters concerning storage, transport, insurance, forward transactions, etc., as well as to regulate baling, ginning, or pressing charges. The open market operations undertaken by these boards were not very frequent and were undertaken only in those years when prices fell to very low levels, owing to a decline in export demand. When the Jute Board faced the need in 1953 to undertake large-scale operations to maintain the support price, it failed to meet the situation adequately in view of limited finance and inadequate storage facilities at its disposal. Both boards suffered losses when they undertook operations on a significant scale. The price support schemes were abandoned in later years, but the idea of buffer stocks has been mooted from time to time.

In the initial years of the operation of the Jute Board, its intervention in the marketing of jute had one beneficial side-effect. The Board's practices of appointing private agents from outside the range of established traders to undertake on its behalf purchases of jute in rural areas enabled newcomers to enter a trade which until then had been dominated by an organized group of balers and shippers who were mostly foreign. It requisitioned baling presses owned by the old established balers for use by its agents (i.e., newcomers) and provided them with liberal credit facilities from the state-sponsored commercial bank (the National Bank of Pakistan), which at the time of its establishment in 1949 had as one of its major responsibilities the task of financing the marketing of jute cotton, and other agricultural cash crops. The Jute Board also attempted to stimulate the growth of co-operative jute marketing societies by appointing them as agents for its purchasing operations and by providing them with financial support through the medium of their apex society, the East Pakistan Provincial Cooperative Jute Marketing Society. This latter society was started in 1952, primarily to undertake pucca baling as well as to sell the baled jute to the indigenous manufacturing industry or to export it abroad. It was granted monopoly rights for the purchase of jute during the years 1952-53 to 1956-57 in the border areas, where jute was usually smuggled out to India. In 1957 the government started a new organization called the Jute Marketing Corporation, which took over many of the functions of the Jute Board in the sphere of internal marketing.[68] At present the main functions of the Jute Board are restricted to the export trade of jute. It is expected to serve as an agent of the government to execute the government's policy regarding the international trade in jute. It is to supervise and regulate all dealings in international trade and make recommendations to the government regarding measures for the promotion of foreign trade, specification of standards and grades, etc. At present there is no attempt at the fixation of a minimum internal price of raw jute, but the Jute Board fixes a minimum export price which is enforced by the State Bank of Pakistan in the course of its control over foreign exchange transactions. The exporters of jute in order to engage in export trade are required to obtain a license from the Board. This enables the Board to keep a record of the business operations of the exporters and maintain a check on the compliance by the exporters with the minimum export price as well as with other regulations concerning grades, qualities, and proper weight. The main objective behind the regulations governing export trade is to build up and maintain the reputation of the Pakistani raw jute in foreign markets. The minimum export price, which is designed to maintain the level of foreign exchange earnings from jute exports, does not guarantee any effective minimum price to the grower. The minimum export price is fixed every year with reference to an estimate of current export demand and supply position. It is not based on a scientific study of demand, both short- and long-run, or of the cost of production. If the domestic price happens to be lower than the minimum export price, the marketing intermediaries usually receive the difference.

[68] "Survey of Jute Marketing in East Pakistan" (manuscript, 1959).

The price received by the growers remains low in spite of a higher export price. However, the new Jute Marketing Corporation is empowered to carry on jute trade in order to stabilize prices of raw jute and to insure a fair price to the growers. The trading operations of the Corporation have not been large enough to make any significant impact on the prices ruling in the market. Its operations, moreover, have so far been more important in the higher stage of marketing, i.e., pucca baling and shipping.[69] Even though its establishment was originally expected to offer an effective competition and thus to counteract any possible monopsonistic action on the part of the balers and shippers, i.e., the intermediaries operating at the higher stages of marketing, where fewness of numbers and consequently the possibility of collusive action is apprehended, the Corporation has in fact turned out to be one of the many other intermediaries with no significant difference in terms of its effect on the market. The Corporation is also expected to establish regulated markets and standard grades by setting up model standards of its own. Furthermore, it is given the responsibility of assisting the growth and development of co-operative societies among the growers, if necessary by means of financial help. In fact it has replaced the provincial co-operative apex society in its role as a co-ordinator and promoter of primary co-operative societies, though the extent of its success has been limited. The Corporation took over from the Co-operative Society the right of monopoly purchase of raw jute in the border areas, which was abolished later on. During the early years of its existence, when it exercised this right of monopoly purchase, its operations were not free from abuses and corruption, often as a result of political interference in its internal affairs. The Corporation has undergone rapid changes in its organization and extent of operations in the past two years. With an improvement in its administration and operational efficiency it is expected to extend the scope of its activities.[70]

There is a great multiplicity of government agencies concerned with the regulation of internal and external trade in jute. These agencies are often under the control of different levels of government, i.e., provincial and central governments, as well as under different government departments. This has not only contributed

[69] *Ibid.*; also, Government of Pakistan, *Report of the Jute Enquiry Commission, 1960* (mimeographed), pp. 157-176.
[70] Government of Pakistan, Ministry of Finance, *Major Commodities of Pakistan; A Review* (Karachi, 1960), pp. 1-32.

to increased costs of administration but also to a certain lack of uniformity and co-ordination in policy and actions. Besides the Jute Board and the Jute Marketing Corporation, which are controlled by the central and provincial governments, respectively, there is yet another agency called the Jute Directorate of the Government of East Pakistan which undertakes registration of dealers and godown-owners. Moreover, it administers the issue of licenses which permit a private dealer or trader to engage in jute trade on the fulfilment of a set of conditions designed to secure compliance by traders with the various government regulations regarding weights, grades, standards, and invoicing of exports.

The state intervention in the marketing of sugar cane is mainly intended to encourage the cultivation of sugar cane in new areas and to insure an adequate and well-timed supply of cane to sugar factories in view of the fact that their operations are seasonal. The government also seeks to regulate the relative quantities of cane available for crushing by modern factories and the indigenous cottage industries. The government fixes the price at which sugar cane is delivered to the factories. The price is usually fixed at a higher level in areas where farmers unused to the cultivation of sugar cane have to be induced for the first time to grow sugar cane in preference to some other crops. This is partly due to the government policy of obtaining a wide geographical distribution of the sugar factories, which has involved their establishment in new areas. The determination of the price of sugar cane by the government is not based on an adequate analysis of the relevant factors, such as the cost of production or the price of competing crops. Political and social considerations as well as local interests have often influenced the level at which price has been fixed.[71] To bring about an orderly supply of sugar cane to factories, sugar cane areas in certain parts of the country are divided into zones, each zone supplying cane to the particular factories within it. The movement of sugar cane by the private traders between different zones is prohibited, except with the permission of the government. The factories within each zone are required to lift either the entire crop or a specific proportion of the total amount offered to them for purchase. In order to regulate the relative quantities of sugar produced by modern factories and cottage in-

[71] Government of Pakistan, *Report of the Pakistan Sugar Commission, 1957-59* (Karachi, 1960), pp. 37, 47-49, 64-76.

dustries in East Pakistan the government specifies the periods in a year in which sugar may be produced by one method or the other. Moreover, it regulates the timing and commencement of the crushing of sugar cane in every factory.[72]

Government intervention has been most extensive in the distribution of food grains, which have frequently been in short supply. The ways in which it has intervened have also affected the production and consequently the supply of food grains. The intervention has included direct state trading and the distribution of food grains under a system of rationing. Under this system the government appoints private dealers as its agents to sell to individual consumers their quotas or rations of mainly such commodities as rice, wheat, and sugar at prices fixed by the government. The supplies of the controlled commodities are provided by the government to dealers out of its own stocks built up either through internal procurement or imports. The imports of food grains, such as wheat and rice, are undertaken directly by the government departments. The internal procurement from the farmers is limited to the surplus areas within the country and is also undertaken by government departments and sometimes by private dealers who are appointed by the government to act as its agents on the basis of commissions.

Rationing has not been universal but has been limited mainly to the urban population and to certain low-income groups in the rural areas. In the case of rice, distribution by rationing has varied from year to year in its coverage. A maximum of 7.5 per cent of the total consumption of rice has been under rationing at any one time. This is a significant proportion in view of the fact that only about 30 per cent of the total food consumption depends on market purchases, the rest being consumed on the farms on which it is produced.[73] In many years in the past food grains were sold under rationing at prices below the cost of procurement or that of imports. The difference was met by a subsidy from the general revenues of the government. In fact, this constituted a transfer of real income to the section of the population which was covered by rationing. In the areas which are under partial rationing open market purchases

[72] Government of East Pakistan, *A Collection of Orders and Notifications Regarding Control on Foodstuffs, etc. 1958*, pp. 137-40.
[73] F. C. Shorter, "Foodgrains Policy in East Pakistan," *Public Policy* (Graduate School of Public Administration, Harvard University, 1959), pp. 107-126; also reprinted in *Pakistan Economic Journal*, Dec. 1958.

and sales are allowed at prices which are higher than controlled prices. However, insofar as the low-income groups in such cases receive rationed food they buy less from the free market. As a result the pressure of demand on the free market is lessened and the free market price tends to be lower than it otherwise would have been.

As far as prices received by the farmers are concerned, the procurement prices have been lower than the selling prices ruling in the market. There were years in the past when there was a compulsory procurement of food grains by the government agencies from the farmers in the surplus areas. This was often combined with "cordoning" of surplus areas, which prevented any movement of crops from the surplus to the deficit areas. This reduced the market price within the cordon walls.[74] In the later years the compulsory procurement of paddy in East Pakistan was abolished, except in the case of border areas. Moreover, in the subsequent years the procurement prices of paddy came to bear a closer relation to market prices, and insofar as the government procured paddy immediately after the harvesting of crops, when the prevailing market price was low, and sold them throughout the year, when the price rose to a higher level, the price differences contributed towards meeting marketing expenses. Internal procurement became increasingly negligible compared with imports.

The procurement prices of food grains have remained low relative to the prices of non-food crops. The latter have risen as a result of the operation of free-market forces under the impact of a rising demand. The unfavorable price ratio for food grains has consequently acted as a dis-incentive to an increased production of food grains. In addition, the terms of trade between food crops and manufactured articles of consumption have most probably moved adversely to the former and thus have further discouraged production of food grains. The food grains policy in the past has been directed towards the prevention of a rise in price. There has been no provision for maintaining a floor price in case market price in certain seasons or years falls to uneconomically low levels. During the period when surplus areas were cordoned off, the greater the extent of success of cordoning, the greater was the fall in prices within the cordon walls and greater was the dis-incentive to sell, with

[74] *Ibid.*

a consequent decline in marketable surplus. It was increasingly recognized that the cost of protecting a small class of consumers, especially in the urban areas, in terms of a higher price to non-rationed population and a dis-incentive to increased production of food grains was too high. These and similar considerations led to the abolition in 1960 of the system of compulsory procurement and rationing in the case of one major food grain, i.e., wheat. The shift in policy is in effect a shift from a policy of distributing real income in favor of a small group to that of affording a greater incentive to increased production, with the expectation that a larger output would ultimately lower price below the level of present-day free market price and benefit a larger section of the population. The cost of operations of government trading has not always been very economical. It is expected that private traders may effect greater economies in the costs of handling and transport, and to the extent that savings in costs may even partly be shared by traders with the consumers the price paid to the former may rise in the short run without a significantly higher penalty to the consumer. The restoration of private trade in wheat has been accompanied by the imposition of a number of restrictions by the central bank on the terms of lending of commercial banks to private dealers in wheat with a view to curbing speculation or hoarding.

Under the new wheat policy the government undertakes to engage in open market operations, i.e., sales and purchases in the free market, in order to stabilize prices within predetermined ceiling and floor prices. The ceiling and floor prices are fixed at such levels as would provide adequate incentives for increased agricultural production and avoid undue hardships to consumers in the years of scarcity. For the purpose of open market operations as well as for such operations to have an effective impact on market prices, the size of the reserve stock is of crucial importance. The government is building up a buffer stock of wheat with the help mainly of imports financed by United States aid and partly from open market purchases at times when market prices fall below floor prices. It stands ready to buy any quantity offered for sale at the floor price. To insure the success of a policy of decontrol in stimulating agricultural production it is not enough that prices are set free from control. It is necessary that prices received by the farmers improve in relation to the prices of other commodities. As past experience with agricultural production has shown, price incentive alone is not successful if supply and cost of inputs in agricultural production such as improved seeds, fertilizers, and equipment are not adequate or commensurate with requirements. No less important is the effective application of the new and better methods of production through proper institutions, such as extension services as well as a provision of ample credit facilities.

In the case of another major food grain, i.e., rice, the present policy is to continue price control and rationing in a very few selected urban areas and partial rationing for certain low-income groups in the rural areas. Recently, in a large number of cities rationing has been abolished. Under the system of partial rationing the selection of the particular rural areas as well as that of specific low-income groups to be covered by rationing is made from time to time by the local administrative authorities on the basis of a judgment about the prevailing scarcity, the magnitude of a rise in prices, and the extent of consequent distress caused to the poorer sections of the population. The level to which prices must rise before rationing is introduced is left to the judgment of the local officials, on the one hand, and, on the other, to the extent of supplies of rice available to the government at the time. The adoption of a policy of price stabilization through open market operations similar to that of wheat is rendered difficult in the absence of a buffer or reserve stock of rice. Unlike wheat, there is no immediate prospect of a guaranteed supply of imports of rice available from foreign sources through foreign aid. Lack of adequate supplies of rice has led the government to introduce increasing quantities of wheat in the rice-eating province.

The regulation of and control over trade and distribution exercised by the government extends considerably beyond the intervention in the marketing of agricultural commodities. Both the internal and external trade are subject to various restrictions and regulations. There is a direct participation of the government in the external trade of the country. For example, the direct imports on government accounts have steadily gone up from 12.7 per cent of the total imports in 1949-50 to 46.8 per cent in 1958-59.[75] This is a reflection of the growing importance of the public sector in the economy of the country as well as of the fact that many materials in

[75] Government of Pakistan, CSO, *Statistical Bulletin*, VIII (Karachi, Feb. 1960), 183-186.

short supply which are used either wholly or substantially in the private sector are also imported by the government for their eventual distribution among private traders. The share of the government in export trade is, however, negligible.

Insofar as private external trade comes under the Imports and Exports (Control) Act of 1950, the government exercises quantitative restrictions on imports and exports by means of a separate licensing of commercial and industrial enterprises. The dealings in foreign exchange are similarly under a strict control. The industrial establishments are permitted to import directly their requirements of equipment and materials without having to pay commercial importers' high profit margins. The commercial importers or import traders are divided into two categories, (a) established importers and (b) newcomers. The former are those who were in business in 1952, i.e., at the end of a period of free imports, popularly called "Open General License." They were assigned a quota of imports based on an average volume of their business prior to 1952. The actual amounts to be imported by them in subsequent years are fixed annually with reference to this basic quota, taking into consideration changes in demand, domestic production, and stocks.[76]

From time to time newcomers are issued licenses to enter import trade on an examination of their genuineness as traders and of their past performance. This usually takes place when a larger volume of imports is permitted as a result of an improvement in the balance of payments, as illustrated in the recent decision to place eleven items on a free import list, i.e., anybody, including an individual consumer, is entitled to import these items directly.[77] Thus entry of new firms into import trade is allowed only insofar as they are expected to cater to a new and expanding import demand, and this insulates the established importers from competition in respect of the existing demand. The current method of distributing import licenses is a crude attempt at maintaining an equilibrium or, more appropriately, a status quo in the relative volume of business of individual importers. A certain amount of arbitrariness is inherent in a replacement of market mechanism by administrative decisions. Recently, the government has undertaken measures to induce importers having import

[76] "Basis of Commercial Licensing for January-June 1959," *Pakistan Trade*, X (May 1959), 58-72.
[77] *Pakistan Observer* (Dacca, March 11, 1962), p. 6.

quotas for a large number of items to merge the comparatively small and uneconomic quotas for many items into bigger quotas for a few such items as constitute their main lines of business. This may result in a greater specialization among importers. For each item there will be a fewer importers, each dealing in a large quantity of individual items, and hence an increase in the imperfection of the market. At the same time it is possible that an amalgamation of quotas may induce economies of specialization and reduce cost. Simultaneously, attempts are being made by the government to encourage a combination among groups of small importers in order to enlarge their scale of operations and to improve efficiency.[78] As in the case of imports, so also in the case of exports there are restrictions on the items which can be exported as well as on their quantities and destinations. Faced with the necessity of stimulating exports and of earning foreign exchange for developmental imports, an export bonus scheme was introduced in 1959. The exporters of almost all the items, except a very few industrial raw materials, are allowed to retain varying percentages of their foreign exchange earnings and to dispose of these titles to foreign exchange either by selling them to other importers at a very high premium or by utilizing them to import directly. This is in fact an indirect form of multiple exchange rates and has succeeded in stimulating foreign exchange earnings.

The extent and intensity of controls on internal trade, distribution, and prices have fluctuated through the years. These controls are based on the Essential Supplies Act of 1946, which was extended and modified in 1953. Under the Act the government may declare any commodity essential and impose such controls as the specification of a number of approved dealers or traders in respect of a controlled article, thereby excluding others from dealing in the commodity, fixing qualities to be sold by importers or producers to approved dealers, specifying maximum quantities which can be held in stock or bought and sold in any transaction by the dealers, and prescribing the method of sales to final consumers. The government may not only fix maximum prices but also may require compulsory submission by producers or importers of information regarding (a) detailed items of cost of production or of import, (b) quantities produced or imported, and (c) the detailed manner of disposing of them. It may also undertake an inspection of books and stocks

[78] *Pakistan Trade*, XI (Feb. 1960), 32-36.

of dealers as well as impose restrictions on the movement of controlled articles.[79] The number of commodities which have been subject to controls and the nature of such controls have varied through the years, depending upon changes in the conditions of supply and in price level. Price control has not always been accompanied by a control of distribution to the level of final consumer. A comprehensive system of control over distribution and price from the point of production or import to that of final consumption needs a complicated administrative apparatus and has been found, as elsewhere, to be very difficult to enforce. It has consequently been limited to a few most essential consumers' goods, such as food grains and some essential intermediate products in short supply, such as cement and iron and steel. The fixing of the price of a controlled item has not always been based on an adequate analysis of costs, differences in efficiency, and quality of products among different producing units. As illustrated in the case of sugar, the level of a controlled price has been manipulated so as to absorb an arbitrarily fixed price of a raw material as well as to subsidize the price of other controlled commodities, i.e., wheat and rice in this case.[80]

In 1953, the first year following the end of a period of liberal imports, fifteen commodities including essential consumers' goods and intermediate goods in short supply were under control. The list of controlled commodities was periodically revised and often expanded. In early 1958 controls were lifted from all commodities, except mechanically propelled vehicles, iron and steel, coal, cement, newsprint, and a few items of food.[81] However, after the abolition of controls prices recorded a substantial rise so that later in the year, with the introduction of martial law, controls were reimposed on a number of items as an anti-inflationary measure. They were particularly tightened in the case of such items as tea and cotton yarn, of which there was a substantial reduction in domestic availability consequent on greatly increased exports under the export bonus scheme. Moreover, in the case of a large number of other articles the government fixed profit margins at 20 per cent over the cost of production. The difference between ex-mill price and retail

[79] Government of Pakistan, Ministry of Industries, *Economic Controls Manual* (Karachi, 1954 and 1959), pp. 1-30.

[80] *Report of the Sugar Commission*, pp. 64-76.

[81] *Economic Controls Manual*; Government of Pakistan, *Report of the Prices Commission*, 1960, pp. 42-51, 70-74.

price, representing the combined profit margins of agents, whole-salers, and retailers, was fixed for each major group of commodities between 20 per cent and 50 per cent. The retailer was to receive 40 to 50 per cent of the combined margins.[82] The regulation of profit margins has been only partially effective, owing to the lack of an adequate administrative machinery to undertake a detailed scrutiny or auditing of costs and prices as reported by producers and dealers. The fixing of profit margins reduces the incentive for economizing in costs, makes inadequate provision for especially risky ventures, and limits further the scope for price competition, which is in any case restricted owing to the existence of oligopoly and product differentiation. The enforcement of profit margins for whole-salers and retailers, of whom there are such a large number and among whom there is a great deal of integration, has been partic-ularly difficult. Subsequently, the number of commodities on which profit margins are regulated has been substantially reduced.

There was a drastic fall in prices on the imposition of various controls backed by the sanction of martial law in late 1958. How-ever, soon afterwards, when all the stocks were sold out at low prices, scarcity reappeared and high prices were substituted by non-availability of goods. Experience has shown that it is only in the case of commodities whose supply is not far short of demand that price controls by themselves, if effective, may allow needier people reasonable chances of obtaining their requirements. In certain cases price controls have the effect of discouraging the production of con-trolled articles and of diverting resources to the production of un-controlled items, as has happened in the case of cotton textiles, thus accentuating the scarcity. The recent trend of the government policy is to relax price and distribution controls and to lay a greater empha-sis on the augmentation of supplies in key sectors as well as on a reduction of excess demand via a higher taxation and a curtailment of unproductive expenditure.

CONCLUSION

The economic system of Pakistan may appropriately be called a mixed economy in which both private and public enterprises coexist in various fields of economic activity. Their relative roles have

[82] Government of Pakistan, *Martial Law Regulations*, No. 42, Dec. 1958 and Aug. 1959; Government of Pakistan, *Press Note*, Aug. 10, 1960.

been governed mainly by the need to accelerate the rate of economic growth in view of the lack of adequate and vigorous private initiative. The emphasis in recent years has shifted towards a greater scope for private enterprise. It is recognized that private enterprise involves a greater degree of decentralization and flexibility than public enterprises. However, its contribution to growth in an underdeveloped economy like that of Pakistan is mainly dependent upon how far it forges ahead with new methods, reduces costs, introduces new products, seeks out talents, and reinvests a significant part of its profits. A sense of social responsibility on the part of private enterprise is as yet undeveloped, so that an exploitation of shortage or of monopolistic position is not uncommon. Social security measures are in their infancy. The government is attempting to evolve a set of minimum working conditions of labor. Trade-unionism and co-operative organizations have not as yet developed any countervailing power.

There are a number of controls on private enterprise, such as controls on prices, profits, production, foreign exchange, trade, etc., intended primarily to protect the real income of particular groups, to relieve the burden of shortage on low-income consumers, and to regulate the allocation of resources and the relative growth of different sectors, in accordance with predetermined priorities. However, over the past years controls have developed in a haphazard manner, on an *ad hoc* basis, often in response to immediate and compelling demands of particular situations, many of which were temporary and had to be considered in isolation, resulting in a certain amount of overlapping and duplication. They have undergone frequent changes, creating uncertainty in the minds of businessmen regarding the future of the government's policy. This has a discouraging effect on long-term commitments on the part of trade and industry. The maintenance of controls has made heavy demands on a limited administrative machinery, diverting the latter from more productive functions. Many controls have been only partially effective owing to inadequate enforcement. The administration of controls affecting considerable fortunes of business has concentrated great powers in the hands of public officials, whose individual incomes can seldom compare favorably with large business gains, and has opened the door to temptation and consequent corruption and abuses. All these limitations tend to interfere with the allocation of scarce resources in a way different from what the very system of controls is intended to serve. To the extent that it encourages illegal transfers of income, it leads to windfall gains and aggravates social injustice. The recent tendency is to rationalize the system of controls, to retain and to administer efficiently a few indispensable ones, and to substitute, if possible, direct, physical controls by taxes and subsidies as regulatory weapons. An improved foreign exchange position enabling an enlargement of domestic supplies has helped the change in emphasis.

The forces of competition and monopoly coexist in the economy of Pakistan. In agriculture, cottage industry, and retail trade competitive forces are stronger, except where state intervention has modified them, whereas concentration of control and restrictions on entry are greater in large-scale industry, financial markets, foreign and domestic wholesale trade, etc. The existing enterprises often get larger businesses. Having an established business in a given line of activity facilitates entry into new lines, since it is easier for the business to muster necessary capital and managerial experience. On the one hand, the managing-agency system and, on the other, accumulation of capital through a reinvestment of profits in existing and new enterprises increase the degree of concentration of control either in management or in financial ownership. The entry of new firms into many of these major areas of activity is regulated by the government and is to a certain extent a matter of the exercise of patronage by state authorities. Though from time to time licenses have been issued to a small number of new entrants, their impact on the competitive situation has not so far been very significant. However, recently there is a stronger emphasis in the government's policy on the encouragement of newcomers and of medium and small entrepreneurs. Within the framework of planning there is a tendency, in view of the limited capital and foreign exchange resources available, to conserve scarce resources already employed in certain lines even if they are not very efficiently utilized and to discourage new entrants, even though it may enlarge the scope of competition, in case capacity already installed is underutilized.

11

The South African Economy

The Relevance of the Competitive Laissez-Faire Model

*O. P. F. Horwood and John R. Burrows**

> The legitimate object of government is to do for the community of people whatever they need to have done, but cannot do at all, or cannot so well do for themselves in their separate and individual capacities. In all that the people can individually do as well themselves, government ought not to interfere.
>
> —ABRAHAM LINCOLN.

In the course of presenting last year's budget to the House of Assembly (March 1961), the South African Minister of Finance made the point that "our economy . . . is based on private enterprise." To understand to what extent the South African economy is characterized by competitive, laissez-faire forces it is necessary to trace, albeit in broad outline, the basic structure of the country and to give some idea of the tremendous growth that has taken place in the economy since the formation of the Union in 1910, and especially since World War II. This is particularly important in any assessment of the role played by government in the economic life of the nation.

The first European settlement took place at the Cape in 1652, when Jan van Riebeeck was sent out by the Dutch East India Company to establish a victualing station and half-way house to the East. One hundred and fifty years later the territory came under British rule. Gradually the hinterland was opened up and colonized until, in 1910, the four colonies then existing, the Cape, Transvaal, Orange Free State, and Natal, came together to constitute the Union of

---

* Professor Horwood is William Hudson Professor of Economics in the University of Natal. Mr. Burrows is Economist to the Department of African Affairs in the Southern Rhodesian Government.

South Africa with dominion status under the British Crown. All tariffs and other restrictions on interprovincial commerce were forthwith abolished.

By 1931 the Union had achieved sovereign independent status, but continued as an original member of the British Commonwealth of Nations. So matters continued for thirty years until 1961, when the decision was made to embrace a republican form of government. No sooner was this done than the Prime Minister severed the country's long connection with the Commonwealth.

South Africa covers an area of some 472,000 square miles, or a little over a sixth of the area of the United States of America. According to the 1960 census, the population comprises 15.8 millions, giving a density of settlement of only thirty-three persons per square mile. On the other hand, one-fifth of the total population (and two-fifths of the White population) reside in the five largest cities.

One result of the size of the country and the relative sparseness of settlement has been that the state has taken upon itself the establishment and running of most of the means of transport and communications. Another effect has been that the main markets have concentrated in the major cities (especially along the Witwatersrand and at Cape Town and Durban), so that the extension of the market-oriented secondary and tertiary industries has further increased the concentration of economic activity and population. Long distances from the main market centers have also tended to reduce the comparative advantage of local sources of raw materials vis-à-vis the imported product, and railway tariff policy has been designed, in part, to counteract this tendency.

Of particular importance to the South African economy is the racial structure of its population, not only because of the declared policy of the present government—which finds expression in the term *apartheid* or "separate development"—but also because many of the most fundamental differences among persons are accentuated in South Africa on racial lines. For instance, while many exceptions may be found to prove the rule, it is generally true that, for many reasons (not all as simple as they might seem), the country has inherited a form of society in which most of the skilled, educated, and well-paid workers are white, and where most of the less skilled, poorly educated, and badly paid workers are black or colored. This divergence of purchasing power on a racial basis leads in turn to marked differences in levels of nutrition, health, housing, and general stand-ards of living.

Over two-thirds (68 per cent) of the population consists of Afri-cans, and a further one-eighth is made up of Coloureds (mainly in the Cape) and Asiatics (mainly in Natal). The Whites account for a little under one-fifth of the total population.

In 1960 the gross national income of South Africa was officially estimated at £2,239 millions, of which 23 per cent was accounted for by manufacturing industries, while 16 per cent came from com-merce and finance and 10-14 per cent each from agriculture, mining, and the public authorities. The average per capita income in 1960 was roughly £141 a year (or £127 per head when allowance is taken of payments made to non-South African factors). While this is much lower than in most Western countries, it represents a standard of living considerably higher than in the rest of Africa.

South Africa's is a dependent economy in the sense that foreign trade and capital play a decisive part in its affairs. Merchandise im-ports and exports, taken together, represent fully 45 per cent of the gross national income. If gold exports are included, the proportion rises to well over half (56 per cent) of the national income.

The structure of the economy is perhaps best viewed in the light of the changes that have taken place since the formation of the Union in 1910. The most noteworthy feature of the fifty years of South Africa's history since Union has been the rapid progress made in almost all sectors of the economy, which for convenience is shown in summary form thus:

			Index
Population of South Africa	1910	5,878,000	100
	1960	15,841,000	269
Urban population	1921	1,934,000	100
	1960	6,970,000	360
Gross national income	1911–12	368	100
(£ million at 1958 prices)	1959–60	2,217	602

Per capita income	1911–12	£61	100
(at 1958 prices)	1959–60	£140	230
Employment on farms	1918	488,062	100
(excluding African farms)	1957	963,622	197
Employment in mines	1910	291,377	100
	1960	605,000	208
Employment on South African Railways	1910	52,595	100
	1960	216,700	412
Employment in manufacturing and	1915–16	97,020	100
construction industries	1960	790,000	814
Net output of manufacturing industries	1915–16	35	100
(£ million at 1958 prices)	1957–58	491	1,404
Electricity generated (KWH million)	1916–17	942	100
	1960	23,259	2,469
Commercial bank deposits (£ million	1913	95	100
at 1958 prices)	1960	565	595
Total government revenue	1911–12	39	100
(£ million at 1958 prices)	1960–61	355	910
Total imports (£ million	1910	95	100
at 1958 prices)	1960	546	575
Total exports (£ million	1910	145*	100
at 1958 prices)	1960	712**	491

* 61 per cent gold.
** 40 per cent gold.

What the economic implications of the fundamental change to a republican form of government outside the Commonwealth will be it is as yet too early to foretell with any precision. But certain tendencies are already apparent. It is, for instance, becoming increasingly uncertain that South Africa will be allowed to continue indefinitely to benefit from the preferential tariffs accorded to many of her products on Commonwealth markets in terms of the Empire Conference at Ottawa in 1932 (the contractual preferences agreed upon there have since been supplemented by certain "non-contractual" preferences). Official declarations that any termination of the existing preferential agreements can be made good by entering into bilateral agreements (with the same or other countries) may or may not be feasible. But the substitution of bilateral for the prevailing multilateral trading arrangements is in itself likely to mean a greater and not a smaller measure of intervention by government.

Another effect—and about this there is no doubt at all—concerns the movement of capital. Traditionally South Africa has always been a highly attractive field for the investment of overseas capital. A recent survey by the Bureau of Census and Statistics disclosed that by the end of 1959 British investment alone in South Africa was of the order of £900 million (of which well over half went to mining and manufacturing industry).

Of late, however, a drastic change has come about. Instead of a continuing inflow there is now (mid-1961) a serious outflow of capital—so serious, indeed, that the government has been impelled to attempt to counter the drain on the country's gold and foreign exchange reserves by intensifying the restrictions on imports (which it has done by way of higher tariffs and a stricter application of quantitative import and exchange controls); and by taking the unprecedented step, for South Africa, of placing an embargo on the withdrawal of external capital, except by special permission. Thus, so far as external trade is concerned the intervention by the state partakes of the nature both of "conformable" (tariffs) and "non-conformable" (import and exchange control) restrictive measures.

Banking and Finance

Perhaps nowhere is the essentially "mixed" nature of the South African economy better exemplified than in its banking and financial institutions. Commercial banking, organized on orthodox British lines, is and always has been in the hands of private enterprise. As in Britain, however, the commercial banks are obliged to conform to legislative enactments governing certain aspects of their operations. Despite the measure of concentration that has taken place as some of the bigger banks amalgamated with the smaller, banking remains clearly competitive. There are at the present time nine commercial banks, as well as a number of "people's banks" and other deposit-receiving institutions in South Africa.

Forty years ago a central bank, the South African Reserve Bank, was established, at a time when the Bank of England was the only central bank in the Commonwealth and the Federal Reserve Banks of the United States the only central banks on the entire American continent. The Reserve Bank was constituted by Act of Parliament as a joint-stock company with limited liability. No restrictions are placed on the ownership of its stock, save that £5,000 out of a capital of £1,000,000 is the maximum holding allowed to any stockholder whose holding did not exceed that figure by the time this provision was enacted in 1944. (Originally the participation of the commercial banks was limited to not more than 50 per cent of the capital stock, the remainder to be offered to the public at par and any unsubscribed balance to be taken up by the Treasury; but subsequent legislation relieved the banks of the obligation to hold Reserve Bank stock.)

The Bank is managed by a board of twelve directors, consisting of a governor, two deputy-governors (who are full-time officers), and three other directors appointed by the government; and six directors elected by the stockholders.

In the Reserve Bank reposes the sole right of note issue in South Africa; and, generally, it is empowered "to perform such other functions of bankers and financial agents as central banks customarily may perform." But its powers are not without restrictions and conditions. Thus, the Bank is required at all times to maintain in gold coin and bullion a reserve of not less than 25 per cent of its note issue and other liabilities to the public (less an amount equal to its foreign assets); and its duties include the obligation to fix and publish from time to time the rates at which it will discount the various classes of bills and to furnish certain prescribed information to the Treasury. Though the Reserve Bank is an autonomous statutory institution, it is, in practice, closely associated with the Treasury in matters of monetary policy.

Over the years the Bank has come to acquire a considerable influence over the discount and interest rates quoted by the commercial banks. "The commercial banks in South Africa," writes Dr. M. H. de Kock, Governor of the Reserve Bank, "usually adopt the local bank rate in the discount of bills which are considered to be eligible for discount by the Reserve Bank, while for other bills they charge higher rates varying according to the currency of the bill and the quality of the name or names thereon; and in respect of loans against gilt-edged securities for periods not exceeding three months, for which the Reserve Bank quotes a rate of ½ per cent above its discount rate, they also adopt that rate as a general rule."[1] This is generally true, though the banks appear to have been less prompt in following bank rate downward than upward.

The monetary authorities in South Africa have not been content to exercise control over credit entirely through bank rate, open market operations (carried out on a relatively limited scale), and moral suasion. To these devices there has recently been added another, which operates through variation of the statutory minimum reserve requirements of the commercial banks. Under the Banking Act of 1942 the commercial banks are required to maintain with the Reserve Bank a liquid reserve of not less than 10 per cent of their demand liabilities and 3 per cent of their time liabilities to the public. By amendment of the Reserve Bank Act, however, the Reserve Bank has since 1956 been empowered to require the commercial banks to increase their reserves above these limits (though this power may be exercised only if deemed in the "national interest" and with the concurrence of the Treasury); and, since 1961, also to reduce their reserves (to 6 per cent of their demand liabilities to the public). In this way moral suasion on the part of the monetary authority has been bolstered by statutory enforcement.

Since World War II concerted efforts have been made to develop an active money market in South Africa. In 1949 the government took the initiative in setting up by Act of Parliament the National Finance Corporation of South Africa. The Corporation is closely associated with the Reserve Bank, with which it shares a common chairman. All its directors are appointed by the government.

[1] M. H. de Kock, *Central Banking* (2nd ed.; London 1946), p. 184.

The Corporation's main function is the acceptance of call money on deposit at interest and the investment of its funds in Treasury bills, bills issued by the Land and Agricultural Bank, short- and medium-term gilt-edged securities and debentures of mining, industrial, and financial houses. It was formed at a time of considerable financial stringency when the government was borrowing freely from the Reserve Bank. A factor in its establishment at that time was no doubt the realization that the existence of such an institution would enable the government, by issuing Treasury bills to the Corporation, to reduce its own indebtedness to the Reserve Bank.

The Corporation is generally regarded as having succeeded in its objective of mobilizing what is loosely called "idle money" in the domestic economy. Its deposits reached nearly £200 million in 1954, though they fell to half that amount in the early part of 1961. In 1959 the aggregate volume of transactions passing through its depositors' accounts exceeded £2,000 million.

Further progress in the evolution of an efficient money market came with the establishment of the first accepting house or merchant bank, Union Acceptance Limited, in 1955 and, two years later, the first discount house, The Discount House of South Africa Limited. Both are modeled on the lines of their British counterparts and both are private undertakings. Parallel with these developments the government, in 1958, brought about further reform by introducing a system of weekly tenders for Treasury bills of ninety-one days' duration. Till then, Treasury bills had been issued at a predetermined rate of interest. In these ways have public and private enterprise gone hand in hand, as it were, to achieve the objective of a modern money market in South Africa.

Apart from the banks and discount houses, other important institutions in the capital market are, so far as public enterprise is concerned, the Land and Agricultural Bank and the Industrial Development Corporation; and, so far as private ownership is concerned, the insurance companies, building societies, mining houses, investment and trust companies, and the (Johannesburg) stock exchange. There are also the pension and social security funds, some of which are publicly administered and some privately; and the Industrial Finance Corporation, the ownership of which is predominantly private.

The Land Bank is a statutory body constituted by Act of Parliament in 1912. All its directors are appointed by the government.

Up to 1959 all its long-term funds were in the form of public monies voted by Parliament but in that year the Land Bank was empowered to issue debentures to the public to augment its capital. This it has subsequently done to the extent of £15 million. The Land Bank's main purpose is to provide credit facilities to farmers and to agricultural co-operatives and regulatory boards in the form of short-, intermediate-, and long-term loans. Its advances were of the order of £290 million at the end of 1960.

The Industrial Development Corporation of South Africa Limited (IDC) is a limited-liability, joint-stock enterprise established by Act of Parliament in 1940. Its entire share capital (at present about £60 million) is subscribed and all its directors are appointed by government. The Corporation's principal object is to assist private enterprise to develop industry on sound business principles by financial participation in industrial undertakings through the medium of loans and shares (both ordinary and preference).

The Act of 1940 enjoins the Corporation to examine every application for assistance "strictly on its economic merits, irrespective of all other considerations whatsoever"; and, "so far as may be practicable, the Corporation shall not be required to provide an unduly large proportion of the capital which is necessary" to give such assistance. Clearly, the original intention was that this public corporation would assist private industry primarily by making good the "gap" in the capital market to which the Macmillan Committee in the United Kingdom had drawn such sharp attention in 1931. (The "gap" relates to the difficulties said to confront small firms in obtaining their capital requirements.) This it proceeded to do by using its capital as a revolving fund to assist a variety of firms each on a relatively small scale. And this policy it adhered to throughout the first decade of its existence.

Once, however, the government decided, in 1950, to establish a large-scale plant to produce oil from coal, this policy went by the board. For the government resolved that the new public utility undertaking, the South African Coal, Oil and Gas Corporation Limited (SASOL), would be registered as a wholly owned subsidiary of the IDC, its entire capital to be provided by government through the agency of the parent corporation (the IDC). Presently the government extended this policy to the production of phosphates when it likewise caused the Phosphate Development Corporation (Pty.)

Ltd. (PHOSCOR) to be registered as a wholly owned subsidiary of the IDC, which took up all its share capital with funds provided by Parliament. In both cases the government appoints the majority of directors to the board, the rest being appointed by the IDC.

The effect of this change of policy has been greatly to extend the IDC's sphere of influence and to canalize the greater part (80 per cent) of its investments into two semi-public corporations, where it constitutes their entire capital, leaving but £13 million with private industry.

Complementing the activities of the IDC is another financial institution, the Industrial Finance Corporation (IFC), set up in 1957 on the initiative of the Reserve Bank and the IDC. Underlying its establishment was the fear that an excessive part of the country's savings was seeking investment in gilt-edged stocks and other relatively risk-free outlets and not enough in industrial equities. The IFC's aim is to assist in the financing of especially the bigger industrial undertakings, in conjunction with other sources of capital. It is clearly envisaged that it will revolve its funds by liquidating its investment in a particular enterprise as soon as that is practicable. The IFC is predominantly privately owned, about two-thirds of its share capital being held by non-government institutional investors like the commercial banks and the mining houses. The balance is held by the Reserve Bank and the IDC.

Insurance is a highly competitive and prosperous business in South Africa and is privately owned. The same applies to the building societies. Both, however, are subject to legislative enactments governing various aspects of their activities. Just as the Banking Act is administered by a senior civil servant, the Registrar of Banks, so are the Insurance and Building Society Acts administered by Registrars of Insurance and of Building Societies, respectively.

Among the more important of the legal restrictions on both insurance and building society operations are those relating to the nature of the assets which they may hold. Thus, every insurer shall retain in South Africa assets of a value not less than the amount of all his liabilities in respect of business carried on in the country. And at least 40 per cent of all his assets covering liabilities shall be made up of officially approved classes of investments (these being predominantly government securities and the stocks of public utilities).

The investment portfolios of the building societies are restricted to various approved classes of liquid assets, loans against deposits and building society shares, advances on the security of urban immovable property, and office premises; and detailed provisions are laid down governing the proportions of their funds that may be held in each class of asset. The Registrars of Insurance and of Building Societies are empowered to investigate the affairs of registered insurers and building societies, respectively.

In order of magnitude the assets of the principal financial institutions at the end of 1960 are, first, those of the commercial banks, followed by building societies, insurance companies, pension and social security funds, the Reserve Bank, trust monies (administered by the various finance houses), the Land and Agricultural Bank, the Post Office Savings Bank and Union Loan Certificates (both government institutions), discount and acceptance houses, the National Finance Corporation, and the hire-purchase finance houses. The figures range from £625 million in the case of the commercial banks to about £50 million in the case of hire purchase.

The Budget

In sympathy with a similar trend in most Western countries the relative importance of government finance has increased in South Africa over the last half century, although the extension in the size and influence of the public sector in this country has been less marked than is sometimes supposed. The increasing power of the central government has been restrained by a determination on the part of successive governments to keep the economy fundamentally in the hands of private enterprise.

One way of measuring the growth in public finance is to express the total expenditure of the government as a percentage of the gross national income. Such a comparison reveals that central government expenditure comprised some 15 per cent of the national income in 1912 and that, despite minor divergences from year to year, it remained at about that level during the whole period between the two wars. From 1941 to 1946 the figure averaged over 26 per cent and remained comparatively high during the early postwar years. During the last decade, however, aggregate expenditure has returned to about 20 per cent of the national income and has shown no indication of an increasing trend.

In the 1959-60 financial year the total expenditure of the central government amounted to some £428 million, which represented 19.1 per cent of the estimated gross national income for that year.[2] The importance of the role of government in the economy of South Africa far exceeds the total expenditure covered by the main budget, however. To the figure of 19 per cent already mentioned should be added the very substantial expenditure of the state-owned railways, airways and harbors, which amounts to almost £270 million in running costs and capital improvements, or a further 12 per cent of the national income.[3]

Table 1 contains these details, together with the comparable figures of fifty years ago.

TABLE 1. *Central Government and Railways Expenditures in South Africa in Relation to Gross National Income, 1911-12 and 1959-60*

	1911-12		1959-60	
	£ million	*Per cent of gross national income*	£ million	*Per cent of gross national income*
Central government expenditure				
Revenue account expenditure	16.5	12.6	302.6	13.5
Capital account expenditure	3.3	2.5	125.4	5.6
Total expenditure	19.8	15.1	428.0	19.1
South African Railways and Harbours Expenditure				
Revenue account expenditure	8.0	6.1	195.3	8.7
Capital account expenditure	1.7	1.3	74.5	3.3
Total SAR&H expenditure	9.7	7.4	269.8	12.0
Grand Total	29.5	22.5	697.8	31.1

Source: Union of South African, *Reports of the Controller and Auditor-General* (Pretoria): South Africa Reserve Bank, *Quarterly Bulletin of Statistics*; and *Official Yearbook of the Union.*

[2] The validity of the comparison between government expenditure and national income in any one year is somewhat reduced by the fact that, whereas the financial year ends on March 31, the national income is calculated for the year ending June 30.

[3] The Constitution (South Africa Act of 1909) provided for two separate budgets—what might be called a main (or central government) budget and a railway budget. For the present purpose, expenditure on Bantu education, which

If, in addition to the foregoing, the annual expenditure of the provincial and local urban authorities is taken into account, the outlay of the public sector rises to over 38 per cent of the national income. Finally, if we include the public corporations,[4] the seventeen agricultural control boards, and the other semi-public institutions and bodies, the total proportion would certainly rise beyond 40 per cent.

Even when this more comprehensive measure of state participation is used, however, it would not seem to show any greatly significant increase in recent years. Although the proportion of the national income falling within the budgets of the central, provincial and local authorities, and the railways, rose from about 35 per cent in 1938 to almost 40 per cent in 1960, there has been no marked upward trend over the last decade.

More indicative of increasing state participation are the figures of the country's gross capital formation, which are available only for the postwar years:

TABLE 2. *Average Annual Gross Capital Formation*

Period	Public Investment (£ million)	Total Investment (£ million)	Per cent Public
1946-49	76.8	251.0	30.6
1950-54	132.0	384.4	34.3
1955-59	206.0	517.6	39.8

Source: South African Reserve Bank, *Quarterly Bulletin of Statistics.*

These figures show that the public sector has accounted for an increasing proportion of the country's gross investment since the war.

A feature of South Africa's public finances in recent years has been the extent of the financing of the government's capital requirements out of current revenues. Thus, since 1953, almost £300 million has been transferred to the capital account out of annual budget surpluses.

since 1956 has had to be kept in a separate account, is included in ordinary revenue expenditure.

[4] E.g., ISCOR, the publicly-owned corporation which produces about 90 per cent of South Africa's steel requirements; ESCOM, which produces the bulk of the country's electricity; SASOL, the oil-from-coal project, and so on.

Some Specific Public Enterprises

The declared policy of successive South African governments has been that the production and distribution of goods and services should be in the hands of private enterprise, and in the main this policy has been adhered to. But in certain fields of activity, where private capital has not been forthcoming, or where for strategic or other reasons Parliament has regarded private enterprise as unsuitable owners or initiators, the state has stepped in as producer or distributor and has not hesitated to reinforce its position with monopolistic powers whenever it has thought that necessary. Some of the more important state-operated enterprises are discussed below.

The South African Railways and Harbours. With the exception of a few small private lines, all rail transport in South Africa is operated by the government-owned railways as a direct department of state. Management is vested in a general manager, and the administration and policy of the railways are controlled by the Minister of Transport in consultation with an advisory board.

The early economic development of South Africa, like that of other large territories, was at first closely tied to the expansion of its system of communications. The development of railways in South Africa really dates from the discovery of diamonds, for, although a short length of line was opened in Durban as early as 1860 and in the Cape a short while after, it was not until the development of important markets on the diamond fields, and later the gold fields, that it became essential to replace the ox-wagon with a faster and cheaper method of transportation. Only after adequate rail linkage to these important markets had been established, did the railway lines branch out laterally to areas of secondary importance.

The latter part of the nineteenth century saw intense rivalry and severe price competition between the Cape and Natal railways, and these conflicts arising over railway policies were some of the most important economic forces working in favor of the eventual union of the four territories now comprising the Republic.

The broad policy of the South African Railways and Harbours is that it should be operated as a non-profit-making public utility, but is expected to run on business lines. An accepted principle of policy provided for in the South Africa Act of 1909 is that the railways should be used to influence the pattern of development of the country, especially towards the opening up of the hinterland. This policy has been reflected not only in the pattern of rail expansion but also in the rating policy.

Apart from the extensive railroad network, the SAR&H owns all the major harbors, together with most of their facilities. The administration also operates a small fleet of coastal steamers. A younger, but rapidly growing branch of the SAR&H is the South African Airways, which controls all the major scheduled internal air services and a modern jet service to Europe.

Two other activities of the SAR&H merit special attention because of the considerable criticism which they arouse among representatives of the private sector of the economy. One is the motor transport section, which operates an extensive service for the movement of both goods and passenger traffic. Existing legislation vests considerable monopolistic powers in the administration as a motor carrier, even to the extent of restricting the right of a manufacturer to transport his own products in certain areas. The second important activity of the administration which has come in for considerable criticism is the processing and servicing of many of its requirements within its own workshops. Many spokesmen of private manufacturing claim that these services can and should be provided by private enterprise.

Posts and Telegraphs. The vast majority of all communications in South Africa is in the hands of the Department of Posts, Telegraphs and Telephones. The Department, which has its own Cabinet minister responsible to Parliament, provides postal services to the whole country, and operates as a member of the African Postal Union. In the 1959-60 financial year the Department's current revenues exceeded £40 million and it employed some 40,000 persons.[5]

Public and Semi-public Corporations and Companies. Holding an important place in the economy of South Africa are those public corporations which, although not government departments or necessarily answerable to Parliament, are nevertheless subject to a greater

[5] Broadcasting is in the hands of the South African Broadcasting Corporation, a public corporation financed entirely from public funds, and the board of directors of which is appointed by the government.

or lesser degree of governmental control. The two public enterprises which undoubtedly have had the greatest influence on the economy as a whole are the South African Iron and Steel Industrial Corporation (ISCOR) and the Electricity Supply Commission (ESCOM).

ISCOR began operations in 1934, and since then its aggregate production of some 20 million ingot tons has been one of the principal factors favoring the rapid development of South African industry, especially engineering projects. The history of ISCOR is a good example of the way in which government in South Africa has sometimes entered business only because private enterprise was not willing to provide what was regarded as a necessary or essentially strategic service. Originally it was intended that the government should own only one-seventh of the total share issue, but the effects of the depression and the disfavor with which the scheme was generally regarded by investors forced the government to take up nearly all of the remaining shares as well.

Today ISCOR produces about 90 per cent of the country's iron and steel output and is planning to increase the production of its two plants to 2,350,000 ingot tons a year. An unusual aspect of ISCOR's activities is that most of its raw material sources are owned either by itself or by associated companies.

ESCOM, whose principal function is quoted in the original Act of 1922 as "the provision of a cheap and abundant supply of electricity," has largely succeeded in its aim. Although many producers and some local authorities generate their own electricity, ESCOM supplies about four-fifths of the country's electrical power, which is a remarkably high proportion when the scattered nature of the population is taken into account. The Commission operates as a non-profit-making public utility, and the commissioners are appointed by the government. In its operations, however, the Commission is free from Parliamentary control and is expected to function very much like a private undertaking. It finances its own development very largely out of loan capital.

The extraction of oil from coal, like the production of iron and steel, was undertaken by the government only after private enterprise had failed, through no fault of its own, to exploit this field of activity. The South African Coal, Oil and Gas Corporation (SASOL) was established in 1950 as a public company, and has been financed to the extent of almost £50 million by the Industrial Development Corporation.

The desirability of establishing an oil-from-coal project seemed to arise from two considerations. On the one hand, government was concerned, from the strategic point of view, at the complete dependence of the economy upon outside sources of supply for all its oil requirements, since there are no known oil reserves in South Africa. On the other hand, the country is especially endowed with coal (the reserves being presently estimated at some 70,000 million tons), and enjoys the lowest pithead prices in the world.

SASOL at present produces petrol, oils, gas, and a considerable range of chemicals, which are sold in competition with the major private oil companies.[6] However, SASOL's production of petrol amounts to only about one-seventh of the country's requirements, and, although the possibility of setting up further plants has been mooted, it is unlikely that such developments will catch up with the country's expanding needs or that South Africa will ever be completely self-sufficient in strategic oils.

Some state-controlled enterprises of lesser importance are the production of super-phosphate fertilizers by PHOSCOR, which was also established for mainly strategic reasons and financed by the Industrial Development Corporation (it produces about a quarter of the country's requirements and expects to make South Africa independent of overseas supplies by 1963); and the ownership of the only factory producing technical DDT and BHC in the country. Other activities in which the state has monopolistic powers include broadcasting, printing for the public service, the sale of guano, and large sectors of education, while it competes with private enterprise in such activities as health services, housing, and saw milling.

Controls Affecting the Utilization and Mobility of Factors of Production

Apart from its direct participation in the processes of production and distribution, the South African Government has its greatest influence on the economy through the operation of numerous and powerful controls which, in toto, directly or indirectly affect the environment in which the private sector is free to operate. Many

---

[6] There is one privately-owned oil refinery in Durban, and another is being constructed in the same city.

of these controls, while differing in detail, are similar to those found elsewhere, but a few, which are particularly severe in their limitations on individual freedoms, are peculiar to South Africa.

Labor. In general, conditions of employment in South Africa are governed by a comprehensive range of legislation providing for minimum wages and conditions of work, industrial conciliation, apprenticeship systems, compensation for injury, unemployment registration and insurance, and so on, over a wide field. It is interesting to note that, up to 1956, very few enactments[7] on the statutes discriminated between workers in South Africa on racial lines, although a *de facto* color bar had arisen in most fields of employment as a result of social custom and the strength of the White labor unions. Such discrimination was not only condoned but also practiced by the state. It is true that an insidious type of discrimination was discernible in the fact that Africans were excluded, by definition, from the terms of certain acts dealing with labor matters, but it was only with the passing of the new Industrial Conciliation Act of 1956 that "job reservation" was introduced as an official policy.

The reservation of jobs on a racial basis has so far been enforced in only a minority of occupations in certain parts of South Africa, but the very existence of such a policy—and its potential extension to further fields of employment—constitutes a serious interference with individual freedom. Whatever the moral, political, or other arguments which may be used to justify the policy of job reservation, no one can deny that it offends laissez-faire principles through an arbitrary, artificial control over the mobility of labor and the freedom of the employer to hire labor.

To a large extent government interference in the South African labor market may be seen as an official ratification of the restrictive practices of the White labor unions. The position in South Africa has always been that the majority of skilled jobs are held by White

[7] The earliest Act embodying a *legal* color bar in South Africa was the Mines and Works Act of 1911, as amended by Act No. 26 of 1926. This provided that certificates of competency issued to certain skilled grades of mine workers could be issued only to Europeans and Coloureds. The Native Building Workers Act of 1951 prohibited employers in the building trade from employing Africans as skilled workers in non-African areas and enabled such controls to be applied to all employers of building artisans in such areas. It also prohibited the employment of White artisans in African areas in circumstances where African skilled workers were also hired.

workers, while most non-Whites are in unskilled categories. The result of this dichotomy is that White artisans have not unnaturally tried—and to a large extent succeeded—in entrenching their privileged position. The implementation of a *de facto* color bar (or more often a "color ceiling") can be seen in most fields of employment. Moreover, the official "civilized labor" and "fair wage" policies, while not manifestly discriminatory on racial lines, effectively operate to reserve skilled work in the public service for White workers. Appropriate clauses in contracts also extend these policies to private firms who tender for government work.

In fact, in those occupations where it applies, the principle of paying the "rate for the job" has had the effect of permanently debarring Africans (and, to a lesser extent Coloureds and Indians) from many of the skilled trades. This trend has been reinforced by other restrictive practices such as the closed-shop principle which, by restricting employees to union members, automatically debars Africans, for whom trade union membership has become increasingly difficult.

The mobility of labor in South Africa is inhibited in two main ways. First, occupational and industrial mobility is reduced, even among Whites, to the extent that the policy of job reservation is implemented, and also affected by certain of the restrictions already mentioned. Second, geographical mobility is curtailed by restrictions on the physical movement of persons and workers, mainly through the operations of the Group Areas Act, the various "pass laws," and certain other legislation.

The Group Areas Act of 1950, with its subsequent amendments, provides for the demarcation of particular areas in the towns for residence by specific racial groups, and to this end sets up controls over the ownership and occupation of land in certain proclaimed areas. This policy not only restricts the mobility of workers by controlling the areas in which they may reside, but also in many cases threatens the workers' livelihood, especially in the case of the Indian community. Many Indians are traders, and in some proclaimed areas these people have been forced to move their businesses out of town to the detriment of their trade.[8]

---

[8] The probable displacement of many of these traders is even more serious than it might at first appear because few of them could hope to find other jobs. There is already a serious unemployment problem among the Indians (mainly in Natal) owing to the restricted range of occupations open to them, their high natural rate

The group areas legislation has had the greatest impact on the lives of the Indian and Coloured sectors of the community since, in the first decade of its operation, comparatively few Whites have been affected by its provisions, while African residence and land ownership in urban areas is already controlled by other enabling legislation on the statutes. The most drastic of the restrictions on the mobility of Africans operate through the provisions of the various "pass laws," and especially through "influx control."

Influx control has its ostensible justification as a means of controlling the movement of Africans from the Reserves into the urban areas and thus avoiding some of the evils of overcrowding, slum formation, unemployment, and human misery which might otherwise accompany a too rapid process of industrialization. Today, however, the policy of influx control appears to have outgrown whatever justification it may have had and represents gross state interference over a wide range of human activity in South Africa.

The influx of Africans into urban areas is controlled according to the estimated demand for labor at the time, and it is the practice, within somewhat flexible limits, to proclaim which particular districts are free to supply each major urban area. In the past, once an African was permitted to enter an urban area and was granted a "permit to seek work" (initially valid for fourteen days), he was free to sell his labor to whomsoever he chose. In terms of a recent decision, however, registered Africans no longer receive such permits automatically, and it is now necessary for employers to lodge all requirements for African labor with the local labor bureau, which endeavors to supply suitable workers.

Except for the small but growing proportion of Africans who were born in the urban area and those who have worked in the area for a considerable time,[9] the temporary residence of Africans in a

of increase, and present slackness in a number of the industries in which they are employed. Trading is one of the few fields of activity in which Indians can operate as independent, self-employed workers.

[9] The Native (Urban Areas) Act of 1945, as amended by the Native Laws Amendment Act of 1957, lays down that no African shall remain in a proclaimed urban area for more than seventy-two hours unless:

(a) he was born and permanently resides there;

(b) he has worked continuously in such an area for the same employer for at least ten years, or has lawfully resided there for at least fifteen years and has continued to reside there and is not employed outside, and has not during either period or thereafter been sentenced to a fine exceeding £50 or to imprisonment for a period exceeding six months:

town is a privilege and not a right, and the refusal to accept what employment is offered to them, or an unsatisfactory history of unstable employment, may result in their being endorsed out of the area. In many cases, this could permanently debar an African from re-entering the area; nor might he be able to obtain permission to seek work anywhere else. This power to withhold from a worker the right to sell his labor in the best market, and which in some cases denies him the right to sell it at all, must be unique in a democratic state except in times of hostility.

One effect of these autocratic powers over African labor is materially to reduce the free mobility of African labor between jobs. While there is still a considerable degree of freedom of choice left to the individual, if no vacancy exists in the occupation of his choice within the specified time, the work-seeker will be faced with the choice of accepting whatever employment is offered to him, or employment in another (probably rural) area, or the termination of his right to be in the area. There are a number of occupations in the urban areas which, because of the very nature of the work involved (e.g., garbage removal), are unpopular among Africans. Instead of the disutility of such work being compensated by a rate of pay higher than in other menial occupations, however, labor is provided from among those work-seekers who would not otherwise be permitted to work in the area at all.

Apart from the restrictions on the free movement of persons and workers in South Africa that have already been mentioned, two final legal bars may be mentioned. The first is the very severe limitation imposed on the inter-provincial movement of Indians in South Africa, which, with very few exceptions, confines them to the province of their birth.[10] Unless ministerial approval is obtained, no Indian may migrate to another province either to live or work, although permits are granted for temporary visits not exceeding six weeks in duration.

This restriction is particularly severe in its effect on Natal, where over 80 per cent of South Africa's Indians live. There is in Natal a

---

(c) he/she is the wife, unmarried daughter, or son of less than taxable age (eighteen years) of any African mentioned in (a) or (b) and who resides with him.

In a recent statement, the Deputy Minister of Bantu Administration and Development suggested that legislation might be passed to insure that *no* Bantu had an automatic right to reside in a "White" urban area.

[10] Immigration Regulation Act No. 22 of 1913.

chronic shortage of employment for Indians and, although there are employment opportunities[11] in other provinces, these legal barriers to the free flow of workers have the effect of perpetuating the depressed conditions in which they are obliged to live and work.

The second additional limitation on the movement of persons in South Africa is the only restriction, apart from the group areas legislation, which affects the White group to any extent, although in the past it has probably had a more detrimental effect on Indians than on Whites. This restriction is the legal bar to settlement or employment in the African areas.

Land and Capital. Government in South Africa has usually left private enterprise as much latitude as possible in capital investment and, until the recent embargo on the withdrawal of foreign-held capital, has been particularly careful to leave the foreign investor free to bring in or withdraw his capital as he wishes. Government interference in investment in South Africa therefore appears in certain isolated fields only.

Some facets of the general structure of the economy which must, of course, affect the flow of investment and the utilization of all resources have already been mentioned. Apart from these indirect controls, which determine the economic climate in which private investment takes place, there are few restrictions on the free flow of capital within the country.

The greatest statutory obstacle to the free investment of capital in South Africa is the restriction on White enterprise in the underdeveloped "Bantu areas" of the country, which accommodate over a quarter of the total population and almost two-fifths of the Africans. In view of the poverty of most of the inhabitants of these areas, it could be expected that the returns on capital would be too low to attract private investment anyway, so that these restrictions may seem unnecessary to protect African interests. It is interesting to note, on the other hand, that Whites are not allowed to hold shares in the new Bantu Investment Corporation, which has been established by the government to foster the development of these areas.

Yet, realizing that European capital and entrepreneurship are necessary if the Reserves are to be developed, the present govern-

[11] One may cite the catering industry, in which Indians are usually favored as employees, as well as trading and certain branches of manufacturing industry.

ment has propounded the policy of "border area industries." This scheme would like to see the establishment of White industries on the edge of the African areas, with the intention of decentralizing industry and developing the Reserves, while at the same time decreasing (or at least halting the increase of) the number of Africans living in the principal urban centers.

As a deliberate policy of encouraging investment in new enterprises the "border areas" scheme does not yet show much promise. Industrialists, strictly on economic considerations, have in the past failed to see any attractions in the border areas as industrial sites and have continued to locate their factories either near their main markets or the source of raw materials.[12]

The exceptions have been a number of concerns (mainly clothing factories with a high proportion of African labor costs) which benefited from the ability to pay lower wages in the previously "uncontrolled" rural areas than in the major industrial areas. Even though wage determinations have now been made for these border areas, the government has accepted the principle that these areas should have lower minimum wage rates than the towns if labor productivity and costs of living are also lower.

Apart from wage differentiation, the government has announced a number of other discriminatory measures in an effort to encourage the development of border industries. These include financial assistance (possibly through the IDC) with the costs of moving existing factories to the border areas or of building new factories there; assistance with the provision of (White) housing; railway rate concessions; and increased capital depreciation allowances for fiscal purposes on factories and plants erected there.

Legislative measures designed to control the occupation and ownership of land in South Africa make a regular appearance in the statutes of the country. The Group Areas Act, which dictates for certain areas the racial occupation and ownership of land and defines the areas in which each racial group can live or earn a living, has already been mentioned. These restrictions have so far affected mainly the Coloureds and Indians in the urban areas. But a much older

---

[12] The Bantu areas fail in both respects. The low purchasing power of the Africans in these areas provides only a very limited and diffused market, while there are very few materials of any sort available for "export" from the Reserves which might form the basis of a processing or manufacturing industry.

and stringent series of enactments[13] (beginning with the Native Land Act of 1913) has shaped the policy in regard to the occupation of land by Africans. Under this legislation, Africans (over two-thirds of the total population) are for the most part debarred from owning land on freehold title. With few exceptions, African ownership of land is restricted to the Native Reserve areas, and even here land tenure is on a tribal basis and the individual has no rights of disposal over the land he holds.

The *occupation* of land and property by Africans is also heavily circumscribed. Outside their own Reserve areas, the Africans are largely confined to the recognized locations and villages set aside for their occupation, to municipal and private hostels and barracks, and to the private accommodation provided for their employees by private householders and, in the rural areas, by White farmers.

Apart from this racial legislation (which has been discussed earlier) and the powers of local planning authorities over the use of land, there are very considerable latent powers vested in the Natural Resources Development Council, in terms of the Natural Resources Development Act of 1947 (as amended). In a number of controlled areas, embracing some 12,000 square miles of territory, no change in the use of land can legally be made without the prior permission of the Minister of Economic Affairs. Most of the delimited land is for mining purposes, but it is clear that the state has the statutory power to extend the provisions of the enabling legislation to other and bigger areas.

COMPETITIVE VS. MONOPOLISTIC CHARACTERISTICS OF THE SOUTH AFRICAN ECONOMY

Structural and Institutional Restrictions on Competition in South Africa

South Africa is a young country, in the economic sense, in which competition is limited by natural environmental conditions. In the first place, in some branches of industry, where modern technological processes demand large capital investments, a single large firm (or

[13] For a fuller description of the legislation see, for example, chaps. vii and xi in *Handbook of Race Relations in South Africa* (Cape Town: Oxford University Press, 1949).

a few firms) may be able to meet the total demand for a product
and do so more efficiently than could a large number of smaller
firms. Moreover, the single producer in South Africa is protected
not only in varying degrees by customs tariffs, but also by geographical separation from the major producing areas in the world.

Second, a degree of natural immunity against competition is afforded to producers by the scattered nature of the market. Although
a large part of the South African market is concentrated in the main
urban areas,[14] their relative dispersion[15] provides the local producer
with a certain amount of protection from his competitors in the other
cities—especially in respect of articles of low specific value.

Evidence of monopolistic practices is no easier to obtain in South
Africa than elsewhere, and for that reason we quote at some length
from the 1951 Report No. 327 of the Board of Trade and Industries
on the Regulation of Monopolistic Conditions. Unfortunately, in
preparing its report, the Board decided against assembling empirical
data on the grounds of shortage of time and staff, but the following
opinions expressed by the Board, on the basis of many years' intimate
association with commerce and industry, must be given considerable
weight:

Judging by the number of complaints received by the Department of
Commerce and Industries, and also by the experience of the Board, such
activities [monopolistic abuses] are fairly common in the Union. Thus,
even in these times of economic prosperity, many trade associations have
exclusive dealing arrangements with local or oversea manufacturers, and
employ these to restrict competition, making it difficult for newcomers to
enter the trade and employing the 'stop list' to cut off recalcitrant members from supplies . . . . Though as a whole the existing system of competition works satisfactorily, there definitely are harmful conditions and
practices . . . . In the Union, with its often limited market, monopolistic
situations are a frequent occurrence, and there has in the past been definite proof that some persons have exploited these situations. It is true
that in due course the expansion of the economy will tend to rectify this,

[14] In 1960 the Witwatersrand (including Pretoria), Cape Town and Durban
accounted for 25 per cent of the South African population and 46 per cent of
the White population. Allowing for the much greater purchasing power of the
Whites, between one-third and two-fifths of the total South African market probably lies in these three areas.

[15] For example, the distances by rail between the three largest markets are:
Johannesburg to Cape Town, 949 Miles; Johannesburg to Durban, 484 miles;
Durban to Cape Town, 1,250 miles.

but progress may be unnecessarily retarded by unwarranted restriction-ism. Moreover, a large proportion of the country's population consists of relatively ignorant consumer-buyers, and the opportunities for exploitation are therefore enhanced.[16]

Apart from the natural conditions favoring restrictive practices, the development of monopolistic powers has been made easier by the passive attitude of government, which has in the past tended to turn a blind eye to all but the worst monopolistic abuses. Governmental policy in this respect has been largely guided by the recommendations of the Board of Trade and Industries, which has steadfastly refused to condemn monopolistic elements *per se,* and which has advocated action only when the monopolistic practices are clearly detrimental to the public interest.

The Board of Trade has also argued the positive aspects of monopoly in a new and expanding economy—such as the attraction of new (and especially foreign) capital to industries showing a higher-than-normal profit and the better utilization of managerial skill and other scarce resources.[17]

Some Examples of Monopolistic Practices in South Africa

The true monopolist is as rare in South Africa as in any other country. But four varieties of monopolistic activity may be taken as typical of a considerable part of the South African economy. First, there is the single and (by South African standards) large firm which, by virtue of its dominant position in the market, must be regarded as a quasi-monopolist. Such an enterprise, which may operate either only one or several plants in the country, is subject to competition only from minor substitutes of smaller firms or from imported products and the potential threat of local competition.

Second, and more common, is the oligopolistic market structure, in which a few medium-sized firms share the market between them. Frequently, but not inevitably, the natural protection provided by the diffusion of the market and other factors is further bolstered by collusive agreements on the regulation of the market. On the other

[16] Board of Trade and Industries, Report No. 327, *On the Regulation of Monopolistic Conditions* (Pretoria, 1951), par. 255-256.

[17] The provisions of anti-monoply legislation in South Africa are discussed below, pp. 497-498.

hand, this group also contains some of the most fiercely competitive branches of economic activity in South Africa.

Third are the large organizations, found in mining and to a lesser extent manufacturing, which carry on a number of diversified activities through a network of affiliated companies. The controlling authority may be a holding-cum-finance company which exerts, through its many-sided interests, considerable power in a number of directions. It is usually difficult for the outside observer to analyze such an organization or to disentangle its intricate financial connections.

The fourth typically restrictive activity is the monopolistic power held by the European farming community in South Africa, exercised through co-operative ventures and the agricultural control boards. These will be discussed in more detail below.

Agriculture. One of the most controversial facets of the South African economy is the monopolistic power granted to the farming community under the Marketing Act of 1937, which, after many years of fluctuating prices and fortunes, consolidated and extended the existing measures aimed at assisting the marketing of agricultural produce. In terms of the Act, machinery is provided for the formation of control boards, which are given considerable powers over the production and distribution of particular commodities. The provisions of the Act are administered by a National Marketing Council, which has at its disposal an advisory consumers' committee.

The original purposes of the Act were to increase the productivity of agriculture, to achieve stability in the prices of agricultural products, and to secure a more efficient marketing system for these products. However, it has been used very largely as a method of advancing the sectional interests of the farming community—mainly by procuring profitable prices—and has not been particularly concerned with the more primary aim of supplying the nutritional needs of the nation at low cost.

The monopolistic powers of the control boards are exercised mainly through the maintenance or enhancement of prices by price control or, if deemed necessary, by restricting output, limiting the number of producers, overseas dumping, or by other methods of restricting competition in the domestic market. These monopolistic practices are made possible by a producers' majority on control boards and exemption from the provisions of the existing anti-monopoly legislation (see pp. 497-498, below).

It is possible that the very considerable power wielded by the agricultural control boards is not generally realized. The seventeen boards now in existence[18] control no less than 70 per cent of the total value of agricultural and pastoral commodities produced in South Africa.[19] Some idea of their power (in comparison, for example, with the power of a large monopolistic manufacturing enterprise) can be gauged by looking at the scale of operations of the Mealie Industry Control Board, which in 1957-58 sold or exported over 36 million bags of maize, valued at some £57 million.

Some of the boards are limited in the extent to which they can control the market by the need to export a large proportion of their particular commodity. This must apply especially to the three fruit control boards. With other products, notably tobacco, the monopolistic powers of the producers are severely restricted by the countervailing power of a semi-monopsonistic market. Yet again, the market for wool—South Africa's most important agricultural product and largest export after gold—is sold on a near-perfect international market. The South African Wool Board (which does not fall under the provisions of the Marketing Act), apart from maintaining an equalization account, limits its functions to research, publicity, and general promotional activities.

There is a considerable measure of disagreement among commentators on how far the South African Marketing Act has achieved its goal. The control of agricultural marketing is a topic that never fails to bring to light the more fundamental question of the proper economic functions of the State, and the diversity of views held partly reflects the controversy between the planners and the champions of laissez faire.[20] While it would appear that the control boards

[18] The commodities falling under the jurisdiction of these boards are: mealies (maize) and kaffircorn (millet); dairying (there is a separate control board to administer the marketing of milk in Cape Town); wheat, barley, oats, rye, and their milling; tobacco; chicory; deciduous fruit; citrus fruit; and dried fruit; oilseeds; lucerne seed; potatoes; dried beans; eggs; livestock and meat; rooibos tea; and bananas.

[19] *Annual Report of the Secretary for Agricultural Economics and Marketing, 1958/59* (Pretoria, 1960), p. 5.

[20] Perhaps the best critical appraisal of the issues involved in the controlled marketing of agricultural products in South Africa is that published by a group of six Cape Town economists in 1940. Cf. W. H. Hutt *et al.*: "Economists' Protest," *South African Journal of Economics*, VIII, no. 1 (1940), 37.

have achieved a greater degree of national self-sufficiency in agricultural and pastoral products, there is no general agreement on whether the monopolistic powers of the boards have led to any increase in the efficiency of the production and distribution of agricultural products. An even more profound difference of opinion exists in regard to the soundness of the very aims of the Marketing Act, especially the apparent disregard for the welfare of consumers and the justification for the end of self-sufficiency.

Apart from the statutory control boards, there are over 300 agricultural co-operatives in South Africa—most of which are primarily designed as marketing organizations, and which had a membership of over 280,000 in 1959. Although the wide range of conditions prevailing permits of no easy characterization of co-operative activity as a whole, one can assume varying degrees of both monopolistic and monopsonistic practices in this field. In a few cases—notably tobacco—there is compulsory marketing through agricultural co-operatives.

Mining. The South African mining industry is dominated by the production of gold and diamonds, which, in turn, are controlled by two vast and quite remarkable organizations—the Transvaal and Orange Free State Chamber of Mines and De Beers Consolidated Mines. Both industries, although in very different ways, approximate in their market structures an extreme example of classical economic theory.

The gold mining industry, through the Chamber of Mines, sells virtually its whole output to the South African Reserve Bank, which in turn disposes of the gold according to the needs of the country's balance of payments and financial position. For some years now, most of South Africa's gold has been sold on the London Gold Market, where it fetches a price higher than the official $35 a fine ounce. The South African gold mining industry, therefore, although producing about half of the world's new gold each year, is faced with what amounts to a perfectly elastic demand curve—or, more exactly, a demand curve that becomes perfectly elastic at the price of $35. The position must be unique for an industry the size of the gold mining industry.[21]

[21] In 1960 the South African gold mines produced gold to the value of £265 million and employed over 455,000 workers.

The result of this peculiar market structure is that the gold producers are completely unable to influence the official price, although they might in theory (but would not try in practice to) increase the free market price by restricting output. Apart from advancing academic arguments in favor of an increase in the price of gold, therefore, the gold producers can only increase their profits by expanding output or increasing efficiency. Costs become of paramount importance and the industry is particularly vulnerable to inflationary tendencies since it cannot pass on higher costs to the consumer.

For these reasons, the monopolistic character of the industry is exercised mainly through its role as South Africa's largest single private consumer, and it tends to be a price leader as a *purchaser* of goods and services. This price leadership has been apparent in the market for explosives and certain other stores as well as the scale of wages paid to certain classes of artisan labor. The shift wages paid to African mine workers especially are often the migrant worker's first experience of contractual labor, whether he comes from within South Africa of from across her borders.

The co-operative arrangements practiced by the gold-mining companies in recruiting and rationing African labor provide the most telling example of labor monopsony in South Africa; though their power to influence wage levels may have been limited somewhat by the growth of the economy as a whole over the last two or three decades—a development which has tended to raise the supply price of African labor generally and probably made the supply to the gold mines more elastic.

The diamond industry, on the other hand, is a classical example of a monopoly controlling the supply of a commodity to preserve a scarcity value. Unlike the gold mines, the diamond industry is not primarily concerned with costs of production, but with adjusting sales to estimated demand.

The De Beers diamond organization, through its Diamond Purchasing and Trading Company and Industrial Distributors Limited, possesses an almost complete monopoly in the world sale of natural gem and industrial diamonds (including even the sale of Russian stones in the free world). Price is maintained by adjusting sales on a quota basis among the associated producers, according to variations in the demand.

Like all monopolies, the De Beers corporation would still be highly vulnerable to new outside competition if such competition were sufficiently large and effective. In this respect, the manufacture of artificial diamonds presents an interesting example of the potential threat which faces most monopolies. So far, however, only the market for industrial diamonds has been affected, as no success has yet been achieved with the manufacture of artificial gem stones.

Since World War II the De Beers group has spread its interests to a greater extent than before and has invested large amounts in other branches of mining and in manufacturing industry. In the process it has become much more than a diamond monopoly.

Monopolistic characteristics are also apparent in other sections of the South African mining industry. Coal mining is an interesting example. To a large extent, coal in South Africa may be regarded as a differentiated product, with the various mines producing and marketing coals of different qualities for different uses. The industry is controlled by three producers' associations, but their power is limited by the fact that 60 per cent of the coal mined in South Africa is consumed by the Electricity Supply Commission and the South African Railways—both of which can exert strong pressure as buyers. A further considerable quantity is consumed by the gold mines.

Manufacturing Industry. A number of factors tend to favor monopolistic market structures in manufacturing in South Africa, the most important of which is the limited size of the market. Restricted demand often results in the market's being supplied either by a comparatively small oligopolistic group of firms, or by one firm operating several plants in different parts of the country, or, sometimes, by one firm operating only a single plant.

The one-firm, one-plant type of monopoly is seldom found in South Africa, particularly in private manufacturing. But there are a number of organizations which operate more than one plant, while many firms, although not the only producers in their field, occupy a dominant position in the industry and must be assumed to exert a considerable influence on the price-setting mechanism. Some examples of industries which, on the face of it, tend towards monopolistic structure are iron and steel, laundry soaps, matches, explosives, alcoholic beverages, insecticides, power generation, drugs and certain chemicals, super phosphates, and paper and board.

More common is the commodity the market for which is shared

among a few large producers, which often have overseas affiliations. Some of the better-known examples of such oligopolistic markets are those for cigarettes, paints, fertilizers, pneumatic tires, oil products, motor vehicles (assembly), confectionery, cement, fruit and vegetable canning, edible oils, toilet requisites, and detergents.

Vertical integration takes place fairly frequently in South African industry, especially (according to the Board of Trade and Industries)[22] in the metal, textile, chemical, and timber industries. Sometimes the extension of a firm's activities to incorporate the production of its raw materials may be an economically desirable development, especially if costs are thereby reduced or if adequate supplies of suitable materials could otherwise not be secured. At other times, a firm may extend its operations merely to increase its monopolistic powers over competitors.

For the reason that their activities are common knowledge, the most conspicuous examples of vertically integrated enterprises in South Africa are the publicly owned corporations such as ISCOR, which owns most of the raw materials (such as iron, coking coal, and manganese) used in the production of its steel, and also markets its products through a subsidiary company. SASOL also owns all the processes of production and distribution from the mining of the raw coal to the sale of the refined petrol and other products. Vertical co-operation, in which the producers and the suppliers join together to restrict entry and control the supplies of materials, is seen in its most effective form in the South African printing industry.[23]

Finally, there are in South Africa the large financial corporations, the ramifications of which often cover a wide range of affiliated companies, especially in mining and to a lesser extent manufacturing. Often these groups take the form of finance and holding companies and are responsible for interconnections (through their common interests) among industries such as gold, paper, and chrome; or gold, coal, cement, and timber; or diamonds, explosives, and fertilizers. While it is impossible in a paper of this length to attempt a satisfactory comment on these organizations, one argument that has been put forward in their favor is that they have a very large prestige

[22] Board of Trade and Industries, *Report No. 327*, par. 206.
[23] Board of Trade and Industries, *Report No. 353* on *The Printing Industry*. (Pretoria, 1955), chap. iii.

value in a young and expanding country—especially in attracting investment capital from overseas.[24] This must certainly be true.

The only statistical data of a structural nature which are available in South Africa come from the annual Censuses of Industrial Establishments. This information reveals that, whereas only 22 per cent of workers employed in secondary industry in 1938 were working in "large" factories (i.e., those employing 500 persons or more), this proportion had risen to 33 per cent by 1953. Moreover, the average labor force of factories over this period increased from 34 to 51 workers. It is doubtful, however, whether this kind of information on the concentration of industry can be used to suggest more than the possibility of a reduction in competition. Especially in a young country, such a trend is likely to be a manifestation of a normal expansion of existing firms in response to a growing market.

Wholesale and Retail Trade. What has already been said about the prevalence of trade associations applies to wholesaling and retailing as well, especially in regard to price fixing and the determination of price margins. Resale price maintenance is prevalent throughout the distributive trade.

On the structural side, the monopolistic elements of the wholesale and retail trade vary, depending largely on the concentration of the market. In the rural areas the far-flung "general store" has a very considerable monopoly power, which is increased the greater variety of miscellaneous commodities it can carry. The rural filling station, chemist, and hotel may enjoy similar advantages from their relative geographical isolation.

In the towns, however, especially in the larger cities, businesses tend to concentrate in a single commercial center, and even separate branches of the retail trade may congregate together. This naturally makes for keen competition and tends to weaken whatever agreements in favor of concerted action that may exist. Active competition is usually noticeable in such branches of the retail trade as general dealers (grocers), filling stations, and furniture dealers in the major urban areas.

Transport and Communications. As described in the section on public enterprise, transport and communications in South Africa are

[24] Board of Trade and Industries, *Report No. 327*, par. 217.

mostly either undertaken or strictly controlled by government enterprises. Thus virtually all rail and air traffic is provided by the state, under statutory monopolistic powers, while competition from motor carrier transport is strictly controlled. In passenger transport, private enterprise is restricted to a number of large bus service companies in the urban areas, with either *de facto* or *de jure* monopoly powers, and to taxi services, air charter companies, and a number of specialized transport services.

Labor. Restrictive practices by organized labor are excluded from the provisions of anti-monopolistic legislation in South Africa, which means that employees are free—within the framework of the Industrial Conciliation Act and other controlling legislation—to apply as many restrictions as their bargaining power will permit. Generally speaking, the European labor force in South Africa is well organized, and the closed shop and other restrictive practices are widespread.[25] The bargaining power of White labor was particularly strengthened during World War II and in the fifteen years immediately afterwards, when over-full employment caused a general shortage of skilled workers and employers were frequently compelled to concede to the demands of organized labor.

This was very clearly brought out in the course of a comprehensive empirical investigation into the effects upon prices (and the position of consumers in general) of industrial and wage legislation in South Africa after World War II.[26] The investigation cited several instances of the embarrassment suffered by employers where they tried to withstand the demands of labor unions; and almost as many where manufacturers, being in a position to exercise price discretion, seemed only too ready to concede the claims for higher wages.

Dealing with certain monopolistic elements in the situation, the investigators argued that "Industrial councils should not be in a

[25] Restrictive practices by labor are seen in an extreme form in South Africa in the printing industry, where the South African Typographical Union has succeeded in obtaining wages and conditions of work for its members which are appreciably better than those in other industries. The Union forced the statutory recognition of the closed-shop principle even before the Great Depression, and has since assumed considerable power in the determination of conditions of work and entry, etc.

[26] O. P. F. Horwood and Sheila T. van der Horst, *Memorandum of Evidence to the Industrial Legislation Commission of Enquiry, 1949* (mimeographed). This memorandum is referred to in the Report of the Commission, published as U. G. no. 62 of 1951 (*The Cape Times*, Cape Town).

position to strike a bargain in secret at the expense of the community"; and they went on to recommend the establishment of "an impartial Industrial Tribunal [which] should exercise some of the present functions of the Minister of Labour with regard to the supervision of Industrial Council and Wage Board agreements and awards." They claimed that "the creation of a tribunal of this kind would tend to remove wage disputes from the political arena and provide a permanent and competent authority to act as arbitrators in disputes." The recommendation found favor with the Commission of Enquiry and was subsequently implemented by government (Industrial Conciliation Act of 1956).

The power of non-White labor is generally much less than that of the Whites. Africans are excluded from the provisions of the Industrial Conciliation Act,[27] and any unions which they may form are not officially recognized and operate under extreme difficulty. The weak bargaining power of the African results chiefly from the prevailing attitude among employers that African workers are homogeneous and largely interchangeable. Even today there still exists a surplus of African labor, residing both in the Reserves and in the towns, and, in the absence of effective union discipline, the occasional strike by Africans is usually broken at once by the mass dismissal and replacement of the strikers.

Those Coloureds and Asiatics who work in skilled or semiskilled occupations are in a better situation and fall under the same legislation as Whites. In terms of the amending Industrial Conciliation Act of 1959, however, no new "mixed" (i.e., inter-racial) trade unions may be registered, while under the influence of the Act many existing unions have broken up into separate unions organized on racial lines. It can be expected that this fragmentation will weaken the whole trade union movement, and especially the non-White unions.

Anti-monopoly Forces

The previous section pointed to some of the reasons why monopolistic and restrictive practices are common in the South African economy and gave some of the more obvious examples of such practices.

[27] Industrial conciliation for Africans is covered by the Native Labour (Settlement of Disputes) Act of 1953.

There are, however, a number of more or less effective curbs to the power and extension of the monopolistic elements in the economy.

Legislation. The first comprehensive legislative measures restricting the scope of monopolistic practices was the Monopolistic Conditions Act of 1955 (as amended). Before this, monopolistic abuses were for the most part left to the courts to control by common law.[28] In terms of the 1955 enactment, the Minister of Economic Affairs may direct the Board of Trade and Industries to investigate any practice which, over a wide field of activity, "restricts competition." On the recommendation of the Board of Trade and Industries, the Minister has considerable powers to control monopolistic practices, mainly through publicity, the potential suspension of custom tariff protection, or by ordering a monopolist to refrain from offensive practices at the risk of moderately heavy penalties.

The Act specifically excludes the operations of agricultural producers' organizations and control boards, and employees' organizations, nor does it cut across the provisions of the Patents Act or the Design, Trade Marks and Copyright Act. An important principle of the Act which has guided the control of monopoly in South Africa is that monopolistic practices should not be condemned per se, but should be curtailed or terminated only if they can be shown to be against the interests of the community as a whole. The Board of Trade and Industries has in the past not been over-anxious to condemn monopolistic elements, and is always willing to concede whatever positive advantages a monopolistic condition may have.[29] One of the Board's contentions is that a high profit margin in a growing economy may be just what is needed to attract new entrants to an industry and hence foster competition.

Up to the present the powers of compulsion provided for in the Act have been exercised on only a few occasions, and the measure serves mainly as a deterrent to the more obvious and harmful abuses

[28] See D. V. Cowen, "A Survey of the Law relating to the Control of Monopoly in South Africa," *South African Journal of Economics*, XVIII, No. 2 (1950), 124-147.

[29] For example, four reports have now been published by the Board of Trade under the Monopolistic Conditions Act, dealing with the manufacture and distribution of tires, liquor, hardware and sanitaryware, and biscuits (including part of the wholesale grocery trade). All four industries revealed malpractices, but the Board felt that the monopolistic conditions existing in the tire and liquor industries were justified because they were in the public's interest.

of monopolistic power. It cannot be said to have affected the great majority of monopolistic elements permeating the South African economy.

Countervailing Forces. Some of the more important countervailing forces operating in the South African economy have already been mentioned from time to time in earlier sections. These revolve mainly around the mines, railways, and agricultural co-operatives as large and powerful consumers of goods and services.

In agriculture, the Marketing Act itself was originally conceived as a means of strengthening the farmers' supposed weak bargaining position vis-à-vis the main purchasers of agricultural output. Under legal protection, the agricultural industry has swung the balance of power so much in its favor, however, that there would seem to be a strong case for providing the consumer with a more effective means of safeguarding his interests.

The South African Railways, with a monopoly on rail transport, are large enough consumers of coal and steel to affect the market for these products, and must also be assumed to influence wage rates over a wide range of occupations. The mines (especially the gold mines), apart from their coal and power requirements, are the largest consumer of explosives, which are produced by a single organization in South Africa. Similarly, the oligopolistic cigarette manufacturing industry is faced with a powerful tobacco producers' organization.

Rate of Expansion. To the extent that certain monopolistic elements in the South African economy are a result of the smallness of the local market, one may expect these elements to wane as the market expands and makes it profitable for new firms to enter. Of course, it is possible that the existing firms with monopolistic powers may be able to entrench some of these powers, and that in certain instances they may be able to keep out competitors and still supply the expanding requirements of the market. In general, however, a rapid rate of growth such as the South African economy has experienced since the late thirties (though there have been signs of a slowing down in the last year or two) would seem to weaken the powers of both monopolists and cartels to the extent of making it easier for a competitor to enter the market with a more or less close substitute.

Competition from Imports. However strong a monopolist may be in his own country, he very seldom has any control over the price, quality, or production of foreign goods, and the imported goods (or the threat of competition from imported goods) is usually a very real factor to be reckoned with in making his price and output decisions. In South Africa, some enterprises such as the railways are complete monopolies in the sense that imports are irrelevant, while others are safeguarded from overseas competition by the low specific value of their product or by import embargoes. Most branches of manufacturing, however, are faced by foreign competition to some degree or other, depending upon the degree of natural immunity afforded by freight charges and the artificial protection granted by tariffs.

The extension of monopolistic conditions in South Africa has, on the whole, been restrained by a liberal trade policy which has, except in periods of particular financial stringency, permitted a substantial inflow of foreign goods, many of which compete with locally produced articles. That neither the tariff structure nor the long distances separating the South African market from the overseas producers has been a serious bar to the importation of commodities is shown by the very high propensity to import in South Africa. In 1960 imports into the country represented almost a quarter of the gross national income, while in the peak year 1948, before import control was resorted to, imports amounted to about 40 per cent of the national income.

Moreover, there still persists a certain prejudice against locally made goods and a preference for the imported product, even when a local article can be bought at a lower price. This attitude is apparently not uncommon in newly industrialized countries and, apart from any other considerations, may be assumed to restrain the local manufacturers' ability to create monopolistic conditions. The countervailing power of a free inflow of imports seems likely to be impaired, however, as a result of a vigorous propaganda campaign now being sponsored by the state and organized commerce and industry, and by an increasing tendency for the government to favor a nationalistic policy towards the production of goods for the home market.

Public Opinion. The general public's attitude towards monopolistic practices is difficult to assess, and to the writers' knowledge, no studies have been carried out in this field in South Africa. It is thought probable that in general there is no strong adverse feeling towards monopolistic practices as such, but that specific abuses would be condemned if the general public were aware of their existence.[30]

More condemnatory attitudes seem to exist towards any extension in the sphere of public enterprise, but even if this is so, it may be because the public is better informed on the practices or malpractices of the state than those of private individuals and companies.

CONCLUSION

The position of the state in the South African economy is anomalous in that, while participation in and direct control over private enterprise appear to be less marked than in some other Western countries, a number of indirect controls, operating mainly against the freedom of the individual, must be viewed as a very severe departure from laissez-faire principles.

On the one hand, we sometimes mark a hesitance—almost a reluctance—on the part of the state to interfere with the activities of private enterprise unless such interference is thought really necessary. Because of this, the economy in many ways remains free to follow market forces, limited only by controlling legislation which is, in the main, common to all Western-type democracies. Thus, for example, the gold mining industry, which has been the cornerstone of the South African economy for so long and in 1960 still paid for more than half of the country's aggregate imports, is left completely in the hands of private enterprise. So too, by and large, is the next biggest exporter, the wool industry.

On the other hand, few other countries in the free world can have legislation on their statutes which imposes as severe restrictions on individual freedoms as do the Industrial Conciliation (Job Reservation) Act, the Group Areas Act, and the laws controlling the movements of Africans and Indians. It is in the light of this kind of anomaly that the degree of competitiveness in the South African economy calls for most critical appraisal.

[30] As the word "monopoly" tends to be emotive, one suspects that more unfavorable attitudes may exist towards the term itself than towards the specific activities which it implies.

12

Competition and Regulation in the West Indies

*W. Arthur Lewis**

General Description

The West Indies consists of a number of islands forming an archipelago which encloses the Caribbean Sea. British islands are intermingled with French, Dutch, American, and independent territories. All the British islands except the Virgin Islands were federated in 1958 under the name "The West Indies."[1] Two mainland territories, British Honduras in Central America and British Guiana in South America, have had close associations with the British islands, and are usually included with the West Indies in discussions of economic and other matters. The Bahama Islands, on the other hand, have never been associated with the other islands and are not included in this paper.

Each of the larger islands has smaller islands associated with it in a single administrative unit which has its own legislature and makes its own laws. The populations of these units, according to the 1960 censuses, are as follows:

Jamaica	1,620,000
Trinidad and Tobago	826,000
Barbados	232,000
Grenada	89,000
St. Lucia	86,000
St. Vincent	80,000
Dominica	60,000
St. Kitts-Nevis	57,000

* The author is Vice-Chancellor of the University of the West Indies.
[1] The Federation of the West Indies has since been dissolved.

Antigua	54,000
Montserrat	12,000
Total, "The West Indies"	3,116,000
British Guiana	559,000
British Honduras	90,000
British Virgin Islands	7,000
Total	3,772,000

Grenada, St. Lucia, St. Vincent, and Dominica are known as the Windward Islands; St. Kitts-Nevis, Antigua, and Montserrat as the Leeward Islands. These were the titles of former administrative groupings, now abandoned.

Agriculture is the largest occupation in the West Indies, even in Trinidad, where the contribution of agriculture to gross domestic product is less than half the contribution of the oil industry. The census details for 1960 are not yet available. The 1946 Census gave the industrial distribution of Trinidad's population as follows:

	per cent
Agriculture, including sugar milling	30
Manufacture	14
Oil mining and refining	5
Construction	10
Transport and communications	6
Trade and finance	9
Services	23
Unclassified	3
	100

Since the end of World War II, the most striking developments have been:

(1) The mechanization of the sugar industry under the pressure of rapidly increasing wage levels. This industry now produces more output but employs fewer workers than in 1946, and this aggravates the employment problem.

(2) The rapid expansion of oil mining in Trinidad and of bauxite mining in British Guiana and Jamaica. Mining contributes relatively little to employment, but its contribution to public revenues in these three territories is now very substantial.

(3) The growth of the tourist industry, most spectacularly in Jamaica and in Barbados, but also to a lesser extent in the other islands.

(4) The growth of manufacturing industry, partly for home consumption and partly for export.

The general effect of these developments has been to diminish the significance of agriculture, even though this still remains the largest sector in terms of employment (unless we lump all "services" together). The 1960 censuses will probably show the proportion of the population engaged in agriculture to be about 20 per cent in Trinidad and between 40 and 50 per cent in the Windward and Leeward Islands. Jamaica, British Guiana, and Barbados come somewhere in between.

As usual, per capita output is much lower in agriculture than in any other sector of the economy. Industrial origin of gross domestic product at factor cost is estimated as follows for Jamaica in 1958:

	per cent
Agriculture	15.5
Mining, including refining	8.8
Manufacture, excluding sugar	10.5
Construction	12.3
Transport and communications	6.4
Other	46.5
	100.0

Per capita income in Jamaica in that year was £108. Real consumption per head was probably up to 25 per cent higher in Trinidad, and possibly 25 per cent lower in the Windward Islands, than in Jamaica. Comparisons in terms of money income are misleading since price levels of consumer goods and services vary between the islands by as much as 50 per cent.

Economic policy is dominated by the fact that the islands are heavily dependent on foreign trade. Thus even in Jamaica, which is the most nearly self-sufficient, the ratio of imports to gross domestic product in 1958 was 32 per cent. Exports from Trinidad, Jamaica, and British Guiana now include a large proportion of minerals, but exports from the other territories are almost wholly agricultural. More thought has been given to ways and means of improving the export markets for agricultural products than to any other economic problem, but in the last five years the problems of industrialization and of the tourist trade have attracted increasing attention.

The Role of Government

Any attempt to describe what West Indian governments do is confused by the number of such governments. Each of the territories makes its own laws. The Federation of 1958 was dissolved in April 1962, Jamaica having voted to secede, by popular referendum. However, even when it existed the Federal Government had few significant economic powers. In general, the island governments pursue similar economic programs. To catalogue the differences would be an immense and unprofitable labor, especially as most of the differences result from the time lag between the adoption of new policies in Trinidad or Jamaica and the decision of the smaller territories to follow suit.

Only a small part of the national income passes through the hands of these governments. They employ very few people and take only a small proportion of the gross national income in taxes— about 14 per cent in Jamaica and 16 per cent in Trinidad. The framework of public services is better developed than in Africa or in Asia, but it is still rudimentary by comparison with Western Europe or North America.

Governments operate some public utilities, but not others. The general pattern on the smaller islands is for the government to operate water, electricity, railway, and telephone services, more because of the difficulty of making these services pay on a small scale than for any ideological reasons. However, in the larger territories the balance is rather with private operation. In Jamaica the telephones, electric power, radio, and most of the bus services are operated by private companies, and the same is true of Trinidad, except that electricity there is now supplied by a public corporation. The question whether these public utilities should not be operated by public boards is ventilated from time to time but seems to raise little public excitement.

There is little demand to nationalize the major industries, such as sugar, oil, or bauxite. The principal political parties have all had nationalization as an item in their programs (except the People's

National Movement, now in power in Trinidad), but they have now all ceased to make an issue of nationalization (except the People's Progressive party, which holds office in British Guiana).

Although government plays such a small role in the economy as an employer, it plays quite a large role as a regulator, especially in agriculture. At the same time the governments are quite active in stimulating production in one way or another. The main reason for this degree of intervention is widespread agreement that entrepreneurship in the West Indies is defective in one way or another, when compared with entrepreneurship in Western Europe or in North America; hence government action is intended to strengthen weak links in the chain.

The most regulated sector is agricultural marketing. This has several purposes and forms.

Export marketing is dominated by the fact that sugar, bananas, and citrus, the leading agricultural exports, are sold in protected markets at prices negotiated by contract with the British government (sugar, citrus) or with monopolistic buyers (Windward Islands' bananas). Rice is also exported from British Guiana to the islands at prices negotiated between the governments. In order to take advantage of these arrangements the producers of these crops are organized into associations for the purpose of bargaining. Normally these associations are of a representative character, recognized by but not appointed by governments. However, in Jamaica for the time being a government-appointed board is the sole exporter of bananas, and in British Guiana a similar board is the sole exporter of rice.

Price negotiation does not necessarily involve organized marketing; sugar is marketed by its producers individually and not through the Sugar Manufacturers' Associations. However, from common bargaining to common marketing is an easy step, which has been taken in a number of other cases, whether voluntarily or under statutory compulsion. The usual reasons are advanced in favor of common marketing—desire to control the quality of the product exported and the reputation of the country in world markets; desire to eliminate middlemen's profits; or desire to stabilize returns to the grower. (Since the marketing organizations do not carry significant financial reserves from year to year, price stability enters into the picture only on a seasonal basis, except where the crop is sold at negotiated prices which fluctuate less than free world prices, e.g., sugar, rice). Common marketing is found for one or other of these reasons even where the crop is sold on the world market at world prices, without organized bargaining, e.g., St. Vincent arrowroot, St. Vincent cotton, and Jamaica cocoa. Much importance is attached to reputation in selling minor products, so it is common to find compulsory grading of exports by government inspectors, even where there is no common marketing.

Negotiated prices lead directly to quotas if the quantity of produce forthcoming at the negotiated price exceeds the quantity which the buyer is willing to take at that price. This is the case in sugar and to a lesser extent in bananas in the Windward Islands. The amount of sugar which the British government will buy at special prices is fixed. Each island has a quota; within each island each sugar factory has a quota, and in some islands each grower also has a quota. In the case of bananas, demand and supply have been more or less in equilibrium at the negotiated prices, which are themselves subject to market fluctuations; buyers are supposed to take all the fruit they are offered but tend to control purchases by raising or lowering the standard of rejects.

Common marketing also makes it possible to discriminate in price between home and export markets. In most of the islands the domestic price of sugar significantly exceeds the export price, thanks to heavy protection. On the other hand in a number of cases, e.g., bananas, domestic prices are lower than export prices because the unexportable surplus is dumped at home.

Price regulation is vertical. The price which the sugar manufacturer gets from Britain is fixed; in turn the price he must pay to the grower of sugar cane is fixed; and in turn the wage which the grower must pay to his workers is fixed. In some cases these prices are fixed by governments, in some cases by negotiations between the parties, and in other cases by governments only when negotiations between the parties break down. Sugar and rice are turbulent industries, where nearly every year one price or another is the subject of a crisis.

The system is at its most elaborate where protected industrialization is based on protected agriculture. Thus, the manufacture of condensed milk is protected in Jamaica, and the factory is also required to use the surplus milk of Jamaican farmers. So the prices

the factory must pay for milk and the prices at which it sells condensed milk are regulated; also regulated are the quantities of
dried milk, condensed milk, and other milk products which may be
imported. Similar controls exist in the case of vegetable oils and
fats. The export of these raw materials from the West Indies is
prohibited by agreement among all the island governments in the
interest of soap and other processing factories. This gives rise to a
series of fixed prices, quotas, and import restrictions for vegetable
oils and for the principal products manufactured therefrom.

Agricultural marketing is the core of the regulative activities of
West Indian governments. Outside the area of marketing, the network of regulations is much smaller than in most countries of Western Europe. Most of the larger towns now have some kind of town
planning authority. Some of the private utilities are subject to price
or profit regulation, but even such powers as exist are not vigorously
exercised. In the banana industry, where plant disease spreads rapidly, some islands have adopted measures of control, usually taking
the form of spraying by teams financed by compulsory levies on the
crop. Jamaica also has compulsory insurance of bananas against hur-
ricane damage. The economic thinking of these islands is oriented
towards supplying agricultural products for export and to protecting
the farmers and wage earners who grow these exports. Entrepreneurs who operate public utilities, factories, or services (except shipping) may do more or less as they please.

Since World War II there has also been a burst of incentive
measures designed to stimulate private investment or to increase
its productivity. In agriculture the seeds of this activity go back
to the beginning of the century. Governments then began to put
increasing sums into agricultural research and extension as well as
to stimulate agricultural credit societies and to lend money to such
societies. Government-financed activities of this sort are now on a
fairly large scale (though in research the biggest activities are the
sugar stations privately financed by the sugar industry and the banana stations of the Jamaica banana industry, which are financed by
direct levy).

A new development, pioneered in Jamaica, is the farm improvement program under which small farmers receive substantial grants
or low-interest loans towards the cost of specific improvements or

additions to fixed capital. This is part of the effort to improve small-settler agriculture and to bring marginal lands under cultivation.

In manufacturing industry and the tourist hotel business incentive measures have been greatly increased within the last five years, again under the leadership of Jamaica. Industrial development corporations are created by governments to advertise the island's suitability for factory development, to create industrial estates, to build factories for renting, to lend debenture capital, and otherwise to assist industrialists. New factories are given "pioneer" status, which entitles them to exemption from income tax for periods of from five to ten years. Potential industries are given substantial protection either by tariff, or in Jamaica (which does not belong to GATT) also by import quota restrictions.

TRADE UNIONS

All the big employers in the West Indies negotiate with trade unions and pay much higher wages and concede much better conditions than are available in non-union employment.

The unions have passed through a phase of great militancy, but they have now subsided into a stage of relative quiescence, where most disputes are settled without strikes. The period of militancy began in the middle 1930's and had ended by 1950; in many cases it was brought to an end by the atmosphere of national unity prevailing during the war.

There were two aspects to this militancy. First, the unions had to struggle for recognition by the employers and for governments to pass adequate industrial legislation. Most West Indian governments and employers looked upon a union as a form of sedition in the 1930's; the atmosphere was not unlike that which prevailed in the United States before World War I. Change was effected partly by the unions' demonstrating power and partly by pressure from the United Kingdom Government which (itself under pressure from the British labor movement) felt bound to concede to West Indian workers much the same privileges as were enjoyed by trade unions in Britain. The war helped by forcing the governments to throw their influence on the side of recognition and conciliation.

The second aspect of militancy arose out of conflicts between different labor leaders seeking power in the same industries. The creation and leadership of unions was a road not only to industrial but also to political power and was fully exploited for this purpose. The two aspects of militancy were not unrelated since, as soon as one leader was recognized by employers and began to practice collective bargaining according to the rules, opportunity was thereby created for a new leader to denounce the old as a pawn of the employees and to try his hand in a new bout of militancy. This phase is nearly finished, since the labor movement has thrown up established leaders over the past twenty-five years, whose authority is not now easily challenged. But the legacy in Jamaica (though not elsewhere) is of three competing leaderships, whose rivalry still occasionally complicates the efforts of employers to reach agreement with their workers.

All the major industries—sugar, oil, bauxite, transport, government employment—and many minor ones as well operate under collective agreements. Most of the large private employers also operate the check-off system, deducting union dues from wage packets by consent. Occasionally disputes flare up which cannot be settled by negotiation, and major strikes are threatened, or may even take place. Most governments have power to impose compulsory arbitration, but this power is exercised with reluctance; more often governments participate in naming arbitrators acceptable to both sides.

The smoothness of collective bargaining has its price in a continuously rising wage level. This process is facilitated by the economic structure of the three leading industries. Oil and bauxite are very capital-intensive; wages are only a small proportion of costs and productivity per man is increasing most of the time through mechanization; so wage increases are easily absorbed. In sugar the process is facilitated by the willingness of the British government to buy sugar at cost, which means that if wages rise to the same extent in all the Commonwealth sources from which the British buy sugar, the cost falls automatically on the British public. The sugar industry has also been mechanizing rapidly, partly due to invention and partly as a response to rising wages.

There are two important consequences. Although there is a very large gap (at least 2 to 1) between wages in the leading industries and wages elsewhere, upward movements at the top induce upward movements lower down, causing costs to rise steadily in all industries where productivity is not increasing *pari passu*. A second consequence is that rapid mechanization of the leading industries throws upon the rest of the economy the burden of coping not only with the steady increase of population, but also with declining employment in the sugar industry. This burden they cannot bear, so most West Indian economies suffer chronic unemployment.

PRIVATE ENTERPRISE

In describing the economic structure of any West Indian territory, one must think in terms not of one economy but of three economies. In nearly every major sector three groups of enterprises exist side by side. These are

(*a*) Large-scale, heavily capitalized, rather efficient firms, for the most part financed from outside the region, as subsidiaries of some of the world's largest corporations, and run by imported managers using the latest managerial techniques.

(*b*) Medium-scale firms, for the most part financed by native capitalists (who may be of any race), insufficiently capitalized to use the latest mechanical equipment and operating for the most part with old-fashioned ideas of labor relations and of labor utilization.

(*c*) Very small enterprises, using very little hired labor, or none, and very little capital.

These three groups, which we here designate for short as foreign capital, domestic capital, and family enterprise, co-exist in agriculture, manufacturing industry, and hotel-keeping. Certain other sectors are almost completely in the hands of the foreign capital, especially mining, banking, and foreign (but not interisland) shipping. Foreign and domestic capital share insurance and mortgage finance. Electricity and telephones, where not publicly owned, are mostly in the hands of domestic capital, though there is also some external participation. Foreign trade (import and export wholesaling) is also more or less confined to domestic capital. Retail distribution, inland transport, and interisland shipping are shared by domestic capital and family enterprise, with little participation by foreign capital.

These three groups of enterprises are not in equilibrium with each other, but the degree of competition is surprisingly small, having regard to the great differences in productive efficiency. Competition between them is retarded by several factors:

(i) Differences in factor remuneration. The foreign group raises capital more cheaply than the others, but it pays much higher wages and salaries and usually pays liberal prices when buying land.

(ii) Custom and prejudice limit the participation of each group in certain sectors. Thus by tradition only the third group grows local foodstuffs for sale (yams, maize, rice—but the prejudice does not extend to cattle). Similarly, foreign capitalists could possibly revolutionize retail distribution but would probably face a public outcry if they moved into this sector in competition with domestic capitalists and family enterprises. The first and second groups could use land more productively than the third group; nevertheless, public pressure is for them to *sell* land to the third group, and they would face serious trouble if they started to buy up the lands of that group, even at generous prices.

(iii) In a few cases competition is limited by government regulation. The most important is the cultivation of sugar cane, from which the third group might by now have disappeared but for the existence of a quota system. Another important example is in manufacturing industry in Jamaica, where substantial tax concessions are offered to factories which sell only in export markets, with the effect of discouraging foreign capitalists from competing in the domestic market.

Though these factors reduce competition, they do not eliminate it altogether. Investment by foreign capitalists has expanded very rapidly during the last fifteen years in sugar, in manufacturing, in mining, and in hotel-keeping. In sugar this has been done by buying estates from the domestic capitalists; but in manufacturing, mining, and hotel-keeping the other groups have not been displaced; the situation has merely been that foreign capitalists have done the lion's share of the pioneering in rapidly expanding sectors, where others have followed their example.

The use of the word "group" is not intended to imply monopolistic behavior or intention. The foreign capitalists operate in different sectors, e.g., sugar, oil, bauxite, banking, hotels, and do not pursue common policies except in so far as within each industry they are compelled by trade unions to have common labor policies for collective bargaining. The sugar firms cannot compete with each other because of the quota system, but in oil, bauxite, banking, manufacturing, insurance, and hotel-keeping, "workable" competition for markets and for concessions prevails to the same extent in the West Indies as it does elsewhere—no less and no more.

The large-scale enterprises are mainly subsidiaries of world-wide corporations, but some of these firms do include some domestic capitalists as shareholders, especially in sugar, in manufacturing, and in hotel-keeping. In some other countries there is a strong prejudice against foreign enterprise, as a result of which foreign capitalists find it prudent to go out of their way to seek partnership or other association with native capitalists. This is not at present the case in the West Indies. Such partnership as exists is mainly due to some of the domestic capitalists displaying such enterprise that they attract participation by foreign capital.

The display of enterprise by the domestic capitalists is a relatively recent phenomenon—post World War II. For a century after emancipation the economy was dominated by domestic capitalists, with participation by foreign capitalists confined more or less to oil, bauxite, banking, and foreign shipping. However, the domestic capitalists showed little enterprise in that time, developing only two major new industries, both agricultural—bananas in Jamaica and cocoa in Trinidad. The energy which this class is now displaying in nearly every sector of the economy—supermarkets, interisland shipping, factories, bananas in the Windward Islands, hotels, mortgage-financing, and so on—is mainly attributable to three factors; to the fact that the West Indies has shared in the world-wide postwar prosperity; to the example set by foreign capitalists, who have shown that money can be made by investing in the West Indies; and to the general psychological buoyancy of these territories, where the prewar sense of hopelessness and defeat has given way, in politics, art, and national self-respect no less than in economic thinking, to sentiments of hope and of self-confidence.

The principal handicap of the domestic capitalists is lack of managerial experience. They have grown up in a world where labor has been not only cheap and abundant but also somewhat contemptuously regarded, partly because of the survival of old-time class attitudes and partly because of racial prejudices. This group therefore tends to use labor wastefully, and its enterprises are not as efficient or as profitable as they could be, given modern managerial attitudes.

The third group, the small family enterprise, is most prominent in agriculture, retail distribution, motor transport, interisland shipping, and workshops. Governments have put a good deal of effort into agricultural extension, but the efficiency of this group continues to be low, lacking as it does both capital and education. To some extent this is a "residual" group, into which people come when displaced from employment activities elsewhere. The West Indies is passing through a stage where the increased demand for wage employment created by population growth and by the displacement of labor by mechanization is less than the increased supply of jobs created by new investment. This is why the numbers in petty retailing and in domestic service are so swollen in the more overpopulated islands, notably Jamaica and Barbados. There is very little "surplus labor" in agriculture, because most of the cultivable land is worked by wage labor on plantations.

We conclude with a brief description of each of the leading industries.

Sugar

Up to the middle of the nineteenth century sugar was grown on estates, each of which had its own factory for milling cane. However, over the last hundred years the economies of large-scale milling have kept on increasing, to the point where what is considered the most efficient size is twenty times as large today as it was a century ago. The number of sugar mills has therefore shrunk very sharply. The number of companies owning mills has shrunk even more, to the point where the twelve remaining mills in British Guiana are owned by only two companies, one of which owns mills also in Trinidad and Jamaica. The only island which has resisted this process of concentration is Barbados, where the average annual output of sugar per mill in 1958 was 7,100 tons, compared with 25,500 tons in British Guiana.

In the course of this development, the ownership of estates and the ownership of mills has been separated. All mill owners (except one) also own estates, which supply cane to their mills. But the great majority of persons who grow cane do not own a mill; they sell to a mill. These growers who do not own mills are known in the West Indies as "cane-farmers."

Cane-farmers may have lands of any size; the category includes estates of ten thousand acres as well as smallholders with one acre. There have been tendencies strengthening both the big and the small. Estates have tended to grow larger for the same reason as mills, namely the economies of large-scale control, which continue to increase as the estates become more mechanized. At the other end of the scale, most West Indian governments adopted measures during the first half of the twentieth century designed to encourage smallholders to grow cane; these measures were particularly successful in Trinidad, in Barbados, and in Jamaica, where the rights of the smallholders are now further preserved by the quota system. British Guiana is a conspicuous exception, where cane-farmers produce only about 1 per cent of the cane (compare Trinidad where the ratio is about one third).

The sugar industry is led by two big companies and three or four of middle size, which own the largest mills and the largest estates. These companies are domiciled in the United Kingdom, where most of their shareholders also live. But there is also a good deal of West Indian capital both in the medium and small factories, and also in medium and small estates. Even the peasant farmer is well represented in the sugar industry. However, the pace of development is set by the biggest companies, which since the war have poured millions of pounds into modernizing the mills, mechanizing the estates, and improving techniques of cultivation. The industry maintains its own first-class research stations.

Since the industry is strictly regulated as to price and output at all stages, competition inside the West Indies takes only the form of the more efficient producers buying out the less efficient at attractive prices. Concentration both of mills and of estates has been rapid since the war and is continuing.

Relations with trade unions were very bad, especially before the war, but are now very good. Mechanization has reduced the labor force and has helped also to reduce seasonal unemployment and casual labor by eliminating the worst of the peaks. The average wage in sugar used to be at or below the average wage in other rural occupations; it now substantially exceeds all other rural occupations except mining.

Bananas

This industry was pioneered by the United Fruit Company in Jamaica. The focal point of monopolistic control was the ownership of refrigerated ships, which are required for regular service. The company owned a number of banana estates in Jamaica, but most of the bananas it carried were bought from other growers, large and small. The growers and the company battled continuously from the beginning of this century until the beginning of World War II, the growers trying to secure and maintain alternative shipping facilities, first by contracting with other shipping companies and later by operating their own ships co-operatively; but the company defeated these efforts one by one.

The upshot today is that the Jamaica government has created a Banana Board which is the sole exporter of bananas from the island. The Board buys from the growers, and sells to wholesalers in the consumer markets. The number of wholesalers handling bananas in the British market is not large, but some degree of "workable" competition exists.

Since World War II bananas have become a major industry in the Windward Islands. The British firm which operates in these islands has contracted to take all the good bananas offered to it at ship side, at a price tied to the price which the Jamaica Banana Board gets in the British market. This contract has proved very profitable both to the growers and to the firm. In each of these islands legislation prescribes that bananas may be exported only by a Banana Association. This Association consists of the growers of bananas and is empowered to make exclusive contracts.

Bananas are grown on farms of all sizes, with farms of less than fifty acres supplying most of the fruit. The main problem is to control epidemic diseases. This is done by levying on the industry to support the cost of teams who move from farm to farm spraying the trees with appropriate mixtures.

Food for Local Consumption

By tradition the local foodstuffs whether cereals (maize, rice), root crops (yams, potatoes, cocoes), or vegetables (cabbages, peas) are grown only by small farmers. Cattle is the single exception;

cattle is also kept by estates. Productivity on small farms is low. Large estates, managed scientifically, could get higher yields but might have difficulty in disposing of their produce, since there is no organized wholesale market in which they could sell. Governments have created public marketing agencies to which growers may sell at fixed prices in the event of gluts, but these agencies have not succeeded in rationalizing the distribution of locally grown foodstuffs. The ruling conception is still that the peasant rides to market with small lots, which he sells to market women, who resell to housewives.

Rice is an exception, because it has to be milled before consumption. Rice is grown in most of the territories, but only in British Guiana is the industry significant. There the industry has suffered from an excessive number of small mills, and rice politics, involving disputes between the growers and the millers and between the large millers and the small millers, have always been turbulent.

British Guiana exports rice to all the islands at prices above world prices; these are negotiated once a year by the governments. The Rice Marketing Board is the sole exporter from British Guiana. It offers a fixed price, based on the price at which it resells, and the stability of the price has done much to reduce the internal temperature of the industry.

Mining

With the exception of some diamond digging, mining is all in the hands of large foreign companies. There are ten oil producers in Trinidad, two of whom also own refineries. These refineries receive all the oil produced in Trinidad and about as much again brought in from Venezuela to be refined and re-exported. Bauxite is mined by four companies, which ship most of what they mine, either as bauxite or as alumina, direct to their aluminum factories in North America. (Small amounts of calcined bauxite and other products are sold in open markets.)

The mining companies compete with each other for concessions and have paid prices for land which are high by West Indian standards. They all recognize trade unions, and they pay the highest wages in the West Indies.

Manufacturing

Growth has been rapid in recent years, especially in Jamaica and in Trinidad. In Jamaica, value added by manufacturing (excluding sugar, oil, and alumina) increased at constant factor cost from £11.5 million in 1953 to £19.3 million in 1958, which is an annual rate of 11 per cent. If this rate were maintained, manufacturing would catch up with agriculture in six or seven years.

Entrepreneurs of all kinds have contributed to this growth; big and small, domestic and foreign. Up to now production for the domestic market has been the main attraction, but governments recognize that, since the islands are overpopulated, they need to make a bid for foreign markets, and they are eager to encourage foreign firms with established markets overseas to establish factories in the islands from which to supply these markets. Jamaica has taken this to the point of offering extra concessions to factories which produce only for foreign markets.

Manufacturing industry is protected by tariffs, and in Jamaica by import quotas as well. The relationship between manufacturers in each island is one of "workable" competition.

Retail Distribution

Shopping has begun to be modernized in recent years. The old general merchandise stores are turning themselves into department stores on modern lines, with modern merchandising practices. Distribution is more competitive in some territories than in others. Distribution is least competitive in Jamaica, where margins are notoriously high; several explanations of this are offered, none convincing. Since consumer co-operatives buying locally from wholesalers have found it difficult to make ends meet, the trouble is probably high wholesale rather than high retail margins. It is not easy to break into the wholesale trade, because all the leading brands for which there is consumer preference are already parceled out among a relatively small number of agents.

The self-service supermarket has arrived and is progressing rapidly in the grocery trade.

Tourism

The hotel industry was pioneered by domestic capitalists, but its success has now attracted a good deal of foreign capital, which is investing in large, modern hotels. Though the high prices of some of the bigger hotels are much talked about, even with awe, West Indian hotels embrace the whole range of price and quality.

INDEX

Date Due